THE OXFORD HA

# PHILOSOPHY IN EARLY MODERN EUROPE

In this Handbook twenty-five leading scholars survey the development of philosophy between the middle of the sixteenth century and the early eighteenth century. The five parts of the book cover metaphysics and natural philosophy; the mind, the passions, and aesthetics; epistemology, logic, mathematics, and language; ethics and political philosophy; and religion.

The period between the publication of Copernicus's *De Revolutionibus* and Berkeley's reflections on Newton and Locke saw one of the most fundamental changes in the history of our way of thinking about the universe. This radical transformation of worldview was partly a response to what we now call the Scientific Revolution; it was equally a reflection of political changes that were no less fundamental, which included the establishment of nation-states and some of the first attempts to formulate a theory of international rights and justice. Finally, the Reformation and its aftermath undermined the apparent unity of the Christian church in Europe and challenged both religious beliefs that had been accepted for centuries and the interpretation of the Bible on which they had been based.

The Handbook surveys a number of the most important developments in the philosophy of the period, as these are expounded both in texts that have since become very familiar and in other philosophical texts that are undeservedly less well-known. It also reaches beyond philosophy to acknowledge the fluidity of its boundaries with what is called science, and to consider the impact on philosophy of historical and political events—explorations, revolutions and reforms, inventions and discoveries. Thus it not only offers a guide to the most important areas of recent research, but also offers some new questions for historians of philosophy to pursue and indicates areas that are ripe for further exploration.

**Desmond M. Clarke** is Professor Emeritus of Philosophy at University College Cork, and a member of the Royal Irish Academy.

**Catherine Wilson** is Anniversary Professor of Philosophy at the University of York, and a member of the Royal Society of Canada.

# THE OXFORD HANDBOOK OF

# PHILOSOPHY IN EARLY MODERN EUROPE

*Edited by*

DESMOND M. CLARKE

*and*

CATHERINE WILSON

OXFORD

UNIVERSITY PRESS

# OXFORD
## UNIVERSITY PRESS

Great Clarendon Street, Oxford OX2 6DP

Oxford University Press is a department of the University of Oxford.
It furthers the University's objective of excellence in research, scholarship,
and education by publishing worldwide.

Oxford is a registered trade mark of Oxford University Press
in the UK and in certain other countries

© The several contributors 2011

The moral rights of the authors have been asserted

First published 2011
First published in paperback 2013

British Library Cataloguing in Publication Data

Data available

Library of Congress Cataloging in Publication Data

Data available

ISBN 978–0–19–955613–7 (Hbk)
ISBN 978–0–19–967164–9 (Pbk)

# CONTENTS

## PART III: EPISTEMOLOGY, LOGIC, MATHEMATICS, AND LANGUAGE

## PART IV: ETHICS AND POLITICAL PHILOSOPHY

## PART V: RELIGION

# Notes on Contributors

**Peter R. Anstey** is Professor of Early Modern Philosophy at the University of Otago, New Zealand. His recent research focused on early modern philosophy and natural philosophy, with special reference to the writings of John Locke and Robert Boyle. He is currently researching the historiography of the philosophy of the seventeenth and eighteenth centuries.

**Gábor Boros** is Professor of Philosophy at Eötvös University, Budapest. He has published widely in Hungarian, English, German, and French. He is author and editor of *The Concept of Love in 17$^{th}$ and 18$^{th}$ Century Philosophy* (Leuven University Press/Eötvös Kiadó Budapest, 2008). His current research focuses on philosophy in the early Enlightenment, and philosophies of emotion.

**Desmond M. Clarke** is Professor (emeritus) of Philosophy at University College Cork, and a member of the Royal Irish Academy. He is general editor (with Karl Ameriks) of *Cambridge Texts in the History of Philosophy*; his recent monographs include *Descartes's Theory of Mind* (Oxford, 2003) and *Descartes: A Biography* (Cambridge, 2006). His translations include a two-volume edition of Descartes for Penguin.

**Stephen Darwall** is Andrew Downey Orrick Professor of Philosophy at Yale University. He has written widely on the foundations and history of ethics. His books include *Impartial Reason, Philosophical Ethics, Welfare and Rational Care*, and, most recently, *The Second-Person Standpoint*. He is the editor, with Allan Gibbard and Peter Railton, of *Moral Discourse and Practice*, and has also edited a number of volumes on normative ethics. He is a founding co-editor, with David Velleman, of *The Philosophers' Imprint*.

**Stephen Gaukroger** is ARC Professorial Fellow and Professor of History of Philosophy and History of Science at the University of Sydney; he is also Professor of Philosophy at the University of Aberdeen. Recent monographs include *Descartes: An Intellectual Biography* (1995), *Francis Bacon and the Transformation of Early-Modern Philosophy* (2001), *Descartes' System of Natural Philosophy* (2002), and *The Emergence of a Scientific Culture: Science and the Shaping of Modernity, 1210–1680* (2006).

**Jean-François Gauvin** is a Mellon Postdoctoral Fellow at McGill University, Montréal, and former Curator at the Collection of Historical Scientific Instruments, Harvard University. His research focuses on instrumentation from the seventeenth to the twentieth centuries. Since 2000, he has co-written and co-edited two prize-winning volumes as well as several articles and book reviews dealing with instruments and instrument making.

**Ursula Goldenbaum** is Associate Professor in the Department of Philosophy, Emory University. She was a member at the *Institute for Advanced Study* at Princeton in 2007/8. She published monographs on Spinoza (Hagen, 1993) and on intellectual public debates in the German Enlightenment (Berlin, 2004), and has edited *Leibniz* (Berlin, 1991) and *Rousseau* (Weimar, 2000). Most recently she co-edited (with Douglas Jesseph) a volume on Leibniz and the metaphysical and mathematical controversy concerning infinitesimals (Berlin, New York, 2006).

**Emily Grosholz** is Professor of Philosophy and a member of the Center for Fundamental Theory/Institute for Gravitation and the Cosmos at the Pennsylvania State University. She is also a member of SPHERE-REHSEIS (University of Paris Denis Diderot–Paris 7 and CNRS). She is the author of *Representation and Productive Ambiguity in Mathematics and the Sciences* (Oxford, 2007).

**Helen Hattab** is an Assistant Professor of Philosophy at the University of Houston. She is the author of *Descartes on Forms and Mechanisms* (Cambridge, 2009) and of articles on the relations between Descartes' philosophy, late Scholastic philosophy, and Renaissance mechanics.

**Philippe Hamou** is *maître de conférences* in philosophy at the University of Paris, Ouest-Nanterre. His publications include *La mutation du visible, essai sur la portée épistémologique des instruments d'optique au XVIIe siècle*, 2 vols. (Presses du Septentrion, 1999–2001); *Voir et Connaître à l'âge classique* (Paris, 2002). He is also the editor of Locke, *Essai sur l'entendement humain*, trans. Pierre Coste (Paris, 2009), and, with Marta Spranzi, of *Galilée: Ecrits coperniciens* (Paris, 2004).

**Ian Hunter** is an Australian Professorial Fellow in the Centre for the History of European Discourses, University of Queensland. His recent publications include *Rival Enlightenments: Civil and Metaphysical Philosophy in Early Modern Germany* (Cambridge, 2001); *The Secularisation of the Confessional State: The Political Thought of Christian Thomasius* (Cambridge, 2007). He has edited *Heresy in Transition: Transforming Ideas of Heresy in Medieval and Early Modern Europe* (London, 2005) (with John Christian Laursen and Cary J. Nederman); *The Philosopher in Early Modern Europe: The Nature of a Contested Identity* (Cambridge, 2006) (with Conal Condren and Stephen Gaukroger).

**P. J. E. Kail,** University Lecturer in the History of Modern Philosophy, University of Oxford, Official Fellow and Tutor in Philosophy, St Peter's College. Peter Kail held posts at Cambridge and Edinburgh before coming to Oxford. He is the author of *Projection and Realism in Hume's Philosophy* (Oxford, 2007), and has written articles on Hutcheson, Hume, and more recently, Nietzsche.

**Jaap Maat** is a lecturer at the Department of Philosophy, University of Amsterdam, a member of the Institute for Logic, Language and Computation (ILLC), and a researcher at the Centre for Linguistics, University of Oxford, where he is preparing a critical edition of John Wallis's *Treatise of Logick* (1685). His publications include *George Dalgarno on Universal Language* (Oxford, 2001; jointly with David Cram), and *Philosophical Languages in the Seventeenth Century: Dalgarno, Wilkins, Leibniz* (Kluwer, 2004).

**José R. Maia Neto** is Professor of Philosophy at the Federal University of Minas Gerais (Belo Horizonte, Brazil). He is the author of numerous articles on early modern scepticism; his monographs include *Machado de Assis, The Brazilian Pyrrhonian* (Purdue University Press, 1994) and *The Christianization of Pyrrhonism* (Kluwer, 1995). He edited, with Richard H. Popkin, *Skepticism: An Anthology* (Prometheus, 2007).

**Philip Milton** is lecturer in law at the University of Leicester. He is the editor (with J. R. Milton) of John Locke, *An Essay concerning Toleration and Other Writings on Law and Politics, 1667–1683* (Oxford, 2006).

**Steven Nadler** is the William H. Hay II Professor of Philosophy at the University of Wisconsin-Madison and the co-editor of *Oxford Studies in Early Modern Philosophy*. His books include *Spinoza: A Life* (Cambridge, 1999) and *The Best of All Possible Worlds: A Story of Philosophers, God and Evil* (Farrar, Straus, Giroux, 2008).

**Eileen O'Neill** is Professor of Philosophy at the University of Massachusetts-Amherst. She published the first modern edition of Margaret Cavendish's *Observations upon Experimental Philosophy* (Cambridge, 2001); co-edited, with Christia Mercer, *Early Modern Philosophy: Mind, Matter and Metaphysics* (Oxford, 2005), and is co-editing, with Marcy Lascano, *Feminist History of Philosophy* (forthcoming, Springer).

**Pauline Phemister** is Reader in Philosophy at the University of Edinburgh and Deputy Director of the Institute for Advanced Studies in the Humanities. She is author of *Leibniz and the Natural World: Activity, passivity and corporeal substances in the philosophy of Leibniz* (Springer, 2005) and *The Rationalists: Descartes, Spinoza and Leibniz* (Polity, 2006).

**Alexander Rueger** is Professor of Philosophy at the University of Alberta. He has published widely in the history and philosophy of physics, and on eighteenth-century aesthetics. He is currently writing a book on Kant's aesthetics in its historical context.

**Paul Russell** is Professor in Philosophy at the University of British Columbia. His published work includes *Freedom and Moral Sentiment: Hume's Way of Naturalizing Responsibility* (Oxford University Press, 1995) and *The Riddle of Hume's Treatise: Skepticism, Naturalism, and Irreligion* (Oxford University Press, 2008). In 2010 he will be Fowler Hamilton Visiting Fellow at Christ Church, Oxford.

**Tad M. Schmaltz** is professor of philosophy at the University of Michigan, Ann Arbor. He is the author of *Descartes on Causation* (2008), *Radical Cartesianism* (Cambridge, 2002), and *Malebranche's Theory of the Soul* (Oxford, 1996), and has edited *Receptions of Descartes* (Routledge, 2005).

**R. W. Serjeantson** is a Fellow and Lecturer in History, Trinity College, Cambridge. He specializes in intellectual history in the early modern period, and is editing (with A. Vine) vol. III of the *Oxford Francis Bacon*. Recent publications include 'Hume's General Rules and the "Chief Business of Philosophers"' (*Impressions of Hume*: Oxford, 2005), and '"Human Understanding" and the Genre of Locke's Essay' (*Intellectual History Review*, 2008).

**Justin E. H. Smith** is associate professor of philosophy at Concordia University, Montreal. He is the author of *Divine Machines: Leibniz's Philosophy of Biology* (Princeton University Press, 2010), and is currently working on a critical edition and translation for the Yale Leibniz series, with François Duchesneau, of Georg Ernst Stahl's *Negotium Otiosum*. His current research concerns the impact of European colonial expansion and exploration in the sixteenth and seventeenth centuries on early modern philosophical reflections about human nature and human difference.

**Mary Tiles** is Professor (emeritus) of Philosophy at the University of Hawaii, Mānoa. She is the author of *Bachelard: Science and Objectivity* (1984), *Introduction to the Philosophy of Set Theory* (1989), *Mathematics and the Image of Reason* (1991), co-author with James Tiles of *The Authority of Knowledge: An Introduction to Historical Epistemology* (1993) and with Hans Oberdiek of *Living in a Technological Culture: Human Tools and Human Values* (1995). Recent research interests include the role of technology in the development of global environmental science.

**Catherine Wilson** is Regius Professor of Moral Philosophy at the University of Aberdeen. She is the author of *Epicureanism at the Origins of Modernity* (Oxford, 2008), *Descartes's Meditations: An Introduction* (Cambridge, 2003), and the recently reprinted *The Invisible World: Early Modern Philosophy and the Invention of the Microscope* (Princeton, 2009). She was editor of *History of Philosophy Quarterly* from 1998 to 2003.

# ABBREVIATIONS

........................................................

A:          Leibniz, Gottfried Wilhelm (1923–). *Sämtliche Schriften und Briefe*. Ed. Deutsche Akademie der Wissenschaften. Multiple vols. in 7 series. Darmstadt/Leipzig/Berlin: Akademie Verlag.

AO:         Arnauld, Antoine (1775–83). *Oeuvres de Messire Antoine Arnauld, docteur de la maison et société de Sorbonne*. 43 vols. Lausanne: Sigismond d'Arnay.

AOP:        Arnauld, Antoine (1843). *Œuvres philosophiques de Antoine Arnauld*. Paris: Adolphe Delahays.

ATF:        Arnauld, Antoine (1990). *On True and False Ideas*. Ed. & trans. Elmar J. Kremer. Lewiston/Queenston/Lampeter: Edwin Mellen Press.

AR:         Aristotle (1984–85). *The Complete Works of Aristotle*. Ed. by Jonathan Barnes. 2 vols. Princeton, NJ: Princeton University Press.

AT:         Descartes, René (1964–76). *Oeuvres de Descartes*. Ed. C. Adam and P. Tannery. 12 vols. Paris: Vrin/CNRS.

B:          *The Works of Robert Boyle* (1999–2000). Ed. M. Hunter and E. B. Davis. 14 vols. London: Pickering and Chatto.

BW:         Berkeley, George (1948–57). *The Works of George Berkeley Bishop of Cloyne*. Ed. A. A. Luce and T. E. Jessop. 9 vols. Edinburgh: Nelson.

CSM:        Descartes, René (1985). *The Philosophical Writings of Descartes*. Ed. and trans. John Cottingham, Robert Stoothoff, and Dugald Murdoch. 2 vols. Cambridge: Cambridge University Press.

CSMK:       Descartes, René (1991). *The Philosophical Writings of Descartes*. Vol. 3. Ed. and trans. John Cottingham, Robert Stoothoff, Dugald Murdoch, and Anthony Kenny. Cambridge: Cambridge University Press.

DJN:        Pufendorf, Samuel (1717). *The Law of Nature and Nations: Or, A General System of Morality, Jurisprudence, and Politics in Eight Books*. Trans. Basil Kennett with an introduction and notes by Jean Barbeyrac. London. Reprinted by the Lawbook Exchange, 2005.

EN:         Galilei, Galileo (1890–1909). *Opere de Galileo Galilei: Edizione nationale*. Ed. Antonio Favaro. Reprint, Florence: G. Barberà (1968).

| | |
|---|---|
| *Essay*: | John Locke (1975). *An Essay concerning Human Understanding*. Ed. Peter H. Nidditch. Oxford: Clarendon Press. |
| GM: | Leibniz, G. W. (1849–63). *Mathematische Schriften*. Ed. C. I. Gerhardt. 7 vols. Berlin and Halle: A. Asher and H. W. Schmidt. |
| GP: | Leibniz, G. W. (1875–90). *Die philosophischen Schriften*. Ed. C. I. Gerhardt. 7 vols. Berlin: Weidmannsche Buchhandlung. |
| HW: | Hobbes, Thomas (1992). *The English Works of Thomas Hobbes*. Ed. W. Molesworth (1839–45). Rprt. ed. J. Rogers. 12 vols. London: Routledge/Thoemmes. |
| KGW: | Kepler, Johannes (1938–98). *Johannes Kepler Gesammelte Werke*. Ed. Kepler-Kommission der Bayerischen Akademie der Wissenschaften. 22 vols. München: C. H. Beck. |
| L: | Hobbes, Thomas (1994). *Leviathan with selected variants from the Latin edition of 1688*. Ed. E. Curley. Indianapolis: Hackett. |
| LAG: | Leibniz, G.W. (1989). *Philosophical Essays*. Ed. and trans. Roger Ariew and Daniel Garber. Indianapolis and Cambridge: Hackett Publishing Company. |
| *Lev.*: | Hobbes, Thomas (1651). *Leviathan*. London. |
| LL: | Leibniz, G.W. (1969). *Philosophical Papers and Letters*. Ed. and trans. Leroy E. Loemker. 2nd edn. Dordrecht: D. Reidel Publishing Company. |
| LN: | (1999). *Hobbes and Bramhall on Liberty and Necessity*. Ed. V. Chappell. Cambridge: Cambridge University Press. |
| LP: | Leibniz, G.W. (1966). *Logical Papers: a selection*. Ed. and trans. G. H. R. Parkinson. Oxford: Clarendon Press. |
| LRB: | Leibniz, G. W. (1996). *New Essays on Human Understanding*. 2nd edn. Ed. and trans. P. Remnant and J. Bennett. Cambridge: Cambridge University Press. |
| LW: | Locke, John (1794). *The Works of John Locke*. 9th edn. 9 vols. London. Rprt. Routledge/Thommes Press, 1997. |
| MLO: | Malebranche, Nicolas (1997). *The Search After Truth*. Ed. and trans. Thomas M. Lennon and Paul J. Olscamp. Cambridge: Cambridge University Press. |
| MS: | Malebranche, Nicolas (1997). *Dialogues on Metaphysics and on Religion*. Ed. Nicholas Jolley. Trans. David Scott. Cambridge: Cambridge University Press. |
| OCM: | Malebranche, Nicolas (1958–76). *Oeuvres complètes de Malebranche*. Ed. André Robinet. 20 vols. Paris: Vrin. |

OD:         *Oeuvres diverses de Mr Pierre Bayle.* 4 vols. The Hague, 1727–31; reprinted Hildesheim 1968.

OL:         Hobbes, Thomas (1839–45). *Thomas Hobbes Malmesburiensis opera philosophica quae latine scripsit omnia.* Ed. W. Molesworth. 5 vols. London. Rprt. Aalen: Scientia Verlag (1961).

*Principia*:   Newton, Isaac (1999). *The PRINCIPIA. Mathematical Principles of Natural Philosophy.* Trans. I. B. Cohen and A. Whitman. Berkeley and Los Angeles: University of California Press [3rd edn. 1726].

S:          Boyle, Robert (1991). *Selected Philosophical Papers of Robert Boyle.* Ed. M. A. Stewart. Indianapolis: Hackett.

SC:         Spinoza, Baruch (1988). *The Collected Works of Spinoza.* Ed. and trans. Edwin Curley. Vol. 1 (2nd corrected printing). Princeton, NJ: Princeton University Press.

SO:         Spinoza, Baruch (1972). *Spinoza Opera.* Ed. Carl Gebhardt. 5 vols. Heidelberg: Carl Winters Universitätsverlag.

ST:         Aquinas, Thomas (1920). *Summa Theologiae.* Trans. by the English Dominicans. 22 vols. London: Oates and Washbourne, 1912–36.

# INTRODUCTION

THE history of philosophy does not provide natural divisions with which to demarcate the scope of this *Handbook*. Nonetheless, the period between the publication of Copernicus's *De Revolutionibus* (1543) and Berkeley's reflections on Newton and Locke in the early eighteenth century coincides with one of the most fundamental changes in the history of our way of thinking about the universe. Accordingly, while alternative boundaries are possible, we have limited the range of these essays to the period from the middle of the sixteenth century to the years immediately before David Hume and the Enlightenment. This radical transformation of worldview was partly a response to what we now call the Scientific Revolution; it was equally a reflection of political changes that were no less fundamental, which included the establishment of nation-states and some of the first attempts to formulate a theory of international rights and justice. Finally, the Reformation and its aftermath undermined the apparent unity of the Christian church in Europe and challenged both religious beliefs that had been accepted for centuries and the interpretation of the Bible on which they had been based.

The volume was conceived with several intentions. We wanted to survey a number of the most important developments in the philosophy of the period, as these are expounded both in texts that have since become very familiar and in other philosophical texts that are undeservedly less well-known. We also wanted to extend the format well beyond that of histories of philosophy that consider only internal and logical relations between philosophical doctrines. Our objective was to make evident the fluid boundaries in the early modern period between deductions from experimental science and philosophical theory, and to consider the impact on philosophy of historical and political events—explorations, revolutions and reforms, inventions and discoveries. By including a number of essays that discuss the impact of scientific innovation and social and political change, we wished to give a more accurate representation of the meaning of philosophical doctrines as their inventors and proponents understood them, and one less distorted by an exclusive focus on a very limited range of questions such as external-world scepticism, mind–body interaction, or necessity and causality. We hope thereby to have suggested some new questions for historians of philosophy to pursue and to have indicated areas that are ripe for further exploration.

Aristotelian metaphysics and philosophy of nature, which dominated teaching in the universities at the beginning of the early modern period, were based on a limited form of experience, which was directed at medium-size objects and their observable properties. Such objects were understood as things (or substances), which were compounded of matter and form and of which various properties—both essential or inessential—were predicated. Proto-scientific insights were codified in syllogisms, in which entailment relations were made manifest. Central to the Aristotelian apparatus were also the notions of natural dominance and subordination that were exemplified throughout the cosmos, including human societies. On such slim foundations the whole of Aristotelian metaphysics, logic, and politics were founded, although the full complexity of their ramifications and subsequent embellishments far exceeds what is summarized in this abbreviated summary.

The contributors to the *Handbook* discuss some of the many ways in which these long-influential ways of describing reality were challenged and eventually replaced. The old categories of 'substance' and 'essence' were treated with special critical scrutiny (Chapter 1), in which the recovery of ancient atomism and the emergence of modern chemistry played a crucial role. Descartes divided substances into only two kinds, extended and thinking (or material and mental), with divine substance existing outside the world and interacting with it only by lending its general concourse to the whole of creation. Other philosophers were ready to abandon the notion of material substance altogether in favour of the term 'matter', by supposing that the world consisted of nothing more than extended, massy particles, of an unimaginable smallness, either separated by a void or filling all of space. Some, such as Hobbes and Locke, suspected that this might be all there was in the universe. However, there were many other variations on this theme of fitting our understanding of reality into a conceptual scheme in which the category of substance was fundamental. Mental substance, the substrate or repository of ideas, might be considered the only substance, as Berkeley and perhaps Leibniz supposed; or, in a throwback to the Aristotelian notion of hylomorphs, living things, tiny bodies ruled by souls, which in turn composed larger hierarchies, might furnish the substance of the world. Alternatively, in Spinoza's scheme, divine substance and extended substance might be considered the same entity, within which all apparent divisions, including individual minds, had the status only of modes. This philosophical inventiveness is typical of the greatest period of metaphysics in our philosophical history.

Other challenges to traditional natural philosophy were motivated by the study of motion and its explanation. This involved a change of perspective in which the local motion of bodies was no longer explained by 'causes', but by patterns in changes in natural phenomena that were described as laws (Chapter 2). Two of the parameters by which motion was specified were space and time, which were reconceptualized on the basis of studies in terrestrial and celestial mechanics, especially by Galileo, Leibniz, and Newton (Chapter 3). The underlying interpretation of the natural world as 'mechanical' is examined in Chapter 4. Although those who used the term 'mechanical' failed to agree on a unique definition, their shared allegiance even to a polyvalent ideal encouraged natural philosophers, from Vesalius to Spinoza, to consider whether living beings, including animals, could be understood as biological machines that did not require a distinct 'principle of life' or soul to explain their complex functioning (Chapter 5). All these innovations can be seen collectively as a gradual substitution of the categorial framework of Aristotle by one derived from the experimental and mathematical sciences. This also involved abandoning the assumption that we perceive reality adequately by means of the unaided senses, and that an ultimate ontological description of reality is expressed exclusively by familiar terms in ordinary language. The traditional epistemic relation between natural philosophy and metaphysics thereby began a long-term reversal.

The Aristotelian tradition accommodated a hierarchy of souls, vegetative, sensitive, and rational, and ascribed life even to the stars, while Christians held the immortality of the soul as an article of faith that was revealed in the New Testament. Both presuppositions were called into question in early modern philosophy, and this opened up a variety of new positions for philosophers. Souls were said by Descartes to be restricted to individual human beings, by Leibniz to be omnipresent in matter, and were even mooted, by Gassendi, Hobbes, and Locke, to be material or products of the activity of matter. Consequently, the immortality of souls was both questioned and vigorously asserted (Chapter 6). Major revisions to the Cartesian doctrine included the notion that all ideas, and not only sensations and emotions, were caused or occasioned by states of the brain, and that other nonhuman animals had ideas in the sense of episodes of awareness and perhaps some rudimentary capacity to reason. Locke argued that the notion of the self did not depend on its being a distinct substance. The self could be grasped either introspectively as a primitive, but momentary datum of awareness, or criteriologically for the purposes of establishing responsibility for past actions.

The seventeenth century can also be seen, in retrospect, as embracing what Bishop Stillingfleet, in his reproach of Locke, called 'the new way of ideas', in which ideas were identified with mental events in human minds—sensory, perceptual, emotional or intellectual. Descartes, Arnauld, and Locke were prominently associated with this innovation. In contrast, Malebranche continued to locate ideas primarily in the divine mind, and to describe human thinking as an activity by which God's ideas are made available, in some way, to human minds (Chapter 7). Thanks, meanwhile, to developments in optics and the theory of vision, qualities, which had been classified as real entities in the Aristotelian scheme, were recognized as products of mind–body interaction that were observer-dependent. This raised the question how the reality behind the appearances was to be described (Chapter 8). Scientific instruments, especially the telescope and microscope, broadened the range of experience and made the conclusion inevitable that the optical images available to human eyes were limited to those of the middle-sized world. The passions could now be treated dispassionately, as possessing anatomical and physiological correlates and as part of the basic equipment of the living creature, and even as useful. Stoic ideals of impassivity and repression, though still important for philosophers like Spinoza, gave way to more favourable treatments of the emotions (Chapter 9). Aesthetics, no longer identified with the formal rules of poetic and dramatic construction and rhetorical technique, became a branch of psychology in which new references to taste, perfection, and harmony reinforced the emphasis on personal experience and judgement that was common to the natural and the human sciences of the period (Chapter 10).

Section III discusses some of the developments in epistemology, logic, language, and mathematics that facilitated or reflected the practices that helped shape the new natural philosophy. Inquirers faced a plethora of information and lore that required sifting to distinguish truth from error or superstition from credible tradition. The popularity of writings by Pierre Charron and Michel de Montaigne in the early seventeenth century provided the immediate inspiration, for authors from Gassendi and Descartes to Bayle, to search for a balance between extreme scepticism and what was often described as the dogmatism of the Schools (Chapter 11). It also motivated others, such as Pascal, to resort to fideism and the conviction that reliable knowledge was available only through divine revelation. The new mechanical philosophy, which was based on the posit of invisible corpuscles and their interactions, no longer provided for knowledge of essences that is derived *a priori*; it was thus impossible to make the transition to the new concept of nature while maintaining an Aristotelian definition of knowledge as 'demonstration'. Hence the added urgency to redefine human knowledge so that uncertainty became one of its inevitable and acceptable features, and certainty was replaced by probability as an adequate achievement in knowledge of the natural world (Chapter 12).

The study of language and its relations to thought occupied many early modern philosophers, beginning with Bacon, who railed against the stilted and empty vocabulary of the Aristotelian Schools and the colourful metaphors of the occult, alchemical philosophy. Philosophers rejected rhetoric, demanding clarity and precision, and sought to convert language into a precise instrument for representing and communicating thoughts (Chapter 13). The concept of a proof or demonstration had been a fundamental feature of Aristotle's logic, on which innumerable commentaries were published and which was taught to generations of students. However, as Galileo had argued, the language in which the natural world was understood in the new sciences was mathematics, and this implied that the logic of the sciences could not be restricted to one that modelled the reasoning of Aristotelian physics. Chapter 14 traces the development of an ideal of 'method' that was inspired by Lull and subsequently found new expressions in many of the proponents of a new science, such as Bacon and Descartes. This required new mathematical methods, and new notations that facilitated developments in algebra and geometry.

The new natural philosophy also required a range of other 'instruments of knowledge' (Chapter 15). They included not just physical instruments, such as the telescope or microscope, but all those epistemological instruments by which human cognitive faculties were trained, extended, or otherwise emended to exploit their innate capacities to acquire knowledge. These instruments included new mathematical techniques that were developed by Descartes, Newton, and Leibniz, and they threw into sharp relief a fundamental issue that could no longer be evaded. The validity of inferences had been traditionally confirmed by their transparency; there was an expectation that one could 'see' how each step in a proof followed from its predecessor. The absence of such transparency or picturability, especially in the infinitesimal calculus, raised a question about whether the validity of mathematical techniques must be tested by comparison with the intuitive inferences of traditional logic, or whether the results achieved by employing such instruments justified their use and thereby extended the scope of what should be described as 'rational' (Chapter 16).

For morals and politics, the new philosophy of nature was equally consequential. Virtue and vice remained fundamental categories for the moralist, and Stoic and ascetic Christian ideals continued to be influential, especially amongst philosophers in the Cartesian tradition. They were softened, however, by an awakening interest in the social emotions, and in the relationship between moral goodness and happiness (Chapter 17). The postulate that human beings were fractious, covetous, and endowed with a strong drive towards self-aggrandizement was associated with Hobbes, and his writings produced a strong counterflow in the form of assertions and demonstrations of altruism and benevolence as natural endowments of human beings (Chapter 18). The doctrine that qualities are perceiver-relative, combined with an increased awareness of other ages and cultures, made moral relativism an attractive position, even while its less attractive implications were grasped at the same time (Chapter 19). The problem of moral and legal responsibility became acute as the mechanical philosophy, thanks especially to Hobbes, was extended to human psychology; as a result human choices, rather than being represented as acts of an autonomous faculty (the will), were explained in terms of desires and preferences, a position that was intolerable to theologians (Chapter 20).

Paradoxically, both scepticism and Cartesianism provided new arguments to establish the equal capabilities and entitlements of women and men (Chapter 21); this conclusion was assuredly not available under the Aristotelian assumption that entities were form–matter composites, and that women were less perfect animals than men and required to be ruled by them. In this debate, traditional metaphysics was seen once again to support prejudices rather than evidence-based arguments. More broadly, the conviction that the theory of government ought to be made independent of theology and metaphysics and derived from the conditions of human flourishing prompted a reexamination of the natural law tradition (Chapter 22), and fostered new accounts of citizenship, subjecthood, and monarchy that laid the groundwork for republican conceptions of the balance of powers and, after centuries of warfare and massacre over religious division, a demand for toleration, liberty of conscience, and free speech (Chapter 23).

The role of faith-transcending reason and the proper attitude to take towards the paradoxes and evidence-transcendent posits of Christianity: transubstantiation, the Trinity, the resurrection, reward and punishment of the dead, heritable original sin, all required rethinking in the early modern period, and the final section considers three issues that were prominent in philosophical discussions of religion. Chapter 24 examines three ways in which God was conceptualized by leading philosophers of the period. The rationalist God was conceived, by Leibniz and Malebranche, by analogy with a rational human being whose actions are explained by their purposes; the voluntarist God, in contrast, was conceived by Descartes and Arnauld, as not being constrained by anything that we might describe as reason. Finally, Spinoza equated God with an eternally existing, infinite nature. The diversity in the objects or content of religious belief was matched by a similar diversity in epistemic descriptions of faith. The challenge to a centralized teaching authority or *magisterium* that originated in the reformed Christian churches coincided with developments in biblical studies that offered new interpretations of the Scriptures, on which Christian teaching had been based for centuries. When combined with parallel reviews of what had formerly been the dominant ideal of knowledge, these revolutionary changes within different Christian churches highlighted the question whether religious belief is a special kind of knowledge, or whether its status should be described in other terms (Chapter 25).

The political implications of the diversity of religious beliefs within emerging nation-states soon became apparent in discussions of religious toleration, especially where it had been accepted that the religious affiliation of rulers should determine that of their subjects. Chapter 26 examines the implications for religious toleration of various non-cognitive views of religious belief, especially those adopted by Hobbes, Spinoza, Locke, and Bayle. Even for those for whom religious belief was a form of knowledge that made claims about transcendent truths, the sheer diversity of churches and creeds, and the obvious consequences of intolerance, helped to foster a form of religious toleration that reflected the theory of limited political authority, based on the consent of citizens, that was defended by Locke at the end of the seventeenth century.

Surveying our volume we are aware that there are important philosophical issues in the early modern period that we were unable to address adequately or indeed at all; correspondingly, it is inevitable that, in a volume such as this, discussions in one chapter will overlap with those of others. We hope that the detection of our omissions will encourage readers to fill those lacunae with new research and future publications, and that cross-references to chapters or pages that discuss related topics will assist readers who consult the book selectively.

# PART I

## METAPHYSICS AND NATURAL PHILOSOPHY

# CHAPTER 1

..............................................................................................................

# ESSENCES AND KINDS

..............................................................................................................

## PETER R. ANSTEY

PHILOSOPHERS, at least since Aristotle, have had a set of ontological categories by which to account for the natures (or essences) of things and to classify them into kinds. To be sure, the Aristotelian categories have been interpreted in various ways and have been augmented and diminished by philosophers. But the notions of substance, attribute, relation, genus, and species have, on the whole, proven to be resilient as tools for the analysis of natures and kinds. This is particularly true of the seventeenth century when, in spite of the remarkable changes that occurred then and the variety of views that were proposed concerning essences and kinds, these categories provided the basic constituents of all analyses.

However, these categories were merely the basic building blocks from which a theory of natures and kinds was to be constructed. For, a moment's reflection brings to bear a host of distinctions and other issues that need to be addressed if one is to understand natures and kinds. First, the phenomena seem to have natural divisions: animate/inanimate; natural/artifactual; animal/vegetable/mineral; parent/offspring; solid/liquid; and so on. Second, there are natural associations within and across these obvious divisions: red flowers and insects; spherical fruit and hailstones; quadrupeds; metals; and so on. Third, there are obvious hierarchies, such as hierarchies of sensitivity and rationality from sensitive plants to conscious humans. Fourth, within each of these classes, divisions, and hierarchies, it seems that each individual, each token cat or rat, each token of gold or pineapple, has its own special nature which makes it what it is in itself. Fifth, every token is subject to change and interacts with other things. Some things have powers while others seem completely passive or inert. Some sorts always behave in the same way, while others are unpredictable. Sixth, it was widely known in the seventeenth century that there are many things that are too small or too far away for us to perceive, and yet these unperceived things also have natures and behave in certain ways. For better or for worse for the early moderns, a theory of essences and a theory of kinds had to provide a comprehensive explanation of all of these phenomena.

If this were not demanding enough, most early modern philosophers also operated within certain constraints, often theological, and they did so in a context in which new phenomena and theories were appearing all the time. For some, a theory of essences had to be compatible with the doctrine of transubstantiation; for others it had to account for the discovery of universal gravity; for still others it had to accommodate the discovery of spermatozoa or new evidence concerning spontaneous generation. It is little wonder then that both theories of essence and theories of kinds (for they almost always went together) that were developed in the seventeenth century are enormously rich and varied and that they provide a kind of gateway into almost every facet of early modern metaphysics and epistemology.

Yet amidst the complexity and diversity of views some players and some theories were more important than others, and this chapter provides an overview of the emergence of the most important and influential approach to essences and kinds. This is the analysis of the essence of all material substances *solely* in terms of corpuscular structure, a structure which, it was claimed, is also the basis for the sorting of token substances into species or kinds. It was the most important type of theory because of its immediate influence and subsequent legacy (Ellis 2001: 55), and because it represented a significant break with the type of scholastic theory that had dominated philosophy of essences and kinds in the late Renaissance. It is the theory associated with René Descartes, Robert Boyle, and John Locke. To be sure, there are other important and interesting theories of essence and species from the period, such as that developed by Spinoza and the series of views developed by Leibniz in the final decades of the century. However, relative to the corpuscular structure theories, they were outliers in terms of impact.

This chapter examines in turn the views of Descartes, Boyle, and Locke, outlining the polemical stances that motivate and direct each of their views and their accounts of essences and kinds. It examines the ontological categories to which they subscribed and their own speculative theories about the actual kinds in the world. The cumulative effect of treating these three philosophers chronologically creates a sense of the organic and integrated nature of the emergence of the theory of essences as corpuscular structures.

# I: The late-Aristotelian theory of substantial forms[1]

There are three questions that any account of essences and kinds has to answer. First, what is it that makes a thing what it is? That is, what is it that gives a thing its specificity or, as Locke put it, what is 'the very being of any thing, whereby it is, what it is'? (*Essay* III. iii. 15). Second, what is it that makes a thing a member of a species or kind? And third, do that which makes a thing what it is and that which accounts for species membership have a role in the generation of members of a species?

By the late Renaissance there was a broad array of answers to these three questions. There were atomist accounts of essence, there were accounts deriving from the new chymical matter theories such as that of Paracelsus, there was a host of views based on Aristotelian categories and matter theory, and there were composite views which explained essences and kinds by appeal both to corpuscular structures and Aristotelian forms. The predominant view, however, was that one particular type of entity was responsible for determining the natures of things and for species membership. This was the substantial form.

Substantial forms were commonly thought to account for the unity of the properties that were necessary for a thing to have the particular nature it in fact has. But substantial forms were not conceived merely as passive bonds or the ontological ground of the unity of an object's properties; they were also used to account for the consistent behaviours of individual things. For example, many substances consistently tend to their 'natural state': the tendency of water to return to the liquid state is explained in terms of the operation of its substantial form. Thus, substantial forms were thought by many to be a kind of internal efficient cause that acted to sustain the integrity of the particular thing and to be the cause of its retaining its specific nature. Finally, substantial forms were thought to be those things which are replicated in generation and destroyed in corruption. But this needed to be balanced with the view held by many, namely, that the underlying elements of material things could transmute into one another.

It is clear then that, for the late Scholastics, substantial forms were called on to do plenty of explanatory work. They were at once the core of essential explanations, of causal explanations of behaviour and change, the *explanans* of modal claims about individuals and species, and they played a role in the definitions of kinds. In all of this they were also subject to the court of observation and experiment. It was primarily this latter constraint, and in particular the phenomena of chymical

---

[1] For more detailed treatments of the late-scholastic theories as background to Descartes see Des Chene 1996, ch. 3; Ariew and Grene 1999; Pasnau 2004.

and generative processes, that led to the proliferation of forms in the beginning of the early modern period. To many a single substantial form could not fulfil all the roles required of it, and pluralist theories emerged. Indeed, the distinction between the pluralists and 'uni-formists' marks a major fault line amongst the proponents of substantial forms in the period leading up to Descartes and his heirs.

# II: DESCARTES

Descartes (1596–1650) was a critic of substantial forms, but he never developed a systematic critique of the scholastic theory. Rather he invested his energies in developing an alternative account of essence and presumed that it would be favoured by his readers on the grounds of comparative plausibility.[2] Moreover, Descartes' theory was not only designed as an alternative to the scholastic view but it was also pitted against atomism. Descartes develops his metaphysics of substance and essence fighting on more than one front.

As for the central questions that define the problem of essence and kinds, the Frenchman was deeply concerned with the first question: What is it that gives a thing with 'real being' its particular nature?[3] Surprisingly, his writings contain no sustained treatment of the second question: he shows little interest in kinds or species. He does, however, address the third question about the replication of substances of particular kinds. His discussions of this issue were strongly empirical, but were only published posthumously and it is clear that he found the problem insoluble. Therefore, our focus here is Descartes' theory of essences.

Descartes' approach to the question of the nature of essence comprises a blend of explanatory, modal, and definitional considerations. He appropriates the main scholastic categories, including the substance/attribute distinction and the category of modes (which he probably derived from Suárez), but puts these categories to his own uses. The result is that Descartes formulates an innovative and influential rival theory to the scholastic account of substantial forms.

Now there has been much controversy over how Descartes' categories are to be interpreted, and space precludes a full justification of the interpretation offered here. It is also clear that Descartes' views changed over time. The following interpretation takes as its starting point the mature view expressed in his *Principles of Philosophy* (1644). Our way into this aspect of Descartes' metaphysics is through

---

[2] The most extended critical discussion is in the letter to Regius, January 1642 (CSMK: 205–9).

[3] Descartes also develops an account of the natures of our ideas that have mere 'objective being', such as geometrical ideas, and an account of the relation between essence and existence. Neither of these Cartesian doctrines is discussed here.

a contemporary approach to the theory of properties. Of course, there is a danger of anachronism in this method, but this is outweighed by its explanatory potential. Indeed, it is now standard practice to use recent developments in the theory of properties, such as the distinction between determinables and determinates, to explicate Descartes' views (see Secada 2000; Chappell 2008).

Turning to Descartes, we find that the central notions in his theory of essence are the attributes of extension and thought. Interestingly, however, he seems to have two conceptions of the nature of extension and thought (Des Chene 1996: 345). On the one hand he seems to conceive of extension in fairly traditional terms as an attribute instantiated by substance. Descartes takes it that there are substances which are bearers of properties. At *Principles* 1 §53 he says,

To each substance there belongs one principal attribute; in the case of mind, this is thought, and in the case of body it is extension.

A substance may indeed be known through any attribute at all; but each substance has one principal property which constitutes its nature and essence, and to which all its other properties are referred.   (CSM I: 210)

The salient relation here is instantiation: substance instantiates the attribute of extension or thought. On this view the substance gives particularity—it is the category that individuates—and extension (or thought) is a principal attribute. The primacy of, say, extension arises from its modes of shape, size, and motion (or rest). This is for two reasons. First, there is a set of tight connections of metaphysical necessity between extension and its modes and the modes themselves. Second, all other properties are reducible to the modes of the primary attributes. It is clear then that, on this view, extension functions like the substantial form of a material substance. Extension is the nature or essence of material substance and the ground of unity of the attributes of that substance.

It is not entirely clear, however, just how the modes stand in relation to the principal attribute. What does Descartes mean when he speaks of the modes and the attributes of extension (*Principles* 1 §§54, 65)? One explanation might be to appeal to higher-order properties. This has proven to be very helpful in clarifying Descartes' conception of the determination of motion which is best analysed as a mode of a mode (McLaughlin 2000).

Let us suppose that first-order properties are those that are instantiated by a substance and that higher-order properties are properties of properties. On some recent theories determinables, such as colour or length, are higher-order properties: being a colour is a property of red, while red is a property of, say, a rose; being a length is a property of one metre, and one metre is a property of, say, a ruler. Thus we have higher-order properties ⇒ first-order properties ⇒ substances (Molnar 2003). Now if Descartes' determinables—shape, size, and motion—are modes of the primary attribute extension, then they seem to be higher-order properties of extension, and extension in turn, as a principal attribute of substance, might be conceived as a first-order property. But this is a strange view indeed. It seems far more natural to view the determinables, shape, size, and motion, as higher-order properties not of extension, but of determinate shapes, sizes, and motions. It also seems that material substances are extended in virtue of having a determinate shape and size, and that extension is just the higher-order disjunctive property of the determinables shape, size, and mobility. If this is correct then the determinables shape, size, and mobility are not properties of extension but are constituents of extension. Our talk of an extended substance is equivalent to talk of a particular thing having some shape, size, and motion or rest.

A more promising approach is Descartes' alternative conception of the primary attributes. In some places Descartes seems to conceive of matter as a kind of stuff such that when he claims that material substance is extension he has in mind the 'is' of constitution. The key passage is *Principles* 1 §63: 'How thought and extension may be distinctly recognized as constituting the nature of mind and of body. Thought and extension can be regarded as constituting the natures of intelligent substance and corporeal substance; they must then be considered as nothing else but thinking substance itself and extended substance itself—that is, as mind and body' (CSM I: 215). On this view substances are individuated by the determinate modes that modify the underlying stuff (Normore 2008). The salient relation here between the primary attribute and its modes is modification. As he puts it in *Principles* 1 §56: 'By *mode*, as used above, we understand exactly the same as what is elsewhere meant by an *attribute* or *quality*. But we employ the term *mode* when we are thinking of a substance as being affected or modified' (CSM I: 211). Extended stuff is modified in so far as it has determinate shape, size, and motion (or rest).

This view seems to make sense of Descartes' claim that shape, size, and motion are modes of extension and of Descartes' claim that there is only a conceptual distinction between substance and extension.

Indeed, it is much easier for us to have an understanding of extended substance or thinking substance than it is for us to understand substance on its own, leaving out the fact that it thinks or is extended. For we have some difficulty in abstracting the notion of substance from the notions of thought and extension, since the distinction between these notions and the notion of substance itself is merely a conceptual distinction. (*Principles* 1 §63; CSM I: 215)

There is, therefore, some vacillation in the *Principles* between instantiation and constitution at the level of principal attributes and between instantiation and modification at the level of modes. This is indicative of the fact that Descartes does not develop the metaphysics of his theory of essence in a systematic manner.

There are four advantages that accrue from establishing extension and thought as principal attributes. First, like the scholastic substantial form, they can account for the unity of the essential or defining properties of the substance. This is because of the necessary connections between the modes of, say, extension. There is a tightly knit group of modes which stand or fall together. They are, in the case of extended substance, shape, size, and motion or rest. Second, in the light of Descartes' identification of space with extended substance, this unity of the determinables can be the basis of two exclusion theses; no other substance can instantiate the modes of extension, and all attributes over and above the determinate shapes, sizes, and motions are accidents.

Furthermore, it is a fact for Descartes that there are just two principal attributes, extension and thought. This, in turn, enables the stipulation of a strict substance dualism and a doctrine of complete concepts—ideas of essences are clear and distinct. This brings us to the third advantage, namely, that the natures of the two types of substance can be grasped by the pure intellect. It is only the determinate shape, size, and motion of a particular material substance that must be perceived by the senses. Each type of substance has a small finite set of modes which necessitate each other and in so doing constitute an exclusive unity that the intellect can conceive as a complete, clear, and distinct concept. Descartes goes so far as to say 'I do not know any other pair of ideas in the whole of nature which are as different from each other as these two' (CSMK: 188). Indeed, according to Descartes, it is the conflation of these two ideas that led to the notion of substantial form in the first place. It is these principal attributes that Descartes calls essences. They are the entities that in Descartes' ontology do the work of substantial forms.

The fourth advantage of making extension a principal attribute is that extension's modes can become the basis for a sparse theory of qualities. As Descartes puts it in the *Principles* 4 §198:

the properties in external objects to which we apply the terms light, colour, smell, taste, sound, heat and cold—as well as the other tactile qualities and even what are called 'substantial forms'—are, so far as we can see, simply various dispositions in the shapes, sizes, positions and movements of their parts which make them able to set up various kinds of motions in our nerves (CSM 1: 285).

On the Cartesian view all qualities are reducible to the determinate shapes, sizes, and motions of the constituent parts of objects. Just as extension can function as an alternative to a substantial form, it can also become the ontological ground for the kind of sparse theory of qualities which is one of the appealing features of atomism. With one cunning move then, Descartes has accrued to his own theory the great strengths of his rivals.

There are some costs, however, and some of these impinge on the adequacy of his metaphysics to answer our three questions about essences and kinds. The first and most pressing cost arises from the fact that there is nothing to the Cartesian notion of essences over and above this dichotomous division between extension and thought. In particular, there is no use for the notion of species over and above the question of which essence (extension or thought) pertains to a particular substance. In Descartes' ontology there are just two species over and above the *sui generis* substance God: matter and minds. But surely there are kinds within nature, kinds that call out for explanation. What are the ontological grounds of the plethora of equivalence classes that we perceive in nature and for which our language has evolved special semantic categories?

Descartes appears to have little interest in the question of species membership, but the resources are there for an account of higher-order essences which will be cashed out in terms of corpuscular arrangement or structure (*Principles* 2 §23; CSM 1: 232–3; Letter to Regius, CSMK: 207). Descartes does not pursue this development of his theory, which was to be the distinguishing feature of Boyle's account of essence. However, Descartes did pursue a separate line of inquiry in his exploration of the phenomena of animal generation. This led him to postulate a theory of *semina* which account for the propagation of species, but in the final analysis, he found this problem insoluble (Aucante 2006).

A second cost is that Descartes' treatment of thought and its modes is developed as an analogue of extended substance, but in the case of thought there is not the same tight modal structure between its modes. In fact, not only is there an asymmetry between Descartes' conceptions of extended and thinking substance, but, ironically, in some places he gestures towards an essentialist analysis of the relationship between the human body and mind that explicitly invokes the terminology of scholastic forms. In fact, the most natural interpretation of the relevant texts is that Descartes has a hylomorphic conception of the union of the body and the soul in which the soul functions as the substantial form of the body (see Hoffman 2009).

# III: ROBERT BOYLE

Robert Boyle (1627–91) was far more polemical in the development of his views on essences and kinds than was Descartes. He tells us in his major treatment of the subject, his *Origin of Forms and Qualities* (1666; 2nd edn 1667), that he has consulted 'both of the more, and of the lesse recent Scholastical Writers about Physicks, and . . . some of the best Metaphysicians to boot, that I might better inform my self, both what their Opinions are, and upon what arguments they are grounded' (B 5, 290 = S 5). *Forms and Qualities* is a sustained critique of the notion of a substantial form (and real qualities) for its lack of explanatory adequacy and ontological economy. Boyle was also far more inclined to bring observational evidence to bear on scholastic metaphysics than his French forebear. Thus, *Forms and Qualities* contains a substantial 'historical' section that is replete with chymical and other observations which, Boyle believes, bear on the question of the nature and origins of forms and qualities. Importantly, the appendix to the second edition of *Forms and Qualities* contains a critique of a prominent pluralist view of substantial forms in the work of Daniel Sennert. Scholars vary in their evaluations of the accuracy and adequacy of Boyle's attack on substantial forms, but what is undeniable is that it is the most sustained and influential case against scholastic essences mounted by a proponent of the new philosophy.

Yet Boyle was also a critic of certain facets of the Cartesian view of essences. To be sure, he accepts Cartesian substance dualism insisting on 'there being but two sorts of Substances, Material, and Immaterial' (B 5, 343 = S 57). However, this was not motivated by Cartesian principles. Instead he viewed Descartes' theory in traditional terms, as stipulating necessary and sufficient conditions for the essential properties of matter. He had serious reservations concerning the sufficiency of extension as the defining property of matter, and inclined to the view that impenetrability was also an essential property of material substance (B 12, 391; 8, 308 = S 202; B 5, 333 = S 50). Thus, he was neutral on the question as to whether matter was continuous and whether vacua are possible. In fact, this neutrality was one of the defining characteristics of his corpuscular philosophy, which was a kind of *via media* between Cartesianism and Gassendi's atomism. Importantly, however, Boyle follows Descartes in making an exception of the human soul from his critique of substantial forms (B 5, 300, 340–3 = S 15, 53–8; B 5, 454). In this respect Boyle retained a limited role for hylomorphism in his philosophy.

The Boylean attack on substantial forms takes the form of a master argument from comparative plausibility and as such it includes a detailed exposition of Boyle's own positive alternative theory. The master argument itself has three components. First, it contains an argument from *comparative intelligibility* which, in turn, is founded on a cluster of claims about the nature of natural philosophical explanation. Second, it contains a critique of various components of the Aristotelian theory that undergirds the doctrine of substantial forms. Boyle criticized the Aristotelian real qualities, the distinctions between art and nature and between natural and violent states, as well as what he took to be the attribution of sentience to matter, but space precludes any discussion of these criticisms here (see Newman 2004: 271–83; Anstey 2000: ch. 5). Third, Boyle's master argument contains extensive interpretations of chymical phenomena which Boyle claims are more consistent with the corpuscularian theory of form than the traditional view. Let us turn then to Boyle's positive theory of forms.

One of Boyle's claims against the doctrine of substantial forms is that material bodies are denominated by their qualities and not by an entity to which we lack epistemic access (B 5, 322–3 = S 38). He then claims that while all qualities are accidents with respect to matter itself, with respect to particular bodies they may well be essential such that 'an Aggregate or Convention of Qualities is enough to make the portion of Matter 'tis found in, what it is, and denominate it of this or that Determinate sort of Bodies.' This is what Boyle calls form: 'such a Convention of Accidents is sufficient to perform the Offices that are necessarily requir'd in what Men call a Forme' (B 5, 324 = S 40; cf. B 5, 461–2). That Boyle has a robust essentialism in mind here is reinforced by the claim that 'though the concurrent Qualities be but Accidental to Matter... yet they are *essentially necessary* to the Particular *Body*, which without those Accidents would not be a Body of that Denomination, as a *Mettal* or a *Stone*, but of some other' (B 5, 334 = S 52). What makes a thing what it is and at the same time renders it a sort of thing is a convention of accidental qualities and nothing more.

However, like Descartes, Boyle has a sparse theory of qualities; he believed that all qualities are reducible to the primary or mechanical affections (not qualities!) of matter, namely, shape, size, motion, and texture. Thus, it is not surprising to find later in *Forms and Qualities* Boyle speaks as if the form is equivalent to the determinate mechanical affections of a body: 'the Form of a Natural Body, being according to us, but an Essential Modification, and, as it were, the *Stamp* of its Matter, or such a convention of the Bigness, Shape, Motion (or Rest), Scituation and Contexture (together with the thence resulting Qualities) of the small parts that compose the Body' (B 5, 353 = S 69). It is clear then that, for Boyle, *form* can be defined in terms of phenomenal qualities or underlying micro-structure, though the weight of textual evidence suggests that it was the qualities rather than mechanical affections which are the primary referent of the term. This is reinforced by the fact that Boyle acknowledges that the boundaries between species can be unclear, and that there is an element of convention in the articulation of that cluster of essential qualities. It is 'very much by a kind of tacit agreement, that Men had distinguish'd the *Species* of Bodies, and that those Distinctions were more Arbitrary then we are wont to be aware of' (B 5, 356 = S 72). The conventional character of our denominations of species arises from the fact that they are made on the basis of phenomenal qualities and not on the basis of an understanding of their underlying structure.

As it stands, this theory of essences and kinds is fairly humdrum and not much of an advance on the Democritean or Epicurean view. But once we begin to unpack the contents of Boyle's master argument and as we explore his own speculative theory and empirical arguments, the theory emerges as a significant rival to the scholastic view. Boyle was committed to a general reduction principle, namely, that all observable phenomena are to be explained by the nature of the unobservable parts of matter. It might be objected that this places him in the same epistemic predicament as the Aristotelian who openly admits that they do not have immediate epistemic access to substantial forms. But Boyle is committed to other explanatory principles which, he argues, place his theory in a stronger position. First, he is committed to the contact criterion, namely, that all change is brought about through collisions of matter in motion. Second, he believes that natural philosophical explanations should proceed by analogy with the functioning of machines. Third, and most importantly, he is committed to what may be called the

Familiarity Condition, that is the explanatory constraint that one can only posit qualities, affections and laws at the unobservable level that one is familiar with at the observable level. And fourth, he is committed to a sparse Cartesian-style theory of qualities such that all qualities, observable and unobservable alike, are reducible to the mechanical affections of shape, size, motion, and texture. The implications of these theses for comparative intelligibility are clear:

I do not remember, that either *Aristotle* himself, (who perhaps scarce ever attempted it,) or any of his Followers, has given a solid and intelligible solution of any one *Phænomenon* of Nature by the help of substantial Forms; which you need not think it strange I should say, since the greatest Patrons of Forms acknowledg their Nature to be unknown to Us, to explain any Effect by a substantial Form, must be to declare (as they speak) *ignotum per ignotius*, or at least *per æquè ignotum*. And indeed to explicate a *Phænomenon*, being to deduce it from something else in Nature more known to Us, then the thing to be explain'd by It, how can the imploying of Incomprehensible (or at least Uncomprehended) substantial Forms help Us to explain intelligibly This or That particular *Phænomenon*? For to say, that such an Effect proceeds not from this or that Quality of the Agent, but from its substantial Form, is to take an easie way to resolve all difficulties in general, without rightly resolving any one in particular; and would make a rare Philosophy, if it were not far more easie then satisfactory   (B 5, 351–2 = S 67–8).

The defender of substantial forms could, of course, run a *modus tollens* argument against Boyle, denying the Familiarity Condition and stressing the explanatory efficacy of substantial forms, in spite of our ignorance of their natures. They could accept that, if the Familiarity Condition were true, there would be no substantial forms. However, we have reason to believe that there are substantial forms because they have such strong explanatory power; therefore, we must deny the consequent and conclude that the Familiarity Condition is false. Yet, Boyle's condition does not stand alone, but is deployed in his empirical, natural philosophical, arguments against substantial forms. Indeed, it was these arguments that constituted, for Boyle, the real polemical power of his corpuscularianism and which clinched the case for comparative plausibility. We need then to turn to Boyle's speculative corpuscular theory.

The central speculative claim in Boyle's philosophy is that the irreducible constituents that function in chymical reactions, that is, the 'chymical atoms' are themselves concretions of an underlying homogeneous matter that retain their structural arrangement through analysis by fire or chymical corrosives (Newman 2009). These allow Boyle to retain a primitive or elementary form within matter and thus to avoid the consequences of a commitment to a completely permissive mereology. Furthermore, Boyle was committed to a conception of laws of nature that, while divinely imposed, could account for the regularities observed in the behaviours of material bodies and thus for one of the functions ascribed to substantial forms.

The details of Boyle's empirical arguments against substantial forms have been carefully explicated by William Newman (Newman 2006). Boyle has three types of empirical argument against substantial forms and in favour of corpuscularian forms. First, he argues from redintegration experiments, particularly the redintegration of nitre, that this is best accounted for by the texture resulting from the recombination of preexistent chymical atoms and not substantial forms. Second, he argues from the reduction to the pristine state for the same conclusion. For example, the process by which gold and silver are fused and then the silver is dissolved out and precipitated such that the silver is reduced to its pristine state, is better explained in corpuscularian terms than by appeal to substantial forms. Third, he argues from the mechanical production and alteration of qualities for the superiority of the corpuscularian theory of qualities and therefore for the hypothesis itself. It will suffice here to give only a summary presentation of one such argument.

The argument against substantial forms from the redintegration of nitre was not the strongest chymical argument that Boyle brought against hylomorphic matter theory, but it was certainly the most important in development of his own views. It is also of historical interest in so far as it is the focal point of Boyle's correspondence (via Henry Oldenburg) with Spinoza, though Spinoza was surprised that Boyle should bother to use it 'to show the weak foundation of the puerile and trivial doctrine of substantial forms and qualities' (Spinoza to Oldenburg, 17 July 1663, Oldenburg 1965–86: 2, 92). The experiment itself involved the resynthesis of saltpetre (potassium carbonate). First the saltpetre is separated into a volatile spirit and a fixed salt and then spirit of nitre (nitric acid) was dropped onto the fixed salt and saltpetre, roughly equal in weight to the original sample, was reconstituted with exactly the same qualities. The natural interpretation of the reaction was that saltpetre had been broken down into its two constituents and then reconstituted again. However, according to the Scholastics saltpetre was a product of nature and therefore had a substantial form. They also believed that once a substantial form is destroyed it is impossible for the matter immediately to instantiate it again without passing through the stages that led to the formation of the original substance in the first place. Boyle's conclusion was that the natural inference is that there is no form of saltpetre but that its qualities arise from the texture which results from the combination of its constituents.

Thus, Boyle had an account of what form is according to the corpuscular philosophy, an account which furnished him with an answer to our first question about what it is that makes a thing what it is. He also had an answer to the question of species membership: members of species are denominated by the same group of essential qualities which arise from the same or similar underlying corpuscular structures. However, Boyle realized that this was not sufficient to provide a full answer to the third question. Boyle needed an explanation of the replication of corpuscular structure and this remained an acute problem for his natural philosophy. The phenomena of spontaneous generation and of the generation of minerals, plants and animals, required further speculative solutions on Boyle's part, speculations which clearly show the limits of his hypothesis.

Like virtually all of his contemporaries, Boyle posited the existence of seminal principles to account for the replication of form. He developed a theory of the origin of these seeds at the creation of the world and then explored, both experimentally and theoretically, the application of the theory of *semina* to mineralogy or petrifaction, the generation of plants and the generation of animals. According to Boyle, at the creation God fashioned protoplasts which he then impregnated with seed. These protoplasts were designed to propagate their own kind in the animal and vegetable kingdoms and possibly the mineral kingdom as well.

It is clear that Boyle conceived of seminal principles as corpuscular structures which, while submicroscopic in size, were, under the right conditions, able to work to replicate the respective protoplasts from which they arose, protoplasts that themselves contained *semina* with the same plastic or formative powers. Boyle even considers them a kind of subordinate form that are 'small parcels of Matter of such a texture, that though whilst they remain associated with the other parts of the compounded body, they are not by sense . . . distinguishable from the rest of the compounded body' (B 5, 457).

Naturally the question arose as to how these seminal principles operate and here Boyle was caught on the horns of a nasty dilemma. On the one hand, if he were to claim that they operate mechanically, this would appear to undermine the reason for which they were introduced in the first place. On the other hand, apart from God's divine concurrence, Boyle was loath to introduce non-mechanical causes into his natural philosophy. In the final analysis, Boyle had to declare his nescience as to the mode of operation of seminal principles, as he puts it in a discussion of the regularity of crystalline bodies in *Certain Physiological Essays* '[w]e deny not then, that these effects depend most commonly upon an internal principle, but the difficulty consists in conceiving how that internal principle produces its effects' (B 2, 192; cf. Anstey 2002).

One such effect which preoccupied Boyle for four decades was the result of the liberation of the seminal agent or internal principle that was responsible for the generation of gold. Boyle aspired to acquire the secrets of chrysopoeia, that is, gold making. His commitment to mercurial transmutational chymistry, which he learned from the American émigré George Starkey, led him on a quest for the Philosophical Mercury which was reputed to be able to 'cleanse' and 'liberate' gold (see Principe 1998; Newman and Principe 2002). Now Boyle's alchemical interests and activities may seem remote from his corpuscular theory of form, but they do imply a commitment to the existence of determinate metalline species and natural, if imperceptible, mechanisms for their replication. More importantly, however, they also provide a link to the philosopher who developed the most elaborate and important theory of essences in the early modern period. This philosopher is John Locke.

# IV: JOHN LOCKE

John Locke (1632–1704) came under the tutelage of Boyle in Oxford around 1659/60 and the latter's influence on Locke was as extensive as it was profound. It is hardly surprising then to find that many of the features of Boyle's views of essences and kinds were adumbrations of the mature theory that Locke lays out in Book Three of his *Essay concerning Human Understanding* (1690; 4th edn 1700). Boyle's muted conventionalism, his sparse theory of qualities, his acceptance of our lack of epistemic access to determinate corpuscular structures, his emphasis on inner corpuscular structure as the foundation of qualities, are all found fully developed in Locke's account of essences and kinds.

Under the influence of Boyle, Locke adhered to a form of mercurialist transmutational chymistry and his recipe for Mercury of Antimony, an essential ingredient in the preparation of the Philosophical Mercury (and given in secret to Boyle), survives among Boyle's papers (Anstey 2010). In fact, Locke's chymical and medical notebooks reveal an implicit commitment to the kind of chymical essentialism entailed by Boyle's chymical atoms, that is, a commitment to stable corpuscular concretions distinguishable into kinds that are not reducible by any known form of analysis.

Moreover, in keeping with the popularity of seminal theories of disease in the mid-1660s in England, Locke explored the possibility that some diseases are caused by 'some small & subtile parcelles of matter which are apt to transmute far greater portions of matter into a new nature & new qualitys'. As to their mode of operation, Locke, like Boyle before him, had to confess his nescience: '[h]ow these small & insensible ferments, this potent Archeus works I confess I cannot satisfactorily comprehend' (Romanell 1984: 207, 208). Locke seems not to have developed the seminal theory of disease much further, but he continued to maintain a belief in seminal principles as theoretical entities which were responsible for some diseases and for the replication of form in minerals, vegetables, and animals. In a short primer on natural philosophy written near the end of his life he claims '[a]ll stones, metals, and minerals, are real vegetables; that is, grow organically from proper seeds, as well as plants' (Locke 1823: 3, 319). It is clear then, that not only did Locke believe that there are species in nature, but that like almost all natural philosophers of the period, he deployed a type of unobservable theoretical entity to explain their generation.

Like Boyle, Locke was also a critic of substantial forms, but his criticism of them in the *Essay* is far less sustained and thorough than that of his mentor. In his scattered comments on scholastic essences he stresses: that only those who have been brought up in the Schools conceive of essences as substantial forms and that for others kinds are identified by their qualities alone (*Essay* III. vi. 24; III. x. 14); that substantial forms are a classic example of people's tendency to reify the referents of general terms (*Essay* III. x. 14); and that the idea of a substantial form lacks any content and so is unintelligible (*Essay* II. xxxi. 6; III. iii. 17; III. vi. 10).

More specifically, what Locke objects to is the 'cookie-cutter' view of essences 'which supposes these *Essences*, as a certain number of Forms or Molds, wherein all natural Things, that exist, are cast' (*Essay* III. iii. 17). He grants that this view is a natural one for those who believe that 'Nature works regularly in the Production of Things, and sets the Boundaries to each of those *Species*, by giving exactly the same real internal Constitution to each individual' (*Essay* III. x. 20). But the 'frequent Productions of Monsters, in all the Species of Animals, and of Changelings' (*Essay* III. iii. 17; cf. III. x. 20–1) undermines this premise. Nature does not reproduce with a cookie-cutter but more organically such that there is variability within a species and such that tokens of a particular species can resemble members of another species more than they do their own. In fact, Locke considers it likely that there is really a continuum of creatures from the lowest to the most perfect wherein 'we see no Chasms, or Gaps' and that there is overlap in the properties of the consecutive links of the chain (*Essay* III. vi. 12). The implication is that the boundaries between species are fuzzy and indeterminate, a reality incompatible with the discrete moulds and casts of cookie-cutter-like substantial forms. This is reinforced by regular exceptions to reproductive isolation: Locke denies that 'the power of propagation in animals by mixture of Male and Female . . . keeps the supposed real *Species* distinct and entire'. He even believed himself to have seen 'the Issue of a Cat and a Rat . . . wherein Nature appear'd to have followed the Pattern of neither sort alone, but to have jumbled them both together' (*Essay* III. vi. 23)!

It is important, however, not to view Locke's strictures against substantial forms as the front line of a more general critique of species essentialism and, by implication, an exercise in ground clearing by way of preparation for an argument for species nominalism. For, as has been pointed out above, Locke himself was committed to a form of Boylean corpuscular essentialism and it is to his positive theory of essences that we now turn.

Locke famously distinguished between nominal and real essences. Nominal essences of substances are those clusters of simple ideas (or that complex, general idea) that are caused by the sensible qualities of objects. By contrast, real essences of substances are the inner constitutions or corpuscular structures of material objects which underlie and are the cause of the perceptible qualities of those objects. Thus 'the *nominal Essence* of *Gold*, is that complex *Idea* the word *Gold* stands for, let it be, for instance, a Body yellow, of a certain weight, malleable, fusible, and fixed. But the *real Essence* is the constitution of the insensible parts of that Body, on which those Qualities, and all other Properties of *Gold* depend' (*Essay* III. vi. 2). Locke even uses the distinctive Boylean term 'texture' to describe real essences (*Essay* III. vi. 9).

According to Locke, we denominate species not by their real essences but by their nominal essences: 'by which of those Essences it is, that *Substances are determined into* Sorts, or *Species*; and that 'tis evident, is *by the nominal Essence*' (*Essay* III. vi. 7). This is because, as Locke is at pains to point out, we do not have epistemic access to the real essences of material substances. Thus, Locke is a conventionalist about kinds, they are the 'Workmanship of the Understanding' (*Essay* III. iii. 12). However, Locke's is a constrained and a convergent conventionalism. It is constrained because the constituent ideas of the nominal essence of each type of substance are partially determined by the real essence of that substance, even though we do not have epistemic access to that real essence. Nominal essences are not formed in an *ad hoc* manner, nor are they arbitrary.

But though these *nominal Essences of Substances* are made by the Mind, they are *not yet made so arbitrarily, as those of mixed Modes*... the Mind, in making its complex *Ideas* of Substances, only follows Nature; and puts none together, which are not supposed to have an <u>union in Nature</u>. No body joins the Voice of a Sheep, with the Shape of a Horse; nor the Colour of Lead, with the Weight and Fixedness of Gold (*Essay* III. vi. 28, underlining added).

It is this 'union in Nature' that is the key notion here. Locke uses this expression frequently in his discussion of the nature of real essences in Book Three of the *Essay*. He also speaks in equivalent terms of '*The real Constitution of Things*, from which all their Properties flow, and <u>in which they all centre</u>' (*Essay* III. ix. 12; underlining added). On Locke's view then, the co-occurrence of the same cluster of ideas in the nominal essence of a substance has its cause in the real essence of the substance which is itself the cause, albeit unknown, of their union in nature.

Where Locke's essentialism departs from that of Boyle is that Locke is committed to the view that, for each sort of substance, there is no individual quality that is an essential characteristic of that kind (*Essay* III. vi. 4–6). Instead he appears to hold that of all of the ideas caused by qualities issuing from the real essence of a substance, some n-tuple of that cluster of ideas is sufficient to constitute the nominal essence of that kind. This is analogous to the homeostatic property cluster view of species first propounded by Richard Boyd (1991) except that, in the case of Locke, we have 'homeostatic idea clusters' that make up the nominal essences of kinds (Anstey 2011, ch. 11). This view allows for the discovery of new properties of kinds, such as the solubility of gold in *Aqua Regis* and for variability in the nominal essences of the same kind between people.

The fact that Locke's view can accommodate the discovery of new properties that belong to a kind is also an indicator that Locke's theory is a form of convergent conventionalism. As we discover more and more qualities of kinds, so our nominal essences come to resemble more accurately the actual real essences of those kinds. This is why Locke believes that it is incumbent upon expert natural philosophers and tradesmen accurately to specify those qualities which belong to particular kinds:

It were therefore to be wished, That Men, versed in physical Enquiries, and acquainted with the several sorts of natural Bodies, would set down those simple *Ideas*, wherein they observe the Individuals of each sort constantly to agree. This would remedy a great deal of that confusion, which comes from several Persons, applying the same Name to a Collection of a smaller, or greater number of sensible Qualities, proportionably as they have been more or less acquainted with, or accurate in examining the Qualities of any sort of Things, which come under one denomination   (*Essay* III. xi. 25).

It is little wonder then that Locke gave pride of place to the Baconian method of natural history in his views on how natural philosophy should be practised.

Now, this interpretation of Locke as a constrained and convergent conventionalist about species differs from a widely accepted interpretation of Locke on species which attributes to Locke a more radical form of conventionalism. According to this more radical view, Locke not only believes that we denominate species by their nominal essences, but that the real essences of material substances are to be relativized to their nominal essences. As Michael Ayers puts it 'real essences could not determine species ontologically because real essences are relative to nominal essences' (Ayers 1991: II, 74). However, this 'relativized real essence' interpretation faces some insurmountable difficulties. For example, Locke frequently speaks evaluatively of nominal essences in so far as they accurately reflect real essences. He tell us,

in Substances, we are not always to rest in the ordinary complex *Idea*, commonly received as the signification of that Word, but must go a little farther, and enquire into the Nature and Properties of the Things themselves, and thereby <u>perfect</u>, as much as we can, our *Ideas* of their distinct Species   (*Essay* III. xi. 24; underlining added).

Locke clearly believes that our *nominal* essences are 'perfected' by inquiring into the 'Natures and Properties of the Things themselves', and would deny that our real essences are modified as our nominal essences change. In fact, the relativized real essence view is but a short step from attributing to Locke an instance of Stove's Gem: the view that the way we carve the world up is purely relative to our own conceptual scheme and that there is ultimately no objective way of determining which categories are superior to any other (Franklin 2004).

Locke's theory of nominal and real essences is rightly seen as the culmination of the emergence of a form of corpuscular essentialism which had diverse sources, but whose most important inspiration was the philosophy of Robert Boyle. Yet there is a very important point of discontinuity with Boyle that must be taken into account in order to complete the picture of Locke's views on essences and kinds. This is his view of the Cartesian theory of essences.

We saw above that Descartes made an exception in his rejection of hylomorphism by allowing that the human soul functioned as a kind of substantial form when it is united to the human body. We also saw that Boyle too excluded the human soul from his critique of the scholastic theory of substantial forms. Locke cautiously, but firmly disagreed. Like Boyle, he took Descartes' theory of essences to be an account of necessary and sufficient qualities for a dualist theory of substance: he missed the tight modal connections that arose from Descartes' primary attribute thesis and led to Descartes' exclusion thesis. Nevertheless, Locke's critique of the Cartesian position is more philosophically astute than Boyle's. Where Boyle was content to accept substance dualism and to query the sufficiency of extension as the sole defining attribute of matter, Locke saw two weaknesses of the popular construal of the Cartesian view.

First, Locke rightly rejected the exclusion thesis, the claim that the properties of thinking substances and the properties of material substances are not able to be mutually instantiated. It seems that many heirs to Descartes' dualism accepted not only the conditional that if something is immaterial then it thinks, but also the biconditional that something thinks *if and only if* it is immaterial. However, the Cartesian distinction between material and immaterial substance, when understood in terms of necessary and sufficient conditions—that extension, say, is necessary and sufficient for a substance to be material—does not entail this biconditional. By suggesting that matter 'fitly disposed' might have the power of thought superadded to it (*Essay* IV. iii. 6), Locke shows that even if extension is an essential property of material substance, this does not preclude material substance from instantiating the power of thought. He puts this very point to Edward Stillingfleet, 'whatever excellency, not contained in its essence, be superadded to matter, it does not destroy the essence of matter, if it leaves it an extended solid substance' (Locke 1823: 4, 460–1).

Second, Locke's critique of Cartesian essentialism did not stop at the exclusion thesis. He not only rejects the Cartesian identification of space with extension (*Essay* II. xiii. 11–14), but also denies the claim that the ideas of extension and thought are clear and distinct. In the *Essay* (II. xxiii. 23–9) he develops an extended argument to show that the notion of extension as 'the cohesion or continuity of solid, separable, movable Parts' (*Essay* II. iv. 5) is itself incoherent.

# CONCLUSION

Locke's theory of essences is the high-water mark of early modern corpuscularian responses to the three questions with which this chapter began. It is more parsimonious than the scholastic view and it is also more intelligible in so far as any explication of the real essences should appeal only to the primary qualities of the corpuscles that make up material substances. It does, however, leave open the questions of the mode of operation of seminal principles and of the underlying cause of the union of the qualities of material substances. There is a sense then in which Locke's real essences perform one of the central functions of the Scholastics' substantial forms, namely, they provide the cause of the union of the qualities that we perceive in particular substances. To this extent, Locke's real essences are just as much of a black box as the substantial forms which they were supposed to replace.

It is this need for an underlying cause of the union of a substance that was a primary motivation for Leibniz (1646–1716) to reintroduce substantial forms in the later stage of the development of his metaphysics. As he explained to Arnauld, bodies 'cannot be true substances without having a true unity, nor have a true unity without having a substantial form' (Leibniz to Arnauld, 4 March 1687, Leibniz 1967: 106). His 'New System' of 1695, while containing a more mature metaphysics, is consistent with the claim that he had earlier made to Arnauld: 'a multiplicity can derive its unity only from *true unities* which come from elsewhere . . . [s]o, in order to get to these *real unities* I had to have recourse to a formal atom'. As a result 'it was necessary to recall and, as it were, to rehabilitate *substantial forms*' (Leibniz 1998: 145). Thus, when commenting on Locke's view of species in his *New Essays on Human Understanding*, his mouthpiece Theophilus says: '[t]here is reason to think that there is an infinity of souls, or more generally of primary entelechies, possessing something analogous to perception and appetite, and that all of them are and forever remain substantial forms of bodies' (LRB 318).

But Leibniz's views on essences and kinds were never to have the influence of those of the corpuscularians and Cartesians. The entry under 'Form' in the fourth edition of Ephraim Chambers' *Cyclopaedia* (1741) is indicative of the shift instigated by Descartes and his corpuscularian heirs. After exposing the 'error' of the proponents of substantial forms he says,

The antient and modern corpuscular philosophers therefore, with the Cartesians, exclude the notion of substantial *Forms*; and shew by many arguments, that the *Form* is only the modus or manner of the body it is inherent in.

And as there are only three primary modes of matter . . . the *Forms* of all bodies they hold to consist therein; and suppose the variation these modes are capable of, sufficient to present all the variety observable in bodies.

# REFERENCES

ANSTEY, P. R. (2000). *The Philosophy of Robert Boyle*. London: Routledge.

ANSTEY, P. R. (2002). 'Boyle on seminal principles'. *Studies in History and Philosophy of Biological and Biomedical Sciences*, 33: 597–630.

ANSTEY, P. R. (2010). 'John Locke and Helmontian medicine', in C. Wolfe and O. Gal (eds), *The Body as Object and Instrument of Knowledge: Embodied Empiricism in Early Modern Science*. Dordrecht: Springer, 93–117.

ANSTEY, P. R. (2011). *John Locke and Natural Philosophy*. Oxford: Oxford University Press.

ARIEW, R. and GRENE, M. (1999). 'The Cartesian Destiny of Form and Matter', in R. Ariew (ed.), *Descartes and the Last Scholastics*. Ithaca: Cornell University Press, 77–96.

AUCANTE, V. (2006). 'Descartes's Experimental Method and the Generation of Animals', in J. E. H. Smith (ed.), *The Problem of Animal Generation in Early Modern Philosophy*. Cambridge: Cambridge University Press, 65–79.

AYERS, M. (1991). *Locke: Epistemology and Ontology*. 2 vols. London: Routledge.

BOYD, R. (1991). 'Realism, anti-foundationalism and the enthusiasm for natural kinds'. *Philosophical Studies*, 61: 127–48.

BOYLE, R. (1991). *Selected Philosophical Papers of Robert Boyle*. Ed. M. A. Stewart. Indianapolis: Hackett.

CHAMBERS, E. (1741). *Cyclopaedia*. 4th edn, 2 vols. London.

CHAPPELL, V. (2008). 'Descartes on Substance', in J. Broughton and J. Carriero (eds), *A Companion to Descartes*. Oxford: Blackwell, 251–70.

DES CHENE, D. (1996). *Physiologia: Natural Philosophy in Late Aristotelian and Cartesian Thought*. Ithaca: Cornell University Press.

ELLIS, B. (2001). *Scientific Essentialism*. Cambridge: Cambridge University Press.

FRANKLIN, J. (2004). 'Stove's Discovery of the Worst Argument in the World'. *Philosophy*, 77: 615–24.

HOFFMAN, P. (2009). *Essays on Descartes*. Oxford: Oxford University Press.

LEIBNIZ, G. W. (1967). *The Leibniz–Arnauld Correspondence*. Ed. H. T. Manson. Manchester: Manchester University Press.

LEIBNIZ, G. W. (1998). *G. W. Leibniz: Philosophical Texts*. Ed. R. S. Woolhouse and R. Francks. Oxford: Oxford University Press.

LOCKE, J. (1823). *The Works of John Locke*, 10 vols. London: Tegg.

MCLAUGHLIN, P. (2000). 'Force, determination and impact', in S. W. Gaukroger, J. Schuster, and J. Sutton (eds), *Descartes' Natural Philosophy*. London: Routledge, 81–112.

MOLNAR, G. (2003). *Powers: A Study in Metaphysics*. Ed. with an introd. by S. Mumford. Oxford: Oxford University Press.

NEWMAN, W. R. (2004). *Promethean Ambitions: Alchemy and the Quest to Perfect Nature*. Chicago: University of Chicago Press.

NEWMAN, W. R. (2006). *Atoms and Alchemy: Chymistry and the Experimental Origins of the Scientific Revolution*. Chicago: University of Chicago Press.

NEWMAN, W. R. (2009). 'The Significance of "Chymical Atomism"'. *Early Science and Medicine*, 14: 248–64.

NEWMAN, W. R. and PRINCIPE, L. M. (2002). *Alchemy Tried in the Fire: Starkey, Boyle, and the Fire of Helmontian Chymistry*. Chicago: University of Chicago Press.

NORMORE, C. G. (2008). 'Descartes and the Metaphysics of Extension', in J. Broughton and J. Carriero (eds), *A Companion to Descartes*. Oxford: Blackwell, 271–87.

OLDENBURG, H. (1965–86). *The Correspondence of Henry Oldenburg*. Ed. A. R. Hall and M. B. Hall. 13 vols. Madison, Milwaukee, and London: University of Wisconsin Press, Mansell, and Taylor and Francis.

PASNAU, R. (2004). 'Form, Substance, and Mechanism'. *Philosophical Review*, 113/1: 31–88.

PRINCIPE, L. M. (1998). *The Aspiring Adept: Robert Boyle and his Alchemical Quest*. Princeton, NJ: Princeton University Press.

ROMANELL, P. (1984). *John Locke and Medicine: A New Key to Locke*. Buffalo, NY: Prometheus Books.

SECADA, J. (2000). *Cartesian Metaphysics: The Late Scholastic Origins of Modern Philosophy*. Cambridge: Cambridge University Press.

# CHAPTER 2

.............................................................................................

# FROM CAUSES
# TO LAWS

.............................................................................................

## TAD M. SCHMALTZ

STILLMAN DRAKE has claimed that 'the search for causes of events in nature' that 'guided science from the time of Aristotle' was superseded at 'the dawn of modern science', starting with the work of Galileo, 'by a quest for laws of nature based on experiment and measurement' (Drake 1981: ix).[1] However, there are complications for the suggestion that there was a 'process by which causes gave way to laws in science' (Drake 1981: xxv). The case of Galileo is complicated not only by the fact that he did not use the notion of laws in his writings on particular issues in mechanics (as noted in Steinle 1995: 320), but also by the fact that he at times claimed to find the real causes of phenomena. For example, he claimed in the Fourth Day of his *Dialogue on the Two Chief World Systems* (Galilei 1997: 282–303) that the motion of the earth is the cause of the tides. Moreover, we will discover that two main proponents of the appeal to laws in Cartesian physics refused to distinguish them sharply from causes.

Even so, I emphasize here a particular development in the early modern period that does reflect a progression to the view that the laws invoked in modern science—what was then called 'natural philosophy' (see Blair 2006)—are merely calculating devices used to save the phenomena. In telling this story, I begin with a consideration of the pre-modern context for the later discussions of causes and laws in natural philosophy. Then I turn to the interrelated discussions of physical

[1] For more on the development of the concept of laws of nature in the early modern period, see Milton (1998) and Joy (2006).

laws in the writings of three overlapping early modern figures: René Descartes (1596–1650), Nicolas Malebranche (1638–1715), and George Berkeley (1685–1753). In contrast to more traditional scholastic discussions, the notion of laws of nature is front and centre in Descartes' physics. There is a prominent reading of his account of laws which suggests the 'occasionalist' position that God is the only real cause of the effects with which Cartesian mechanistic physics is concerned. Occasionalism itself dates back to eleventh-century Islamic thought (as documented in Perler and Rudolph 2000), and it was prominent in later Cartesianism, particularly in the work of Malebranche. However, I defend a non-occasionalist interpretation of Descartes in which he took physical laws to reflect the nature of the powers that bodies have to bring about changes in motion due to collision. Though Malebranche did give an occasionalist turn to this view in Descartes, on my reading the former identified laws with the general volitions in God that are causally responsible for the effects of bodily collisions. For Malebranche, then, as for Descartes, laws are not to be separated from causes. Berkeley offered his own distinctive version of Malebranchean occasionalism in physics, but he also accepted the view—which he claimed to find in the work of Isaac Newton—that physics involves laws that are mere 'mathematical principles' detached from any concern with causes. In contrast to Descartes and Malebranche (and, in fact, to Newton), Berkeley holds that the natural philosopher works with physical laws that are involved in non-causal explanations, and that the consideration of real causes should be restricted to the distinct discipline of metaphysics.

It will become clear that the cross currents in the history of science are too strong to support Drake's thesis of a clear process in modern science by which causes gave way to laws. However, we do find such a process in the particular historical current that runs from Descartes, through Malebranche, to Berkeley.

## I. Causes and laws in context

At the beginning of the seventeenth century, the notion of law was not central to the investigations of nature that dominated discussions in the schools. Rather, the agenda for scholastic investigations was set by the account of causes in Aristotle's *Physics*. This account starts from a hylomorphism according to which material substances are composed of matter and form, and it distinguishes four different causes, namely, material, formal, efficient, and final. This basic account was complicated by centuries of scholastic commentary, resulting in the distinction between, on the one hand, the substantial form that unites with prime matter to compose each composite material substance and, on the other, the accidental forms of various qualities that inhere in a material substance and serve as the main immediate sources of natural change. Moreover, scholastic commentaries increasingly emphasized the importance of efficient causation, even in the case of the substantial forms that serve as the formal causes of material substances. Such an emphasis is reflected, for instance, in the *Disputationes Metaphysicae* (1597) of the Jesuit scholastic Francisco Suárez (1548–1617), where he argues that an efficient cause most properly fits the definition of a cause as something that is a 'principle from which being flows into another' (*principium . . . influens esse in aliud*), since this particular sort of cause 'most properly inflows being' (Suárez 1856–78: 25, 952). For Suárez, material and formal causes are 'intrinsic' causes that contribute their own being to their effects, and thus inflow being 'into another' only in an attenuated sense, whereas final causes can produce their effects in another only by means of the activity of efficient causes (Carraud 2002: ch. 1; Schmaltz 2008a: §1.2). This explains the fact that, in the section of the *Disputationes* devoted to the formal causality of substantial forms, Suárez emphasizes an argument for the existence of such forms that appeals to their activity as efficient causes of effects (Suárez 1856–78: 25, 500).

Finally, in marked contrast to the case of Aristotle's writings, the notion of final causality in nature became increasingly problematic in later scholasticism. The source of the problems is the sense that a cause that acts for an end must be able to cognize that end, and thus that causes in nature that cannot cognize ends could not properly be said to be final causes. Their final causality was attributed instead to the *concursus* that God contributes to the actions of all natural agents (Des Chene 1996: ch. 6).

This last point concerning final causality helps to explain the relative absence of an appeal to physical laws in scholastic natural philosophy. As in the case of final causes, the notion of a law was widely believed to apply most properly to the case of agents capable of cognition, and more specifically in this case to those agents capable of cognizing and obeying that law. Here again Suárez reflects this current of thought when he states, in a treatise on law, that since strictly speaking laws can apply only in cases where they can be recognized and obeyed, the notion of a law is applicable only 'metaphorically' (*per metaphoram*) to beings that are not capable of cognition (Suárez 1856–78: 5, 1). For Suárez and other later scholastics, the regularities that involve such beings are to be attributed not to the instantiation of laws, but rather to the (primarily efficient) causal activity of accidental and substantial forms.

However, prior to the seventeenth century the notion of law did gain something of a foothold in the disciplines of optics and astronomy, which fall on the periphery of scholastic natural philosophy. These disciplines belong to 'mixed mathematics', which on the traditional Aristotelian view differs from pure mathematics insofar as it considers quantity as it is in bodies and not as a mere abstraction, but differs also from natural philosophy proper insofar as it does not consider internal principles of change. Already in the thirteenth century, for instance, one finds in works on optics by Roger Bacon (*c.*1210–*c.*1292) references to the 'laws [*leges*] of reflection', the 'laws of refraction' and the 'laws of the multiplication of species'. Here the notion of law is interchangeable with that of rules (*regula*) governing optical phenomena (Ruby 1995: 292–301).[2] Bacon's work had a continuing influence on later work on optics, and one finds references to laws in the optical writings of Lorenzo Ghiberti (1378–1455), Regiomantanus (1436–76), Francisco Maurolic (1494–1575), and Giambattista della Porta (1535–1615) (Ruby, 1995: 302–3). The relevance of laws to astronomy is even more obvious given that the name itself is based on the Greek term for law, *nomos*. Indeed, in 1551 Caspar Peucer (1522–1603) defined astronomy as 'the science of the motions of the heavenly bodies and of the fixed and perpetual successions and laws of motions' (*motuumque certis et perpetuis vicibus ac legibus*) (Ruby 1995: 309–10).

There are thus precedents in the tradition of mixed mathematics for the appeal to physical laws in the early modern period. It is not totally coincidental, therefore, that as these disciplines displaced the more traditional Aristotelian accounts of nature during the early modern period, the notion of natural laws also came to play a more central role in natural philosophy. The link is indicated by Newton's remark in the preface to his *Philosophiae Naturalis Principia Mathematica* that 'the moderns—rejecting substantial forms and occult qualities—have undertaken to reduce the phenomena of nature to mathematical laws' (*Principia* 381). Even so, it perhaps goes too far to say, as Jane Ruby does in her impressive survey of pre-modern appeals to laws of nature, that by 1540 'all of the familiar modern scientific uses of "law" were in place' (Ruby 1995: 312). At least, it cannot be said that all of the *early* modern uses of the term were in place then. What is missing, in particular, is a clear connection of laws to the immediate causes of natural phenomena. We will see that this connection is important to Descartes, who was one of the first to make the notion of law central to causal explanation in physics.

## II. DESCARTES: LAWS AS SECONDARY CAUSES

In a passage from article 36 in the second part of his *Principia Philosophiae* (1644), Descartes claims that God acts as the 'universal and primary cause of motion' in conserving the total quantity of motion and rest he initially created in the universe by means of his 'ordinary *concursus*' (AT VIII-1: 61). Later, Descartes explains that

---

[2] As Ruby notes (1995: 296), Bacon cites in this context an exceptional reference to laws in Aristotle's *De Caelo*, where Aristotle states that he has taken divisibility in three dimensions as one of the 'so to speak laws' of nature (268a, 13–14).

God conserves the material world 'by the same action and in accordance with the same laws as when he first created it' (AT VIII-1: 66). The identification of God's act of creation with his act of conservation is supposed to reveal that God conserves the same quantity of motion and rest that he initially created.

It is not unusual for commentators to read Descartes as affirming here the occasionalist position that God is the only real cause of motion that derives from bodily collision, with the colliding bodies serving as mere 'occasions' for divine action. For instance, Daniel Garber asserts that 'it seems to me *as clear as anything* that, for Descartes, God is the only cause of motion in the inanimate world of bodies, that bodies themselves cannot be genuine causes of change in the physical world of extended substance' (Garber 1993: 12; cf. Hatfield 1979).

However, the claim that Descartes accepted an occasionalist account of the causation of motion in physics seems to be based less on the textual evidence than on intuitions about what his ontology of the material world requires. Descartes' own persistent suggestion—even in passages that emphasize the role of God as the primary cause of motion—is that bodies are genuine causes (Della Rocca 1999: 58–62).[3] Thus, in article 36 Descartes contrasts God's action as universal and primary cause with the 'particular' cause that 'makes singular parts acquire motion that they did not have previously' (AT VIII-1: 61). The indication here is that God's conservation of the quantity of motion and rest by means of his ordinary *concursus* must be distinguished from the production of *changes* in the motions of particular parts of matter. Moreover, Descartes notes that the law governing transfers of motion in collision covers 'the causes of all particular changes . . . at least those [causes] that are corporeal' (AT VIII-1: 65).

In his translation of this passage, John Cottingham takes Descartes to say that the law 'covers all changes which are themselves corporeal' (CSM 1: 242). The passage, so translated, involves no commitment to bodily causes. However, the issue is somewhat unclear, since the Latin text speaks only of the law's covering 'those that are themselves corporeal' (*eae quae ipsae corporeae sunt*). Cottingham takes the demonstrative pronoun '*eae*' to refer to the *mutationes* rather than the *causae particulares mutationum* mentioned earlier in the passage. As Della Rocca (1999: 53) observes, however, it would be odd to emphasize that a law governing motion is restricted to bodily changes. It would make more sense to claim that the law is restricted to changes deriving from bodily (as opposed to mental) causes.

It is true that when Descartes identifies the 'particular causes' of changes in motion, he cites not bodies but rather 'certain rules or laws of nature' (AT VIII-1: 62). Even so, his discussion of the laws indicates clearly enough that it is features of bodies that are supposed to be doing (at least part of) the causal work. Thus, the

---

[3] Cf. the attempts in Pessin (2003) and Hattab (2007) to provide a 'concurrentist' alternative to occasionalist readings of Descartes' physics. For a defence of a more radical 'conservationist' reading of Descartes, see Schmaltz (2008*a*).

first of his three laws of nature states that 'each and every thing, insofar as it is in itself [*quantum in se est*], always perseveres in the same state' (AT VIII-1: 62). By the seventeenth century, there was a tradition of using the phrase *quantum in se est* to indicate that which derives from the nature (*ex natura sua*), internal force (*sua vi*) or spontaneity (*sponte sua*) of an object.[4] The first law thus suggests that causation in the material world involves not only God's immutable action but also a certain nature in a body that explains its tendency to persist in its same state *quantum in se est.*

It might seem that we do not yet have a particular cause in Descartes' sense, namely, something that makes singular parts acquire new motions. However, the first law can be called a particular cause in virtue of its connection to the third law of motion, which directly concerns changes in motion. According to the third law:

> Where a body that moves encounters another, if it has a lesser force for proceeding [*vim pergendum*] in a straight line than the other has for resisting [*resistendum*] it, then it is deflected in another direction, and retaining its motion gives up only the determination of motion; but if it has greater, then it moves the other body with it, and the quantity of its motion it gives to the other it also loses.   (AT VIII-1: 65)

We have the view here that changes in the motions of material parts are produced by various 'forces' for proceeding in or resisting motion. Descartes emphasizes that these forces just consist in the fact 'that each and every thing tends, insofar as it is in itself, to persist in the same state it is in, as posited in the first law' (AT VIII-1: 66). For Descartes, therefore, it is what is contained in a body *quantum in se est* that explains the force it has to produce new motions.

I take the suggestion to be that, given the first law, bodies have a tendency to persist in their states of motion and rest if left to themselves. This persistence has varying strengths, which, in the case of motion, depend on the quantity of the motion (measured by the product of volume and speed). So what explains the fact that a moving body gives to the body with which it collides a new motion is the fact that the former has a tendency to persist in its state of motion that is stronger than, and thus overcomes, the tendency of the latter to persist in its state (Schmaltz 2008a: §3.2.2). This interpretation is a development of a 'causal realist' reading of Descartes' physics that is found in Gueroult (1980) and Gabbey (1980), which has provided the main alternative in the literature to the occasionalist reading of Descartes.

On this non-occasionalist reading, then, the claim that the laws are particular causes indicates merely that the laws express features of bodies that themselves are the causes of changes in motion. There is a presumption that God continues to

---

4 See Cohen (1964), which traces the phrase back to Lucretius.

conserve the same overall quantity of motion and rest, but the changes derive directly from what each body possesses *quantum in se est*.[5]

If this reading is correct, there is a complication for a popular view of Descartes' introduction of laws into his physics. As indicated previously, there was a tradition of appealing to laws in the disciplines of mixed mathematics, and Newton's remarks indicate that the use of laws in early modern physics is explained by the increasing importance of 'mathematical principles' in that discipline. But on one interpretation another important factor was the new tendency—which Edgar Zilsel attributed in his classic article to the rise of the modern nation-state (Zilsel 1942)— to conceive of nature in terms of the way in which a king reigns over his kingdom. In contrast to earlier conceptions of nature, God is now held to impose laws by his will that nature must obey. This view is reflected in Francis Oakley's claim:

So central, indeed, was this notion [of divine legislation] for Descartes himself that he portrayed God, on the analogy of a mighty king, as the omnipotent legislator and, as such, the efficient cause of the laws he imposed on nature—not merely, that is, the laws of motion and inertia upon which the mechanistic physics rested, but, more startlingly, the laws of mathematics and logic.   (Oakley 2005: 41)

The comment regarding Descartes' view of the laws of mathematics and logic refers to his doctrine of the creation of the eternal truths (pp. 530–4). According to this doctrine, as described in the 1630 correspondence with Mersenne in which Descartes introduced it, such truths 'have been laid down by God and depend on him no less than the rest of his creatures' (AT I 145). The political analogy is even clearer in another text in which Descartes notes that God can be said to be the efficient cause of eternal truths 'in the sense that a king may be called an efficient cause of a law' (AT VII 436). On Oakley's view, it is this conception of God as legislator of eternal truths that led Descartes to introduce laws into his physics.

Although this view finds some support in the texts, there is an important disanalogy between Descartes' account of eternal truths and physical laws. The truths are said to derive directly and eternally from the divine will. There is no appeal here to God's continuing conservation of the world. By contrast, the laws are said to hold only insofar as God conserves the world by means of his ordinary *concursus*. Moreover, the laws derive directly not from that *concursus*, but rather from the fact that the bodies God conserves have certain internal forces.[6]

---

[5] In this respect Descartes' position seems to be similar to the suggestion in the work of Francis Bacon that laws are to be identified with the internal 'forms' of bodies. For discussion of Bacon's position, see Steinle (1995: 329–34). But cf. Milton's conclusion that 'no one has ever succeeded in subsuming everything that Bacon said about laws and forms into a single coherent account, and one may reasonably suspect that the enterprise is impossible' (Milton 1998: 686).

[6] Cf. Janet Broughton's claim that for Descartes 'what makes eternal truths true is God's timeless decree; what makes [a] law of motion true is God's preservation of the world from moment to moment by the same activity by which he created it' (Broughton 1987: 212). My account differs from Broughton's in emphasizing that the laws depend as well on what is in each body *quantum in se est*.

We can understand the significance of this difference in terms of a distinction that Oakley himself invokes to criticize Zilsel. Zilsel takes the early modern notion of law to be the application to the realm of nature of a notion of natural law that the Stoics had previously restricted for the most part to the moral sphere (Zilsel 1942: 251–2). Oakley's objection is that, according to the Stoics, law is 'conceived as immanent in the very structure of the world and springing from the very natures of beings that compose it', whereas on the early modern conception, particularly as found in Descartes, laws are taken to be 'behavior patterns imposed on the world from without and reflecting the mandates of an omnipotent creator' (Oakley 2005: 43–4). If the preceding analysis is correct, however, Descartes' notion of a law of nature is in fact closer to the Stoic conception of natural law as Oakley conceives it, insofar as Descartes' laws reflect immanent features of bodies that are the immediate source of changes in motion due to collision. Of course, Descartes' doctrine of the divine creation of the eternal truths requires that God is the cause of immutable and eternal truths concerning body. But once God has created those truths, the laws follow simply from his creation and conservation of the bodies in the material world that are conditioned by the truths.

## III. MALEBRANCHE: LAWS AS GENERAL VOLITIONS

Malebranche's views fit Oakley's story concerning the early modern appeal to laws of nature in a more straightforward manner. For in Malebranche, it is clear that God imposes laws on the material world, and indeed that he is the only causal agent involved in the changes in motion that occur in a Cartesian universe (Pellegrin 2006). Moreover, the laws themselves are contingent on the divine will; thus Malebranche notes both that the truth concerning the laws of motion 'is arbitrary and depends on the volitions of the Creator' (OCM 17-1: 45), and that 'God could without doubt have established other laws than those we see of the communication of motions' (OCM 17-1: 581).

We have seen the suggestion in Descartes that there are other material causes with which God 'concurs'. However, Malebranche firmly rejects any appeal to a divine *concursus*, insisting instead on his occasionalist position that it is God alone who acts in the production of motion. Thus, in the fifteenth of the Eclaircissements of his *Recherche de la verité*—first published with the *Recherche* in 1678—Malebranche writes:

To concur [*Concourir*] in contrary actions, is to give contrary concurrences, and by consequence to perform contrary actions. To concur with the action of creatures that resist each other is to act against oneself. To concur with useless motions is to act uselessly. But God does nothing uselessly; he produces no contrary actions; he does not struggle against himself. Thus he does not concur in the action of creatures, which often destroy each other and produce useless actions or motions.   (OCM 3: 216)

Changes in nature are to be attributed not to divine *concursus*, but rather to God's production of changes in accord with natural laws. In this Eclaircissement, Malebranche describes two laws of motion that are central to his version of Cartesian physics. The first dictates that unimpeded motion is rectilinear, whereas the second holds that transfers of motion in collisions occur in proportion to the sizes of the colliding bodies and in a way that conserves the total quantity of speed. Significantly, Malebranche does not follow Descartes in appealing to what is in each body *quantum in se est*, but rather holds that bodily collisions serve as mere 'occasions' for God to produce the relevant effects (OCM 3: 216).

Bodily collision therefore is in Malebranche's terms an 'occasional cause' that merely prompts God's production of natural changes in motion that follow from the two laws of nature. As indicated below, however, Malebranche held that occasional causes do not merely prompt but also 'determine' God's action in a non-causal manner. For Malebranche, the 'general volitions' in God that serve to establish these laws are the real causes of such changes. God's production of these changes contrasts with his production of miraculous events. God is said to produce the latter by means of 'particular volitions' that are restricted to particular circumstances, and such volitions do not establish the sort of general law-like relations between occasional causes and their effects that derive from general volitions.

There is admittedly some question concerning the precise manner in which Malebranche conceived of the relation of the laws governing motion to the corresponding general volitions in God (Schmaltz 2003: 747–8). In the course of a polemic with Malebranche during the 1680s, fellow-Cartesian Antoine Arnauld read him as identifying the laws with God's volitions, and then objected that such an identification illicitly conflates acting *by means of* laws with acting *according to* laws (AO 39: 175).[7] However, Steven Nadler has responded that this line of objection involves a misunderstanding of Malebranche's position. For Nadler, 'Malebranche's God must be directly and immediately responsible for each and every particular effect in nature' (Nadler 1993: 41). His argument for this claim emphasizes the position—which is prominent in Malebranche's discussion of occasionalism in his *Entretiens sur la métaphysique* (1688)—that God brings about effects of motion in the material world by means of his continuous creation of bodies (OCM 12: 157). Thus, God moves a body by willing that it exist successively in different places. As Nadler sees it, Malebranche held that God wills the existence of a body in a place by means of 'a discrete and temporalized volition with

---

[7] On Arnauld's discussion here, see Black (1997: 33–7). Cf. Jolley (2002: 245–7).

a particular content (e.g., "Let this body move now thus")'. This volition is general simply in the sense—which Arnauld allowed—that it is in accord with a general law (Nadler 1993: 43).

The stress in the *Entretiens* on continuous creation may seem to indicate that God causes effects by means of 'an infinite number of discrete temporalized acts', as Nadler puts it (Nadler 1993: 43). By 'temporalized acts', Nadler means acts that, though not themselves temporal, are indexed to particular times (e.g., 'Let body A exist at place P at time $t_5$'). The claim in Nadler that there is 'an infinite number' of such acts seems to conflict, however, with Malebranche's emphasis in the *Entretiens* on the fact that 'the conservation of creatures is, on the part of God, only a continued creation, simply the *same* volition that subsists and operates unceasingly' (OCM 12: 160; emphasis added). Here he was simply following Descartes' claim that conservation is distinct from creation only by reason, a claim, as we have seen, that underlies the view in Descartes' *Principia* that God conserves motion 'by the same action' with which he created it. But if Malebranche accepted Descartes' point that it is the very same volition that creates and conserves motion, as the passage from the *Entretiens* seems to indicate, then *pace* Nadler, he could not have held that God brings about motion by means of a series of discrete law-like volitions.[8]

There are further difficulties for Nadler's reading in Malebranche's own insistence to Arnauld that 'God must act through laws or general volitions, the efficacy of which is determined by the action of natural or occasional causes' (OCM 8: 667). One obvious problem is that this claim seems to indicate that laws are to be *identified* with God's general volitions (*loix ou des volontez générales*). Yet there is another, and in some respects more significant, difficulty that derives from the claim that natural or occasional causes 'determine' the efficacy of laws or general volitions. If the general volitions had a particular content (e.g., 'Let this body move now thus'), the efficacy of the volitions would seem to be fixed by this content alone. However, if the content of the general volitions were exhausted by general laws (e.g., 'Let motion be communicated after collisions in a manner that is proportional to the sizes of the bodies and that conserves the total quantity of speed'), these volitions by themselves would not dictate any particular effect. What would be required in addition are particular bodies with particular sizes and states of motion and rest that, together with the laws or general volitions, yield the determinate results (cf. the exchange in Clarke 1995 and Nadler 1995).

I take Malebranche to follow Descartes in thinking that the laws are inextricably linked to causation, with the difference being that Descartes takes the laws to reflect internal features of bodies responsible for changes in motion, whereas Malebranche takes the laws to be identified with the divine volitions that produce such changes.

[8] For a similar objection to Nadler's position, see Black (1997: 39). Black offers the related objection that Nadler cannot accommodate the position in Malebranche (e.g., at OCM 5: 31) that God reduces as much as possible the number of volitions required to bring about natural effects (Black 1997: 40).

Even so, there is a way of drawing from Malebranche an account on which laws are mere generalizations rather than real causes. Consider his comment in Eclaircissement XV:

I grant that recourse to God or the universal cause should not be had when the explanation of particular effects is sought. For we would be ridiculous were we to say, for example, that it is God who dries the roads or who freezes the water of the rivers. We should say that the air dries the earth because it stirs or raises with it the water that soaks the earth, and that the air or subtle matter freezes the river because in this season it ceases to communicate enough motion to the parts of which the water is composed to make it fluid. In a word, we must give, if we can, the natural and particular cause of the effects in question.   (OCM 3: 213)

Insofar as physics emphasizes only the natural and particular (read: occasional) causes of effects, and pushes God's activity as the 'universal cause' into the background, the laws invoked in explanations of natural phenomena could not be identified with God's general volitions. Rather, they would be generalizations that concern not real causal activity, but mere correlations between occasional causes and their effects. Though Malebranche was too focused on the identification of laws with general volitions to offer this conception of laws, such a conception is front and centre in Berkeley's version of Newtonian physics.

# IV. BERKELEY: LAWS AS MATHEMATICAL PRINCIPLES

Malebranche endorsed an occasionalist version of the position in Descartes that the terrestrial effects of gravity, as well as the facts concerning planetary motion, are to be explained in terms of the vortical motions of 'subtle matter'.[9] Newton subjected this position to a searching critique in the *Principia Mathematica*, first published in 1687. In particular, he argued in precise detail that vortices could not provide an adequate explanation of either celestial or terrestrial phenomena. Newton also claimed—in a General Scholium to the third book that was added in the second edition of his *Principia* (1713)—that he 'feigns no hypotheses' (*hypotheses non fingo*) concerning the 'cause of gravity', concentrating instead on deducing from phenomena laws that have been 'made general by induction' (*Principia* 943). Newton thus proposed to replace the hypothetical 'principles' of Cartesian physics with the 'mathematical principles' that he took to derive from this sort of induction.

---

[9] On appeals to vortices in early modern physics, see Aiton (1972).

Malebranche shared in the judgement common on the Continent that, though Newton's *Principia* displays impressive mathematical acumen, it fails to count as a treatise in natural philosophy insofar as it excludes a study of the mechanisms required for an explanation of the sensible effects. Thus, in a 1707 letter, Malebranche offers the following back-handed comment regarding the first edition of Newton's text: 'Although Mr. Newton is not a physicist, his book is very curious and very useful to those who have good principles of physics; he is, moreover, an excellent geometer' (OCM 19: 771–2).

In contrast, Berkeley claimed around the same time in his *Principles of Human Knowledge* (1710) that Newton's 'celebrated treatise on mechanics' is 'the best key for . . . natural science' (*PHK* §110, BW 2: 89).[10] To be sure, Berkeley continues by criticizing the notions of absolute space and motion that Newton's theory invokes. In particular, he argues that absolute motion is inconceivable since conceiving of motion involves conceiving of relations of distance involving more than one body, and since it is impossible to conceive of pure space independent of all bodies (Brook 1973: 125–45). However, he has no difficulty with the fact that Newton explained gravity without providing a mechanical cause, and indeed notes that 'it depends entirely on the will of the *governing spirit*, who causes certain bodies to cleave together, or tend towards each other, according to various laws, whilst he keeps others at a fixed distance; and to some he gives a quite contrary tendency to fly asunder, just as he sees convenient' (*PHK* §106: BW 2: 87). Berkeley's claim that laws reflect merely how God has decided to act suggests that there is nothing to prevent God from bringing it about that bodies at a distance attract one another in accordance with Newtonian laws, without the assistance of any intervening bodies.

This suggestion seems to be at odds with Newton's claim, in a famous passage from a 1692/93 letter to Bentley, 'that one body may act on another at a distance through a vacuum without the mediation of anything else, by and through which their action or force may be conveyed from one to another, is to me so great an absurdity, that I believe no man who has in philosophical matters a competent faculty of thinking can ever fall into it' (Newton 2004: 102). As we will see, Berkeley is committed to rejecting the view that bodies have any 'action or force' at all. However, he also seems to have no qualms in holding that changes involving gravitational attraction can occur even though there is nothing in the physical world that mediates that attraction.

In contrast to Newton, there is a connection to Malebranche's occasionalism in Berkeley that is indicated by his claim in the *Principles* that 'the connexion of ideas does not imply the relation of *cause* and *effect*, but only of a mark or *sign* with the thing *signified*. The fire I see is not the cause of the pain I suffer on my approaching it, but the mark that forewarns me of it' (*PHK* §65: BW 2: 69). However, Berkeley

---

[10] On Berkeley's appropriation of Newton, see McMullin (2001: 299–301).

also insists in this text on the 'immaterialist' position that the sensible objects with which the natural philosopher is concerned are nothing beyond collections of sensible ideas, and such a position is at odds with Malebranche's own view that mind-independent bodies serve as occasional causes in physics.

There is a question whether Berkeley allowed for a form of mechanistic 'corpuscularianism' that is consistent with his immaterialistic reduction of bodies to sensible ideas. Garber (1982) argues that such an immaterialistic corpuscularianism is suggested by Berkeley's discussion of the 'curious organization' of the 'internal parts' of bodies in *Principles* §§60–66 (BW 2: 66–70), whereas Wilson (1985) argues that this discussion does not suggest so strong a position. As Downing notes (2005*a*: 234–5), Berkeley's own preference for Newtonian attractionism over the mechanism of Descartes seems to support Wilson's position. Though this preference is implicit in Berkeley's earlier works, it is explicit in his last major text, *Siris* (1743), where he claims that 'Nature seems better known and explained by attractions and repulsions, than by those other mechanical principles of size, figure and the like: that is by Sir Isaac Newton, than Descartes' (§243: BW 5: 116).

Though Berkeley's embrace of both immaterialism and Newtonian attraction distinguishes him from Malebranche, he nonetheless agrees with Malebranche in holding that law-like connections in nature are grounded not in natural causes but rather in the divine will. Just as Malebranche claimed that 'the study of nature is false and vain in every way when true causes are sought in it other than in the volitions of the Almighty, or the general laws according to which he acts' (OCM 3: 213), so Berkeley concludes that 'endeavouring to understand those [laws] instituted by the Author of Nature . . . ought to be the employment of the natural philosopher, and not the pretending to explain things by corporeal causes' (*PHK* §66: BW 2: 70).

Berkeley understood his occasionalism to complement his Newtonianism.[11] This is clear from the discussion of Newton in Berkeley's *De Motu*, which dates from 1721, roughly thirty-four years after the initial publication of Newton's *Principia* and seventy-seven years after the publication of Descartes' *Principia*. In contrast to the case of his *Principles*, Berkeley's immaterialism is hidden in *De Motu*. Berkeley submitted the latter text for an essay competition at the Paris Académie des sciences (Stock 1989, 1: 19), and it would be understandable that he would not have wanted to distract his Cartesian judges by drawing attention to an aspect of his position that they would consider untenable. However, we do find in *De Motu* the view that occasionalism provides crucial support for what Berkeley

---

[11] Indeed, Lisa Downing (2005*b*: 214) has gone so far as to claim that that 'Berkeley's openness to attractionism seems to flow naturally from the occasionalism shared by Malebranche and Berkeley'. For the argument that there are differences between the occasionalisms of Malebranche and Berkeley that serve to explain why the former rejected the sort of attractionism that allows an occasionalist 'action at a distance', see Schmaltz (2008*b*).

takes to be the correct Newtonian account of the phenomena. In this text, Berkeley cites the position of the 'Cartesian philosophers' that God is 'the principle of natural motions' (*DM* §32: BW 4: 18/39). Drawing on the account in Malebranche of the divine conservation of motion, Berkeley holds that such a position requires that God is the only 'cause of the successive existence of the body in different parts of space', and thus the only 'cause whence is derived the successive existence of the same body in different parts of time' (*DM* §34: BW 4: 19/40). This view might seem to be contradicted by the Newtonian appeal to gravitational forces to explain the effects of attraction. However, Berkeley insists that attraction 'was certainly introduced by Newton, not as a true, physical quality, but only as a mathematical hypothesis' (*DM* §17: BW 4: 15/35). Thus, mechanistic critics of Newton who reject 'the mathematical principles of physics on the ground that they do not assign the efficient causes of things' fail to recognize that 'it is not . . . in fact the business of physics or mechanics to establish efficient causes, but only the rules of impulsions and attractions, and, in a word, the laws of motions, and from the established laws to assign the solution, not the efficient cause, of particular phenomena' (*DM* §35: BW 4: 19/40).

Berkeley thus endorses an instrumentalist interpretation of Newton's *Principia*, according to which Newtonian laws of nature are merely calculating devices for deducing kinematic effects. Though Berkeley is not alone in reading the *Principia* in this manner, there is reason to doubt that such a reading tracks Newton's own intentions. After all, Newton indicated in his *Principia* that even though we should not speculate concerning the cause of gravity, 'it is enough that gravity really exists and acts according to the laws that we have set forth and suffices for all the motions of the heavenly bodies and of our sea' (*Principia* 943; translation altered). The view here, it seems, is that gravity is a real cause of gravitational phenomena. To be sure, Newton does claim in the first book of the *Principia* that his concept of force is 'purely mathematical', and emphasizes that 'I am not now considering the physical causes and sites of forces' (*Principia* 407). One can understand why a reader such as Berkeley would have taken Newton to distinguish gravitational forces from real efficient causes. However, Newton's suggestion is that, whereas his consideration of gravity is 'purely mathematical' insofar as it abstracts from the underlying physical 'sites of forces', he nonetheless is committed to the conclusion that gravity itself is a real cause that is somehow instantiated in nature (though concerning the precise nature of that instantiation: *hypotheses non fingo*).[12]

---

[12] For an interpretation of Newton's claim to provide a mathematical treatment of gravity that attempts to reconcile it with a 'causal realist' account of gravitational force, see Janiak (2008: ch. 3). But cf. McMullin's contention that Newton offered a 'dynamic' form of explanation that lies between strong agent-causal sorts of explanations, on the one hand, and weak forms of explanation that involve mere subsumption under a general law, on the other (McMullin 2001: 298).

In contrast, Berkeley is concerned in *De Motu* to distinguish 'mathematical principles' from another sort of principle that is bound up with causation. Thus he noted that though God, as 'the true, efficient and conserving cause of all things', is properly called 'their fount and principle', the principles of 'experimental philosophy' are principles in the sense that they serve as the foundation 'not of their existence but of our knowledge of corporeal things'. In Berkeley's view, then, Newtonian laws are not metaphysical principles that serve as causes of the existence of phenomena. Rather, the laws are merely epistemological principles, something from which 'are derived both general mechanical theorems and particular explanations of the phenomena' (*DM* §36: BW 2: 20/40–41).

With this division between two kinds of principles comes a distinction between metaphysics and natural philosophy. According to Berkeley, when we follow the Cartesian occasionalists in considering God as 'the principle of natural motions', we are more in 'the province of first philosophy or metaphysics and theology than of natural philosophy, which today is almost entirely confined to experiments and mechanics' (*DM* §34: BW 2: 19/40). What is emerging here is a conception of natural philosophy on which its principles are sharply distinguished from the metaphysical principles involved in causal explanation (on Berkeley's conception of metaphysics, see Bardout, 2008). This sort of sharp distinction can be found neither in Descartes nor Newton. Nor is there any explicit endorsement of such a distinction in Malebranche although, as I have suggested, it can be linked to his claim that we should have recourse only to occasional causes in providing 'the explanation of particular effects'.

One might think that Berkeley had the option of following Malebranche in identifying laws with the divine volitions that are responsible for effects in the sensible world. However, it is clear that he was led by his reading of Newton to identify the laws with 'mathematical principles' that are not concerned with real efficient causes. In a sense, Berkeley was returning to a traditional Aristotelian understanding of the status of laws in mixed mathematics, according to which they abstract from real causes. Nonetheless, Berkeley rejected the orthodox Aristotelian view that the disciplines of mixed mathematics are peripheral to natural philosophy insofar as the latter is concerned with real causes. In effect, Berkeley took the invocation in mixed mathematics of non-causal laws to serve as the model for natural philosophy, and assigned the task in Aristotelian natural philosophy of providing causal explanations to metaphysics.

In Berkeley, then, we see the completion of one sort of progression in the history of science from causes to laws. This progression started when Descartes, in a deviation from past scholastic practice, made laws central to physics. However, the indication in Descartes is that laws are not to be contrasted with causes; indeed, he identified them with secondary causes of changes in motion that are grounded in internal features of bodies. The next step was made by Malebranche, who took real causality out of the material world and placed it in God. Even here, though, the progression is not complete, since Malebranche identified the laws not with mere correlations in the material world, but rather with God's efficacious volitions. What was required to complete the progression was Berkeley's view that we are to follow Newton in identifying the laws of physics with mathematical principles that do not concern the real causes of motion.

# CONCLUSION

Drake's remark—that there has been a progression in modern science from causes to laws—may suggest that there was a decisive and permanent transition to Berkeley's view that explanation in terms of scientific laws involves a mere subsumption of particular events under inductive generalizations, as opposed to an inference to metaphysically robust causal structures. And indeed, there are remnants of Berkeley's view in the instrumentalist accounts of scientific explanation that one finds in the twentieth century. There is, for instance, Werner Heisenberg's claim—in the 1927 paper that expresses his celebrated 'uncertainty principle'—that 'speculations' concerning 'a "real" world in which causality holds' are 'fruitless and senseless', and that 'physics ought to describe only the correlation of observations' (Dear 2006: 153). There is some irony here since this comment reflects an antipathy toward metaphysics, whereas Berkeley took his instrumentalist physics to be supported by the occasionalist conclusion of his metaphysics that God is the only cause of the alterations of sensible objects of concern to physics. But in this respect Berkeley is not all that distinctive, since the general concern in the early modern period to supplement an account of scientific laws with a metaphysical account of God's causal activity has disappeared from contemporary philosophy of science.

Even so, it is important to recognize that from the beginning, in Descartes, explanations that invoke scientific laws were seen as involving inferences to real causes. The survival of this view of explanation in contemporary versions of 'scientific realism' can itself be explained in terms of the continuing influence of the stress in traditional natural philosophy—which Peter Dear has highlighted—on the goal of revealing the 'intelligibility' of nature (Dear 2006). Dear notes that the stress on intelligibility is often coupled, though at times competes, with a stress on the 'instrumentality' of science, on its pragmatic success. Traditional mixed mathematics provides an example of a case in which the goal of instrumentality pulls apart from the goal of causal intelligibility, and by appealing in effect to the account of laws in these disciplines, Berkeley was offering the former goal in his physics to the exclusion of the latter. Certainly there is no going back now to an

Aristotelian account of causation in nature; developments in science triggered by the work of Descartes and Newton, among others, have seen to that. However, these developments have not effaced the project in Aristotelian natural philosophy of rendering intelligible causal interactions in nature. And even if the details of Descartes' physics have been consigned to the dustbin of history, what remains influential is his sense that physical laws need to be linked to those features of bodily causes that serve to explain why they have the effects that they do.[13]

## REFERENCES

AITON, E. J. (1972). *The Vortex Theory of Planetary Motions*. London: Macdonald.

BARDOUT, J.-CH. (2008). 'Berkeley devant les métaphysiques de son temps'. *Journal of the History of Philosophy*, 46: 119–39.

BLACK, A. (1997). 'Malebranche's Theodicy'. *Journal of the History of Philosophy*, 103: 639–67.

BLAIR, A. (2006). 'Natural Philosophy', in K. Park and L. Daston (eds), *The Cambridge History of Science, Vol. 3: Early Modern Science*. Cambridge: Cambridge University Press, 365–406.

BROOK, R. J. (1973). *Berkeley's Philosophy of Science*. The Hague: Nijhoff.

BROUGHTON, J. (1987). 'Necessity and Physical Laws in Descartes's Philosophy'. *Pacific Philosophical Quarterly*, 68: 205–21.

CARRAUD, V. (2002). *Causa sive ratio. La raison de la cause, de Suarez à Leibniz*. Paris: Presses Universitaires de France.

CLARKE, D. (1995). 'Malebranche and Occasionalism: A Reply to Steven Nadler'. *Journal of the History of Philosophy*, 33: 499–504.

COHEN, I. B. (1964). '"Quantum in se est": Newton's Concept of Inertia in Relation to Descartes and Lucretius'. *Notes and Records of the Royal Society of London*, 19: 131–55.

DEAR, P. (2006). *The Intelligibility of Nature: How Science Makes Sense of the World*. Chicago: University of Chicago Press.

DELLA ROCCA, M. (1999). '"If a Body Meet a Body": Descartes on Body–Body Causation', in R. Gennaro and C. Huenemann (eds), *New Essays on the Rationalists*. New York: Oxford University Press, 48–81.

DES CHENE, D. (1996). *Physiologia: Natural Philosophy in Late Aristotelian and Cartesian Thought*. Ithaca, NY: Cornell University Press.

DOWNING, L. (2005a). 'Berkeley's Natural Philosophy and Philosophy of Science', in K. Winkler (ed.), *The Cambridge Companion to Berkeley*. Cambridge: Cambridge University Press, 230–65.

DOWNING, L. (2005b). 'Occasionalism and Strict Mechanism: Malebranche, Berkeley, Fontenelle', in C. Mercer and E. O'Neill (eds), *Early Modern Philosophy: Matter and Metaphysics*. New York: Oxford University Press, 206–30.

[13] Thanks to the audience at the Department of Physics and Physical Oceanography, University of North Carolina, Wilmington, for helpful discussion of an earlier version of this chapter. I am indebted as well to Des Clarke, May Domski, Andrew Janiak, and Eric Watkins for their helpful comments on this chapter.

DRAKE, S. (1981). *Cause, Experiment and Science.* Chicago: University of Chicago Press.

GABBEY, A. (1980). 'Force and Intertia in the Seventeenth Century: Descartes and Newton', in S. Gaukroger (ed.), *Descartes: Philosophy, Mathematics, Physics.* Sussex: Harvester Press, 230–320.

GALILEI, G. (1997). *Galileo on the World Systems.* Trans. and ed. M. A. Finocchiaro. Berkeley: University of California Press.

GARBER, D. (1982). 'Locke, Berkeley, and Corpuscular Scepticism', in C. Turbayne (ed.), *Berkeley: Critical and Interpretive Essays.* Minneapolis: University of Minnesota Press, 174–93.

GARBER, D. (1992). *Descartes' Metaphysical Physics.* Chicago: University of Chicago Press.

GARBER, D. (1993). 'Descartes and Occasionalism', in S. Nadler (ed.), *Causation in Early Modern Philosophy.* University Park: Pennsylvania State University Press, 9–26.

GUEROULT, M. (1980). 'The Metaphysics and Physics of Force in Descartes', in S. Gaukroger (ed.), *Descartes: Philosophy, Mathematics, Physics.* Sussex: Harvester Press, 196–229.

HATFIELD, G. (1979). 'Force (God) in Descartes' Physics'. *Studies in History and Philosophy of Science,* 10: 113–40.

HATTAB, H. (2007). 'Concurrence or Divergence? Reconciling Descartes's Physics with his Metaphysics'. *Journal of the History of Philosophy,* 45: 49–78.

JANIAK, A. (2008). *Newton as Philosopher.* Cambridge: Cambridge University Press.

JOLLEY, N. (2002). 'Occasionalism and Efficacious Laws in Malebranche', in P. A. French, H. K. Wettstein, and B. Silver (eds), *Renaissance and Early Modern Philosophy, Midwest Studies in Philosophy.* Malden, MA: Blackwell, 26: 245–57.

JOY, L. (2006). 'Scientific Explanations from Formal Causes to Laws of Nature', in K. Park and L. Daston (eds), *The Cambridge History of Science, Vol. 3: Early Modern Science.* Cambridge: Cambridge University Press, 70–105.

MCMULLIN, E. (2001). 'The Impact of Newton's *Principia* on the Philosophy of Science'. *Philosophy of Science,* 68: 279–310.

MILTON, J. R. (1998). 'Laws of Nature', in D. Garber and M. Ayers (eds), *The Cambridge History of Seventeenth-Century Philosophy.* Cambridge: Cambridge University Press, 1: 680–701.

NADLER, S. (1993). 'Occasionalism and the General Will in Malebranche'. *Journal of the History of Philosophy,* 31: 31–47.

NADLER, S. (1995). 'Malebranche and Occasionalism: A Reply to Clarke'. *Journal of the History of Philosophy,* 33: 505–8.

NEWTON, I. (2004). *Philosophical Writings.* Ed. A. Janiak. Cambridge: Cambridge University Press.

OAKLEY, F. (2005). *Natural Law, Laws of Nature, Natural Rights: Continuity and Discontinuity in the History of Ideas.* New York: Continuum.

PELLEGRIN, M.-F. (2006). *Le Système de la loi de Nicolas Malebranche.* Paris: Vrin.

PERLER, D. and RUDOLPH, U. (2000). *Occasionalisus: Theorien der Kausalität im arabisch-islamischen und im europäischen Denken.* Göttingen: Vandenhoeck & Rup.

PESSIN, A. (2001). 'Malebranche's Distinction between General and Particular Volitions'. *Journal of the History of Philosophy,* 39: 77–99.

PESSIN, A. (2003). 'Descartes's Nomic Concurrentism: Finite Causation and Divine Concurrence'. *Journal of the History of Philosophy,* 41: 25–50.

RUBY, J. E. (1995). 'The Origins of Scientific "Law"', in F. Weinert (ed.), *Laws of Nature: Essays on the Philosophical, Scientific and Historical Dimensions.* Berlin: Walter de Gruyter, 289–315.

SCHMALTZ, T. M. (2003). 'Cartesian Causation: Body–Body Interaction, Motion, and Eternal Truths'. *Studies in History and Philosophy of Science*, 34: 737–62.

SCHMALTZ, T. M. (2008a). *Descartes on Causation*. New York: Oxford University Press.

SCHMALTZ, T. M. (2008b). 'Occasionalism and Mechanism: Fontenelle's Objections to Malebranche'. *British Journal for the History of Philosophy*, 16: 293–313.

STEINLE, F. (1995). 'The Amalgamation of a Concept—Laws of Nature in the New Sciences', in F. Weinert (ed.), *Laws of Nature: Essays on the Philosophical, Scientific and Historical Dimensions*. Berlin: Walter de Gruyter, 316–68.

STOCK, J. (1989). 'An Account of the Life of George Berkeley', in D. Berman (ed.), *George Berkeley: Eighteenth Century Responses*. New York: Garland, 1: 1–94.

SUÁREZ, F. (1856–78). *Opera Omnia*. Ed. D. André and C. Berton. 26 vols. Paris: Vivès.

WILSON, M. (1985). 'Berkeley and the Essences of the Corpuscularians', in J. Foster and H. Robinson (eds), *Essays on Berkeley: A Tercentennial Celebration*. Oxford: Oxford University Press, 131–47.

ZILSEL, E. (1942). 'The Genesis of the Concept of Physical Law'. *Philosophical Review*, 3: 245–79.

C H A P T E R 3

# SPACE AND TIME

## EMILY GROSHOLZ

SPACE and time have cast a spell over philosophers for two thousand years. No other pair of metaphysical items has proved so elusive and yet accessible to reason, so impalpable and yet obviously *there*. The philosophical treatment of space and time raises questions about the finite and the infinite, thought and perception, the nature of the continuum, and the reality of change. Around 1600, philosophers began to question the metaphysical framework of the late Middle Ages, which combined Aristotle's doctrines with Christian cosmogony and eschatology, and their questions led to heated and novel debates about space and time. The revision of natural philosophy, mathematics, and theology both provoked and retrospectively justified profound transformations in the way that human beings understood the spatio-temporal framework of their world. Of course, the enchantment of space and time has never really been broken: we still find that seventeenth-century debates are taken up and refined, but not resolved, in present-day cosmological disputes.

The central debate about space and time in the early modern period was the celebrated exchange between Leibniz and Newton, recorded in the Leibniz/Clarke correspondence. Samuel Clarke was Newton's mouthpiece; he was Newton's friend and the translator into Latin of his *Opticks*. Both sides of the correspondence take up almost a hundred pages in *Die Philosophische Schriften* of Leibniz; Clarke wrote in English, and Leibniz responded in French. Thus, this chapter is organized around the Leibniz/Clarke correspondence. In the first section, I give a brief account of Galileo's critique of medieval cosmology, the finite, two-sphere cosmos with fixed places as well as a beginning and an end in time, the related account of motion as finite and in need of an external agent, and the too-limited use of geometry in mechanics. Galileo's critique leads into the doctrines of Descartes, which I review in the second section; these include his account of space, time, and motion, which are given their most authoritative expression in the *Principia Philosophiae*. The work of Henry More forms a noteworthy bridge between the metaphysical speculations of Descartes and Newton's ideas about space and time, and so is reviewed in the third section, while Newton's positing of absolute space and time is discussed in section IV.

In section V I review in some detail the achievements of Leibniz and Newton, primarily in order to make clear the differences in their views about space and time, construed in mathematical, metaphysical, and physical terms as they emerged in the Leibniz/Clarke correspondence. Leibniz defends his relativist theory of space and time against the absolutist Newtonian account, as well as the principle of sufficient reason, which was closely tied to his conception of God. Modern commentators tend to emphasize either the scientific or the metaphysical dimensions of the debate, depending on their philosophical orientation; however, both dimensions are essential in the seventeenth century. I end with some brief reflections on the debt of modern cosmology to this debate.

# I: GALILEO

The origins of theories of space and time in Early Modern Europe lie in Greek cosmology and the cosmology of the Christian world. The atomists (Leucippus and Democritus) held that what exists are material atoms in an infinite void, which collide by chance, move in vortices, and sort themselves out according to their size. The world thus exists by chance, falling into its vortical arrangement for no reason, and at no assignable place or time, and the infinite void itself has no structure. Plato attacks atomism in the *Laws* (889b) on the grounds that it fails to explain the apparent order and harmony of the world, and he proposes the myth of the *Timaeus* (27c–91c) where a creator god (demiurge) constructs the world out of triangular elements according to a method, and as a result of which the study of nature may proceed as an organized science. Since this long account in the *Timaeus* is a myth, its status as knowledge is problematic; however, it testifies to Plato's fidelity to the principle of sufficient reason and to a rather Pythagorean belief that the structure of things (including space and time) can be represented by mathematics (Gregory 2008; Pyle 1995).

Aristotle sides with the great rival of the atomists, Parmenides, in rejecting cosmogony altogether and positing the 'two-sphere universe' with its distinctive spatial structure, but without a temporal beginning or end. It consists of the earth at the centre and the sphere of the fixed stars which turns around it on the celestial pole every twenty-four hours; in between lie the homocentric aetherial spheres that carry the moon, the sun, and the planets. Thus for Aristotle, space is finite, not homogeneous, and not isotropic: it has places and directions. It is also a plenum, without void: his doctrine of the five elements, which under-writes causal explanations in the *Physics*, is an articulation of the places of space: earth belongs at the centre, followed by concentric shells of water, air, fire, and aether. Thus a bit of earth thrown upwards will fall back down, seeking the centre of the cosmos, its rightful place; water will float on earth, and air and fire will rise above both, though the four elements below the aetherial heavens tend to get mixed together due to processes of generation and corruption. Aristotle's doctrine of time concerns only the realm of the first four elements, the realm of change; since change has the structure of continuous magnitude (between any two points on a line there can always be another point—the decomposition of the line produces only further lines, not points), so does time (Coope 2005: chs 2, 6).

Christian cosmology, by contrast, is derived from Genesis, in the Old Testament, in which God creates the material world at the beginning of time, and the Apocalypse of the Book of Revelation in the New Testament, St John's vision of the end of time. These two events are reproduced in many churches in Christen-dom during the thousand years of the medieval period. Thus Saint Thomas Aquinas' doctrine of space and time in the thirteenth century is syncretic. Christian doctrine was expressed in terms of a finite two-sphere universe that had a begin-ning in time and would be dismantled again at the end of time. But Aquinas also borrows Aristotle's definition of time as the measure of continuous change, which is understood by the human mind as a succession of parts; and he views the outermost sphere as determinative of the places within it. For Aquinas and his followers, the motion of a body is referred to its place, understood in relation to the cosmos (whose centre and poles are fixed) as a whole. This view is countered by Duns Scotus, who argues that place is just the relation of one body to another: Scotist doctrine holds that the motion of a body must be defined as a relation among bodies. Thus even though late Scholastics agree that time and space conceived as outside the created world must be purely imaginary, so that real time and space are not independent of bodies, the debate over absolute versus relative time and space has its origins in philosophical disputes of the late Middle Ages (Ariew 1999: ch. 2). However, an issue central to the philosophy of time—how to account for temporal asymmetry—does not emerge at this point. To say that time is asymmetric means that time flows in one direction, and that our descrip-tions of the world should not remain true if the arrow of time is reversed. Since Aristotle treats time as dependent on change, asymmetry is explained by the analysis of change as the actualization of a potency: potencies become actual, not vice versa. And since Christian time is the realization of divine intention, temporality exhibits the before and after of intentionality. The issue emerges, as such, only after Galileo makes space, time, and motion (uniform and accelerated) geometrical.

Copernicus upsets the scheme of the Aristotelian two-sphere universe by arguing, in *De revolutionibus orbium coelestium* (1543), that the sun, not the earth, stands at the centre of the solar system. This challenge was supported by the revival of Democritean materialism in Renaissance Italy, the discovery of numerical rules for (heliocentric) planetary motion by Kepler on the basis of Tyco Brahe's improved empirical data, and by the assault on the Aristotelian worldview by Galileo Galilei in the following century. In the *Dialogo sopra i due massimi sistemi del mondo* (1632), and *Discorsi e Dimostrazioni Matematiche, intorno a due nuove Scienze* (1638), Galileo introduced a challenge at once theoretical, mathematical, and empirical. Two classic studies on this transition (and its aftermath) were published in the middle of the twentieth century: Koyré's *From the Closed World to the Infinite Universe* (1957) and Kuhn's *The Copernican Revolution* (1957).

Galileo is often cited as the thinker who gave the world the concept of inertial motion. Whereas Aristotelian bodies move in ways that are causally determined by their material essence and the places of the cosmos, Galilean bodies are indifferent to motion. Moreover, unaccelerated motion is indistinguishable from rest; Galileo argues this point in two different ways. He appeals to empirical experience: sailors shut up in the hull of a smoothly sailing boat cannot tell whether they are moving or at rest, for all physical interactions within the hull go on just as they would if the boat were at rest. He also appeals to a thought experiment, in which a perfectly spherical ball is rolled down a frictionless inclined plane (gathering speed) to a frictionless horizontal plane, where it must keep on going forever since it will never lose the speed it has acquired, unless it is forced to lose speed by going up another inclined plane. Since Galileo's plane here is an idealized version of the surface of the earth, it must be admitted that he takes inertial paths to be sections of great circles, rather than straight lines, but Descartes corrects this Aristotelian throwback (Westfall 1971: ch. 1; Cushing 1998: ch. 6).

Galileo uses the thought experiment of a sailor shut up in the hull of a ship in uniform motion to explain why the inhabitants of the earth might think the earth was at rest. On the Second Day of the *Dialogo*, Salviati observes: 'Whatever motion comes to be attributed to the earth must necessarily remain imperceptible to us and as if nonexistent, so long as we look only at terrestrial objects: for as inhabitants of the earth, we consequently participate in the same motion' (Galilei 1967: 114). That is, the earth is our inertial frame of reference. The Aristotelian argument that if the earth turned we would be scoured off the earth's surface is thus discredited. It follows that, for Salviati, the motion of the heavens may be just as well explained by the (to us imperceptible) turning of the earth:

Now there is one motion which is most general and supreme over all, and it is that by which the sun, moon, and all other planets and fixed stars—in a word, the whole universe, the earth alone excepted—appear to be moved as a unit from east to west in the space of twenty-four hours. This, in so far as first appearances are concerned, may just as logically belong to the earth alone as to the rest of the universe... (Galilei 1967: 114)

Galileo's analysis of motion has major consequences not only for astronomy but also for terrestrial mechanics. It indicates that the scientist investigating a body in motion should ask not what keeps it going, but what makes it stop or alter, and what results when two or more different motions are 'compounded' in a single body, a possibility opened by the indifference of Galilean bodies to motion. This striking conceptual change—along with the inspired insights that time, like distance and displacement, can be represented by a straight line, and the distance traversed by a body in uniformly accelerated motion by the area of a triangle—set the stage for Galileo's geometrical models of free fall and of projectile motion as the parabolic combination of free fall and inertial motion. Thus although Galileo may be credited with the first scientifically pertinent account of an inertial frame of reference, which is then used by Descartes to motivate a relativistic account of space, his geometrization of motion also suggests that physical space is Euclidean, and so is absolute, homogeneous, and isotropic (Petkov 2009: chs 2–3; Grosholz 2007: ch. 1).

Galileo's brilliant representation of time as a straight line, justly celebrated by Koyré, has other repercussions as well. First, it suggests that temporality is space-like. Precisely because it allows one to exhibit temporal (and eventually dynamic) relations in a diagram, it downplays two distinctive features of temporality, unidirectionality and open-endedness, the way the relation of the present to the future is unlike the relation of the present to the past. Since their aim is to make determinate predictions, the creators of seventeenth-century mechanics are disposed in any case to downplay the indeterminacy of the future. Indeed, the processes of Newtonian mechanics are supposed to be symmetrical with respect to time: they can run as easily backwards as forwards. Second, Galileo's representation suggests that the line of time is composed of points rather than linear intervals. When he constructs the triangle that represents the distance traversed by a body in uniformly accelerated motion (free fall), he performs an operation that is the precursor of integration with respect to time, something like the infinite sum of the product of every $f(x)$ with every $dx$ on the interval, though not under that description. Though Leibniz treats $dx$ as if it were a tiny line rather than a point, the effect of the introduction of the infinitesimal calculus in the long run is the point-decomposition of the line (and therefore here of time) beloved of set theory.

This representation also downplays an important feature of temporality as experienced by human beings; for us, experienced temporality always has an indeterminate spread into both the past and the future, because human action (what characterizes us as long as we are conscious) is intentional. Whether the things that carry out physical processes exhibit anything like rudimentary intentionality is highly debatable, though it is much less debatable that rudimentary intentionality characterizes living things, even the very small and simple ones studied by molecular biology. Biological function is a middle term between physico-chemical events and human action. In any case, physical science has still not solved the problem of how to represent properly the apparent unidirectionality and open-endedness of time, and (perhaps) the temporal spread or topological open-set-like nature of the present.[1]

# II: DESCARTES

In Part II of *Principia Philosophiae*, Descartes characterizes the physical realm as a three-dimensional Euclidean plenum of *res extensa*, matter which is both impenetrable and divisible; like Aristotle, he denies the possibility of the void. His first law of nature states that, 'each and every thing, in so far as it can, always continues in the same state; and thus what is once in motion always continues to move' (AT viii 62: CSM I 240). The second law, correcting Galileo, states that, 'all motion is in itself rectilinear' (AT viii 63: CSM I 241). The parts of a unified body will thus strive to retain, with the persistence of inertial motion, their state of common motion or common rest. For Descartes, the persistence of inertial motion leads to the third law, the conservation of 'quantity of motion' in collisions, where *mv* is taken to mean the product of 'bulk' or quantity of matter with speed (construed as a scalar). It should also be noted that, for Descartes, inertial motion is ideal or virtual; it is never realized in the plenum though constitutive of the discursive, imaginative, three-dimensional Euclidean space which the plenum makes physically real. The uniform motion of a particle is always disrupted in the 'real world' of Descartes, Huygens, and Leibniz, because it is always deflected by other particles jostling it in the plenum, and it continues to be virtual in the 'real world' of Newton, because it is always deflected by the attraction of nearby centres of force. In Cartesian mechanics, the jostling of particles produces circular swirls in the plenum, called 'vortices'. In Newton's diagrams, inertial motion becomes one linear component of curvilinear, accelerated motion.

Descartes' third law states that, 'if a body collides with another body that is stronger than itself, it loses none of its motion; but if it collides with a weaker body, it loses a quantity of motion equal to that which it imparts to the other body' (AT

---

[1] For an alternative view, see Dainton (2001: chs 3–6) and Maudlin (2007: ch. 4).

viii 65: CSM I 242). It is articulated into seven rules governing collisions of various kinds, which Descartes intends to be a coherent and complete set of rules, though as Huygens, Leibniz, and others variously pointed out later, it is neither. Thus for Descartes mathematical space is three-dimensional Euclidean space, which his new analytic geometry provides with axes and so a centre, and with novel methods that in *La Géométrie* are applied mostly to two-dimensional Euclidean space. The space of Cartesian physics is a plenum of matter which is taken to instantiate the space of geometry. It is not infinite but 'indefinitely extended', without an intrinsic centre or axes; one might say it is homogeneous and isotropic in the sense that, according to the third law, bits of matter have the same effects irrespective of where they are or in what direction they are moving. Descartes claims that *res extensa* differs from geometric (Euclidean) space only as the individual differs from the genus: they share the same relational structure. And indeed Descartes' physics is curiously atemporal and undynamic, far more so than that of Galileo, whose concern for and mathematical articulation of the temporality of motion leads directly to the sophisticated consideration of dynamical systems in the writings of Torricelli (and then Newton). There is in fact no accelerated motion in Descartes' account of collision, since 'quantity of motion' is supposed to be transferred instantaneously, and *pari passu* there is no infinitesimalistic reasoning in his *Principia* (Gaukroger 1995: ch. 7–9; Grosholz 1991: ch. 3–4).

Thus Descartes' invocation of Euclidean geometrical structure, which might lead us to expect from him an absolute conception of space if not of time, includes a strong relativism in his account of space. His definition of motion is 'the transfer of one piece of matter, or one body, from the vicinity of the other bodies which are in immediate contact with it, and which are regarded as being at rest, to the vicinity of other bodies' (AT viii 53: CSM I 233). Given that motion takes place in a plenum, the choice of which bodies are to be considered at rest is arbitrary. He writes: 'We cannot understand that a body AB is transferred from the vicinity of a body CD without simultaneously understanding that CD is transferred from the vicinity of AB' (AT viii 55: CSM I 235). Thus, motion and rest can be defined only as a difference in velocity or acceleration among bodies; no absolute determination of motion or rest is possible. Descartes' relativism can be interpreted as retrospective, that is as indebted to neo-Scholastic doctrine, or as prospective, that is as linked to his commitment to the radically un-Aristotelian concept of inertial motion. But his definition of motion is quite radical. It not only raised the question whether a given particle is at rest or in uniform, rectilinear motion, but also whether its trajectory should be considered uniform and rectilinear or accelerated and curvilinear. Descartes seems unaware of or unconcerned by how radical his relativism is, or that it makes the determination of inertial motion strictly impossible. Perhaps since there is no accelerated motion in his physics (because all causal interaction is the instantaneous transfer of *mv* in his schema for the collision of particles), the issue of the relativity or absoluteness of accelerated motion as well as of uniform motion just does not arise for him (Garber 1992: chs 7, 8; Des Chene 1996: ch 8).

It is hard to say what Descartes thought about the cosmological significance of time, because of his well-justified fear of antagonizing the Catholic Church; he had provided a cosmogony in *Le Monde* (1632), but carefully denied it any real significance and then suppressed the whole treatise. In the *Principia Philosophiae*, Descartes presents the physical world as the creation of God and its orderliness as an expression of God's perfection, which would presuppose a genesis (very unlike the Biblical *Genesis*), but there is no suggestion that future time is either finite or infinite. It is, like space, 'indefinitely extended'.

# III: HENRY MORE

Henry More, a theologian and philosopher, is the central figure in the group known as the Cambridge Platonists. He reads the *Principia Philosophiae* in 1646, and enters into a brief correspondence with Descartes. More objects to Descartes' metaphysics on a variety of grounds. He argues that spirit as well as matter must be extended, since God is omnipresent in the universe; thus the defining feature of matter is not extension but impenetrability. Rejecting Descartes' identification of matter and space and invoking the authority of the classical atomists, he argues that the universe is not a plenum and that void space is possible. Indeed, space itself must be infinite, not merely 'indefinite in extent', since it is an aspect of the divine essence; More spends many years struggling to define the precise sense in which space could be considered an aspect of God.

Descartes defends his notion of a transcendent God in his first reply to More, distinguishing between the 'vastness of this bodily extension' and 'the vastness of the divine substance or essence', which is not extended: 'And so I call the latter simply "infinite", and the former "indefinite"' (AT v 275: CSMK 364). More counters that the world is either finite or infinite; since God is infinite and everywhere present, the world itself must be infinite. In his second reply, Descartes asserts the relativity of time: if there were no world, there would be no time either. Supposing the existence of time before or after this world would make God subject to succession or temporality. Descartes' God radically transcends the material universe; More seeks to bring God into closer relation with this world (Koyré 1957: ch. 4; Hall 2002: ch. 8).

After Descartes' death, More continues to wrestle with Cartesianism, defending the infinity of space while vacillating over the question whether matter is finite or infinite. Twenty years later, the *Enchiridium metaphysicum* presents his final system. All substance is extended or diffused; extension is a necessary condition of existence. Matter is impenetrable and occupies space; the idea of matter without space is unthinkable, but the idea of space without matter is thinkable and indeed necessary. The mechanical philosophy cannot explain many important features of the world, foremost among them light, magnetism, and gravity. In order to account for these phenomena, More adds another middle term, the 'spirit of nature', distinct from pure immaterial extension. While his use of this notion is often fanciful, More is correct to point out that Descartes' mechanical philosophy cannot explain the physical effects of light or magnetism, why bodies persist as unities, or why bodies adhere to the surface of the earth. Infinite space he identifies with the 'Immensity of Divine Essence'.

More also criticizes Descartes' relativism on related grounds. He rightly objects to the implied generalization of the relativity of motion from inertial motion to rotation, and he argues by *reductio ad absurdum*: 'That the Cartesian definition of motion is rather the description of site and that, if it were of motion, the reciprocal nature of it argues one body to be moved by two contrary motions, indeed to be moved and not moved at the same time' (More 1671: 56; More 1995: I, 47). In other words, if we assume (as More does) that space is absolute, then the Cartesian definition of motion would lead us to claim that a body remained in the same place (defined as a well-defined locus in absolute space) and did not remain there at the same time. More believes that motion can ultimately be understood only on the basis of absolute space; and so he argues at cross purposes with the Cartesians, as Clarke would later argue at cross purposes with Leibniz.

More agrees with Descartes that space must be the attribute of something, but denies that it is an attribute of matter. Rather it is an attribute of spirit and indeed, as the condition of all existence, an attribute of God. Space thus becomes divine, an organ by means of which God creates the world and maintains it in order. In the end, More decides that the material universe while immense is still finite, in contrast to the infinite temporal duration and spatial amplitude of God, the sole infinite existent. This allows him to avoid the appearance that God might be immanent in the created world; as infinite, God still transcends the world while being omnipresent to it (Koyré 1957: ch. 6; Hall 2002: ch. 10).


# IV: ISAAC NEWTON

Newton rarely mentions Henry More (see Power 1970). However, the intellectual debt of Newton (who did not like to admit to metaphysical influences) to More has been traced by scholars ever since the publication of the *Opticks* (1704), where it is especially clear. Newton was known to have visited More in Christ's College, Cambridge, to discuss theological matters, and may well have read the *Enchidirion metaphysicum*. Like More, Newton invokes absolute space and time (an invocation which in fact proves problematic for the reception of his ideas), and views space as an attribute and organ of God. Newton claims in the *Opticks* that the wonderful uniformity of the planetary system 'can be the effect of nothing else than the Wisdom and Skill of a powerful ever-living Agent, who being in all Places, is more able by his Will to move the Bodies within his boundless uniform Sensorium, and thereby to form and reform the Parts of the Universe' (Newton 1952: 403). The study of natural philosophy thus leads us to an apprehension of God. More's metaphysical influence, including his critical opposition to Descartes on many points, may be discerned throughout Newton's works.

Newton's *Principia* (1687) begins with eight definitions concerning matter and force, and a Scholium on time, space, and motion, as well as three laws of motion. It will be useful for the following discussion to review the three laws of motion.

Law I. Every body perseveres in its state of being at rest or of moving uniformly straight-forward, except insofar as it is compelled to change its state by forces impressed.

Law II. A change in motion is proportional to the motive force impressed and takes place along the right line in which that force is impressed.

Law III. To any action there is always an opposite and equal reaction; in other words, the actions of two bodies upon each other are always equal and opposite in direction. (*Principia* 416, 417)

He defines quantity of matter as the product of volume and density, and the quantity of motion as the product of quantity of matter times velocity (a vector); his definitions then distinguish among the innate force of matter (*vis insita* or *vis inertiae*), impressed force, and centripetal force. Definition V runs: 'Centripetal force is the force by which bodies are drawn from all sides, are impelled, or in any way tend, towards some point as to a center' (*Principia* 405), and the last three definitions elaborate on that definition. Newton's method is geometrical. His proof that the law governing a centre of force which deflects a satellite from its inertial path into an elliptical orbit is an inverse square law, for example, depends on the famous diagram of an articulated ellipse with a centre of force at one of its two foci, the inertial path of the satellite drawn as a tangent to the curve, and a short line QR representing an 'impulse' of force. The argument proceeds by Euclidean reasoning about proportions among elements in the diagram, modified by Newton's method of ultimate ratios to accommodate infinitesimalistic reasoning (De Gandt 1995: ch. 3).

The Scholium says this about space and time.

I. Absolute, true, and mathematical time, in and of itself and of its own nature, without reference to anything external, flows uniformly and by another name is called duration. Relative, apparent, and common time is any sensible and external measure (precise or imprecise) of duration by the means of motion; such a measure—for example an hour, a day, a month, a year—is commonly used instead of true time.

II. Absolute space, of its own nature, without reference to anything external, always remains homogeneous and immovable. Relative space is any movable measure or dimension of this absolute space; such a measure or dimension is determined by our senses from the situation of the space with respect to bodies and is popularly used for immovable space, as in the case of space under the earth or in the air or in the heavens, where the dimension is determined from the situation of the space with respect to the earth. (*Principia* 408)

It follows from these definitions that absolute motion can be defined as the translation of a body from one absolute place (at a point in absolute time) to another. But since, as Newton admits, absolute space and time cannot be directly indicated, how can we empirically distinguish true absolute motion from what is only motion relative to things we can measure? Newton's answer is that forces, and their effects, are real and can be measured; he offers two thought experiments in defence of this claim.

First, suppose that a vessel, filled with water, is hung by a long cord. If it simply hangs there, the surface of the water remains flat; but if the cord is twisted and then released, so that the vessel spins, the surface of the water will form a concave figure, depressed in the middle and creeping up the sides of the vessel. This change indicates the 'impression of force' on the vessel and the reality of its accelerated, spinning motion. Second, suppose there are two globes connected by a cord in empty space, 'in an immense vacuum, where nothing external and sensible existed with which the balls could be compared' (*Principia* 414). If the globes were at rest with respect to each other, there would be no tension on the cord; but if they were revolving around their common centre of gravity, a tension would exist in the cord which, being measurable, would allow us to measure the 'endeavor of the balls to recede from the axis of motion' and therefore their true rotational, accelerated motion (*Principia* 414).

Thus for Newton, forces are real and measurable, and the presence of forces is the sign of true (accelerated) motion. And in Book III of the *Principia*, where he treats the solar system as an elaborate case study that exhibits the power and usefulness of his theory, Newton writes,

Hypothesis I: The center of the system of the world is at rest.
Proposition 11, Theorem 11: The common center of gravity of the earth, the sun, and all the planets is at rest.   (*Principia* 816)

Taken together, these claims offer a strikingly absolutist position that makes not only accelerated motion, but also uniform motion, absolute with respect to a Euclidean space that has been posited to exist independently of any bodies within it, and which is also provided with a centre and axes! In his attempt to save the cogency of the distinction between straight line motion at a constant velocity from accelerated (straight or curvilinear) motion, Newton has sacrificed the equivalence of inertial reference frames and thus his own first law. He has also postulated a spatio-temporal structure that cannot be empirically verified, which violates his own methodological principle of not invoking merely metaphysical hypotheses.

Newton criticizes a relativistic account of space and time in the Scholium on space and time in the first edition of the *Principia* (1687) and in the General Scholium in the second edition (1713); but his discussion in *De gravitatione*, published only in the twentieth century, reveals that the doctrine he is attacking is that of Descartes' *Principia*. Since in Cartesian vortex mechanics all bodies are constantly shifting their relative positions with the passage of time, Newton argues, 'It follows indubitably that Cartesian motion is not motion, for it has no velocity, no definition, and there is no space or distance traversed by it. So it is necessary that the definition of places, and hence of local motion, be referred to some motionless thing such as extension alone or space in so far as it is seen to be truly distinct from bodies' (Hall and Hall 1962: 131). In other words, Descartes' central concept of inertial motion is incompatible with his claim that spatial relations must be defined relativistically, so that all motion is relative in a very strong sense. Because Descartes' relativism is so strongly stated, it entails the relativity not only of uniform motion, but also of accelerated motion (Dainton 2001: ch. 11; Slowick 2002: ch. 2).This must be a problem for Descartes, because the conceptual basis of *La Géométrie* is the priority and distinction of straight lines, and Descartes claims that his physics is materialized geometry. Moreover, given his conception of method as an order of reasons proceeding from simple elements to complexes constructed from them, if he cannot establish the status of the simple elements (particles in unilinear motion at a constant speed), he could not construct his physics. Since a body's line of motion and velocity cannot be determined in a Cartesian universe, Newton concludes, Descartes' science of mechanics is contradictory, and we cannot avoid the hypothesis of absolute space and time. Newton's bold claim is disputed almost as soon as he makes it, and Cartesianism persists even after the reception of Newton's mechanics on the Continent (Bertoloni Meli 1993: ch. 9; Maglo 2007).

# V: G. W. Leibniz and Samuel Clarke

Leibniz is interested in natural philosophy from an early age; his *Hypothesis Physica Nova*, a response to Hobbes' *De Corpore*, is published in 1671. But it is his invention of the infinitesimal calculus during his sojourn in Paris (1672–6) and his study of the work of Kepler, Galileo, Torricelli, Huygens, and Descartes, that deepens his understanding of mechanical problems. In 1688, while in Vienna on his way to Rome, Leibniz reads Newton's *Principia*, and writes extensive notes on it and then a series of papers, culminating in the *Tentamen de Motuum Coelestium Causis*, which is published in the *Acta Eruditorum* in February 1689. In this work, Leibniz uses the notation of his infinitesimal calculus to frame differential equations that would correctly characterize planetary motion, since he sees clearly that differential equations will be the language of mechanics. Leibniz combines finite and infinitesimal variables in the study of motion, whereas the variables used by Newton are finite, because he sidesteps the problem of infinitesimals by using finite ratios between vanishing or 'evanescent' quantities. Newton's notation does not lend itself to the development of differential equations. Leibniz in the *Tentamen* also combines Cartesian vortex theory with Newton's recasting of Kepler's three laws, in order to furnish an acceptable physical explanation of the laws governing central forces and to avoid the quandary of action at a distance. For Leibniz, the setting of celestial motion is fluid orbs, whereas for Newton it is empty space. While Newton thinks that his radically novel, geometrized, concept of force provides an explanation for planetary motion, Leibniz argues that the concept of force itself requires explanation (Bertoloni Meli 1993: ch. 4; Futch 2008: chs 1, 2).

A brief exchange of letters between Leibniz and Newton takes place in 1693, where Leibniz charges that Newton has failed to locate the cause of gravity, a cause that must follow from bits of matter in motion that transfer motion through collisions. Newton replies that he has successfully identified *gravity* as the cause of celestial motion: forces (gravity is one such force) are the cause of changes in states of motion of material bodies. After the Englishman John Keill in 1708 accuses Leibniz of stealing the infinitesimal calculus, the interchanges between Leibniz and Newton are indirect and embittered. The letters between Leibniz and Clarke, for all their interest, are unfortunately a polemical reduction of the more interesting exchange that might have taken place directly between the two great thinkers if politics had not intervened.

Philosophical reflection on this exchange in the latter half of the twentieth century, up until the present day, can be traced back to Alexander Koyré's masterful discussion of the metaphysical issues involved, in *From the Closed World to the Infinite Universe* (1957: ch. 11), and Hans Reichenbach's equally influential invocation of the debate in *The Philosophy of Space and Time* (1957), where he claims Leibniz as the philosophical source for the ideas of Mach and Einstein, and therefore of relativity theory. Young philosophers who return to the Leibniz/Clarke correspondence based on reading essays that stem from Reichenbach's interpretation will be puzzled to find no discussion of the nature of God, a topic that was both metaphysically and politically important for both philosophers. Those who come to the debate from the more historical perspective may not discern the technical issues, which are also important. On the one hand, Newton does not need and is not entitled to the hypothesis of absolute space provided with an origin and axes, nor that of absolute time; on the other hand, Leibniz (like Descartes) cannot in fact reconcile the indispensable concept of inertial motion with his relativistic account of space and time.

A year before his death, in November 1715, Leibniz reproaches Newton and his followers for supposing that space is the organ that God uses to perceive created things, which seems to make God corporeal. Here the ambiguous relation of Newton to More is revived. He also complains that Newton's God must from time to time re-wind the great timepiece of the universe, rather than supposing that nature is a 'pre-established order' (GP vii 352). Clarke in his first reply spends a long paragraph trying to save Newton from the threat of materialism.

And in the Universe, he [Newton] doth not consider Things as if they were Pictures, formed by certain Means, or Organs; but as real Things, form'd by God himself, and seen by him in all Places wherever they are, without the Intervention of any Medium at all. And this Similitude is all that he means when he supposes Infinite Space to be (as it were) the Sensorium of the Omnipresent Being.   (GP vii 354)

Clarke also argues that, as God is the maker of the world-clock, it cannot go on without his continual 'government and inspection', and suggests that Leibniz might be aligned with the sceptics, who suppose the world has no creation or author (GP vii 354). Clearly, Leibniz and Clarke were sharply divided in the way they understood God's intervention in the world. According to Leibniz, Newton's God is arbitrary and inconsistent whereas, in his view, God must always have sufficient reason for His choices. According to Clarke, Leibniz's God is no more than a mechanism; thus the cosmos is doomed to necessity. The conflict between Leibniz's rationalism and Newton's voluntarism could not be more apparent (Bouquiaux 2008).

In Leibniz's second letter, he hastens to distance himself from the materialists, and claims that mathematics alone cannot construct principles that will successfully oppose them. Mathematics requires the aid of metaphysics: the principle of contradiction must be supplemented by the principle of sufficient reason. There must always be a reason why things are as they are, rather than otherwise. Since observed facts must always underdetermine theory, a true physics will combine mathematics and empirical observation under the guidance of metaphysics. The world must be explained as the product not just of God's power, but also of His wisdom and perfection; this means, among other things, that there is no such thing as the void, empty space (GP vii 355–9).

Clarke responds to Leibniz's rationalism with an emphatic, English, Scotist, voluntarism: yes, there is always a reason why something happens, but 'this sufficient Reason is oft-times no other, than the mere Will of God.' So, for example, why this particular system of matter should be in the place it is (space being indifferent to matter), is explained by the claim that God decided by *fiat* to put it there. He adds that our solar system is not eternal, but will sooner or later 'fall into Confusion', and that it will last only as long as God wants it to last. God conserves things only as long as it seems fitting to him (GP vii 359–62). In his third letter, Leibniz counters by insisting that notions like cause and effect are governed by metaphysical, not just mathematical, principles, and that in particular the purely geometrical concept of space is an idol of the tribe, in Bacon's sense. Space, like time, is relative: space is an order of coexisting—logically compatible—things, as time is an order of successive—logically incompatible as well as asymmetrical—things. Here we should recall that for Leibniz, ideas are possibles, with genuine ontological status even if they will never be realized. God surveys the infinite ranges of *possibilia* and chooses, in accord with the principle of perfection (a version of the principle of sufficient reason), the best one to create. The creation of this world as nested infinities of ensouled material unities brings about the creation of space and time. Thus for Leibniz, logical relations of mutual compatibility among ideas are metaphysically prior to space, and logical relations of asymmetrical incompatibility are metaphysically prior to time. The extent of space and the successiveness of time are not fundamental, but must be explained by metaphysics (aided by logic).

Leibniz then turns to one of his famous thought experiments: suppose the universe sat in Newton's space; then suppose that East and West were switched and everything was backwards, but maintaining the same mutual relations. There would be no discernible difference between the first and the second universe. Therefore, by the principle of the identity of indiscernibles, they cannot be distinct. We cannot ask why God would prefer one to the other, because they are the same. Moreover, to say that God acts by *fiat* is to impugn the wisdom and goodness of God; God is not a tyrant but a wise monarch. So we must not say that the world needs an occasional tune-up; because then either God acts transcendently by miracle, or God is immanent in the world as a cause, and we are left with Spinozism (GP vii 363–7). Clarke replies with his own thought experiment, reminiscent of the way in which More used a *reductio ad absurdum* argument to attack the relativism of Descartes on the basis of his own absolutist conception of space and time. If the solar system were placed where the remotest stars are now, but everything preserved its order and distance, then according to Leibniz's relativism they would be in the same place then as they are now. Likewise, if God suddenly moved everything in a straight line 'with any swiftness whatsoever', Leibniz would have to say that everything continued in the same place. Or, if God had created the world millions of ages sooner than he did, Leibniz would have to say it was created at the same time as ours. Clarke finds all these conclusions absurd, and infers that they discredit Leibniz's relativism. Clarke also tries to clarify the Newtonian conception of infinite, indivisible space and time in relation to God: they are consequences of the existence of an infinite and eternal Being, in virtue of the fact that God is omnipresent to every thing at every time (GP vii 367–71). The significance of these thought experiments, along with Newton's 'bucket' thought experiments, are reviewed in Stein (1977), Friedman (1986), Earman (1992) and Dainton (2001).

Leibniz's fourth letter reiterates the importance of the principle of sufficient reason and the principle of the identity of indiscernibles. He claims that Clarke's thought experiments are without merit because they violate those principles, and that he is able to derive a contradiction because he has himself put a contradiction into the premises of the argument. Moreover, space and time cannot be due to God's awareness of all things at all times: space is the place of things, not of God's ideas of things. In a postscript, Leibniz adds that those who believe in the void and in atoms, violating as they do the two principles, are led astray by imagination rather than guided by reason. The amount of matter in the world as well as the degree of subdivision cannot be bounded, except arbitrarily, and God does nothing without reason (GP vii 371–81). Clarke responds with vehemence: 'This Notion leads to universal Necessity and Fate,' because they compare God's motives and judgement to the weights on a balance. And even if no two leaves can be found exactly alike, two small bits of matter could well be such: if they were in two different places, it would be absurd to say they were the same bit of matter. 'Two things, by being exactly alike, do not cease to be Two. The parts of Time, are as exactly like to each other, as those of Space. Yet two Points of Time, are not the same Point of Time' (GP vii 382). Clarke repeats his claim that space and time are consequences or properties of God's existence; space and time contain not just all things but all ideas as well. The action-at-a-distance of gravity is not a miracle; the real miracle—and an imaginative rejection of reason—would be Leibniz's pre-established harmony. Even if the action of gravity cannot be explained by 'mechanical' means, he concludes, it must be called natural because it is regular and constant (GP vii 381–8).[2]

Leibniz's long fifth letter responds in detail to each of Clarke's objections; Leibniz seems especially stung by the accusation of necessitarianism, to which he was often subject. He makes a distinction between absolute and hypothetical necessity, which depends on his according to *possibilia* a robust ontological status. In the case of an absolute necessity, there is no alternative because the only alternative is a contradiction, that is, nothing. However, when God chooses to create the best of all possible worlds, he sets aside other possible worlds that are

---

[2] For judicious reviews of this debate, see Wilson (1989: ch. 6), Cover and O'Leary-Hawthorne (1999: ch. 5).

not nothing; the choice is a real choice. A possible world is a collection of ideas in merely logical relation; only by creating this one world does God create material-spiritual unified things (monads), whose relations precipitate space and time. Clarke mistakes the incomplete, imaginary notions of mathematics for physical realities. To pursue mechanics successfully, we must treat space and time as completely filled by the things that exist: space and matter differ as do time and movement. And we must always supplement the principle of contradiction with the ampliative principle of sufficient reason, which entails that no entity can be admitted in physics that is in principle unobservable. It also entails that, in the best of all possible worlds, the universe of creatures constantly increases in perfection. Thus the spatially unbounded world has a temporal beginning point, but no end. The world is not the awareness of God, but the harmony of perspectives of all created things, for each monad is a 'living mirror' of the universe, according to its point of view. Thus the universal harmony is not a miracle, but a natural consequence of the mutual awareness of the things that exist (GP vii 389–420; see Adams 1998).

Clarke's equally long reply, the last letter in the series, is mostly a review of differences and alleged incomprehensions. Universal harmony does not seem to work very well for Leibniz and Newton! Clarke denies Leibniz's distinction between absolute and hypothetical necessity: 'Necessity, in Philosophical Questions, always signifies absolute Necessity.' He reiterated the claim that two bits of matter, exactly alike, could indeed exist in two different places, and argues that the exact likeness of two parts of mathematical space counts against the principle of the identity of indistinguishables. He re-asserts that the space occupied by a body is not the extension of the body, but that rather the extended body exists in space; and that God's existence causes space and time. He urges Leibniz to acknowledge the distinction between absolute real motion and relative motion, dismisses the principle of sufficient reason as unphilosophical, and says that he doesn't understand at all what the doctrine of universal harmony could mean. Finally, once again, he claims that gravitational attraction is a fact, the truth of which is not called into question by the failure of philosophers to find a mechanical cause for it (GP vii 421–40). Koyré's final analysis of this impasse is both funny and sobering: in the end, the two philosophers and the scientific revolution they generated between them, manage to do away with God (in his various rationalist and hermetic guises) altogether: 'The infinite Universe of the New Cosmology, infinite in Duration as well as Extension, in which eternal matter in accordance with eternal and necessary laws moves endlessly and aimlessly in eternal space, inherited all the ontological attributes of Divinity. Yet only those—all the others the departed God took away with him' (Koyré 1957: 276).

# CONCLUSION

The seventeenth-century debates about space and time seem to reach an impasse. On the one hand, relativists like Descartes and Leibniz cannot distinguish in a satisfactory way between inertial motion and other kinds of accelerated motion, despite the fact that inertial motion is defined as a central feature of their mechanics. On the other hand, Newton's absolutist doctrine of space and time is too strong; it makes all motion absolute, so that the physical equivalence of rest and inertial motion, and of motion in different inertial frames, is lost; but this equivalence, on which depends the 'Galilean invariance' of physical laws, is central to his mechanics. This doctrinal tension pervades debates throughout the eighteenth century about the reality of force, the reality of time, and the relation of space and time, until it finds precise expression in the scientific revisions of electromagnetic theory and thermodynamics in the nineteenth century, and the revolutions of special and general relativity, and quantum mechanics in the twentieth.

Contemporary philosophers and physicists concerned with modern cosmology have likewise found very few conclusions and a great deal of speculation in modern science, and quite often go back to the seventeenth century to get their bearings. Smolin begins Part 4 of *The Life of the Cosmos* (1997) with a review of the debate between Leibniz and Newton, and cites both thinkers throughout the book. Dainton begins the discussion of space in his comprehensive survey *Time and Space* (2001) with a review of Galileo, Descartes, and the debate between Leibniz and Newton. He observes that, to save the integrity of inertial motion, Newton posits absolute acceleration, but in so doing also posits absolute velocity, even though his own theory assumes Galilean invariance: his theory thus distinguishes empirically indistinguishable states of affairs. Some twentieth-century philosophers try to avoid this problem by re-casting Newtonian mechanics in terms of spacetime, and by attributing a novel structure to it; the result is 'neo-Newtonian spacetime'. In neo-Newtonian spacetime, while the temporal relations among hyperplanes remain intact, the concept 'same place' cannot be applied over time, since spatial relations obtain only among points that are simultaneous; and this seems obviously counterintuitive.

Similar variants have been described by other philosophers. Tim Maudlin proposed a relationist version of neo-Newtonian spacetime, and Edward Slowik a Cartesian spacetime. (Maudlin 1994: ch. 2; Slowik 2002: Part III). It is worth recalling that, in special relativity theory, Minkowski spacetime is also designed to abolish absolute velocity while retaining absolute acceleration. Whereas neo-Newtonian spacetime abandons spatial relations over time but retains a rigid temporal framework, Minkowski spacetime makes temporal separation relative to the frame of the observer, so that the notion of a temporal interval between events is not well defined, and the concept 'same time' loses its meaning. Moreover, while neo-Newtonian spacetime allows for the assignment of a magnitude to absolute acceleration, Minkowski spacetime does not, though it distinguishes between zero and non-zero acceleration (Sklar 1974: ch. 3; Dainton 2001: ch. 16). All of these models have consequences that run counter to our quotidian experience of space and time, and have consequently met with renewed and intensified criticism from other philosophers. Moreover, spacetime models of the cosmos assimilate time to space and thus fail to capture the essential asymmetry of temporality. The spell of space and time apparently remains unbroken in the enchanted, or haunted, wood of the twenty-first century.

# REFERENCES

ADAMS, R. (1998). *Leibniz: Determinist, Theist, Idealist.* Oxford: Oxford University Press.

ARIEW, R. (1999). *Descartes and the Last Scholastics.* Ithaca, NY: Cornell University Press.

BERTOLONI MELI, D. (1993). *Equivalence and Priority, Newton versus Leibniz.* Oxford: Oxford University Press.

BOUQUIAUX, L. (2008). 'Leibniz Against the Unreasonable Newtonian Physics,' in M. Dascal (ed.), *Leibniz: What Kind of Rationalist?* Heidelberg: Springer Verlag, 99–110.

COOPE, U. (2005). *Time for Aristotle.* Oxford: Oxford University Press.

COVER, J. A. and O'LEARY-HAWTHORNE, J. (1999). *Substance and Individuation in Leibniz.* Cambridge: Cambridge University Press.

CUSHING, J. T. (1998). *Philosophical Concepts in Physics. The Historical Relation between Philosophy and Scientific Theories.* Cambridge: Cambridge University Press.

DAINTON, B. (2001). *Space and Time.* Montreal and Kingston, CA: McGill-Queen's University Press.

DASCAL, M. (ed.) (2008). *Leibniz: What Kind of Rationalist?* Heidelberg: Springer Verlag.

DE GANDT, F. (1995). *Force and Geometry in Newton's Principia.* Princeton, NJ: Princeton University Press.

DES CHENE, D. (1996). *Physiologia: Natural Philosophy in Late Aristotelian and Cartesian Thought.* Ithaca: Cornell University Press.

EARMAN, J. (1992). *World Enough and Space–Time: Absolute versus Relational Theories of Space and Time.* Cambridge, MA: MIT Press.

EARMAN, J., GLYMOUR, C. N., and STRACHEL, J. J. (eds) (1977). *Foundations of Space–Time Theories.* Minneapolis: University of Minnesota Press.

FRIEDMAN, M. (1986). *Foundations of Space–Time Theories: Relativistic Physics and the Philosophy of Science.* Princeton, NJ: Princeton University Press.

FUTCH, M. (2008). *Leibniz's Metaphysics of Space and Time.* Boston Studies in the Philosophy of Science 258. Heidelberg: Springer Verlag.

GALILEI, G. (1967). *Dialogue Concerning the Two Chief World Systems.* Trans. S. Drake. Berkeley: University of California Press.

GARBER, D. (1992). *Descartes' Metaphysical Physics.* Chicago: University of Chicago Press.

GAUKROGER, S. (1995). *Descartes: An Intellectual Biography.* Oxford: Oxford University Press.

GREGORY, A. (2008). *Ancient Greek Cosmogony*. London: Duckworth.

GROSHOLZ, E. (1991). *Cartesian Method and the Problem of Reduction*. Oxford: Oxford University Press.

GROSHOLZ, E. (2007). *Representation and Productive Ambiguity in Mathematics and the Sciences*. Oxford: Oxford University Press.

HALL, A. R. (2002). *Henry More and the Scientific Revolution*. Cambridge: Cambridge University Press.

HALL, A. R. and HALL, M. B. (eds) (1962). *Unpublished Scientific Papers of Isaac Newton*. Cambridge: Cambridge University Press.

KOYRÉ, A. (1957). *From the Closed World to the Infinite Universe*. Baltimore, MD and London: Johns Hopkins University Press.

KUHN, T. (1957). *The Copernican Revolution*. Cambridge, MA: Harvard University Press.

MAGLO, K. (2007). 'Force, Mathematics, and Physics in Newton's *Principia*: A New Approach to Enduring Issues', *Science in Context*, vol. 4. Cambridge: Cambridge University Press.

MAUDLIN, T. (1993). 'Buckets of water and waves of space: Why spacetime is probably a substance'. *Philosophy of Science*, 60: 183–203.

MAUDLIN, T. (1994). *Quantum Non-Locality and Relativity*. Oxford: Blackwell.

MAUDLIN, T. (2007). *The Metaphysics Within Physics*. Oxford: Oxford University Press.

MORE, H. (1671). *Enchiridium metaphysicum*. London.

MORE, H. (1995). *Henry More's Manual of Metaphysics*. Trans. A. Jacob and A. Zuerich. New York: Georg Olms.

NEWTON, I. (1952). *Opticks*. Ed. I. B. Cohen. New York: Dover Publications [1st edn. 1704].

PETKOV, V. (2009). *Relativity and the Nature of Spacetime*. Berlin and New York: Springer Verlag.

POWER, J. E. (1970). 'Henry More and Isaac Newton on absolute space'. *Journal of the History of Ideas*, 31: 289–96.

PYLE, A. (1995). *Atomism and its Critics: From Democritus to Newton*. South Bend, IN: St Augustine's Press.

REICHENBACH, H. (1957). *The Philosophy of Space and Time*. Mineola, NY: Dover Publications.

SKLAR, L. (1974). *Space, Time, and Spacetime*. Berkeley, CA: University of California Press.

SLOWICK, E. (2002). *Cartesian Spacetime: Descartes' Physics and the Relational Theory of Space and Motion*. Dordrecht: Kluwer.

SMOLIN, L. (1997). *The Life of the Cosmos*. Oxford: Oxford University Press.

STEIN, H. (1977). 'Some Philosophical Prehistory of General Relativity', in J. Earman, C. N. Glymour, and J. J. Strachel (eds), *Foundations of Space–Time Theories*. Minneapolis: University of Minnesota Press, 3–49.

WESTFALL, R. (1971). *The Construction of Modern Science: Mechanisms and Mechanics*. Hoboken, NJ: John Wiley.

WILSON, C. (1989). *Leibniz's Metaphysics: A Historical and Comparative Study*. Princeton, NJ: Princeton University Press.

CHAPTER 4

# THE MECHANICAL PHILOSOPHY

## HELEN HATTAB

IF one were to ask a group of experts which early modern philosophers counted as sceptics or idealists, one would hear the same handful of names from each respondent. It is not so with the mechanical philosophy, or mechanism, as it is often called. Self-described proponents of the mechanical philosophy include figures as diverse as Descartes, More, the young Leibniz, Boyle, and Hooke. Moreover, different experts in the history of philosophy and science have argued that diverse subsets of the following figures comprise the mechanists: Bacon, Beeckman, Galileo, Mersenne, Gassendi, Charlton, Digby, Descartes, More, Hobbes, Cordemoy, La Forge, Malebranche, Régis, Rohault, Huygens, Spinoza, Boyle, Locke, Hooke, Leibniz and, under some descriptions, even Newton.[1] The list

---

[1] For instance, Marie Boas Hall traces mechanism back to ancient atomism and associates it primarily with atomist matter theory, claiming that modern mechanists added the variations of the motions of particles to atomist explanatory principles (Boas Hall 1981: 434–5). J. A. Bennett, by contrast, contends that many accounts of mechanism are too quick to embrace a radical divide between theoretical science (high science) and practical crafts (low science), leading them mistakenly to locate the inspiration for mechanical philosophy in ancient atomism (Bennett 1986: 1–4). Some scholars seek to reconcile theoretical and practical approaches by distinguishing between 'strict mechanism' or 'mechanism as ontology' which, like atomism, adopts a strict reduction of matter to primary qualities, and 'loose mechanism' or 'mechanism as method' which allows for the reinjection of active principles into matter (Janiak 2009: 52; Des Chene 2005: 246; Downing 2005). Others suggest that since the mechanical philosophy consists in a 'legitimatory program' it must not be confused with the more practical fields of mechanics and experimental philosophy, which unlike mechanism, did not entail a reductive theory of matter (Gaukroger 2006: 253–6).

expands significantly if one also includes less well-known early modern figures. A more apt title for this chapter might have been 'Mechanical Philosophies'. Just as the label 'Aristotelian' came, over time, to include a bewildering variety of doctrines and approaches, the term 'mechanical' when applied to natural philosophy came to function as an equally wide-ranging umbrella, encompassing a variety of distinct alternatives to both Aristotelian and animistic natural philosophies. The notion that the leading anti-Aristotelian modern philosophers all practised a clearly identifiable type of philosophy that we call 'mechanistic' is a historical construct that originated in the works of Robert Boyle and was perpetuated by subsequent historians.[2] That is not to say that there were no such philosophers who considered their endeavours 'mechanical' in some sense of the word. Clearly, there were. However, as I will show, to be a *mechanical* philosopher meant different things in different contexts.

Henry More appears to have been the first to use the term 'mechanical philosophy' but Robert Boyle popularized it, using two terms more or less interchangeably, '*Corpuscular* or *Mechanical* philosophy' (Anstey 2000: 12). Boyle distinguished his natural philosophy from Epicurean atomism and a deist interpretation of the Cartesian creation story, and claimed that God, after creating matter 'so guided the various motions of the parts of it so as to contrive them into the world he designed they should compose ... and established those *rules of motion*, and that order amongst things corporeal, which we are wont to call the *laws of nature*' (S: 139). God's 'incessant concourse and general providence' implies that 'the phenomena of the world thus constituted are physically produced by the mechanical affections of the parts of matter, and that they operate upon one another according to mechanical laws' (S: 139). Having emphasized the intelligibility and clarity of mechanical explanations and principles, Boyle praised their economy: 'there cannot be *fewer* principles than the two grand ones of the Mechanical philosophy—*matter* and *motion*' (S: 141). Once he introduced the primary qualities of matter: motion, figure, size, posture, rest, order, and texture, he claimed that the 'innumerable diversifications that compositions and decompositions make of a small number' provide mechanical explanations in statics, hydrostatics, and astronomy, and even in the invisible parts of matter (S: 142).

Following Boyle, the mechanical philosophy is most often associated with a reductive theory of matter, according to which the parts of matter are defined by geometrical properties, and move in accordance with universal, mathematizable laws of motion. Hence, all physical phenomena, including all forces and qualities of matter, can be explained in terms of two principles: matter and motion. However, since these motions occur at the unobservable, corpuscular level, scientific

[2] I wish to acknowledge receipt of a Summer Undergraduate Research Fellowship from the University of Houston, which supported a research assistant, Casey Johnson, for the extensive research for this chapter.

explanation must consist in certain forms of structural explanations whereby the geometrical properties and mathematical laws that hold of everyday observable phenomena are transferred, by analogy, to unobservable phenomena, the ultimate goal being mathematical demonstrations of the phenomena in question (Gabbey 2001). Historically, these crucial elements of Boyle's 'mechanical philosophy' rarely all come together in the works of so-called mechanists; some concentrate on providing metaphysical accounts of matter, whereas others adjust their accounts of matter to fit the best available explanations of specific phenomena.

For example, Descartes and Hobbes were among the most consistent mechanists with respect to matter theory, since both upheld the strict reduction of matter to the properties of extension, denying intrinsic forces to matter and the possibility of vacua. And yet, we do not look to either as shining examples of the kinds of mathematical explanations associated with the mechanical philosophy. For Hobbes, as for Aristotelians of this time, physics still consists in the identification of material and efficient causes of effects, although he redefines both of the latter: 'The aggregate of accidents in the agent or agents, requisite for the production of the effect, the effect being produced, is called the *efficient cause* thereof; and the aggregate of accidents in the patient, the effect being produced, is usually called the *material cause...*' (HW I: 122, 4). Descartes envisions a *cosmos* governed by universal laws, but his rules of collision are notoriously false, and most of his scientific explanations consist in hasty inferences from observed effects to the supposed geometrical properties and arrangements of unobservable material particles. Representative is his structural explanation of salt, which he recommends to Regius: 'Essential forms explained in our fashion, on the other hand, give manifest and mathematical reasons for natural actions, as can be seen with regard to the common form of salt in my *Meteorology*' (AT III 507). Descartes' 'manifest and mathematical' explanation consists merely in claiming that since we observe salt grains to be square, they must be made up of oblong shaped particles arranged side by side, to form a square. This is fairly typical of Cartesian explanations.

On the other hand, Beeckman, whose 'physico-mathematics' is regarded as an early instance of mechanism, was successful in articulating mathematical laws of motion but far less consistent when it came to metaphysical matter theory. For Beeckman, the ability to conceive or mentally picture how something occurs is key to explanation. In 1613 he rejects the Aristotelian impetus theory of motion: 'Who can form a mental conception of what that power would be, how it keeps the stone in motion, in which part of the stone it resides? However, it is very easy to form a mental conception that motion never comes to rest in a vacuum because no cause occurs to change the motion, for nothing is changed without any cause of change' (Beeckman 1939: I, 24–5). Similarly, in a contemporaneous exchange with Jeremiah van Laren, he defends small vacua on the grounds that otherwise there could be no motion and challenges Van Laren to prove by reason that matter can rarify and densify without a vacuum rather than appealing to God's power to infuse it with rarifying and densifying powers (Beeckman 1953: IV, 27–8). By 1618 Beeckman holds the view that 'all things consist in atoms of diverse forms and at different distances from each other, that is by empty intermediate spaces...' (1953: I, 201). He elsewhere specifies that there are four shapes of atoms from which the elements themselves are composed and concludes that 'The forms and natures of things are made of these first bodies' (1953: I, 153). Van Berkel shows that Beeckman was led to atomism not through an initial encounter with classical atomism, but via his engagement with the mechanical explanations of Hero of Alexandria's *Pneumatica*, some of which appealed to interstitial vacua (Van Berkel 1983: 167–8). Beeckman is thus driven eventually to formulate an atomist matter theory not primarily on metaphysical grounds, but because it fits the intelligible mechanical explanations he seeks. Consequently, he confronted head on the contradiction between the definition of atoms as absolutely hard and the requirement that they must be elastic so as to explain the fact that they bounce off each other (Beeckman 1942 II: 100–1). Different attempts to resolve this problem in various parts of Beeckman's *Journal* make it unclear whether he was a consistent atomist.

In the face of historical instances of the 'mechanical philosophy' Boyle's criteria are at once too broad and too narrow. They are too broad, when he claims to write 'rather for the Corpuscularians in general, than any party of them' (S: 7); he treats the mechanical philosophy as a hypothesis that is neutral about the metaphysical nature of matter:

I have forborne to employ arguments that are either grounded on, or suppose, indivisible corpuscles called *atoms*, or any *innate motion* belonging to them; or that the essence of bodies consists in extension; or that a vacuum is impossible; or that there are such *globuli caelestes*, or such a *materia subtilis*, as the Cartesians employ to explicate most of the phenomena of nature.   (S: 7)

Boyle conflates two competing natural philosophies grounded in distinct theories of matter under the label 'mechanical or corpuscularian philosophy', namely, Gassendist atomism and Cartesian mechanism.[3] But this is unwarranted since to be an atomist need not imply a commitment to the mechanical demonstrations that Descartes envisioned and vice versa.[4]

---

[3] That the Cartesians considered themselves first and foremost as rivals to the atomists is clear from the fact that Jacques Rohault even goes so far as to align the Cartesian philosophy with Aristotle in opposition to Epicurus (Rohault 1978: 151). Lynn Sumida Joy highlights key differences between Boyle's conciliatory aims and the distinct metaphysical programmes of Descartes and Gassendi (Joy 1992).

[4] E.g. the Dutch philosopher David van Goorle (aka Gorlaeus) had developed a comprehensive atomist theory as early as 1610, but his major work, the *Exercitationes Philosophicae* (published posthumously in 1620) shows no hint of mechanical explanations of natural phenomena. Furthermore, Lolordo points out that Gassendi had no interest in mechanics, and compared nature to a machine about as often as he compared it to an army (2007: 154).

Boyle's criteria are also too narrow because, eschewing metaphysical speculation, he adds the evidentiary requirement of experimental confirmation, which is lacking in many of the explanations advanced by early mechanists.

That, then, which I chiefly aim at is to make it probable to you by experiments (which I think hath not yet been done) that almost all sorts of qualities, most of which have been by the Schools either left unexplicated, or generally referred to I know not what incomprehensible substantial forms, *may* be produced mechanically—I mean by such corporeal agents as do not appear either to work otherwise than by virtue of the motion, size, figure, and contrivance, of their own parts (which attributes I call the *mechanical affectations* of matter, because to them men willingly refer the various operations of mechanical engines); or to produce the new qualities, exhibited by those bodies their action changes, by any other way than by changing the *texture,* or *motion,* or some other *mechanical affection,* of the body wrought upon.   (S: 17)

Hence I propose that we not take Boyle's rather unique amalgam of atomist and other corpuscularian matter theories, mechanical explanations, and experimentalism as definitive of all mechanical philosophies and instead examine different kinds of early modern natural philosophy that were regarded as 'mechanical' in some sense.

To identify all the forms that such philosophies took is a gargantuan task not feasible in a chapter of this length. What I propose is to provide a starting point for further studies. I begin with a characterization of what I will call the 'mechanical ideal'. This broader ideal lies at the origin of and provides the stimulus for the development of various mechanical philosophies, and persists throughout various reinterpretations of what it means to be a 'mechanical philosopher'. I then focus on three cases involving important (re)interpretations of the philosophical implications of this ideal. I do not pretend that these cases are exhaustive, nor that the philosophers examined capture the range of philosophical responses to the issues at stake. However, they provide us with useful examples of antagonistic responses to the same problem. Each case thus highlights a bifurcation that occurred at a crucial juncture among philosophers who shared the mechanical ideal. I take no position regarding which side of the bifurcation has the better claim to represent the mechanical philosophy, since this would require a neutral and clear definition, which we still lack.

# I: THE MECHANICAL IDEAL

In its earliest, inchoate expressions, the mechanical ideal aligns itself with a Platonist, as opposed to Aristotelian, conception of the true essence of the universe, and strives for the certainty of geometrical demonstrations found in the newly revitalized ancient science of machines as opposed to the syllogistic demonstrations of natural causes that prevailed in Aristotelian physics. While Christian appropriations of Plato's geometer God who fashions the universe according to 'number, measure and order' are at least as old as St Augustine, in the Renaissance, the success enjoyed by geometrical explanations of the workings of simple machines prompted the addition of mechanical skill to the divine artificer's geometrical penchant. Ramus's student and teacher of mathematics, Henri de Monantheuil, proclaims:

Indeed with these great and numerous things which were manifestly in the eyes of all both made and conserved by man . . . it is most easy [for] whoever has a mind to believe, know, and grasp, that this world, certainly the greatest work of works, was made and conserved . . . not by any man, but by another 'maker of machines' surpassing man by as much excellence, wisdom and power, indeed infinitely, as the amount by which this machine of the world surpasses and is superior to the machines of all men, even of the Archimedeans.    (1599: 6–7)

The image of the universe as the most intricate of machines created by the divine mechanic was not unique to anti-Aristotelian philosophers. The Jesuit priest, Giovanni de Guevara, draws on it in his commentary on the Aristotelian *Quaestiones Mechanicae*, to account for the God-like power mechanics gives us over nature: 'Whence, just as the human mind itself reflects the image of divine wisdom and providence so long as it arranges everything correctly, so also the hand of man expresses in a certain fashion the omnipotence of the creator, so long as the so various and remarkable things are brought to completion with mechanical thought as the leader' (De Guevara 1627: 3–4).

The superiority of the mathematical demonstrations employed in mechanics over the demonstrations of other sciences is clearly articulated by another Jesuit, Josephus Blancanus:

In demonstrations from signs [*a signo*], from which other sciences frequently start, only the cognition of the name of the subject is required, but not the essential definition, for its essence, which is hidden, is investigated by its accidents and its properties, from what is posterior [*a posteriori*]; and then, once the essence is detected, we return to the distinct and scientific demonstrations of its properties. However, if the perfect cognition of the object were given in the first place, as is the case with mathematical objects on account of their perfect definitions, we would proceed according to the most beautiful order of nature, from the essence of the object to the demonstration of its properties, as it happens in demonstrations from the cause [*a causa*], as are almost all geometrical and arithmetical demonstrations . . .    (Blancanus 1996: 194).

But no one envisioned the potential for a unified, certain science modelled after the geometrical demonstrations found in mechanics in more vivid detail than Descartes. Responding to Fromondus' criticism, he writes:

If my philosophy seems too 'crass' for him, because, like mechanics, it considers shapes and sizes and motions, he is condemning what seems to me its most praiseworthy feature, of which I am particularly proud. I mean that in my kind of philosophy I use no reasoning which is not mathematical and evident, and all my conclusions are confirmed by true observational data.   (AT I 421: CSMK 64)

To facilitate the application of mathematical demonstrations to nature, Descartes also firmly established the identification of nature with a divinely fashioned machine, stating that there is no essential difference between machines of human origins and the parts of nature. Natural objects are not merely *like* machines; they *are* simply more complex machines. Responding to Morin, Descartes writes: 'I know that you will say that the form of the clock is only an artificial form, while the form of the sun is natural and substantial; but I reply that this distinction concerns only the cause of these forms, and not at all their nature . . .' (AT II 367: CSMK 122). He also advised Regius in 1642 to respond to Voetius by making the identification in the other direction: 'I would like to explain in what way even automata are works of nature and men in making them do nothing but apply the active to the passive' (AT III: 504). He then claims that 'there is no essential difference' but only one of degree between them (AT III: 504).

Descartes' scientific writings are rife with analogies between parts of nature and human artefacts: the particles of light move through a medium like a tennis ball, planets follow circular paths just like a stone rotated in a sling, the diseased human body follows the laws of nature as much as a clock that does not tell the right time, the heart is like a furnace, magnetic matter consists in particles shaped like screws, and the human body is a machine that resembles a fountain or an organ. Some analogies, most notably the comparison of the motions of planets to bodies carried around in a water vortex, are not direct analogies to machines but are inspired by problems for which the Aristotelian *Quaestiones Mechanicae* gives geometrical explanations (AR II, 1317–18).[5] *Post* Descartes, both the general nature/machine analogy and more specific analogies are appropriated by Cartesians and experimentalist philosophers alike. The identification of nature and artefact serves both to reinforce the broader ideal of a universe that is as intelligible as the workings of a machine, and to generate mechanical explanations of specific unobservable natural processes through the construction of observable models.

One analogy that seems to have been particularly fruitful in the second regard is the analogy between water vortices and the heavens. While Descartes does not invoke it in his published writings, in various letters he makes a specific comparison to an observable reproduction of a water vortex in order to justify his explanation of gravity:

[5] Sixteenth- and seventeenth-century commentators developed the geometrical explanation given in the Aristotelian text in ways that illuminate Descartes' account of heavenly vortices (Hattab 2005).

In order to understand how the subtle matter which revolves around the earth chases heavy bodies towards the centre of the earth, fill some round vessel with tiny lead pellets, and mix in some larger pieces of wood or other material that is lighter than lead. Now spin the vessel round very quickly. In this way you will demonstrate that the pellets drive the pieces of wood or other such material towards the centre of the vessel, just as subtle matter drives terrestrial bodies towards the centre of the earth.    (AT II 593–4: CSMK 138–9)

Christiaan Huygens echoes Descartes' view that to 'search for an intelligible cause of gravity, one must see how it can be done, while supposing that there are in nature nothing but bodies made of the same matter in which one considers no quality nor inclination to approach one another, but only different sizes, shapes and movements...' (Huygens 1937: 631). He then notes that Descartes' version of the experiment does not rule out that the motion of the pieces of wood towards the centre could be due to the difference in the heaviness of the wood and the lead.[6] Huygens thus devises another version in which a circular dish, filled with water and containing some pieces of wax only slightly denser than the water, is spun around on a rotating table top until the water shares in the motion of the dish. When the dish's motion is suddenly stopped, the pieces of wax collide with the bottom of the dish, after which they move more slowly than the surrounding water and gather at the centre of the dish. To rule out causal interference by collisions between the wax and the bottom of the dish, Huygens fastens a ball of wax so that it can slide up and down strings spanning the diameter of the dish (1937: 632–3). The ball still slides down the string to the centre of the bowl when the dish's motion is suddenly stopped. In Huygens' hands, the mechanically produced water vortex serves to demonstrate that an intelligible, purely mechanical explanation of natural gravity can be given. The successful mechanical explanation of the observed effect of gravity, in turn, reinforces the general analogy between the heavens and water vortices.

However, the analogies that form part of the mechanical ideal do not always give rise to explanations modelled after demonstrations of mechanical devices, nor does a commitment to some form of mechanical explanation in physics always imply a commitment to the view that the universe is, by its very essence, just a machine made up of passive bits of matter activated by an external source of power. Hence one still finds in the mature Leibniz, a commitment to the image of the divine mechanic that originated in the Renaissance: 'Thus each organized body of a living being is a kind of divine machine or natural automaton, which infinitely surpasses all artificial automata.... But natural machines, that is, living bodies, are still machines in their least parts, to infinity. That is the difference between nature and art, that is, between divine art and our art' (LAG 221). However, his idealist metaphysics precludes explanations at the ground level

---

[6] See Dear (2005) for a more detailed discussion of the differences between Descartes' and Huygens's uses of the experiment.

from being mechanical in nature: 'Moreover, we must confess that the *perception*, and what depends on it, is *inexplicable in terms of mechanical reasons*, that is, through shapes and motions' (LAG 215). By contrast, in his Preface to the *Principia Mathematica* Newton traces the mathematical science by which he explains the mathematical principles of nature back to an ancient science of mechanics, implying that his explanations are still mechanical, albeit in a different sense than Leibniz's:

> Since the ancients (according to *Pappus*) considered *mechanics* to be of the greatest importance in the investigation of nature and science and the moderns—rejecting substantial forms and occult qualities—have undertaken to reduce the phenomena of nature to mathematical laws, it has seemed best in this treatise to concentrate on *mathematics* as it relates to natural philosophy ... *geometry* is founded on mechanical practice and is nothing other than that part of *universal mechanics* which reduces the art of measuring to exact propositions and demonstrations. But since the manual arts are applied especially to making bodies move, *geometry* is commonly used in reference to magnitude, and *mechanics* in reference to motion. In this sense *rational mechanics* will be the science, expressed in exact propositions and demonstrations, of the motions that result from any forces whatever and of the forces that are required for any motions whatever.   (*Principia*: 381, 382)

Newton thus saw his mathematical demonstrations as 'mechanical' in a sense that did not imply an underlying metaphysics of matter that reduced all physical actions to contact.

While the figures on our list of possible mechanical philosophers, from Beeckman to Newton, minimally share some version of the mechanical *ideal* originating in the Renaissance, it is not clear at which point a mechanical *philosophy* comes into being; nor is it evident when natural philosophy ceases to be *mechanical*. If the universe/machine analogy is taken to imply a certain type of matter theory (i.e. matter is a passive, extended substance, divided into minute particles and set in motion by an external force) then the mechanical philosophy begins with the revival of atomist matter theory (e.g. Bacon) and ends with the reintroduction of active powers and forces into matter (e.g. More, Leibniz, Newton, and on some accounts, Boyle). On the other hand, if the mechanical ideal is first and foremost a commitment to mathematical demonstrations as found in the science of machines, rather than to a specific matter theory, then experimentalist philosophers and mathematicians who were not systematic (e.g. Beeckman, Mersenne, Galileo, Huygens, and Hooke) displace more systematic philosophers from the list who did little to advance mathematical explanations modelled after mechanics (e.g. Bacon, Hobbes, Rohault, and Locke). As indicated, there is no historical reason beyond the authority of Boyle or later historians to privilege any one interpretation of what the ideal entails. Hence, I will remain neutral on these questions and limit myself to three instances illustrating how the mechanical ideal was, in different contexts, implemented in opposing ways by its proponents.

# II: FOUNDATIONALISM VERSUS
## MITIGATED SCEPTICISM

Mersenne and Descartes shared the mechanical ideal, and in the 1630s each advanced a mathematical approach to scientific explanation. However, whereas Descartes' clear and distinct perceptions penetrated to the metaphysical essence of the nature machine, Mersenne held that our best hope for scientific knowledge was limited to devising possible models to explain the observed phenomena. Mersenne seems to have preferred mechanical models and explanations mainly because of their utility. He expresses his scepticism regarding our ability to know the true essence of God's creation in several places. The following passage from *Les Questions Theologiques, Physiques, Morales, et Mathematiques* (1634) indicates a theological motivation:

> For one can say that we see only the bark and the surface of nature without being able to enter inside, and that we will never have any other science but that of its external effects, without being able to penetrate to the reasons, and without knowing the way in which it acts, until it pleases God to deliver us from this misery and open our eyes by the light which he reserves for his true worshippers    (Mersenne 1634: 217).

In the *Questions Inouyes* he reasons that we can neither know the elements necessary for the composition of the world, nor what is necessary for its establishment and conservation (Mersenne 1634: 51). We are hence limited by observation to two visible elements: earth, which is hard, firm, and opaque and air or water, which is soft, fluid, and diaphanous (1634: 51). Mersenne criticizes the alchemists for pretending to have penetrated to the ultimate elements and true substance of the world. He objects that their three elements could just as well be further reducible to more basic principles, whether these be Aristotelian matter and form, atoms, Anaxagoras' homœomery, Anaximenes' universal mind, the Ideas of the Academicians, Patricius' light and the hot and cold, dense and rare of Telesio and Campanella. Mersenne thus rejects all the competing metaphysical theories and urges those who wish to contribute to the establishment of the true philosophy to 'draw up faithful memories of their observations and experiences' (Mersenne 1634: 78).

Mersenne is equally sceptical about the ability of mathematics to yield knowledge of real essences and causes. For him, pure mathematics, like metaphysics, is a science of the imagination or pure intelligence which is concerned only with possible objects. Mathematics, he claims, rests entirely on the possibility of quantity. Without this foundation, mathematicians are limited to the lowest grade of demonstration, namely, *a posteriori* demonstrations which reason from observed effects back to cause(s). In other words, whether their subject or object is possible or not, mathematicians can reason hypothetically, that if it is possible to make a right angled triangle, then the Pythagorean theorem holds (Mersenne 1634: 54). Nonetheless, Mersenne champions the cause of practical mathematics by highlighting the usefulness of calendar reform and chronology to Theology, and of various mathematical propositions to Physics. For example, mathematics allows us to explain that smaller animals are less hurt when they fall from a height because they have more surface area in proportion to their solidity and hence fall less quickly (1634: 79–80). He claims that the underlying mathematical ratio can provide useful explanations of countless other physical phenomena, and so his commitment to seeing the world as a machine whose functions can be explained mathematically stems from the utility of such explanations rather than any special insight into nature's essence through mathematical and mechanical principles.

Descartes adopts the opposite view in respect of mathematical demonstrations. When faced with the merely possible objects of mathematics, and the inscrutable essence of God's creation, Mersenne retreats into an experimentalist, pragmatic approach to science. Descartes, by contrast, renders the possible objects of mathematics actual by redefining bodies as geometrical objects made real. In this way he places mathematical demonstrations about physical objects on a firm foundation. While earlier proponents of the mechanical ideal did not entirely discard the standard Aristotelian divisions between nature and art, and between physical and mathematical objects, Descartes' identification of nature and machine allowed him to regard the mathematical principles of mechanics as fundamental truths capturing the essence of God's creation. Hence Descartes claimed that, in his *Discourse on the Method,* he had deduced observed meteorological effects from principles borrowed from geometry.

And the principles or premises from which I deduce these conclusions, are only the axioms that the demonstrations of the geometers depend on, such as, 'the whole is greater than the part', 'if you take away equals from equals, the remaining ones will be equal', etc., not, however, abstracted from all sensible matter, as with the Geometers, but applied to various experiences known by sense and undoubted, as when from the fact that the particles of salt are oblong and inflexible, I deduced the square shape of its morsels, and many others which are evident to the senses . . .    (AT I 476).

Similarities between Descartes' deductions and those found in Aristotelian works in the mathematical science of machines appear to underlie his confident claim that 'my entire physics is nothing but mechanics' (AT II 542: CSMK 135).[7] Thus Descartes conceives of his physics as mechanical and of his explanations as mathematical, not because they are necessarily quantitative but rather because, as in Aristotelian mechanics, they consist in *a priori* demonstrations (i.e. proofs that proceed from cause to effect) from the principles of geometry applied to sensible matter to observed effects.

Descartes' actual scientific explanations fell short of this deductivist ideal on several fronts, causing considerable confusion both in the seventeenth century and

---

[7] I discuss this in more detail in *Descartes on Forms and Mechanisms* (Hattab 2009: ch. 6).

subsequently regarding what he meant by 'mechanical demonstration'. Descartes later retreated from his ambitious aim of deducing his entire physics from the principles of geometry (which are also the principles of mechanics) and settled, in his *Principles of Philosophy*, for suppositions regarding matter's properties in its initial state of creation; even though

all the bodies which compose the universe are formed of one [sort of] matter . . . we have not been able to determine . . . the size of the parts into which this matter is divided, nor at what speed they move, nor what circles they describe. For, seeing that these parts could have been regulated by God in an infinity of diverse ways; experience alone should teach us which of all these ways He chose. That is why we are now at liberty to assume anything we please, provided that everything we shall deduce from it is {entirely} in conformity with experience    (Descartes 1983: 106).

Descartes' hypothesis regarding the sizes, shapes, and motions that God imparts to matter at the beginning is then supposed to be confirmed by the sheer number of observable phenomena one can deduce from it. Unfortunately, his suppositions regarding certain kinds of unobservable microstructures to account for observable effects are often taken to exhaust the extent of his mechanical form of demonstration. This has the effect of confusing certain types of structural explanations, which Descartes employs hypothetically, with the *a priori* deductions he had envisioned but had managed only to sketch in the *Discourse*.

This much is clear: Descartes' nature/machine analogy could not have gone beyond mere metaphor, nor could he have ever hoped to offer *a priori* mathematical demonstrations of observable physical effects, had he not reduced the qualities of parts of matter to geometrical properties of size, shape, and motion. This reduction is accomplished via the identification of extension as the essence of material substance, and the replacement of the Aristotelian substance/accident ontology with a substance/mode ontology. The mere redefinition of matter as essentially extended does not suffice for Descartes' deductive scientific ideal because, according to an Aristotelian substance/accident ontology, accidental properties are separable from, and in no way logically derivable from, the essence of the substance in which they inhere, regardless of how one defines that substance. For example, I could lose my tallness because this accidental form does not follow logically from my essential forms of rationality and animality; similarly, my body could lose power since this property does not flow from its extended essence. However, on the substance/mode ontology that was adopted by Descartes, all properties are mere modes or modifications of the substance and, as such, are both inseparable and derivable from its essence. This, in turn, allows for the possibility of deducing the particular modes of matter from its essence of extension in the same way that the properties of a mathematical figure were thought to follow logically from its essence.

Descartes' reductive theory of matter is thus inextricably linked to his identification of natural objects with machines, and his aim to provide mechanical demonstrations of natural causes grounded in the principles of geometry. Armed with an epistemology that gives us direct insight into the essence of matter through clear and distinct ideas of the intellect, Descartes thought, in the 1630s, that he could provide a secure foundation for *a priori* mathematical demonstrations of natural phenomena which the more sceptical Mersenne considered beyond our reach.

## III: ANIMATED MACHINES VERSUS MECHANICAL ANIMATIONS

By the end of the seventeenth century, mathematical explanations of the kind used in mechanics, which had been successfully applied to the science of motion, were extended not only to the domains of cosmology and chemistry, but also to biology (see Chapter 5). The year 1680 marked the publication of two remarkable works in physiology: Alfonso Borelli's *De Motu Animalium* and Claude Perrault's *La Mécanique des Animaux*. Both exemplify the mechanical ideal by treating the organs of animals as machines and explaining their functions by means of geometrical demonstrations of simple mechanical devices. Borelli and Perrault each provide mathematical demonstrations of muscle structures and functions by equating their shapes with geometrical figures. Borelli sees the arm literally as a lever and describes the arm muscle's specific geometrical structure. This, in turn, allows him to apply the principle of the lever and calculate exactly how much weight the arm of a young man can carry.[8] In his *Cours entier de philosophie* of 1691, the Cartesian philosopher Pierre-Sylvain Régis took up Perrault's anatomical discoveries and geometrical explanations of muscles but insisted on an important difference between his approach and Perrault's and, by implication, Borelli's.

Neither Perrault nor Borelli ground their geometrical explanations of the functions of muscles and other organs in a strict reduction of nonhuman animals to machines. Borelli divides his treatise into two parts; the first part deals exclusively with the observable motions of the external parts of animals, and the second part discusses the internal motions and causes of the motions of muscles. Each requires a different method: 'With respect to the first, we proceed not according to the order of things, but according to the requirement of the clearer teaching, by searching

---

[8] Borelli 1680: 10–13, 34–5. See also Perrault (1680: 78–9) who makes an analogy between the antagonistic muscles of a limb and the shrouds of a boat. Dennis Des Chene and Sophie Roux have made detailed studies of Borelli's and Perrault's mechanical explanations of muscle functions (Des Chene 2005; Roux forthcoming).

after the construction of the muscle and by demonstrating by how much motive force and by which mechanical organs the parts of animals are agitated' (Borelli 1680: Proemium 2). The second part, which presumably follows the order of things or nature rather than teaching, deals not only with involuntary internal motions but also with spirits and sensations. Borelli is able to proceed geometrically in the first part by separating the source of animal motion (the spirits which the will sets in motion) from its quantifiable effects. Perrault explicitly distances himself from the Cartesian *bête machine*; lest the title of his work should give the impression that all animals are pure machines, he clarifies that he means by 'animal':

a being which has feeling, and which is capable of exerting the functions of life by a principle which one calls the Soul, and that the soul uses the organs of the body, which are true machines, as the principal cause of the action of each piece of the machine, and that even though the disposition which each of the parts has in relation to the others hardly does anything else by means of the soul than what it does in pure machines, nevertheless, the whole machine still needs to be moved and directed by the soul just as an organ, which is capable of producing different sounds by the disposition of the pieces that compose it, will never do so without the direction of the soul    (Perrault 1680: 1).

By contrast, Régis reduces even apparent acts of will in an animal to strictly mechanical processes:

When this same dog chases a hare, this highly regulated movement depends on nothing but the fact that his brain, which is a mechanical organ, is so disturbed by the insensible parts which the body of the hare continually gives off, that it determines the animal spirits to flow precisely into the muscles which serve, following the order of nature, to produce the motions necessary for this chase.    (Régis 1691: 609)

Both approaches fit the mechanical ideal and, for all practical purposes, the successful application of mechanical explanations to physiology does not rest on the Cartesian reduction of nonhuman animals to pure machines. And yet there is more than a doctrinal issue at stake in the dispute between Perrault and Régis. At least from Régis' point of view, what is at stake is the very structure of science. Perrault is himself responding to a prior dispute and maintains a certain agnosticism so as not to fall prey to the excesses of either sect. To the philosophers he attributes the view that nature must be regarded as a cause without intelligence which conducts itself only by chance. Perrault says he will not follow this path confessing, rather sarcastically, that he does not count himself among those who claim to know by a special light and are capable of placing themselves above everything which subjugates reason. While he also rejects the new sect, which is completely opposed to the old (presumably the philosophical sect), it is less repugnant to Perrault because it does not distrust all the knowledge of which humans are capable (Perrault 1680: 3–4). It is unclear exactly whom Perrault is targeting; it is ambiguous whether he attributes the view that mechanics can explain everything pertaining to animals to the old sect or new sect (though the reference to distrust of human knowledge suggests that the Philosophers might include Cartesians). What is clear is that Perrault carefully maintains his neutrality on the question of whether the underlying principles of nature are strictly mechanical. He does so by distinguishing physics from mechanics on the grounds that purely physical things are not as accessible to the senses as those of mechanics, and hence can only be treated by means of problems. Unlike those sciences (like mechanics) which admit only what is certain and demonstrative, 'physics must receive all that is probable' (Perrault 1680: 6). Perrault thus remains neutral when it comes to purely physical matters; he claims that mechanical objects 'depend on a composition which one can know without knowing the true causes of the parts which enter into this composition', whereas in Physics 'several probable Systems, some more so than others, are worth more than the most probable one alone; because in the end, there would not be a single one that was sufficient for solving all the difficulties which one encounters in the investigation of the secrets of nature' (1680: 5–6).

Régis explicitly rejects Perrault's view, naming him, and arguing that one system grounded in the first truths of nature is worth more than several probable ones. Like Perrault, he considers a physical body to be 'composed of several insensible parts' but adds 'of a certain shape and arranged in such a way that one can explain all the properties that depend on this body by their configuration and arrangement' (Régis 1691: 273). He characterizes a mechanical body as 'composed of large, sensible and palpable parts, which being joined together, can by their shape and position, augment or diminish the movement of bodies to which the mechanical body applies itself' (1691: 273). He agrees with Perrault that, whereas it is easy to deduce the properties of a mathematical body from its simple and intelligible nature, and easy to explain the effects of machines if its springs and relations are readily observable, we do not perceive the insensible parts and arrangements of physical bodies and it is therefore difficult to determine them from their effects. Unlike Perrault, however, Régis considers mechanics and physics to be linked via the reduction of both the mechanical and physical body to the mathematical body by means of an 'abstraction of the size, shape and arrangement of the parts of these bodies and by the sole consideration that their extension is comprised under some regular figure, such as the cube or the cylinder etc.' (1691: 274). Hence physical explanations and mechanical explanations are both grounded in the first truths that follow from the extended nature of matter.

Given Régis' commitment to certain indubitable first truths of nature, physics for him is not a purely speculative enterprise that proposes different probable systems. The most perfect physics comprises both a practical part, which deals with the careful observation of the effects of various bodies, and a speculative part which consists in various reasonings for discovering the causes of the effects. Despite the fact that the speculative branch of physics consists in problems rather than demonstrations, since nature always acts by the most simple means, its actions are best explained by a single system that allows us to deduce all the effects of a given body from its distinctly known properties (Régis 1691: 274–5). Régis makes it clear that connecting observed effects back to the insensible properties of bodies requires that we adopt, and remain open to correcting, hypotheses regarding the particular shapes, sizes, and arrangement of a body's parts. Nonetheless, these hypotheses must always depend on the first truths, which include that there exists a corporeal nature, that it has quantity, that quantity is divisible by nature, and actually divided by motion, that local motion follows certain rules, that according to these rules the parts of quantity acquire certain shapes etc. (1691: 276–7). Because he regards a system 'not as one single hypothesis, but a collection of many hypotheses, depending on one another, and so joined to the first truths, that they are just like consequences necessarily depending on them', there can be but one system that successfully unites all domains, despite the fact that individual hypotheses are subject to correction (1691: 276). This system is the Cartesian system, and hence mechanical explanations of the functions of organs are not separable from the reduction of nonhuman animals to machines, and ultimately, of all bodies to the properties of extension.

The source of contention between Perrault and Régis is different from the question that engaged Mersenne and Descartes in the 1630s. Both Perrault and Régis accept that, since the parts of physical bodies are insensible, the demonstrations of mathematics and mechanics are not transferable to physical phenomena. Both agree that physics must proceed by means of problems and hypotheses rather than mathematical demonstrations. What is at stake in their reinterpretations of the mechanical ideal is whether the mathematical explanations of mechanics, when applied to specific phenomena, such as the functions of organs, are neutral with respect to different systems of physics, or whether they follow from, and form and integral whole with, the first truths of nature and their consequences. As shown above, Perrault regards his mechanical explanations as compatible with different systems and remains agnostic in regards to physical foundations, whereas Régis maintains their inseparability from Cartesian physics and metaphysics. This invites the question whether Cartesian first truths could themselves count merely as probable hypotheses.

## IV: THE MECHANICAL HYPOTHESIS: EPISTEMIC OPTIMISM VERSUS PESSIMISM

Descartes' philosophy was very influential, albeit not uncontroversial, in seventeenth-century England (Laudan 1966; Henry 1986; Anstey 2000: 4, 11; Anstey 2005). Cartesian mechanism, when transplanted to English soil, was influenced by the philosophical and religious preconceptions that prevailed there and, as a result, it underwent a significant transformation. Those, like Boyle, Glanvill, and Locke, who adopted Descartes' clock/nature analogy and were inspired by his scientific method, were also committed to Baconian experimentalism (Laudan 1966: 73–6). Hence they came to reject key features of both Bacon's and Descartes' methods so as to synthesize the two. Whereas Laudan points to the hypothetical nature of English natural philosophy and traces this back to the method found in Descartes' *Principles of Philosophy* (Laudan 1966: 85, 97; Laudan 1967: 218–19), Anstey cautions against identifying the Lockean sense of 'hypothesis' with today's meaning and highlights a pervasive division between speculative philosophy based on hypotheses (normally identified with Cartesianism and regarded with distrust) and experimental philosophy found in English natural philosophy of the late seventeenth century (Anstey 2003: 2005).

The use of active principles precedes Newton and is typical of seventeenth-century English mechanical philosophy.[9] But rather than focus on matter theory and take the debate between strict reductionists and those who attributed forces to matter as definitive of the mechanist and non-mechanist camps, it may be instructive to see how Boyle's and Locke's characterization of mechanism as a 'hypothesis' permanently disfigured the 'mechanical philosophy' as interpreted by Cartesians. In Boyle's case, the transformation was immensely fruitful, laying the foundations for the scientific method we still employ today. In Locke's case, its epistemological roots seem to have engendered an overly pessimistic view of our capacity for scientific knowledge.

Unlike Hobbes, Boyle was committed to the existence of incorporeal entities that lay beyond the scope of mechanism. Indeed, from 1658 onwards he adopted many Cartesian categories; however, for Boyle the mechanical philosophy functioned as 'a comprehensive heuristic for the explanation of all corporeal phenomena' rather than a metaphysical foundation (Anstey 2000: 4, 11). As indicated in the passages quoted earlier, Boyle, like Descartes, was committed to a reductive matter theory, and sought explanations of all natural phenomena that followed the model of mechanical explanations, and rested only on primary qualities. He also accepted the view that all motions were governed by universal laws of motion. However, unlike Descartes, who built up his natural philosophy from indubitable metaphysical

---

[9] Henry traces this back to the primacy of experimentalism over Cartesian matter theory in English mechanical philosophies: since completely passive matter could not save the observed phenomena, it was necessary to posit active, occult principles (Henry 1986: 352–66). The reintroduction of active principles also served to combat charges of atheism that were provoked by the image of a clockwork universe capable of functioning independently of its maker (Henry 1986: 338). McGuire likewise defends the thesis that 'the "mechanical philosophy" of Boyle and other seventeenth-century thinkers was, in part, a reformulation of a nominalist ontology arising mainly from the reformed theology of the Calvinists' (McGuire 1972: 525).

principles grounded in clear and distinct ideas, Boyle characterized mechanism as a hypothesis.

The term 'hypothesis' had a range of meanings in England at this time, including a causal explanation, a metaphysical principle or maxim, an inductive generalization or a theory of doctrines (Anstey 2005: 223–4). Early modern English philosophers regarded hypotheses as following from experience, in that they were deduced from, or illustrated and explained, experiments and observations. To formulate hypotheses without recourse to experience was to engage in speculative philosophy and to build castles in the air, as the Cartesians were accused of doing. Hence, for Boyle, mechanism captures experience better than any other hypothesis, and yet it also functions to delimit, in advance, what counts as an intelligible explanation. For example, all occult qualities are, in principle, explicable in mechanical terms, even though we do not yet possess mechanical explanations for many of them. By characterizing the mechanical philosophy itself as a hypothesis, Boyle limits himself from the beginning to what McMullin calls structural explanations (McMullin 1978: 139).

But why should we suppose, in advance, that the underlying structure will conform to the mechanical hypothesis, especially since hypotheses are supposed to follow from experience, and we do not observe the microstructures of bodies? Boyle adopted the familiarity condition of explanation, whereby unfamiliar phenomena or those that are difficult to understand are to be reduced to ones that are familiar and easy to understand. The mechanical or corpuscular philosophy is unique in this regard, since it is so easy for us to understand the size, shape, local motion, rest, order, position, and texture of material substances and to deduce things from them.

Due to Boyle's defence of mechanism as the most excellent hypothesis rather than a metaphysical truth, certain tensions and ambiguities arise at the ground level of his philosophy. Despite the general assumption that all non-mechanical properties are reducible to mechanical ones, it is difficult to determine which exact properties he counts among those that we would call the primary qualities of matter (pp. 161–79). For Boyle there are three different levels of matter: the smallest, insensible corpuscles (atoms), insensible compound corpuscles (molecules and seminal principles), and observable bodies (Anstey 2000: 41). The second level, reminiscent of Bacon's natural philosophy, is the key to his causal explanations, but it also poses a barrier to Boyle's assumed reductive theory of matter. At this level, one is dealing with textures, which on a strict reductionist view should be reducible to the properties of the constituent atoms and their relations. However, in practice, Boyle did not always take such strict reductions to mechanical properties to be feasible or desirable.

Boyle's experiments with nitre illustrate this problem. Boyle's distillation of nitre into spirit of nitre and fixed nitre, and his recombination of the two into the same nitre, shows that nitre is a compound of two distinct substances with different natures (Boyle 1669: 130–4). Spinoza, who insisted on a strict reduction to mechanical properties, objected that the experiment was consistent with the claim that the two parts of the nitre differed only mechanically, that is, the acid taste of the spirit of nitre could be accounted for by the fact that the particles of the nitre were now in motion (SO IV: 17).[10] The reply that Boyle made via Oldenburg indicates that he did not take their differing tastes and colours to be deducible from the shape or size of their corpuscles alone but rather that one must invoke their different textures (Clericuzio 1990: 575).

Why did Boyle, in this case and others, resist a strict reduction to mechanical properties? Boyle provides no clear answer to the question whether sensible qualities, such as the acidity of the nitre, insofar as they are powers, are ontologically reducible to relations among corpuscles; nor is it clear whether these relations are ultimately reducible to their *relata*, namely, the mechanical affections of matter (Anstey 2000: ch. 4). We are left, then, with irresolvable tensions and ambiguities at the heart of Boyle's apparent commitment to a reductive theory of matter and mechanical explanations. This can be attributed, in large part, to Boyle's adoption of mechanism as a hypothesis. As a hypothesis, it was subordinate to experience, and this gave Boyle a certain flexibility that the Cartesian metaphysical approach to matter theory lacked. Boyle could appeal to textures and their resultant powers as intermediate causes of phenomena without addressing their ontological status in a way that proved fruitful to scientific discovery. In other words, Boyle's mechanism as an hypothesis allowed scientific inquiry to be guided by mechanistic principles without being overly constrained by them.

While Boyle appears optimistic that, in the long run, sensible qualities will be reduced to mechanical affections, the epistemology that underpins Locke's discussions of the mechanical hypothesis precludes this. Briefly, Locke lists three main kinds of knowledge. The first consists in the direct agreement or disagreement between ideas (*Essay* IV. iii. 8). This is intuition and consists, for example, in the agreement between one idea of a square shape and another idea of square shape.

The second type of knowledge consists in the agreement or disagreement of our ideas in co-existence (*Essay* IV. iii. 9). In this case, either intuitively or by demonstration, the mind perceives both a visible connection and a necessary dependence, for example, between the idea of shape and the idea of extension on which it depends. The other example Locke gives is that the reception or communication of motion depends on solidity (*Essay* IV. iii. 14). While he does not specify this, it must be kept in mind that since knowledge involves the agreement or disagreement of ideas, Locke is speaking of our *ideas* of motion and solidity and their connections. It is not clear what these necessary dependencies and connections consist in, but they appear to involve both logical and causal relations. The absence of such

---

[10] For further details on this controversy between Boyle and Spinoza, see Clericuzio 1990: 576–7.

connections in the case of the vast majority of our ideas is illustrated by the example of our complex idea of gold: since we do not know the size, figure, and texture of the insensible parts of the gold that cause the sensible qualities of its yellow colour, its weight and malleability, we cannot determine which qualities are logically consistent or inconsistent with its constitution (*Essay* IV. iii. 11). Hence, our scientific investigations into the powers of substances are normally limited to experience (which does not count as proper knowledge for Locke) of sets of properties that we sense to coincide with one another without any understanding of their logical and causal relations. Locke concludes his discussion of the second kind of knowledge by stating:

I have here instanced the corpuscularian Hypothesis, as that which is thought to go farthest in an intelligible Explication of the Qualities of Bodies; and I fear the Weakness of humane understanding is scarce able to substitute another, which will afford us a fuller and clearer discovery of the necessary Connexion, and *Co-existence*, of the Powers, which are to be observed united in several sorts of them. This at least is certain, that which ever Hypothesis be clearest and truest, (for of that it is not my business to determine,) our Knowledge concerning corporeal Substances, will be very little advanced by any of them, till we are made to see, what Qualities and Powers of bodies have a *necessary Connexion or Repugnancy* one with another; which in the present State of Philosophy, I think, we know but to a very small degree: And I doubt, whether with those Faculties we have, we shall ever be able to carry our general Knowledge (I say not particular Experience) in this part much farther. Experience is that, which in this part we must depend on. And it were to be wish'd, that it were more improved.    (*Essay* IV. iii. 16)

This passage suggests that Locke starts from metaphysical notions of real essence and primary quality and that, since mechanical explanations are uniquely intelligible and natural to us, he regards Boyle's corpuscularian hypothesis merely as the best illustration and support for his otherwise sparse metaphysics (Downing 1998). However, it must be noted that Locke here employs the corpuscularian hypothesis only as the best illustration of how knowledge of the second kind is accomplished, and that he still considers it woefully inadequate given the small number of ideas of qualities that can be connected in this way. His ultimate conclusion is not that one must rely on the corpuscular hypothesis because it is clearer and truer than other hypotheses, but that experience is the best that we can hope for in science, and so we must rely on that rather than any particular hypothesis.

There is yet a third kind of knowledge which may prove relevant to Locke's views on scientific knowledge. This knowledge consists in the agreement or disagreement of ideas in any other relation (besides the dependency relation). Locke points out that this is the largest area of our knowledge, making it difficult to determine how far such relations might extend (*Essay* IV. iii. 18). *Prima facie* then, the extension of such relations among ideas to the scientific realm is possible. Locke's prime example of such knowledge is mathematics; for example, via intermediate concepts, we can grasp the agreement between a right-angled triangle and the equality of its angles to two right angles (*Essay* IV. iii. 29). For a variety of reasons, mathematical ideas are best suited to this process of 'finding intermediate *Ideas*, that may shew the *Relations* and *Habitudes* of *Ideas*, whose Co-existence is not considered' (*Essay* IV. iii. 18, 19).

Locke thinks this form of knowledge can be extended to morality: 'The *Relation* of other *Modes* may certainly be perceived, as well as those of Number and Extension: and I cannot see, why they should not also be capable of Demonstration, if due Methods were thought on to examine, or pursue their Agreement or Disagreement. *Where there is no Property, there is no Injustice*, is a Proposition as certain as any Demonstration in *Euclid*' (*Essay* IV. iii. 18). Locke's model for this type of knowledge is not Euclidean geometry but algebra. After listing all the disadvantages we face in the domain of morality in contrast to the advantages of mathematics, he comments: 'And what method *Algebra*, or something of that kind, may hereafter suggest, to remove the other difficulties, is not easy to fore-tell' (*Essay* IV. iii. 20). This is the only glimmer of optimism we find in Locke, but the point is not developed. However, it could explain why Locke, after writing the *Essay*, came to embrace Newton's theory of gravity, despite the negative implications that the attractive forces it attributed to matter had for the mechanical hypothesis. The mechanical hypothesis may be the best example we have of knowledge of the second kind in science, but by mathematically establishing the law of gravity, Newton was able to account for relations that obtain among bodies in motion, regardless of his inability to derive gravity from the primary qualities of the mechanical hypothesis. In other words, this third kind of knowledge can exist independently of our ability to discover a necessary connection between sensible and primary qualities and provides an alternative to purely experiential science.

It seems, however, that Locke either failed to recognize, or failed to develop, the possibility of the third type of knowledge in natural science. Instead, he concentrates his efforts in the *Essay* on highlighting the fact that 'we are not capable of *scientifical Knowledge*' since 'having no *Ideas* of the particular primary Qualities of the minute parts of either of these Plants, nor of other Bodies which we would apply them to, we cannot tell what effects they will produce' (*Essay* IV. iii. 26). The *Essay* reveals the limitations of the Boylean corpuscular/mechanical hypothesis in that it shows that mental properties and operations, gravity, and the coherence and continuity of matter are inexplicable in mechanistic terms.[11] Indeed, there is an ongoing debate regarding whether or not Locke is a consistent mechanist.[12] Before

[11] Margaret Wilson and Lisa Downing discuss these issues in detail (Wilson 1979: Downing 1998: 406–14). Downing suggests that Locke's refusal to abandon the traditional model of science as demonstrative knowledge of causes may also have led him to moderate scepticism (Downing 1998: 412).

[12] Against Wilson, Ayers focuses primarily on Locke's hypothesis that God could have superadded thought to matter and argues that, despite some weaknesses, Locke did present a systematic, mechanistic account which contemporary readers have failed to appreciate, in part, because they

this issue can be resolved, it must first be determined what role the mechanical hypothesis, and hypotheses in general, played for Locke. Locke's discussion of the different types of knowledge in the *Essay* suggests that, at least in this context, the mechanical hypothesis was a negative example, designed to convince us just how limited our scientific knowledge is, and how much we must depend on experience rather than our best theories about the ultimate qualities of matter.[13]

Given the ambiguities and apparent inconsistencies in various texts Locke wrote at different times, determining his overall stance towards mechanism would require a more comprehensive study of his philosophy than the purpose of this chapter permits (Farr 1987). Nonetheless, it is clear that the characterization of the mechanical philosophy as a hypothesis forever changed the course of philosophy and science in Europe. Coupled with Boyle's optimism, the mechanical hypothesis guided scientific inquiry in fruitful ways. Coupled with Locke's epistemic pessimism, it served to bolster the scepticism so characteristic of British empiricism.

# CONCLUSION

The mechanical ideal raised new problems in different contexts and inspired antagonistic views of its philosophical implications in proponents who operated within the same intellectual context. Within Mersenne's circle of the 1630s, it raised questions regarding the nature of mathematical demonstrations, specifically, whether or not there could be essentialist accounts of natural phenomena based on mathematics. Mersenne and Descartes took opposing positions; yet both extended the mathematical explanations of mechanics to physics. By the century's end, Descartes' French followers had abandoned the quest for mathematical *demonstrations* in physics. Instead, Régis defends the superiority of one unified scientific system (Cartesianism) that grounds mechanical explanations in physical hypotheses deriving from the first truths of nature, against Perrault's claim that mechanical explanations fit a plurality of probable physical systems. One is hard pressed to pronounce one of these philosophies of science more genuinely 'mechanical' than the other, unless one already presupposes Cartesian foundationalism to define mechanism. Finally, in late seventeenth-century England, Boyle and Locke treat the principles of Cartesian mechanism as the mechanical or

---

failed to understand what 'superaddition' meant in the seventeenth-century context (Ayers 1981). McCann (1985), on somewhat different grounds, argues that Locke is not only a consistent, but a sophisticated mechanist, given seventeenth-century standards.

[13] See also Anstey's discussion of the rather limited role that hypotheses play in Locke's overall approach to scientific inquiry (2003: 29–33).

corpuscular *hypothesis*. Both regard Cartesian first truths of nature as subject to experience and as not indubitable. However, Boyle appears optimistic that they will, in due course, be confirmed by experiments, whereas Locke's epistemology entails a sceptical retreat to experience and to explanations based on weaker relations between ideas than the dependencies demanded by mechanical explanations. It is difficult to discern what features all these so-called mechanists shared other than an acceptance of the mechanical ideal, however that was interpreted and however attainable (or unattainable) it was thought to be. Perhaps more extensive study is required before the main features and boundaries of the mechanical philosophy can be delineated or perhaps it will reveal itself as a fluid category that constantly reinvents itself. The jury is still out.

## REFERENCES

ANSTEY, P. (2000). *The Philosophy of Robert Boyle*. London and New York: Routledge.

ANSTEY, P. (2002). 'Robert Boyle and the heuristic value of mechanism'. *Studies in History and Philosophy of Science*, 33: 161–74.

ANSTEY, P. (2003). 'Locke on Method in Natural Philosophy', in Peter R. Anstey (ed.), *The Philosophy of John Locke*. London: Routledge, 26–42.

ANSTEY, P. (2005). 'Experimental versus Speculative Natural Philosophy', in P. R. Anstey and J. A. Schuster (eds), *The Science of Nature in the Seventeenth Century*. Dordrecht: Springer, 215–42.

AYERS, M. R. (1981). 'Mechanism, superaddition and the proof of God's existence in Locke's Essay'. *The Philosophical Review*, 90: 210–51.

BEECKMAN, I. (1939–53). *Journal tenu par Isaac Beeckman*. Ed. C. de Waard. The Hague: Martinus Nijhoff.

BENNETT, J. A. (1986). 'The mechanics' philosophy and the mechanical philosophy'. *History of Science*, 24: 1–28.

BERKEL, K. VAN (1983). *Beeckman en de Mechanizeering van het Wereldbeeld*. Amsterdam: Rodolphi.

BLANCANUS, J. (1996). *De Mathematicarum Natura Dissertatio*, Gyula Klima (trans.), in P. Mancosu (ed.), *Philosophy of Mathematics and Mathematical Practice in the Seventeenth Century*. Oxford and New York: Oxford University Press.

BOAS HALL, M. (1981). *The Mechanical Philosophy*. New York: Arno Press.

BORELLI, A. (1680). *De Motu Animalium*. Rome: Angeli Bernabo.

BOYLE, R. (1669). *Certain Physiological Essays*. London: Henry Herringman.

CLERICUZIO, A. (1990). 'A redefinition of Boyle's chemistry and corpuscular philosophy'. *Annals of Science*, 47: 561–89.

DEAR, P. (2005). 'Circular Argument: Descartes' Vortices and Their Crafting as Explanations of Gravity', in P. R. Anstey and J. A. Schuster (eds), *The Science of Nature in the Seventeenth Century*. Dordrecht: Springer, 81–97.

DESCARTES, R. (1983). *Principles of Philosophy*. Trans. V. R. Miller and R. P. Miller. Dordrecht: Reidel.

DES CHENE, D. (2005). 'Mechanisms of Life in the Seventeenth Century: Borelli, Perrault, Régis'. *Studies in History and Philosophy of Biological and Biomedical Sciences*, 36: 245–60.

DOWNING, L. (1998). 'The status of mechanism in Locke's Essay'. *The Philosophical Review*, 107: 381–441.

DOWNING, L. (2005). 'Occasionalism and Strict Mechanism: Malebranche, Berkeley, Fontenelle', in C. Mercer and E. O'Neill (eds), *Early Modern Philosophy*. Oxford: Oxford University Press, 206–30.

FARR, J. (1987). 'The way of hypotheses: Locke on method'. *Journal of the History of Ideas*, 48/1: 51–72.

GABBEY, A. (2001). 'Mechanical Philosophies and Their Explanations', in C. Lüthy, J. E. Murdoch, and W. R. Newman (eds), *Late Medieval and Early Modern Corpuscular Theory*. Leiden: Brill, 441–64.

GAUKROGER, S. (2006). *The Emergence of a Scientific Culture: Science and the Shaping of Modernity: 1210–1685*. Oxford: Oxford University Press.

GUEVARA, I. DE (1627). *In Aristotelis Mechanicas Commentarij una cum Additionibus Quibusdam*. Rome: Jacob Mascardus.

HATTAB, H. (2005). 'From Mechanics to Mechanism: The *Quaestiones Mechanicae* and Descartes' Physics', in Peter R. Anstey and John A. Schuster (eds), *The Science of Nature in the Seventeenth Century: Patterns of Natural Change in Early Modern Natural Philosophy*. Dordrecht: Springer, 99–129.

HATTAB, H. (2009). *Descartes on Forms and Mechanisms*. Cambridge: Cambridge University Press.

HENRY, J. (1986). 'Occult qualities and the experimental philosophy active principles in pre-Newtonian matter theory'. *History of Science*, 24: 335–81.

HUTCHINSON, K. (1983). 'Supernaturalism and the mechanical philosophy'. *History of Science*, 21: 297–333.

HUYGENS, C. (1937). *Oeuvres Complètes*. Vol. 19. The Hague: Martinus Nijhoff.

JANIAK, A. (2009). *Newton as Philosopher*. Cambridge: Cambridge University Press.

JOY, L. S. (1992). 'The Conflict of Mechanisms and Its Empiricist Outcome', in V. Chappell (ed.), *Essays on Early Modern Philosophers: Grotius to Gassendi*. London: Garland, 222–38.

LAUDAN, L. (1966). 'The clock metaphor and probabilism: The impact of Descartes on English methodological thought, 1650–1665'. *Annals of Science*, 22: 73–104.

LAUDAN, L. (1967). 'The nature and sources of Locke's views on hypotheses'. *Journal of the History of Ideas*, 28: 211–23.

LOLORDO, A. (2007). *Pierre Gassendi and the Birth of Early Modern Philosophy*. Cambridge: Cambridge University Press.

MCCANN, E. (1985). 'Lockean Mechanism', in A. J. Holland (ed.), *Philosophy, Its History and Historiography*. Dordrecht: Reidel, 209–31.

MCGUIRE, J. E. (1972). 'Boyle's conception of nature'. *Journal of the History of Ideas*, 3/4: 523–42.

MCMULLIN, E. (1978). 'Structural Explanation'. *American Philosophical Quarterly*, 15, 2: 139–47.

MERSENNE, M. (1634). *Questions Inouyes* and *Les Questions Theologiques, Physiques, Morales et Mathematiques*. Reprinted Paris: Fayard, 1985.

MONANTHEUIL, H. DE (1599). *Aristotelis Mechanica Graeca, emendata, Latina facta & Commentariis illustrata*. Paris.

PERRAULT, C. (1680). *Mécanique des Animaux*, in *Essais de Physique*. Paris: Jean Baptiste Coignard.

RÉGIS, P.-S. (1691). *Cours entier de philosophie*. Amsterdam.

ROHAULT, J. (1978). *Entretiens sur la Philosophie*, in *Recherches sur le XVIIe Siècle 3*, A. Robinet (ed.). Paris: Centre National de la Recherche Scientifique.

ROUX, S. (forthcoming). 'Quelles Machines pour quels animaux? Jacques Rohault, Claude Perrault, Giovanni Alfonso Borelli', in A. Gaillard *et al.* (eds), *L'Automate: Machine, Modèle, Merveille*. Bordeaux: Presses Universitaires de Bordeaux.

WILSON, M. D. (1979). 'Superadded properties: The limits of mechanism in Locke'. *American Philosophical Quarterly*, 26: 143–50.

........................................

# CHAPTER 5

# MACHINES, SOULS, AND VITAL PRINCIPLES

........................................

## JUSTIN E. H. SMITH

## I: FROM ANIMALS TO BRUTES

........................................

Before the early modern period, to deny souls to animals would have been to deal in paradox. The word 'animal', after all, is simply an adjectivized form of the Latin noun '*anima*', which is to say 'soul'. There is no such etymological connection between 'animal' and 'soul' in Greek, yet the conceptual link is just as strong as in later Latinity. As Aristotle writes in *On the Parts of Animals*, the study of animal nature necessarily involves study of the soul: '[I]nasmuch as it is the presence of the soul that enables matter to constitute the animal nature, much more than it is the presence of matter which so enables the soul, the inquirer into nature is bound to treat of the soul rather than of the matter' (AR I, 998: 641a 28–31). He notes, though, that if it is the whole soul that the student of nature must treat, 'then there is no place for any other philosophy beside it' (AR I, 998: 641a 35–6). Thus, in the study of animals, we must limit our scope to that part of the soul that is responsible for growth (which is a property of plants, animals, and humans alike) and that part that is responsible for locomotion (shared by animals and humans), while leaving out that part that is responsible for intellect and is had by humans alone.

The radical reconceptualization of animals that takes place in the modern period and is most often associated with the name of René Descartes might be taken to imply that *only* those inquirers interested in intellect are bound to treat of the soul, while inquirers into nature, in contrast, can explain everything in their field of interest, including generation, growth, and locomotion, by appeal to the properties of matter. From the earlier emphasis laid upon what humans and animals share—namely, a certain type of ensouledness—early modern natural philosophy came to identify animals as 'brutes' (or, just as often, '*animalia bruta*'), a designation which highlights the faculties they lack rather than those they possess.

For Descartes, an animal is a particular kind of machine, which is fundamentally no different from the machines that human beings are capable of building, as is also the human body considered independently of its ensouledness. The collapse of the ontological distinction between the natural and the artificial is, one might argue, the central principle of Descartes' natural philosophy, in virtue of which he may be called a mechanist *par excellence* (Gaukroger 2002). However, one might also argue that to speak of the machine *model* of animals is to be concerned with epistemology rather than with natural philosophy; on this line of reasoning, mechanism had less to do with deeming animals to be merely machines than with attempting to *understand* animals by seeing how far one could go in conceptualizing them in terms borrowed from mechanics (Duchesneau 1998).

Far from holding that animals are entirely explicable in the same terms as a human-designed artefact, there are in fact many passages in which Descartes seems to ascribe not only life but also sensation to animals (AT V 278), denying that they think, but leaving the question of awareness vague. Thus he writes that he 'cannot share the opinion of Montaigne and others who attribute understanding and thought to animals' (AT IV 573: CSMK 302). He evidently shares the majority opinion of his time that animals are irrational or subrational, against an influential, but certainly a minority view, promoted not only by Montaigne, but also by other representatives of scepticism such as Hieronymus Rorarius.

In any event, Descartes parts ways with the traditional approach to animals in maintaining that the life and sensation of brutes is an entirely corporeal process, while it is only the thinking of human beings that must be explained in terms of the inherence of an incorporeal soul. He reasons that if animals 'thought as we do, they would have an immortal soul like us' (AT IV 576: CSMK 304), and since the possibility of eternal life for animals is both implausible and heretical, it follows that animals do not think. 'Lower' functions that were traditionally attributed to the soul, by contrast, can be accounted for without invoking an immortal principle to cause these functions in the body. For Descartes, that means not invoking a soul at all.

Whether principally intended as an ontological theory or as an epistemological model, one important implication of Descartes' picture of the animal-machine is the collapse of the traditional distinction in natural philosophy between being made and being born, that is, between manufacture and generation. Descartes seems to have well understood that the success of his theory of the animal-machine depended on his ability successfully to account for the origins of animals 'in the same style as the rest, namely, by demonstrating effects from causes' (AT VI 45–6). He could not provide such an account, and it is for precisely this reason that Descartes' embryology appears in retrospect to be wildly speculative and ungrounded, even if he himself believed that his own, epigenetic account of embryogenesis through thermo-mechanical causes must be true for deep philosophical reasons. His attempt to provide a mechanical account of generation was often derided, and his failures often explicitly cited by later seventeenth-century philosophers who wished to reintroduce into their own ontologies the vital principles that had been banished by earlier mechanism, in order to account for the phenomena of conception and development. There is an amusing example of such a view of mechanist generation theory in John Ray (1627–1705), who writes in his *Wisdom of God Manifested in the Works of His Creation* that generation

is so admirable and unaccountable, that neither the Atheists nor Mechanick Philosophers have attempted to declare the manner and process of it; but have (as I noted before) very cautiously and prudently broke off their Systems of Natural Philosophy here, and left this Point untoucht; and those Accounts which some of them have attempted to give of the Formation of a few of the Parts, are so excessively absurd and ridiculous, that they need no other Confutation than *ha, ha, he*.   (Ray 1717: 67)

Whether in need of it or not, Descartes' doctrine received a much more thorough confutation than this. Indeed, a good number of the theories of natural growth, motion, and change of the second half of the seventeenth century (including Ray's own work) amounts to a sustained argument against what Ray here simply laughs off.

It is important to chart these confutations not only for the sake of understanding the relatively (though perhaps unjustly) obscure history of early modern philosophy of biology, but also in order to understand the eventual triumph of more or less materialistic theories of the mind–body relationship in the eighteenth century. Although these theories did not enjoy an unchallenged reign since then, they at least ensured that subsequent accounts of this relationship would be expected to hew as closely as possible to whatever natural science has to tell about the corporeal correlate or, depending on how one sees things, the corporeal substrate of thinking.

In the end, Descartes' insistence that perceiving, self-moving animals are generated by purely natural causes, while thinking souls come into the world by causes of an entirely different order, would prove untenable. As Leibniz would sharply note, one has to be very skilled in self-delusion in order not to see all the different respects in which animals are like us in their behaviour, and presumably in their internal lives. This means that our origins need to be accounted for in the same terms as theirs, and the prospect that we are elaborate machines needs to be taken just as seriously as the prospect that they are. Ultimately, this means that the prospect that matter can think needs to be taken seriously. If John Locke chose only to entertain such a possibility without committing himself to it in his *Essay*, the Pandora's box was by then open. One might suppose that an important stage in its opening was the growing uneasiness with supernaturalistic accounts of the origins of human thought, together with the naturalistic hand-waving of theories of the origins of animals with lower vital functions, which were being proposed in the absence of any knowledge of the actual mechanisms of genetics that might render a naturalistic account theoretically compelling.

The concept of *origins* invoked in the previous sentence requires a brief comment. Too often, basic philosophical problems about 'the body', among which one certainly must include the mind–body problem, are addressed as though the body is always some pre-given entity that bears or does not bear some timeless relationship to 'the mind', without any consideration for the way in which this relationship, or appearance of a relationship, might have got started in the first place. Yet it is clear enough that, in the seventeenth century, any author who was interested in the body and its connection to apparently non-bodily capacities was for that reason intensely interested in the problems of generation. We may suppose they assumed that, if there is a relationship, then it is one that had to get started at some point, and we may perhaps unravel the mystery of that relationship by tracing it back to its starting point.

With this in mind, then, let us turn to some largely unfamiliar aspects of the debate about the nature and origins of machines, and about the difference, if any, between natural and artificial machines.

## II: SOURCES OF THE EARLY MODERN MACHINE CONCEPT

The doctrine of the animal-machine should be called 'Cartesian' only if one bears in mind that the French philosopher did not propose an entirely new conception of the nature, structure, and motion of animals. Nor does he deserve to be singled out for blame for the subsequent objectification of animals in, for example, medical experiments and factory farming (Regan 1982; for an alternative view, Sorell 2005). Rather, there are important continuities between pre-Cartesian and post-Cartesian models of animal bodies and animal motion. This is shown by the following brief survey of some of the sixteenth-century sources of the animal-machine doctrine, by their reworking in various categories of machine in seventeenth-century science, and by the overlap between the field of mechanics on the one hand and medicine and chemistry on the other.

Machines, it should be noted, came in many varieties, as the *Hydraulico-pneumatic Mechanics* of Kaspar (or Gaspar) Schott (1608–1666), makes evident. Far from rejecting the 'magical' thinking of the pre-mechanist, Renaissance worldview, Schott identifies mechanics itself as a branch of magic, alongside 'magnetic, gnomonic, static, optical . . . sympathetic, steganological, cryptographic, divinatory, kabbalistic, hieroglyphic', and, finally, 'holy magic' (Schott 1657: unpaginated Preface). This is a motley grouping that does not fit easily with our standard picture of mechanics as rejecting, for example, sympathetic magic, rather than as existing alongside it. However, the subject of this particular study by Schott is 'mechanical magic', and even more narrowly a particular branch of mechanics, whose study is not machines in general, but only a very special kind of machine. As Schott succinctly explains: 'I say hydraulico-pneumatic, while you say aquatico-spiritual: that is, driven by water and air' (Schott 1657: Preface). By means of these two basic natural elements, Schott enthuses, one is able to make statues that are 'hurled into the air by the violent force of the compressed air trapped inside, letting pipes and tubes swell up, imitating the motion and song of birds and other animals, and producing other such wonderful and exotic effects, that one can hardly understand how this could be done by the human spirit of invention' (Schott 1657: Preface). Schott's fascination with machines of this sort is heavily influenced by the work of his fellow Jesuit Athanasius Kircher, though Schott himself traces it back to the Roman author Hero (or Heron) of Alexandria (10–70 CE), the author of *Pneumatica*, and purportedly the inventor of the first steam engine (Boas 1949: 38).

Earlier, Andreas Vesalius (1514–64), the Belgian anatomist active in the Padua school of anatomy and the author of *On the fabric of the human body* (1543), had proposed that a living body could be organized as a '*fabrica*'. This term had been reserved mostly for institutions, workshops, and manufactories, though this came with the explicit disavowal of any interest in the working of animal bodies, for in Vesalius's view, only autopsies conducted on human corpses could be of relevance to the science of anatomy. His preferred source of analogies for the structure of the human body was the deeply rooted tradition of architecture. For instance, he notes that the source of the name of the ginglymus or 'hinge joint' would become clear 'if you compared this species of joint with the hinges of doors in which the iron driven into the wall receives that which is attached to the door, and the iron from the wall enters up into that of the door' (Vesalius 1543: 14).[1] As Vivian Nutton explains: '[Vesalius] describes the fabrica of the human body in all senses of the Latin word, as the structure that underlies the body, as the created fabric that constitutes it, and as the "workshop" that allows humankind to function properly' (2003: no page numbers).

---

[1] The page number given here from the 1543 edition, but the translation is from Garrison's version, which is available online without page numbers.

The 'mechanical' approach to anatomy was thus already evident in the mid-sixteenth century, and the view that animal growth, organization, and locomotion could be accounted for in terms of automatic stimuli and responses was not unknown.[2] Gómez Pereira (1500–1567), in his *Antoniana Margarita* (1554), maintains that 'if the animal senses, then necessarily it makes judgments; if it judges, then it reflects; if it reflects, then it forms universal propositions: then there is no essential distinction between it and man, an inadmissible and absurd conclusion' (Pereira 1554: 57). For Pereira, as for Descartes subsequently, to admit that an animal has *any* of the powers attributed in the Aristotelian tradition to the lower parts of the soul is already to open up the possibility that it has *all* of the soul-powers enjoyed by human beings. Pierre-Daniel Huet (1630–1721) would argue later, in his *Censura philosophiae cartesianae* (1689), that Descartes plagiarized Pereira directly. There is no need to take sides in this dispute in order to agree that Descartes' model of the animal-machine is not entirely new. What is novel in Descartes, in any case, is the confluence of philosophical arguments against animal ensouledness, such as one sees in Pereira, with the attempt to identify processes such as digestion, respiration, and muscular contraction with analogous processes in mechanical devices. However, each of these two strands of the Cartesian doctrine is capable of existing independently.

Neither Schott nor Pereira were principally interested in biomechanics—that is, the modelling of living bodies according to mechanical principles; yet many philosophers, following Descartes, would appropriate the hydraulico-pneumatic machine model for conceptualizing animal bodies. Robert Boyle, for example, writes in his *Free Inquiry into the received Notion of Nature* (1686):

I look not on a human body, as on a watch or a hand-mill, i.e., as a machine made up only of solid, or at least consistent parts; but as an hydraulical, or rather hydraulico-pneumatical engine, that consists not only of solid and stable parts, but of fluids, and those in organical motion: and not only so, but I consider that these fluids, the liquors and spirits, are in a living man so constituted, that in certain circumstances the liquors are disposed to be put into a fermentation or commotion . . .    (B: X, 540)

Boyle maintains that fermentation or explosiveness needs to be added to fluidity, and that both of these need to be added to mechanicity, in order to get at the true nature of the animal-machine. Leibniz expresses a similar view more succinctly when he claims that the animal body is in fact a 'hydraulico-pneumatico-pyrotechnical machine' (Smith 2007b: 161). As Enrico Pasini has argued, this addition to the list of subvarieties of machine may be traced back to the metallurgical work of Vannoccio

---

[2] In the sixteenth century some argued that it is precisely the automatism of animals, or the fact that they proceed directly to action without any time-consuming deliberation, that proves that they are more rational than humans. This was one of the themes of Rorarius (1647). This publication would give rise to a lively debate in the late seventeenth century, which resulted from the article on 'Rorarius' in Bayle's *Dictionnaire historique et critique* (1697).

Biringuccio, and particularly to his *Pirotechnia* of 1540, which describes the production of bombs and explosives. Pasini explains that over the following century 'the field of application of pyrotechnics ends up corresponding in substance . . . to chemical reactions. Leibniz, with his neologism, wishes to emphasize the dynamic character which imbues the animal machine with its active principle, whether this is a matter of effervescence, which . . . was capable of producing heat and ebullition, or of a fire without light as Descartes had already maintained, or, finally, of little explosions similar to those of gunpowder' (Pasini 1995: 119).

Meanwhile, the physiological modelling of animal bodies after the manner of gear- and lever-driven contraptions would continue alongside more complicated varieties of machine, such as those envisioned by Boyle and Leibniz. Giovanni Alfonso Borelli's (1608–1679) *On the motion of animals*, a treatise posthumously published in 1680, might perhaps seem a 'fantastic work of the analogical imagination' (Wilson 1995: 13). Yet Borelli's *models* were just that, and do not seem to have implied any ontological commitment to the view that living bodies are in fact machines. Besides, in spite of the partial usefulness of modelling living bodies after what Scott terms 'tractoric' machines—those that accomplish their tasks 'through the forces of weights and wheels' (Schott 1657: Preface)—Borelli also relies heavily on iatrochemical explanations, that is, explanations that account for physiological processes such as the contraction of the muscles in terms of minute chemical reactions. By Borelli's time, basic chemical processes such as effervescence, ebullition, fermentation, and the like had come to be seen as ineliminable in the explanation of animal growth and motion. Indeed, some recent studies (e.g. Clericuzio 2000), have argued that in the seventeenth century the line between iatromechanism and iatrochemistry—between, on the one hand, the treatment of the body by doctors and anatomists as a tractoric machine and, on the other, as a machine that is also driven by chemical processes—is not nearly so clear as was previously thought.[3] Descartes himself believed that the animal-machine was kept alive thanks to the heat of the heart, which was, in the end, the result of fermentation, a chemical process *par excellence*.

Another important addition to the machine model was the micromechanics of Marcello Malpighi (1628–94) and of others working in the domain of so-called 'subtle anatomy'. Malpighi's innovation consisted largely in the fact that his method, unlike Descartes' reliance on 'analogical models intended to account for global functions', instead '[gave] pride of place to analysis, and [was] limited to

---

[3] As the first half of both the terms 'iatromechanism' and 'iatrochemistry' indicate, debates about the causes of bodily processes in the seventeenth century were conducted to no small extent in the field of medicine. Even those who have been classified in history as philosophers, who were concerned with the ontology of body and with the nature of causality in bodily processes, saw their own interest in these topics as motivated by a desire to contribute to medicine itself. On Descartes' interest in the advancement of medicine, see Carter (1983), Aucante (2004); on Leibniz's interest in the same, see Smith (2010).

observable entities and processes' (Duchesneau 1998: 199–200). Malpighi's preferred instrument of research was the microscope, and by its use he was able to
discover the capillaries, among other subtle structures.[4] As Malpighi vividly describes his approach to the study of the body:

> We make progress… in forming hypotheses about the rainbow, the rain, ice, and even
> lightning, which we unfortunately experience as being more cruel than other natural
> phenomena. We may make the same assertions concerning the machines of our body
> that form the basis of medicine: for these are composed of threads, of filaments, of joists,
> of levers, of webs, of stagnant fluids, of tanks, of canals, of filters, of sieves, and other like
> machines. In examining these parts with the help of anatomy, philosophy, and mechanics,
> man is made the possessor of their structure and their function.    (Malpighi 1967: 512–13)

One of the most pressing questions for seventeenth-century physiologists, and one
that was best investigated at the level of subtle anatomy, concerned the nature of
muscle contraction and expansion. This was the physiological process that was seen
to underlie animal locomotion, which in turn had traditionally been cited as the
primary activity of the sensitive soul common to all animals. Nicolaus Steno (Niels
Stensen, 1638–86) argued, most importantly in his *Specimen of the Elements of
Myology, or A Geometrical Description of the Muscle* (1667), that the nerves and
muscles alike contract and expand without the influx or efflux of any new material.
Here Steno is effectively attempting to demonstrate the mechanism of contraction
*more geometrico*, namely, by showing how the shortening of the fibres that constitute the muscles is alone sufficient to account for muscular contraction. The Swiss
physician Johann Bernoulli (1667–1748) for his part sought to explain the contraction of muscle tissue [*crispatio*] in terms of mechanical effervescence. In his view,
active corpuscles become lodged in the angles of other corpuscles, which causes
them to explode and set free the bubbles of elastic air that they had contained. This
in turn creates an effervescence leading to the expansion of the muscle and, finally,
the motion of the animal.

   In Johann Bernoulli and Leibniz, we see the remarkable malleability of mechanism in the latter half of the seventeenth century. Both insist that they remain
faithful to the mechanist principle that everything in nature must be explained in
terms of mass, figure, and motion. Nonetheless, they supplement the minimal
programme of iatromechanism with ebullition, effervescence, and other chemical
processes for which no reductive atomistic account is available. Leibniz, moreover,

---

[4] For a comprehensive treatment of the impact of the microscope in early modern natural
philosophy, see Wilson (1995). One of the most important consequences of microscopic research
was the discovery, not only of the subtle anatomy of large organisms, but that autonomous organic
units or microscopic animals exist on a vastly smaller scale than previously suspected. The extent to
which this discovery influenced philosophical debates about the nature of corporeal substance has
been widely debated, particularly in connection with the philosophy of Leibniz. See Canguilhem
(1992); Wilson (1997); Smith (2007a).

identifies the 'mechanical' simply as that which is immediately knowable by quantitative means, while nonetheless reserving a place in nature for physical processes that are known to occur and yet that cannot be adequately explained in mechanical terms. Leibniz's earliest writings on medicine are marked by an enthusiasm about the possibility of what he himself describes as the 'mathematization' of medicine. By the dawn of the eighteenth century, however, Leibniz is much more sceptical about the possibility of such a mathematization. He writes to Bernoulli:

You know that at present there are many disputes in England, Holland, and France concerning the use of mechanics in medicine: some deny that all things are done mechanically by means of actions in our bodies, in whose ranks is Stahl himself, who quarrels with me in his letters, but whom I do not believe sufficiently understand this. Certain people on the contrary suppose all things to be able to be explained by us mechanically. I agree with neither. All things certainly arise mechanically, but we are not yet so advanced in this respect that we should be able to explain all things mechanically. In the meanwhile, this study of mechanics is not to be disdained, but on the contrary is to be more and more developed. (GM III/2: 884)

Leibniz writes similarly to Michelotti, in his letter on animal secretion of 1715: 'There may be many mechanical causes that explain secretion. I suspect however that one should sooner explain the thing in terms of physical causes. Even if in the final analysis all physical causes lead back to mechanical causes, nonetheless I am in the habit of calling "physical" those causes of which the mechanism is hidden' (Leibniz 1768: II 2, 91). Here, 'physical' contrasts with 'mechanical' to the extent that the latter lends itself to immediate mathematization, given the state of our knowledge and our capacity for observation, whereas 'physical' explanation remains avowedly hypothetical.

Leibniz chose to model human and animal *bodies* after machines without however arguing that humans or animals *themselves* are lacking souls, soul-like principles, or ends. And while Descartes, for his part, thought that to give a mechanical account of animals was *eo ipso* to deny that they have functional unity (Des Chene 2001; for an alternative account, see Simmons 2001), for Leibniz and others, to identify a given entity as a machine was not at all to deny its end-directedness. Leibniz is fully ready to say that the body-machine is best understood in terms of its ends. 'Any machine', he writes in the early 1680s *The human body, like that of any animal, is a sort of machine,*

is best defined in terms of its final cause, so that in the description of the parts it is therefore apparent in what way each of them is coordinated with the others for the intended use. Thus one who is to describe a given clock will say that it is a Machine made to display equal divisions of time, and therefore the function of a clock-hand lies in its uniform motion for some period of time.    (LH III 1, 2; Smith 2007b: 151)

But if a clock is a time-telling machine, what sort of machine is an animal? It is, in the first place and most generally for Leibniz, a perpetual-motion machine, which is superior to the artificial approximations of such machines because: (i) it is able to move itself so as to find and consume new fuel; and (ii) before it ceases to function as an individual machine, it can transmit its likeness to another, similar, machine through sexual reproduction. The animal is not only a perpetual-motion machine (of sorts) capable of nourishing and reproducing itself; it is also, depending on its kind membership, a machine that carries out an activity or cluster of activities peculiar to that kind. Leibniz explains in the same text:

[T]he Bodies of Animals are Machines of perpetual motion, or, to put it more clearly, they are machines comparable to a certain fixed and singular species of perpetual organic motion that is always maintained in the world. Thus for as long as there are spiders there will be weaving machines, for as long as there are bees there will be honey-producing machines, and for as long as there are squirrels there will be leaping machines.    (LH III 1, 2; Smith 2007b, 153)

Leibniz seems to be speaking of perpetuity in two distinct senses here. The first is that of continuing to exist, either through the 'refuelling' that is nutrition or, since an individual animal-machine cannot be sustained in this way forever, through transmission of the animal's likeness, with the same animal ends, to other animal-machines through sexual reproduction. When Leibniz begins in the late 1670s to plan to develop wind-based energy sources for everything from the winding of clocks to the ventilation of mines, he nonetheless insists that 'this invention will have the effect and the advantage of perpetual motion, even though there is none: for this perpetual motion, in the form in which it is sought, is impossible' (A I ii 90). Leibniz harshly criticizes contemporaries, such as Joachim Becher (1635–82), for claiming to have designed perpetual-motion machines that nonetheless require an external energy source such as water.

[I]n order that men should obtain . . . durability of action in their machines, they now add to them a quasi-perpetual machine that is made by nature, which is of course man himself, the pilot, who repairs what is weakened or broken down in time, who applies an external force, bringing agents together with patients . . . or in some other way conserves the power of the Machine.    (LH III 1, 2; Smith 2007b: 155)

In other words, artificial machines are able to continue running only because a certain kind of natural machine, viz. a human being, tends to them by bringing them new fuel. But natural machines themselves require no such attendance: 'Nature . . . brings it about that her Machine is able to do this very thing on its own, that is, that it be able now to be nourished, whereby worn-down parts and forces are renewed' (LH III 1, 2; Smith 2007b: 155). And even if the individual animal will eventually cease functioning, in death, it is still capable of a sort of perpetuity to the extent that it is capable of reproduction: 'Machines of this sort are able to produce others similar to themselves' (LH III 1, 2; Smith 2007b: 155).

In short, a fermenting, exploding, end-directed machine of quasi-perpetual motion is a far cry from the sort of gear-driven contraption that mechanical philosophers are supposed to have taken animals to be. Most mechanists agreed with Descartes that everything is either a body or a soul, but that does not settle the question as to what exactly bodies are capable of doing on their own. Let us consider this last point in more detail.

## III: ANIMAL SPIRITS AND THE PROBLEM OF INTERMEDIATE PRINCIPLES

As indicated above, mechanical theories of living bodies allowed earlier ideas about vital principles to live on in the form of irreducible chemical processes (such as fermentation) from the very beginning of the early modern period. Nonetheless, at least by Descartes' own explicit avowal, there was nothing spiritual about fermentation: it was just as wholly a corporeal phenomenon as anything in the domain of tractorics. Still, the mechanist either/or dichotomy would not reign supreme for long. Cheung (2008) has argued that the Cartesian split between *res extensa* and *res cogitans* would quickly prove to be untenable, and would give rise to a further split, between *res cogitans* and *res vivens* or 'living stuff'. Banished from the domain of the soul, which has now been entirely taken over by thinking, yet unable to be accounted for merely in terms of extension, a *tertium quid* emerges to account for the once soul-based natural phenomena of generation, growth, self-organization, and motion in living beings.

One common candidate for the role of *tertium quid* was the 'animal spirits'. In the mid-sixteenth century, Jean Fernel offered the following traditional definition of 'spirit':

The proper sense of the word 'spirit' is, in all languages, breath, wind. As wind brings about very powerful effects and yet is not visible, the name 'spirit' is given to any corporeal or incorporeal thing that does not enter into the senses . . . To the extent that it brings about its effects, spirit seems to have some affinity with bodies; to the extent that it does not produce these, it is an incorporeal substance. It is thus mixed and intermediate between the corporeal and the incorporeal. All immaterial substances that escape the senses exercise their influence on material bodies by means of spirit.   (Fernel 2005: II, 7)

Animal spirits had traditionally been conceived as the most rarefied part of the blood. For this reason, theories of the nature and purpose of the blood were intimately connected, from antiquity to the seventeenth century, with animal ensouledness, and it was just this sort of view against which Descartes argued when he declared: 'What I call "spirits" here are just bodies' (AT XI 334). William Harvey, in sharp contrast, argued that the blood *is* the soul of the animal. Harvey assumed that the body is anything but a machine in the tractoric sense, and that the return of blood to the heart could be explained only in terms of its inherent drive to return 'home'. The non-mechanistic context of the discovery of the circulation of the blood, however, did not prevent the subsequent study of circulation from contributing to the machine model of animal bodies. Experiments conducted by the Royal Society throughout the 1660s (Guerrini 1989: 2003) were undertaken in the hope that the very nature of species differences could be unravelled through the experimental study of intra- and inter-species transfusion. Thus we learn in the *Philosophical Transactions* (February 11, 1666) of

Tryals Proposed by Mr. Boyle to Dr. Lower, to Be Made by Him for the Improvement of Transfusing Blood Out of One Live Animal into Another. Queries: Whether a fierce dog, by being quite new stocked with the blood of a cowardly dog, may not become more tame or vice versa? Whether a transfused dog will recognize his master? Whether characteristics peculiar to a breed (e.g., the scent of bloodhounds) will be abolished or impaired if a spaniel's blood is transfused into a bloodhound? Whether rejuvenation will occur if an old, feeble dog is given the blood of a young, vigorous one? Whether the blood of one animal may be safely transferred into another, as a calf into a dog, or a cold animal, as a fish, frog, or tortoise, into a hot animal, and vice versa? Whether, by frequent transfusion, something tending to a degree of change of species may be accomplished?

Richard Lower (1631–91), the doctor referred to in the above passage, denounced the view that the possibility of blood transfusion is nothing more than 'an old fable of Pythagoras, and like another ridiculous metempsychosis' (Lower 1669: 182). The reason for holding such a belief seems to have resulted from the intense and widespread association of the blood with the animal soul, either because the animal spirits were seen as the most rarefied product of the blood, or were accepted (as in the case of Harvey) as the soul itself. Transfusion, on such a view, much like cloning today, was an intervention in nature that seemed to overturn many of our most basic metaphysical distinctions. But it was in part precisely these distinctions, and the need to either corroborate them or reject them, that drove such experiments. Some involved human subjects. Lower, for example, describes an experiment performed 'on a certain A[rthur] C[oga], who had a harmless sort of madness, and into whose arm, in the presence of the Royal Society, we injected at various times a few ounces of sheep's blood, without causing him any harm ... But he eluded our aims, preferring his own inclination to debauchery to the pursuit of healing' (Lower 1669: 200). The idea that sheep's blood could make a sick horse healthy or an insane man sane is evidently premised on the supposed moral character of the sheep, which in turn is rooted in a long history of religious iconography and allegory.

Lower believed that, 'just as the illustrious Harvey was the first to teach that the blood that circulates outside of its own vessels conserved the life of the body', he himself had been the first to discover that blood transferred out of an animal can rehabilitate the health of another body (Lower 1669: 203). These experiments, and others like them, could have been an important factor in the emergence of a view of life and health, not as properties of individuals, but as diffuse quantities that might be shared or exchanged. Such a view was common to the vitalistic materialism of the eighteenth century. However, concerns about the criteria for the persistence of the identity of organisms begin already in the seventeenth century. John Locke (*Essay* II. xxvii. 3–6) in particular was very concerned to articulate criteria by which one could assert that an individual organism remains the same over time. While some would attribute the ensouling function to the blood that courses throughout the entire body, others would argue that the soul animates and conserves each portion of the body directly. Georg Ernst Stahl (1659–1734) identifies life with the power to conserve the organization of the body. He explains that 'all actions in the body that pertain both to its structure as well as to the conservation of its mixture are supported by the soul itself, and on account of its uses and ends' (Stahl 1708: I, i, § 8, 204). As Duchesneau explains, even if the movements of an organic body are for Stahl in the end acts of the soul corresponding to the soul's intentions, they correspond perfectly to the nature of organic bodies, 'of which they guarantee the special structuring, vital conservation, and functional processes' (Duchesneau 1998: 296).

In the course of a bitter and contentious debate, Leibniz mocked Stahl's view of the soul as having a body-preserving function by comparing the soul's role in the body to that of salt in cured ham, a comparison that was originally made by the third-century Stoic philosopher Chrysippus: 'The very celebrated author identifies [the role of the soul] with the power of preserving the body from its own tending towards death, since otherwise the bodies of living things would decompose, so that future life would have the value of salt, as was said in jest of the soul of a pig' (Stahl 1720: 11). In other words, if the body-preserving account of the soul were correct, salt could just as easily be brought in to take over the role of the porcine soul once the pig has been slaughtered, since it would keep the flesh from rotting. Leibniz, in contrast, was optimistic about the possibility of deducing the vegetative force that preserves the body 'from the structure of the machine itself' (Stahl 1720: 11). The nutrition, metabolism, and excretion of wastes through which this preservation is effected is fundamentally little different from the manner in which a flame avoids extinction by burning up surrounding matter. 'That life preserves itself in casting off alien substances and in conserving the substances that it appropriates to itself does not rule out mechanism any more than the fact that the flame attracts air and sends off smoke' (Stahl 1720: 14). And a flame, Leibniz insists, is patently not a living thing.

The comparison between life and a flame is central to Leibniz's polemic against Stahl. In Leibniz's view, it shows that there is no sound reason for cordoning living beings off from a mechanistic explanation on the grounds that their capacity for self-preservation cannot be explained without appeal to the inherence of a soul. Leibniz cites experiments by Boyle to corroborate his view that an animal, like a flame, is in perpetual flux, and is nothing in itself without the constant appropriation of materials from the surrounding environment. Leibniz denounces the soul–body relation imagined by Stahl as one of obedience through violence, whereas Leibniz himself envisions an obedience through accord [*ex consensus*] (Stahl 1720: 18). The soul cannot impose anything upon the bodily machine that the machine is not capable of producing spontaneously. The body is thus an automaton, as is the soul (by analogy with the body), in that both move from one state to the following state entirely in accordance with their own laws. The soul need not constantly 'worry about the body' (Stahl 1720: 221) in order for the body to do what it has been made to do. To hold that there can be some sort of 'proportion' between soul and body, and thus a causal influence from the one to the other, as does Stahl's animistic theory of animal economy, is, Leibniz thinks, to do nothing more than to 'substitute the soul for the animal spirits by a change of name', a move Leibniz derides as 'resting on I-don't-know-what incoherent principles lacking in any value' (Stahl 1720: 221).

For Leibniz, a crucial component of the true mechanistic theory of bodies, including ensouled bodies, is that there can be no intermediate principle between the soul and the body that facilitates their cooperation. Such third entities merely complicate the existing problem of interaction between entities that belong to fundamentally different ontological categories. Over the course of the second half of the seventeenth century, particularly in English natural philosophy, intermediate principles in bodies that would explain their observable vital properties were gradually rejected in favour of the view that matter *itself* is capable of having the properties associated with life. This might be described as a shift away from pananimistic vitalism towards vitalist materialism, a school of thought that would ultimately come to flourish only after the seventeenth century.

## IV: FROM VITAL PRINCIPLES IN MATTER
## TO THE VITALITY OF MATTER

The figures associated with the school of Cambridge Platonism, while differing one from another, maintained that matter was inherently incapable of action or of any sort of natural change or motion that is associated with life. Henry More (1614–87) is a dualist of sorts, who divided the world into body and spirit and thus distinguishes himself from the psychopyrists, hylozoists, and others who would wish to impart vital properties to matter. Yet he understands the essence of spirit not as a *res cogitans* but rather as a substance that is *penetrable and indiscerpible.* Thus, by Descartes' standards, More attributes to spirit more of a share in the bodily than is acceptable or even coherent. In the *Immortality of the Soul*, More justifies this definition as follows: 'The fitness of [this] Definition will be the better understood, if we divide *Substance* in generall into these first kindes, *viz. Body* and *Spirit*, and then define *Body* to be *A Substance impenetrable and discerpible*. Whence the contrary kind to this is fitly defined, *A Substance penetrable and indiscerpible*' (More 1667: 21). Although More sees spirit and body as two entirely distinct kinds of substance, for him spirit shares in one important feature of the corporeal, *viz.* it is extended, and is thus wholly unlike what Descartes imagined the non-bodily to be. But for More, Descartes' dualism could not work, since it posited two absolutely distinct realms, mind and extension, while holding that the one could, in spite of its absolute distinctness, communicate motion to the other. More, while holding that spirit and body are, in a sense, absolutely distinct, avoids Descartes' interaction problem by maintaining that spirit moves body not by transference of motion but instead by permeating and activating body from within.

More believes that nobler human activities, such as cogitation, result from the motion of the animal spirits rather than from the brain, since 'the very consistency [of the latter] is so clammy and sluggish', and thus unsuitable for such fine and subtle activities as geometry. It is no more fit to serve as the seat of the soul than is 'a Cake of Sewet or a Bowl of Curds' (More 1653: 34). More identifies these spirits with the heavenly or ethereal matter that Ficino held to constitute heaven, and with 'the Fire which Trismegist affirms is the inward vehicle of the Mind, and the instrument that God used in the forging of the world, and which the Soul of the world, wherever she acts, does most certainly still use' (More 1667: 127f.). He does not explicate this 'fire' in the chemical terms in which his contemporaries understood the fermenting 'fire without light' that keeps the body alive; but in his view the life of a body is in some broad sense 'pyrotechnical'. Indeed, More's notion of the Archaeus, which posits a singular plastic or animating faculty belonging to a world-soul, appears to originate in the Paracelsian tradition, where it is conceptually quite close to the notion of ferment. The principal difference between More's view and that of Leibniz, in this respect, is that the English thinker conceives the 'fire' of the body in a largely metaphorical sense, while Leibniz seeks to invoke pyrotechnics as one of the branches of mechanics, which in turn enables one to model the living body in exhaustive detail.

More's Cambridge contemporary, Ralph Cudworth (1617–88), also insisted that there must be some innate principle in matter that activates it. One of the most important philosophical concepts developed in his *True Intellectual System of the Universe* is that of 'plastic nature'. For Cudworth, the plastic nature of the world is nothing other than an 'Inferior and Subordinate Instrument' of God, which 'doth Drudgingly Execute that Part of his Providence, which consists in the Regular and Orderly Motion of Matter' (Cudworth 1678: 150). This universal plastic nature is what keeps the dead or inorganic world moving in accordance with natural laws. Expressing his commitment to the first of two sorts of plastic nature, Cudworth writes that 'there is a *Mixture* of *Life* or *Plastick Nature* together with *Mechanism*, which runs through the whole Corporeal Universe' (Cudworth 1678: 148). He also often writes of particular plastic *natures*, in the plural, each belonging to a particular creature. While acting as 'God's instruments', plastic natures unconsciously bring about changes in extended matter, just as minds or souls do consciously (Cudworth 1678: 158–9). The unconscious powers within each individual living creature mean that each moves in accordance with God's will without being moved directly by God (Jacob 1970: 110–14).

More and Cudworth were the core members of the Cambridge Platonist school, and as such were averse to the sort of naturalistic explanation of motion and change preferred by a philosopher such as Spinoza. For the Platonists, it was crucial that the causes of natural change should lie ultimately outside the natural sphere altogether. Yet many other English philosophers of the same period would argue that there is indeed a vital element in matter, but this is something intrinsic to matter, a natural property of it, rather than something incorporeal derived from a supernatural source. Thus for example the English Gassendist, Walter Charleton, writes '[t]hat same motive virtue, therefore, wherewith every Compound Bodie is naturally endowed, must owe its origine to the innate and co-essential Mobility of its component particles' (Charleton 1654: 126, 269). Henry Power, too, would argue that motion 'is as inseparable an attribute to bodies, as well as Extension is' (Power 1664: 61; cited in Henry 1986: 342). Indeed, as John Henry has compellingly argued, the sort of theory of active spirit defended by Power and the majority of his English contemporaries 'is unequivocally materialistic' (Henry 1986: 343).

Another fine example of a thoroughgoing naturalistic—a term preferred here to 'materialistic', which suggests a reductivism or eliminativism that does not seem to be in the spirit of the thinkers under consideration—vitalism is to be found in Francis Glisson (1597–1677). He argues, in his *Treatise on the energetic nature of substance*, that there is an 'energetic nature' at work in all bodies. Living bodies are distinguished from dead ones to the extent that the energetic nature, which to some extent defines all bodies, brings about an organized interconnection of their parts. Glisson seeks to articulate a principle of individuation beyond the difference between the bodily and the immaterial, and, according to Cheung (2008), ultimately finds it in a 'process ontology' which 'connects stimulus, differentiation, and reaction with one another in a corporeally delimitable unity'. As Cheung explains, 'energetic nature is the "vital principle" of living, corruptible bodies, and at the same time it is the immanent principle of the differentiation of unitary substance' (Cheung 2008: 135).

Glisson describes this dual role of energetic nature as 'biusia', a term compounded from the Greek words *bios*, 'life', and *ousia*, 'being' (Glisson 1672: 207), which is likely the first modern usage of some form of the prefix '*bio*'. The term 'biology' would not come into use until the nineteenth century, and it is perhaps significant that the prefix is first used, not to describe some particular portion of the natural world (as biology would later do), thereby leaving the vastly greater part of the world for study by physics alone, but rather to characterize nature as such. As we learn from an elegant 'accompt' published as a supplement to the *Philosophical Transactions* (1672): 'The famous Author of this Philosophical Treatise endeavors to make it out, that matter is the Prime and Radical subject of Life; or, that Life is the inmost essence of matter, and inseparable from the same' (1672: 5076).

Glisson's metaphysics is in the end monistic, while nonetheless making room for a wide variety in nature, and, crucially, a distinction between living and non-living. According to Guido Giglioni, 'Glisson bridges the gap between monism and pluralism, between prime matter and individual "modes", by viewing matter as a whole individuum in the constant process of increasing its self-organization and individuation' (2002: 33). For Glisson, 'distinctions and differences are the result of a development internal to the nature of substance. Substance itself is a tendency towards growing distinctions and individuality' (Giglioni 2002: 33). Spinoza is a better-known metaphysician to whom this or a similar characterization would also apply. Glisson with his 'biusia', no less than Spinoza with his '*natura naturans*', offers a thoroughly naturalistic account of the diversity of beings in the natural world to the extent that he traces back the principle that individuates and activates them to a single basic feature of all of material nature, rather than to a non-natural property superadded to certain things in nature but not to others.

At least since the important work of John Henry we have known that, in Henry's words, 'the use of active principles in pre-Newtonian matter theory represents a clear and undeniable tradition in English mechanical philosophy and cannot be dismissed as nothing more than a series of minor aberrations by the writers involved' (Henry 1986: 338). Where Stahl argues that it is the soul that directly animates the body, and Cudworth that plastic natures are somewhat mind-like principles in bodies in addition to their matter, the English *res vivens* theorists (to adopt Cheung's apt phrase) agree, that activity is intrinsic to matter. They appear to be searching for a way of setting matter in motion by positing an active principle within matter, without for that identifying this principle directly with a soul or mind.

# CONCLUSION

Early modern natural philosophy by and large rejects the Aristotelian attribution of biological phenomena such as generation, growth, nutrition, and locomotion to the activity of a vegetative and sensitive soul. These phenomena were generally redescribed in terms of the activity of the body (though there is substantial evidence that Aristotle himself understood the functions of the lower soul as functions of a *corporeal* soul). This body was sometimes conceived by analogy with a machine, but the category of 'machine' was far more capacious than what is suggested by the well-known figure of the clock with its gears. Machines ran on hydraulic, chemical, and thermal as well as 'tractoric' processes, and the wholes made out of such assemblages might be regarded as having true functional unity.

Dissatisfaction with mechanism, even in its more complicated forms, motivated a return on the part of some theorists to a resident soul, or to intermediate principles that would, so to speak, move between an incorporeal soul and the body, serving as their line of communication. But many who believed in a vital principle in nature believed that it was body *itself* that was vital, rather than that there was some *tertium quid* between soul and body. This view places these thinkers much closer to the vitalistic materialists of the century to follow than to their own vitalist contemporaries such as Stahl, though neither of these labels would have had any meaning for these thinkers themselves. Their speculations paved the way for the views associated most closely, not with English thinkers, but rather with French philosophers such as Julien Offray de La Mettrie, Denis Diderot, and Paul-Joseph Barthez. Vitalism and materialism are often thought to be two very distinct schools of thought. Yet it is but one small step from the view that all of nature is imbued with a vital principle to the view that material nature itself has within it the requisites for all of the phenomena that we associate with life.

# References

*An Accompt of Some Books*, 1672, Number 87: *Tractatus de Natura Substantiae Energetica, seu de Vita Naturae, ejusq; Tribus primis Facultatibus; Perceptiva, Appetitiva, Motiva, &c. Jeremiae Horroccii Angli Opera Posthuma: una cum Guil. Crabtraei Observationibus Coelestibus; nec non Joh. Flamstedii de Temporis Aequatione Diatriba, Numerisq; Lunaribus ad Novam LUNAE Systema Horroccii*, in *Philosophical Transactions* (1665–78), Volume 7, 5076–82.

AUCANTE, V. (2004). *La philosophie médicale chez Descartes*. Paris: Presses Universitaires de France.

BOAS, M. (1949). 'Hero's *Pneumatica*: a study of its transmission and influence'. *Isis*, 40: 38–48.

CANGUILHEM, G. (1992). 'Note sur les rapports de la théorie cellulaire et de la philosophie de Leibniz', in *La connaissance de la vie*. Paris: Vrin, 240–2.

CARTER, R. B. (1983). *Descartes' Medical Philosophy: The Organic Solution to the Mind–Body Problem*. Baltimore, MD: Johns Hopkins University Press.

CHARLETON, W. (1654). *Physiologia Epicuro-Gassendo-Charltoniana: Or a fabrick of science natural upon the hypothesis of atoms*. London.

CHEUNG, T. (2008). *Res vivens: Agentenmodelle organischer Ordnung 1600–1800*. Freiburg: Rombach Verlag.

CLERICUZIO, A. (2000). *Elements, Principles, and Corpuscles: A Study of Atomism and Chemistry in the Seventeenth Century*. Dordrecht: Springer.

CUDWORTH, R. (1678). *The True Intellectual System of the Universe*. London.

DAWSON, V. P. (1987). *Nature's Enigma: The Problem of the Polyp in the Letters of Bonnet, Trembley and Réaumur*. Philadelphia, PA: American Philosophical Society.

DES CHENE, D. (2001). *Spirits & Clocks: Machine and Organism in Descartes*. Ithaca, NY: Cornell University Press.

DUCHESNEAU, F. (1998). *Les modèles du vivant de Descartes à Leibniz*. Paris: Vrin.

FERNEL, J. (2005). *De abditis rerum causis*. Ed. John M. Forrester. Leiden: Brill.

GARRISON, D. (2003). 'Metaphor and analogy in Vesalian anatomy'. http://vesalius.northwestern.edu.

GAUKROGER, S. (2002). *Descartes' System of Natural Philosophy*. Cambridge: Cambridge University Press.

GIGLIONI, G. (2002). *The Genesis of Francis Glisson's Philosophy of Life*. Ph.D. Dissertation: The Johns Hopkins University.

GLISSON, F. (1672). *Tractatus de natura substantiae energetica, seu De vita naturae, ejusque tribus primis facultatibus, I. Perceptiva, II. Appetitiva, & III. Motiva, naturalibus &c.* London: H. Brome.

GUERRINI, A. (1989). 'The ethics of animal experimentation in 17th-century England'. *Journal of the History of Ideas*, 50: 391–407.

GUERRINI, A. (2003). *Experimenting with Humans and Animals: From Galen to Animal Rights*. Baltimore, MD: Johns Hopkins University Press.

HENRY, J. (1986). 'Occult qualities and the experimental philosophy: active principles in pre-Newtonian matter theory'. *History of Science*, 24: 335–81.

HUET, P.-D. (1689). *Censura philosophiae cartesianae*. Paris.

JACOB, F. (1970). *La logique du vivant. Une histoire de l'hérédité*. Paris: Gallimard.

LEIBNIZ, G. W. (1768). *Gothofredi Guilelmi Leibnitii Opera Omnia*. Ed. Louis Dutens. 6 vols. Geneva: De Tournes.

LOWER, R. (1669). *Tractatus de corde. Item de motu & colore sanguinis et chyli in eum transitu*. London: Jacob Allestry.

MALPIGHI, M. (1967). *Opere scelte di Marcello Malpighi*. Ed. L. Belloni. Turin: UTET.

MORE, H. (1653). *An antidote against atheism*, in *A collection of Several Philosophical Writings* (1662) [repr. New York and London: Garland, 1978].

MORE, H. (1667). *The Immortality of the Soul*, in *A Collection of Several Philosophical Writings*. London: J. Fleisher.

MORRIS, K. (2000). 'Bête-machines', in S. Gaukroger, J. Schuster, and J. Sutton, (eds), *Descartes' Natural Philosophy*. London: Routledge, 401–19.

NUTTON, V. (2003). 'Introduction' to Andreas Vesalius, *Of the Fabric of the Human Body*. Ed. and tr. Daniel Garrison and Malcom Hast. http://vesalius.northwestern.edu.

PASINI, E. (1995). *Corpo e funzioni cognitive in Leibniz*. Milan: Franco Angeli.

PEREIRA, G. (1554). *Antoniana Margarita, opus nempe physicis medicis et theologis non minus utile quam necessarium*. Medina.

POWER, H. (1664). *Experimental philosophy in three books: containing new experiments, microscophical, mercurial, magnetical*. London.

RAY, J. (1717). *The wisdom of God manifested in the works of His Creation*. London: Harbin.

REGAN, T. (1982). *All that Dwell Therein: Animal Rights and Environmental Ethics*. Berkeley, CA: University of California Press.

RORARIUS, H. (1648). *Quod animalia bruta ratione utantur melius homine.* Paris.

SCHOTT, K. (1657). *Mechanica hydraulico-pneumatica, Qua praeterquam quod Aquei Elementi natura, proprietas, vis motrix, atque occultus cum aere conflictus.* Francoforti: Sumptu Heredum Joannis Godofredi Schönwetteri.

SIMMONS, A. (2001). 'Sensible ends: latent teleology in Descartes' account of sensation'. *Journal of the History of Philosophy,* 39: 49–75.

SMITH, J. E. H. (2007*a*). 'Leibniz on spermatozoa and immortality'. *Archiv für Geschichte der Philosophie,* 89: 264–82.

SMITH, J. E. H. (2007*b*). 'The body-machine in Leibniz's early physiological writings: a selection of texts with commentary'. *The Leibniz Review,* 17: 141–79.

SMITH, J. E. H. (2011). *Divine Machines: Leibniz and the Sciences of Life.* Princeton, NJ: Princeton University Press.

SORELL, T. (2005). *Descartes Reinvented.* Cambridge: Cambridge University Press.

STAHL, G. E. (1708). *Theoria medica vera: physiologiam & pathologiam, tanquam doctrinae medicae partes vere contemplativas.* Halle: Literis Orphanotrophei.

STAHL, G. E. (1720). *Georgii Ernesti Stahlii Negotium otiosum: Seu Σκιαμαχια adversus positiones aliquas fundamentales* Theoriae verae medicae. Halle: Impensis Orphanotrophei.

VESALIUS, A. (1543). *De humani corporis fabrica.* Basel.

WILSON, C. (1995). *The Invisible World: Early Modern Philosophy and the Invention of the Microscope.* Princeton, NJ: Princeton University Press.

WILSON, C. (1997). 'Leibniz and the Animalcula', in M. A. Stewart (ed.), *Studies in Seventeenth-Century European Philosophy.* Oxford: Clarendon Press, 153–76.

# PART II

## THE MIND,
## THE PASSIONS,
## AND AESTHETICS

# CHAPTER 6

........................................................................

# THE SOUL

........................................................................

## R. W. SERJEANTSON

THE soul has not been a prominent object of philosophical investigation since the eighteenth century; indeed its demise as a philosophical subject is owing, in good part, to a historical transformation that will be elaborated here. But in European philosophy of the early modern period the soul was a central preoccupation of philosophers of widely differing philosophical and religious commitments, whether Christian, freethinking, or Judaic. There seems, accordingly, no need to pursue a case for the potential relevance of the subject to contemporary philosophy. What a history of philosophical discussions of the soul in the early modern period may hope to achieve, instead, is the task of explanation: explaining why the soul had such an important place in philosophical speculation in pre-modern Europe, and how it became— gradually and hesitantly—a questionable object of philosophical inquiry. The goals of this chapter, therefore, are twofold. The first is to offer an account of some significant aspects of the philosophy of the soul in the early modern period and of its transformation across that period. But the second and perhaps more far-reaching purpose is to offer a thesis about the place of the soul in early modern conceptions of what it meant to be a human animal, and, ultimately, to trace the contribution of the early modern philosophy of the soul to the enlightened 'science of human nature'.

## I: THE SOUL IN NATURAL PHILOSOPHY

........................................................................

The soul certainly played a role in all the major disciplines of early modern philosophy: logic, metaphysics, natural philosophy, and moral philosophy. In particular, every student of logic learnt that the essential definition of 'man' (*homo*) was 'rational animal' (*animal rationale*) (Crane 1962): the human possession of a rational soul, that is to say, was the attribute that distinguished unequivocally and exactly the human animal from its brutal cousins. But the discipline in which the soul was principally treated was natural philosophy. This was an Aristotelian legacy, for the founding document of the early modern study of the soul was Aristotle's *De anima* (*On the Soul*). Within the Aristotelian corpus that formed the basis of later-medieval and early-modern pedagogy in natural philosophy, that work had taken on an undisputed place among the so-called *libri naturales* (Blair 2006: 366–7). This situation was well founded in Aristotle's own text, for the opening of the *De anima* had asserted that knowledge of the soul above all contributes to the understanding of nature and gave reasons for supposing that its province was the science of nature (*De anima*, I. i). In respect of the soul, therefore, as in many other areas, the history of philosophy in the early modern period is inseparable from the history of the natural sciences.

Hence until the middle years of the seventeenth century, the principal forums for philosophical discussion of the soul took their starting-point, in one way or another, from Aristotle's *De anima*. Editions, translations (into Latin), and commentaries, and sometimes all three together, were widespread. Commentaries on the *De anima*, as on most other Aristotelian philosophical texts, were a particular speciality of members of the Jesuit order, with notable contributions by the commentators associated with the University of Coimbra (1609), Antonio Rubio (1611), and Francisco Suárez (1621) (Simmons 1999). Protestant authors tended to prefer to produce more monographic treatments of the subject. Here they followed the lead of the magisterial reformer Philipp Melanchthon's influential *Book on the Soul* (1540, 1553) (Kusukawa 1995: 75–123), and indeed several late-Renaissance Protestant treatments of the soul take the form of commentaries or elaborations upon Melanchthon's book (Strigel 1590; Magirus 1603).

However, after an efflorescence of scholarly interest in the Greek text at the turn of the sixteenth century, traditions of commentary and interpretation of the text of the *De anima* fell into a decline. For pedagogical purposes, textual commentaries were increasingly being replaced by a genre of writings that had already begun to gather strength in the sixteenth century: compendia that treated the whole field of natural philosophy in a systematic fashion (Schmitt 1988). Yet across this genre— which was very broad, stretching from works of the most schematic puerility to ambitious and elaborate treatises—the soul retained its central place in the field of natural philosophy. As Eustachius a Sancto Paulo (1573–1640) put it in his *Summa of Philosophy* (1609), 'consideration of the soul has become a special branch of physics' (1998: 83). Characteristically, in fact, the soul formed the culmination of a course in natural philosophy. After making their way through topics such as nature, local motion, generation and corruption, meteors, and the parts of animals, these books tend to culminate in an account of the soul, including its powers of sensation and locomotion, and concluding with the rational soul and its powers of understanding and will (e.g. Fox Morcillo 1560: 235–381; Magirus 1619: 437–662; Sanderson 1671: 113–16). Even John Locke, for all that he attacked the prominence of the soul 'in some sort of natural Philosophy' in his *Essay Concerning Humane Understanding* of 1690 (*Essay* IV. viii. 9), nonetheless adopted precisely this schema in his own little *Elements of Natural Philosophy*, written in 1698 for the twelve-year-old Frank Masham: here Locke passes from animals, through the senses, to the 'understanding of man' (Locke 1720: 211–30). This somewhat surprising observation indicates what will be a theme of this study: that although Aristotle's book itself ceased to sit at the centre of the web of investigations into the soul, the *de anima* tradition was subsequently transformed rather than straightforwardly rejected.

With all this said, one must acknowledge that the soul's place in natural philosophy in the early modern period was not unquestioned. *Physica* or natural philosophy was, in a common definition, 'the knowledge of natural bodies, insofar as they are natural' (Sanderson 1671: 2). Yet the nature—though not the existence—of the soul was widely acknowledged to be, to a greater or lesser extent, uncertain, and knowledge of it was difficult to obtain (McCracken 1998). It may therefore appear somewhat paradoxical that the soul should have been a part of this science of the body. In fact, the question of whether the contemplation of the soul properly pertained to the study of natural philosophy was one that was raised fairly prominently. The interlocutors, for instance, of Jean Bodin's (1530–96) *Theatre of Universal Nature*, first published in 1596, open their account of the soul in the penultimate fifth book of his dialogue with a discussion of whether the human soul 'belongs to the knowledge of nature' (Bodin 1605: 431–2). From a more orthodox Aristotelian (and Catholic) perspective the Jesuit commentator Antonio Rubio (1548–1615) also noted that while the vegetative and sensitive souls derived from matter, the rational soul, especially when separated from the body, belonged more properly to 'first philosophy', or metaphysics, than to natural philosophy (Rubio 1621: 2–3, 517).

Yet even for those natural philosophers who remained relatively faithful to an understanding of the soul as part of nature, certain complications arose of which they were well aware, and which commentators often sought to resolve. It was an inescapable and increasingly pressing fact that, in Christian Europe, theological requirements had accreted themselves to the exclusively natural-philosophical account available from Aristotle. The Fifth Lateran Council (1512–17) had mandated that philosophers demonstrate the immortality of the soul by the light of reason as well as that of faith. This optimistic requirement was rapidly flouted by Pietro Pomponazzi in an episode that remained notorious throughout the early modern period. Pomponazzi's *Treatise on the Immortality of the Soul* (1516), for all that it ultimately arrived at the orthodox fideistic conclusion that doctrine known by faith trumped the conclusions of reason, judged arguments for immortality to be 'absurdities and contrary to the principles of philosophy', and noted that 'no natural reasons' could be found for it (Pomponazzi 1948: 321, 379). The papal condemnation of Pomponazzi's work meant that, as Eustachius (1998: 89) put it, 'a Christian may not doubt that rational souls are spiritual and immortal', and throughout our period it was by no means only Catholic philosophers who thought their reason must arrive at this conclusion. For example, when Leibniz was writing his *New Essays on the Understanding* in the very early eighteenth century, he regarded it as 'infinitely more useful' to religion and morality 'to show that souls are naturally immortal' than to maintain the (potentially suspicious) fideistic position that their continued existence depended upon a divine promise (LRB 68).

Yet for all this, theological considerations must not be over-emphasized when considering the soul as an object of early modern philosophical inquiry. The intellectual life of the period tended to observe strong disciplinary divisions, and at least before the mid-point of the seventeenth century, writers on the soul remained strongly conscious that the province of the philosopher was distinct from that of the physician or the theologian. These distinctions were reinforced by the faculty-structure of the universities, with their strong differentiation between the undergraduate study of the arts, in which philosophy took a central place, and graduate training in the three professions of medicine, law, and divinity. The different disciplines and faculties did of course share presuppositions and arguments—the study of philosophy was after all a necessary preliminary to the pursuit of a profession—but natural philosophers, particularly those in Italy, where theologians inhabited their own separate institutions, enjoyed a good deal of autonomy. The soul was first and foremost an object of philosophical, not of theological knowledge.

# II: The soul and life

What the soul explained above all was life (Garber *et al.* 1998). Indeed, on one definition the soul was simply 'life itself' (Goclenius 1613: 103). In the Aristotelian conception of the soul its fundamental role within natural philosophy was to explain the observable phenomena of life: growth, sensation, locomotion, appetition, and even understanding (Aristotle, *De anima*, II. 3; Des Chene 2000). As the principle of animal life, the soul could be regarded as 'the chief of all the faculties and operations which one finds in animate body', that by which 'we live and feel and understand' (Eustachius 1640: 247, 248). Not every kind of being that possessed a soul was capable of each of these faculties—understanding, in particular, was reserved for the human animal—but taken together they were 'the general powers of living things', as Eustachius put it (1998: 85).

Indeed, a less tightly Aristotelian tradition was even willing to extend the scope of the life-giving soul both to the bowels of the earth and the starry heavens above. Girolamo Cardano, Tommaso Campanella, Jean Bodin, and Johannes Kepler were criticized by later seventeenth-century philosophers for proposing that stones and metals might have a form of life imparted by their own souls in the manner of plants and animals (Froidmont 1649: 10). Leibniz similarly identified a tradition of 'spiritualizing authors' including Cardano, Campanella, Anne Conway, Franciscus Mercurius van Helmont, and Henry More who put 'life and perception into everything' (LRB 72). Early modern authors were also conscious of neo-Platonic traditions that attributed souls and even mind to the stars (Goclenius 1613: 103; Froidmont 1649: 23–8). The most significant early modern philosopher to take up such thoughts, Johannes Kepler (1571–1630), went so far as to suggest that the earth itself possessed in its bowels a soul with a 'formative power' which was, as he went on, 'similar to that which is in females' (Kepler 1618: 125); the knowledge of geometry possessed by this soul explained the beautiful regularities of snowflakes (Sakamoto 2009: 78). Nonetheless, in the second edition of the *Mysterium Cosmographicum* (1621) the mature Kepler rejected his earlier view (derived, as he acknowledged, from the ideas of Julius Caesar Scaliger) that 'the cause which moves the planets' was a soul (Escobar 2008: 26).

Most philosophers of the soul, however, restricted themselves to the consideration of more proximate animal life, and followed the Aristotelian and Thomist (*Summa theologiae*, I. q. 78) legacy in developing an account that identified three different and distinct kinds of soul (Park 1988). The first and lowest of these was the vegetative soul, which was concerned with nutrition, growth, and generation; these were fundamental properties that were possessed and shared by all living things. This lowest form of soul, nonetheless, was 'neighbouring and akin to' the form of inanimate things (Froidmont 1649: 83). The second type of soul, possession of which was restricted to animals, was sensitive or organic: it was concerned with perception or sensation. The senses and faculties with which this soul was concerned were the five external senses (touch, taste, smell, hearing, sight), and also the 'internal senses'; the common sense, which integrated the information provided by the external senses; and the faculties of (at the least) memory and imagination. This sensitive soul in its turn might be held to 'approach more closely to spiritual form than the vegetative soul' (Froidmont 1649: 83).

Finally, there was the rational or intellective soul, possessed only by human beings. Accounts of its nature and faculties—'a pleasant, but a doubtful Subject' (Burton 1621: 39)—were elaborately developed in the earlier part of our period. Its details were extensively debated, but it was very generally agreed that its principal faculties were two: the understanding and the will. The understanding was what gave humans their unique powers of reason, generally conceived in syllogistic terms; its task was principally contemplative. The will, by contrast, was practical, and governed moral action. It was by means of the rational soul that the world was made intelligible, through its power to transform the singulars of sensory experience into the universals of knowledge (*scientia*).

Throughout the early modern period the possession of a rational soul was therefore intimately bound up with what it meant to be a human being. The Marburg philosopher Rudolph Goclenius identified a disparity in this matter between the 'Platonists', who held that human beings, properly speaking, *were* their souls; and the 'Aristotelians', who held that the soul was rather a constituent part of what it meant to be human (Goclenius 1613: 105). Among natural philosophers, who tended to the latter view, the soul was the form of the body; hence human nature consisted of these two elements, which were undivided until the moment of death. Moreover, the soul had no special seat within the body: 'It truly actuates and informs the body in all its parts' (Eustachius 1998: 84). Above all, as we have seen, the definition of 'man' as the 'rational animal' was universally known.

This rational soul was very widely held to be immaterial. Indeed, philosophers who were willing to countenance the possibility that body alone, of whatever sort, might be capable of the complex operations of thought—apprehension, composition and division, ratiocination, reflexion—are extremely rare, especially in the earlier part of the period. The capacity of the understanding to perceive and judge universals as well as singular sense-perceptions, in particular, provided one of the strongest arguments for the soul's immateriality, since it was widely held that matter was incapable of such abstraction.

The immateriality of the rational soul, in its turn, was widely held to be one of the strongest arguments for its immortality (e.g. Eustachius 1998: 85). Seth Ward (1617–89) put this case in the form of a very bald syllogism, in the *Philosophicall Essay* (1652) that he published to distance himself from Thomas Hobbes following publication of the incendiary *Leviathan* (1651): 'Whatsoever substance is incorporeall it is immortall. But the souls of men are incorporeall substances, *Ergò* [the souls of men are immortal]' (Ward 1652: 35). This rich possession of immortality, with the soul as its vessel, was almost universally taken as a central (although not a defining) quality of human nature. Indeed, immortality was, as the Jesuit philosopher Guy Holland (1585–1660) put it in the title of his anti-mortalist treatise of 1653, *The Grand Prerogative of Humane Nature.*

The possession of a rational soul thus provided philosophers with a powerful and widespread means of identifying and defining the nature and limits of what was human, both in death and in life. This is a significant preoccupation, for instance, of the Liégeois philosopher Libert Froidmont (Libertus Fromondus, 1578–1653) in his *Four Books of Christian Philosophy on the Soul* (1649), a work published a decade after he had criticized Descartes' account of animal life in the *Discourse on the Method* (CSMK 60–6; Ariew 1992: 70; Byers 2006: 753–4). The widespread early modern legal penalty of decapitation meant that experience of the behaviour of severed heads was reasonably widespread, and for Froidmont as for others this naturally raised questions of important philosophical interest. Froidmont recounts how he had heard from a reliable witness of an execution in Antwerp at which a dog, in the course of licking the blood from the neck of a cleanly severed head, had been greatly surprised when the victim's teeth (forgivably enough, perhaps, in the circumstances) fastened themselves to its ear, causing the dog to flee howling from the room with the head still dangling from it. For Froidmont this account served as proof of the Thomist doctrine that the souls of perfect animals are wholly present in the whole body and all its parts (Froidmont 1649: 98, and cf. 803–4). For René Descartes, by contrast, the capacity of 'severed heads' to 'continue to move about and bite the earth although they are no longer alive' had proved the power of animal spirits, rather than the soul, to animate the body (CSM I 139).

Froidmont was similarly exercised by problems posed to human nature by the existence of cynocephalics (i.e. people with the heads of dogs), monosceli (or sciapods; one-footed people), pygmies, arimaspi (people with a single eye in the centre of their foreheads), and satyrs. These and other doubtful forms between brutes and men, he reassured his reader, belonged to the genus of *simiae* (monkeys and apes), unless of course stories of such beings were fables: 'For Seneca justly calls philosophers a "a credulous lot".' Yet even if these beings were fabulous, Froidmont was well aware that sometimes 'monsters' (*monstra*) might be born to parents who themselves 'were not monstrous at all'. (Though a *Belgus* himself, Froidmont was willing to countenance Juan-Luis Vives's thought that Belgian women were prone to this, on account of the quantities of cabbage and beer that they consumed.) While the birth of such prodigies meant that it could not be the case, as physicians such as Giovanni Argenterio mistakenly supposed, that it was the rational soul that 'conforms and informs' the parental seed, Froidmont—like Descartes (CSM I 140)—was nonetheless persuaded by the thought that the ability of such equivocal beings to speak meant that it could not be the lack of a rational soul that separated them from us (Froidmont 1649: 87, 47, 88).

In these instances, the rational soul was used to define and delineate the nature of 'man', the 'rational animal'. In fact, however, such a soul was also possessed by what John Locke called the 'superior Ranks of Spirits', who populated the early modern philosophical world so richly (*Essay* IV. iii. 6; Yolton 2004). Such spirits often provided philosophers with a touchstone for the powers of the understanding, for although even in its separated form the human soul's powers of perception and understanding were inferior to theirs, they differed in degree rather than kind. Humans might not reason as perfectly as such beings, and they might not see so clearly the best way to achieve their ends; but in the celerity and freedom of their powers of decision, they approximated to those of the angels (Froidmont 1649: 905–6).

One further capacity of the rational soul was very commonly invoked to prove the nobility of its operations and the immateriality of its nature: reflexion, the soul's capacity to reflect upon and understand itself. This was a subject very widely treated by Renaissance and seventeenth-century philosophers. One account of this question that remained particularly influential into the seventeenth century, no doubt because of the importance that his book subsequently took on for the teaching of natural philosophy in Protestant Europe, was that provided by Julius Caesar Scaliger (1484–1558), in the 307th of his *Exoteric Exercitations On Subtlety* (1557). The *Exercitations* were primarily directed against Girolamo Cardano, but here Scaliger also took occasion to attack the views of another important early modern theorist of the soul, Juan-Luis Vives (Maclean 2008). Vives had treated the theme of reflexion in his *On the Soul and Life* (1538), arguing that the reason it was so difficult for the mind to know itself was that there was no superior mind to serve as a vantage point to scrutinize our own. Scaliger treated Vives' discussion with characteristic scorn. He pointed out that it was perfectly possible for superior intelligences (such as angels and God) to be comprehended by inferior ones; and therefore there was no reason why the mind might not apprehend itself (Scaliger 1557: fo. 388$^{r-v}$). Scaliger's solution to the problem of how the understanding might understand itself involved making a distinction between the perception of the external and of the internal world. He noted that the understanding operated not only by means of information ultimately derived from the external world, but also by reflection upon itself. The first mode of understanding he called 'direct' (*recta*); the second, by which the understanding truly grasped the thing understood, he called 'reflexive' (*reflexa*) (Scaliger 1557: fo. 390$^r$).

Scaliger's emphasis upon the reflexive faculty of the soul, and his solution to Vives' difficulty, was an argument that a good number of subsequent philosophers found persuasive long afterwards (e.g. Sanches [1581] 1988: 132; Burgersdijk 1631: 96; Sennert 1618: 601; [Anon.] 1655: 30–1; Stillingfleet 1702: 99); indeed, as we shall see at the end, its legacy ultimately stretches into the human sciences of the eighteenth century.

# III: THE SOUL AND THE MIND

Thus far we have been considering the soul within the philosophical world of the late Renaissance; an intellectual world that contained strong elements of humanistic eloquence, neo-Platonism, Italian naturalism (Ingegno 1988), and even a tentatively emerging Epicureanism (Hill 1601), but which was above all Aristotelian in its assumptions, vocabulary, and fields of investigation. I turn at this point, however, to offer an account of the fortunes and slow supersession of the Aristotelian *De anima* tradition in relation to the increasingly prominent investigation of 'human nature' as a distinct and discrete area of philosophical inquiry.

There was no text in the Aristotelian corpus that took the human being *per se* as its subject. Increasingly throughout the Renaissance, however, the *de anima* tradition took on this role. In particular, the legacy of Melanchthon's *Book on the Soul* encouraged a generic development that would have important consequences for its treatment by early modern philosophers: the treatise 'on man' (*de homine*). Whereas the Aristotelian treatment of the soul considered soul (although in different ways) as the possession of plants and animals as much as of men, this new, un-Aristotelian, and generally (although not exclusively) Protestant genre considered the human being in bipartite terms, as the possessor of both a body and a soul. Contributions to this form of inquiry were made, in rather different ways, in Italy by the heretic Agostino Doni (1581), and in the German-speaking lands by Otto Casmann (1594) and Gregor Horst (1612). Francis Bacon, a reader of both Doni and of his teacher Bernardino Telesio (Spruit 1997), had also called in the *Advancement of Learning* (1605) for a general and extensive consideration of 'HVMANE NATVRE' which would be emancipated from other branches of learning and 'made a knowledge by it self' (Bacon 2000: 93–4). More generally, one also finds at this time a tendency to provide treatises 'on man' within comprehensive treatments of natural philosophy, such as that comprised by book VIII of Daniel Sennert's *Epitome of Natural Knowledge* (1618).

If philosophers had to work to emancipate the philosophy of human nature, they were certainly encouraged by the example of a profession predisposed by its very subject matter to think in these terms: the physicians of the learned medical tradition, all of whom used the philosophical teachings of the undergraduate arts course as a starting-point, or in some cases as a foil, for their own investigations (Maclean 2001: 101–205). Medical writers in general were particularly motivated to look for physiological explanations of mental as well as bodily functions, and physicians such as Giovanni Argenterio and Ambroise Paré in the later sixteenth century, and André du Laurens, Daniel Sennert, and Thomas Willis in the seventeenth, explored the soul from a physiological perspective. They willingly developed somatic explanations, often in terms of the motion of super-subtle 'animal spirits' (Walker 1984), for all manner of mental functions up to, but not including, pure understanding. The philosophers' rational soul remained off-limits, even if its borders were encroached upon.

The Portuguese physician Francisco Sanches (1551–1623), who taught philosophy and medicine at the University of Toulouse, is a particularly notable example of a physician willing to apply the implications of his medical learning to philosophical questions about the soul. While Sanches's insistence on the combined functioning of body and soul was not unique, his insistent and emphatic defence of the unitary nature of the human being is unusually strident:

the human soul, the most perfect of all things created by God, needs a wholly perfect body in order to perform the most perfect of all the actions of which it is capable, namely perfect understanding. 'What!' you will say. 'Understanding does not depend on the body, nor is it in any way helped by it, but it is produced by the mind alone.' This . . . is false. It is futile to say that the mind understands, just as it is to say that the mind hears. It is the *human being* who does both, using both body *and* mind in both instances, and performing any other action whatsoever with the aid of both of these at once.    (Sanches 1988: 262)

Seventeenth- and eighteenth-century debates over the 'Epicurean' thesis of the materiality of the soul (Wilson 2008: 142–55), therefore, had their precedents in these slightly early medical speculations, and the arguments of seventeenth-century mortalists such as Richard Overton rested in part upon speculations he had found in medical writings (1643: 13–16). Yet, while such physicians often acquired equivocal reputations for orthodoxy, and while physicians' encroachment on the territory of philosophers was sometimes looked upon with suspicion by the latter (Froidmont 1649: 46–7; Holland 1653: 21), the medical tradition did not ultimately give rise to the controversies that mortalism or materialism provoked. One reason for this probably lies in the two traditions' shared assumptions—a relationship encapsulated in the maxim *ubi desinit philosophus ibi incipit medicus* ('where the philosopher ends, the physician begins') (Maclean 2001: 80–2). But a deeper reason probably lies in the reluctance of physicians, by contrast with the willingness of more heterodox philosophers, to extend the implications of their speculations into the territory of theology.

That extension went hand-in-hand with new conceptions of natural philosophy, and the fight to bring about the abandonment of the framework supplied by the *libri naturales*. This was above all the case in respect of doctrines of matter. The Aristotelian definition of 'body' relied upon a distinction between (on the one hand) formless matter, out of which natural bodies 'are made and composed', and (on the other) immaterial form, which 'assigns an essence and a name' to natural things. Moreover, from this doctrine of 'substantial form' it was a natural step to regard the soul as the 'form of the body' and indeed the noblest of all causes (Magirus 1619: 29–30, 446). Such thoughtful contemporary observers of the 'new philosophy' as the Scottish language-reformer George Dalgarno (*c*.1620–87) regarded its principal tenet as being the rejection of this distinction between matter and form. On this view, the forms of things 'were nothing else . . . but a multitude of modes of matter' (Dalgarno 2001: 367–8). What the new natural philosopher had to understand was no longer an essential quality that gave a body its form, but rather the configuration, motion, and interaction of bodies themselves. This mechanical vision of the operations of the natural world had dramatic consequences for conceptions of the soul, not least because the soul itself increasingly served philosophers as a principal means for demarcating the limits, or aggrandizing the extent, of natural knowledge.

One consequence of the new philosophies of body (Garber *et al.* 1998) was that the distinction between substance and body tended to collapse. Aristotelian natural philosophy permitted the argument that while the rational soul was certainly not corporeal, it was nonetheless a substance and not an accident. The development of mechanical and corpuscularian philosophies in the seventeenth century brought this distinction into disrepute: the basic quality of 'body' came to be seen in terms of extension, and the class of 'incorporeal substance' that had previously accommodated the soul became more problematic. By the early eighteenth century this stark new contrast between the material and the spiritual realms had sharpened and aggravated debates over the soul such that the principal question about it became whether or not it was material in nature (Thomson 2008). This in turn brought even more to the fore than it had been in the late Renaissance (Colerus 1587) the question of the soul's immortality.

The philosopher who first pursued the consequences of these new doctrines of matter to one of their possible conclusions was thus also one of the earliest mechanists: René Descartes (1596–1650). Descartes, as he put it in his *Discourse on the Method of Rightly Conducting One's Reason and Seeking Truth in the Sciences* (1637), regarded 'the laws of mechanics' as being 'identical with the laws of nature' (CSM I 139). His physics was accordingly profoundly motivated by a rejection of the doctrine of substantial form (Garber 1992: 287). This rejection is in turn reflected in his sharp hostility to the view that the soul is the form of the body. Descartes' physical commitments therefore led his account of human nature into its notoriously stark dualism, a dualism that he developed across his unpublished *Treatise on Man* (part of *The World*, 1629–33), first outlined in print in part V of the *Discourse on the Method*, and further elaborated in his *Meditations on First Philosophy* (1641).

On this account the body should be regarded purely as 'a machine . . . made by the hands of God'. The soul, by contrast, 'cannot be derived in any way from the potentiality of matter, but must be specially created'. Moreover, the soul of which Descartes spoke is exclusively a rational soul, whose purpose 'is simply to think'. It possesses none of the organic and sensitive functions which even the human soul was previously regarded as sharing with animals. This is why, when Descartes introduces his account of animate bodies in part V of the *Discourse*, he supposes that 'the body of a man exactly like our own' might perform all the functions 'which may occur in us without our thinking of them', even though it had not (yet) been infused by God with 'any rational soul'. Nor, more strikingly, does this body require the infusion of 'any other thing to serve as a vegetative and sensitive soul' (CSM I 139, 141, 134). The hitherto dominant typology of the soul was being systematically dismantled and a new anthropology put in its place.

Descartes therefore used the doctrine of mechanism to push against conventional doctrines of the soul as life. Discussing the physical mechanisms of the body—its five external senses, and also the functions previously ascribed to the 'internal senses' of the soul, such as the *sensus communis* in which ideas are received from the external senses, the corporeal imagination, and the memory—he insisted that they were all capable of moving that body 'without being guided by the will', that is, by a rational soul (CSM I 139; see also *The World*: AT XI 202). To this extent Descartes regarded the bodies of humans and animals as cognate, sharing the same mechanisms. But in another crucial respect humans were distinguished from animals by means of their possession of the 'universal instrument' of reason. It was 'impossible', asserted Descartes, 'for a machine to have enough different organs to make it act . . . in the way in which our reason makes us act'. Animals can neither give voice to this reason in words, nor show 'any intelligence' at all (CSM I 140–1).

Both in his rigorous denial of any power of communication to animals, and in his separation of humans from the other animals on account of their possession of a rational soul, Descartes can be seen as taking to an extreme views that were already well-established in his intellectual culture (Serjeantson 2001). What is striking about these views is that Descartes defined them so strongly in terms of the nature of the soul: 'For after the error of those who deny God . . . there is none that leads weak minds further from the straight path of virtue than that of imagining that the souls of the beasts are of the same nature as ours' (CSM I 141). For Descartes, the soul is no longer part of organic life.

Descartes' restriction of 'soul' to human beings alone came to a head in the debate he had with the neo-Epicurean philosopher Pierre Gassendi (1592–1655), which focused on the second of his *Meditations on First Philosophy* (1641). In that meditation, Descartes had explicitly stripped from the soul the powers conventionally attributed to it: nutrition, movement, and sense-perception (CSM II 18). Gassendi, in his set of *Objections*, interpreted this as an attempt to redefine human nature itself: in asking 'What is a man?', Descartes' answer had led him to 'deliberately dismiss' the 'common definitions' of man (CSM II 181). This just charge recognized that, in terms of logic or natural philosophy, Descartes was no longer willing to acknowledge 'man' as the 'rational animal' who shared with the other animals a sensitive soul that conferred life.

Descartes' strikingly disembodied conception of humanity led Gassendi into an equal and opposite corporeal response, asserting—to an unusual and striking degree—the animality of human nature. He raised the possibility that the 'power of sensation possessed by animals' might also 'deserve to be called "thought"', since it is not dissimilar to your own'; that the difference between human and animal reason was 'merely one of degree'; that even though animals 'do not produce human speech', they do produce 'their own kind of language'; and ultimately that 'although man is the foremost of the animals, he still belongs to the class of animals' (CSM II 188). Gassendi's polemically corporealist view of human nature was not widely taken up, and even he later retreated from it (Michael and Michael 1988); as we shall see, although in certain respects Thomas Hobbes developed some of Gassendi's themes, he did not choose to do so on the basis of the specifically animal qualities of the human being.

What was fundamentally at stake here was the question of the role of the soul in defining human nature, and Descartes recognized this clearly in his somewhat intemperate *Replies* to Gassendi's objections. The word 'soul', he argued, was ambiguous. Drawing upon the humanist commonplace that language took its meaning from common usage rather than from the definitions of philosophers, Descartes suggested that it had taken its original meaning from 'the ignorant', who had illegitimately applied the same term both to the 'principle by which we are nourished and grow' and to the apparently quite different 'principle in virtue of which we think'. Descartes at this point drew tactically, and strictly temporarily, upon the schools' received definition of the soul as the 'principal form of man' to assert that it was now thought alone that should be regarded as this form. For which reason, he went on: 'I have so far as possible used the term "mind" for this. For I consider the mind not as a part of the soul but as the thinking soul in its entirety' (CSM II 246). Descartes was thus engaged in a polemical restriction of the notion of 'soul' (*anima*) to what previous philosophers had also called 'mind' (*mens*). In order to make this point quite clear, he also used the word 'mind' in this respect. But unlike earlier philosophy of the mind—such as Jacopo Zabarella's *De mente humana*—Descartes simultaneously ceased to speak of the 'soul' in any other context. Here we may find both the end of one tradition: of the soul as the source of life (Des Chene 2001); and the beginning of another: the investigation of the human mind on Cartesian principles (La Forge [1666] 1997; Le Grand 1672, pt. VII).

Descartes returned to the question of human nature in his last book, *The Passions of the Soul* (1649): part I of this work is concerned with 'the passions in general, and incidentally the whole nature of man'. As the title of the book suggests, Descartes allowed himself here to speak of the 'soul' rather than rigorously of the mind, but he continued to distinguish strictly between soul and body, to deny the 'very serious error' that it is the soul that gives life to bodies, and to insist that 'a passion in the soul is usually an action in the body' (CSM II 328–9). On the whole, therefore, those attracted by Descartes' ideas did not require the posthumous publication of his *Treatise on Man* (which appeared in Latin translation in 1662 and in its original French in 1664 and 1677) to appreciate the scope and significance of his reorientation of human nature away from having its source in a life-giving soul.

One of the first philosophers whose work on the soul was given direction by that of Descartes was the English Catholic exile Kenelm Digby (1603–65), who wrote of Descartes that he 'hath left us no excuse for being ignorant of any thing worth the knowing' (Digby 1644: 275, I. xxxii. 1). Digby's *Two Treatises* were first published in Paris in 1644 and reprinted several times in the following quarter-century both in their original English and in Latin. The very division of his book, into a first treatise on 'the Nature of Bodies', and a second of 'the Nature of Mans Soule', betrays the impact of Descartes, first by its consideration as an aspect of living bodies those functions (such as 'the retentiue, the secretiue, the concoctiue, and the expulsiue faculty') which would hitherto have been regarded as falling within the scope of the sensitive soul (Digby 1644: 289, I. xxxiv. 3); and second by its restriction of 'soul' specifically to the human soul. Many of the doctrines that Digby ascribes to that soul, however, and particularly his conviction that the three principal operations of the mind reflect the structure of the syllogism (Digby 1644: 353 and II. i–iii), manifest a rather less dramatic break with teachings of the schools than Descartes himself succeeded in effecting.

Another philosopher who, in the wake of Descartes' ideas, turned his attention specifically to human nature and the human soul was the French natural philosopher Honoré Fabri, SJ (Honoratius Faber, 1607–88). Fabri published his *Two Treatises* in 1666; the first of these is on plants and the generation of animals, the second 'on man', and specifically on those functions possessed by humans in their capacity as a more-than-animal 'composite' of a feeling body and a rational soul (Fabri 1666: 198). In the context of his Jesuit predecessors, Fabri's work feels innovative in its preoccupation with 'man' in particular, and his concern to distinguish the ensouled human animal from other animals. In other respects, however, his account of the soul is a self-consciously reactionary one: in particular, the rational soul 'truly is the form of man; for what else would it be?' (Fabri 1666: 66 *bis*).

It seems possible that Fabri's work on human nature is one of the targets of the studies of the soul by the English physician Thomas Willis (1621–75), whose lectures at Oxford as Sedleian Professor of Natural Philosophy are likely to have been attended by the young John Locke. Having published a notable account of the anatomy of the brain, Willis turned to develop his preoccupation with the physiology of the soul in his *De anima brutorum* (1672; translated as *Two Discourses concerning the Soul of Brutes* in 1683). Willis's approach in the first of these treatises was physiological, arising from his dissection of silkworms, oysters, and sheep. Willis was well aware of Descartes' views, and shared with him the thought that the animating principle in animals was corporeal and fiery in nature. But Willis, for his own reasons, wished to preserve the continuity between animal and human nature that was provided by their shared possession of a vital and sensitive soul. For this reason, too, Willis was critical of the view (which he claims has 'prevailed in our Schools') that the rational soul performed not only the functions of understanding and reasoning, 'but also the other Offices of Sense and Life, yea...the whole Oeconomy of Nature' (Willis 1683: 40). Fabri, by contrast, and no doubt others with him, had argued that strictly speaking human sensitive powers possessed a rational quality, and that formally the rational soul was also sensitive and vegetative (Fabri 1666: 198, 67 *bis*).

Willis's opposite interest in the contiguity of human and animal nature is further strongly suggested by the second of his treatises on the 'soul of brutes', which turns from considerations of physiology to those of pathology. Although he is ostensibly still speaking of the animal soul it is clear that Willis's accounts of the diseases to which the soul is subject are much more human than animal in orientation. Among others, he is concerned with the all-too-human phenomena of headache, melancholy, and stupidity. Here, in a most un-Cartesian way, an existing philosophical tradition of the sensitive animal soul is being turned, pointedly, towards the pathologization of non-conformist religiosity (Martensen 2004).

Descartes therefore offered one important way in which accounts of the soul derived from the *De anima* were transmuted under the impact of the mechanical philosophy into more strictly physiological studies on the one hand, and towards more abstract questions of knowledge and of metaphysics on the other. The impact of this separation was felt strongly, not only by Cartesians of different stripes such as Antoine Arnauld and Nicolas Malebranche (Jolley 2000), but also by the former Cartesian Baruch Spinoza and—for all the local quarrels that he pursues with Cartesianism in the *Essay Concerning Humane Understanding* (1690)—by John Locke (1632–1704).

Locke's philosophy of the soul was sceptical and doubtful. An important aspect of the significance of his *Essay* is that it treats a subject—the understanding—that had hitherto principally been the province of logic and natural philosophy in a way that is neither natural philosophical (he disclaims to 'meddle with the Physical Consideration of the Mind') nor that of syllogistic logic (*Essay* I. i. 1). As such he extended into unrecognizability the Renaissance tradition of monographic treatments of the *intellectus*, from Girolamo Fracastoro to Jacopo Zabarella; superseded the efforts of his contemporaries, such as Jean-Baptiste du Hamel, to extend the implications of Baconian experimental philosophy into the study of the human mind (*De mente humana*, 1672); and laid the groundwork for a new philosophy of the mind in the eighteenth century (Serjeantson 2008).

Locke's foremost thought about the soul, which for him is now unequivocally only the human soul, is the anti-Cartesian one that emphasizes 'Our ignorance about it' (*Essay* II. xxvii. 27). Locke speaks of 'that ignorance we are in of the Nature of that thinking thing that is in us' (*Essay* II. xxvii. 27); and elsewhere he regards the soul as having been 'put out of the reach of our Knowledge' (*Essay* IV. iii. 6). When he wished to criticize 'Trifling Propositions' of excessively logical modes of philosophical argument, Locke picked up on the example of '*a Soul is a Soul*' as his example of the vacuity of identical propositions (*Essay* IV. viii. 3). And he went on in the same chapter to use philosophical discourse about the soul as an example of how one may use words—'*Substance, Man, Animal, Form, Soul, Vegetative, Sensitive, Rational*'—to 'make several undoubted Propositions', yet 'without knowing at all what the Soul really is' (*Essay* IV. viii. 9; Yolton 2004: 54).

Yet Locke's scepticism about our ability to have knowledge of the soul is not a scepticism about its existence, only about its nature. His thought that the soul has been 'put out of the reach of our Knowledge' clearly implies that this is a decision taken by a creator; it also perhaps suggests that this ignorance might not be permanent. Moreover, at a few points in the *Essay*, although never systematically, Locke canvasses a range of hypotheses about the soul's nature, raising possible counterarguments to the ordinary view that soul is an immaterial substance independent from matter. Is it 'tied to a certain System of fleeting Animal Spirits'? Can it 'perform its Operations of Thinking and Memory out of a Body organized as ours is'? And has it 'pleased God that no one such Spirit shall ever be united to any but one such Body, upon the right Constitution of whose Organs its Memory should depend'?

The first question arises out of the naturalistic tradition that was willing to conceive the operations of the soul in terms of animal spirits; the other two were relatively long-standing questions (usually answered in the affirmative) among early modern philosophers of the soul. But there is more than a tinge of parodic *reductio ad absurdum* in the suggestion that Locke goes on to make: 'taking, as we ordinarily now do (in the dark concerning these Matters), the Soul of a Man for an immaterial Substance, independent from Matter, and indifferent alike to it all' there was no reason not to suppose that 'a part of a Sheep's Body yesterday should be a part of a Man's Body to-morrow, and in that union make a vital part of *Meliboeus* himself, as well as it did of his Ram' (*Essay* II. xxvii. 27). Nevertheless, it was not this burlesque passage, but a later one in Book IV, Chapter iii, in which Locke suggested that God might if he chose 'superadd to Matter a Faculty of Thinking' that continued to provoke controversy well into the eighteenth century over whether matter in motion might think (*Essay* IV. iii. 6; Yolton 1984).

As we have seen, one of the principal motivations for maintaining the philosophical doctrine of the immateriality of the soul was that it was taken to support the ultimately theological doctrine of its immortality. Locke never denied this doctrine; the evidence of the *Letter Concerning Toleration* (1689), in particular, is that he regarded the doctrine of a future state as essential for social life as well as personal happiness. Yet this did not prevent him finding this long-standing association of immateriality and immortality unsatisfactory. In a private journal entry from 20 February 1682 he observed: 'The usuall physicall proofe (as I may soe call it) of the immortality of the soul is this, Matter cannot thinke ergo the soule is immateriall, noe thing can naturally destroy an immaterial thing ergo the soul is naturally immortall.' Yet this, Locke went on, proved 'noe other immortality of the soule then what belongs to one of Epicurus's atoms, viz. that it perpetually exists but has noe sense either of happynesse or misery' (Locke 1936: 121–2).

## IV: HUMAN NATURE WITHOUT A SOUL

Descartes' denial of a sensitive soul to animals, and his transformation of 'soul' into a 'mind' that was 'entirely independent' (CSM I 141) of extended matter with which it has 'nothing in common' (CSM II 124), can be seen as one kind of response to a physical universe that consisted of matter in motion, albeit perhaps a provisional response (Clarke 2003). The opposite response, which was also to cease speaking of the soul, but to insist that even the mind is material, was taken by Hobbes (1588–1679). Indeed, comparably to Gassendi, it was in his objections to Descartes' second Meditation that Hobbes argued that 'a thinking thing is something corporeal' (CSM II 122). However, whereas Descartes was concerned above all with the implications for metaphysics of his rejection of previous stories about the soul, Hobbes asked what these implications were for moral and political philosophy.

It would be misleading to speak in terms of Hobbes's theory of the soul, for it is clear that he no longer wishes us to have one. To an even greater extent than Descartes, and perhaps even from before he first encountered Cartesian ideas (Tuck 1988), Hobbes declines to speak of the 'soul', preferring instead the language of 'mind'. In Hobbes's *Elements of Law* (published in manuscript, 1640), the term 'soul' is almost always reserved for specifically theological uses (Hobbes 1994, I. xi. 5, I. xviii. 2, II. vi. 6; but see also II. ii. 4). Similarly in *Leviathan* (1651), Hobbes's first reference to the 'soule' is in the context of ignorant and fearful pagan beliefs (*Lev.* 53). Hobbes knew the alternative stories perfectly well: he alludes derisively to those 'Doctors that hold there be three Soules in a man'. He was also happy to use the conventional *de anima* theory for metaphorical purposes, describing the power of levying money as the 'Nutritive faculty' of civil government, and even speaking of the sovereign as the 'publique Soul, giving life and motion to the Common-wealth' (*Lev.* 171, 172, 174). But it is clear that he no longer seriously credited such theories.

The evidence for this is the alternative accounts of human sensation, imagination, and cognition that Hobbes provided in each version of his moral and political theory: the *Elements of Law* in 1640; *Leviathan* in 1651; and the third part of his *Elements of Philosophy*, the *De homine* of 1658. In each of these works Hobbes offers an account of the faculties of the human mind which both follows through into his moral and political theory, and which also presents a deeply polemical and damaging alternative to the doctrine taught by 'the Philosophy-schooles, through all the Universities of Christendome, grounded upon certain Texts of Aristotle' (*Lev.* 4).

If aspects of Hobbes's natural philosophy can be understood as 'the mechanisation of Aristotelianism' (Leijenhorst 2002), it seems clear that the impetus behind Hobbes's revisionary account of the human soul lies in rather more anti-Aristotelian traditions (Leijenhorst 1997). Whether or not Hobbes (Schuhmann 1995; Leijenhorst 1996) or his friend Robert Payne (Raylor 2001; Malcolm 2002b) was the author of the manuscript known as the 'Short Tract' (and the latter is more likely), that work is indicative of Hobbes's involvement in a philosophical culture that drew upon anti-Aristotelian Italian naturalism to develop a naturalistic account of the motion of 'animal spirits' to explain all the functions of the soul, from perception right through to 'the Act of understanding' (British Library, MS Add. 6797: fo. 308[r]). A more conventional stimulus behind Hobbes's ideas is the post-Melanchthonian Protestant endeavour to provide a complete account of 'human nature' in terms of the faculties of the body and of the soul. Hobbes clearly signalled that this was his purpose in the opening chapter of *The Elements of Law* when he spoke of 'Man's nature' as 'the sum of his natural faculties and powers, as the faculties of nutrition, motion, generation, sense, reason, &c.' These powers 'are contained in the definition of man, under these words, animal and rational'. Hobbes goes on to divide the human faculties 'according to the two principal parts of man', 'faculties of the body, and faculties of the mind' (Hobbes 1994: 21–2, I. i. 1–5).

If this general programme is so far familiar, then Hobbes's doctrines of the faculties of the mind are much less so. The most startling aspect of his theory of cognition, from the perspective of the tradition he is rejecting, is the scope he accords to the imagination. In *Leviathan* (he is less explicitly imperial in the *Elements of Law*) Hobbes makes this corporeal faculty responsible for everything from external sensation to 'that we generally call *Understanding*' (*Lev.* 8). Behind this lies Hobbes's conclusion that talk of '*Immateriall Substances*' (of which the soul was the chief exemplar) was '*Non-sense*' (*Lev.* 19), a conclusion for which Hobbes had prepared the ground by his nominalist insistence that there is 'nothing in the world Universall but Names' (*Lev.* 13). This dramatic curtailing of the traditional panoply of the faculties of the mind was nonetheless not unprecedented. In particular, Hobbes had been preceded in similar claims by his contemporary and friend, Pierre Gassendi. In his *Paradoxical Exercitations Against the Aristotelians* (1624), Gassendi had asserted that there is 'no distinction between the understanding and the imagination' (Gassendi 1972: 25). And even in his later *Syntagma philosophicum* (published posthumously in 1658), in which Gassendi drew back from his earlier assertions of the corporeality of the soul (Osler 1985), he still accorded the imagination a capacity even for syllogistic modes of reasoning (Gassendi 1658b: II, 413–14).

It was the stimulus (although not necessarily the direct influence) of Hobbes that placed the idea of 'human nature' so firmly as the foundation for both moral and political philosophy in the later seventeenth and earlier eighteenth centuries. The mediation of Samuel Pufendorf was central here, for he took up a distinctly Hobbesian story (Malcolm 2002a) about the significance of 'human nature' to the new theory of the state offered in his *On the Law of Nature and Nations* (1672). (It is even possible that the broad legacy I have argued for here of Hobbes's account in post-Melanchthonian Lutheran accounts of the *natura hominis* helped in turn to make it attractive to the Lutheran Pufendorf.)

Pufendorf's writings were central documents in the teaching of moral and political philosophy in the fifty years or so after they were published. They helped institutionalize a 'natural law' tradition of political philosophy that took Hugo Grotius' *On the Laws of War and Peace* (1625) as its founding document (Tuck 1987; Hochstrasser 2000). However, Pufendorf's writings also helped formalize the thought that moral philosophy should begin from an analysis, not of the nature of virtue or even of right, but of 'man'. And although commonly ascribed to Grotius (Smith 1995, 1997; Wood 2003: 808), it seems rather more out of this Pufendorfian programme that the 'science of the man' in the eighteenth-century took its origin (Hont 1987).

Pufendorf's impact was particularly prominent in early eighteenth-century Scotland. Francis Hutcheson (1694–1746), who praised Gershom Carmichael's 1718 edition of Pufendorf's *Duty of Man* (first published 1673), also produced his own *Philosophiae Moralis Institutio Compendaria* (1742; translated as *A Short Introduction to Moral Philosophy* in 1747) which founds the subject on human nature conceived as a composite of body and soul (2007: 24–5). Hutcheson has reverted, as Pufendorf did before him, to speaking of the 'soul', and many aspects of his account, particularly his primary division of its powers (*vires*; no longer the discredited 'faculties') into understanding and will are instantly recognizable as standing at the end of a long tradition of *de anima*-type analysis. Less stereotyped, but more interesting for what it suggests about the longevity of early modern Protestant traditions of the analysis of the soul, is that Hutcheson also draws a distinction between 'direct' (*directa*) and 'reflex' (*reflexa*) perceptions of the understanding (2007: 27, 32–43; 1. i. 8–14). We first encountered this distinction, and noted its influence, in Julius Caesar Scaliger's *Exotericae exercitationes* of 1557, where it served as a distinction between the simple apprehension of something and the understanding of it. In Hutcheson's hands, however, the 'reflex' acts of the soul have become the (innate) 'internal senses' of sympathy, conscience, honour, and shame, upon which Hutcheson's moral sense philosophy is founded. Thus, by the intermediation of the late Renaissance study of the 'nature of man', the soul has been transformed from an object of Aristotelian natural science to become the starting-point for the moral and historical 'science of human nature' of the Enlightenment.

## REFERENCES

[ANON.] (1655). *Anthropologie Abstracted: Or the idea of humane nature reflected in briefe philosophicall, and anatomicall collections.* London.

ARIEW, R. (1992). 'Descartes and scholasticism: the intellectual background to Descartes' thought', in J. Cottingham (ed.), *The Cambridge Companion to Descartes.* Cambridge: Cambridge University Press, 58–90.

BACON, F. (2000). *The Advancement of Learning*, ed. M. Kiernan. The Oxford Francis Bacon, vol. IV. Oxford: Clarendon Press.

BLAIR, A. (2006). 'Natural philosophy', in L. Daston and K. Park (eds), *The Cambridge History of Science*, vol. III: *Early Modern Science.* Cambridge: Cambridge University Press, 365–406.

BODIN, J. (1605). *Universae naturae theatrum.* Hanau.

BURGERSDIJK, F. (1631). *Idea philosophiae tum naturalis, tum moralis.* 3rd edn. Oxford.

[BURTON, R.] ('Democritus Junior') (1621). *The Anatomy of Melancholy.* Oxford.

BYERS, S. (2006). 'Life as "self-motion": Descartes and "the Aristotelians" on the soul as the life of the body', *The Review of Metaphysics*, 59: 723–55.

CASMANN, O. (1594). *Psychologia anthropologica; sive animae humanae doctrina.* Hanau.

CLARKE, D. M. (2003). *Descartes's Theory of Mind.* Oxford: Clarendon Press.

COLERUS, J. (1587). *De animarum immortalitate.* Wittenberg.

CRANE, R. S. (1962). 'The Houyhnhnms, the Yahoos, and the history of ideas', in J. A. Mazzeo (ed.), *Reason and the Imagination: Studies in the history of ideas 1600–1800*, New York: Columbia University Press, 231–53.

DALGARNO, G. (2001). 'The autobiographical treatise' [*c*.1684], in D. Cram and J. Maat (eds), *George Dalgarno on Universal Language: The Art of Signs (1661), The Deaf and Dumb Man's Tutor (1680), and the Unpublished Papers.* Oxford: Oxford University Press, 353–90.

DES CHENE, D. (2000). *Life's Form: Late Aristotelian conceptions of the soul.* Ithaca, NY: Cornell University Press.

DES CHENE, D. (2001). *Spirits and Clocks: Machine & Organism in Descartes.* Ithaca, NY: Cornell University Press.

DIGBY, SIR K. (1644). *Two Treatises. In the one of which, the nature of bodies; in the other, the nature of mans soule; is looked into: in way of discovery of the immortality of reasonable souls.* Paris.

DONI, A. (1581). *De natura hominis libri duo.* Basel.

ESCOBAR, J. M. (2008). 'Kepler's theory of the soul: a study on epistemology', *Studies in History and Philosophy of Science*, 39: 15–41.

EUSTACHIUS A SANCTO PAULO (1640) [first publ. 1609]. *Summa philosophiae quadripartita, de rebus dialecticis, ethicis, physicis, & metaphysicis.* Cambridge.

EUSTACHIUS A SANCTO PAULO (1998). 'A compendium of philosophy in four parts [*Summa philosophiae quadripartita*, 1609]', trans. John Cottingham, in R. Ariew, *et al.* (eds), *Descartes' Meditations: Background Source Materials.* Cambridge: Cambridge University Press, 68–96.

FABRI, H. (1666). *Tractatus duo: quorum prior est de plantis, et de generatione animalium; posterior de homine.* Paris.

FROIDMONT, L. (1649). *Philosophiae Christianae de anima, libri quatuor.* Louvain.

GARBER, D. (1992). 'Descartes' physics', in J. Cottingham (ed.), *The Cambridge Companion to Descartes.* Cambridge: Cambridge University Press, 286–334.

GARBER, D., HENRY, J., JOY, LYNN and GABBEY, A. (1998). 'New doctrines of body and its powers, place, and space', in D. Garber and M. Ayers (eds), *The Cambridge History of Seventeenth-Century Philosophy*, 2 vols. Cambridge: Cambridge University Press, I: 553–623.

GASSENDI, P. (1658*a*). 'Disquisitio metaphysica' [1644], in *Opera omnia*, 6 vols., vol. III. Lyons.

GASSENDI, P. (1658*b*). 'Syntagma philosophicum', in *Opera omnia*, 6 vols. Vols. I–II. Lyons.

GASSENDI, P. (1972). 'Exercises against the Aristotelians [1624]', *The Selected Works*, trans. C. B. Brush. New York: Johnson Reprint, 9–108.

GOCLENIUS, R. (1597). *Psychologia, hoc est de hominis perfectione, animo et in primis ortu hujus.* Marburg.

GOCLENIUS, R. (1613). *Lexicon philosophicum quo tanquam clave philosophiae fores aperiuntur.* Frankfurt am Main.

HILL, N. (1601). *Philosophia Epicurea, Democritiana, Theophrastica proposita simpliciter non edocta.* Paris.

HOBBES, T. (1994). *The Elements of Law Natural and Politic,* ed. J. C. A. Gaskin. Oxford: Oxford University Press.

HOCHSTRASSER, T. J. (2000). *Natural Law Theories in the Early Enlightenment.* Cambridge: Cambridge University Press.

[HOLLAND, G.] (1653). *The Grand Prerogative of Humane Nature.* London. (2nd revised edition of *The Prerogative of Man.* [Oxford], 1645.)

HONT, I. (1987). 'The language of sociability and commerce: Samuel Pufendorf and the theoretical foundations of the "four-stages theory"', in A. Pagden (ed.), *The Languages of Political Theory in Early-Modern Europe.* Cambridge: Cambridge University Press, 253–76.

H[ORST], G[REGOR] (1612). *De natura humana libri duo, quorum prior de corporis structura, posterior de anima tractat.* Frankfurt am Main.

HUTCHESON, F. (2007). *Philosophiae Moralis Institutio Compendaria with A Short Introduction to Moral Philosophy.* Ed. Luigi Turco, trans. Michael Silverthorne. Indianapolis: Liberty Fund.

INGEGNO, A. (1988). 'The new philosophy of nature', in C. B. Schmitt, *et al.* (eds), *The Cambridge History of Renaissance Philosophy.* Cambridge: Cambridge University Press, 236–63.

JOLLEY, N. (2000). 'Malebranche on the soul', in S. Nadler (ed.), *The Cambridge Companion to Malebranche.* Cambridge: Cambridge University Press, 31–58.

KEPLER, J. (1618). *Epitome astronomiae Copernicanae.* Lenz.

KUSUKAWA, S. (1995). *The Transformation of Natural Philosophy: The Case of Philip Melanchthon.* Cambridge: Cambridge University Press.

LA FORGE, L. DE (1997). *Treatise on the Human Mind (1666).* Ed. and trans. Desmond M. Clarke. Dordrecht: Kluwer.

LE GRAND, A. (1672). *Institutio philosophiæ, secundum principia Domini Renati Descartes.* London.

LEIJENHORST, C. (1996). 'Hobbes and Fracastoro', *Hobbes Studies,* 9: 98–128.

LEIJENHORST, C. (1997). 'Motion, monks and golden mountains: Campanella and Hobbes on perception and cognition', *Bruniana & Campanelliana,* 3: 93–121.

LEIJENHORST, C. (2002). *The Mechanization of Aristotelianism: The late Aristotelian setting of Thomas Hobbes' natural philosophy.* Leiden: Brill.

LOCKE, J. (1720). 'Elements of Natural Philosophy', in *A Collection of Several Pieces . . . never before printed.* London, 178–230.

LOCKE, J. (1936). *An Early Draft of Locke's Essay Together with Excerpts from his Journals.* Ed. by R. I. Aaron and J. Gibb. Oxford: Clarendon Press.

MACLEAN, I. (2001). *Logic, Signs and Nature in the Renaissance: The case of learned medicine.* Cambridge: Cambridge University Press.

MACLEAN, I. (2008). 'Cardano's eclectic psychology and its critique by Julius Caesar Scaliger', *Vivarium,* 46: 392–417.

McCRACKEN, C. J. (1998). 'Knowledge of the Soul', in D. Garber and M. Ayers (eds), *The Cambridge History of Seventeenth-Century Philosophy.* 2 vols. Cambridge: Cambridge University Press, I: 796–832.

MAGIRUS, J. (1603). *Anthropologia, hoc est: commentarius eruditissimus in aureum Philippi Melanchthonis libellum de anima.* Frankfurt am Main.

MAGIRUS, J. (1619). *Physiologiae peripateticae libri sex cum commentariis.* London.

MALCOLM, N. (2002a). 'Hobbes and the European republic of letters', *Aspects of Hobbes.* Oxford: Clarendon Press, 457–545.

MALCOLM, N. (2002b). 'Robert Payne, the Hobbes manuscripts, and the "Short Tract"', *Aspects of Hobbes.* Oxford: Clarendon Press, 80–145.

MARTENSEN, R. L. (2004). 'Willis, Thomas (1621–1675)', *Oxford Dictionary of National Biography,* Oxford University Press, Sept 2004; online edn, October 2007. http://www. oxforddnb.com/view/article/29587.

MICHAEL, F. S. and MICHAEL, E. (1988). 'Gassendi on sensation and reflection: a non-Cartesian dualism', *History of European Ideas,* 9: 583–95.

MORCILLO, S. F. (1560). *De naturæ philosophia, seu, De Platonis, & Aristotelis consensione libri V.* Paris.

OSLER, M. J. (1985). 'Baptizing Epicurean atomism: Pierre Gassendi on the immortality of the soul', in M. J. Osler and P. L. Farber (eds), *Religion, Science and Worldview.* Cambridge: Cambridge University Press, 163–84.

O[VERTON], R[ICHARD] (1643). *Mans Mortallitie.* 'Amsterdam' [i.e. London].

PARK, K. (1988). 'The organic soul', in C. B. Schmitt, *et al.* (eds), *The Cambridge History of Renaissance Philosophy.* Cambridge: Cambridge University Press, 464–84.

POMPONAZZI, P. (1948). *On the Immortality of the Soul* [1516], in E. Cassirer, *et al.* (eds), *The Renaissance Philosophy of Man.* Chicago: University of Chicago Press, 255–381.

RAYLOR, T. (2001). 'Hobbes, Payne, and *A Short Tract on First Principles*', *Historical Journal,* 44: 29–58.

RUBIO, A., SJ (1621). *Commentarii in libros Aristotelis de anima, una cum dubiis et quaestionibus hac tempestate in scholis agitari solitis.* Cologne [1st edn. 1611].

SAKAMOTO, K. (2009). 'The German Hercules's heir: Pierre Gassendi's reception of Keplerian ideas', *Journal of the History of Ideas,* 70: 69–92.

SANCHES, F. (1988). *That Nothing is Known (Qvod nihil scitvr)* [1581], ed. Elaine Limbrick, trans. Douglas F. S. Thomson. Cambridge: Cambridge University Press.

SANDERSON, R. (1671). *Physicae scientiae compendium.* Oxford.

SCALIGER, J. C. (1557). *Exotericarum exercitationum liber quintus decimus, de subtilitate, ad Hieronymum Cardanum.* Paris.

SCHMITT, C. B. (1988). 'The rise of the philosophical textbook', in C. B. Schmitt, *et al.* (eds), *The Cambridge History of Renaissance Philosophy.* Cambridge: Cambridge University Press, 792–804.

SCHUHMANN, K. (1995), 'Le Short Tract, première oeuvre philosophique de Hobbes', *Hobbes Studies,* 8, 3–36.

SENNERT, D. (1618). *Epitome naturalis scientiae.* Wittenberg.

SERJEANTSON, R. W. (2001). 'The passions and animal language, 1540–1700', *Journal of the History of Ideas,* 62: 425–44.

SERJEANTSON, R. W. (2008). '"Human understanding" and the genre of Locke's *Essay*', *Intellectual History Review,* 18: 157–71.

SIMMONS, A. (1999). 'Jesuit Aristotelian education: the *De anima* Commentaries', in J. W. O'Malley, SJ, *et al.* (eds), *The Jesuits: Cultures, Sciences and the Arts 1540–1773.* Toronto: University of Toronto Press, 522–37.

SMITH, R. (1995). 'The language of human nature', in C. Fox, *et al.* (eds), *Inventing Human Science: Eighteenth-century Domains*. Berkeley: University of California Press, 88–111.

SMITH, R. (1997). *The Fontana History of the Human Sciences*. London: Fontana.

SPRUIT, L. (1997). 'Telesio's Reform of the Philosophy of Mind', *Bruniana & Campanelliana*, 3, 123–43.

STILLINGFLEET, E. (1702). *Origines Sacrae: or A rational account of the grounds of natural and revealed religion. The seventh edition. To which is now added part of another book upon the same subject written A.D. MDCXCVII*. Cambridge.

STRIGEL, V. (1590). *In Philippi Melanchthonis libellum de anima notae breves et eruditae*. Leipzig.

THOMSON, A. (2008). *Bodies of Thought: Science, religion, and the soul in the early Enlightenment*. Oxford: Oxford University Press.

TUCK, R. (1987). 'The "modern" theory of natural law', in A. Pagden (ed.), *The Languages of Political Theory in Early-Modern Europe*. Cambridge: Cambridge University Press, 99–119.

TUCK, R. (1988). 'Hobbes and Descartes', in G. A. J. Rogers and A. Ryan (eds), *Perspectives on Thomas Hobbes*. Oxford: Clarendon Press, 11–41.

VIVES, J. L. (1538). *De anima et vita*. Basel.

WALKER, D. P. (1984). 'Medical spirits and God and the soul', in M. Fattori and M. Bianchi (eds), *Spiritus, atti del IV Colloquio Internazionale del Lessico Intelletuale Europeo*. Rome: Edizione dell'Ateneo, 222–44.

[WARD, SETH] (1652). *A Philosophicall Essay towards an Eviction of the Being and Attributes of God, the Immortality of the Souls of Men, the Truth and Authority of Scripture*. Oxford.

WILLIS, T. (1672). *De anima brutorum. Quæ hominis vitalis ac sensitiva est, exercitationes duae*. Oxford.

WILLIS, T. (1683). *Two Discourses concerning the Soul of Brutes, which is that of the Vital and Sensitive of Man*. London.

WILSON, C. (2008). *Epicureanism at the Origins of Modernity*. Oxford: Oxford University Press.

WOOD, P. B. (2003). 'Science, philosophy and the mind', in R. Porter (ed.), *The Cambridge History of Science*, vol. IV: *Eighteenth Century Science*. Cambridge: Cambridge University Press, 800–24.

YOLTON, J. W. (1984). *Thinking Matter: Materialism in eighteenth-century Britain*. Oxford: Blackwell.

YOLTON, J. W. (2004). *The Two Intellectual Worlds of John Locke: Man, person, and spirits in the Essay*. Ithaca, NY: Cornell University Press.

ZABARELLA, J. (1617). *De rebus naturalibus libri XXX*. Frankfurt [1st edn 1590].

CHAPTER 7

......................................................................

# IDEAS

......................................................................

## PAULINE PHEMISTER

[T]out ce bruit qu'on fait aujourd'hui des idées vient des meditations d'un
homme ingenieux et pensif (Des Cartes).

(Leibniz: compte rendu de la Vindication de Stillingfleet
et de la lettre de Locke: A VI vi. 20)

Thomas Reid, in his notes on the history of the term 'idea', claimed that the
Scholastics employed the term solely in theological contexts. 'Previous to the age
of Descartes', he thought, 'as a philosophical term, ["idea"] was employed exclusively by the Platonists—at least exclusively in a Platonic meaning' (1863: II, 925),
that is to say, as referring to 'archetypes in the divine intellect' (Kenny 1968: 97).
Reid's conjecture was not entirely accurate. Francisco Suárez, citing Seneca, employed the term 'idea' to mean the exemplar that would guide either God or a
human artisan in the making of an object.[1] Nevertheless, Descartes, as Robert
McRae remarks, 'intentionally took an old philosophical term, idea, and put it to a
new use' (1965: 175), and the great 'noise' about ideas in the early modern period
was prompted by this change. Reid identified his countryman, David Buchanan, as
the first both to use the term 'idea' to refer to objects in the human, as opposed to
the divine, intellect and to extend the term to include the objects of memory,
imagination, and sensation (1863: II, 926).[2] But Descartes also extended the term

---

[1] I am grateful to Stephen Menn for pointing this out.
[2] Reid cites Buchanan's Historia Animae Humanae (Paris, 1636), the year before the appearance of
Descartes' Discourse on Method. Non-philosophical references to ideas as located in human rather than
divine minds occur even earlier: for example, Brinsley (1968: 84) and Bullokar (1967, entry on 'idea').

'idea' in the manner of Buchanan to sensation, imagination, and memory, and while he admitted to Hobbes that he had 'used the word "idea" because it was the standard philosophical term used to refer to the forms of perception belonging to the divine mind' (AT VII 181; CSM II 127), he, like Buchanan, also located ideas in the human intellect. It was, moreover, through Descartes' transfer of the concept rather than Buchanan's, that the notion of ideas as resident in the human mind gained common currency.

The implications of this shift were wide-ranging. Philosophical enquiry could now take as its starting point the exploration of the contents of the human mind. Armed with a clear and distinct idea of his mind as a thinking thing, obtained by reflecting on his mind's acts of thinking, Descartes proceeded to certain knowledge of external reality from an examination of other ideas in his mind. He began with his innate idea of God and ended with knowledge of the existence of bodies, of other minds, and of the substantial union of the mind and the body. While Descartes held ideas to be the immediate objects of human perception, he also regarded them as acts of perceiving or thinking. In the former sense, ideas have objective reality insofar as they have intentional or representational content; in the latter sense, they have formal reality insofar as they are modes (or states) of minds (AT VII 40; CSM II 28).

Locke too regarded ideas both as perceptions or acts of perceiving, and as the immediate objects considered by minds in these perceptual states (e.g. *Essay* I. i. 8; II. i. 9). In this way, he wholeheartedly embraced Descartes' placement of ideas in human minds. However, such had been the impact of Descartes' thought on the philosophical landscape that, by the 1690s, Locke, when charged with novelty by Edward Stillingfleet, refused to accept that his use of the term 'idea' was *new*. To Stillingfleet's description of his 'way of ideas' as 'new', Locke retorted that he was doing no more than putting an old philosophical term to a new use; he added that 'if it be *new*, it is but a new History of an old Thing' (*Essay* I. i. 8 note). However, what Locke described as his use of an old philosophical term was the still relatively new Cartesian usage. The newness of Locke's 'way of ideas' resides, by his own reckoning, in his account of how the mind makes use of these immediate objects in the performance of its characteristic activities, as for instance, its acts of thinking, reasoning, believing, and knowing (*Essay* I. i. 8 note). In this, Locke may be read as having extended Descartes' philosophy by conducting a thorough analysis of the 'mechanics' of the mind's construction of complex ideas through the comparison and combination of simple ideas, and its construction of general ideas by a process of abstraction in which '*Ideas* taken from particular Beings, become general Representatives of all of the same kind' (*Essay* II. xi. 9).

By no means all the philosophers of the period accepted these Cartesian innovations. Among the resistors, Spinoza and Malebranche were the most prominent. Far from locating ideas in substantial human minds, Spinoza viewed ideas as modes of God insofar as God possesses the attribute of thought. He considered the human mind as no more than a collection of those particular mode-ideas which are the ideas of its human body. Malebranche too insisted on retaining the pre-Cartesian opinion that ideas exist in God and not in human minds. Although Malebranche presented his theory as a 'new philosophy of ideas' in a letter to Arnauld (OCM VI: 80), it can be seen as new only when contrasted with Descartes' characterization of ideas as modes of human minds. Malebranche's theory harkened back to the older, pre-Cartesian tradition in which ideas were regarded as existing in a divine realm independently of human minds. Malebranche drew heavily on the Augustinian doctrine (Schmaltz 2000: 60–8) that 'we live and move and have our being in God', and developed an original theory of the vision in God, in which we perceive external objects through the conjunction of (i) our perception of ideas of intelligible extension, which exist as objects in God's mind and are made visible to us by divine illumination; and (ii) sensations of colour and other sensory qualities, which God produces as modes of our minds when the appropriate occasions arise.

Pierre Bayle's detailed and closely argued critique of Spinoza highlighted problems in locating all ideas in God, not the least being that such a god would inevitably contain ideas that contradict each other (1991: 308–10). Antoine Arnauld was Malebranche's most vigorous opponent. The publication of Arnauld's *On True and False Ideas* (1683) began a public and acrimonious debate between them that continued even beyond Arnauld's death in 1694, and came finally to an end with a response from Malebranche in 1699 (Nadler 1989: 79). Leibniz declared his position *vis-à-vis* the debate in the *Acta Eruditorum* in 1684, in which he published his *Meditations on Knowledge, Truth, and Ideas* (GP IV 422–6), although he had not yet fully studied the controversy at this point in time (LL 291). Leibniz negotiated a middle path between the two disputants, while Locke took a critical stance against Malebranchean ideas in *Of P. Malebranche's Opinion Of Seeing All Things in God*, which was published posthumously in 1706 (LW VIII 211–54).

Arnauld's objections seem to have been motivated primarily by theological concerns. Although Malebranche had published his theory of ideas in his *Search After Truth* in 1674/75, Arnauld did not react to it until after the publication in 1680 of Malebranche's *Treatise on Nature and Grace*. In this work, the Oratorian proposed that God acts only by His general volition and not by particular volitions on specific occasions. On this view, the salvation of individual souls depends on whether it follows naturally from the operation of the divinely decreed and inviolable general laws and not, as Arnauld preferred, on God's dispensing grace on a case by case basis (Malebranche 1992: 15–51). Since Malebranche claimed that his *Treatise of Nature and Grace* is understood properly only in the light of 'his doctrine *on the nature of ideas*' (AOP 28: ATF 2), Arnauld objected directly to the latter as an indirect critique of Malebranche's views on nature and grace.

# I: IDEAS: OBJECTS OR PERCEPTIONS

Malebranche offered a number of arguments to support the claim that ideas exist as objects in God's mind. Although he also wrote, especially in the early chapters of the *Search*, of sensations as sensible ideas, our discussion here is confined to the intelligible ideas had by God. In Book 3, part 2, chapter 1 of the *Search After Truth*, Malebranche describes an idea as the 'immediate object, or the object closest to the mind, when it perceives something' (OCM I 414; MLO 217). Confusingly, he also claimed that an idea 'affects and modifies the mind'. This contradicts claims made elsewhere in the *Search*. For instance, in Book I, chapter 1 (OCM I 42; MLO 2), he described two types of perceptions of ideas: pure perceptions, which do not sensibly modify the soul, and sensations, which do modify the soul. Even if pure perceptions modify the soul in some non-sensible manner, it is the perceptions or perceptual states, not the ideas themselves, which are the modifications of the soul. The claim (III. 2. i) that ideas are efficacious in bringing about modifications of the soul—that they bring about pure perceptions—appeared only in the 1712 edition of the *Search* (Schmaltz 2000).

Malebranche's fundamental insight, that ideas are the immediate objects of perception, led him to argue that this role could not be played by external, physical objects, which are, in a sense, too far away. The soul cannot, as it were, get outside itself, to enter the material world. Yet, there must be some object before the mind when it perceives. Ideas fulfil that role. This is clearly so when we think of things that do not exist. In imagination, dreams, and hallucinations, the material things of which we think do not exist. When we think of a golden mountain, for example, the object of our thought is the *idea* of a golden mountain, and not any actual golden mountain (OCM I 414; MLO 217). The objects of perception in such cases are not physical things, but only ideas. Even in those cases where the physical things do exist, there is a misalignment between the way that we perceive them and the way they really are. Although we often judge that objects exist just as we see them, in fact, this never happens (ibid.). Once again, the immediate object 'closest' to the mind is an idea, not the actual external material thing. One might note in passing that the mind presumably also reaches beyond itself when it perceives ideas in God, and there is therefore a question as to why Malebranche did not consider God's ideas, like physical bodies, as too far away for humans to perceive directly.

Descartes, Arnauld, and Locke agreed that ideas are the immediate objects of the mind when it perceives, but insisted, contra Malebranche, that these objects are found in human minds. Descartes, for instance, reasoned from the content of his own mind to the intelligible idea of the essence of body as *res extensa*. Malebranche, however, considered it impossible that a finite mind should contain such an idea. Only God can encompass the infinity contained in the idea of intelligible extension, which includes ideas of the infinitely many modifications (innumerable shapes and sizes) that matter may assume. Human minds can perceive the infinite, but cannot hold the infinite idea in their own minds. As he explains in the *Search*,

being neither actually infinite nor capable of infinite modifications simultaneously, it is absolutely impossible for the mind to see in itself what is not there. It does not see the essence of things, therefore, by considering its own perfections or by modifying itself in different ways.   (OCM I 435; MLO 229)

Instead, we see the essence of things through seeing the perfections that are in God.[3] The 'perfect simplicity' of the infinite, indivisible God 'includes all beings' (OCM I 439; MLO 231). In the tenth Elucidation, he explained further that God 'contains within Himself in an intelligible fashion the perfection of all the beings He has created or can create' (OCM III 136; MLO 617). God's ideas are ideas of intelligible perfections, among which there are infinitely many degrees of perfection, insofar as these ideas represent possible or created beings (OCM III 137; MLO 618) and a 'necessary and immutable order' of these degrees (ibid.). According to Malebranche's doctrine of the vision in God, finite minds see God's infinite ideas in the universal or Sovereign Reason that is 'coeternal and consubstantial' with God (OCM III 131; MLO 614).

Although we may agree with Malebranche's claim in the *Dialogues on Metaphysics and Religion* that 'nothing finite can contain an infinite reality' (OCM XII 51; MS 21), it is not clear that the inability of the mind to contain infinity need prevent it from having in itself ideas that represent the infinite. Could not the soul contain an idea that represents the infinite without itself being infinite? Arnauld maintained as much to Malebranche, by appealing to a suggestion he attributed to Pierre-Sylvain Régis that ideas can be 'finite *in essendo*' while at the same time 'infinite *in repræsentando*' (AO XL 88–9; cf. Schmaltz 2000: 73; Nadler 1992: 40–4).

This was by no means the only objection Arnauld raised against Malebranche's doctrine of the vision in God. He ridiculed the theory at length in *On True and False Ideas*, and reserved especial scorn for Malebranche's image of the soul that is not free to leave its body in order to stroll through the heavens to see the sun directly. He accused Malebranche of misunderstanding the 'closeness' of ideas to the mind in terms of a physical proximity (as local presence) that is misplaced in the context of the relation of ideas to the mind (AOP 73–4; ATF 37). Compounding the error, he had turned ideas into mind-independent objects that serve as substitutes for the physical objects that the mind cannot reach. Parodying Malebranche, Arnauld wrote:

---

[3] In Book 3, Part 2, chapters 2–5 of the *Search*, Malebranche rejected various alternative accounts of human perception of ideas. Following this process of elimination, he then advanced the theory of the vision in God in chapter 6. He offered no argument that all possible alternatives had been considered (Schmaltz 2000: 69–71; Pyle 2003: 50–7).

Our soul can see only the objects that are present to it; that is indubitable. But the sun is distant from our soul by more than thirty million leagues, according to Casini. Therefore, before the soul can see the sun, either it must be approached by the sun, or the sun by it. But you do not believe that your soul has left your body to go looking for the sun or that the sun has left the sky to be united intimately with your soul. Therefore you are dreaming when you say that you see the sun. But do not be upset. We are going to save you from that difficulty and give you a way to see the sun. In place of the sun, which would not seem to leave its place so often (that would be too great a difficulty) we have very cleverly discovered a certain *representative* being to take its place and to make up for its absence by being intimately united to our souls. We have given the name of *idea* or *species* to that *being which is representative* of the sun (whatever the nature and origin of that entity may be, for we have not yet agreed among ourselves about that).    (AOP 71–2; ATF 36)

Arnauld considered it totally unnecessary to postulate representative ideas as entities that exist in God, external to the soul, in order to explain our perception of material bodies. Such ideas do not constitute the simplest way for God to make bodies visible to us. Worse, according to Arnauld, Malebranche's theory entails that we do not perceive bodies at all. All that we really perceive are God's ideas. We see only the intelligible ideas of bodies, not the bodies themselves. Malebranche had created a disjunct between the idea of a body and the body itself. Arnauld himself thought that representative ideas do exist in finite souls and are the means by which we perceive material things. Moreover, since Malebranche and Arnauld agreed that God always acts by the simplest means, the latter was able to argue that God should give us our own ideas of bodies as a far simpler way of ensuring that we perceive external bodies than, as on Malebranche's view, giving us our own sensations and then, in addition, making His intellectual ideas visible to us.

For Arnauld, then, ideas exist in human minds. Indirect realist interpretations understand these as 'objects' in the mind, distinct, though not separable from, the acts of perceiving (Nadler 1989: 104–7, 111–12). However, some commentators have recently offered direct realist interpretations whereby Arnauld is understood to have advanced an 'act theory of ideas' (Yolton 1984: 62–5; Nadler 1989: 107–26). According to this reading, Arnauld's ideas are acts of thought whose representative content is neither separable nor distinct from the act of thought or perception itself. By means of such perception-ideas, we perceive external things directly, for our perceptions of bodies *are* ideas of them. The idea-perception act is a modification that has two relations—one to the mind, the other to the body. Whether we call this act a perception or an idea depends upon which relation we emphasize: 'perception' when the relation is to the soul, and 'idea' when the relation is to the external object (Nadler 1989: 109).

This internal distinction is reminiscent of Descartes' distinction between the formal and objective reality of ideas. For this reason Descartes too is sometimes taken to be an act-theorist about ideas (cf. Nadler 1989: 126–30). Locke too can be read in this way. He didn't mark a distinction between ideas as actual perceptions

(*Essay* I. iv. 21; II. i. 9; II. x. 2; II. xxiii. 1; II. xxxii. 3), and ideas as objects (*Essay* I. i. 8; II. viii. 8), and even, on occasion, described ideas in both ways in the same section of the *Essay*, as for instance at II. viii. 8: 'Whatsoever the Mind perceives in it self, or is the immediate object of Perception, Thought, or Understanding, that I call *Idea*...as they are Sensations, or Perceptions, in our Understandings, I call them *Ideas*.' There is no contradiction involved in ideas being both immediate objects of perception and themselves perceptions, so long as the perceiving-idea act of mind is a perception that is conscious of itself as its immediate object. This is Locke's position. He believed that we are always conscious of what passes in our minds, although this consciousness may be so weak (or 'scarce') that it does not amount to awareness or attention (Kulstad 1984: 154–5). Similarly, no contradiction arises so long as the idea as object is understood on Cartesian lines as the idea's representational content.

Nonetheless, act theories of ideas are not unproblematic. Leibniz objected to Locke's treatment of object-ideas as perceptions on the ground that ideas as objects of thought must subsist in some way even when they are not being consciously thought. This cannot be so if ideas are actual perceptions: 'If the idea were the *form* of the thought, it would come into and go out of existence with the actual thoughts which correspond to it, but since it is the *object* of thought it can exist before and after the thoughts' (LRB 109). If, as Locke and Arnauld contended, ideas exist only in the mind as perceptions or modifications, then, as Leibniz indicates here in the *New Essays*, they are fleeting and temporary and last only as long as does the perception. Such ideas lack the permanence required for thought. It becomes impossible to have the same idea at different times or to be confident that we are thinking about the same thing today as yesterday, or even from one moment to the next.

Locke maintained that the ideas the mind acquires from either sensory or reflective experience are retained in some sense by the mind even when it no longer actively perceives them. Once experience has imprinted ideas on the mind, it retains them in its memory, which serves as a 'store-house' of ideas (*Essay* II. x. 2). If these ideas are later revived, or refreshed, they are imprinted more strongly; if not, they tend to lapse and eventually we forget them altogether. Might this model address Leibniz's worry about the act theory of ideas? Might ideas be retained in the memory as objects with some degree of permanence or persistence? Locke denied that this is so. The 'laying up' of ideas in the memory consists in nothing more than the acquisition of the ability to have the ideas (as a perception) again, though on future occasions the idea occurs together with a perception that the idea had already been had before.

But our *Ideas* being nothing, but actual Perceptions in the Mind, which cease to be any thing, when there is no perception of them, this *laying up* of our *Ideas* in the Repository of the Memory, signifies no more but this, that the Mind has a Power in many cases, to revive

Perceptions, which it has once had, with this additional Perception annexed to them, that it has had them before. And in this Sense it is, that our *Ideas* are said to be in our Memories, when indeed, they are actually no where, but only there is an ability in the Mind, when it will, to revive them again.    (*Essay* II. x. 2)

Desmond Clarke (2003: 93–9) finds a similar account of the memory of sensory ideas in Descartes.

According to the Cartesian hypothesis, what is stored in the brain is merely a disposition to give rise to other ideas that are similar to, and occur subsequent to, the perceptual impression that initially affected the brain. In this sense, what is stored is not so much an idea but a capacity or disposition to come to have similar ideas at a subsequent time.    (Clarke 2003: 96)

Locke agreed that external objects create impressions on our bodily senses (e.g. *Essay* II. i. 21; II. i. 23; II. xix. 1; II. xxi. 1), but he did not call these bodily states 'ideas'. He reserved that term for the perceptions in the mind caused by these impressions (*Essay* II. viii. 8, but cf. *Essay* II. viii. 7). Nonetheless, Locke did agree with Descartes insofar as he believed (i) that impressions are sometimes retained in the brain in such a way that the mind can appeal to them as it recalls past idea-perceptions, and (ii) that such restored memories bring with them an awareness of their having been in the mind previously (AT V 220; *Essay* I. iv. 20; Clarke 2003: 103–5). Most importantly in the present context, on both Descartes' and Locke's accounts, ideas are stored in the memory dispositionally. They are not objects and when they are revived, as actual perceptions, they are not exactly the same as their originals. Given this, Leibniz's objections to the act theory of ideas still stand. Ideas understood as perceptions 'come into and go out of existence' as actual thoughts do, never to recur. At best, revived ideas resemble the original perceptions. Certain knowledge of the resemblance remains beyond our grasp, since *ex hypothesi* we can never hold both the original and the remembered idea together in the mind to compare them.

Locke negotiated the chasm that separates Malebranche and Arnauld on the nature of ideas by siding with Arnauld; he viewed ideas as perceptions and rejected the notion that ideas exist as objects separate from the perceptual act. Leibniz, however, steered a course that attempted to mediate the dispute between the two priests, arguing with Malebranche for ideas that are separate from human perception and exist as objects in God and, with Arnauld, that ideas are perceptions (affections or modifications) in human minds. This middle way is clearly expressed in *Meditations on Knowledge, Truth, and Ideas*:

As to the controversy over whether we see everything in God (which is certainly an old opinion and should not be rejected completely, if it is understood properly) or whether we have our own ideas, one must understand that, even if we were to see everything in God, it would nevertheless be necessary that we also have our own ideas, that is, not little copies of God's, as it were, but affections or modifications of our mind corresponding to that very thing we perceived in God. For certainly there must be some change in our mind when we have some thoughts and then others, and, in fact, the ideas of things that we are not actually thinking about are in our mind as the shape of Hercules is in rough marble.    (GP IV 426; LAG 27; see also *Discourse on Metaphysics*, GP IV 454; LAG 60)

Leibniz considered his *Meditations on Knowledge, Truth, and Ideas* as an authoritative statement of his position and he held the example of the statue of Hercules in particularly high regard. In the *New Essays*, he often referred Locke back to the *Meditations* (e.g. LRB 219, 254, 266, 296, 407, 437) and, in the preface, he invoked the Hercules statue to illustrate the way in which all ideas in humans are innate. They are so as 'dispositions, tendencies, or natural potentialities' (LRB 51) which are ready to be brought into consciousness as our essences unfold in time, just as the shape of Hercules in the marble is revealed by the sculptor. But if all ideas are innate in us, they cannot all be held consciously in the mind. The vast majority are in the mind only as dispositions, tendencies, or natural potentialities. Ideas are in us as 'natural potentialities, and not as actions; although these potentialities are always accompanied by certain actions, often insensible ones, which correspond to them' (LRB 51). Potential or dispositional ideas are perceived so insensibly that we are not consciously aware of them, although some of them may surface into consciousness in due course.

That even dispositional ideas are perceived, albeit insensibly, is an essential part of Leibniz's metaphysical doctrine, according to which every substance mirrors or expresses the whole universe, as well as all possibilities and all essences at every moment. In 1686, with a discrete reference to Malebranche, he commented in the *Discourse on Metaphysics*:

I am not of the opinion of certain able philosophers who seem to maintain that our very ideas are in God and not at all in us. In my opinion, this arises from the fact that they have not yet considered sufficiently either what we have just explained about substances or the full extent and independence of our soul, which makes it contain everything that happens to it, and makes it express God and, with him, all possible and actual beings, just as an effect expresses its cause.    (GP IV 453–4; LAG 60)[4]

Two years earlier, in the *Meditations on Knowledge, Truth, and Ideas*, he had insisted that our ideas are not copies of God's ideas (GP IV 426; LAG 27). Whereas divine ideas are essences or concepts of things, our ideas are either modifications of the soul or mere dispositions. Earlier still, in 1678, in a paper entitled *What is an Idea?*, he had regarded an idea only as 'something which is in our mind' that '*consists, not in some act, but in the faculty of thinking, and we are said to have an idea of a thing even if we do not think of it, if only, on a given occasion, we can think of it*' (GP VII

---

[4] As we shall see, not all of our ideas express reality with the highest degree of accuracy. Leibniz had offered an early definition of 'expression' in *What is an Idea?* (GP VII 263–4; LL 207–8). Leibnizian expression is not restricted to the expression of essences by ideas (McRae 1976: 20–4; Kulstad 1977). In language, ideas are expressed by words, as Descartes explained in the Second Set of Replies (AT VII 160; CSM II 113). Leibniz (LRB 142) and Locke (*Essay* II. i. 2; III. ii. 2) were of the same opinion.

263; LL 207). 'That the ideas of things are in us means therefore nothing but that God, the creator alike of the things and of the mind, has impressed a power of thinking upon the mind so that it can by its own operations derive what corresponds perfectly to the nature of things' (GP VII 264; LL 208). Leibniz had not yet arrived at the *New Essays'* position that all our ideas are innate as dispositions, though the step to the later view is short. In the early piece, he attributed to minds a 'remote' faculty for thinking about all things, but believed that it is only when we have a 'near' faculty that we actually have the ideas—that is, the ability to think about some one thing (GP VII 263; LL 207).

# II: Representation

In the second of his *Meditations on First Philosophy*, Descartes took the view that, when we consider our ideas as modifications of our minds, 'solely in themselves' and without reference to anything beyond themselves, they 'cannot strictly speaking be false; for whether it is a goat or a chimera that I am imagining, it is just as true that I imagine the former as the latter' (AT VII 37; CSM II 26). All are equally states of mind, or acts of perceiving minds (AT VII 40; CSM II 27). However, Descartes also thought that ideas could be discriminated and arranged in a hierarchical order according to their objective reality or representational content. They may be ideas of other modifications (such as an idea of an idea), or they may be ideas of contingently existing things (for instance, an idea of a man), or they may be ideas of necessarily existing things (as is the idea of God). When arranged in hierarchical order, ideas of modifications have less objective reality than ideas of contingent things, and these in turn have less objective reality than the ideas of the necessary, infinite, divine substance (AT VII 40; CSM II 28). In addition, the representational contents of ideas represent their objects with differing degrees of success, which suggests a further ordering of ideas according to their respective degrees of clarity and distinctness.

In large part, Descartes' immediate successors followed his analysis of the relationship between the representational content of our ideas (or in the case of Malebranche, the degrees with which we perceive God's ideas) and their truth. Typically, early modern philosophers took the clarity and distinctness of ideas as a divinely guaranteed indication of their truth. In doing so, they followed Descartes' position as expounded in his *Fifth Meditation* (AT VII 70; CSM II 48) and the *Principles of Philosophy* (AT VIIIA 16; CSM I 203). There was also broad agreement, following Descartes, about the meanings of the terms 'clear' and 'distinct' and the associated terms, 'obscure', 'confused', 'adequate', and 'inadequate', although, as would be expected, there were also nuanced differences. Descartes wrote in the *Principles of Philosophy* that a perception is clear when 'it is present and accessible to the attentive mind' (AT VIIIA 22; CSM I 207). Perceptions of pain, for instance, are often clear and demand the soul's attention. But they are not always also distinct perceptions since the nature of the pain itself might not be clearly perceived. The sensation is clear, but may be accompanied by an 'obscure' judgement that locates the pain in the body when in fact it resides in the mind (AT VIIIA 22; CSM I 208). Arnauld and Nicole offered essentially the same account, using the same example as illustration (1996: 48–9).

A perception (or idea) is distinct when 'as well as being clear, it is so sharply separated from all other perceptions that it contains within itself only what is clear' (AT VIIIA 22; CSM I 207–8). Descartes' definition appears to conflate clear and distinct ideas with Leibniz's definition of an 'adequate idea'.[5] For Leibniz, an idea (or notion) is clear when the object cognized can be re-cognized on a later occasion. When reasons can be given to justify this recognition, that is, when marks (*nota*) that differentiate the object from others are identified, the idea is distinct; however, only when *all* the differentiating marks are listed is the idea not only clear and distinct, but also adequate (GP IV 422; LAG 23–4).[6] Some of the ideas Descartes identified as clear and distinct conform to Leibniz's definition of adequate ideas because they are ideas that involve a small and finite number of primitive ideas that do not admit of further analysis. The classic case is Descartes' clear and distinct idea of his mind as a thinking thing. This comprises only the primitive ideas of existence and thought. Unlike Leibniz, Descartes also considered the idea of body as *res extensa* as a primitive idea; extension, in Descartes' opinion, was nothing more than extendedness in length, breadth, and depth. The truth of such ideas is indubitable and known by intuition, defined as 'the conception of a clear and attentive mind, which is so easy and distinct that there can be no room for doubt about what we are understanding' (AT X 368; CSM I 14).

Spinoza distinguished adequate ideas and true ideas. In the *Ethics*, he defined an adequate idea as having 'all the properties, or intrinsic denominations of a true idea', but as differing from a true idea because an adequate idea is one that is only 'considered in itself, without relation to an [external] object' (SO II 85; SC 447). True ideas, in contrast, are related to, and indeed in agreement with, their objects (SO II 47; SC 410). In Spinoza's system, all ideas are God's ideas; all are modes of

---

[5] Descartes occasionally employed the Leibnizian meaning of 'adequacy' of ideas, as, for instance, when replying to Arnauld's Objections (AT VII 220; CSM II 155). Arnauld also understood adequate knowledge as inclusive of all the features of the object known, equating this with 'complete' knowledge, as he did in the Fourth Set of Objections to Descartes' *Meditations* (AT VII 200–1; CSM II 141). In reply to Arnauld, Descartes distinguished adequacy and completeness, redefining the latter as knowledge of an object as a 'complete thing' (AT VII 221; CSM II 156).

[6] Leibniz uses the term 'notion' rather than 'idea' here, but in the *New Essays* (LRB 255–6), he offered the same account while substituting 'idea' for 'notion'.

God's essence insofar as this is expressed under God's attribute of thought. Of these, those that are ideas of our human bodies constitute our human minds (SO II 96; SC 457). Our true ideas are those within the composite set of ideas that make up our individual minds that correspond exactly to ideas that are adequate in God, that is with no consideration of an external object. Thus, our true ideas are those that are 'adequate in God insofar as he is explained through the nature of the human Mind' (SO II 123; SC 479), and the human mind is 'part of the infinite intellect of God' (SO II 94; SC 456).

Locke too stressed the relation of adequate ideas to truth and explicated adequacy in terms of correspondence to the object to which the idea refers. Ideas are adequate when they 'perfectly represent those Archetypes, which the mind supposes them taken from; which it intends them to stand for, and to which it refers them' (*Essay* II. xxxi. 1). But Locke was wary of references to true ideas. Properly speaking, truth relates to propositions, not to single ideas (*Essay* II. xxxii. 1). When the archetype to which an idea in our minds refers is an external thing—for instance, a physical object, a quality of a physical object, or an immaterial being, such as God—the idea is a *real* idea. On Locke's view, all simple ideas are 'real ideas', by which he meant that they 'all agree to the reality of things' even though they may not exactly represent or resemble that reality. For others of our ideas, as, for instance, the idea of a triangle or the idea of murder,[7] the idea itself is the archetype (*Essay* III. vi. 44). With no external archetype, these ideas are not 'real', but they are always adequate because they represent their objects perfectly. Such ideas are their own patterns and cannot fail to represent themselves. My idea of murder cannot fail to correspond perfectly to the archetypal idea of murder that my mind has constructed (*Essay* II. xxxi. 3), though of course my idea of murder may fail to represent adequately the idea of murder in another's mind (*Essay* III. ix. 7).

Although Locke held that adequate ideas are those that 'perfectly represent' their archetypes (*Essay* II. xxxi. 1), he interpreted perfect representation very loosely in the case of our simple ideas. For Locke, all our simple ideas of sensation, such as the ideas of the whiteness and sweetness of sugar, are adequate ideas because they are the effects of powers in the objects to cause these ideas in us. Although we do not know exactly how these powers operate so as to produce the ideas, and in spite of the fact that our ideas of secondary qualities do *not* resemble the qualities as they exist in the object (namely, as powers residing in the primary qualities of the component particles), our sensation-ideas, as effects of these causes, must 'be correspondent, and adequate to those Powers' (*Essay* II. xxxi. 1).

In not insisting on perfect resemblance to the external archetype for the adequacy of ideas, Locke diverged sharply from Descartes and Leibniz. His view that simple

---

[7] Locke called these 'mixed modes' because they combine ideas of different kinds; 'simple modes' combine ideas of the same type (*Essay* II. xii. 5).

ideas of sensation are adequate even though they may not actually resemble their physical, external causes legitimated sensory experience as a source of knowledge of the external world. For the most part, Locke allowed that sense experience provides us with ideas that are clear, distinct, *and* adequate. Nonetheless, even he admitted that some sensory ideas are obscure and confused. As with his exposition of clear ideas, he invoked the analogy with vision: 'we shall best understand what is meant by *Clear*, and *Obscure* in our *Ideas*, by reflecting on what we call *Clear* and *Obscure* in the Objects of Sight' (*Essay* II. xxix. 2). We can see the figures and colours of objects clearly in broad daylight, but are often unable to perceive them clearly in the dark. The reasons for the obscurity of our ideas, however, lie not in the deficiency of light, but in deficiencies in our sense organs or in defective memory (*Essay* II. xxix. 3). Thus Locke agreed with Descartes that confused ideas may be clear but do not contain sufficient distinguishing marks to enable us to differentiate such ideas from others (*Essay* II. xxix. 4). But he noted that since every idea is identical with itself and easily identifiable as such, the definition seems to allow very few, if any, confused ideas (*Essay* II. xxix. 5). Instead, he proposed that confusion arises with the assigning of names to ideas (*Essay* II. xxix. 6–12).

Among Locke's rationalist predecessors and contemporaries, however, there was unanimity that our sense experiences provide us, at best, with confused ideas. Sensory ideas cannot be adequate since they are not clear and distinct. They do not provide us with the distinguishing marks of objects. Hence, sensory experience is not a source of adequate ideas. Confused sensations, while implicated in knowledge, do not constitute it. Sense experience gives us no clear and distinct ideas of external reality and cannot be a reliable source of knowledge of the nature of the external world. For Malebranche, sensations take us into the realm of material things and divorce us from the intelligible ideas and truths that reside only in God. In the *Dialogues on Metaphysics and on Religion*, he sided with Descartes in claiming that sensations, while useful for the preservation of life, are not conduits of truth (OCM XII 280–1; MS 219).[8] Sensations correspond only arbitrarily to the physical reality of extended moving bodies. In contrast, Leibniz insisted upon a non-arbitrary correspondence. There is an intelligible relation between the composition of our sensations and the composition of bodies, as befits its creation by a supremely rational God. Still, our perceptions of the infinitely small parts of material things are insensible and the composite perception of them confused. Hence, in direct opposition to Locke, Leibniz considered the sensation of green as a confused idea in which the blue and yellow components are not distinguished (*Meditations on Knowledge, Truth, and Ideas*: GP IV 426; LAG 27; *New Essays*, LRB 403). Against Locke, he argued that our ideas of sensation are far from simple and adequate, for our sensations do not give us distinct and adequate knowledge of

---

[8] Malebranche sometimes admitted that sensation plays a role, in the intellectual vision in God, in the perception or knowledge of intelligible extension (OCM XII 46; MS 17).

their causes, of the organized structure of microscopic particles that comprise perceived objects.

While Locke agreed that our sensations do not give us knowledge of the microscopic composition of bodies (we do not know bodies' real essences), he saw in this no reason to deny their adequacy as representatives of external reality. He admitted that our lack of knowledge of bodies' microscopic structures limits our knowledge of the external world, but he did not take this as a reason to reject ideas of sensation and reflection as the basis of all human knowledge. Sensation and reflection are necessary for us to have ideas, and the perception of the various agreements and disagreements (of identity; relation; co-existence or necessary connexion; and real existence) among our ideas constitutes knowledge, by Locke's definition (*Essay* IV. i. 2–3). When we intuitively or demonstratively perceive these relations, we can be said to have knowledge. In all cases where the archetype is a human-constructed idea, certain knowledge is possible. For instance, when the mind combines the ideas of 'straight lines', 'three', and 'enclosed figure' and thereby constructs the idea of a triangle, demonstrative reasoning can establish necessary connections between this idea and others, such as the idea of the sum of the angles of this figure. In mathematical (and, for Locke, moral) knowledge, there is no external reality to which our ideas must conform. However, where the archetype is an external reality, for instance, a material or an immaterial substance, human knowledge is restricted.

# III: Empiricism and rationalism

The demarcation between rationalists, such as Descartes, Spinoza, Arnauld, Malebranche, and Leibniz, and empiricists like Hobbes, Locke, and Berkeley, is sometimes said to lie in the appeal to innate ideas by the former and their rejection by the latter. The criterion is not entirely reliable because some rationalists, notably Malebranche and Spinoza, did not espouse a doctrine of innate ideas. However, innatism aside, when we investigate particular ideas and the form that they take in the philosophies of the early modern period, the familiar empiricist–rationalist distinction begins to emerge more clearly.

Even though Leibniz held that, strictly speaking, all our ideas are innate, he accepted that some ideas do seem to enter the mind via our sense organs, which in this respect serve as intermediaries through which we have access to the external world. So, in the *New Essays*, he consented to speak as if sensible ideas come via the sense organs so that he could more easily engage with Locke's philosophy (LRB 74). However, other ideas—intellectual ideas—cannot be conceived as grounded in sense experience. A list provided in the preface to the *New Essays* includes, among others, intellectual ideas of 'Being, Unity, Substance, Duration, Change, Action, Perception, Pleasure', which all derive from reflection, understood as 'attention to what is within us' (LRB 52). As a passage from *On What is Independent of Sense and of Matter* makes clear, he believed that sense experience grants, at best, inductive knowledge and is incapable of leading to knowledge of eternal or necessary truths:

It is true that the mathematical sciences would not be demonstrative and would consist only in simple induction or observation (which would never assure us of the perfect generality of the truths found there) if something higher, something that intelligence alone can provide, did not come to the aid of *imagination* and *senses*.   (GP VI 501; LAG 188)

The intellect's knowledge of necessary truths is dependent on knowledge of the self. The passage just quoted continues:

Therefore, there are objects of still another nature which are not in any way included in what we notice among the objects of either the particular senses or common sense, and which, consequently, are not objects of the imagination either. Thus, besides the *sensible* and the *imaginable*, there is that which is only *intelligible*, the *object of the understanding alone*; and such is the object of my thought when I think of myself.   (GP VI 502; LAG 188)

Knowledge of the 'I' brings with it knowledge of metaphysical notions of substance in general, as well as 'of cause, effect, action, similarity, etc.' (ibid.). The issue was taken up again in the *Monadology*, where Leibniz explained that self-knowledge also gives us access to logical and ethical notions. Self-reflective acts,

enable us to think of that which is called 'I' and enable us to consider that this or that is in us. And thus, in thinking of ourselves, we think of being, of substance, of the simple and of the composite, of the immaterial and of God himself, by conceiving that that which is limited in us is limitless in him. And these reflective acts furnish the principal objects of our reasonings.   (GP VI 612; LAG 217)

We might add that, since knowledge of absolutely necessary truths depends upon an understanding of the principle of contradiction, and because this requires knowledge of sameness or identity and difference, which is acquired in gaining knowledge of the 'I', self-knowledge is essential to knowledge of any eternal, absolutely necessary truth whatsoever. Sometimes, however, Leibniz argued in favour of purely intellectual ideas by using a version of Descartes' dream argument. Hence, in *On What is Independent of Sense and of Matter*, he proposed that intellectual truths, such as those of mathematics and geometry, transcend what is known by means of the senses and experience, and claimed that we know them to be independent of sense experience because they remain true even if we are dreaming or hallucinating (GP VI 503: LAG 189). Nevertheless, sensation and imagination do play a role in knowledge acquisition. We apply our understandings to the data acquired first from sensation and imagination. 'Thus', Leibniz concluded, 'it can be said that there is nothing in the understanding that did not come from the senses, except the understanding itself, or that which understands' (GP VI 502; LAG 188; cf. *New Essays*, LRB 111).

Descartes, of course, had founded all knowledge in the innate knowledge of the self as a thinking thing; his one indubitable Archimedean point, from which he proceeded to re-build the edifice of knowledge after sceptical doubt had been taken to the furthest horizon. It may even be said that Descartes, as later would Leibniz (*Monadology*: GP VI 612; LAG 217), derived knowledge of God from the knowledge of the self, for Descartes' starting point in his first cosmological proof is the innate idea of God that he finds when he examines the contents of his mind.

Although other rationalists granted purely intelligible ideas, they did not always ground them in the idea of the self. Malebranche, for instance, explicitly denied that we have any idea of the self. Spinoza granted an idea of the self, but did not establish it as foundational for the attainment of the intellectual idea of God towards which we strive. Spinoza grounded his philosophical system in the idea of substance and through this in the knowledge, and intellectual love, of the existence and nature of the one Substance, God or Nature.

The key intellectual ideas identified by Leibniz, writing in response to Locke's *Essay*, were those of being, unity, substance, duration, change, action, perception, and pleasure (LRB 52; cf. LRB 111). These ideas are all premised on the idea of the self, which is gained by reflection. Locke offered an alternative account of the acquisition of all but one of these ideas. He agreed that they could be obtained from reflection, though some could also be acquired from sensation. Thus, the idea of perception is an idea of reflection (*Essay* II. ix). The ideas of pleasure, existence (i.e. being), unity, and power or action (*Essay* II. xxii. 10–12) may come from either reflection or from sensation (*Essay* II. vii. 1). The same holds for the idea of succession, although it most commonly comes from reflection (*Essay* II. vii. 9; cf. II. xiv. 6). The idea of duration is an idea of reflection since we acquire the idea of duration from observing the succession of ideas in our minds (*Essay* II. xiv. 3–4). Locke did not discuss the idea of change, but it is surely implicated in the idea of 'cause', which is a kind of power (*Essay* II. xxii. 11) or in the idea of succession.

However, for Locke, in contrast to Leibniz, the reflective experience from which these ideas are acquired is not necessarily an experience of the self. We do not need to have an idea of the self, and specifically the idea of the self as a substance, in order to have ideas of pleasure, existence, and so on. Even the idea of unity can be acquired by reflection on the unity of our ideas rather than on the unity of our selves as substances. In fact, Locke denied we have any clear idea of substance as a substratum: 'The *Idea* then we have, to which we give the general name Substance, being nothing, but the supposed, but unknown support of those Qualities, we find existing which we imagine cannot subsist, *sine re substante*, without something to support them, we call that Support *Substantia*' (*Essay* II. xxiii. 2). We have only an 'obscure and relative Idea of Substance in general' (*Essay* II. xxiii. 3) and hence only an obscure and relative idea of our selves as the substrata of our experiences. Locke discussed the idea of the self late in the *Essay* (and not at all in the first edition), and then only in the form of the idea of personhood. The idea of a person is premised, not on the idea of substance, but rather on the idea of identity, and specifically on the idea of the identity of consciousness (*Essay* II. xxvii. 19).

George Berkeley went even further than Locke in denying ideas of substance. In the *Three Dialogues between Hylas and Philonous*, he suggested that the idea of a material substratum that supports the qualities of bodies is not just obscure and relative, but not a positive idea at all (BW II 197–9). In the *Treatise concerning the Principles of Human Knowledge*, he denied any idea of the self, as a soul or a spirit, but for a different reason: 'A spirit is one simple, undivided, active being', an 'active incorporeal substance' (BW II 52). Since ideas are passive and inert perceived things rather than active perceivers, they are incapable of representing 'by way of image or likeness' any active being or substance (BW II 52, 103–5). Hobbes, in the Third Set of Objections to Descartes' *Meditations*, had taken the same stance and denied that we have any idea of substance, or any idea of God or of the soul (AT VII 185; CSM II 130).

Descartes, Spinoza, Arnauld, Malebranche, and Leibniz, on the rationalist side, all admitted the idea of substance, whether they found it innately through examination of their own minds, as did Descartes, Arnauld, and Leibniz, or through their intellectual knowledge of, or access to the ideas of, God, as did Spinoza and Malebranche. The acceptance or denial of the idea of substance thus appears as one, although not necessarily the only, distinctive mark of the separation between the rationalist and empiricist traditions and one that is entirely understandable given the empiricists' appeal to fleeting and temporary experiences as their philosophical starting point, as well as their rejection of intellectual ideas, either innately in finite minds or visible in God. Only with Kant would the rationalist insistence on the validity of *a priori* and experience-transcending ideas and the empiricist insistence on the 'bounds of sense' find their way into a single philosophy.

## References

Arnauld, A. and Nicole, P. (1996). *Logic or the Art of Thinking*. Trans. J. V. Buroker. Cambridge: Cambridge University Press [1st edn, 1662].

Bayle, P. (1991). *Historical and Critical Dictionary: Selections*. Ed. and trans. R. Popkin. Indianapolis: Hackett Publishing Company.

Brinsley, J. (1968). *Ludus Literarius*. London: Man; Facsimile edn Menston, England: Scolar Press [1st edn 1612].

Bullokar, J. (1967). *An English Expositor*. Cambridge: Cambridge University Press. Facsimile edn Menston, England: Scolar Press [1st edn. 1616].

Clarke, D. (2003). *Descartes's Theory of Mind*. Oxford: Clarendon Press.

JOLLEY, N. (1990). *The Light of the Soul: Theories of Ideas in Leibniz, Malebranche, and Descartes.* Oxford: Clarendon Press.

KENNY, A. (1968). *Descartes: A Study of his Philosophy.* New York: Random House.

KULSTAD, M. (1977). 'Leibniz's conception of expression'. *Studia Leibnitiana,* 9: 55–76.

KULSTAD, M. (1984). 'Locke on consciousness and reflection'. *Studia Leibnitiana,* 16: 143–67.

McRAE, R. (1965). '"Idea" as a philosophical term in the seventeenth century'. *Journal of the History of Ideas,* 26(2): 175–90.

McRAE, R. (1976). *Leibniz: Perception, Apperception and Thought.* Toronto: University of Toronto Press.

MALEBRANCHE, N. (1992). *Treatise on Nature and Grace.* Ed. and trans. P. Riley. Oxford: Clarendon Press.

NACHTOMY, O. (2007). *Possibility, Agency, and Individuality in Leibniz's Metaphysics.* Dordrecht: Springer.

NADLER, S. (1989). *Arnauld and the Cartesian Philosophy of Ideas.* Princeton, NJ: Princeton University Press.

NADLER S. (1992). *Malebranche and Ideas.* Oxford: Oxford University Press.

NADLER, S. (ed.) (2000). *The Cambridge Companion to Malebranche.* Cambridge: Cambridge University Press.

PYLE, A. (2003). *Malebranche.* Abingdon, Oxford: Routledge.

REID, T. (1863). *The Works of Thomas Reid.* Ed. W. Hamilton. 2 vols. 6th edn, Edinburgh: Maclachan and Stewart; London: Longman, Green.

SCHMALTZ, T. (2000). 'Malebranche on Ideas and the Vision in God', in S. Nadler (ed.), *The Cambridge Companion to Malebranche.* Cambridge: Cambridge University Press, 59–86.

YOLTON, J. W. (1984). *Perceptual Acquaintance from Descartes to Reid.* Oxford: Basil Blackwell.

CHAPTER 8

······················································

# QUALITIES AND SENSORY PERCEPTION

······················································

## PHILIPPE HAMOU

IN his *Treatise of Human Nature*, Hume contrasted the ancient metaphysics of substantial forms and occult qualities with the metaphysics of the Moderns, which he characterized as follows: 'The fundamental principle of that philosophy is the opinion concerning colours, sounds, tastes, smells, heat and cold; which it asserts to be nothing but impressions in the mind, deriv'd from the operation of external objects, and without any resemblance to the qualities of the objects' (Hume 1985: 275). Hume evidently had in mind the definition of secondary qualities that is given in Locke's *Essay*. Locke had distinguished two kinds of qualities that may be considered in bodies: (i) '*original* or *primary Qualities*', that is, qualities 'utterly inseparable from the Body', such as 'Solidity, Extension, Figure, Motion or Rest'; (ii) '*secondary Qualities*', such as colours, sounds, or tastes, 'which in truth are nothing in the Objects themselves, but Powers to produce various Sensations in us by their *primary Qualities, i.e.* by the Bulk, Figure, Texture, and Motion of their insensible parts' (*Essay* II. viii. 9–10). Locke had also explained that, in contrast with ideas of primary qualities, the '*Ideas, produced* in us by these *Secondary Qualities, have no resemblance* of them (the qualities of bodies) at all' (*Essay* II. viii. 15). Although Hume's own appreciation of the doctrine is rather critical, it is striking that he describes it as the 'fundamental principle' of 'the modern philosophy'. I shall argue in what follows that Hume was fundamentally correct, and that the doctrine of secondary qualities is indeed a distinctively modern doctrine that captures something of the very essence of the new philosophical age.

Hume was not the only author of the eighteenth century who believed that 'modern philosophy' was deeply committed to the theory of secondary qualities. The opinion was implicit in many writings of the time, and especially in popular accounts of science and philosophy intended for ladies or for philosophically uneducated people. There is a telling example in a famous article by Joseph Addison, in the *Spectator*. There Addison invokes 'that great modern discovery . . . namely, that light and colours, as apprehended by the imagination, are only ideas in the mind, and not qualities that have any existence in matter.' Following this discovery, Addison invites his reader to meditate on the 'secret spell' that governs our lives:

In short, our souls are at present delightfully lost and bewildered in a pleasing delusion and we walk about like the enchanted hero of a romance who sees beautiful castles, woods, and meadows, and at the same time hears the warbling of birds and the purling of streams; but upon the finishing of some secret spell the fantastic scene breaks up, and the disconsolate knight finds himself on a barren heath or in a solitary desert.   (Addison 1712)

This image captures a distinctive feature of the modern mind. The modern philosopher, having recognized the spell of the senses, has to face the barren nature of the physical world. There is no longer room for the qualities that make human existence pleasing or beautiful. One may accept this with equanimity, as Addison seems to have done, and accept the fact that all the beauty of the world is a mere creation of the imagination. Alternatively, one may lament this new state of affairs and see in the doctrine of qualities the seeds of modern despair and scepticism. This was Berkeley's motive for rejecting modern philosophy in general and Locke's doctrine of secondary qualities in particular, and this line of thought is still well represented in our time.

# I: MODERN QUALITIES: THE PHILOSOPHICAL CORE

What then is the doctrine of qualities to which Hume and his contemporaries refer (for complaint or for praise) as the great principle of 'modern philosophy'? Part of the answer is found in Locke's *Essay*, where the doctrine is stated in its full force and with the greatest detail. However, as we shall see, Locke's theory is in many respects more specific than the general doctrine it exemplifies and promotes. The core of the doctrine had been expressed in various philosophical contexts during the seventeenth century, long before Locke stamped the now received terminology of 'primary and secondary qualities'.[1]

Many authors who defend one form or another of the doctrine rely on a strange piece of hypothesizing. Suppose that human beings and all other sensible beings were entirely annihilated. The question is then asked: what could still be said of the remaining material world, the bodies and corpuscles it comprises? Or what is it like for something (say a body, a material substance) to exist unperceived, without the mind? Does it make sense to say that it is solid and extended, red or green, warm or cold, where there are no eyes to see, no flesh to feel? The 'modern' answer is twofold: were all animals annihilated, insensitive corporeal things would continue to exist unperceived with *some sort* of qualities, such as extension, motion, or contexture of parts (the exact list is open to discussion), but there is also a set of 'sensory' qualities usually attributed to them, such as colours or tastes (this list is also open to discussion), that would simply vanish. As Locke says in the *Essay* (II. xxxi. 2): 'there would yet be no more Light, or Heat in the World, than there would be Pain if there were no sensible Creature to feel it, though the Sun should continue just as it is now, and Mount *Aetna* flame higher than ever it did.' A similar argument is found in Galileo: 'if the living creature were removed, all these qualities would be removed and annihilated' (E.N. VI, 347; Shea 1977: 100), and in Boyle: 'if there were no Sensitive Beings those Bodies that are now the Objects of our Senses would be but dispositively, if I may so speak, endow'd with Colours, Tasts, and the like; and actually, but onely with those more Catholick Affections of Bodies, Figure, Motion, Texture, etc.' (B: V, 319).

Whatever the subtle distinctions one may find between these quotations, Galileo, Boyle, and Locke share an assumption that the question they ask is both meaningful and answerable. Not only does it make sense to ask questions about 'things unperceived' (a point that Berkeley will deny[2]), but it is also possible to give a probable account of the intrinsic *qualities* of such things, as they are *in themselves* (a point that Kant will deny (Allais 2008)). We may call this the *accessibility thesis*, although it might be said that it is no more or no less than crude 'pre-critical' metaphysical realism (cf. Meillassoux 2006: 13–38).

A second common assumption, of equal importance, is what may be called the *discrepancy thesis*. It says that things external to the mind do not resemble the way

---

[1] The expression 'secondary quality' is very rare in Boyle (Anstey 2000: 39), and is not used in Locke's meaning. The same holds for Malebranche. Both authors still use the phrase 'secondary qualities' in a rather traditional manner to signify compound qualities that are constructed out of 'elementary' ones. According to Rodis-Lewis (Malebranche 1979: 1487) the usual categorization of qualities, into primary ('elementary'), secondary, occult, and specific virtues originates in Galen, and receives its canonical form in Jean Fernel's *Universa medicina* (1567).

[2] Berkeley contends that the very conception of something unperceived entails a contradiction: 'when we do our utmost to conceive the existence of external bodies, we are all the while only contemplating our own ideas' (BW II, 50).

they are in the mind, when we perceive them or imagine them. When we perceive them, we tend to attribute to them qualities that exist only because the things are related to us or perceived by us, but these are not their intrinsic or real qualities. Such additional qualities are usually called 'secondary qualities' in Locke's idiom, but they may as well be called (as they are once in Locke's *Essay* II. viii. 22) 'imputed qualities'. Things just *look like* such. As a consequence, there is a deep epistemological divide between two images of the world: one presents the world *as it looks*—the commonsensical world of ordinary experience, coloured, tasteful, and humanized; the other presents it *as it is*, that is, *sub specie aeternitatis*, in its pristine and inexorable existence. This latter is what we may call, borrowing Wilfrid Sellars' famous phrase, the early modern 'scientific image' (Sellars 1963: 19–20).

## II: Cosmological context

Before considering more closely these assumptions, and in order better to understand their true import and modernity, we shall focus a little more on the thought experiment from which they stem, namely: what would it be like for something material to exist in a world that is entirely devoid of living sensible habitants? Although it may seem a strange question to ask, the fascination it exerted on the Moderns is undeniable and understandable. The question captures in a somewhat radical fashion the metaphysical uneasiness that accompanied recent discoveries and speculations of natural philosophy. Microscopes and telescopes, those epoch-making instruments, had shown that there are many things in the world that had existed unperceived since the beginnings of humanity, and they also suggested that there were probably many more situated in the recesses of the universe, well beyond the capacity of our best instruments. These newly discovered (or speculated) 'invisible worlds' had a significant influence on the modern attitude toward nature (Wilson 1995; Hamou 1999–2001). They suggested that the whole Creation is not proportionate to, nor intended for, human existence, human perception, or human thought.

A similar insight arose from new cosmological speculations which considered infinite spaces (real or imaginary) situated beyond the scope of our senses, or infinite times (real or imaginary) displayed before or after the existence of mankind. Although a majority of philosophers in the seventeenth century still accepted as literally true the biblical chronology, which assigned a beginning and end not only to human existence but also to the material world created for men's use, there was a growing tendency to think that Creation would be better understood if we could extend its genetic development in a longer imaginary ancestral time. *La fable du monde*, the *cosmogenesis* described in Descartes' *Traité de la lumière*, is probably the best example of the way modern philosophers, who pretended to believe in the literal meaning of the seven days of Creation, indulged in such fictional narratives (AT XI 31–2; CSM I 90). This potential extension of space and time well beyond human or sensitive existence was an important sequel to the Copernican revolution. Although some Copernicans of the first generation, such as Kepler (KGW IV 309; Kepler 1965: 46), still held that the new position and movement of the Earth among its sister planets is best suited to realize man's destination as Contemplator of nature, this anthropocentric confidence faltered when it became apparent, by the mid-seventeenth century, that the system of the Sun had no cosmic privilege at all but was a very small, local, and peripheral part of the universe (Van Helden 1985).

These ideas also gained strength from their association with some features of the newly rediscovered Epicurean cosmology, which had a deep hold on the imagination of the Moderns, even on those who most vehemently objected to it (Wilson 2008). Among those Epicurean theses was the idea that the world, as we know it here and now, is the temporary result of a long process of atomic collisions and concatenations, which has already produced and destroyed many worlds before the first living being was even produced. Because of such considerations, it was easy to transmute the annihilation thought-experiment into other questions more clearly attuned to the scientific preoccupations of the time. How, for example, shall we describe the reality of a bare planet, revolving in a deserted part of the universe, much too far away for the best instrument to capture its image, or much too *ancestral* for any living creature to contemplate it? Or what sort of reality shall we attribute to the minutest parts of matter, which even the best microscope cannot access?

Of course the 'new theory of qualities' is not directly deducible from this cosmological context. The modern sensitivity to worlds beyond our perception only makes room for a doctrine that conjugates, in a rather intricate manner, a new ontology and epistemology. The modern doctrine of qualities is an ontological doctrine, which deals with the very being or essence of material substances. It is also an epistemological doctrine about the way we get *access* to that intrinsic nature, and the reasons why we *usually mistake* that nature and impute to it qualities that do not exist.

# III: Ontology

The term 'quality' still retains, for an early modern ear, some of its Aristotelian overtones. For Aristotle, quality is one of the ten categories, a mode of being. Aristotle defines it in general as that in virtue of which things, substances, people, are said to be such and such. Thus, the qualities are those inherent and more or less lasting features, habits, or dispositions of substances that specify them, and allow for such or such denomination and predication. More specifically, the qualities that Aristotle called 'affective (or sensory) qualities' are those features of a substance that allow such and such denomination, because of the way the senses are affected when the substance is presented to them. For example 'Socrates is white' means that there is in Socrates an intrinsic feature called 'whiteness' that makes us see Socrates as a white man. In short, a quality-name is, in the ancient doctrine, a term whose meaning captures something of the true, intrinsic nature of the thing, so that the particular that is qualified (e.g. Socrates' whiteness) can be considered as a true instantiation of the qualifying genus (the 'form': white), and may be legitimately called by its name, through what Aristotle called 'paronymy' (AR I, 3).

Part of this ontological description still makes sense for modern philosophers, for whom a quality is, generally speaking, the *cause* why something is qualified in such and such a manner. So it is legitimate to say that a substance, like porphyry, is red *because* it has certain intrinsic features that cause us to perceive it as red. Some Moderns would say that porphyry has 'a rubrific property' (Newton 1721: 108), or a 'power' to produce a perception of red (Locke *Essay* II. viii), or again a 'disposition' to appear red (Boyle B, V 319). An Aristotelian would have no qualms with these denominations: redness, in peripatetic philosophy, is certainly a *potentia*, a *rubrific* property: it makes people see red. However, for Aristotle, redness is more than that. It is a real quality that shares not only its name but also its essence with the form perceived; 'red' is an integral part of the real essence of a substance that is perceived as red. This real feature is embodied in porphyry and exists whether the porphyry is actually perceived or not. This is the point at which the ancients and moderns diverge.

In the modern theory of qualities, an affective or secondary quality receives its name *only* because of the causal relation between the sensible and the sentient. This process is 'metonymic'; as Leibniz says, we name the cause after the effect (A VI/VI: 135), and there is room for equivocation here. In principle, cause and effect are distinct. There is no reason to assume, simply because of the causal relation, that there exists a likeness between a given quality and its perceptual effect or that the one should be a particular instance of the other. For example, although it is proper to say that porphyry is red, this does not necessarily mean that something, among the intrinsic features of porphyry, is an instance of 'redness' or a likeness of that sensation that I receive in my mind when I perceive red things. Most of the moderns think that there is something else (not 'redness', but some sort of texture or disposition of parts) in porphyry that causes us to perceive it as red and to name it accordingly. If so, redness is not a real quality, in the strictest Aristotelian sense of the term; it is, as Locke says, *only* a power to produce a perception of red or, as Galileo puts it, *only a name* for something in porphyry that is not red but which makes porphyry look red.

The moderns' critique of the peripatetic doctrine of 'real qualities' is well expressed by Malebranche when he says that the ancients failed to acknowledge that 'their physics was nothing but a kind of logic'.

It is clear to anyone who has read a little that practically all books of science . . . are full of argument based on elementary qualities and on secondary qualities such as attractive, retentive, concoctives, expulsives, and other such items, on other qualities they call occult, on specific virtues, and on several other entities men compose from the general idea of being and the idea of the cause of the effect they observe. . . . If these ordinary philosophers contented themselves with offering their physics simply as a logic that might furnish appropriate terms for discussing the things of nature . . . we would find no complaint in what they do. But they pretend to explain nature through their general and abstract terms, as if nature were abstract.   (OCM III 458–9: MLO 242)

This was the same sort of error as occurred with the so-called 'occult qualities'. Opium makes one sleep and, as a consequence, it may be said to have a 'dormitive power'. The fire heats things, and so there must be something in fire (call it 'heat') that causes this effect. In general, from any sentence expressing a causal action, one may abstract a substantive predicate (a quality) that can be attributed to the subject.

But this is grammar (or logic), not physics. The peripatetic quality, as Malebranche says, 'did not arouse other ideas in our minds than the ideas of being and cause in general' (OCM III 458; MLO 242). In naming the quality we just describe the fact that there is something in the object that causes some effect (AT VIII-1 34; CSM I 218), but we do not thereby explain anything. 'Heat', 'gravity', 'dormitive power', or even 'redness' do not explain the actions of heating, weighing, inducing sleep, or making one see red; they merely name them. The mistake occurs when one substantiates the referents of these terms by considering them as real or formal entities.

Of course the critic of the ancient doctrine of qualities does not rely entirely on this alleged confusion between grammar and physics. After all, it *might* be the case that things such as 'real qualities' exist in matter, even though the mere fact that we have sensory impressions is not a good argument for that. So the disagreement between the Ancients and the Moderns is deeper. What is at stake is the general picture of the physical world that each accepts: what kind of physical entities should we reckon as making up the furniture of the world? What are those that really explain the behaviour of matter and, in particular, the fact that matter makes itself perceptible? For various reasons the Moderns do not think that the Aristotelian 'real qualities' are good candidates.

First, there are too many of them. One important argument invokes some version of Ockham's razor: one must not multiply entities without necessity. The ancients believe that there are as many real qualities, either manifest or occult, as we have names for the various effects of matter. But one should expect from a good explanatory principle that it allow for some degree of reduction, that it attributes a greater number of effects to a lesser number of causes—the fewer the causes, the better the explanation. In contrast, the ancients' real qualities are explanatory in a piecemeal and *ad hoc* manner. In particular, sensory qualities, such as colour, do not seem to have any function other than to explain why things should appear to us such and such (Smith 1990: 225), which is clearly anthropocentric. To a mind attuned to the new cosmological insights, it should not be the case that material things possess certain real intrinsic features whose unique *ratio essendi* is to make them perceptible to animal beings.

Although it had been commonly voiced among early modern philosophers, such criticism does not do justice to the Aristotelian doctrine of matter, which was strongly reductive. Some affective qualities, such as heat and cold, dry and moist, were considered as primary and essential, and were paired in every material substance (AR 539). Other qualities (including colours) were, in various degrees, derivative, compound, and accidental ('secondary' in this sense). Besides, some qualities had an active causal power, while others were only passive. Thus when the moderns criticized the lack of explanatory power of real qualities, it was not solely on account of Ockam's razor, although they certainly considered their own doctrine of matter as simpler and more parsimonious. Their criticism aimed also at the nature of the explanation itself, at its very intelligibility.

Aristotelian physics requires that at least some affective qualities possess active powers, and that they be thus able to produce qualitative changes in matter through specific kinds of causation, such as assimilation or alteration, corruption or genesis. These types of changes are *sui generis* and irreducible. For example, sensory perception is considered in *De Anima* as a type of alteration; it affects the internal qualities of the sensing body and forces it to assume the form of the sensed body (AR 663, 674). For the Moderns this kind of causal action does not make sense any more. There is only one intelligible way to explain changes in matter, viz. through mechanical causality: bodies pushing or pulling other bodies, motion communicated through impulse and impact, and differentiated according to the variety of the shapes and quantity of matter. One explains a given change only when it has been reduced to such simple mechanical motions.

This mechanical reductionism is closely related to a new metaphysical conception of matter. Matter, the stuff which underlies all kinds of bodies, is no longer conceived as a pure indeterminate *substratum*, whose elusive existence is grasped only by abstracting it from the cluster of real qualities embodied in it. For a Modern, matter is an actual entity, fully determined, and possessed with 'catholick affections' such as shapes and movements. In consideration of those 'primary' qualities, matter is one and the same in all its manifestations. One may not be able to see this at the level of our ordinary experience, where bodies seem to belong to various classes according to the possession of some, apparently irreducible, qualities and powers. But a common assumption among the moderns is that these specific differences are all produced by the various arrangements and motions of a universal matter that is wholly undifferentiated.

This also explains why the new mechanical philosophy has to assume the form of a *corpuscular* philosophy (of which atomism is only one type, and not necessarily the most favoured one). If the variety of material substances depends only on the various arrangements and movements of its constitutive parts, there must be some point in the division of a material substance where the specific properties produced by the texture or arrangement of parts will entirely disappear. At the sub-microscopic level of the 'corpuscle', there should be no more composition of parts to be considered: matter should appear fully homogeneous and possess only its truly 'catholick' affections. This is the significance of Locke's somewhat puzzling 'division' argument, when he explains that the primary qualities are those that a body constantly keeps, whatever the changes it undergoes through division of parts.

For division (which is all that a Mill, or Pestel, or any other Body, does upon another, in reducing it to insensible parts) can never take away either Solidity, Extension, Figure, or Mobility from any Body, but only makes two, or more distinct separate masses of Matter, of that which was but one before... (*Essay* II. viii. 9)

This has often been represented (and criticized) as an empirical argument for the distinction of primary and secondary qualities, according to which invariance through division would be a criterion for primary qualities. That argument would be subject to the objection that, as long as the divided parts are still perceptible (or visible in a microscope), they retain *some* secondary qualities such as colours; when they are no longer visible, it begs the question to assert that those qualities would necessarily disappear. The fact that division cannot in principle affect the determinable spatial properties, such as the possession of shape or mobility, but somehow presupposes them, is irrelevant to the demonstration and cannot serve as a criterion for the distinction. However, Locke's point was not to provide a justification for primary qualities; he used the physical and mental division rather as an explanatory device to show what sort of thing a primary or inseparable quality is. What is implicit here is not so much a new physics, but its ontological underlying core: the conception of matter as a fully actualized being, completely undifferentiated at the corpuscular level. On this view, it is true that only the properties that can be ascribed to the constitutive undifferentiated parts of matter should be considered as utterly inseparable qualities of body in the most general sense of the term.[3]

---

[3] One may see here an illustration of a 'transdiction' principle. The term has been devised by M. Mandelbaum (1964: 61). It refers to the (perhaps dubious) inference in virtue of which we extend to the characterization of invisible bodies properties that have been universally found in the visible ones—a practice which, according to Mandelbaum, characterizes Early-modern corpuscular philosophy, and constitutes a distinctive feature of Modern realism. Newton, in his third methodological rule, gave to this transdictive principle its canonical formulation: 'the qualities of bodies that cannot be intended and remitted...and that belong to all bodies on which experiments can be made should be taken as qualities of all bodies universally' (*Principia* 795).

The contrast, then, between the ancients and the moderns reflects a deep ontological disagreement concerning the furniture of the physical world, and the nature of what may count as explanatory entities for natural philosophy. For the ancients, sensory qualities are reckoned among the ingredients of material reality, deeply inscribed in its elemental nature, constitutive of its substantial form, and in some cases (such as heat and cold) causally responsible for its activity. For the Moderns, they are nothing of the sort. They are attached to their subject, just as names are attached to the things named—that is, in virtue of an extrinsic relation to a living being who is endowed with sense and language. What truly exists in nature is a universal matter, whose constitutive parts (the corpuscles) are variously arranged and composed, but otherwise wholly undifferentiated, and which possesses the only qualities that the mechanical philosophy considers as requisite for an intelligible explanation of whatever appears in this world.

# IV: Epistemology

The ontological distinction between real intrinsic features of the physical world and features that are only nominal and extrinsic has no immediate epistemological basis. In both cases quality-predication is imposed on us by the very *fact* of sensory perception: things appear to be coloured, just as they appear to be extended or solid. This fact is well expressed in Locke's conception of simple ideas as all equally positive, whatever the reality of their possible cause (*Essay* II. viii. 7). It seems natural to assume that the same sort of ontological and causal structure underlies both appearances. To justify the distinction, therefore, one needs to loosen the grip of sense and to make oneself, so to speak, blind, in order to see beyond the surface or to see 'without the eyes', if such a feat were ever possible.

The doctrine of a distinction of qualities was widely shared in the seventeenth century, by philosophers (such as Descartes) who considered that knowledge in general is gained through an 'intellectual vision', and by so-called empiricist philosophers (such as Gassendi and Locke), for whom all knowledge of corporeal things originates in sensory experience. Consequently, each of them required some sort of access to the distinction in question. This access might be (a) direct, if one can find, in the very experience we have of bodies, reasons to think that some qualities are primary and original; or it may be (b) indirect, through some sort of hypothetical reasoning and inference to the best explanation.

## (a) The direct road to the distinction

One of the *direct* arguments is expressed in a famous page of Galileo's *Assayer* (1623), probably the first fully fledged statement of the modern doctrine of qualities:

As soon as I think of a material object or a corporeal substance, I immediately feel the need to conceive simultaneously that it is bounded and has this or that shape, that it is big or small in relation to others, that it is in this or that place at a given time, that it moves or stays still, that it does or does not touch another body and that it is one, few or many. I cannot separate it from these conditions by any stretch of imagination. But my mind feels no compulsion to understand as necessary accompaniments that it should be white or red, bitter or sweet, noisy or silent, of sweet or of foul odour. For that reason, I think that tastes, odors, colors and so forth are no more than mere names, so far as pertains to the subject wherein they seem to reside, and that they only reside in the body that perceives them. Thus, if the living creature were removed, all these qualities would be removed and annihilated.    (E.N. VI, 347; Shea 1977: 100)

The distinction is presented here, in a first-person narrative, as the result of a pure thought-experiment. The question is not about existing, sensible corporeal substances, but about constraints and strictures of consciousness. It asks: what is going on in *my* mind when I think of a 'body'? It appears that, on the one hand, there is a mental necessity or compulsion to link the concept of body with other concepts, such as shape or motion and rest; on the other hand, when one comes to other determinable qualities such as colour or taste, no such need is felt. The mental link between the concept of body and these latter sensory qualities is experienced as contingent. For example, it is possible to think of a tasteless or colourless body, but not of a body without shape. The mental process involved in this experience of separability or inseparability is a sort of abstraction. Through this mental process, it seems that I can detach the concept of body from some conditions or circumstances of its familiar existence, but not from others, and I conclude that the detachable conditions would never be attributed to the body if I were not endowed with corporeal senses.

The argument is puzzling. The necessity Galileo tries to capture through the mental experience is not merely analytical. The essential features of bodies cannot be essential simply because they are included in a nominal or conventional definition of bodies. They are supposed to be inseparable in *res* and not only in *words*, and this suggests a number of possible objections. Berkeley identified one of them when he contended that the modern distinction between primary and secondary qualities relies on an undue confidence in the abstracting powers of the mind (BW II 45). Is it really possible to think of an extended body without giving it a colour? It seems clear that one cannot think of a colour without giving it an extension, and so one still has to explain why and in what sense the extended colour does not pertain to the body, whereas the uncoloured extension does.

Another problem is how far this method of mental analysis should be considered as capable of securing an exhaustive list of primary or essential qualities. Shall we say that what holds true for extension, number, or shape, holds true as well for solidity, cohesion, or gravity? Or shall we count these latter qualities among the ones that would simply vanish when unperceived? One may therefore wonder whether it is impossible to consider at least some of those other qualities as 'secondary' in an Aristotelian (not Lockean) sense, that is, as *real qualities* resulting from certain combinations or interactions of primary qualities. But once this possibility is admitted, it seems that there is nothing in our mental experience to prevent us from drawing the same conclusion about other sensory qualities, such as colours, and treating them as *real* secondary qualities, rather than illusory ones. Last, but not least: Galileo doesn't even try to explain or justify why a conceptual necessity, captured through a purely mental process, should describe adequately the world as it is. Such a justification would require much more metaphysical or epistemological theorizing than Galileo was willing to provide.

Descartes, another proponent of *the direct method*, was more alive to the metaphysical underpinnings of the doctrine. In the *Meditations* he argued that, provided that one succeeds in leading the mind away from the senses, it is possible to access a purely intellectual mode of thinking, which provides clear and distinct ideas. Since God exists and does not deceive, such ideas must be considered as representing truly their objects; otherwise our very nature would be deceitful. Extension, the object of geometry, is one of these purely intellectual ideas, and it is the only idea of this sort that we have when we try to get a pure intellectual conception of the external material substance. Thus, the essence of matter appears to the mind as pure quantity diffused in length, breadth, and depth. In contrast, ideas of the sense do not show the intrinsic possibility of what they exhibit and they include a 'material falsity', a structural defect that gives occasion to false judgements (AT VII 43; CSM II 30).

However, the distinction drawn in the *Meditations* between the clear and distinct ideas of extension and its modes on the one hand, and the confused and obscure ideas of sense on the other, is not identical with the distinction of primary and secondary qualities. We have sensory (confused) ideas of determinate extensions, shapes, and movements that can be as deceitful as our ideas of sounds, colours, or tactile qualities. Thus the argument that focuses on the fact that our senses are not the source of our knowledge of bodies but are, at the very best, an occasion for it, does not directly address the distinction between real and imputed qualities. However, it serves as an important basis for a direct argument that is found rather inconspicuously in the *Principles*.

If, whenever our hands moved in a given direction, all the bodies in that area were to move away at the same speed as that of our approaching hands, we should never have any sensation of hardness. And since it is quite unintelligible to suppose that, if bodies did move away in this fashion, they would thereby lose their bodily nature, it follows that this nature cannot consist in hardness. By the same reasoning it can be shown that weight, colour, and all other such qualities that are perceived by the senses as being in corporeal matter, can be removed from it, while the matter itself remains intact; it thus follows that its nature does not depend on any of these qualities. (AT VIII-1 42; CSM I 224)

The argument is similar to the one Galileo had devised in the *Assayer*: in both cases a thought experiment serves as a test for the mental separability or inseparability of qualities. But here the distinction of qualities is the result of an *active* (although purely mental) process in which we consider the partly confused ideas that we have of particular bodies and, so to speak, put them mentally to a test. We submit the particular body, invested with its various apparent qualities, to some imaginary actions, such as moving it or moving with it, dividing it, etc. These actions, whose effects are mentally anticipated through what Gareth Evans has aptly called 'a natively given primitive mechanics' (Evans 1996: 271), allow us to grasp what is really inseparable from bodies (e.g. spatial properties, aptness to move) and what is not (e.g. hardness).

Besides, the Cartesian version of the thought experiment can stand on a firmer metaphysical basis. To this end the *Meditations* had provided at least three important elements: (i) the very possibility of a pure intellectual consideration of bodies has been secured through radical doubt; even though we do not have any body or organs to sense material things, we might still be able to know them. This is a sophisticated version of the animal-annihilation hypothesis. 'I shall consider myself as not having hands or eyes, or flesh or blood or senses, but as falsely believing that I have all these things' (AT VII 23; CSM II 15); (ii) God's veracity allows us to adopt the rule that whatever is clearly and distinctly conceived of something may be said truly of that thing. This implies that whatever is conceived clearly and distinctly as belonging to a particular body either exists, or at least *can* exist as a genuine intrinsic property of that body; (iii) finally, the doctrine of confused ideas and of material falsity is important at least negatively, in that it shows why, whenever the question of the essence of matter is at stake, we must not rely on the ideas of sense, which are apt to represent to us what is not as if it were something.

## (b) The direct road: empiricist strategies, and empiricist critics

In the *Essay* (II. viii), Locke mentioned a number of facts which have often been considered as 'empirical motives' for adopting the distinction between real and imputed qualities. For example, the same flame at different distances produces in us sensations of warmth or pain (§16); the same water is cold to one hand and hot to another (§21); porphyry ceases to appear red and white whenever light is prevented from striking on it (§19); an almond changes its colour and taste when it is reduced to powder (§20). Several other similar facts (including facts about diseases that affect our perception of tastes or colours) are mentioned in the early modern literature on qualities. They suggest that there are some qualities that can be altered radically and even converted into their contrary (such as hot and cold), or affected with contrary existential value (such as agreeable and painful) on account of a mere circumstantial change, such as the location of the sensible object in relation to the percipient, the internal disposition of the sensitive body, the illumination of the object, or its state of division.

These changes are circumstantial because, whereas they affect significantly our sensory ideas, they cannot (with the possible exception of the ground almond) be reasonably thought of as affecting the internal structure of the body in question, which, to all appearances, remains the same. It is not only that the same object appears under different perspectives at different times, or to different persons— since perspectival relativity applies first and foremost to primary qualities, it cannot function as a possible criterion; it also causes us to attribute incompatible properties to the body. This strong relativity would be understandable if the ideas of those qualities were not instantiations of 'real qualities' possessed by the bodies themselves but rather (as is commonly thought of pain) if they were only effects of the bodies on our sensory organs, with no resemblance whatsoever with their cause.

However, it is not enough to show that at least some secondary qualities in given couples of contraries (such as hot and cold, sweet and sour) are necessarily without an archetype (external resemblance) and as such are purely mental; one has also to understand that it is a common feature of both contraries and of all secondary qualities whatsoever. Since we know that any sensation may be without an arche- type, and since there is no phenomenal feature in sensations themselves that may justify us in saying, for example, that warmth is more real than cold, both may proceed from the same sort of cause: what has appeared *necessarily* true of the one should also be true of the other.

If thus construed, the empiricist argument about secondary qualities does not prove what it is supposed to prove. Or rather, it proves too much. On empiricist standards, such as the ones Berkeley thought he shared with Locke, we do not have any idea of an extended body except through the sensory ideas (or impressions) that we have of its minimal parts of coloured extension or tangible (solid) extension. So if the demonstration quoted above were both empirically grounded and valid, it must apply not only to colour or other secondary qualities considered *in abstracto*, but also to whatever cannot be thought of *but as coloured or tangible*, that is, to the very primary properties that the modern doctrine of qualities considered as existing independently of us. Hume summarized the unavoidable conclusion: 'instead of explaining the operation of external objects by its [the doctrine of qualities] means, we utterly annihilate all these objects, and reduce ourselves to the opinions of the most extravagant skepticism concerning them' (Hume 1985: 277). The very argument adduced to prove the modern theory of qualities leads us to conclusions that are directly opposite to the convictions the doctrine was supposed to express and ground: the external reality of primary qualities and the modern scientific image.

In summary, the direct road has proved a difficult one. In both forms (as a result of a thought experiment, or as a conclusion from empirical facts about our sensations), it reveals severe weaknesses. One may conclude that it was probably not because of such arguments that the modern mind found the theory of qualities so convincing.

## (c)  The indirect road: sense-perception and mechanism

Although the standard interpretation of Locke construes his discussion as providing empirical arguments for the distinction of qualities, there is a growing consensus among scholars in favour of an alternative reading (Mandelbaum 1964; Curley 1972; Alexander 1985). The *Essay* is now generally read against the background of Boyle's mechanical and corpuscular hypothesis, and the putative empirical arguments outlined above are now considered rather as 'clarifying examples of the power of corpuscularian explanations' (Wilson 1992: 220). That hypothesis explains why it may be possible for the same water to appear hot to one hand and cold to another because of the mechanical interactions, at the corpuscular level, between external bodies and the senses.

Locke himself had presented his discussion of qualities as a digression into physical considerations, whose aim was to make the reader understand the nature of sensation and the important distinction between ideas and qualities (*Essay* II. viii. 22). This digression shows how, according to the corpuscular hypothesis, ideas (of the senses) are produced in the mind through the action of external objects. According to the mechanical philosophy, action through contact and impulse is the only intelligible way bodies can be conceived to operate one upon the other (*Essay* II. viii. 11). Whenever it seems that such contact is missing, one has to postulate some invisible threads, corpuscles, or effluvia that connect the cause and the effects. In the case of vision (in which sensory perception seems to occur at a distance), this contact action is effected by light, whose corpuscles, variously reflected by the surface structures of the bodies, affect the retina with various motions and forces. This affection can then be propagated to the brain, either through vibrations of an internal fluid or by direct impulse, and can contribute to form there some sort of image or, in Newton's language, a 'motional picture' (Newton 1959–97, II: Letter 264). The mental counterpart of this process takes place at the very end of it, when cerebral motions or pictures, acting, so to speak, directly 'against' the soul, cause the mind to have various 'ideas' or 'sentiments'.

Such description of the mechanism of sensory perception owes much to the theories of visual perception devised in the first half of the century in the optical works of Kepler and Descartes. Kepler, through geometrical analysis and insights from contemporary anatomists (such as Felix Plater or Fabrizio d'Aquapendente) discovered that the eye functions as a 'camera obscura': the crystalline is a lens, refracting the rays of light, and the retina is a screen, receiving a two dimensional picture of the external visual hemisphere (KGW II: 151; Crombie 1964: 147). Unlike the 'sensible species' of the ancient theories, this *pictura* is not some sort of specular image of the external hemisphere, floating as it were in the transparent parts of the eye, and then transmitted through the supposedly hollow canal of the optic nerve to the inner cells of the 'ultimate sentient'. Recent anatomical observations had shown that there was no canal of any sort inside the optic nerve that would allow for such transmission. Rather, the retinal picture is a 'penetrating affection', which affects the 'animal spirits'[4] filling the optic nerve in a fully physical way, described in Kepler's *Dioptrics* as a kind of combustion (KGW IV 372). Such analysis made clear that the image produced in the eye, to which our conscious vision is congruent, is, in many ways, distinct from the external object producing it. One important difference is the fact that one dimension is lost: the picture is a perspective image projected on a curved surface, and as such submitted to a number of geometrical distortions. However, this discrepancy is no obstacle to representation. As Descartes will say: 'the perfection of an image often depends on its not resembling its object as much as it might' (AT VII 113; CSM I 165). Thus, just as in perspective painting, the retinal picture provides the judgement with indirect signs for tri-dimensional visual properties. Such analysis reveals that the eye is no longer a mere receptor of the form of the sensible; it plays an active role in reshaping the information transmitted by the rays of light, disfiguring it or rather encoding it, so that the input from the external world is converted into something that can adequately move the material spirits circulating in the nerve connecting the retina to the brain, and there properly affect the seat of sensation.

It is possible that Kepler was not himself fully conscious of the conceptual change involved in his new theory of vision, but Descartes, who extensively drew on Kepler's descriptions, definitely was. According to Descartes' *Dioptrics*, sensory

---

[4] In order to account for the various actions and passions of the animal body, the Renaissance physiologists had devised the concept of *spiritus*, or animal spirit, a subtle fluid infused from the brain into the nerves to the various parts of the body, allowing sensation to take place whenever this *spiritus* is touched or affected. By the end of the sixteenth century, through the works of Jean Fernel, Pierre Severin, and Tommaso Campanella, the *spiritus* has been progressively unified, naturalized, and conceived sometimes in atomistic terms. But it is only in the physiological works of Isaac Beeckmann, Descartes' friend and mentor in the formative years, that the *spiritus* was for the first time understood in a fully mechanistic sense. Beeckmann provided a hydro-dynamical model that Descartes took over and refined. This physiological part of the story (de Calan 2008) is of crucial importance to understand the genesis of the modern concept of 'sensation'.

perception does not require that any resemblances or '*images voltigeantes*' issue from things and then pass through the organs of vision to the seat of sensation. All that is required is that some movement or pressure be communicated to the organ and appropriately transmitted to the brain, where it gives 'occasion' to the mind to have various ideas. In such a theory, there is no reason why the (mental) effect should resemble the (physical) cause. One has only to suppose, in accordance with the doctrine of mind–body union, that the motion in the brain is constituted by nature in such a way that it regularly produces the mental effect: 'It can also be proved that the nature of our mind is such that the mere occurrence of certain motions in the body can stimulate it to have all manner of thoughts which have no likeness to the movements in question. This is especially true of the confused thoughts we call sensations or feelings' (AT VIII-1 320; CSM 1 284). Thus, the relation between cerebral movements and sensory ideas is a causal relation, not a cognitive one. Its *nomological* structure is the result of an arbitrary (although natural) institution connecting a mind to a body. Without such an institution, the soul, by its own nature, would not be able to react to the motions produced in the brain to which it is present, any more than it is actually able to read similar motions in other brains, or directly in the external world.

We are now in position to formulate the indirect argument for the new theory of qualities. It stands on two connected grounds. On the one hand, there is the causal analysis of sensory perception that we have just outlined. The organs of sense are not neutral receptacles of the sensible form, but rather mechanical devices whose function is to transmit corpuscular motions from the outer world and convert them into physiological events and cerebral configurations, to which the soul reacts in a constrained manner. Thus, the mere fact that we have sensory experiences is no longer a good reason for endowing objects with secondary qualities that resemble them. The only conclusion to which we are entitled is that the external bodies possess some (causal) powers or dispositions to produce certain ideas in us.[5]

On the other hand there is the superior heuristic value of the mechanical hypothesis, its explanatory success and promise. Reducing matter to its mechanical (or primary) properties alone will allow us to satisfy the need for a pervasive explanatory principle in physics, a principle that is both simpler and more intelligible than the real qualities of the Ancients. It will also offer side-benefits, of no slight import, such as the one mentioned by Malebranche in the *Search after Truth*: if we suppose that there exist in matter other intrinsic qualities of which we know

---

[5] However, Locke, following a tradition that originated in Gassendist physics and had been transmitted to him through the works of William Digby, Walter Charleton, Thomas Willis, and Robert Boyle, is taking a step beyond this strict conclusion when he contends that those powers are each of them causally dependent on specific arrangements of the particles of the bodies (see *Essay* II. viii. 13). So (and one may see here an important specificity of this tradition) each secondary quality has a true individualized correlate in the physical world, a corpuscular texture, or molecular composition, exerting a specific 'chemical' action on the spirits (de Calan 2008: 270–393).

nothing, then how shall we answer libertines and atheists who argue that the matter of the brain can think in virtue of some unknown power (OCM III 466; MLO 246).

So goes the indirect argument: the modern scientific image and its new ontology of qualities will provide us with the best explanation of the physical world; and sensory experience no longer provides any objection to this image. On the contrary, the causal process involved in sensation is an almost ordinary instance of mechanical action through local contact and 'impulse', and its final result, the mental effect, no longer belongs to the physical realm.

The hypothetical or indirect road towards the modern theory of qualities appears to have been the one most trodden in early modern philosophy. Even philosophers who devised *a priori* arguments for the distinction appear to have done it in order to give a metaphysical basis to a conviction that was first framed by considering the superior heuristic value of the mechanical hypothesis. This is especially apparent in Descartes' early physics, in texts such as the *Treatise of the World* and the *Treatise of Man*, which make extensive use of a hypothetical method (the 'fable'). There Descartes asserts that, in a hypothetical world of matter conceived as pure quantity, consisting of extended parts of various shapes and sizes, subject to a small number of basic mechanical laws, any effect that is ordinarily attributed to the so-called real qualities of bodies, either occult or manifest, active or passive, can be intelligibly produced and explained (AT IX 25–6; CSM I 89). In the *Treatise of Man* in particular, one can see that the whole range of known animal reactions and behaviours may be explained if the organs of sense are mechanically affected by matter in its various arrangements and motions in as many ways as there are secondary qualities that affect us differently.

## (d)  The false imputation of the sense

One last question is in order: how can the false imputation of the senses be explained, justified, and accounted for within the general scheme of God's Providence, to which most philosophers in the early modern period were still so deeply attached?

At the end of Part I of the *Principles*, Descartes offers a plausible psycho-genetic explanation of why we falsely attribute to things sensations that do not accurately represent anything in them.

It is here that the first and main cause of all our errors may be recognized. In our early childhood the mind was so closely tied to the body that it had no leisure for any thoughts except those by means of which it had sensory awareness of what was happening to the body. It did not refer these thoughts to anything outside itself, but merely felt pain when something harmful was happening to the body and felt pleasure when something beneficial occurred. And when nothing very beneficial or harmful was happening to the body, the mind had various sensations corresponding to the different areas where, and ways in which, the body was being stimulated . . . sensations which do not represent anything located outside our thought. At the same time the mind perceived sizes, shapes, motions and so on, which were presented to it not as sensations but as things, or modes of things, existing (or at least capable of existing) outside thought, although it was not yet aware of the difference between things and sensations. The next stage arose when the mechanism of the body . . . twisted around aimlessly in all directions in its random attempts to pursue the beneficial and avoid the harmful; at this point the mind that was attached to the body began to notice that the objects of this pursuit or avoidance had an existence outside itself. And it attributed to them not only sizes, shapes, motions and the like, which it perceived as things or modes of things, but also tastes, smells and so on, the sensations of which were, it realized, produced by the objects in question.    (AT VIII-1 35–6; CSM I 218–19)

Descartes here proposes an empirical description of the way we acquired our ideas (and prejudices) about the external world. The false imputation of secondary qualities is said to result from the very order in which ideas are acquired—an order that is imposed on us by the biological fact that we were infants before becoming adults. Prejudices are acquired in childhood, because the mind is too tied to the body; they are maintained through a consequent lack of right (pure) reasoning and by the effect of natural processes, such as the association of ideas. So error is almost unavoidable. It is inscribed in the very process of men's maturation. How shall we evaluate this fact? On the one hand, its frequent denunciation by modern philosophers is justifiable. Obscure ideas, however acquired, should never be considered as reliable grounds for judgement and, for that reason, men are genuinely accountable for the false imputation of secondary qualities. Whatever the incorrigibility of our error, God's veracity is not really at stake.

On the other hand, for Descartes as for many of his successors, the 'error' of the senses, because it is natural, must be understood in a providential setting. According to the genetic description, sensory qualities are usually related to objects that may affect our bodies with either beneficial or harmful effects. One is naturally led therefore to use them to acknowledge, and take advantage of, these biologically prominent features of the external world. One may go even further in evaluating this functional status of the senses, following a line of argument developed by Arnauld in *On True and False Ideas*. By allowing us to distinguish things according to qualitative differences that are easy to recognize, such as differences of colour, our senses as currently constituted are indeed much more efficient than they would be if they gave us direct access to the corpuscular correlates of our sensations in the physical world—that is, to subtle differences in quantity of motion, arrangement, or shapes. Our soul 'would find it too difficult to discern the difference in these stimulations, which is only one of degree' (Arnauld 1990: 132). It has been argued (Beyssade 2001: 165–73) that, in this new perspective, secondary qualities are no longer what hinders our perception of primary ones; instead, they constitute a most useful key for interpreting them. Arnauld compares secondary qualities to the 'rough pattern' used in tapestry-work in order to avoid error in the composition of what are often very slightly differing shades: 'just as tapestry workers have a pattern, which they call a "rough pattern", where the various shades of the same colour are indicated by completely different colours, so that they are less liable to mistake them' (Arnauld 1990: 132). On this characterization, the ontological predication itself is perhaps no longer at fault: 'Thus it was due to our making language match the intentions of the Author of Nature that we call bodies white, black, or putrid . . . the intention of the Author of Nature is that our soul attach colours to them (objects) and apply them to bodies in some way, in order to distinguish between them more easily' (Arnauld 1990: 174–5).

Malebranche on the one hand, and Locke and Berkeley on the other, expressed similar ideas: they also thought that the organization of sense perception (not only the sensory qualities, but also the natural judgements we tend to make while perceiving) constitute an important argument in favour of the providential disposition of things. Malebranche added a religious dimension to the argument. God provides secondary qualities (and the spontaneous natural judgements that result) in order to alleviate the burden of the human mind, so that it can devote itself to its proper objects of contemplation, the spiritual goods (OCM XII 98–9).

For Locke, ideas of sense are exactly correlated to powers in things, and serve as 'distinguishing characters' enabling us to know them. In consequence all simple ideas, including ideas of secondary qualities, can be said to be real and adequate, despite the fact that they do not all resemble their objects:

For these several Appearances, being designed to be the Marks, whereby we are to know, and distinguish Things, which we have to do with; our *Ideas* do as well serve us to that purpose, and are as real distinguishing Characters, whether they be only constant Effects, or else exact Resemblances of something in the things themselves: the reality lying in that steady correspondence, they have with the distinct Constitutions of real Beings. But whether they answer to those Constitutions, as to Causes, or Patterns, it matters not; it suffices, that they are constantly produced by them.    (*Essay* II. xxx. 2)

Berkeley will draw on this, pushing the Lockean argument to its extreme: the sensory qualities are not only provided by God as tools for deciphering the world; they are the very language with which God chose to address us, designed for directing us in our lives and our knowledge (BW I 231). The agreement of our sensory ideas with the inner constitution of a putative external material substance is no longer relevant. The world of sensory qualities is the only world in which we live; there is no other to be looked for. Once again the theory of qualities seems, by its own virtue, to revert to its contrary.

## REFERENCES

ADDISON, J. (1712). *Spectator*, 413, 24 June 1712.

ALEXANDER, P. (1985). *Ideas, Qualities and Corpuscles: Locke and Boyle on the External World*. Cambridge: Cambridge University Press.

ALLAIS, L. (2007). 'Kant idealism and the secondary quality analogy'. *Journal of the History of Ideas*, 45: 459–84.

ANSTEY, P. R. (2000). *The Philosophy of Robert Boyle*. London and New York: Routledge.

ARNAULD, A. (1990). *On True and False Ideas*. Trans. S. Gaukroger. Manchester and New York: Manchester University Press.

BEYSSADE, J.-M. (2001). 'Sensation et Idées: le patron rude de Descartes à Arnauld', in *Etudes sur Descartes. L'histoire d'un esprit*. Paris: Editions du Seuil.

CROMBIE, A. C. (1964). 'Kepler: De Modo Visionis. A translation from the Latin of *Ad Vitellionem Paralipomena*, V, 2, and related passages on the formation of the retinal image', in *L'Aventure de la Science, Mélanges Alexandre Koyré*. Paris: Hermann.

CURLEY, E. M. (1972). 'Locke, Boyle and the distinction between primary and secondary qualities'. *The Philosophical Review*, 81: 438–64.

DE CALAN, R. (2008). *Généalogie de la Sensation Physique, physiologie et Psychologie en Europe, de Fernel à Locke*. Thèse de doctorat de Philosophie, Ecole Normale Supérieure LSH, Lyon.

EVANS, G. (1996). 'Things without the Mind', in *Collected Papers*. Oxford: Oxford University Press.

HAMOU, P. (1999–2001). *La Mutation du visible, essai sur la portée épistémologique des instruments d'optique au XVIIe siècle*. 2 vols. Villeneuve d'Ascq: Presses Universitaires du Septentrion.

HUME, D. (1985). *A Treatise of Human Nature*. Ed. E. C. Mossner. London: Penguin Classics.

KEPLER (1965). *Kepler's Conversation with Galileo's Sidereal Messenger*. Trans. Edward Rosen. The Sources of Science, No. 5. New York: Johnson Reprint Corp.

MALEBRANCHE, N. (1979). *Oeuvres I*. Ed. G. Rodis-Lewis. Bibliothèque de la Pléiade. Paris: Gallimard.

MANDELBAUM, M. (1964). *Philosophy, Science and Sense-Perception: Historical and Critical Studies*. Baltimore: Johns Hopkins University Press.

MEILLASSOUX, Q. (2006). *Après la finitude. Essai sur la nécessité de la contingence*. Paris: Editions du Seuil.

NEWTON, I. (1721). *Opticks, or A Treatise of the Reflections, Refractions, Inflections & Colours of Light*. 3rd edn. London.

NEWTON, I. (1959–77). *The Correspondence of Isaac Newton*. Ed. H. J. Turnbull. 7 vols. Cambridge: Cambridge University Press.

SELLARS, W. (1963). *Science, Perception and Reality*. London: Routledge & Kegan Paul.

SHEA, W. (1977). *Galileo's Intellectual Revolution. Middle Period: 1610–1632*. New York: Science History Publications.

SIMMONS, A. (2003). 'Descartes on the cognitive structure of sensory experience'. *Philosophy and Phenomenological Research*, 67: 549–79.

SMITH, A. D. (1990). 'Of primary and secondary qualities'. *The Philosophical Review*, 99: 221–54.

VAN HELDEN, A. (1985). *Measuring the Universe: Cosmic Dimensions from Aristarchus to Halley*. Chicago: The Chicago University Press.

WILSON, C. (1995). *The Invisible World: Early Modern Philosophy and the Invention of the Microscope.* Princeton, NJ: Princeton University Press.

WILSON, C. (2008). *Epicureanism at the Origins of Modernity.* Oxford: Oxford University Press.

WILSON, M. D. (1992). 'History of philosophy in philosophy today; and the case of the sensible qualities'. *The Philosophical Review,* 101: 191–243.

# CHAPTER 9

...............................................................

# THE PASSIONS

...............................................................

## GABOR BOROS

AT the beginning of the seventeenth century the word 'passion', which had formerly been used to denote all phenomena of the emotional sphere, began to narrow in meaning down to the more intense emotions and especially the amorous emotions. In a parallel development, the word 'emotion' was given a new meaning in at least two vernacular languages, French and English. 'Emotion' had hitherto been used almost exclusively to denote revolution-like political events;[1] now it began to appear as the new, neutral term for emotional phenomena. The key figure in the rearrangement of the semantic field of passion was Michel de Montaigne whose *Essais*, as well as their English translation by John Florio, bear witness to the new meaning of 'emotion'.[2]

The generally accepted view in the historiography of philosophy until recently was that the seventeenth century was a rationalistic age in which the emotions and especially the passions were seen as deserving suppression or even extirpation. This generalization is no longer tenable, and it has become increasingly evident that the seventeenth century was far less Stoic in its general attitude than had been supposed earlier (James 1997; Wilson 2008*b*). Neither the Stoic nor the Christian moral code determined the overall frame of the theories of passions in any of the main thinkers, and the nature and significance of the passions was as

---

[1] The *OED* includes the following definition of 'emotion': 'a political or social agitation; a tumult, popular disturbance'. There is an example of the older use in Montaigne: *lors de l'émotion de Catilina*' (Montaigne 1969: 1, 326).

[2] I am indebted to Gabor Soós, *Passions in the Culture of the Mind: Early Modern Configurations* (unpublished PhD thesis at Eötvös University, Budapest), which shed light on this development for me. See Diller (2005).

lively a field of research and debate as were theories of substance or of knowledge. As is the case with these traditional subjects, the starting point is to be found in Descartes' *œuvre*, and it is helpful to think in terms of the period which begins with Descartes' *Passions of the Soul* (1649) and Hobbes's *Leviathan* (1651), and embraces the later contributions of Spinoza, Pascal, Malebranche, Locke, and Leibniz.

As a consequence of his preoccupations with physics and physiology, Descartes—far from simply taking over traditional treatments of the passions—reconstructed the theory of the emotions by providing a mechanical 'basement' for the traditional phenomenal part of the theory, leaving aside the moral-theological evaluative parts. Yet while Descartes' and Hobbes' *caveats* pushed into the background any serious attempt to deal with theological questions in the frame of the new philosophy, theology and philosophy came into a new alliance in a way that was significant for the evolution of the theory of the passions, beginning with Dutch Cartesians like Abraham Heidanus, Johannes Coccejus, and Christoph Wittich, and continuing with Nicolas Malebranche and Gottfried Wilhelm Leibniz.

In this chapter I will focus first on the significance of the two main concepts 'passion' and 'action', before considering some specific features of individual theories.

# I: Passion and action

The word 'passion' stems from the Latin *patior*, the general meaning of which is that something undergoes something; the patient becomes the object of an action involuntarily. Therefore, when analysing a particular theory of passions, it is important to see who or what undergoes what sort of action and who or what, according to the theory, is the agent. Descartes writes that 'we are not aware of any subject which acts more directly upon our soul [*contre nostre ame*] than the body to which it is joined. Consequently we should recognize that what is a passion in the soul is usually an action in the body' (AT XI 328; CSM 1 328). This view reflects the assumption that changes in the body have a direct impact on the soul. However, Descartes' considered view, at least from his *Meditations* onwards, is that the body as pure matter cannot exert an influence on the soul. It is solely as a continuously changing portion of the matter informed by the soul—that is as soul-like in its own, peculiar, not quite clear way—that the body is able to influence the soul taken in itself. The two antagonists of the theory of passions in Descartes, body and soul, are both, in reality, within the realm of the soul (Guenancia 2000: 238–319; Hoffman 1986; Shapiro 2003).

Before examining the details of Descartes' theory of the emotions and how philosophers of the next generation developed further the core Cartesian concepts, altering their understanding of the concepts of activity and passivity in ways that reflected their own metaphysical innovations, a survey of Hobbes' rival approach to the passions is essential.

Hobbes developed a reductionist analysis of cognition and the formation of affects on the basis of his corporealistic metaphysics and theory of knowledge, as well as his concept of *conatus*, which plays a fundamental role in the physics and psychology of *De corpore* and *Leviathan*.[3] In diametrical opposition to the metaphysical theory of knowledge-acquisition in Descartes' *Meditations*, Hobbes construes the process of learning as a series of pure physical events.

The cause of sense, is the externall body, or object, which presseth the organ proper to each sense, either immediately... or mediately... which pressure, by the mediation of nerves, and other strings, and membranes of the body, continued inwards to the brain, and heart, causeth there a resistance, or counter-pressure, or endeavour of the heart, to deliver itself: which endeavour because outward, seemeth to be some matter without. And this seeming, or fancy, is that which men call sense.   (HW III: 1)

Thus, Hobbes replaces the functions traditionally attributed to the soul with the newly discovered functions of the body or, in any case, functions that he himself attributes to the body, *corpus*, considered as the only type of real being. Hobbes accomplishes this task by introducing the concept of *conatus* or 'endeavour' in order to introduce a source of motion and change into this corporeal universe. Originally and pre-scientifically, this concept characterized the effort of the more or less consciously striving soul. However, Descartes had already transferred it to the realm of the physical when referring to the striving of each body to move in a straight line as opposed to their realized motion, which always differs from a straight line (AT VIII-1 63, 108; CSM 1 241, 259).

In Chapter 6 of *Leviathan*, Hobbes applies the *conatus* concept explicitly to the theory of passions.

And because going, speaking, and the like voluntary motions depend always upon a precedent thought of whither, which way, and what, it is evident that the imagination is the first internal beginning of all voluntary motion.... These small beginnings of Motion within the body of Man, before they appear in walking, speaking, striking, and other visible actions, are commonly called Endeavour.... This Endeavour, when it is toward something which causes it, is called Appetite or Desire.... And when the Endeavour is fromward something, it is generally called Aversion.   (HW 3: 38)

---

[3] Cf. the official definition in the *De corpore*: 'Primo definiemus *conatum esse motum per spatium et tempus minus quam quod datur, id est, determinatur, sive expositione vel numero assignatur*, id est, *per punctum*' (OL I 177).

In this passage, *conatus* is first applied to purely bodily events—'small beginnings of Motion within the body of Man'—but it is then reinstated in its original, psychological sense one sentence later, where it is identified with appetite, desire, and aversion. However, it is now deprived of its traditional relationship with a substantial, incorporeal soul. Accordingly, in Hobbes' theory of the passivity of passions, both the actor and the acted-upon are of a bodily nature, and the moving force behind them both is nothing but a physically construed *conatus* or endeavour. The experienced passions are actions occurring within the body.

The philosophers of the next generation were in an appropriate position to compare and combine both the viewpoints and the views of Descartes and Hobbes. Among them, Spinoza is unrivalled for the profundity of his theory of passions, which is contained mainly in Parts 3–5 of his *Ethics*, as well as in his theological and political works *passim*. Although he was far from being a Cartesian in his theory of substance and his philosophical theology, Spinoza made use of the Cartesian rather than the Hobbesian framework for developing his own metaphysically-based theory of passions or *affects*, as he terms emotional phenomena. There is, however, a noteworthy exception to this generalization, *viz.* Spinoza's appropriation of the concept of *conatus*.

Spinoza was convinced that the Cartesian doctrine of three substances, mind, body, and God, was mistaken. The view that there is but one substance, which is not identified with either the body or the soul/mind, implies already that there can be no plurality of substances such that one of them is able to act upon another. Therefore, passivity and activity had to be redefined if they were to be retained in his system at all.

Spinoza's ingenious solution set out from his basic metaphysical concept of every individual's essential striving to remain in its own being. To the extent that an individual succeeds in maintaining its own being, it can be said to be active in a broad sense, whereas its passivity consists in its being acted upon through the overwhelming 'potency-in-act', that is, strivings of the other individuals of nature, in the sense of *natura naturata*. Spinoza broadens this notion of activity by going on to identify it with adequate causality. Now, no finite human individual can be an adequate cause of anything, according to Spinoza, except its own adequate (i.e. true, clear, and distinct) ideas. True human activity is therefore limited to obtaining true, assured knowledge via the two higher kinds of cognition: reason, and intuitive science. Consequently, passivity must also be understood in epistemic terms, and Spinoza analyses it as inadequate causality, that is, as having inadequate (false, obscure, and truncated) ideas.

Leibniz faced much the same problem. Because he rejected Cartesian interaction between mind and body, he had to construct an account of activity and passivity that did not depend on this framework. Yet he was loath to accept either Hobbes's corporeal analysis of action or Spinoza's one-substance theory, and this complicated his task considerably.

A permanent element within Leibniz's metaphysics is his idea that, far from being able to act on something on its own, body in and of itself is not a real entity as it is not a true unity. Bodies need something else that is non-corporeal in order to be substantial; hence (and here Leibniz agrees with Spinoza), a Cartesian body would be incapable of performing any action 'upon' (*contre*) its soul. What makes body real and so active is, paradoxically, something that has no bodily character, something that has the nature of a soul. Consequently, it is always in the soul (i.e., in the individual substance or monad) that the passivity of a passion, and the activity of an action, originate. 'It must be said that, on a rigorous definition, the soul has within it the principles of all its actions, and even of all its passions, and that the same is true in all the simple substances scattered throughout Nature, although there be freedom only in those that are intelligent' (Leibniz 1966: 57). Having excluded the possibility that the essence of a substance is constituted by its primary bodily qualities, the only possible solution for Leibniz is that action and passion are features of the internal life of a monad. As Spinoza had ultimately interpreted these concepts in terms of cognition, Leibniz interprets them in terms of distinct and confused expressions or perceptions.

If there is some reality, we cannot search for it but in the power of performing or under-going an action, and this is what constitutes the substance of the body like matter and form. . . . The substance has metaphysical matter or passive force as far as it expresses something confusedly, and it has active force as far as it expresses something distinctly.   (*De modo distinguendi* . . . , A VI/4/B 1504; my translation)

It might seem as though Leibniz's theory of substance could commit him only to a radically Stoic theory, in which activity and passivity correspond only to two sorts of perception, clear and confused. Given that, in Leibniz's thought, the dominant aspect of reality is the mental, it is hardly surprising that it is cognition or perception that determines the basic quality of our affects. If we could ever achieve a state devoid of confused perceptions, we would become divine beings living without passions, and an omniscient divine sage would be necessarily exempt from all passions, that is, all emotive states. 'For there is in the soul not only an order of distinct perceptions, forming its dominion, but also a series of confused perceptions or passions, forming its bondage: and there is no need for astonishment at that; the soul would be a Divinity if it had none but distinct perceptions' (Leibniz 1966: 56). At first glance, it seems that Leibniz, contrary to Spinoza, does not admit the possibility of *active affects*, that is, affective states directed by distinct, not confused perceptions. However, the expressions 'passive *force*' and 'active *force*', which occur constantly in his metaphysical and physical writings from the time of *Specimen Dynamicum* (1690) onwards, suggest that Leibniz's stoicism is a fundamentally modified one. Moreover, core terms like *force* or *appetition* even point to the presence of a theory of *conatus* in Leibniz's philosophy, indicating that he has combined the cognition-based Stoic elements with characteristic Epicurean ones—in this case, the notion of spontaneous activity, deriving from the substance itself.

As one might expect, the source of this spontaneous activity cannot but be the concept of *conatus* Leibniz took over from Hobbes.[4] But we must hasten to add to this assertion that Leibniz's conception of *conatus* is diametrically opposed to the one we have seen in Hobbes, where it underwrites his corporealism. For Leibniz, the *conatus* helps us to identify the real difference between the body and the soul, where the latter is construed as the only real substance or the only entity capable of conferring substantiality on matter. In a letter to Arnauld at the beginning of November 1671, Leibniz elaborates on the role of the *conatus* in both the body and the soul:

All bodies can be understood as momentary minds, but lacking memory. No endeavour in bodies can be destroyed with regard to its determination; in the mind, it cannot be destroyed with regard to its degree of speed either. As the body consists in the course of motions, the mind consists in the harmony of endeavours. The present motion of the body originates in the composition of the preceding endeavours, whereas the present endeavour of the mind, that is, the will, is from the composition of the preceding harmonies in a new harmony, that is, by way of pleasure; yet if the harmony of this pleasure gets disturbed by the intrusion of another endeavour, pain results.   (A II/1 173; my translation)

*Conatus* conceptually connects and separates body and soul at the same time. The soul's ability to retain its past *conatus* is, for Leibniz, the feature that distinguishes it from the body, an ability anchored in the substantial character of the soul.

With this background in mind, it is easier to understand the details of Leibniz's theory of passion and action. In response to Locke's *Essay* (II. xxi. 5), he introduces the concept of *conatus* in the *New Essays* in a way that removes all uncertainty about his ongoing commitment to the notion.

I shall say that volition is the effort or endeavour (*conatus*) to move towards what one finds good and away from what one finds bad, the endeavour arising immediately out of one's awareness of those things. This definition has as a corollary the famous axiom that from will and power together, action follows; since any endeavour results in action unless it is prevented. So it is not only the voluntary inner acts of our minds which follow from this *conatus*, but outer ones as well, i.e., voluntary movements of our bodies, thanks to the union of body and soul which I have explained elsewhere. There are other efforts, arising from insensible perceptions, which we are not aware of; I prefer to call these 'appetitions' rather than volitions, for one describes as 'voluntary' only actions one can be aware of and can reflect upon when they arise from some consideration of good and bad; though there are also appetitions of which one can be aware.   (LRB 172)

Now a passion (or affect or emotion) is at the very least a state of mind immediately preceding an action, including the suppression of an action. However important the Stoic-cognitive component in Leibniz's theory of the passions might be, the real basis of the mind's affective states is the *conatus*. In this respect, it would be

---

[4] As is witnessed by the only letter Leibniz wrote to Hobbes (13/23 July 1670).

a mistake to ascribe to him a purely Stoic theory of the passions. His explicit definition of passion in the *New Essays* stresses the element that distinguishes his theory from Stoic ones, according to which passions are merely opinions.

The Stoics took the passions to be beliefs: thus for them hope was the belief in a future good, and fear the belief in a future evil. But I would rather say that the passions are not contentments or displeasures or beliefs, but endeavours—or rather modifications of endeavour—which arise from beliefs or opinions and are accompanied by pleasure or displeasure.   (LRB 167)

The passions are endeavours modified by confused perceptions that the soul possesses before everything else. This is the way we can best interpret the famous 'uneasiness' (*inquiétude/Unruhe*) in the same chapter of the *New Essays*. Leibniz certainly agrees with Locke that, '[t]he chief if not only spur to human industry and action is uneasiness' (*Essay* II. xx. 9). But he dismisses as mistaken the way in which Locke continues his argument, namely, that uneasiness urges us to acquire that thing through the absence of something that carries with it displeasure or pain. Contrary to this Lockean view, Leibniz suggests that uneasiness is nothing but a small, imperceptible pain, which is, at worst, a matter of indifference for us. We 'enjoy the advantage of evil without enduring its inconveniences', and:

[O]ur continual victory over these semi-sufferings—a victory we feel when we follow our desires and somehow satisfy this or that appetite or itch—provides us with many semi-pleasures; and the continuation and accumulation of these (as with the continuing thrust of a heavy body gaining impetus as it falls) eventually becomes a whole, genuine pleasure. In fact, without these semi-sufferings there would be no pleasure at all, nor any way of being aware that something is helping and relieving us by removing obstacles which stand between us and our ease. This also exhibits that affinity of pleasure with suffering which Socrates comments on in Plato's *Phaedo* [606c], when his feet are itching.   (LRB 165)

Therefore, the fundamental structure of the Leibnizean soul consists in an infinity of small, confused perceptions directing an infinity of imperceptible endeavours, which, on the one hand, become condensed into various desires and, on the other hand, accumulate to become perceptible pains and pleasures.

This raises the question, important to seventeenth-century theologians and philosophers, whether love of God should be considered a passion, and if so, whether it is intrinsically confused. The most promising way for a philosopher to approach God, according to Leibniz, is by increasing their knowledge of His attributes, which leads us inevitably to an ever increasing love of Him as the most perfect thing. Accordingly, it is not plausible to think of the love of God as a passion coming from a confused perception. Even a superficial analysis leads us to the supposition of a twofold concept of love: one is a passion, defined by the lack of knowledge; the other is an action, defined by the increase and plenitude of knowledge. This latter conception is remarkably close to the Spinozan conception of an *active affect* originating from an adequate idea.

## II: The systematic character
## of theories of passions

Descartes advocated the bifurcated method of analysis and synthesis. Amongst the complex phenomena he proposed to analyse into their constituents were the phenomenally experienced emotions—for example, the ones mentioned in the correspondence with Princess Elisabeth, which was the starting point (together with the *Passions of the Soul*) for Descartes' elaboration of a theory of emotional experience. For this method to work, there must be a point where the analysis of the original data comes to its end, and the synthesis, which is the re-composition of the analysed data, can proceed. The general definition of passion may be accepted as such a philosophical turning point, which leads from the analysis to the synthesis of the passions. 'After having considered in what respects the passions of the soul differ from all its other thoughts, it seems to me that we may define them generally as those perceptions, sensations or emotions of the soul which we refer particularly to it, and which are caused, maintained and strengthened by some movement of the spirits' (AT XI 349; CSM 1 338).

The whole first part of the *Passions* is condensed in this definition: the 'spirits' are the fine bodies that mediate all the body's actions on the soul. Descartes uses extremely strong words here—causation, maintenance, strengthening—in order to stress the importance of the bodily component of any passions. Even in the extreme case of the love of God, which is an *émotion intérieure*, an emotion close to an active affect in Spinoza's sense, Descartes is anxiously looking for a way to assure the reader of the bodily ingredients of this emotion. But the most important feature of a passionate human being is the phenomenally evident capacity of the mind to interfere with the natural default settings of the inner bodily mechanisms that let the whole body function in the same way that beast-machines or other machines operate. Descartes' official explication for the 'hardware' of this interference involves the artifice of an extremely fine thread keeping the so-called pineal gland in balance, and enabling the soul to influence some of the bodily reactions to the bodily stimuli, that is, to re-arrange those original connections that nature set between sense perception and action (or at least some of them). However, the question of the software remains to be asked, namely: what authorizes the human mind to change the nature-God-given settings, and in which way, to what aim, should this intervention take place? (Boros 2005.) Where the first question is concerned, it is obviously God who authorizes the mind to alter the initial settings during a human being's lifetime. Second, the aim is one that God himself set up; although we cannot know the purposes of God, according to Descartes, one can say that it is most probably the good, the well-being of the mind–body composite. Here there is an obvious parallel with the theory of knowledge of the *Meditations*:

the human propensities to factual and moral error have no explanation, but they do have remedies.

The passions are, moreover, divine reminders, as it were, that a human being is a unity of mind and body instead of a juxtaposition of them. Neither the good of the body nor that of the mind is to be considered and pursued as the main aim of human life, but that of the composite, the real unity of the two. From this perspective, the passions are all good, because they fulfil this principal task, teaching us to consider ourselves as composite and unified beings. As Descartes puts it at the end of the *Passions*:

> Now that we are acquainted with all the passions, we have much less reason for anxiety about them than we had before. For we see that they are all by nature good, and that we have nothing to avoid but their misuse or their excess, against which the remedies I have explained might be sufficient, ... For the rest, the soul can have pleasures of its own. But the pleasures common to it and the body depend entirely on the passions, so that persons whom the passions can move most deeply are capable of enjoying the sweetest pleasures of this life. It is true that they may also experience the most bitterness when they do not know how to put these passions to good use and when fortune works against them. But the chief use of wisdom lies in its teaching us to be masters of our passions and to control them with such skill that the evils which they cause are quite bearable, and even become a source of joy.   (AT XI 485–8; CSM 1 403–4)

Descartes assuredly does not despise the passions, and neither Hobbes, nor Spinoza, nor Leibniz praises an ascetic ideal in the Stoic or the Christian sense. However weak Descartes' foundation (i.e. the theory of 'animal spirits') might seem in the light of the discoveries of modern neurosciences, it is indisputable that he laid the basis for the methodological self-understanding of all modern sciences of the brain. It was he who broke consciously with moral-theological, that is negatively evaluating, approaches of the past, which he accomplished by introducing the ideal of value-neutral inquiry. He makes clear, in the short letter preceding the *Passions*, what his intention was when compiling it: 'I have changed nothing in the style, whose simplicity and brevity will reveal that my intention was to explain the passions only as a natural philosopher [*en physicien*], and not as a rhetorician or even as a moral philosopher' (AT XI 326; CSM 1 327).

Spinoza shares this Cartesian ideal of a value-neutral inquiry, even if his own methodological ideal is slightly different. In the preface to the third book of his *Ethics*, he sums up the methodology of the subsequent treatment of affects as follows.

> For now I wish to return to those who prefer to curse or laugh at the Affects and actions of men, rather than understand them. To them it will doubtless seem strange that I should undertake to treat men's vices and absurdities in the Geometric style, and that I should wish to demonstrate by certain reasoning things which are contrary to reason, and which they proclaim to be empty, absurd, and horrible ...

The Affects, therefore, of hate, anger, envy, etc., considered in themselves, follow from the same necessity and force of nature as the other singular things. And therefore they acknowledge certain causes, through which they are understood, and have certain properties, as worthy of our knowledge as the properties of any other thing, by the mere contemplation of which we are pleased. Therefore, I shall treat the nature and powers of the Affects, and the power of the Mind over them, by the same Method by which, in the preceding parts, I treated God and the Mind, and I shall consider human actions and appetites just as if it were a Question of lines, planes, and bodies.   (SC 492)

This quotation shows that there is an important difference between the Cartesian theory, modelled on physics, and the Spinozan theory, modelled on geometry, notwithstanding their shared view on the value of an objective philosophical-scientific inquiry into the emotions. This difference is also evident in their divergence about the relation of mind and body. Geometry does not call for some tiny bit of extended stuff, the pineal gland, to be involved in the explanation of a mysterious connection between thinking and extension. For the philosopher who proceeds *more geometrico* looks at the difference between thinking and extension as existing on the level of attributes, not on the level of substance. Mind and body have their identities and differences, and no special tools are needed to explain how they can go hand in hand.

Descartes, Hobbes, and Spinoza, nevertheless share the ideal of an inquiry free from traditional values and assumptions. They try to establish the new moral ideal of a reason-based dwelling in the world, where reason-regulated passions, affects, play a decisive role. We have seen Descartes' final judgement on the passions' sweetest pleasures. Hobbes lets the passion of fear move people to join together and establish the state in a rational manner, whereas Spinoza makes an even greater and more extended use of the passions and the affects induced or transformed in us by reason or intellect. Before examining the role of the passions in social and political life, I need to comment on the systematic features of their respective theories of emotion and their relationship to a geometrical-Ramistic ideal of classification.

Descartes, Hobbes, and Spinoza were devout admirers of the *Elements* of Euclid. Each of them tried to shape his system of emotions following the Euclidean model combined with the Ramistic ideal of bi-partition. Each begins with a set of elementary passions or affects, in order to construe all the derivative ones on the basis of the primitives. Descartes enumerates six such passions, wonder, desire, joy, sadness, love, and hatred, whereas the systems of Hobbes and Spinoza have a more 'elementary' character. Both acknowledge only three basic affects—endeavour, desire, and aversion in Hobbes; and, in Spinoza, desire, joy, and sadness. Both Hobbesian endeavour and Spinozean desire have a special role to play: they accompany all the derivative affects of desire and aversion, respectively joy and sadness.

Evidently, bi-partition is not only the consequence of Ramus's influential teaching method; it also represents the philosophical transposition of an everyday partition of all emotions into positive and negative types. In general, an emotion arises when a person perceives an event as relevant concerning something salient for her. The emotion is positive if the event favours a positively valued thing, negative if it hinders its realization. Although Descartes introduces wonder and desire, which do not have pair-emotions, he enumerates two pairs of positive-negative emotions: joy and sadness, love and hatred. Hobbes's scheme in the *Leviathan* (Chapter 6) is already clearly structured by only one pair of positive-negative emotions; as we have seen, he emphasizes the small beginnings of voluntary motions that follow upon the fancy of an object or event retained in what he terms the 'imagination'. So voluntary motions are elicited by a memory trace of an event that we deem to further or to hinder the realization of what we think is salient for us.

In Spinoza's carefully constructed introduction to the theory of affects, desire is regarded as the general motivational force behind all emotions. Afterwards, Spinoza differentiates between joy and sadness, positive and negative emotional desires. They are, as it were, the genera of all the emotions, and it is in them that elementary consciousness of both ourselves and the objects affecting us get articulated.[5] Although Spinoza refuses to follow Descartes by assigning a distinguished position to wonder (which is a state of mind that he does not respect and considers theologically pernicious), he does connect the affects to wonder in the Scholium to Prop. 52 of Part 3 (while denying that wonder is itself an affect).

The composition of the theory of affects in Spinoza's *Ethics* is very sophisticated. It does not follow the scheme of only one line of bipartition. The very first bipartition, that of passion and action under the general concept of affect, is followed by a second distinction within passions: joy and sadness are distinguished, though not symmetrically: sadness is more common—given the whole of nature's overwhelming potency-in-act. Nevertheless, joy is conducive to active affects, and even a passive joy is more useful than sadness, which cannot but be passive. The active affects, based on adequate knowledge and conceived as 'strength of character', have their own bipartition: one sort relates to the good of the individual, the other to that of fellow human beings.

All actions that follow from affects related to the Mind insofar as it understands I relate to Strength of character, which I divide into Tenacity and Nobility (*generositas*). For by Tenacity I understand the Desire by which each one strives, solely from the dictate of reason, to preserve his being. By Nobility I understand the Desire by which each one strives, solely from the dictate of reason, to aid other men and join them to him in friendship.   (SC 529)

I will return later to the importance of nobility (*generositas*) for Spinoza's philosophy as a whole and its relation to Descartes' most positive passion, the virtue he terms *generosité*.

---

[5] See the definitions and explications of desire in *The Ethics* (Book 3, Prop. 9), as well as the first of the Definitions of Affects.

The most important Spinozan distinction within the whole realm of affects is between the 'objective' and the 'imitative' affects, which possibly follows a hint of Descartes' and prepares the ground for Hume's concept of sympathy (Moreau 2006). The objective affects are aroused when their proper objects crop up and influence the individual in their proper way. The class of the imitative affects, which are aroused by what might be called 'improper objects', is itself bifurcated. These affects can be elicited on the basis of similarity. Both the similarity to the object of an earlier—objective or imitative—affect and the similarity to an individual having a certain affect can elicit in us an affect whose proper object does not influence us on the spot. Prop. 16 of Book 3 lays the groundwork: 'From the mere fact that we imagine a thing to have some likeness to an object that usually affects the Mind with Joy or Sadness, we love it or hate it, even though that in which the thing is like the object is not the efficient cause of these affects' (SC 503). This discovery helps Spinoza to explain the familiar *odi et amo* experience, which he does in the following proposition. But more to the present point is his claim in Prop. 27 of Part 3: 'If we imagine a thing like us, toward which we have had no affect, to be affected with some affect, we are thereby affected with a like affect' (SC 508).

With this proposition, a new subsystem of other-directedness begins to unfold. The imitation of the affects of another involves only a minimum of cognitive activity: at this level, it corresponds to the everyday idea of natural empathy. The next level is reached in the propositions 21 to 24, dedicated to the transfer of affects. On this level we are already 'tuned up' emotionally: we love or hate a thing according to its effects on other things we antecedently love or hate. 'He who imagines what he loves to be affected with Joy or Sadness will also be affected with Joy or Sadness; and each of those affects will be greater or lesser in the lover as they are greater or lesser in the thing loved' (Prop. 21).

Spinoza complicates this subsystem once again when he mentions that, when someone hates someone else, she finds joy in the other's grief. This is a disturbing conclusion since, ethically speaking, hatred and misfortune should not be a cause of joy. Spinoza deals with this difficulty by reminding the reader that 'this Joy can hardly be enduring and without any conflict of mind. For (as I shall show immediately in P27), insofar as one imagines a thing like oneself to be affected with an affect of Sadness, one must be saddened. And the opposite, if one imagines the same thing to be affected with Joy' (SC 507). After the first level of emotional experience as a response to good or bad events in one's own life, and the second level of emotional experience as a response to good or bad events in the lives of others with whom one has some emotional relationship, a third level comes into play. Here, there is no concession made to the inevitably passive affect of hatred evolving from inadequate ideas. Even if we are afflicted by some wrong on the part of another, the hate that arises from this is 'to be conquered by love, or generosity, not by repaying it with Hate in return'.

Locke and Leibniz attend to the classification of the emotions in Book 2, Ch. 20 of the *Essay*, and in the corresponding passages in the *New Essays*. Locke's general standpoint is interesting enough in so far as he reduces to the minimum the cognitive component in the concept of a passion. Being an idea, the passion is in the mind. But it is there neither as a concept nor as a judgement. Rather than desire and aversion, or joy and sorrow, the concepts of pleasure and pain organize the general bifurcation of the passions. They cannot be described or their names defined, since they are simple ideas of sensation that are grasped through experience. At first, the notions of good and bad are grasped in connection with pleasure and pain, and this gives a slightly hedonistic flavour to Locke's ethics. However, since, according to Locke, the basics of a successful human life are unalterably given by God, the highest good, the hedonistic concept of good and bad is not normative but only descriptive-phenomenological.

From the systematic point of view, we may miss in Locke that concept which plays such an important role in the systematic accounts of Hobbes and Spinoza, namely *conatus* in the guise of endeavour or desire. However, Locke did feel the need to introduce a general motivational concept into the framework of his theory of passion too, for one of his most famous concepts, that of *uneasiness*, whose function in human life is explored at length in Book 2, Ch. 21, fulfils precisely this task. 'The uneasiness a man finds in himself upon the absence of anything, whose present enjoyment carries the idea of delight with it, is that we call desire . . . the chief, if not only spur to human industry and action, is uneasiness' (*Essay* II. xx. 6). Superficially, Book 2, Ch. 20 of the *Essay* does not seem to be very systematic in form. However, when Locke speaks about love and hatred, it becomes evident that he intended to provide systematic outlines for a theory of the passions. First, he gives a definition tightly connected to those 'hinges on which our passions turn', that is, the simple ideas of pleasure and pain. 'The thought he has of the delight, which any present or absent thing is apt to produce in him, is the idea we call love, [and] . . . the thought of the pain, which anything present or absent is apt to produce in us, is what we call hatred' (*Essay* II. xx. 4–5). Next, Locke gives us a hint of the general direction of the seventeenth-century philosophical concept of love that I address later.

Were it my business here to enquire any farther than into the bare ideas of our passions, as they depend on different modifications of pleasure and pain, I should remark, that our love and hatred of inanimate insensible beings, is commonly founded on that pleasure and pain which we receive from their use and application any way to our senses, though with their destruction: But hatred or love, to beings capable of happiness or misery, is often the uneasiness or delight, which we find in ourselves arising from a consideration of their very being or happiness. Thus the being and welfare of a man's children or friends, producing constant delight in him, he is said constantly to love them. (*Essay* II. xx. 5)

# III. THEOLOGICO-PHILOSOPHICAL APPROACHES
## TO THE EMOTIONS

The last decades of the seventeenth century witnessed a remarkable change of outlook, when more rather than fewer theological elements were introduced into philosophical theorizing than had been the case. Earlier in the century, there had been a lively debate on the properly Christian form of love, beginning with the publication of the *Traité de l'amour de Dieu* of François de Sales in 1615. Largely neglected by philosophers for the first two-thirds of the century, it came to attention again towards the end of the century when philosophy began to be permeated by theological questions in the writings of Malebranche, Leibniz, John Norris, Damaris Masham, and others.

It was Nicolas Malebranche, the Catholic friar, who produced the first significant philosophical contribution to the theological debate on *amour pur*, which was taking place between, among others, François de Salignac de la Mothe Fénelon, who maintained that one must love God disinterestedly without fear of punishment or hope for reward, and the authoritarian Jacques Bossuet. Malebranche tried to find a middle course in his own *Traité de l'amour de Dieu* between a sort of egoistic self-concerned love and a pure love that excluded all consideration of the lover's own interest. John Norris took over Malebranche's main theses, both those that pertained to philosophy in general and those that were specifically devoted to love, while Lady Masham, daughter of the English Platonist Ralph Cudworth, a friend and pupil of Locke, contested them in a book based on both biblical-theological and philosophical arguments.

Like Descartes and Spinoza before him, Malebranche grounded his theory of the passions in something not yet really passionate; Descartes had chosen wonder, and Spinoza had opted for desire. Malebranche claimed that God implanted in human beings a fundamental inclination toward Himself, which was the real happiness of the human being. 'Thus God unceasingly imprints in us a love like His own...' (MLO 267). In a world not corrupted by the Fall, this general inclination would occupy the place of the passions of the actual (corrupted) world, playing a somewhat similar, although theologically-based, role to that of the active affects in Spinoza. At the same time, due to an inclination toward the highest or general good that is not clearly understood, we start desiring and looking for particular finite goods that are mistakenly identified with the infinite real good. Taken in this role, the inclination resembles rather the Spinozan concept of desire, a sort of guided action-readiness. '... He also provides us with all those natural inclinations that do not depend on our choice, and that necessarily dispose us toward preserving our own being and the being of those with whom we live... if God... did not continuously impress upon man's soul a love like His own... we would will nothing, and as a result, we would be without a will' (MLO 267, 337). It is in this sense that Malebranche stresses the essential (if hidden) dependence of the passions (i.e. sensible emotions) on the natural inclinations, even if the definition and the treatment of the passions cannot but be based on the post-lapsarian dependence of men on the body: 'Only because God loves Himself do we love anything, and if God did not love Himself, or if He did not continuously impress upon man's soul a love like His own, i.e., the impulse of love that we feel toward the good in general, we would love nothing, we would will nothing, and as a result, we would be without a will . . .' (MLO 337).

Thus Malebranche's perspective is basically Augustinian. This becomes evident when we consider his deep suspicion of the role of the passions in human life. Norris accepted both Malebranche's occasionalist claim that God is the sole real cause in the universe, and the connected claim that His love—in the double sense of this love being *His* love, and a love *toward Himself*—is the only real and legitimate love. He concluded that, since we cannot love God with the love of benevolence, given His perfect being, we must love him with the love of desire; second, created things do not deserve to be loved with our love as desire. Masham's arguments in her *A Discourse concerning the Love of God* defend Locke's account of the love of creatures, and she claims that a philosophy supported by the Catholic dogmas cannot prove to be useful for Protestant thinkers. But she also argues philosophically that Malebranche is wrong when he assumes that God is the only real cause of everything, and that we cannot see things except through Him. She uses also her own interpretation of the main Bible citations concerning love against the cleric-philosopher Norris.

## IV: LOVE AS A COUNTERWEIGHT TO SOLIPSISM

The passion or affect of love was also seen by early modern philosophers as overcoming the threat of solipsism. Descartes had numbered love among the primary passions, and Spinoza too considered love to be the first affect after the primary ones. In his *Ethics*, the cognitive aspect dominated, whereas his *Theological-Political Treatise* considered 'love towards others' as part and parcel of the divine word ('reason' in Spinoza's vocabulary) imprinted in everybody's heart. But this later concept too remained a purely philosophical as opposed to a theological one. Even for the theology-oriented Leibniz, love as 'the charity of the wise'—as he defined justice—was a key philosophical concept, a combination of juristically rationalized Christianity and Platonic philosophy that was aimed at the improvement of the living conditions of humankind.

Love and the benevolence assumed to flow from it were regarded as an important emotion by early modern authors precisely because, without it, the metaphysical character of their systems would have remained solipsistic or egoistic, as Hobbes's system appeared to be, much to his discredit. For those involved in its renewal in the seventeenth century, philosophy had a certain double tendency: first, exploring the characteristics of the ego, and its perpetuation; second, ascertaining the way out to other egos. The second tendency itself involved two moments: first, models had to be constructed for new institutions for directing individuals to as much human perfection as possible; second, the emotional basis for such institutions, that is emotional reasons why it would make sense for the individuals to join them and to keep company within them had to be discovered. In the early modern period, therefore, love played a crucial role in explaining how human societies and communities have come about, how they can continue functioning, and how they can be improved.

Descartes offered a general definition of love in Article 79 of the *Passions*: 'Love is an emotion of the soul caused by a movement of the spirits, which impels the soul to join itself willingly to objects that appear to be agreeable to it' (AT XI 387; CSM I 356). The definition is clearly modelled on the general definition of passions: the movement of the spirits causes, maintains, and strengthens also this passion of the soul. Descartes goes on to assign special names to the three possible combinations of the relation between lover and beloved:

We may, I think . . . distinguish kinds of love according to the esteem which we have for the object we love, as compared with ourselves. For when we have less esteem for it than for ourselves, we have only a simple affection for it; when we esteem it equally with ourselves, that is called 'friendship'; and when we have more esteem for it, our passion may be called 'devotion'. (AT XI 390; CSM 1 357)

In all three kinds of love-relation, 'we consider ourselves as joined and united to the thing loved, and so we are always ready to abandon the lesser part of the whole that we compose with it so as to preserve the other part' (ibid.).

There is much to say about the first two sorts of love. But the general point can best be highlighted by considering love *qua* devotion: 'In the case of devotion . . . we prefer the thing loved so strongly that we are not afraid to die in order to preserve it' (ibid.). 'We may also have devotion', Descartes remarks, 'for our sovereign, our country, our town, and even for a particular person when we have much more esteem for him than for ourselves. . . . We have often seen examples of such devotion in those who have exposed themselves to certain death in defence of their sovereign or their city, or sometimes even for particular persons to whom they were devoted' (ibid.).

The main effect of devotion is that the lesser part of the whole feels emotionally obliged to sacrifice itself for the good of the other entity. For Descartes, the most appropriate object of love *qua* devotion is God or our prince; in other words, this sort of love is eminently theological-political in character. God and the sovereign who leads and represents our political community are the two principal others to whom the metaphysical ego reaches towards. But we can find traces of the notion of a devotion to society in Descartes, which is closer to the idea of a new institution for a small number of chosen people—philosophers of the new type—than to that of a political community, namely, a society constituted by the kind of gratitude generous friends feel towards each other.

> I complain of the world being too big in relation to how few reliable people are to be found there; I would like them to come together and settle down in one town, and then it would be easy for me to leave my seclusion to go and live with them, in case they accepted me in their company. For although I escape from the multitude due to the usual impertinence, I continue thinking that the best thing in life is the joy we gain from the conversation with people we respect.   (Descartes 1989: 242; my translation)

This *civitas amicorum* (city of friends) anticipates the intellectual friendships of the later academies of sciences and arts. Leibniz, too, envisions such a gathering of the like-minded in his 1669 fragment on the *societas philadelphica*, which exists in two forms. One kind is established like a religious community *cohabitatione et quasi communione* (with cohabitation and almost communion), whereas the other is founded *connexione tantum* (A IV/1, 553), that is, without living together as in a monastery.[6]

The first move of Cartesian philosophy, keeping a distance from the opinions of others both in theoretical and in practical philosophy, does not therefore issue in a solipsistic withdrawal. On the contrary, the argument of the *Passions* for the thesis that 'generosity prevents us from having contempt for others' excludes any solipsistic or egoistic interpretation of Descartes' main ethical tenets. Descartes emphasizes that philosophical clarity and confidence preclude any feelings of personal superiority: 'Those who possess this knowledge and this feeling about themselves readily come to believe that any other person can have the same knowledge and feeling about himself, because this involves nothing which depends on someone else. That is why such people never have contempt for anyone' (AT XI 446; CSM 1 384). Descartes was convinced that 'the final fruit' of his true philosophical ethics would guarantee perfect solidarity among those who acquired it and that it could never get lost or corrupted in defiance of what might seem to follow from the inevitable metaphysical solitude of the *ego cogitans*. Because enlightened philosophers 'esteem nothing more highly than doing good to others and disregarding their own self-interest, they are always perfectly courteous, gracious and obliging to everyone' (AT XI 448; CSM 1 385).

In Spinoza, the fact that there is no good will either on the human or the divine level does not imply that generous people are not friendly to one another in the technical sense of the word, even if this friendship has no foundation in the inborn faculty of a free will, as in Descartes. The last propositions of the fourth part of the

---

[6] We know that for a while Descartes would have appreciated the continuous presence of friends like Isaac Beeckman or Claude Mydorge.

*Ethics*, about the 'free man', clearly state that liberty does not necessarily have to be founded on the freedom to dispose our volitions indifferently to cement human society. In Prop. 71, we find all the ingredients of a theory of generosity and gratitude, even if Spinoza does not employ the term *generositas* for this affect of the free men, in his claim that 'Only free men are very thankful to one another'. The demonstration tells us that: 'Only free men are very useful to one another, are joined to one another by the greatest necessity of friendship [*maxima amicitiae necessitudine*] (by P35 and P35C1), and strive to benefit one another with equal eagerness for love [*parique amoris studio*] (by P37)' (Spinoza 1985: 586). Civic affection thus implies reciprocity and equality in the relationship of free men. Spinoza refers to the first corollary of Prop. 35 of the fourth part, where he maintains that living under the guidance of reason makes people live harmoniously, that is, renders them the most useful for one another. Spinozan generosity does not, however, depend on a God endowed with good will, who invested us with benevolence similar to his own good will, and who at the same time established a domain in the universe where it is possible to act according to the free decisions of this good will.

# CONCLUSION

One of the trademarks of philosophy in the early modern period is the renewal of the theory of passions on the basis of the new mechanical-corpuscular philosophy, which Descartes regarded as his signal contribution to ethics. However, this is not a naturalistic renewal, either in the sense of being anti-metaphysical or in the sense of being morally nihilistic. What was at stake is rather the introduction of new, non-theological values for guiding both the individual and society in the novel social and political conditions of early modernity. This general thesis remains true even if, in the second half of the seventeenth century, the theological perspective on the passions once again became relevant for philosophical inquiries.[7]

## REFERENCES

BOROS, G. (2005). '*Dieu ou la nature*: Die Umkehrung des cartesianischen Naturbegriffs im Spätwerk Descartes', in T. Leinkauf and K. Hartbecke (eds), *Der Naturbegriff in der Frühen Neuzeit. Semantische Perspektiven zwischen 1500 und 1700*. Tübingen: Niemeyer.

[7] Research for this chapter was supported by the research project of OTKA 67798.

BOROS, G., MOORS, M. and DE DIJN, H. (eds) (2008). *The Concept of Love in the Seventeenth- and Eighteenth-Century Philosophy*. Budapest: Eötvös Kiadó/Leuven: Leuven University Press.

DESCARTES, R. (1649). *Les passions de l'âme*. Paris.

DESCARTES, R. (1989). *Correspondance avec Élisabeth et autres letters*. Paris: GF-Flammarion.

DILLER, H.-J. (2005). 'Affection, passion, feeling, stirring: Towards a pre-history of the category "emotion"', in P. Michel (ed.), *Unmitte(i)lbarkeit: Gestaltungen und Lesbarkeit von Emotionen*. Zürich: PANO Verlag.

GUENANCIA, P. (2000). *Lire Descartes*. Paris: Gallimard.

HOFFMANN, P. (1986). 'The unity of Descartes' man'. *The Philosophical Review*, 95: 339–70.

JAMES, S. (1997). *Passion and Action. The Emotions in Seventeenth-Century Philosophy*. Oxford: Clarendon.

LEIBNIZ, G. (1765). *Nouveaux essais sur l'entendement humain*. Ed. R. E. Raspe. Amsterdam and Leipzig.

LEIBNIZ, G. (1966). *Theodicy*. Trans. E. M. Huggard. Ontario: Dent.

MASHAM, D. C. (1696). *A Discourse concerning the Love of God*. London.

MONTAIGNE, M. DE (1969). *Essais*. Paris: Garnier-Flammarion.

MOREAU, P.-F. (2006). 'Spinoza et les problèmes des passions', in P.-F. Moreau (ed.), *Les passions à l'âge classique*. Paris: Presses Universitaires de France, 147–58.

SPINOZA, B. DE (1677). *Ethica more geometrico demonstrata*, in *Opera posthuma*. Amsterdam.

SHAPIRO, L. (2003). 'The Structure of the Passions of the Soul', in A. Gombay and B. Williston (eds), *Passion and Virtue in Descartes*. Buffalo: Prometheus/Humanity Books, 31–79.

WILSON, C. (2008a). 'The Theory and Regulation of Love in 17th Century Philosophy', in G. Boros, M. Moors and H. De Dijn, (eds), *The Concept of Love in the Seventeenth- and Eighteenth-Century Philosophy*. Budapest: Eötvös Kiadó/Leuven: Leuven University Press, 63–79.

WILSON, C. (2008b). *Epicureanism at the Origins of Modernity*. Oxford: Clarendon Press.

# CHAPTER 10

# AESTHETICS

## ALEXANDER RUEGER

ALTHOUGH it was only after Baumgarten's writings, from 1735 on, that the discipline of aesthetics was gradually recognized under this name (1954: 78; 1988: 3), its origins are usually dated to the years around 1700. With authors like Joseph Addison, who has been credited with undertaking 'the first effort . . . to build up a real aesthetic' (Monk 1935: 57; Stolniz 1961: 187f.), aesthetic experiences—the 'pleasures of the imagination'—were clearly separated from other pleasurable experiences, in particular, from the 'pleasures of the understanding'. The delightful experience of an object for its own sake, unrelated to the achievement of further goals like instruction, came to characterize a distinct mode of apprehension; early aesthetic theorists did not restrict their attention to the experience of beauty but also considered delight in the sublime, in novelty, and sometimes in the horrible. These various occasions for enjoying the pleasures of the imagination highlight the focus on a special sort of experience, which is not strictly defined through its object.

The early modern literature on the arts before 1700, by contrast, does not seem to focus on a special sort of delight. Neither in theory nor in practice was there a conscious distinction between the pleasure provided by what would later be called the fine arts and the delight experienced in the products of other arts, for example, in the ingenious products of mechanics or the natural curiosities displayed, along with art works, in the *Wunderkammern* of the Baroque era. Gentlemen travellers like John Evelyn inspected ancient monuments and sculptures, Renaissance paintings, and Baroque churches, and described their reactions in terms that did not differ from those they used when visiting collections of rare coins or unusually shaped rocks. If there was a characteristic common to these responses, it would be the emotion of wonder, admiration, or astonishment, as in Evelyn's use of words such as 'admirable' or 'stupendous' to report experiences on his visit to Florence (1955: II, 186–200). Wonder, the response to the novel or marvellous, indeed played a prominent role in art theoretical debates of the period. Theories of the arts in the seventeenth century were concerned with efficient ways of stimulating and managing various passions in the audience, drawing on the rich corpus of theories that ancient and Renaissance rhetoric provided on this topic. This rhetorical framework is visible as the background of debates in art theory throughout the seventeenth century. In considerations of the causes and the control of the passions the interests of art theorists and philosophers met—much more so than in speculations about the nature of beauty, which remained very much in the background during the early modern period. All parties, philosophers, artists, and art theorists, drew on the same resources for this topic, the treatises on rhetoric.

The debates in art theory centred on questions of the legitimacy of artistic innovations in style and genre, and were based on interpretations of the ancient texts of rhetoric and poetics. In the case of painting, there was an emphasis on efforts to reconstruct guidelines for painters from ancient writers, in analogy with the poetic and rhetoric manuals; prominent artists like Rubens and Poussin actively involved themselves in this task. New literary genres like the romance (Ariosto, Tasso), the tragicomedy (Corneille), or the novel (Cervantes, Gracian), and forms that combined several arts (the emblem, opera) stimulated extended theoretical efforts to show, or reject, their claims to become incorporated into the classical canon.

This chapter discusses two themes from these debates. One is the discussion of the role of imagination, judgement, and taste which involved the art theorists in more general issues concerning the passions and their management. In this context, Platonic and Neoplatonic views on the imagination were attractive because they provided a strategy for raising the status of the artist, but such efforts also had to be carefully balanced against common suspicions against poetic fury and enthusiasm. The second theme is the debates about the marvellous in art as an especially effective means of stimulating the audience's passions, that is, its sense of wonder. Central to these discussions was the problem of distinguishing between legitimate and illegitimate uses and forms of wonder—a problem that has an almost exact parallel in the attempts of natural philosophers of the period to find an adequate attitude towards wonders in nature (Daston and Park 1998, chs. viii–ix; Kenseth 1991).

In showing the relevance of these two aspects for the development of aesthetics, one has to resist the temptation to impose on the early modern debates reconstructions of problems in terms that achieved their meaning only much later. The rhetorical background against which the debates were conducted therefore has to be kept in sight. This framework itself showed a Janus face in the transition to the next century: on the one hand, the setting did not encourage a theoretical focus on beauty or on a special sort of experience; on the other hand, the transformation of tensions and debates within the framework did lead to the new focus on 'aesthetic experience'. Instrumental in this transformation was the increased interest in the sublime from the last quarter of the seventeenth century on. Initially conceived not as a contrast to but as an intensification of beauty, the sublime emerged out of the debates about the legitimacy of wonder as the respectable form of the marvellous in art.

# I: THE QUESTION OF AESTHETICS PRIOR
## TO THE EIGHTEENTH CENTURY

Tatarkiewicz (1974: xvii) summarizes the view that, between antiquity and the beginning of the eighteenth century, there was in aesthetics 'nothing more than one great gap'. How is the apparent lack of interest in philosophical analyses of beauty and the absence of the subject matter of aesthetics in the seventeenth century to be explained? According to a widely accepted account of the phenomenon by Kristeller (1965), aesthetics as an identifiable area of philosophical discussion could only be established once the 'fine arts', the primary concern of the new discipline, had been separated as a distinct group of practices from the rest of the traditional 'arts'. Only when poetry, painting, sculpture, music, and architecture were recognized as fundamentally different from, say, the 'arts' of optics, mechanics, or astronomy, did a new subject matter arise, which was unified by the aim of producing beauty. This process of differentiation, Kristeller claimed, was completed only in the mid-eighteenth century; therefore, an aesthetics in the customary sense could not exist prior to this time. The main role in this development, he argued, was played by the extended 'Battle of the Ancients and the Moderns' which, although much older, entered an especially lively phase in France in the 1680s and had repercussions all over the rest of Europe. In the course of the *Querelle des anciens et des modernes*, it became clear to all parties that, with respect to certain arts, the Moderns could demonstrate progress over the state these arts had reached in classical antiquity; with other arts, such demonstrations were much more controversial. The dividing line between clearly progressive arts and the rest fell between the sciences and mechanical arts on the one hand and the 'fine arts' on the other. Additional confirmation for Kristeller's claim for the significance of the *Querelle* comes from the fact that only in the eighteenth century did the Baroque cabinets of curiosities, the collections of specimens of *all* the arts and of nature, dissolve into separate museums for the 'fine arts' and scientific collections (Bredekamp 1993; Daston and Park 1998).

Kristeller's thesis seems to make it plausible that an age that classified mechanics and poetry under the same title 'art' could not have thought about beauty and the fine arts in the same way as later authors did. Although this view has been contested (e.g. Halliwell 2002, 7 f., 289; Porter 2009), the fact remains that the *grand siècle* did not produce any treatises devoted to a philosophical analysis of beauty. Instead, we have a variety of discussions of separate arts, books with titles that are variations of *ars poetica*, treatises on painting, etc. Insofar as there is overlap between such treatments of the different arts, it does not stem from a common interest in beauty but from the framework that informs all these discussions—the framework of rhetoric as it had been developed from antiquity to the Renaissance. These 'theories of the arts', which are concerned with the nature, the causes, and the regulation of various emotions induced by different arts, are distinguished from a 'theory of beauty', which is interested in the nature of beauty without focusing on its manifestation in the arts (Panofksy 1968; Baeumler 1972). This distinction helps to capture the different perspective that the seventeenth-century theorists brought to issues which, with hindsight, one would expect to be discussed under the label 'aesthetics'. The fact that there was little attention to the theory of beauty during the period (Tocanne 1978: 325), and much emphasis on the work of art and its effects, appears as part of a tradition in which the metaphysical formulas for beauty—unity amidst variety, proportion, harmony, etc.—formed the more or less fixed background against which the theories of art developed. Unsurprisingly, the innovations in the process in which seventeenth-century rhetoric and art theory were transformed into eighteenth-century theories of 'aesthetic experience' came from investigations into the emotional effects of artworks. They included the move away from efforts to identify the efficient causes of aesthetic delight in objects, which had prevailed among the empiricist theorists.

## II: The rhetorical framework: ## rules, decorum, imitation

The modern, post-Kantian distinction between the tasks of rhetoric and those of aesthetics has been succinctly summarized by Hegel: the former is the art of speech for a 'practical final purpose' while the latter deals with the 'free poetic work of art' (1970: 261ff.). For the early modern period, however, works of art and of poetry in particular are not understood in terms of such freedom from purposes; on the contrary, poetry shares with rhetoric the final purpose of *persuading* the audience.[1] Given this general aim of persuasion, the art theorist designs adequate or optimal

---

[1] For basic concepts of rhetoric see Lausberg (1998), and the entries in Ueding *et al.* (1992–).

means for reaching it in the form of rules. Although the rules are, in the first place, aides for the orator or poet, they characterize at the same time the expected responses of the audience. From this basic structure it follows that what the author does cannot be regarded as a 'free, creative process', or an expression of subjectivity.

Jacopo Zabarella provides a typical classification of the sciences and arts along Aristotelian principles from the late sixteenth century (Edwards 1969), which shows how closely related rhetoric and poetry were in their tasks as well as in their instruments. In this classification, poetry and rhetoric are branches of logic. Like logic in general, poetry is not a proper science; it is not concerned with acquiring knowledge, which is rather the business of metaphysics, mathematics, the mechanical arts, and moral philosophy. Logic rather is an instrumental discipline, an *organon* for all proper sciences. Poetry falls under *logica specialis* where we learn not only how to apply the syllogism to gain necessary knowledge or merely probable knowledge but also, through rhetoric, how to use incomplete syllogisms (enthymemes) to achieve persuasion. As its specific form of argument, poetry uses 'incomplete induction', that is, *exempla*, for the same effect of persuasion. The audience should infer from one single case, the *exemplum* on the stage, to another, the recipient's own case, on the basis of similitude. This is how the Aristotelian characterization of tragedy as providing the 'imitation of an action' was understood: the poet presents an action on the stage so that the spectator can relate his own situation to it, *per analogiam*, and can recognize it as an *exemplum* of a general (moral) doctrine. Both rhetoric and poetry are thus directed at inducing action or moral improvement in the audience; therefore they are associated with the 'active sciences', with moral philosophy. Concerns about poetic language (*elocutio*)—the use of figures and tropes, etc.—are subsumed under the ways of making the *exemplum* evident and appealing to emotion.

The classification of poetry as a branch of logic, as an art of giving arguments of a specific kind, straightforwardly explains why there is no 'theory of beauty' in poetics or why such a theory would have nothing to do with poetics. A set of rules for applying a form of argument, a part of the *Organon*, cannot be expected to deal with the nature of beauty which would be found, perhaps, in metaphysics. Accordingly, the rules that figure in so much of the seventeenth-century discussion of art are not rules for producing or judging beauty but guidelines for bringing about an intended effect in the audience, viz., persuasion in its three modes, instruction, delight, and movement. In their evaluative role the rules allow for judgements about how well an author has succeeded in achieving this aim. The process can succeed only if the orator or poet takes into account the audience's opinions, expectations, and moral views. These views, therefore, have a significant role to play in determining the adequacy of the artistic means to the intended effect; *decorum*—the summary name for the rules—had to be observed by the successful poet.

Thus the most familiar requirements for poetic effect and for judging a work of literature, *vraisemblance* and *bienséance* in their French version, are motivated by the aim of poetry: the spectator can successfully relate to the *exemplum* only if what is presented in the work is believable (or probable or verisimilar), and if the general message and its way of presentation conforms to what is generally (socially and morally) accepted. The postulate of the unities of place, time, and action for tragedy, for example, could be justified by the requirement of *vraisemblance* because the action on stage should have a believable relation to the audience's actual experience of space and time during the performance; *bienséance* determined that certain ways of speaking (styles) are appropriate only for persons of certain social ranks, or for certain subject matters or genres. On the basis of these requirements, the notion of the 'imitation of nature', as has often been noticed, effectively reduced to observing *decorum*: if what is presented has to be probable, that is, believable to the audience, 'nature' cannot mean much more than what is believed by everybody, or by most, or by the wise (Patey 1984). If the latter interpretation of 'probability' is used, 'imitation of nature' becomes *imitatio veterum*, that is, the poet follows the example of the eminent ancient authors.

Many discussions of art in the seventeenth century focused on tensions that developed within the framework of *decorum*. The *Querelle du Cid* (1637 ff.), the *Querelle du merveilleux* (1657 ff), the *Querelle des anciens et des modernes* (1687 ff.), and the controversy over drawing and colour in the *Académie Royale de Peinture* (1673 ff.), were debates about the general question of whether certain artistic (or rhetorical) techniques that appeared to be effective, in the sense that they moved and delighted the audience, could be reconciled with the established rules of *decorum* (Weinberg 1961, for earlier Italian quarrels). These quarrels have a paradoxical structure because, on the one hand, *decorum* was supposed to ensure the intended effect on the audience, while, on the other hand, the techniques at issue seemed to achieve the effect but contradicted *decorum*. For example, if the marvellous in poetry—either in terms of *res* (marvellous events or figures) or in terms of *verba* (marvellous style)—was known to be especially effective in moving and delighting the audience, could it be allowed as a poetic technique when it also seemed, by definition, to violate the requirement of probability?

The marvellous in art, in poetry or painting, in subject matter or in style, aims at wonder or admiration. Arcimboldo's 'monstrous' paintings, epics and plays with supernatural interventions by devils or angels, Giambattista Marino's poems with their farfetched 'conceits' (metaphors) and 'witty' phrases, are examples of the kind of Baroque art that a growing critical consensus, usually labelled Neoclassicism, turned against. Early in the century, Marino himself was explicit that 'the poet's aim is the marvellous' and his task is to amaze the reader (Mirollo 1963: 116–20; 167–74). Guez de Balzac complained in 1639 about contemporary comedies in a way that would be echoed in the writings of later neoclassicist critics like Boileau, Rapin (1970a: 107), Racine (1960: 413 f.) or Dryden: 'One wanted embellished portraits, not those that resemble. . . . We saw on stage unnatural men, borrowed passions, and artificial actions'. Only the vulgar could delight in such plays: 'the crowd likes prodigies [the marvellous] and . . . comets receive more attention than the sun.' These illegitimately successful works did not 'stimulate the beautiful passions [*belles passions*] . . . [but] resemble the illusions of magic that astonish the imagination and satisfy only bad curiosity [*mauvaises curiositez*]' (Guez de Balzac 1971: ii, 509; 516 f.) All the listed defects were evidently violations of *decorum*.

Despite these attacks on the use of the marvellous as a means of instructing and delighting the audience, the Neoclassicists were aware that wonder was a necessary ingredient in art without which it would lose much of its effectiveness. Corneille (1987) had to fend off such criticisms, and he developed complex distinctions within the concept of *vraisemblance* in order to show that the marvellous could be combined with the probable and the imitation requirement. Such a balance of *decorum* with the marvellous was the standard neoclassicist prescription: 'The admirable is all that which is against the ordinary course of nature', said René Rapin, and the 'probable is whatever suits with common opinion.' But most poets, 'by [the] too great a passion they have to create admiration, take not sufficient care to temper it with probability' (Rapin 1970b: 288). This might make it sound as if a compromise was possible because one could take 'the ordinary course of nature' to be distinct from 'common opinion'. But the problem remained because, in order for the violation of the 'course of nature' to be admirable, 'common opinion' had to be aware of nature's regular behaviour, which could not be counted on.

Several strategies of dealing with the difficulty of tempering the marvellous with the probable were pursued. The notion of probability could be relativized: an event or an action that violates the ordinary course of nature could become probable if, as Rapin put it, an agent is introduced on account of 'whose power this change was possible' (1970b: 288). Common opinion is satisfied if the cause of the marvellous event itself is beyond the ordinary course of nature; an angel can do things that are impossible for human agents. Although Corneille himself had adopted this manoeuvre, it had already been pointed out by Tasso that it succeeds only for supernatural agents with a Christian pedigree in whose existence everybody had to believe; pagan deities, supernatural agents in the exemplary works of the ancient poets, could not be rescued in this way (Tasso 1973: 38f.). Alternatively, the notion of imitation, always closely linked to probability, could be modified in a Neoplatonic sense.

Again, Tasso had already employed this strategy when he claimed, against Plato's understanding of mimesis, that the poet should imitate not objects or actions in the empirical world but 'ideas' since these, in the Platonic view, have more reality than the empirical world. What exists, Tasso asked, 'the intelligible or the visible? Surely the intelligible, in the opinion of Plato too, who put visible things in the genus of non-being and only the intelligible in the genus of being. Thus the images of the angels that Dionysius [the pseudo-Aeropagite] describes are of existences more real than all things human' (1973: 32). While Tasso may have thought to develop a Platonic theme, the Neoclassicists developed a version of the same thought with a more Aristotelian flavour to justify poetic violations of what to common opinion *appears* to be the ordinary course of nature in the name of a higher truth. Imitating what is true (nature as it is or commonly thought to be) is, as the *Poetics* taught, not the aim of the poet because 'truth represents things only as they are, but probability renders them as they ought to be. Truth is wellnigh always defective by the mixture of particular conditions that compose it. Nothing is brought into the world that is not remote from the perfection of its idea from the very birth. Originals and models are to be searched for in probability and in the universal principles of things, where nothing that is material and singular enters to corrupt them' (Rapin 1970*b*: 288). The poet's imitation of 'the probable', understood in the sense of the 'idea' or 'original' of ordinary, corrupt nature, thus could well produce marvellous effects because the originals are not known to common opinion. The artwork could be marvellous by going against common opinion and still be probable in this modified sense.

But the compromise is deeply problematic. While probability at first, in Rapin's own definition, referred to common opinion, it now pointed to the world of ideas, an uncorrupted reality into which the poet has special insight. The traditional concept of *vraisemblance*, the accordance with the opinion of the audience, coexisted now with an in principle audience-independent notion that was claimed to be based on *raison* or nature. Anticipating Pope's later famous phrase, Rapin declared that the rules of poetry are 'made only to reduce nature into method, to trace it step by step, and not suffer the least mark of it to escape us'. These rules, the observation of *decorum*, maintain 'the verisimility in fictions...which is the soul of poesy... they are founded upon good sense and sound reason rather than on authority and example' (1970*b*: 284).

In later authors like John Dennis and the Abbé Dubos, who emphasized that art above all has to speak to the passions, the recourse to 'nature' rather than to the audience's opinion led to a further development of the notion of imitation. Probability, the result of imitation, was now defined by Dubos as the requirement that artworks have to 'produce an effect similar to that which would naturally arise from [what the artists] imitate ...' This applies to poetry and painting as well as to music and, in the latter case, allows the composer to 'imitate' sounds we have never heard—like 'the bellowing of the Earth when Pluto rushed forth from Hell'—by producing musical sounds that conform to our 'confused idea' of the unheard sounds 'by a relation to known sounds' (Dubos 1748: I, 370f.). Marvellous events which violate the order of nature can thus be rendered probable, in the new sense, and considered as products of imitation if their effects on the audience are, more or less vaguely, related to the effects of known phenomena. But the original tension reconstitutes itself in this new setting. On the one hand, authors like Dennis and Dubos insist that the audience's emotional response should be 'fair and just', and should be such that reason can approve of it, if only with hindsight (see Section IV).

However, the most intense effects of art come about when reason is suspended, when the effect is 'immediate': 'For the warmer the Imagination is', wrote Dennis, 'the less able we are to reflect, and consequently the things are more present to us of which we draw the Images; and therefore when the Imagination is so inflam'd, as to render the Soul utterly incapable of reflecting, there is no difference between the Images and the Things themselves' (1939: I, 363).

## III: Two models of delight

The tension within the rhetorical framework, or within the notion of *decorum* itself, the conflict between what is, empirically, most effective with the audience and what is required by *decorum* or reason, has been illustrated with the debates about the use of marvellous *res* and *verba*. In the philosophical tradition, the marvellous had been defined as that of which we do not know the causes (Cunningham 1976: 53 ff.). It stirs the noble passion of admiration (or wonder) and thus is closely connected with novelty, the principal cause of admiration. Feeling admiration is always pleasurable; as Descartes put it, admiration has no contrary (AT XI 373; CSM I 350). Following Aristotle, philosophers tried to justify this pleasure by linking it to the desire for knowledge, the wish to learn, which is aroused by the experience of the marvellous. These attempts, however, faced an objection that Aristotle himself already noticed: we seem to desire to know those things most intensely of which we can in principle not acquire much knowledge because they are too 'distant' from us and which we therefore admire most (Trimpi 1983: 97 ff.; Cunningham 1976, 70 ff.). Thus the pleasure we feel about the marvellous seemed to be connected with our lack of knowledge rather than with the beginning of an actual investigation into the causes of wonder. In 1701 Dennis characterized the issue succinctly when he defined 'the chief Thing' in superior poetry as 'Enthusia-stick Passion', and pointed out that this is 'a Passion . . . whose Cause is not compre-hended by us' (1939: I, 217).

This basic tension within the art theoretical discussions of the seventeenth century is reflected in two philosophical models of how delight in art is produced. The first model specifies that the feeling of delight is connected to an especially suitable, easy way of perceiving the object; I call this the *facilitation model*. It can be found, for instance, in Aquinas' doctrine that objects which are 'convenient' to the way we apprehend them stimulate delight; that is, the sensory impressions the objects make have to be proportioned to the specific sense that receives the impressions (Eco 1988: 93 f., 50 ff.). In the mid-sixteenth century, Cardano gave a version of the model: 'Truly, every sense especially enjoys things which are recognized; those recognized things are called consonance when heard, beauty when seen . . . Thus, whatever is commensurate is beautiful, and wont to delight' (cit. Reiss 1999: 514).

Such views about the proportion between objects and our senses and the convenience of apprehension were taken up in the seventeenth century, for example in Descartes' early *Compendium musicae* (1618). He argued that in order for one of our senses to experience delight, 'there is required a certain proportion of the object with its sense. . . . The object must be such that it does not befall sense too difficultly and confusedly' (AT X 91f.; Sepper 1996: 38–40). In the 1690s, Leibniz gave another account of aesthetic pleasure along the lines of the facilitation model. Delight, he said, is the sensation of a perfection, and music provides an illustration of the general thesis: we are delighted by the perfection, the order of the vibrations of a string, even though we don't clearly perceive this order (an 'invisible order'), as we often fail to do in other works of art. 'All order is purposive for the soul' and hence pleasurable—presumably because perceptions themselves are understood as a certain unity within a manifold, an order (Leibniz 1924: 492; cf. also 1915: ii. 21). In the facilitation model, the connection of pleasure with certain characteristics of the object is important since the model is oriented towards our ability to know an object, or at least to detect features of the object through sensation if not through understanding. Baumgarten's *Aesthetica* (1750) is the culmination of the facilitation approach: as '*scientia cognitionis sensitiva*', his theory has as its aim the 'perfection of sensate cognition as such', which perfection he calls beauty (1988: 2, 11).

The other model of response, the *stimulation model*, lacks this focus on cognition; in fact, it provides an account of pleasure that is virtually dissociated from the object. This model too can be illustrated by views Descartes held after he had become sceptical about his earlier facilitation model. In the 1630s he questioned whether there is a connection between musical consonances and the passions, and conjectured that all one could say about beauty is that it is what pleases most people (18. iii. 1630; AT I 132–4; CSMK 19f.). In the *Passions of the Soul*, he gave a very brief though influential account of aesthetic response (AT XI 399; CSM I 362), a view he had already expressed earlier to Princess Elizabeth: 'in general the soul is pleased to feel passions arise in itself no matter what they are, provided it remains in control of them' (6. x. 1645; AT IV 309; CSMK 270). Thus, the pleasure we experience from art is based on an agitation of the soul, a movement which, under the conditions specified, is necessarily pleasurable because the soul likes to be in motion rather than to be idle. The difference to the earlier facilitation model is obvious: the soul is delighted when moved, but there are no claims about the nature of the motion, that it be correlated with motions in other bodies. On the facilitation account, the mind is pleased because one of its highest interests has been satisfied, viz., to achieve cognition of the object; in the stimulation model, the pleasure is due to an interest of the soul in its own entertainment which consists in the relief from stasis or, as Dubos will later say, from boredom.

The remarks which Descartes made in the context of a discussion of the old problem of why we find pleasure in tragedy were brief and unspecific. But they were soon generalized by others or independently formulated. In 1674, Rapin seemed to refer to them when he explained that poetry 'labours to move the passions, all whose motions are delightful, because nothing is more sweet to the soul than agitation' (1970*b*: 281). For the Italian art theorist Emanuele Tesauro, humans, as opposed to animals and angels, have a natural tendency to develop 'a certain nausea for ordinary affairs, however beneficial they may be', from whence they crave stimulation by art, by ornament and 'novelty of style' in particular (1968: 122; cf. Montgomery 1992, 22 f.). In 1719, the most influential formulation of the stimulation account was presented by Dubos: 'one of the greatest wants of man is to have his mind incessantly occupied. The heaviness [*ennui*, boredom] which quickly attends the inactivity of the mind, is a situation so very disagreeable to man, that he frequently chuses to expose himself to the most painful exercises, rather than be troubled with it' (1748: I, 5).

The stimulation model allows, of course, for the combination of stimulation with instruction as another, or superior, aim of art. Likewise, it allows imitation among the instruments for achieving the intended effect, because imitation tends to produce probability, which may be needed for successful stimulation but the model does not in principle require it. Indeed, as shown in Section IV, the model can be applied to account for artworks that focus on admiration, the marvellous, novelty—effects that tend to be generated when imitation and probability recede into the background.

What is the relation of the models to the rhetorical framework? The facilitation account, it would seem, could not be straightforwardly applied to works of poetry unless these were understood as generating delight merely by the sound of the words. But the requirements of the unity of action, time, and place, for instance, could be interpreted as means to make a play more convenient to grasp (cf. Dennis 1939: I, 57); and that the poet should give *evidentia* or *enargeia* to his descriptions so that they represent their subject matter vividly and 'place it before the eyes', was easily understood in terms of facilitation. These same rhetorical tools, of course, have their place in the stimulation account. But here the emphasis is not on *evidentia* as a verbal means to reach the *res* but instead as a tool for stimulating the passions of the audience.[2]

---

[2] The late seventeenth-century debate in the *Académie de peinture et de sculpture* over the comparative significance of colour (defended by the *Rubenistes*) and drawing (defended by the *Poussinistes*) illustrates a clash of the two models of delight. For the Rubenists, 'the rhetorical force of their paintings does not come from the way in which they represent passions [the Poussinists' facilitation view] but from the effectiveness with which they provoke them [the stimulation model]' (Lichtenstein 1993: 209).

# IV: IMAGINATION, JUDGEMENT, TASTE

Observing *decorum* on the part of the artist (but also on the part of the audience that is supposed to respond appropriately to the artwork) is, as we have seen, a balancing act between the requirements of believability and the stimulation of emotions. What enables the artist to perform such an act? By the end of the seventeenth century, there is a consensus that a peculiar combination of two faculties is necessary: the imagination or fancy, and judgement. The artist's work requires a division of labour between the operations of a faculty that is 'inventive' (in a sense to be clarified), that produces plots and images, and a faculty that is able to enforce the requirements of *vraisemblance* and *bienséance*. With eighteenth-century hindsight one is tempted to recognize here the cooperation between 'genius' and 'taste'. This view, however, distorts the seventeenth-century developments, in particular, the emergence of the notion of 'taste'.

The rhetorical tradition distinguished different stages in the poet's (and orator's) work as *inventio, dispositio*, and *elocutio*. The first of these meant the finding, the discovery, of themes and arguments (*res*) appropriate to the artist's aim of persuasion. This is an *intellectual* activity and has little to do with inventing or creating *images*. Furthermore, *inventio* is defined as finding true or probable *res*; there is no sense in which judgement decides, *after* the invention, about whether the themes are probable or not. It was only from the sixteenth century onwards that the intellectual business of invention became associated with the imagination or fancy. But even then, the task was still understood as 'finding' suitable items—'to recouer or resummon that which wee already knowe', as Bacon defines it—rather than as 'creating' them. Bacon compared invention to 'a Chase as well of Deere in an inclosed Parke, as in a Forrest at large' (2000: 111), an image still used by Dryden (1962: I, 98).

How did this change in the office of the imagination come about? (Patey 1984, 1997: 45; Bundy 1930; Rossky 1958). A plausible speculation seeks the cause in the Neoplatonic view of the poet that had been adopted, for instance, by the French *Pléiade* in the sixteenth century. Ronsard, the most famous representative of this movement, claimed in 1565 that '*inventio* is nothing but an inborn good power of imagination that takes in the ideas and forms of all imaginable things . . . in order to then represent, describe and imitate them' (1950: 999). While there was a traditional division of labour between the intellect, which finds the *res* in *inventio*, and the imagination, which represents them in images in *elocutio*, the Neoplatonic understanding of the poet as inspired by *furor poeticus* tends to see the two tasks together and attribute them to the imagination alone, the faculty that genuinely participates in the fury. What the Neoplatonist theoreticians call the imagination thus is an intuitive as well as intellectual capacity, a faculty that, while 'fantasizing', produces 'probable' representations. 'The fantasy', says Mazzoni in his defence of

Dante, 'is the power of the soul common to dreams *and* to poetic verisimilitude' (1971: 190; emphasis added).

When Puttenham and Sidney adopted features of this elevated view of the poet at the end of the sixteenth century, they were careful to distinguish the way imagination operates in the poet from pathological states like madness and fever; they indicated that imagination on its own, undistorted, is in accordance with the intellective power (Puttenham 1968: 15). Although it may not be clear to what extent Puttenham and Sidney, besides cautiously using Neoplatonic images to elevate the status of the poet, were committed to an intellective imagination in the artist, the next generation of theorists in England made a sharp distinction between imagination and judgement, and attributed a natural tendency towards distortion to the former. Bacon expressed such a view (2004: 91) and it found its canonical formulation in Hobbes. He separated fancy, the unruly but productive faculty, from judgement and claimed that wit, the talent needed for poetry, consists of a combination of the two with an emphasis on judgement: '[W]here wit is wanting, it is not fancy that is wanting, but discretion. Judgment therefore without fancy is wit, but fancy without judgment is not' (1946: 45). Fancy detects similarities or connections between things; hence it 'begets the ornaments of a Poem', while judgement discerns differences and thus 'begets the strength and structure' of a work (Hobbes 1908: 59). This distinction became standard in Locke (*Essay* II. xi. 2) and Dryden (1962: II, 244; cf. Ustick and Hudson 1935).

If the imagination is regarded as unreliable, as unruly, and hence as incapable of intellective functions on its own, it needs an instance that checks on it, that is, judgement. It is judgement that decides about the probability of the products of the imagination which, left to itself, would produce nonsense, monstrosities or, at best, indecorous marvels. The introduction of the concept of *taste* into debates about art in France since the mid-century responds to this separation of fancy and judgement. The origins of taste, in what is called its 'metaphorical sense' well into the eighteenth century, seem to lie in treatises about correct and prudent behaviour at court (Castiglione, Gracian). In this context, taste meant an ability to manage one's action and demeanour so as not to offend while still pursuing one's own interests, or, to use a rhetorical formula: an art that hides its own artfulness (cf. Frankowiak 1994). This social skill was both productive, in guiding behaviour, and receptive, in judging the appearance of others, in detecting perfection and flaws. The way the concept was used in discourses on art was strictly analogous; it played its main role as an instrument for condemning art that seemed 'in bad taste', art that somehow violated *decorum*. Medieval art was so judged and so was Baroque poetry in the style of Marino by the Neoclassicists.

But if judgement decided on the extent to which the poet's fancy remained in accordance with the rules of *decorum*, a special ability to judge, taste, might seem superfluous. Almost simultaneously with taste, however, a further famous notion appeared prominently in French discussions: the *je ne sais quoi*. Like taste, this concept had application far beyond art, that is, to social behaviour and appearance. With respect to this ineffable quality, taste reveals its rationale.

The *je ne sais quoi*, said Dominique Bouhours in the widely read *Entretiens d'Ariste et d'Eugène*, 'is a pleasing effect which animates beauty and other natural perfections... it is a charm and an air which blends with all actions and expressions [*paroles*]' (1962: 141). Its effect is immediate, it strikes us in the 'shortest possible moment' (143), and 'evades reason' and the control of our will (147). If we think we know why art pleases because we are familiar with the rules that connect features of the artwork with the effect in the audience, we are mistaken, explains Ariste. The great artists discovered 'that nothing pleases more in nature than that which does so without our knowing why' and they 'sought to make their works pleasing by concealing their art with great care and artifice' (148). The connection between work and effect thus becomes mysterious and the audience's response is ascribed to an 'occult quality', a term Bouhours himself uses. In the end, then, the *je ne sais quoi* re-describes the traditional definition of the wonderful: its effect is the pleasure whose cause we don't know. Judgement, understood as the ability to check whether *decorum* has been observed, cannot operate because the ineffable effect comes about, as it were, too quickly and without an identifiable cause.

This appears to be the problem to which the theorists responded by postulating taste, a kind of judgement that is appropriate to the *je ne sais quoi* because it matches the latter's immediacy and quickness. Taste is a judgement by instinct, not mediated by the deliberations of reason: 'Some people, when faced with a matter of judgment, always choose the right side by a kind of instinct, without knowing why. Such people display more taste than intelligence' (La Rochefoucault 2007: 214). Bouhours, in another of his dialogues from 1687, discussed approvingly a characterization of taste as 'a natural Sensation of the Soul... which is independent from all the Sciences that one can acquire... [I]in short the good Taste is the first Motion or a sort of Instinct of right Reason that draws it, with Rapidity, and who Conducts it more surely then all the Reasons it can make' (Bouhours 1705: ii, 106). Taste, then, is an intuitive judgement, a short-cut which comes to conclusions more quickly than reason or science but these conclusions are such that they can afterwards be ratified by reason.

This conviction that the judgement of taste can, in principle, be ratified by reason if given enough time, is important because it compensates for the unreliability of the imagination. Taste, in this understanding, fills the gap that has opened up once the imagination has lost its intellective quality: the gap between the immediacy of the aesthetic effect (on the imagination) and the slow workings of judgement. It is the same gap, under a different description, that separates cause and effect in the case of the *je ne sais quoi* where the cause cannot be identified anymore. When Addison opened the series of essays on the 'pleasures of the imagination' as an 'Account' of the notion of 'the fine Taste' (1965: III, 527), he characterized it according to the results of the French discussion; and Dubos, in his

*Reflections* of 1719 similarly understood taste as a judgement which has nothing to do with reason because it is immediate like a sense impression; only after the fact can we try to find reasons for why we judged in this way (1748: II, 238–49).[3]

As long as *decorum* is the generally accepted measure of judgements of art, the problem of a 'standard of taste', which exercised the eighteenth-century theorists, could not arise as a serious issue. Even the recognition of ineffable qualities of art did not change this situation as long as it was generally accepted that taste is an intuitive judgement that can, in principle, be ratified by reason. It seems nevertheless plausible that the introduction of 'occult causes' prepared, within the theory of art, the ground for Hume's problem, an issue that only became serious, he claimed, when a new 'species of Philosophy' separated ideas or sentiments from their external causes (Hume 1875: 268 f.).

It is tempting to connect these discussions of the ineffable in art with developments in rhetoric. The Port-Royal *Logic* (1662), though officially not concerned with rhetoric, made the important observation that a word often, 'in addition to the main idea which is considered its proper meaning . . . may prompt several other ideas—which may be called incidental [or accessory] ideas—without our realizing it.' A speaker's tone of voice, gestures, but also metaphors and figures of speech 'connect to our words countless ideas diversifying, changing . . . and augmenting their meaning, by joining to them the image of the speaker's emotions', thereby producing a more vivid impression in the audience's mind than plain speech (Arnauld and Nicole 1996: 66 f.). Of this mechanism we are not, or are barely, aware and its effects are so powerful precisely because it is concealed from us (cf. Carr 1990: 75 ff.). Although I am not aware of any attempts to employ this doctrine in discussions of the *je ne sais quoi*, it seems obvious that the theory of accessory ideas could have been used in this way. Indeed, a later theory which appears like a faint echo and a generalization of the Port-Royal view, has explicit links with the *je ne sais quoi*. Leibniz's doctrine of *petites perceptions*, which he worked out in the 1680s, claimed that our conscious perceptions are composed of innumerable other perceptions of which we are not, or are barely, aware—as is evident, he explained in an often repeated example, in the sound of the ocean which we are conscious of without ever becoming aware of the *petites perceptions* of the individual waves (e.g. Leibniz 1924: 182). He claimed, without further elaboration, that 'the *je ne sais quoi* and our taste' were based on such effects (Leibniz 1915: 11; cf. Barnouw 1993).

The same principle of saying much with few words underlies the notion of *délicatesse* which Bouhours employed. 'True delicacy', he explained, 'consists [in] not to say all upon certain subjects, but slide over, rather than dwell upon them; in one Word, to leave more to the Reader's Thoughts than we have said of them' (Bouhours 1705: i, 115). This idea of delicacy of taste, which expresses one of the

---

[3] Félibien's (2000: 220 f.) discussion of 'grace' in painting is another example of the *je ne sais quoi* (though the concept in art theory is much older).

various meanings the term 'simplicity' in art took on during the second half of the seventeenth century, points forward to one of the central notions in Baumgarten's aesthetics, the claim that poetic discourse is characterized by 'extensive clarity', that is, by clear but non-distinct representations that somehow 'represent more' than other (non-poetic) representations (1954: 43; cf. von Stein 1886: 86 ff.). But *délicatesse* is also connected with the early modern predilection for 'devices', emblems, and *impresa*, a form of art to which many prominent theorists contributed lengthy treatises (Klein 1979; Gombrich 1972). A device, one could say, is an intensified metaphor, because it combines two ingredients, the motto and the picture, each of which on their own may appear like metaphors but which achieve the intended meaning only in combination, in the interaction of picture and words. The enthusiasm for this art form united Baroque and at least some Neoclassicist authors, and indicates that the device was close to the heart of seventeenth-century aesthetic sensibility. In the *Entretiens* of 1671, Bouhours devoted considerable space to a discussion of devices and repeatedly referred to the work of Emanuele Tesauro which constituted, next to Gracian's writings, the most ambitious and comprehensive theory of Baroque art.

Tesauro, like Bouhours of Jesuit extraction, published the *Cannocchiale Aristotelico* in 1655 as a general theory of the arts. Artistic production, for Tesauro, was based on a faculty that unified intellect and imagination (*ingegno*). He found the nature of the work of art *in general* in metaphorical expression, and he characterized the response to art as *one* emotion, viz., admiration or wonder. The significance of this work consists in its Janus face: on the one hand it is often regarded as a *summa* of Baroque aesthetic sensibility—in this respect it was a target of Neoclassicist criticism; on the other hand, the *Cannocchiale*, with its emphasis on unification, anticipates later concerns with a special aesthetic experience, the characteristic response to the fine arts (Tatarkiewicz 1974: 391).

In Tesauro's view of the *ingegno*, the intellective imagination became significant again for a short time in the middle of the seventeenth century. This faculty of the mind combined the two functions that the common view, represented by Hobbes, kept clearly distinguished: *perspicacia* which 'probes the most remote and minute circumstances hidden within things' and *versabilità* which 'rapidly brings together all these circumstances, tentatively joining or dividing them' (Tesauro 1968: 82; cf. van Hook 1986: 28). Tesauro unhesitatingly compared the poet to God (1968: 82 f.), and one is tempted to find in his work a theory of creative genius in the eighteenth-century sense. But this is mistaken because the very aim of the work was to assist the poet in finding surprising metaphors, for example by providing long lists of items that can be combined into 'strange' conceits. The attraction of such conceits, for Tesauro, consisted in their effect on the audience: at first, the reader or viewer is deceived before she recognizes the deception, the artist's 'lie', and then responds with delight at the artist's ingenious deceit. The delight is thus based on the admiration of the artist's ability to give the false appearance of the true. That the *ingegno* becomes especially pertinent and visible when the audience's mind is engaged in apprehending the artfulness of 'lies' may seem perverted, as it did to Neoclassicist critics. But for Tesauro, the apparent perversion is based on the fact that the truth itself, the '*Ragioni vere*', is boring—'*senza novità, senz' acume*' (1968: 492)—and that what is to be represented here, the glory of the mind, cannot straightforwardly be presented in imitations of the truth.

All the arts, from poetry, painting, and dance to tournaments and masquerades, are based on metaphorical expression (Tesauro 1968: 731 ff.). While metaphors, from an Aristotelian point of view, can be incorporated into the tools that assist poetic imitation because finding metaphors requires the poet to recognize similarities between things, Tesauro's account emphasizes metaphors based on dissimilarities. He claimed that such *concordia discors* were especially effective because most surprising and hence admirable. The *Cannocchiale* therefore provides an especially clear instance of the stimulation model of aesthetic response. The emphasis on wonder, which neglects the various other emotions traditionally considered as effects of art, provides a unification of the arts because it ascribes one dominant aim to them.

## V: THE MARVELLOUS, THE SUBLIME, 'AESTHETIC EXPERIENCE'

The transformation of the marvellous, as a display of the artist's *ingegno*, into the basic principle of all art was offensive to the Neoclassicist critics of the later seventeenth and early eighteenth centuries; it was an example of the bad taste for 'turns of Wit and forced Conceits', 'this *Gothic* Taste', which Addison aimed to banish (1965: III, 530). Excessive lust for wonder and novelty was a defect, not a virtue, of which Descartes, though he described admiration as the first of the passions of the soul, as a 'disinterested' pleasure, had warned: when admiration turns into astonishment, it paralyses reason and blocks the progress to knowledge (AT XI 385 f.; CSM I 355 f.). This state of astonishment in the audience seemed to correspond to the poetic fury on the side of the author and was regarded with the same reservations. Tesauro, by contrast, had given an unrestricted, positive characterization of this state as the ultimate effect the artist should aim at. The Neoclassicist banishing of this bad taste, however, took on the form of a transformation of the marvellous into a legitimate artistic tool: the sublime.

As a special quality of poetic (and oratorical) discourse, the sublime had been characterized in the Hellenistic tract *On Sublimity*, attributed to (Pseudo-)Longinus, through its extraordinary effect on the audience: it 'produces ecstasy rather than persuasion in the hearer', said Longinus, 'and the combination of wonder and astonishment always proves superior to the merely persuasive and pleasant' (Longinus 1972: 462). Although French authors like Montaigne and Guez de Balzac were aware of this work, it was only with Nicolas Boileau's annotated translation, published as the *Traité du sublime* (1674), that the sublime turned into a main theme of literary discussion. Boileau included the *Traité* together with his *Art poétique* in the same volume—a decision that has caused some consternation. While the *Art poétique*, a versified poetics, is often regarded as the canonical expression of the Neoclassicist moderated stance towards the conditions of the poet and the response of the audience, the *Traité* appeared to break with Neoclassicist rules of *decorum* and emphasized poetic tools that aimed at audience responses that were suspicious: rapture, transport, elevation (e.g. Litman 1971: 70; Zelle 1995). And given the eighteenth-century development of the concept of the sublime, it certainly seems plausible that Boileau was, consciously or not, undermining the Neoclassicist position he supposedly articulated in the *Art poétique*.

For Boileau and his followers, however, the situation must have looked different (Borgerhoff 1950; Brody 1958; Cronk 2002). They understood and used the sublime as a weapon with which to defend the position of the Ancients in the *Querelle*: the special nature of the sublime experience, as well as its ancient pedigree in Longinus's treatise, seemed to predestine it as an example of good taste that was recognized at all times and that stood in no danger of being surpassed by modern achievements. As the title of Boileau's translation clearly indicated, it was a treatise on 'the marvellous in discourse' ('*du merveilleux dans le discours*') and should be understood as an attempt to transform the old concept of the marvellous, which had always been recognized as one of the most effective poetic tools, into a notion acceptable to Neoclassicist expectations about art. Boileau was far from making the marvellous the constitutive feature of poetry but, in the form of the sublime, he thought it could achieve especially intense effects which did not fall under the verdict against the vulgar, Baroque understanding of wonder. And the differences to the Baroque rhetorician's views were plainly visible: Boileau's sublime was explicitly distinguished from the traditional *genus sublime*, a style of writing rich in ornaments, and was, by contrast, introduced as a form of simplicity of discourse. By the sublime is not meant, Boileau explained, 'what Orators call the *Sublime Stile*, but something *extraordinary* and *marvellous* that strikes us in a Discourse and makes it elevate, ravish and transport us' (1972: 15). A favourite illustration of this *simplicité majestueuse* of the sublime, both in Longinus and in Boileau's comments, is the beginning of the book of Genesis, the *fiat lux*. If somebody were to deny the sublime in these words, Boileau claimed, 'we ought not to study for Reasons to demonstrate the contrary to him; but pity his Incapacity and want of Taste, which hinders him from feeling what every body is instantly sensible of' (1972: 62). Hence the significance of the sublime in literary debates: its appeal is universal and it works its effect without requiring 'reasons'.

What made the emotion of wonder, the response to the sublime, legitimate were the dignity of the object, the content of the sublime thought, and its expression, which was opposed to any bombast or superfluous ornament (and also, perhaps, the exemplary character of the poet). Both of these aspects, *res* and *verba*, however, can be called marvellous in the traditional sense. The object is wonderful because it is so elevated above our common knowledge that we do not quite grasp the cause of the effect it has on us. In Longinus' example, such an object is the infinite power of God, expressed in the *fiat lux*. From this unapproachable nature of the object it follows that its poetic representation will tend to be 'indirect', in the sense that the unachievable similarity between object and representation has to be substituted for by the adequacy of the effect of the representation to the status of the object (Trimpi 1983: 97 ff.; Shuger 1988). The simplicity of the sublime expression, the *verba*, is itself marvellous because it appears to stand in contrast to the intensity of the effect, a contrast that is especially vivid against the traditional understanding of the *genus sublime*. Remaining at a critical distance from the '*Messieurs du Sublime*', Bouhours maintained that 'the great and sublime are . . . not natural, nor can they be, for the Natural carries in it somewhat low, or less elevated' (1705: I, 156), a remark which illustrates how extraordinary Boileau's combination of the sublime with simplicity of expression must have been. Since simplicity was generally associated at the time with naturalness, he attempted to bring together what did not seem to go together: the marvellous and the natural.

This astonishing combination focused the art theoretic discussion on an experience of art as an extraordinary one, distinguished from the large variety of emotions that the rhetorical tradition was interested in. The experience of beauty, however, was included in this process of re-focusing. Although we are accustomed to separating beauty and sublimity because the latter is associated with the feeling of terror, this separation was not part of Boileau's programme, nor was it common in earlier discussions of the sublime in rhetoric (Shuger 1988: 190). Dennis, who first introduced the sublime into English literary discourse, did refer to terror but only, it seems, to characterize the sublime as an intensified experience of beauty; Dennis' 'sublime is simply the highest beauty, not a separate experience, different from one's perception of the beautiful' (Monk 1935: 54; Barnouw 1983). Addison, who has also been credited with distinguishing the beautiful from the sublime, praised Milton by showing 'how some passages are beautiful by being sublime' (1965: III, 392). Similar views can be found in theorists of painting (Richardson 2000: 409 f.; Ten Kate 2000: 411). Thus the sublime, in its early career, was clearly seen as intensified beauty. It was only Burke, in 1757, who established the separation of the notions that became canonical (Litman 1971: 241).

The close association of beauty and sublimity had a further important consequence. Given the necessary lack of resemblance and the emphasis on the intensity of the effect, it became conceivable that the delight in the sublime could be occasioned by poetic discourse that violated the traditional standards of beauty, harmony, order, and proportion. Longinus had mentioned Pindar's odes as examples of sublime writing, and the *Art poétique* traced their effect to a '*beau désordre*' of poetic discourse (Boileau 1966: 164). Although this was an isolated remark in Boileau, its consequences were considerable. That disorder could bring about aesthetic delight of a more intense quality than the pleasure we find in order may well have confirmed the suspicion that the ultimate causes of this delight in the objects are inscrutable, for both beauty and the sublime. It was central to Boileau's message that the sublime could not be defined in terms of its cause but only characterized through its effects: 'The Sublime is not properly a Thing to be prov'd and demonstrated; but...it is a certain Marvellousness which seizes us, strikes us, and makes it self be felt' (1972: 62). This was the reason, for Boileau as well as for Hume, why the 'test of time' had to play a central role in the theory of art; it is a criterion that looks only at effects. Dubos was similarly frank about his ignorance of the grounds for the efficacy of certain rules: 'It would be to no purpose to ask me the physical reasons for these fitnesses or agreements; I can allege none but the instinct which suggests them to us' (1748: I, 91 f.). And Addison officially excluded the search for efficient causes from his discussion of the pleasures of the imagination: '[W]e must own that it is impossible for us to assign the necessary Cause of this Pleasure...all that we can do...is to reflect on those Operations of the Soul that are most agreeable...without being able to trace out the several necessary and efficient Causes from whence the Pleasure or Displeasure arises' (1965: III, 544 f.).

The 'new way of ideas' was certainly in the background of Addison's and Dubos' views, but just as significant was the art theoretical discussion of aesthetic effects that are confusing because they can arise from objects that satisfy the traditional notions of order and symmetry *and* from objects that defy them, the '*beau désordre*'. Boileau's respectable marvellous set the stage for the eighteenth-century notion of a special aesthetic experience as well as for the problem of the standard of taste.[4]

REFERENCES

ADDISON, J. (1965). *The Spectator*. Ed. D. F. Bond. Vol. III. Oxford: Oxford University Press.
ARNAULD, A. and NICOLE, P. (1996). *Logic or the Art of Thinking*. Trans. J. Burocker. Cambridge: Cambridge University Press [1st edn. 1662].
BACON, F. (2000). *The Advancement of Learning*. Ed. M. Kiernan. [=*The Oxford Francis Bacon*, vol. IV]. Oxford University Press [1st edn. 1605].

---

[4]  Unless I quote from translated works, all translations are my own.

BACON, F. (2004). *The Instauratio Magna. Part 2: Novum Organum.* Ed. G. Rhees [= *The Oxford Francis Bacon*, vol. XI]. Oxford University Press [1st edn. 1620].

BAEUMLER, A. (1972). *Ästhetik.* Reprint Darmstadt: WBG [1st edn. 1934].

BARNOUW, J. (1983). 'The morality of the sublime: To John Dennis'. *Comparative Literature*, 35: 21–42.

BARNOUW, J. (1993). 'The Beginnings of "Aesthetics" and the Leibnizian Conception of Sensation', in P. Mattick (ed.), *Eighteenth-Century Aesthetics and the Reconstruction of Art.* Cambridge: Cambridge University Press, 52–95.

BAUMGARTEN, A. (1954). *Reflections on Poetry.* Trans. K. Aschenbrenner and W. B. Holther. Berkeley, CA: University of California Press [1st edn. 1735].

BAUMGARTEN, A. (1988). *Theoretische Ästhetik.* Ed. H. R. Schweitzer. Hamburg: Meiner [1st edn. 1750].

BOILEAU, N. (1966). *Oeuvres Complètes.* Ed. A. Adam and F. Escal. Paris: Gallimard.

BOILEAU, N. (1972). *Boileau on Longinus.* Transl. J. Ozell [1713]. University of Sheffield: Department of English Literature.

BORGERHOFF, E. B. O. (1950). *The Freedom of French Classicism.* Princeton. NJ: Princeton University Press.

BOUHOURS, D. (1705). *The Art of Criticism.* London.

BOUHOURS, D. (1962). *Les Entretiens d'Ariste et d'Eugène.* Ed. F. Brunot. Paris: Colin [1st edn. 1671].

BREDEKAMP, H. (1993). *Antikensehnsucht und Maschinenglauben.* Berlin: Wagenbach.

BRODY, J. (1958). *Boileau and Longinus.* Geneva: Droz.

BUNDY, M. W. (1930). '"Invention" and "Imagination" in the Renaissance'. *Journal of English and Germanic Philology*, 29: 535–45.

CARR, T. M. (1990). *Descartes and the Resilience of Rhetoric.* Carbondale, IL: Southern Illinois University Press.

CORNEILLE, P. (1987). 'Discours de la Tragédie', in G. Couton (ed.), *Oeuvres complètes.* vol. III. Paris: Gallimard, 142–73 [1st edn. 1660].

CRONK, N. (2002). *The Classical Sublime.* Charlottesville, NC: Rockwood Press.

CUNNINGHAM, J. V. (1976). *Collected Essays of J. V. Cunnigham.* Chicago: Swallow Press.

DASTON, L. and PARK, K. (1998). *Wonders and the Order of Nature.* New York: Zone Books.

DENNIS, J. (1939). *The Critical Works of John Dennis.* 2 vols. Ed. E. N. Hooker. Baltimore, MD: Johns Hopkins University Press.

DRYDEN, J. (1962). *Of Dramatic Poesy and Other Critical Essays.* 2 vols. Ed. G. Watson. London: Dent.

DUBOS, J. B. (1748). *Critical Reflections on Poetry, Painting and Music.* 3 vols. Trans. T. Nugent. London: J. Nourse [1st edn. 1719].

ECO, U. (1988). *The Aesthetics of Thomas Aquinas.* Cambridge, MA: Harvard University Press.

EDWARDS, W. F. (1969). 'Jacopo Zabarella: A Renaissance Aristotelian's View of Rhetoric and Poetry and Their Relation to Philosophy', in: *Arts Libéraux et Philosophie au Moyen Age.* Montreal: Institut d'études médiévales, 843–54.

EVELYN, J. (1955). *The Diary of John Evelyn.* Ed. E. S. de Beer. 6 vols. Oxford: Clarendon Press.

FÉLIBIEN, A. (2000). *Conversations on the Lives and Works of the Most Excellent Ancient and Modern Painters* [excerpt], in C. Harrison *et al.* (eds), *Art in Theory 1648–1815.* Oxford: Blackwell, 220–2 [1st edn. 1666].

FRANKOWIAK, U. (1994). *Der gute Geschmack. Studien zur Entwicklung des Geschmacksbegriffs.* München: Fink.

GOMBRICH, E. (1972). *Symbolic Images.* Chicago: University of Chicago Press.

GUEZ DE BALZAC, J.-L. (1971). 'Réponse à deux questions, ou du caractère et de l'instruction de la comédie', in *Oeuvres.* Vol. 2. Reprint. Genève: Slatkine, 509–19 [1st edn. 1665].

HALLIWELL, S. (2002). *The Aesthetics of Mimesis.* Princeton, NJ: Princeton University Press.

HEGEL, G. W. F. (1970). *Vorlesungen über die Äesthetik III.* (=*Werke in zwanzig Bänden.* Vol. 15.) Ed. E. Moldenhauer/K. M. Michel. Frankfurt: Suhrkamp.

HOBBES, T. (1946). *Leviathan.* Ed. M. Oakeshott. Oxford: Blackwell [1st edn. 1651].

HOBBES, T. (1908). 'Answer to Davenant's Preface to *Gondibert*', in J. E. Springarn (ed.), *Critical Essays of the Seventeenth Century.* Oxford: Oxford University Press, II, 54–67.

HUME, D. (1875). 'On the Standard of Taste', in T. H. Green and T. H. Grose (eds), *Essays, Moral, Political and Literary.* London: Longmans, I, 266–84 [1st edn. 1757].

KENSETH, J. (ed.) (1991). *The Age of the Marvellous.* Hanover, NH: Hood Museum of Art.

KLEIN, R. (1979). *Form and Meaning.* New York: Viking.

KRISTELLER, P. O. (1965). 'The Modern System of the Arts', in Kristeller, *Renaissance Thought II.* New York: Harper, 163–227.

LAUSBERG, H. (1998). *Handbook of Literary Rhetoric.* Trans. M. T. Bliss *et al.* Leiden: Brill.

LEIBNIZ, G. W. (1915). *Neue Abhandlungen über den menschlichen Verstand.* Transl. E. Cassirer. Leipzig: Meiner.

LEIBNIZ, G. W. (1924). 'Metaphysische Abhandlung', in A. Buchenau, trans. *Hauptschriften zur Grundlegung des Philosophie.* Leipzig: Meiner, II, 135–88 [1st edn. 1686].

LICHTENSTEIN, J. (1993). *The Eloquence of Color.* Berkeley, CA: University of California Press.

LITMAN, T. A. (1971). *Le Sublime en France (1660–1714).* Paris: Nizet.

LONGINUS (1972). 'On Sublimity', in D. A. Russell and M. Winterbottom (eds), *Ancient Literary Criticism.* Oxford: Clarendon Press, 462–503.

MAZZONI, J. (1971). *On the Defense of the 'Comedy' of Dante* [excerpts], in H. Adams (ed.), *Critical Theory Since Plato.* San Diego, CA: Hartcourt, 179–91 [1st edn. 1587].

MIROLLO, J. (1963). *The Poet of the Marvellous: Giambattista Marino.* New York: Columbia University Press.

MONK, S. H. (1935). *The Sublime.* New York: Modern Languages Association.

MONTGOMERY, R. L. (1992). *Terms of Response.* University Park, PA: Pennsylvania State University Press.

PANOFSKY, E. (1968). *Idea. A Concept in Art Theory.* New York: Harper.

PATEY, D. L. (1984). *Probability and Literary Form.* Cambridge: Cambridge University Press.

PATEY, D. L. (1997). 'Ancients and Moderns', in *Cambridge History of Literary Criticism IV.* Cambridge: Cambridge University Press, 32–71.

PORTER, J. I. (2009). 'Is art modern? Kristeller's "Modern System of the Arts" reconsidered'. *British Journal of Aesthetics,* 49: 1–24.

PUTTENHAM, G. (1968). *The Arte of English Poesie.* Rprt. Menston: Scolar Press [1st edn. 1589].

RACINE, J. (1960). 'Discours prononcé a l'Académie Française...', in R. Picard (ed.), *Oeuvres complètes.* Paris: Gallimard, II, 344–50 [1st edn. 1685].

RAPIN, R. (1970a). *Les Réflexions sur la poétique de ce temps...* Ed. E. T. Dubos. Genève: Droz [1st edn. 1675].

RAPIN, R. (1970*b*). 'Reflections on Aristotle's Treatise of Poesy', in S. Elledge and D. Schier (eds), *The Continental Model*. Rev. edn. Ithaca, NY: Cornell Unversity Press, 279–306 [1st edn. 1674].

REISS, T. J. (1999). 'Cartesian Aesthetics', in *Cambridge History of Literary Criticism III*. Cambridge: Cambridge University Press, 511–21.

RICHARDSON, J. (2000). 'Of the Sublime', in C. Harrison *et al.* (eds), *Art in Theory 1648–1815*. Oxford: Blackwell, 409–10 [1st edn. 1725].

LA ROCHEFOUCAULT (2007). *Collected Maxims and Other Reflections*. Trans. E. H. Blackmore *et al.* Oxford: Oxford University Press.

RONSARD, P. DE (1950). *Abrégé de l'Art poétique françois*, in G. Cohen (ed.), *Oeuvres complètes*. Paris: Gallimard, II, 995–1009 [1st edn. 1565].

ROSSKY, W. (1958). 'Imagination in the English Renaissance'. *Studies in the Renaissance*, 5: 49–73.

SEPPER, D. L. (1996). *Descartes's Imagination*. Berkeley, CA: University of California Press.

SHUGER, D. K. (1988). *Sacred Rhetoric*. Princeton, NJ: Princeton University Press.

VON STEIN, K. H. (1886). *Die Entstehung der neueren Aesthetik*. Stuttgart: Cotta.

STOLNIZ, J. (1961). '"Beauty": Some stages in the history of an idea'. *Journal of the History of Ideas*, 22: 185–204.

TASSO, T. (1973). *Discourses on the Heroic Poem*. Trans. M. Cavalchini and I. Samuel. Oxford: Oxford University Press.

TATARKIEWICZ, W. (1974). *History of Aesthetics*. Vol. II. The Hague: Mouton.

TEN KATE, L. H. (2000). 'The Beau Ideal', in C. Harrison *et al.* (eds), *Art in Theory 1648–1815*. Oxford: Blackwell, 410–12 [1st edn. 1728].

TESAURO, E. (1968). *Il Cannocchiale Aristotelico . . .* Ed. A. Buck. Bad Homburg: Gehlen [1st edn. 1654/70].

TOCANNE, B. (1978). *L'idée de nature en France . . .* Paris: Klincksieck.

TRIMPI, W. (1983). *Muses of One Mind*. Princeton, NJ: Princeton University Press.

UEDING, G. *et al.* (eds) (1992–). *Historisches Wörterbuch der Rhetorik*. Tübingen: Niemeyer.

USTICK, W. L. and HUDSON, H. H. (1935). 'Wit, "Mixed Wit", and the bee in amber'. *Huntington Library Bulletin*, 8: 103–30.

VAN HOOK, J. W. (1986). '"Concupiscence of Witt": The metaphysical conceit in Baroque poetics'. *Modern Philology*, 84: 24–38.

WEINBERG, B. (1961). *A History of Literary Criticism in the Italian Renaissance*. 2 vols. Chicago: University of Chicago Press.

ZELLE, C. (1995). *Die doppelte Ästhetik der Moderne*. Stuttgart: Metzler.

# PART III

## EPISTEMOLOGY, LOGIC, MATHEMATICS, AND LANGUAGE

CHAPTER 11

...........................................................................................

# SCEPTICISM

...........................................................................................

## JOSÉ R. MAIA NETO

DESCARTES' discussion of doubt in the *Meditations* drew attention to a significant revival of interest in scepticism in early modern philosophy. This chapter is accordingly divided into three sections. The first discusses the revival of scepticism in the Renaissance and early seventeenth-century philosophy. Section II explores some of Descartes' connections to this early modern sceptical context. Section III shows the impact of Cartesian doubt in late seventeenth- and early eighteenth-century scepticism.

## I: EARLY MODERN PRE-CARTESIAN SCEPTICISM
...........................................................................................

There were two branches of scepticism: Academic and Pyrrhonian. The first is the philosophy held by the members of Plato's Academy from Arcesilaus to Philo of Larissa, whose major sources—Cicero and Plutarch—were influential from the sixteenth to the eighteenth centuries. Academic scepticism was also diffused by Lactantius and Augustine, whose first philosophical work was *Against the Academics*. Despite Augustine's title, which indicated a confrontation with Cicero's *Academics*, both Church Fathers believed that scepticism could have a role in Christian apologetics insofar as it challenged all pagan dogmatic philosophies. The main sources of the second branch of ancient scepticism, that is Pyrrhonism, were two complete works of Sextus Empiricus, the only ancient Pyrrhonian whose works survived, and the chapter on Pyrrho in Diogenes Laertius' *Lives of Eminent Philosophers*. These Greek sources were translated into Latin and, together with the Latin sources, they nurtured innovative (mainly anti-Aristotelian) philosophical thought in the sixteenth and seventeenth centuries.

Of all the Renaissance philosophers who recovered or discussed ancient scepticism, Montaigne was the most important one. Unlike others, he presented a coherent and personal scepticism rather than merely used the ancient school for aims alien to scepticism itself, such as combating Aristotelianism. The coherence and radicalism of Montaigne's scepticism, when compared to that held by other Renaissance sceptics, has been partially attributed to the fact that he used extensively Sextus's Pyrrhonian sources that had been recently made available in Latin translations. In the 'Apology for Raymond Sebond' (*Essays* II.12), Montaigne explores the Pyrrhonian problem of justifying a criterion of truth and the ten modes (PH II 20 and M I; for the ten modes, PH I 36–163[1]). He argues that we have no access to the nature of things themselves, since our own 'form', our senses and other intellectual faculties, alter in an incorrigible way our cognitive access to things (Paganini 2008: 31–52). Montaigne dealt with this epistemological problem in a remarkably subjective and personal way, showing, for example, how his judgement shifts among contrary views on account of a variety of non-epistemic causes.

There has been much controversy on the nature and scope of Montaigne's scepticism and its relations to the Christian religion and theology. Popkin's view (2003: 47–56) is that Montaigne exemplifies the typical appropriation of ancient scepticism in the period in order to prepare for a non-rational acceptance of religious faith (fideism), by showing that human natural faculties cannot attain the truth. By removing false, merely human beliefs, scepticism prepares the mind to receive the revealed truths of Scripture. In contrast, Brahami (1997: 73–78; 2001: 33–7) argues that Montaigne's scepticism is not a preparation for faith but one of the consequences of faith. It is because the Christian God, where truth lies, is wholly transcendent that scepticism obtains. Third, at least some of Montaigne's sceptical arguments have been linked to the Ockamist discussions of the consequences for human rationality and for negative theology of God's *potentia absoluta* (Miernowski 1998; Popkin 2003: 50; Carraud 2004). Finally, others have argued in the opposite direction that Montaigne's scepticism tends to atheism and libertinism (Giocanti 2001: 241–55 and 2004; Naya 2006: 33–9; Cardoso 2009).

Seventeenth-century scepticism begins with Pierre Charron, whose widely influential work, *De la Sagesse*, was published in 1601. Although Charron was strongly influenced by Montaigne, his scepticism differs from Montaigne's in at least two important ways. First, *Of Wisdom* presents scepticism as the epistemological and

---

[1] Throughout the chapter, the *Outlines of Pyrrhonism* are cited as PH and the *Adversus Mathematicos* as M (Sextus 1987).

moral position which accomplishes the limited perfection of human nature, which is naturally incapable of truth (Charron 1986: 138). Montaigne's view of the ancient sceptic as the sole philosopher who renounced the vanity of pretending to have the truth, but whose position was hard to sustain because it was self-referential and because of the inconstancy of human reason, becomes in Charron the ideal position of the wise man, for whom wisdom is hard to achieve fully but nonetheless possible. The second major difference is that Charron's sceptical wisdom is much more Socratic and Academic than Pyrrhonian. Wisdom's slogan is '*Je ne sçais*' (I do not know), in clear polemics against Montaigne's Pyrrhonian one: '*Que sais-je?*' (What do I know?), which does not express the self-assurance and stability required for the wise man.

*Of Wisdom* has three books. The first focuses on human nature and presents the self-knowledge which is a requirement for the achievement of wisdom. Only after pointing to human epistemic and moral predicaments can one follow the rules of wisdom presented in Book II, and then apply them to the many circumstances of life according to Book III. In the chapter on the understanding, in Book I, Charron claims that the very feature that makes reason the most important faculty we have, namely, its boundless capacity to consider everything, makes it a major source of error, given its tendency promptly to assent even in the absence of evidence.

Charron thus reappraises ancient Academic sceptical wisdom as it was presented in Cicero's *Academica*.[2] Since we cannot find the truth, which is hidden in God with whom we have no proportion, what we can do is to avoid error, whose sources are various: the weakness of the senses (as compared to those of other animals), the limits that our senses impose on our apprehension of the vast nature of things, the bias that our passions impose on our understanding, and the tyranny to which our understanding is submitted through superstition, vulgar opinions, and scholastic (Aristotelian) science. The way to avoid error is to follow the rules of wisdom presented in Book II, of which the most fundamental one is to examine everything and assent to nothing as certain truth. The two aspects work in conjunction in what could be characterized as a virtuous circle. On the one hand, an absence of any previously held belief is required for unbiased rational investigation.

On the other hand, universal investigation is required to maintain a suspended judgement, because an open, endless, and rigorous examination will inevitably undermine the plausibility of any belief or doctrine to which one might feel inclined to adhere (Charron 1986: 387–8). Charron founds his wisdom on Cicero's notion of intellectual integrity, '*integra nobis judicandi potestas*' (Ac II 8), which has not only the normative sense of restricting assent to what is evident but also a moral and anthropological sense. The integrity of man's capacity for rational examination is maintained in *epoche*. It is therefore in *epoche* that reason (and

---

[2] Cicero (1994) *De Natura Deorum and Academica* is henceforth cited as Ac.

consequently the human being) attains its fully fledged perfection and excellence (Maia Neto 2009).

In the frontispiece of *De la Sagesse*, Charron represents the four enemies of Wisdom as four women: Opinion, Science, Superstition, and Passion, who are enchained to Wisdom's pedestal. This picture represents the battle over scepticism in seventeenth-century French philosophy up to the time of Descartes and Pascal. The major philosophers of the period would focus either on science or on vulgar opinion and superstition; they would develop and detail sceptical wisdom by criticizing these enemies further than Charron, or by presenting a new science (Descartes) or a new apology for the Christian religion (Pascal), which would entitle them to take over the pedestal of Charron's sceptical wisdom.

Bacon refers to the kind of Academic scepticism adopted by Charron, in the preface to the *Novum Organum*. He contrasts those who pretend 'to lay down the law of nature' with those 'who have taken a contrary course, and asserted that absolutely nothing can be known' (Bacon 1875: 39). Bacon claims that the position held by the second group is partly similar to his own point of departure.

Commentators have shown the influence of scepticism in Bacon's attack on the idols, that is false beliefs (errors) that lie in the way of science (Granada 2006; Eva 2006). The elimination of such idols through scepticism would thus be a means of establishing a new science. The Idols of the Tribe are those derived from human faculties. Here Bacon follows Montaigne, who rehearses the sceptical mode of mixtures (PH I 124–8), in claiming that we do not apprehend things themselves but the result of the mixture of our senses and the external things (Bacon 1875: 41). The understanding is also naturally prone to jump to conclusions, in the form of general truths, before fully and carefully considering them. This is why Bacon says that the understanding 'must not . . . be supplied with wings, but rather hung with weights, to keep it from leaping and flying' (Bacon 1875: 104).[3] He also denounces our attachment to previously held opinions (Bacon 1875: 45), and to affections and passions (Bacon 1875: 49), which compromise the objectivity of our inquiries. The Idols of the Cave are those which derive from contingent situations of individuals, such as their education, which also compromise intellectual integrity. The Idols of the Market are those derived from language. They are transmitted by the vulgar and are extremely contagious, as Charron illustrates 'Opinion' at the frontispiece of *De la Sagesse*. Finally, the Idols of the Theatre are philosophical and scientific doctrines about nature. Bacon concludes his exposition by recalling the opposition between dogmatists (the Aristotelians) and Academic sceptics (Bacon 1875: 67).

He thus rehearses some of the criticisms the latter present to the former but also warns that 'by far the greatest obstacle to the progress of science [is] . . . that men despair and think things impossible. For wise and serious men are wont in these

---

[3] See Charron 1986: 16: '[*l'esprit*] *a besoin d'estre retenu, plus besoin de plomb que d'aisles*'.

matters to be altogether distrustful; considering with themselves the obscurity of nature, the shortness of life, the deceitfulness of the senses, the weakness of the judgment.' Bacon cites here Cicero's explanation of why the Academics became sceptics (Ac I 43–6), which he sees as justifying Charron's view that wisdom lies in avoiding error (suspending judgement) and not in pretending to have the truth. Because of Bacon's anti-sceptical rhetoric, some commentators claim that sceptical arguments are for him, as they are for Descartes, only a means to destroy Aristotelian science and establish a new dogmatism (Popkin 2003: 41–2; Van Leewen 1963: 1–12). However, Manzo (2009) argues that Bacon's anti-scepticism is much more present in his (ideal) view of science than in his practice of science, and Oliveira and Maia Neto (2009) claim that Bacon's new science is not inconsistent with a kind of mitigated scepticism and that it was so interpreted by members of the Royal Society such as Joseph Glanvill.

Since Montaigne and Charron were the two Renaissance thinkers who, respectively, developed the most radical scepticism and who most practically focused on the intellectual world of the time, it was natural that seventeenth-century scepticism was more influential in France than elsewhere in Europe and Great Britain. The title of Gassendi's first book is *Exercitationes paradoxicae adversus aristoteleos, in quibus . . . opiniones vero aut novae, aut ex veteribus obsoletae, stabiliuntur* (1624). Gassendi's anti-Aristotelianism and his later Epicureanism have been cited as evidence that scepticism played only a secondary and merely instrumental role in early modern philosophy, as a means of debunking Aristotelianism (Brundell 1987: 15–29; Larmore 1998: 1158). However, the ancient philosophy that Gassendi wanted to rehabilitate, as indicated in the subtitle of the *Exercitationes*, is ancient scepticism. In the preface, he claims that it was his reading of Vives and Charron which gave him the courage to confront the Aristotelians. As indicated above, science, which was understood as Aristotelian science, is one of the four enemies of Academic sceptical Wisdom portrayed in the frontispiece of Charron's book.

Gassendi defends intellectual integrity—*libertas philosophandi*—against the way of philosophizing of scholastic Aristotelians who, according to Gassendi, induce their students only to defend and never to attack Aristotle. This method was contrary to Aristotle's own pedagogy (Gassendi 1959: 8). As Gassendi claims in the title of his book, his main quarrel is with the Aristotelians (not with Aristotle himself), whose sectarianism is contrary to Academic sceptical wisdom (Charron 1986: 401). The exercise which generated the *Exercitationes* was an exercise of intellectual integrity. It grew out of Gassendi's classes on Aristotle in Aix-en-Provence. After presenting Aristotle's view, intellectual integrity obliged him to argue *in utramque partem* (on both sides). Arguing both ways was a method to teach the students epistemic caution, combating harshness in philosophical inquiry (Gassendi 1959: 9). The exercise is thus the exercise of reason, which is the nature of philosophy to promote, but which dogmatic commitment to some philosophical school compromises, in Gassendi's time, especially with Aristotelianism.

Besides defending the *libertas philosophandi*, Gassendi points out 'omissions, superfluities, errors and contradictions' in the Aristotelian *corpus*. He uses materials, which were prepared by two other Renaissance authors whom he mentions in the preface, Ramus and Gianfrancesco Picco, to develop the programme laid down by Charron (1986: 42). *Exercitatio* 3 aims at re-establishing philosophical *diaphonia* by arguing that there is no rational justification for preferring Aristotelian philosophy over competing dogmatic ones. *Exercitatio* 8 details the internal contradictions in the Aristotelian *corpus*, and Aristotle's errors—those cited by Charron and many others—fill in the content of *Exercitatio* 7.

A second book, against Aristotle's logic, appeared only in 1654. Gassendi shows that Aristotle's logic is useless as a logic of discovery and he raises a number of objections to Aristotelian science. Its failure shows the 'weakness and uncertainty of human knowledge' and 'establishes the foundations of Pyrrhonism' (Gassendi 1959: 13). The same Pyrrhonian arguments that challenge dogmatic knowledge about the nature of things establish the possibility of phenomenal knowledge. We can no more say that honey is sweet than it is sour, but we can say that it appears sweet under certain circumstances and sour under others. 'It follows from the preceding that a science exists, but an experimental science . . . grounded on appearances' (Gassendi 1959: 505). True, Gassendi develops this science, which is announced here, through a reappraisal of Epicureanism and this implies the need to break with ancient Pyrrhonism. But even at this point, he proposes his philosophy as a *via media* between dogmatism and scepticism.[4]

A friend of Gassendi's, La Mothe Le Vayer, openly upheld sceptical views on various topics in a number of publications, but his more radical sceptical views were published secretly under the pseudonym of Orasius Tubero in the *Dialogues faits à l'imitation des anciens* (1630–1). Orasius qualifies Sextus Empiricus as divine, the ten modes as 'our decalogue', and Pyrrhonism as 'our sacred philosophy' (La Mothe 1988: 82–3). La Mothe endeavours to establish the enlarged mind of the wise man in the exercise of the tenth mode, which deals with the variations of laws, habits, values, and beliefs (PH I 145–63). He uses both ancient ethnographic views and more recent reports by travellers who describe customs of various people from America, Africa, and the East, to feed the tenth mode. By showing the lack of epistemic justification for a choice out of this diversity, he attacks the opinions and superstitions of his contemporaries. Christian doctrines, rituals, and mysteries are not excluded from La Mothe's Pyrrhonian *zetesis*. But, following Montaigne and Charron, fideism precludes this *zetesis* from leading to *epoche*: 'we assent to the

---

[4] Gassendi breaks with Pyrrhonism to the extent that, in his *Syntagma Philosophici*, he attacks Sextus's arguments against indicative signs. However, Popkin (2003: 122) argues that Gassendi remains partially a sceptic because he views science as hypothetical and probabilistic. See also Fisher (2005: 19–53). For the role of Gassendi in the reappraisal of Epicureanism in early modern philosophy, see Wilson 2008.

divine principles [of theology] through the pure command of our will . . . submitting to the things which it does not see nor understand' (La Mothe 1988: 306). Such 'submission' does not compromise the intellectual integrity of the wise man who verifies the epistemic equipollence between Christian and pagan religious beliefs.

If La Mothe's *zetesis* proceeds through the tenth mode, targeting above all superstition (one of the four enemies of Charron's sceptical wisdom), *epoche* is presented as the *esprit fort*'s alternative to 'opinion' (another enemy of Charron's wisdom). The weak or dogmatic mind assents to a mere appearance and becomes a sectarian of this opinion. This sectarianism compromises intellectual integrity, which is here understood, as in Montaigne and Charron, not only as intellectual honesty but also as the fully fledged exercise of the intellectual faculties. The full force of the mind, the *esprit fort*, is preserved in *epoche*. 'Those of our family [the Pyrrhonians], who [unlike the dogmatists] make the convenient reflections about the probability of all propositions, rather than weakly letting themselves be carried to a party, generously stand themselves upon their own forces, between the extremities of so many different opinions, which is the most beautiful and happiest position for a philosophical mind' (La Mothe 1988: 386). La Mothe's *epoche* differs from the ancient Pyrrhonian to the extent that detachment from beliefs does not lead just to *ataraxia* but discloses an emancipated subjectivity, constitutive of the *ethos* of the wise man (Giocanti 2001).

## II: CARTESIAN DOUBT AND SCEPTICISM

Whereas Gassendi develops and details Charron's attack on dogmatic science, Descartes builds partially on Charron to develop a new science that could replace Charron's sceptical wisdom. Popkin relates Descartes' methodic doubt to this debate about scepticism among early modern French philosophers. The sceptics of the time had used doubt to deprive the mind of erroneous human beliefs, and to prepare the field for God's supernatural intervention. Descartes made a similar use of doubt but, in his case, he used it to disclose innate ideas: the *cogito*, God, and extension (Popkin 2003: 143–57). According to this interpretation, Descartes' doubt would be an innovative use of scepticism to refute scepticism itself, thus enabling the foundation of a new mathematical-mechanical science through establishing the mind–body distinction.

Besides providing the foundation of the new science, according to Gouhier (1954), Descartes' method would provide, against the sceptical fideist challenge, a renewal of the Thomist view of the role of reason or philosophy as *preambulum fidei*. In the dedicatory letter of the *Meditations*, Descartes rejects fideism as an apologetic strategy (CSM II 3–4). Since the traditional Thomist arguments were discredited, thanks to the collapse of Aristotelianism, methodic doubt would lead to new and indubitable proofs of God and the immateriality of the soul. Popkin and Gouhier support their interpretations of Descartes' philosophical project by reference to Descartes' meeting with Bérulle in Paris in 1627 or 1628, in a gathering of learned men which included Mersenne and Villebressieu (AT I 213; CSMK 32–3). They had gathered to hear the chemist Pierre Chandoux's new philosophy, which was critical of Aristotle's. Descartes' rejection of Chandoux's philosophy, because it could not provide the certainty that his method claimed, caught the interest of the powerful Cardinal Bérulle who exhorted him to apply his method to develop a new metaphysics that would be capable of replacing Aristotle's.

Although Popkin's view of Descartes as engaged in refuting scepticism predominates in Anglo-American Cartesian studies, it has been challenged. According to a more recent view, Descartes was not disturbed by the sceptical threat, and his doubt was neither sceptical nor genuine, but a means to validate reason and/or to combat Aristotelianism (Frankfurt 1968; Carriero 1997; Menn 1998; Larmore 1998). The Chandoux episode itself is alleged against Popkin's interpretation for, according to these critics, it does not reveal any epistemological discussion (Gaukroger 1995: 181–6; Secada 2000: 38–41). Lennon (2008: 55–77) persuasively shows that Descartes despised the sceptics and that refuting them was not one of his main concerns. However, it is undeniable that Descartes saw such a refutation as at least a welcome byproduct of his philosophy (Descartes' replies to Hobbes and Bourdin: CSM II 121, 374; and *Notae in programma*: CSM I 309). Moreover, the scepticism of the time, in particular that of Charron, was decisive in Descartes' philosophical trajectory. The Chandoux episode is indicative of this influence. According to the report of his biographer, Adrien Baillet, Descartes showed that what the audience picked as an instance of something very probable could, by small steps, be shown to be quite improbable and vice versa (Baillet 1691: I, 162). This is a typical application of sorites, one of the traditional Academic arguments. Descartes' aim was to show the danger of accepting probability as truth; Chandoux's and all current philosophy was only probable, and the distinctive feature of probability is to induce assent to something that, being only probable, might be false and so compromise intellectual integrity. Probability must thus be combated because it is a major source of errors.

In discrediting probability in philosophy, although it is indispensable in practical life, Descartes follows Montaigne and Charron. In the 'Apology for Raymond Sebond', Montaigne had attacked Academic probability on two grounds. First, epistemically (as Augustine took probability to be, namely, as something similar to the truth, *verisimilis*), the concept is not sceptically coherent. Montaigne prefers Pyrrhonian scepticism, which does not recognize any dissimilarity among representations with respect to degrees of probability (Montaigne 1991: 632–3). Second, even when considered merely as a practical guide, Montaigne found probability inappropriate because it does not give a stable rule of action. What seems probable now to a person may seem improbable later on (and vice versa), depending on the dialectical or rhetorical skill of a philosopher or theologian. In the 'Apology for Raymond Sebond', Montaigne suggested that this shifting was precisely what had happened in the court of Marguerite de Valois, a Catholic queen subjected to the rhetorical skills of Reformer apologists who argued that Calvinism was more probable than Roman Catholicism (Montaigne 1991: 490, 630). What appears more probable may be false, given the weakness of reason. Therefore, crucial decisions in one's life (in particular the Queen's), such as conversion to another religion, should not be based on variable and precarious probability. The safer stand in this context of epistemic weakness is to remain in the ancient religion in which one was born.

Charron continues the fight against probability, not in the strict practical sense that is compatible with the suspension of judgement, but in the epistemic sense. To accept probability as truth is to sin against intellectual integrity, which is sustained only in *epoche*. Charron argues that one must be an *esprit fort*, that is one must have willpower, to remain suspended in the face of probability, given that the probable is precisely that which induces assent. The sceptical view of Descartes' time was that probability is all we can get, since the truth about the nature of things is hidden. The sceptics thus deployed sceptical arguments against those who pretended to have the truth, and they supported a fallibilist assent to the probable. However, to accept the probable as true is to risk holding erroneous beliefs, which the wise man should avoid above all else.

While Descartes accepted the sceptics' view that we should not take the probable as true, he did think that we could have certain truth, which we achieve by first radicalizing the sceptical attack on probability. 'Although the Pyrrhonists reached no certain conclusion from their doubts, it does not follow that no one can' (to Reneri, April or May 1638: CSMK 99). While the ancient Pyrrhonians did not conclude anything certain from their doubt, Charron denies that the *epoche* of his wise man is Pyrrhonian, and claims that Academic *epoche* is 'the science of sciences, the certitude of certitudes' (Charron 1986: 859).

The most striking echo of Charron in Descartes appears in the opening passage of *La Recherche de la Vérité*. It gives textual evidence of Charron's influence on Descartes' methodic doubt and suggests that Descartes thought that even the first truth of Cartesianism is already present in Charron, although Charron and his sceptical followers did not notice it. In describing the original position of the philosophical inquirer, Descartes observes that

[H]e came into the world in ignorance, and since the knowledge which he had as a child was based solely on the weak foundations of the senses and the authority of his teachers, it was virtually inevitable that his imagination should be filled with innumerable false thoughts before reason could guide his conduct. So later on he needs to have very great natural talent, or else the instruction of a wise teacher [*un tres grand naturel, ou bien des instructions de quelque sage*], in order *both* to rid himself of the bad doctrines that have filled his mind *and* to lay the foundations for a solid science.   (AT X 496; CSM II 400; translation modified).

This sage is Charron, the instructions are those presented in Book II *Of Wisdom*, whose title is precisely '*instructions et regles generales de Sagesse*', from which Descartes borrows most of his Charronian passages (Maia Neto 2003). Charron's instructions are required to eliminate previously held opinions because the basic cognitive attitude of the wise man is to examine everything and assent to nothing (Charron 1986: 389–401). Descartes says that Charron's instructions are also necessary 'to lay the foundations for a solid science'. Charron's instructions appear here as delivering Descartes' *cogito*. The crucial passage of Charron's to which Descartes alluded distinguishes three kinds of spirits: the vulgar, the scholastic pedant, and those who can achieve wisdom thanks to their own nature or through the rules and instructions of wisdom displayed in Book II (cf. *Regulae*: CSM I 50; *Discourse*: CSM I 118; and Replies to Bourdin: CSM II 320).

This . . . distinction . . . arises both from the natural and from the acquired, by which there are three kinds of people in the world. . . . In the third and highest place there are the men bestowed with an alive and clear mind, strong, solid and firm judgment, who do not rest content with hearsay and are not trapped by commonly received opinions, but examine everything, investigating passionlessly causes down to their roots. [These men] prefer to doubt and suspend their belief rather than, out of a too weak and loose easiness, or rashness or precipitation of judgment, accept falsities and affirm or become assured of something of which they can have no certain reason.   (Charron 1986: 291–2)

We find in this passage the background of Descartes' first methodic rule: 'never to accept anything as true if I did not have evident knowledge of its truth: that is, carefully to avoid precipitate conclusions and preconceptions' (CSM I 120). As far as philosophy is concerned, Descartes follows Charron: it is better to suspend judgement than assent to probability.[5] Descartes' position is contrary to the Jesuit teaching he received at La Flèche. As Maryks (2008: 83–105) points out, from 1599 Jesuit education became very influenced by Ciceronian humanism, in particular by Cicero's rhetoric, which is epistemologically grounded on his Academic probabilism. In philosophy as in everyday life, one had to argue in a way that established the probable, since the truth was not available to fallible human beings (Jardine 1983). This is consistent with Descartes' claims in the *Regulae* and in the *Discourse* (CSM I: 11, 113, 115) that the philosophy he learned in school was merely probable and was therefore uncertain (Dear 1988: 21).

---

[5] See also the *Regulae*: 'in accordance with this Rule [II], we reject all such merely probable cognition and resolve to believe only what is perfectly known and incapable of being doubted' (CSM I 10).

Bourdin's reaction to Descartes' doubt in the Seventh Objections is typical of Jesuit probabilism. Most of Bourdin's criticism targets Descartes' attack on probability as a means to acquire knowledge. Since the Jesuit thinks that probability is all we can get, to attack it is to deprive us of the only means to have acceptable (limited) knowledge. Consequently, he argues, Descartes' method leads to Pyrrhonism. Descartes replies that 'it may happen that a claim which we do not recognize as possessing complete certainty may in fact be quite false, however probable it may appear. To make the foundations of all knowledge rest on a claim that we recognize as being possibly false would not be a sensible way to philosophize. If someone proceeds in this way, how can he answer the sceptics who go beyond all the boundaries of doubt?' (CSM II 374)[6] These sceptics are the Pyrrhonians who have the skill to establish equipollence even with respect to what looks most probable. This is precisely what Descartes himself did by using sorites with Chandoux's audience, in order to make the point that any philosophy based only on probability, though powerful enough to attract the assent of weak minds like those of the audience, could not resist the sceptic who was able to transform the strongest into the weakest probability.

Descartes' attack on probability is mostly deployed in the *Meditations*. In order to find certainty, we must resist assenting to what is probable by bringing forth sceptical arguments which show that the probable may be false. Furthermore, sceptical doubts must be contrived to fight probability directly. Here lies the novelty of Descartes' sceptical arguments, which aim at doubting what is most probable, such as that there are bodies, and that two plus two equals four. These arguments imply a substantial and decisive expansion of the scope of *epoche vis-à-vis* that of Charron and of all previous sceptics. When Charron says that the wise man should doubt everything, he means everything *doubtful* (philosophical doctrines and ordinary beliefs), not the existence of an external material world which would include the very body of the wise man. Wisdom comprises above all the perfection of the mind (intellectual integrity) but also the integrity of the body (Charron 1986: 28). When Descartes replaces the practical doubt of the sceptics of his time by hyperbolic doubt, the firmness and assurance of the *epoche* exhibited by the wise man becomes metaphysical (dogmatic) assurance. Furthermore, scepticism itself, construed hyperbolically in the Cartesian fashion, becomes incapable of implementation, for it includes in its scope elements that the traditional sceptics left outside the scope of doubt that secured their practical lives. Descartes' refutation of scepticism has therefore a sceptical base, *epoche*. It is not that an abstract sceptic would be forced to agree on the truth of the *cogito*. The sceptic's practical position itself already exhibits it. Charron's doubt contains a philosophical treasure he does not perceive because of his strictly practical concern. What is missing in Charron is the philosophical

---

[6] Paganini (2008: 248–63) takes this passage as revealing the importance of combating the sceptics in Descartes' project. He identifies the latter as libertine or atheist sceptics such as La Mothe Le Vayer.

universality (beyond the practical frame that restricted it) of his claim that the wise man must doubt all things, that his doubt must be universal.

If Charron could not react to Descartes' subversion of his *epoche*, it was possible for one of his disciples who did so. Gassendi's reaction to Descartes' sceptical arguments is most revealing. He begins by praising Descartes' goal of eliminating prejudices (which is Charronian) but rejects the way he attempts to do it, that is, through hyperbolic doubt (CSM II 180). Gassendi understands that Descartes' move is anti-sceptical, for it allows him to claim that what he could not doubt is the truth. He rejects Descartes' sceptical arguments based on the evil genius, the deceiver god, and dreaming, on the grounds that they are artificial (note that Gassendi's doubt is a doubt to be lived by) and deviated from tradition. Gassendi sees well that Descartes' anti-scepticism begins with his doubt and he denounces it here as elsewhere in his *Disquisitio* (Gassendi 1962: 31–59; cf. Gouhier 1987; Williams 1986).

Another important criticism of Gassendi's is that Descartes did not manage to reestablish beyond any doubt the existence of an external material world. This is what Descartes called Gassendi's 'objection of objections' (CSM II 275; Popkin 2003: 167–8; Lennon 2008: 183–200). The problem of the existence of an external material world is the price Descartes had to pay for his attack on probability. Descartes himself acknowledged that, since the proof of the existence of an external material world relies on the union of the mind with the body, that is, on sense perception, it cannot have the same epistemic status as those of the other doctrines established in the *Meditations*. Apparently, unlike his proofs for the existence of God, for example, Descartes did not consider his argument in Meditation VI as a demonstration, but only as probable.

[I]n the Sixth Meditation . . . there is a presentation of all the arguments which enable the existence of material things to be inferred. The great benefit of these arguments is not, in my view, that they prove what they establish . . . [but that make us] realize that they are not as solid or as transparent as the arguments which lead us to knowledge of our own minds and of God, so that the latter are the most certain and evident of all possible objects of knowledge for the human intellect.   (CSM II 11)

Most post-Cartesian early modern philosophers rejected Descartes' proof of the existence of an external material world. I limit the following discussion to the impact of this problem, following Descartes, in the early modern period.


# III: Post-Cartesian scepticism

Pascal and Glanvill developed sceptical views under the impact of Cartesian doubt, but their main reference in the sceptical tradition was still Charron and Gassendi and, in Pascal's case, Montaigne. Neither was a sceptic properly speaking, but both held a kind of mitigated scepticism; they were sceptical as far as metaphysics is concerned, but supported a fallibilist experimental view of science. Furthermore, both used scepticism: the Frenchman to attack the irreligious scepticism that libertines derived from Montaigne and above all from Charron, the Englishman to attack Aristotelianism and vindicate the experimental and hypothetical kind of science practised by the Royal Society. Both also considered scepticism as one of the results of original sin, reconstructing the ancient philosophical school within the framework of the anthropological Christian view of fallen men.

Glanvill shows great admiration for Descartes but implicitly charges him with Pelagianism (the heretical doctrine combated by Augustine, which denies the consequences of original sin, or mitigates it in the case of semi-Pelagianism). Glanvill claims that Descartes' methodical doubt would be the only way to certain science, if the latter were possible. 'A third reason of our Ignorance and Error, *viz.*, the impostures and deceits of our Senses. The way to rectifie these misinformations propounded. Descartes his method the only way to Science. The difficulty of exact performance' (Glanvill 1978: ch. 10). The reasons given by Glanvill for the impossibility of attaining certain knowledge in our present state derive from Descartes' physiology: '[W]hen we want to fix our attention for some time on some particular object, this volition keeps the gland [which directs the animal spirits] leaning in one particular direction during that time' (CSM I 344). However, Adam alone could fully observe Descartes' rule of assenting only to what is clearly and distinctly perceived, since the mind's control of the body, by means of the control of the pineal gland over the animal spirits, no longer obtains in the present fallen state. In the later essay 'Of Scepticism and Certainty' (1676), Glanvill argues that Descartes' alleged metaphysical certainty in the *Meditations* is ungrounded given the (metaphysical) uncertainty of the human faculties established in Meditation I. But the moral certainty we can have is all that we need in ordinary life and science (Glanvill 1978: 47–8; see Talmor 1981; Brahami 2008). Glanvill is the first early-modern sceptic to deprive Cartesian doubt of its metaphysical context in the *Meditations* and to recognize its crucial value as a methodological device as it appears in the second part of the *Discourse*.

Glanvill has also been cited as a possible source for Hume's scepticism about causality. One of the sceptical arguments and sources of errors presented in *Scepsis Scientifica* is that we never perceive the cause of effects; we perceive only similar effects following from similar causes. 'We cannot conclude, any thing to be the cause of another; but from its continual accompanying it: for the causality it self is insensible. But now to argue from a concomitancy to a causality, is not infallibly conclusive' (Glanvill 1978: 142; see Popkin 1953). Glanvill's arguments are not meant to establish a general scepticism that is similar to what Hume calls Pyrrhonian or excessive scepticism. They were intended to teach modesty, detachment from strongly held opinions, and an attitude of open-mindedness and tolerance, like the scepticism that Hume (1975: 161) calls Academic. In the last chapter of *Scepsis Scientifica*, Glanvill presents his *scepsis* as the remedy for the moral defects of dogmatism; '(1) 'tis the effect of Ignorance. (2) It inhabits with untamed passions, and ungovern'd Spirit. (3) It is the great Disturber of the World. (4) It is ill manners, and immodesty. (5) It holds men captive in Error. (6) It betrays a narrowness of Spirit' (Glanvill 1978: 165–72). This involved a moral (pre-Cartesian) view of scepticism similar to Charron's, whom Glanvill cites in the concluding paragraph of the book: '[T]he wise Monseur Charron hath fully discourst of this Universal liberty, and sav'd me the labour of enlarging. Upon the Review of my former considerations, I cannot quarrel with his Motto: in a sense *Je ne scay,* is a justifiable Scepticism, and not mis-becoming a Candidate of wisdom' (Glanvill 1978: 172).

Unlike Glanvill and like Descartes, Pascal targets Charron's sceptical wisdom, not to introduce a new philosophical one in its place but to show that Christian wisdom is the only viable wisdom, thereby combating the French free thought of his time. Fragment La 6 of the *Pensées* resumes Pascal's projected apology for the Christian religion.[7] 'First part: Wretchedness of man without God. Second part: Happiness of man with God. Otherwise. First part: Nature is corrupt, proved by nature itself. Second part: There is a Redeemer, proved by Scripture.' The corruption of man is naturally verified above all by the scepticism exhibited by Montaigne, and by Charron in the first book of *Of Wisdom*.[8] For Pascal, the predicaments pointed out by Charron, misery, weakness, inconstancy, etc., are effects whose cause (the fall of man) and especially whose cure (grace) can be found only in revelation. So while he builds on Book I of *Of Wisdom* for the diagnosis of the human predicament, Pascal denies that Book II provides a viable solution to them. This solution cannot be the purely human sceptical wisdom that Charron proposes in Book II, but depends on the revealed Christian wisdom which would be the object of the second part of the apology.

In order to attack Charron's sceptical wisdom, Pascal reconstructs the sceptical position with elements from Montaigne and Cartesian doubt. In fragment La 131, Pascal says that the strongest of the sceptical arguments are based on the uncertainty of our origins and the verisimilitude of dreams. The certainty we have concerning the first principles of nature—extension, movement, and time—is a feeling. As we cannot establish by reason whether we were created by a benevolent

---

[7] Pascal (1966). *Pensées* is henceforth cited in the text as La, followed by the number of the fragment.

[8] Pascal bases his description of man's moral wretchedness above all on Charrron's fourth '*consideration de l'homme morale*' (Charron 1986: 227–80), which has five aspects: '*Vanité, Foiblesse, Inconstance, Misère, et Présomption.*' '*Vanité*' is the title of one of the sections planned by Pascal for the first part of his apology and figures as the title of fragments La 23, 32, and 46. '*Foiblesse*' is the title of La 28, '*Inconstance*' of La 54 and 55, and '*Misère*' of another section of the *Pensées* and also of La 69 in this section. '*Présomption*' does not figure as the title of any fragment, even though there is a related one: '*orgueil*'.

God, an evil demon, or by chance, we cannot be certain (apart from Revelation) whether these feelings are true, false, or uncertain. There is no rational way to refute these hypotheses, but the inability of reason to prove the principles cannot lead to the suspension of judgement about them. Nature imposes such beliefs. The upshot is that one cannot be a consistent sceptic (since *epoche* is not viable) or a consistent dogmatist (since reason cannot justify one's beliefs). 'Nature confounds the sceptics . . . and reason confounds the dogmatist. What then will become of you, man, seeking to discover your true condition through natural reason?' (La 131)

This means that the only two possible philosophical wisdoms, the dogmatic and the sceptic, are not viable. Since these two positions are the only possible natural philosophical positions, philosophy is excluded and only Christian revelation, and specifically the doctrine of the Fall, can explain the contradiction of scepticism and dogmatism. Pascal thus strikes at Charron's sceptical rationalism. Charron's wise man judges everything and assents to nothing. But as assent cannot be suspended, this sceptical reason that would like to judge everything and assent to nothing, because nothing is sufficiently warranted, is humiliated to the extent that it is forced by nature to assent. Charron champions the autonomy of philosophy vis-à-vis theology, claiming that [sceptical wisdom] is '*l'excellence et perfection de l'homme comme homme . . . celuy est homme sage qui sçait bien et excellemment faire l'homme*' (Charron 1986: 32). Pascal claims that the explanation of man's contradictory nature is 'beyond dogmatism and scepticism, beyond all human philosophy. Man transcends man' (La 131).

Later scepticism is deeply marked by Cartesian doubt and by the debates concerning Cartesianism. Pierre-Daniel Huet's most sceptical work, the *Traité philosophique de la foiblesse de l'esprit humain*, was published posthumously in 1723.[9] The *Traité* presents the view that our intellectual faculties cannot reach metaphysical certainty. Among the various arguments given by Huet to support this view, those derived from Descartes figure preeminently. The sceptical argument Huet finds most decisive is the veil of ideas. The physiology of the nerves and the animal spirits, together with the mind–body distinction, leave us completely in the dark as to whether our sense perceptions correspond or not to the material things that cause them (Huet 1974: 32–52). He rehearses the Pyrrhonian modes (PH I 40–123) dealing with perceptual variations (due to different percipient beings, to different senses, to different conditions of the perception and so on) in terms of different compositions of the brain and nerves and, crucially, the break in the mechanism of perception from the movement in the brain to the perception in the mind. Huet thereby updates ancient Pyrrhonian and Academic sceptical criticism of Stoic epistemology, whose purpose was to show the obscurity

---

[9] I discovered at the Bibliothèque Nationale, Paris, a Latin manuscript of this work, BN Ms Lat 11443, in which it figures as the first book of a much larger work, which also included the *Censura Philosophiae Cartesianae*, Book II (Paris, 1689), and the *Quaestiones Alnetanae*, Book III (Paris, 1690).

of things from the point of view of sense perception (the point of view considered in the Academics' debate with the Stoics) (Cicero Ac: I. 44).

Another central sceptical argument for Huet begins from Descartes' doubt about our origins. He builds on Pascal's view (La 131) that, 'apart from faith and revelation', we cannot tell whether the things we feel as indubitable truths are in fact true, because the credibility of our feelings depends on our nature and its origin.[10] Huet's aim is to show that philosophy cannot provide metaphysical certainty and that in order to have it we must rely on revelation. Once this point has been established, Book II of the original work (the *Censurae*) purports to show that the most fashionable philosophy of the time—that is, Descartes'—failed to provide metaphysical certainty. Huet praises Descartes' decision to begin with doubt but argues that the *cogito* and the proofs for the existence of God are undermined by the doubts raised in the First Meditation. Descartes began philosophizing as one must, by doubting everything, but when he advanced his positive metaphysical views he sinned against the intellectual integrity which he championed at the outset of his philosophy. According to Huet, the coherent conclusion of the First Meditation is the sceptical scenario alluded to by Descartes at its end, when he writes: 'if it is not in my power to know any truth, I shall at least do what is in my power, that is, resolutely guard against assenting to any falsehoods' (CSM II 15). According to Huet, the two objectives of 'the art of doubting' are 'to avoid error' and to 'prepare the mind to receive the faith' (Huet 1974: 209). Once he has established that the human cognitive faculties are incapable of certain knowledge and that the Cartesian attempt has failed, Huet moves on in Book III to argue that the Christian revelation is supported by historical and philological arguments which, although deprived of metaphysical certainty, are solidly grounded on the history of mankind. Because the *Traité* was published apart from these other works, it was wrongly interpreted as supporting Pyrrhonism and blind fideism (Maia Neto 2008).

Simon Foucher, a friend of Huet's, undertook the philosophical project of rehabilitating the Academic tradition. Foucher's relation to Descartes may have been similar to Arcesilaus' relation to Plato. As Arcesilaus, according to Cicero (Ac I 15–18), assumed *epoche* to contravene the Stoic dogmatic development of Plato, so Foucher reacted to contemporary Cartesians, notably Nicolas Malebranche, who was developing dogmatic views from Descartes. Foucher thus endeavoured to preserve the non-dogmatic aspect of Descartes in a way similar to Arcesilaus' endeavour concerning Plato. Foucher's Academic rules of philosophizing correspond approximately to Descartes' methodical rules (Foucher 1687: 5–8). But, according to Foucher, Descartes himself followed these rules only to the point of establishing the *cogito*. From there on he could not avoid precipitation, above all in

---

[10] Huet's reading marks in his copy of the *Pensées* discloses his source (Maia Neto 2006).

believing that he could prove the existence of an external material world. He says that if one ever has 'courage and patience to follow these [Academic] rules with exactitude one can hope for success greater than one can imagine, so much the more so that the truth discovered in recent centuries will add new sources of light to the ancient meditations' (Foucher 1995: 15).

This truth discovered in recent times is the view that the so-called secondary qualities are in the mind. The progress one can achieve with respect to this truth by following more thoroughly the Academic rules than Descartes did is the discovery that the so-called primary qualities are also in the mind. All this, concludes Foucher, sheds new light on the 'ancient meditations' that exposed sense error, corroborating scepticism about the material world and opening the way for the discovery of intellectual truths.[11] Foucher claims that an Academic can provide a proof of God by following the Platonic principle that 'everything we can know through the senses cannot subsist without an antecedent thought or understanding which gives being to all things' (Foucher 1687: 131). This principle shows how far Foucher is from materialism and how close he is to Leibniz. Foucher applauds Leibniz's view that matter is not pure extension and that it must have some kind of mental nature.[12] Popkin and Richard Watson have pointed out how Foucher's attack on the distinction between primary and secondary qualities, which was conveyed above all through the 'Pyrrho' article in Pierre Bayle's *Dictionnaire*, was historically important to Berkeley's idealism and to Hume's scepticism about the senses (Popkin 2003: 276; Watson 1969: xxix–xxx).

Foucher might have welcomed Berkeley's idealism if he had been able to regard it as consistent with the Academic laws of inquiry. He does not claim, however, that there is no matter, probably because of his adherence to the Academic classical tradition that emphasizes the obscurity of things. According to Foucher, Descartes himself is unconsciously an Academic, though only in intention. He failed mainly because he pretended that (what he perceived as) his clear and distinct idea of extension corresponded to what exists externally in the material world. Descartes fails to implement the Academic method (which was also his own) out of precipitation, thereby betraying his own project of philosophizing in order to detach the

---

[11] For Foucher, doubt is a method to eliminate prejudices and to prepare the mind for the truth. He attributes this position to the Academics: 'they doubted only provisionally in order to become better disposed to receive knowledge of the truth' (Foucher 1687: 154). This interpretation is based on the legend diffused by Sextus and Augustine, and which is denied by most contemporary scholars, that the Academics were secret Platonists who doubted the sensualist and materialist philosophy of the Stoics and Epicureans in order to preserve the Platonic truths.

[12] In a letter of 30 May 1691 to Leibniz, Foucher says that '*pour ce qui est de l'essence de la matiere, il y a longtems que je me suis declaré sur ce point dans ma Critique et ailleurs où je pretends que l'on se trompe de pretendre que toute étendue soit materielle. Je suis bien aise de voir que vous vous accordez avec moy en ce point*' (GP I 399).

mind from the material world. Because Foucher considers the idea of extension as sense-based, just like those of colour and taste, he saw Descartes failing in a way similar to the way in which, according to Descartes in the Letter-Preface to the French translation of the *Principles*, Aristotle and his scholastic disciples failed by departing from the Academic tradition.[13] So Foucher took as his mission to revive and update Academic prudence and vigilance against precipitation, extending doubt to the so-called 'primary qualities' and thereby fully realizing its liberating potential.

Bayle, like Foucher, developed sceptical arguments about the existence of an external material world in the footsteps of Malebranche, who claimed, based on Cartesian metaphysical principles, that only faith can assure us of such existence (Remark B of 'Pyrrho', and Remark H of 'Zeno of Elea': Bayle 1984). He argues that the new philosophy establishes Pyrrhonism in an assertive way, for the modern philosophers do not just suspend judgement about whether things have a certain colour or taste. They positively show that they have none. He claims that the same arguments apply to the so-called primary qualities (Remark B of 'Pyrrho'). Criticizing Descartes' proof of the existence of an external material world in Meditation VI, Bayle says that if Descartes claims that God does not deceive us when we commit the mistake of affirming that things are coloured, odoriferous, etc., why would He be a deceiver if our belief in external material extended bodies were false? Bayle goes further than Foucher to the extent that his arguments are not only epistemological but also metaphysical. He shows the paradoxes that reason encounters when it tries to understand extension ('Zeno of Elea') and the paradoxes that result from Descartes' doctrine of the creation of the eternal truths (Paganini 2000).

It is also in Remark B of his dictionary article 'Pyrrho' that Bayle sets forth the famous dialogue between two abbots, one of whom claims that the Christian mysteries abolish the validity of the most self-evident truths. The Trinity destroys the principle of the excluded middle, the Eucharist destroys the principles of non-contradiction and identity, Transubstantiation denies the metaphysical principle that modes cannot exist without a substance, and the Fall of Man makes null our most basic ethical principles. In Remark C, Bayle gives a fideist solution to these doubts, which has been the object of much controversy. Whereas Popkin (2003: 283–302) and Hickson and Lennon (2009) find no reason not to take Bayle at face value, Mori (1999) has attempted to reestablish the Enlightenment view of Bayle as

---

[13] Descartes says that 'although [Aristotle] had been Plato's disciple for twenty years, and possessed no principles apart from those of Plato, he completely changed the method of stating them and put them forward as true and certain' (CSM I 181). Putting it in Foucher's terms, Aristotle broke with the (sceptical) Academy (which was the right way to philosophize) by assenting to what is not evident; that is, he did not avoid precipitate conclusions. Aristotle's disciples, continues Descartes, recognized that some things were certain but mistook those things for sense perception: 'certainty does not lie in the senses but solely in the understanding, when it possesses evident perceptions' (CSM I 182).

an anti-Christian rationalist: the opposition of the Christian mysteries to the rational principles show the falsity and absurdity of the former. The safest view is that the abbots' paradoxes reveal neither a Christian fideist nor an atheist in Bayle, but rather his denial of any kind of natural theology, and his belief in the irreconcilable opposition between faith and reason. 'If you do not want to believe anything but what is evident and in conformity with the common notions, choose philosophy and leave Christianity. If you are willing to believe the incomprehensible mysteries of religion, choose Christianity and leave philosophy' (Bayle 1991: 429). This is consistent with other positions held by Bayle, notably his attack on theodicy, by claiming that reason cannot reconcile Christianity with the existence of evil ('Manicheans' in Bayle 1991).

Though Bayle denied any role for reason in Christianity, which is supernatural, he considered reason crucial in all natural things. He joins Foucher in rejecting Descartes' metaphysical doubts of the First Meditation, because they serve to show only the abyss into which metaphysical reason can lead us. However, he endorses Cartesian methodic doubt as it is presented in the rules of Part II of the *Discourse*. The key to Bayle's view of scepticism is not to be found in his article on 'Pyrrho' but in 'Remark G' of the article on a major adversary of the Academic sceptics, the Stoic Chrisippus. Bayle says that Chrisippus and the dogmatists in general are not philosophers fully committed to intellectual integrity because their philosophizing is prejudiced by their attempt to conceal the weak features of their own systems. Bayle then distinguishes two kinds of philosophers: '*avocats*' and '*rapporteurs*'. 'The former, in proving their Opinions, hid the weak side of their Cause, and the strong of their Adversaries, as much as they could. The latter, to wit, the Sceptics or Academics, represented the strong and the weak Arguments of the two opposite Parties, faithfully, and without any Partiality' (Bayle 1984: II, 487). Pointing out that Christians as Christians cannot be merely *rapporteurs*, Bayle tells a theologian who charged him with defending heretical views that, as a historian, and not as a Christian he 'may, and ought, faithfully to represent the most specious things that the worst Sects can allege in their own vindication, or against Orthodoxy' (Bayle 1984: II, 487). In 'Dissertation on the project of the Dictionary', Bayle uses the same term '*rapporteur*' to characterize his own method as a historian. Labrousse (1964: II, 57) says that Bayle applies Descartes' method to the historical field, although in Bayle the Cartesian method is 'reduced to the first rule, and severed from its metaphysical consequences'. This is entirely consistent with Foucher's claim that Descartes is Academic as far as the first rule of his method is concerned: 'carefully to avoid precipitate conclusions and preconceptions' (CSM I 120). This rule is emphasized by Foucher in opposition to its abandonment by the major Cartesians and it is crucial in his effort to recover the sceptical side of Cartesianism, which was neglected by Descartes' followers who developed the doctrinaire aspects of Cartesian philosophy.

Post-Cartesian early modern scepticism is mostly Academic. By sceptically incorporating some aspects of Descartes' philosophy, Huet, Foucher, and Bayle attempt to undo Descartes' subversion of Charron's academic sceptical wisdom.[14]

## REFERENCES

BACON, F. (1875). *The New Organon*, in *The Works*, vol. IV, ed. J. Spedding, R. Ellis, and D. Heath. London: Longmans.

BAILLET, A. (1691). *La Vie de M. Descartes*. Paris: Daniel Horthemels.

BAYLE, P. (1984). *The Dictionary Historical and Critical*. 5 vols, reprint of the 1734–8 English edn. New York: Garland.

BAYLE, P. (1991). *Historical and Critical Dictionary: Selections*. Ed. and trans. R. Popkin. Indianapolis, IN: Hackett.

BRAHAMI, F. (1997). *Le Scepticisme de Montaigne*. Paris: PUF.

BRAHAMI, F. (2001). *Le Travail du Scepticisme. Montaigne, Bayle, Hume*. Paris: PUF.

BRAHAMI, F. (2008). 'Au fil conducteur du scepticisme: science et métaphysique chez Glanvill'. *Philosophiques*, 35: 207–22.

BRUNDELL, B. (1987). *Pierre Gassendi. From Aristotelianism to a New Natural Philosophy*. Dordrecht: Reidel.

CARDOSO, S. (2009). 'On Skeptical Fideism in Montaigne's *Apology for Raymond Sebond*', in J. Maia Neto, G. Paganini, and J. C. Laursen (eds), *Skepticism in the Modern Age. Building on the work of Richard H. Popkin*. Leiden: Brill, 71–82.

CARRAUD, V. (2004). 'L'imaginer inimaginable: le Dieu de Montaigne', in Vincent Carraud and Jean-Luc Marion (eds), *Montaigne: scepticisme, métaphysique, théologie*. Paris: PUF, 137–71.

CARRIERO, J. (1997). 'The First Meditation', in V. Chappell (ed.), *Descartes's Meditations: Critical Essays*. Lanham: Rowman & Littlefield, 1–31.

CHARRON, P. (1986). *De la Sagesse*. Ed. Barbara de Negroni. Paris: Fayard.

CICERO, M. T. (1994). *De Natura Deorum and Academica*. Trans. and ed. H. Rackham. Loeb Classical Library. Cambridge, MA: Harvard University Press. First edition 1933.

DEAR, P. (1988). *Mersenne and the Learning of the Schools*. Ithaca, NY: Cornell University Press.

EVA, L. (2006). 'Sobre as afinidades entre a filosofia de Francis Bacon e o ceticismo'. *Kriterion*, 47: 73–97.

FISHER, S. (2005). *Gassendi's Philosophy of Science. Atomism for Empiricists*. Leiden: Brill.

FOUCHER, S. (1687). *Dissertation sur la Recherche de la Verité contenant l'Apologie des Academiciens. Où l'on fait voir que leur maniere de Philosopher est plus utile pour la Religion, & la plus conforme au bon sens. Pour servir de Réponse à la Critique de la Critique, &c. Avec plusieurs remarkes sur les ERREURS des SENS & sur l'Origine de la Philosophie de Monsieur Descartes*. Paris: Estinne Michallet.

FOUCHER, S. (1995). *Critique [of Nicolas Malebranche] Of the Search for the Truth in which is examined at the same time a part of the Principles of Mr. Descartes. Letter by an*

[14] This work benefited from research grants from CNPQ and FAPEMIG.

*Academician*, tr. Richard A. Watson. In R. Watson and M. Grene (eds), *Malebranche's First and Last Critics*. Carbondale: Southern Illinois University Press.

FRANKFURT, H. (1968). 'Descartes's Validation of Reason', in W. Doney (ed.), *Descartes*. Garden City, NY: Doubleday.

GASSENDI, P. (1959). *Exercitationes paradoxicae adversus aristoteleos*, ed. and tr. Bernard Rochot. Paris: Vrin.

GASSENDI, P. (1962). *Disquisitio Metaphysica seu dubitationes et instantiae adversus Renati Cartesii metaphysicam et Responsa*. Ed. and tr. Bernard Rochot. Paris: J. Vrin.

GAUKROGER, S. (1995). *Descartes: An Intellectual Biography*. Oxford: Clarendon Press.

GIOCANTI, S. (2001). *Penser l'Irrésolution. Montaigne, Pascal, La Mothe Le Vayer. Trois itinéraires sceptiques*. Paris: Honoré Champion.

GIOCANTI, S. (2004). 'Quelle place pour Dieu au sein du discours sceptique de Montaigne?' in M.-L. Demonet and A. Legros (eds), *L'Écriture du scepticisme chez Montaigne*. Paris: Droz, 63–76.

GLANVILL, J. (1978). *Scepsis Scientifica*. New York & London: Garland.

GOUHIER, H. (1954). 'La crise de la théologie au temps de Descartes'. *Revue de Théologie et de Philosophie*, 3e Série, 4: 19–54.

GOUHIER, H. (1987). *La Pensée métaphysique de Descartes*. Paris: Vrin.

GRANADA, M. (2006). 'Bacon and skepticism'. *Nouvelles de la république des letters*, 26: 91–5.

HICKSON, M. and LENNON, T. (2009). 'The real significance of Bayle's authorship of the *Avis*'. *British Journal for the History of Philosophy*, 17: 191–205.

HUET, P.-D. (1974). *Traité philosophique de la foiblesse de l'esprit humain*. Hildesheim: Olms [Rprt. of the 1723 Amsterdam edition].

HUME, D. (1975). *An Inquiry Concerning Human Understanding*, ed. L. A. Selby-Bigge. 3rd edn. P. H. Nidditch. Oxford: Clarendon.

JARDINE, L. (1983). 'Lorenzo Valla: Academic Skepticism and the New Humanist Dialectic', in M. Burnyeat (ed.), *The Skeptical Tradition*. Berkeley and Los Angeles: University of California Press, 253–86.

LA MOTHE LE VAYER, F. DE (1988). *Dialogues faits à l'imitation des anciens*. Ed. A. Pessel. Paris: Fayard.

LABROUSSE, E. (1964). *Pierre Bayle*. 2 vols. La Haye: Martinus Nijhoff.

LARMORE, C. (1998). 'Scepticism', in D. Garber and M. Ayers (eds), *The Cambridge History of Seventeenth-Century Philosophy*. Cambridge: Cambridge University Press, 1145–92.

LENNON, T. (2008). *The Plain Truth. Descartes, Huet and Skepticism*. Leiden: Brill.

MAIA NETO, J. (2003). 'Charron's *epoche* and Descartes's *cogito*: the sceptical base of Descartes's refutation of scepticism', in G. Paganini (ed.), *The Return of Scepticism from Hobbes and Descartes to Bayle*. Dordrecht: Kluwer, 81–113.

MAIA NETO, J. (2006). '"As principais forças dos pirrônicos" (La 131) e sua apropriação por Huet'. *Kriterion*, 114: 237–57.

MAIA NETO, J. (2008). 'Huet n'est pas un *sceptique Chrétien*'. *Les Etudes Philosophiques*, 2: 209–22.

MAIA NETO, J. (2009). 'Charron's Academic Sceptical Wisdom', in G. Paganini and J. Maia Neto (eds), *Renaissance Scepticisms*. Dordrecht: Springer, 213–27.

MANZO, S. (2009). 'Probability, Certainty, and Facts in Francis Bacon's Natural Histories. A Double Attitude Towards Skepticism', in J. Maia Neto, G. Paganini, and J. Laursen (eds), *Skepticism in the Modern Age*. Leiden: Brill, 123–38.

MARYKS, R. (2008). *Saint Cicero and the Jesuits. The Influence of the Liberal Arts on the Adoption of Moral Probabilism.* Hampshire: Ashgate.

MENN, S. (1998). *Descartes and Augustine.* Cambridge: Cambridge University Press.

MIERNOWSKI, J. (1998). *L'Ontologie de la contradiction sceptique.* Paris: Honoré Champion.

MONTAIGNE, M. DE (1991). *The Complete Essays.* Trans. M. A. Screech. London: Penguin.

MORI, G. (1999). *Bayle Philosophe.* Paris: Honoré Champion.

NAYA, E. (2006). *Essais de Michel Seigneur de Montaigne.* Paris: Ellipses.

OLIVEIRA, B. J. DE, and MAIA NETO, J. R. (2009). 'The Sceptical Evaluation of *Technê* and Baconian Science', in G. Paganini and J. Maia Neto (eds), *Renaissance Scepticisms.* Dordrecht: Springer, 249–73.

PAGANINI, G. (2000). 'Apogée et déclin de la toute-puissance: Pierre Bayle et les querelles post-cartésiennes', in G. Canziani, M. A. Granada, and Y. Ch. Zarka (eds), *Potentia Dei. L'onnipotenza nel pensiero dei secoli XVI e XVII.* Milan: Angeli, 589–630.

PAGANINI, G. (2008). *Skepsis. Le Débat des Modernes sur le Scepticisme.* Paris: Vrin.

PASCAL, B. (1966). *Pensées.* Trans. A. J. Krailsheimer. London: Penguin.

POPKIN, R. (1953). 'Joseph Glanvill: A Precursor of Hume'. *Journal of the History of Ideas*, 14: 292–303.

POPKIN, R. (2003). *The History of Scepticism from Savonarola to Bayle.* 3rd edn. Oxford: Oxford University Press.

SECADA, J. (2000). *Cartesian Metaphysics. The Late Scholastic Origins of Modern Philosophy.* Cambridge: Cambridge University Press.

SEXTUS E. (1987). *Outlines of Pyrrhonism* and *Adversus Mathematicos.* Trans. and ed. R. G. Bury. Loeb Classical Library. Cambridge, MA: Harvard University Press.

TALMOR, S. (1981). *Glanvill: The Uses and Abuses of Skepticism.* Oxford: Pergamon.

VAN LEEWEN, H. (1963). *The Problem of Certainty in English Thought 1630–1690.* The Hague: Martinus Nijhoff.

WATSON, R. (1969). 'Introduction', in S. Foucher's *Critique de la Recherche de la Verité.* New York: Johnson Reprint.

WILLIAMS, M. (1986). 'Descartes and the Metaphysics of Doubt', in Amelie Rorty (ed.), *Essays on Descartes's Meditations.* Berkeley: The University of California Press, 117–39.

WILSON, C. (2008). *Epicureanism at the Origins of Modernity.* Oxford: Oxford University Press.

# CHAPTER 12

....................................................................................

# HYPOTHESES

....................................................................................

## DESMOND M. CLARKE

I have not as yet been able to deduce from phenomena the reason for
these properties of gravity, and I do not feign [*fingo*] hypotheses. For
whatever is not deduced from the phenomena is to be called a hypothesis; and hypotheses, whether metaphysical or physical, or based on occult
qualities, or mechanical, have no place in experimental philosophy.

(*Principia* 943)

Isaac Newton wrote this famous disclaimer, for the second edition (1713), to correct
what he regarded as misinterpretations of *The Mathematical Principles of Natural
Philosophy*. Newton's deep-seated rejection of hypotheses, and the assumption that
their use in natural philosophy would compromise its status as genuine scientific
knowledge, reflects the complexity of a discussion that had been carried on for
more than a century before Newton. Throughout that period, it was assumed that
certainty is a necessary condition for knowledge, despite variations in the source
and definition of such certainty. Explicit challenges to that assumption began
following publication of Copernicus' *On the Revolutions*; the role and epistemic
status of hypotheses in scientific theory were central to that book's foreword, which
was subsequently discovered to have been written by Andreas Osiander (Jardine
1984: 150; Gingerich 2004: 158–64).

Osiander informed readers that, since an astronomer 'cannot in any way attain
to the true causes [of planetary motions], he will adopt whatever suppositions
enable the motions to be computed correctly from the principles of geometry for
the future as well as for the past' (Copernicus 1992: xx). He claimed that the
hypotheses proposed by Copernicus 'need not be true nor even probable', and

that 'they merely provide a reliable basis for computation' of planetary motions (Copernicus 1992: xx), although it is very doubtful that Copernicus had shared this antirealist interpretation of his work. For Osiander, astronomical hypotheses were mere mathematical devices for calculating the positions of the planets, and the question of their truth or otherwise did not arise.

During the following century, however, natural philosophers constructed theories in a wide range of fields such as magnetism, physiology, chemistry, meteorology, and optics—disciplines in which it was difficult to understand hypotheses as mere computational devices, because they involved postulating physical causes of observed phenomena. The proliferation of causal hypotheses during the seventeenth century and their function in a new understanding of scientific explanation eventually resulted in a redefinition of knowledge that was as fundamental as the Aristotelian definition that it replaced.

This reconceptualization of knowledge was inhibited for a long time by the apparent obviousness of the arguments by which Aristotle, following Plato, had distinguished between (i) mere opinions or plausible beliefs, and (ii) demonstrated truths, and had aligned the concept of knowledge unhesitatingly with the latter. Aristotle had explained scientific knowledge in the *Posterior Analytics* as follows: 'We think we understand a thing *simpliciter* (and not in the sophistic fashion accidentally) whenever we think we are aware both that the explanation because of which the object is is its explanation, and that it is not possible for this to be otherwise' (AR: 115). Aristotle claimed that scientific knowledge is inferred by valid syllogisms from primitive truths that are known by intuition and are necessarily true. The pattern of reasoning involved was called a 'demonstration' (pp. 299–300). This Aristotelian ideal of genuine knowledge generated a lengthy tradition of commentaries for almost two thousand years. During that period, although the meanings of key terms may have evolved, the fundamental division between 'demonstrated' knowledge-claims and other opinions remained as unchallenged as it had appeared evident to Aristotle. As a result, many of the natural philosophers who made key contributions to the Scientific Revolution struggled unsuccessfully with two incompatible convictions: (i) that it was impossible, without hypotheses, to construct scientific explanations of natural phenomena that were consistent with the new corpuscularian worldview; (ii) if Aristotle's definition of knowledge were relaxed, it would breach a self-evident distinction between genuine knowledge and mere opinion.

Despite these obstacles, however, fundamental developments in scientific knowledge eventually precipitated a correspondingly radical redefinition of what counts as knowledge and, in the period between Kepler's reply to Ursus in 1601 (Jardine 1984) and the publication of Huygens' *Treatise on Light* in 1690, many philosophers significantly adjusted their epistemic intuitions to their laboratory practices. This was a case in which practice preceded theory, or in which conceptual change was shaped by the success of a new kind of experimentally-based practice.

# I: Realism and instrumentalism

The history of astronomy up to the sixteenth century provided a uniquely appropriate subject matter for an instrumentalist interpretation of science. The sheer complexity of the motions that were assigned to planets, including epicyles and eccentric circles, together with the absence of any physical explanation of why planets moved in those apparent ways, made plausible the suggestion that the function of mathematical astronomy was to predict accurately the positions of planets vis-à-vis observers rather than to describe the actual paths by which they moved. Pierre Duhem (1969) summarized this history, somewhat simplistically, as the parallel development of two models of astronomy. One, characteristically exemplified by Ptolemy, constructed mathematical models which predicted the motions of the planets without purporting to represent their real motions. The other alternative was either to claim with Aristotle and his followers that we can identify the true causes of planetary motions in physics, or to adopt the sceptical attitude of Proclus that it is impossible for human beings to achieve the kind of understanding to which Aristotle aspired. The sceptics and Aristotelians were united in their agreement about the limitations of mathematical astronomy: 'The geometric contrivances we use to save the phenomena are neither true nor likely. They are purely conceptual . . . Very different hypotheses may yield identical conclusions, one saving the appearances as well as the other' (Duhem 1969: 21).

The conviction that hypothetical causes, such as planetary motions, could never be confirmed by the observational evidence to which they conform was motivated by the realization that 'affirming the consequent' is a logical fallacy. If one finds the body of Murphy dead, and if one then reasons: 'had A murdered Murphy, the latter would be dead; Murphy is dead; therefore A murdered him', it was obvious from at least the time of Aristotle that the conclusion does not follow, and that Murphy would be equally dead had he died from natural causes, had someone else dispatched him, etc. The awareness of this fallacy prevented astronomers from concluding that an astronomical hypothesis must be true simply because its implications correspond with our observations of apparent planetary motions. As Aquinas wrote, reflecting the established tradition of commentaries on Aristotle: 'The assumptions of the astronomers are not necessarily true. Although these hypotheses appear to save the phenomena, one ought not affirm that they are true, for one might conceivably be able to explain the apparent motions of the stars in some other way' (quoted in Duhem 1969: 41).

The two models of astronomy were both represented in Copernicus' *Revolutions* and in Osiander's anonymous preface. Johannes Kepler subsequently addressed many of the epistemological assumptions of the latter in reply to an instrumentalist tract written by Nicolaus Ursus (Nicolai Baer), entitled *A Tract concerning Astronomical Hypotheses*. Kepler's reply was completed in 1601, although it remained unpublished until 1858. Ursus had defined 'hypothesis' as 'a fictitious supposition that is a portrayal contrived out of certain imaginary circles or an imaginary form of the world-system, and thought up, adopted, and introduced for the purpose of keeping track of and saving the motions of the heavenly bodies and forming a method for calculating them' (Jardine 1984: 41). He thus included the falsehood of hypotheses in the very definition of the term. In reply, Kepler deployed a whole series of objections, beginning with an alternative definition of the term 'hypothesis'.

Kepler challenged the assumption that all hypotheses are false as 'a perverse understanding of the original sense' of the term, 'which seems to Ursus to be the same as "to feign"' (Jardine 1984: 144); for example, 'hypotheses' in geometry include axioms that are assumed to be true. The Latin term used here, *fingere*, was the same one chosen by Newton, in 1713, in the passage quoted in the epigraph above. Kepler also distinguished between the use of mathematical and physical hypotheses. 'Even if the conclusions of two hypotheses coincide in the geometrical realm, each hypothesis will have its own peculiar corollary in the physical realm' (Jardine 1984: 141–2), and he argued that the physical differences between hypotheses would provide reasons for choosing between them. Third, Kepler challenged the assumption that two different hypotheses could have exactly the same observational implications if they are integrated into a comprehensive theory and checked against a wide range of phenomena. He argued that, if those two conditions were satisfied, a false hypothesis would eventually 'betray itself' (Jardine 1984: 140). Finally, he compared the methods used in astronomy with other disciplines in which causal hypotheses are constructed to explain observations. In astronomy, 'we first of all perceive with our eyes the various positions of the planets at different times, and reasoning then imposes itself on these observations and leads the mind to recognition of the form of the universe' (Jardine 1984: 144). While the logic of this mental 'leading' remained unspecified, it was significant to recognize that the starting-point for constructing hypotheses was observation. Kepler emphasized that the same method is used when a physician reasons from symptoms to the identification of a disease, or when William Gilbert proposed an explanation of magnetic phenomena by 'first collecting observations in the study of magnets' (Jardine 1984: 146).

Kepler thus opened up a wider discussion than was envisaged if one merely compared how alternative mathematical hypotheses 'save the phenomena'. He openly acknowledged one of the factors that would recur frequently in subsequent discussions, namely, that hypotheses designed to explain natural phenomena must involve some degree of conjecture:

I shall also do the same where, as is customary in the physical sciences, I mingle the probable [*probabilia*] with the necessary and draw a plausible [*probabilem*] conclusion from the mixture. Since I have mingled celestial physics with astronomy in this work, no one should be surprised at a certain amount of conjecture [*conjecturas*]. This is the nature of physics, of medicine, and of all the sciences which make use of other axioms besides the most certain evidence of the eyes.    (Kepler 1992: 47)[1]

---

[1] Kepler refers in *Astronomia Nova* to a causal hypothesis as a 'physical conjecture' [*conjectura physica*] (1992: 52, 53).

The choice between Ptolemy and Copernicus could not be made simply by discovering which hypothesis best saves the phenomena, but by deciding which one best *explains* the observed motions of the planets, and in that judgement the simplicity of competing hypotheses, and the plausibility of the proposed cause, were relevant criteria (Westman 1972). Kepler's legacy included, therefore, not just an elegant mathematical description of planetary motions that matched our observations, but an attempt to provide a hypothetical causal explanation of those motions by reference to a universal solar force that was conceived by analogy with magnetic force.

## II: INSTRUMENTALISM AND THE CHURCHES

While Osiander's unauthorized foreword to *On the Revolutions* contrasted what he described as the mathematical fictions invented by astronomers with the attempt by philosophers to seek at least 'the semblance of truth', he also claimed that neither astronomers nor philosophers 'will understand or state anything certain, unless it has been divinely revealed' (Copernicus 1992: xx). Osiander thereby introduced one of the unquestioned assumptions of the period: that what is revealed in sacred scriptures enjoys the highest degree of certainty, as if God's omniscience could be transmitted through human texts without compromise or dilution (p. 552). Unless one adopted some version of a 'two truths' doctrine—that it is possible to hold inconsistent truths that result from different sources, such as reason and religious faith—the simplest solution to apparent conflicts between revelation and scientific knowledge was to distinguish, as Osiander had suggested, between the certainty of revelation and the relative uncertainty of scientific views, and to conclude that revealed truths effectively trump all other claims that are inconsistent with them. Thus, if *On the Revolutions* were understood as nothing more than a mathematical hypothesis for computing planetary positions, it could be tolerated for the same reasons as Ptolemy or any other similar hypothesis, and the apparent conflict between heliocentrism and revealed Christian doctrine was resolved by reducing the former to 'mere hypotheses'. The alternative solution, evidently, was to argue in the opposite direction—to query the certainty with which theologians interpreted biblical texts, and to adjust such interpretations in the light of new scientific developments.

Kepler was among the first to propose the latter solution. He did so as a Lutheran, under the protection of the Holy Roman emperor at Prague. The Imperial Mathematician concluded that, among the three competing theories of planetary motions, those of Ptolemy, Copernicus, and Brahe, 'only Copernicus' opinion concerning the world (with a few small changes) is true, and the other two are false' (Kepler 1992: 48). Kepler recognized that a literal interpretation of some biblical texts implied that the sun moved around the earth, rather than vice versa, and he addressed this question directly in the *New Astronomy* (1609): 'Now the Holy Scriptures, too, when treating of common things ... speak with humans in the human manner, in order to be understood by them. They make use of what is generally acknowledged, in order to weave in other things that are more lofty and divine' (Kepler 1992: 60). In other words, the Bible was not written to teach astronomy and, in the course of expressing views about God or morality (which is its primary function), it assumed the pre-scientific views of the times in which its various books were written. This attempt to reconcile the Bible and heliocentrism was even more notoriously adopted by Galileo.

Galileo, however, had to contend with a less receptive ecclesiastical and political authority in the Roman Catholic Church. Osiander's instrumentalist interpretation of Copernicanism was endorsed by Bellarmine in 1614:

> To say that assuming the earth moves and the sun stands still saves all the appearances better than eccentrics and epicycles is to speak well. This has no danger in it, and it suffices for mathematicians. But to wish to affirm that the sun is really fixed in the centre of the heavens and merely turns upon itself without travelling from east to west, and that the earth is situated in the third sphere and revolves very swiftly around the sun, is a very dangerous thing, not only by irritating all the theologians and scholastic philosophers, but also by injuring our holy faith and making the sacred Scripture false. . . . To demonstrate that the appearances are saved by assuming the sun at the centre and the earth in the heavens is not the same thing as to demonstrate that in fact the sun is in the centre and the earth in the heavens.   (Drake 1957: 163–4)

Galileo addressed this challenge in the *Letter to the Grand Duchess Christina* in 1615, in which he engaged in a dialectical discussion of the warrant for his own astronomical theory and of the uncertainty of the Church's biblical interpretation. Although he conceded that astronomical hypotheses need to be 'demonstrated', he claimed that his own theories had been confirmed by observational evidence. In parallel, he argued, as Kepler had done, that the Bible 'was not written to teach us astronomy' (Drake 1957: 212). Therefore, rather than look to the Bible for astronomical theories, Galileo argued that such theories should be based on 'sense-experiences and necessary demonstrations' (Drake 1957: 182). Having conceded that his own theories should be demonstrated, he had to admit that 'probable arguments' (183) would not be enough to outweigh the authority of the scriptures even about issues that are not matters of faith.[2] His attempts to specify the

---

[2] Galileo appealed numerous times, in the same *Letter*, to 'necessary demonstrations and sense experiences' and to 'manifest sense and necessary demonstrations' (186), and he distinguished between merely 'probable conjectures' and 'propositions of which we have ... positive assurances through experiments, long observation, and rigorous demonstration' (197). He classified heliocentrism among the latter. Galileo's efforts to limit the authority of the scriptures to matters of faith, and to defend Copernicanism as 'demonstrated', are examined in detail in McMullin (2005: 150–90).

epistemic status of astronomical hypotheses was doomed to failure as long as he framed the discussion, as did his Church critics, within the limits of the Aristotelian concept of demonstration (McMullin 2005: 88–116).

The condemnation of Galileo cast a very long shadow over discussions of the relative boundaries of science and religion in the early modern period. For example, Descartes heard about the condemnation in 1633, just as he made final preparations to publish his first book on natural philosophy, *Le Monde*, in which he had also defended heliocentrism. He promptly suppressed the book and left it unpublished for the rest of his life. His subsequent attempts to placate church authorities were obvious when he requested prior approval for the *Meditations* from the theology faculty at the University of Paris, and when he concluded the *Principles of Philosophy* in 1644 with these words: 'However, mindful of my weakness, I make no claims, but I submit all these opinions both to the authority of the Catholic Church and the judgment of those who are more wise' (AT VIII-1 329).

Following Galileo, the theological motivation for supporting instrumentalism was less prominently invoked against natural philosophers during much of the seventeenth century, although the power of the churches to suppress dissent provided an implicit boundary beyond which astute natural philosophers did not stray. In some countries, in which the dominant Christian churches were reformed, the argument ran in the opposite direction and the uncertainty of science fostered theological latitudinarianism (Shapiro 1983: 74–118). The defensive posture did emerge, however, in a renewed guise in the Church of Ireland in the early eighteenth century, in the work of George Berkeley. Berkeley contrasted the uncertainty of scientific theories with the certainty of sensory observations or conclusions that were inductively or deductively inferred from them. This represented a shift in the rationale for instrumentalism, although the conclusion remained the same, *viz.* that knowledge is limited by definition to what is certain, and divine revelation and (with Berkeley) what we perceive are much more certain than scientific hypotheses.

# III: The logic of explanation and confirmation

Descartes is often held responsible, especially in a negative sense, for the profusion of speculative hypotheses that some of his successors classified as unsupported conjectures. He rejected completely contemporary scholastic explanations in terms of forms and qualities and, by implication, the natural philosophy to which the Holy Office appealed in its condemnation of Galileo (Clarke 1992). In its place, he proposed that there is only one matter in the universe rather than two (*viz.* celestial and terrestrial), that it is divisible into indefinitely many small parts of varying sizes, shapes, and motions, and that a specification of the properties of such particles could provide an explanation of any natural phenomenon. Since the particles in question were unobservable or, at least, unobservable to Descartes despite the incipient development of optical instruments, the only way to construct such explanations was to hypothesize an appropriate combination of small particles and their motions that could give rise to a particular phenomenon. This understanding of explanation was evidently open to the familiar objection that more than one such hypothesis may be compatible with the same observational evidence. That point was put directly to Descartes in 1638 by Jean-Baptiste Morin, who had earlier defended the traditional view that the earth is stationary at the centre of the universe (Morin 1631).

You know very well that the appearance of celestial movements results equally certainly from the assumption that the earth is at rest as from the assumption that it is in motion. Therefore, the experience of this appearance is not sufficient to prove which of these two causes just mentioned is the true cause.... There is nothing easier than to adjust some cause to a given effect, and you know that this is familiar to astronomers, who by means of different hypotheses, of circles and ellipses, come to the same conclusion.   (AT I 538–9)

Descartes replied that, in principle, 'there are many effects to which it is easy to adjust different causes.' He had already intimated, in the *Discourse on Method* (to which Morin was objecting), that it should be possible to choose the most plausible hypothesis from among alternative possible explanations by conducting crucial experiments. 'I know of no other way of doing this except by then looking for some experiences such that their occurrence is not the same if the effect should be explained in one rather than another of these ways' (AT VI 65). Morin's objection prompted him to appeal to a number of other factors, such as the simplicity and intelligibility of hypotheses, and the disparate range of phenomena that they explained, as evidence that his proposed explanations were more likely to be correct than those offered by other philosophers.

If one compares the assumptions of other philosophers with mine ... and if one compares what I have deduced from my assumptions concerning vision, salt, the winds, the clouds, snow, thunder, the rainbow, and similar things, with what others have derived from theirs about the same phenomena, I hope that this will be enough to persuade those who are not too prejudiced that the effects that I explain have no other causes apart from those from which I deduced them.   (AT II 200)

Descartes also identified another element of what would eventually be adopted as a solution to this problem, in reply to Mersenne, when he clarified what was reasonable to expect in this type of inquiry. The Minim friar had asked whether Descartes' speculations amounted to a 'demonstration', by which he meant an Aristotelian demonstration. The Cartesian reply reintroduced a distinction that had been made by Kepler: that the term 'demonstration' means different things in physics and mathematics.

You ask whether I believe that what I have written about refraction is a demonstration. I believe it is, at least insofar as it is possible to provide a demonstration in this subject matter without having first demonstrated the principles of physics by means of metaphysics . . . and in so far as any other question in mechanics, or optics, or astronomy, or any subject which is not purely geometrical or arithmetical, has ever been demonstrated. But to demand geometrical demonstrations from me, in something which depends on physics, is to expect me to do the impossible.   (AT II 141–2)

This illustrates Descartes' unresolved ambivalence about the methods used in his scientific essays in 1637. On the one hand, he admits that the distinctive character of explanations in natural philosophy makes it impossible to produce proofs that realize the logic or certainty of mathematics. At the same time, he implies that it would have been possible in principle to ground his physical assumptions in metaphysical principles and that, with such extra foundations, his natural philosophy would achieve the certainty of a classical demonstration.

Descartes also acknowledged the apparent circularity involved when, beginning from observations, one imagines hypothetical causes that may explain them, and then confirms the hypotheses because they are consistent with the observational effects for which they were postulated as causes. He addressed this issue in Part VI of the *Discourse on Method*: 'I take my reasonings to be so closely interconnected that just as the last are proved by the first, which are their causes, so the first are proved by the last, which are their effects.' However, he denied that this reasoning process is formally circular: 'There is a big difference between proving and explaining. To this I add that one can use the word "demonstrate" to mean one or the other, at least if one understands it according to common usage and not according to the special meaning which philosophers give it' (AT II 198). Thus, while observed phenomena are 'explained' by hypothetical causes, the latter are 'proved' or confirmed by the former.

Pascal provided a famous example of this style of reasoning when he requested his brother-in-law, Florin Périer, to test his hypothesis that the weight of air is the cause of variations in the height of mercury in a Torricelli tube. The phenomenon that was observed at ground-level was not in dispute; the mercury in a Torricelli tube rises to a height of approximately thirty inches and does not flow out of the tube. What was at issue was the explanation of this phenomenon. Pascal wished to prove that the cause was not nature's fear of a vacuum, but the weight of the air in the atmosphere that pressed down on the surface of the mercury in the dish. He proposed that his hypothesis be tested by carrying a sample of the experiment up the side of a mountain. As one ascends, the column of air weighing down on the mercury surface should decrease and the height of the mercury in the tube should decrease proportionately; likewise, on returning to the bottom of the mountain, the column of mercury should recover its original height. Since Pascal was too ill to perform the experiment himself, Périer did so on his behalf (19 September 1648), on the puy-de-Dôme, and all the results (at least as reported) matched exactly Pascal's predictions (Pascal 1998: I, 426–35).

It was obvious that Pascal was not interested merely in recording variations in atmospheric pressure at different heights or correlating them with the heights above sea-level at which the readings were taken. Pascal designed the 'famous experiment' to confirm a causal hypothesis; if the anticipated correlation were observed between the height of the mercury column and the height of the instrument above sea-level, he wanted to conclude that its cause is the pressure of the atmosphere on the surface of the dish of mercury. When he claimed that his causal hypothesis had been confirmed, he failed to understand the complexity of the reasoning involved in confirming hypotheses.

In contrast, Pascal displayed a prescient understanding of the factors that may interfere with attempts to disconfirm hypotheses experimentally. For example, he argued in the posthumously published *Treatise on the Weight of the Mass of Air* that a balloon filled with air should expand as it is carried up a mountain, because the weight of air that compresses it reduces in proportion to the height one climbs. If that result were found in practice, he argued, that would 'prove absolutely that the air has weight'. However, 'if there were no expansion in the balloon on top of the highest mountains, that would not destroy what I have deduced, for I could say that the mountains were not high enough to cause a perceptible difference' (Pascal 1998: I, 492). This anticipated what is now called the Duhem–Quine thesis, *viz.* that the experimental testing of a hypothesis presupposes other hypotheses, so that a failure to achieve an expected result may be attributed to one or more of the latter. The ways in which experimental tests may fail, without disconfirming an hypothesis that is being tested, were also discussed by Boyle (B: I, 35 ff.). However, in Pascal's case, he used the argument almost exclusively to claim a degree of certainty for the hypothesis about the weight of air that was not warranted by the evidence.

# IV: CERTAINTY AND PROBABILITY

The intuition that originated with Plato and Aristotle, that knowledge implies beliefs that are certain, seemed for centuries to be both self-evident and incapable of qualification. It also assumed that any given belief was either certain or uncertain, and that there were no degrees of certainty within which beliefs could qualify as 'knowledge'. The eventual though reluctant acceptance of scientific hypotheses as knowledge, therefore, presupposed the development of a concept of epistemic probability that admitted degrees of more or less certainty.

Descartes struggled unsuccessfully with this issue. Although conscious of the unsatisfiable demands of the traditional definition of knowledge, he claimed that at least the first principles of his natural philosophy were 'absolutely certain'. Nonetheless, he also conceded that many explanations of specific natural phenomena that depended on those principles were no more than 'morally certain':

> There are some claims, even in relation to natural phenomena, which we regard as absolutely, and more than morally, certain. . . . These include mathematical demonstrations, the knowledge that material things exist, and all evident reasoning about material things. Perhaps those who consider them will also admit into this class even those conclusions of mine [in the *Principia*] that have been deduced in a continuous sequence from the first and simplest principles of human knowledge . . . once those claims are accepted, it would seem as if all other natural phenomena can be understood, at least what I have written about the more general features of the universe and the earth, which can hardly be explained otherwise than as I have explained them.    (AT VIII-1 328–9)

Even this summary statement, at the conclusion of the *Principia Philosophiae*, reflects ambivalence in the face of a stark choice between absolute certainty and mere probability. In other contexts, however, Descartes conceded that while his principles may not have been certain they provided better explanations than those offered by other natural philosophers. It was almost as if an increase in explanatory success compensated for unavoidable uncertainty. 'I would not dare claim that those [principles] are the true principles of nature. All I claim is that, by assuming them as principles, I have satisfied myself in explaining all the many things which depend on them' (AT IV 690). Although Hacking claims that Descartes' philosophy 'had no room for probability' (1975: 46), it would be more accurate to acknowledge the frequent use of that term in his work while he struggled to find a middle ground between the certainty of *scientia* and the uncertainty of mere opinion.[3]

The intellectual effort to identify features of hypotheses that confirm their plausibility, in the four decades between Kepler and Descartes' *Principia*, began to accumulate a range of factors, such as: the intelligibility of hypotheses (compared, for example, with scholastic forms and qualities); the fact that a few primary principles could explain a large number of disparate natural phenomena; the quantification or mathematical expression of hypotheses, so that the agreement between hypotheses and observed phenomena could be subject to measurement; and the lack of alternative hypotheses which could compete with the apparent success of corpuscularian natural philosophy. Many of these intuitions were

---

[3] Hacking (1975: 45) emphasizes that Descartes 'had no truck with the nascent concept of probability.' However, as long as one is concerned with a 'nascent' concept of probability, Descartes' contribution should not be excluded as if the concept appeared for the first time in the 1660s. Shapiro

summarized by Robert Boyle, whose record of results as an experimental natural philosopher was unchallenged during the 1660s.

Boyle summarized much of the discussion from the previous decades in two unpublished manuscripts, in which he distinguished between good and excellent hypotheses. He listed some of the conditions for a 'good hypothesis' as follows:

1. That it be intelligible.
2. That it contain nothing impossible or manifestly false.
3. That it suppose not any thing that is either unintelligible, impossible, or absurd.
4. That it be fit and sufficient to explicate the phenomena, especially the chief.
5. That it be at least consistent with the rest of the phenomena it particularly relates to, and do not contradict any other known phenomena of nature, or manifest physical truth.

Boyle then listed some of the features of an 'excellent hypothesis':

1. That it be not precarious, but have sufficient grounds in the nature of the thing itself, or at least be well recommended by some auxiliary proofs.
2. That it be the simplest of all the good ones we are able to frame, at least containing nothing that is superfluous or impertinent.
3. That it be the only hypothesis that can explicate the phenomena, or at least that does explicate them so well.
4. That it enable a skilful naturalist to foretell future phenomena, by their congruity or incongruity to it, and especially the events of such experiments as are aptly devised to examine it, as things that ought or ought not to be consequent to it (S: 119).[4]

Efforts such as Boyle's to find a middle ground between absolute certainty and mere opinion were facilitated, during the seventeenth century, by the emergence of various concepts of probability (Hacking 1975; Shapiro 1983; Daston 1998). These developments originated in a revival of interest in ancient pyrrhonism, especially in the work of Montaigne, which implied an almost universal uncertainty about all opinions, and by the widespread uncertainty about religious dogmas that was precipitated by the Reformation. Independent developments in the understanding of historical and judicial evidence suggested that human agents are often required, not only to make judgements in conditions of uncertainty, but to act on those judgements. When applied to scientific hypotheses, therefore, it seemed unreasonable that one could not accept an apparently successful explanatory hypothesis

---

(1983: 38) likewise claims that 'neither Descartes nor Bacon had any interest in a probabilistic natural science.'

[4] A similar account is found in a previously unpublished Boyle manuscript, 'The Requisites of a Good Hypothesis breefly consider'd in a Dialogue, between Carneades, Eleutherius, Themistius, & Zosimus' (B: XIII, 270–2). See Hunter (2009: 119, 120).

until one had succeeded in 'demonstrating' its truth. Blaise Pascal was a significant contributor to this conceptual development.

Pascal rejected the theological theory of probabilism, according to which 'anything approved by well-known authors is probable and safe in conscience' (Pascal 1967: 204), even if there were more probable opinions available from other authorities. In contrast with probabilism, which relied exclusively on the authority of authors to decide which opinions were credible, the newly emerging theories of probability focused on objective evidence to decide the degree of warrant of an opinion. Here, as elsewhere, conceptual developments went hand in hand with innovative practices, although the full fruits of their interaction appeared only much later than the early modern period.

Different concepts of probability were articulated in response to a number of conceptually distinct problems. The latter included the kind of decision-making in conditions of uncertainty of which Pascal's wager about the existence of God was a famous example; the calculation of future values for annuities, which had become a recognized method of funding state-sponsored developments in the United Provinces; the analysis of rates of mortality in times of plague, and the likelihood of infection if alternative strategies for avoidance were adopted; and the reasonableness of belief in future events, depending on the 'probability' of their occurrence, to which the *Port Royal Logic* devoted its final chapters in 1662 (Arnauld and Nicole 1981: 338–55).

In parallel with the tentative steps taken by Pascal and others, many natural philosophers began to recognize that it was inappropriate to gauge the credibility of scientific explanations by comparing them with the certainty of purely formal disciplines such as mathematics or the allegedly incontestable truths of divine revelation. The uncertainty that characterizes explanations in natural philosophy could be explained by religious believers by reference to the limits of post-lapsarian human understanding. Since the 'fall' resulted in both moral weakness and intellectual impairment, human beings have no reason to expect that they could acquire absolutely certain knowledge. Similar limited expectations were explained by others, however, as the inevitable consequence of the logic of explanation.

Pierre-Sylvain Régis, for example, adopted the second option, when he expanded the reply that Descartes had given more than fifty years earlier to Mersenne. Régis distinguished two parts in physics: what he called 'practical physics' which is concerned with knowledge of observable effects, and 'speculative physics', which is concerned with knowledge of causes. He acknowledged the indirect manner in which one hypothesizes the unobservable causes of observable phenomena and concluded, in the *Cours entier de philosophie*:

Although speculative physics can be pursued only in a problematic way, and while nothing that is specifically demonstrative belongs to it, one must acknowledge that this part of physics, however uncertain it is, still holds one of the highest places in human knowledge.

For despite the fact that one is not entirely certain of what it teaches, one can still believe that one has learned everything which the human mind can know about a physical body if one succeeds in conceiving of a certain disposition, a certain figure and a certain arrangement of its parts from which one can easily deduce all the effects of the body. This implies that it would be equally unreasonable to demand demonstrations in physics as to be content with probabilities in mathematics; just as the latter should admit only what is certain and demonstrated, the former must accept what is merely probable, on condition that it is deduced from a single system based on the first truths of nature.   (Régis 1690: I, 275)

The same conclusion was reached by Christiaan Huygens, in a work that was published in the same year and was equally inspired by Descartes. Huygens had published the first textbook on probability in 1657. Although it was concerned with games of chance rather than with epistemic probability, it seemed like a short step from one to the other in the conceptual obscurity in which various theories of probability were developing. Huygens made the transition without friction when drafting the *Treatise on Light*. In the Preface to that work, he made a sharp distinction between the axioms used in mathematics and the observational evidence on which explanations in natural philosophy are based, and an equally clear distinction between the kinds of inference used in each discipline:

There will be seen in it [the *Treatise*] demonstrations of those kinds which do not produce as great a certitude as those of geometry, and which even differ much therefrom, since whereas geometers prove their propositions by fixed and incontestable principles, here the principles are verified by the conclusions to be drawn from them; the nature of these things not allowing of this being done otherwise. It is always possible to attain thereby to a degree of probability which very often is scarcely less than complete proof. To wit, when things which have been demonstrated by the principles that have been assumed correspond perfectly to the phenomena which experiment has brought under observation; especially when there are a great number of them, and further, principally, when one can imagine and foresee new phenomena which ought to follow from the hypotheses which one employs and when one finds that therein the fact corresponds to our prevision.   (Huygens 1962: vi–vii)

While the term 'complete proof' retains connotations of an Aristotelian 'demonstration', Huygens had creatively adapted insights from Descartes and Boyle to reflect accurately the methodology adopted in his *Treatise*. It was impossible to construct the kind of causal explanation that Huygens wished to discover except by constructing hypotheses and then testing, not only that they corresponded with already known observations, but also that they correctly predicted new experimental results.

Despite the development of elementary mathematical theories of probability and their application to the frequency with which similar events occur, which permitted the quantification of the probability that an event would occur (given various assumptions), there was no similar progress in quantifying the epistemic probability of hypotheses. That remained qualitative rather than quantitative. Thus, although there were signs in the final decades of the seventeenth century that degrees of probability are degrees of certainty, the fundamental disagreement of earlier decades concerning merely probable beliefs was still evident in Locke and Leibniz.

Locke repeated the claims made by Descartes in the *Rules*, before the latter had begun to do natural philosophy, that genuine knowledge is realized only by intuition or demonstration. 'These two, (*viz.*) Intuition and Demonstration, are the degrees of our Knowledge; whatever comes short of one of these, with what assurance soever embraced, is but Faith, or Opinion, but not Knowledge, at least in all general Truths' (*Essay* IV. ii. 14). Since Locke defined knowledge in terms of certainty, he contrasted probability negatively with the latter. '*Probability* is likeliness to be true, the very notation of the Word signifying such a Proposition, for which there be Arguments or Proofs, to make it pass or be received for true' (*Essay* IV. xv. 3). He was forced to conclude that certainty is realized only in purely formal disciplines, such as mathematics or morality, and that the efforts of natural philosophers to know the underlying causes of observable phenomena are doomed to failure.

'tis impossible we should know, which [primary qualities] have a necessary union or inconsistency one with another. . . . Besides this ignorance of the primary Qualities of the insensible Parts of Bodies, on which depend all their secondary Qualities, there is yet another and more incurable part of Ignorance, which sets us more remote from a certain Knowledge of the *Co-existence*, or *Inco-existence* (if I may so say) of different *Ideas* in the same Subject; and that is, that there is no discoverable connection between any *secondary Quality, and those primary Qualities* that it depends on.   (*Essay* IV. iii. 11, 12)

Locke thus assumed that the observable properties of natural phenomena depend on unobservable corpuscles, and since beliefs about the latter were expressed only in more or less probable causal hypotheses, he had to conclude that it is impossible in principle to acquire genuine knowledge either of the unobservable particles or their connection with observable properties. He concluded that 'how far soever humane Industry may advance . . . *scientifical* [philosophy] will still be out of our reach . . . as to a perfect *Science* of natural Bodies . . . we are, I think so far from being capable of any such thing, that I conclude it lost labour to seek after it' (*Essay* IV. iii. 26, 29).

Leibniz came to the opposite conclusion when he composed the *New Essays on Human Understanding* in 1705 (published in 1765), and disagreed fundamentally with Locke's evaluation of probability. 'Perhaps opinion, based on likelihood, also deserves the name knowledge; otherwise nearly all historical knowledge will collapse, and a good deal more . . . I maintain that the study of the degrees of probability would be very valuable and is still lacking' (LRB IV. ii. 14). Leibniz also disagreed with Locke's comment that the grounds of probability are 'the conformity of any thing with our own knowledge, observation, and experience' and 'the testimony of others' (*Essay* IV. xv. 4); he maintained that probability 'is always grounded in likelihood or in conformity with the truth', and that the 'testimony of others is something else' (LRB IV. xv. 4). Accordingly, he concluded that heliocentrism 'at the time when Copernicus was almost alone in his opinion, [it] was still incomparably more likely than that of all the rest of the human race' (LRB IV. xv. 4). The probability of an opinion, for Leibniz, was evidently not a function of the authority or the relative number of people who adopted it, but of the objective evidence that supported it.

Jakob Bernoulli summarized in 1705 the intuitions about epistemic probability that had been developing since Pascal, in his *Ars Conjectandi*. Bernoulli distinguished between what he called 'objective certainty', which applies to things, and 'subjective certainty', which applies to our knowledge of things. He recognized that the latter is 'not the same in respect of all things but varies, more or less, in many ways' (Bernoulli 1969: III, 239). Bernoulli defined probability as 'a degree of certainty, which differs from certainty as a part from the whole' (1969: III, 239). While one might query his definition of something as 'morally certain, whose probability is almost equal to complete certainty' (Bernoulli 1969: 240), one finds here, in the early eighteenth century, an acceptance of various degrees of certainty within human knowledge and the term 'probability' is used to describe that spectrum.

# V: NEWTON AND POSITIVISM

By the time Newton began to draft the *Principia* in 1684, the experimental work that characterized the culture of the Royal Society had completely displaced the model of science proposed in Aristotle's *Posterior Analytics*. There was also widespread concern that some Cartesians had tolerated many assumptions for which there was almost no empirical warrant. The alleged proliferation of unwarranted hypotheses seemed to confirm that, if the traditional definition of *scientia* as demonstration were relaxed, it would generate a slippery slope on which the distinction between mere guesswork and plausible hypotheses would be eliminated.

Rather than embark on that path, however, there were two other alternatives available in the 1680s, both of which had previously been adopted by Pascal. First, Descartes' distinction between the certainty of mathematics and the probability of physical hypotheses was intended to justify acceptance of the latter *faute de mieux*. However, the contrast could as easily have been used to select a new model of certainty in physical science, namely mathematics. Second, many of those who had contributed to the new scientific culture had also identified sensory observations as certain. Even Pascal was confident in claiming that 'matters of fact can only be proved by the senses' (1967: 295), and he used that criterion (mistakenly) to criticize the Jesuits' opposition to Galileo. These two features of the new science—a focus on sensory observations as certain, and the expression of scientific claims in mathematical terms—provided a novel opportunity for those who still demanded certainty in natural philosophy to present their work as depending exclusively on these secure foundations. In this context, hypotheses would be acceptable only if they were derived from observation by mathematical deductions. Newton was foremost in making this claim, and in attempting to apply it in natural philosophy.

Had Newton reflected explicitly on the kinds of reasoning used within scientific methods during the preceding century, he would have noticed three options. The most familiar was deduction which, when validly performed, preserved and transmitted the truth of premises to all their conclusions. The *Port Royal Logic* made familiar to a new generation of philosophers, in the 1660s, many of the valid deductive patterns of syllogistic reasoning that had been identified over a period of centuries. However, Newton would also have classified the reasoning used in geometry and, in general, in mathematics, as deductive in the sense that it was truth-preserving.

Newton was also aware of the inductive methods that had been championed by Bacon and implemented with such success by Boyle. In the case of Boyle's discovery of his eponymous law, he reported observing a correlation between the 'spring' of the air in a closed tube and its temperature. Of course, even such apparently simple observations could not have been recorded without an appropriate conceptualization of what to look for and how to measure it. Boyle noticed a covariance between observable values of what we now call the volume, pressure, and temperature of air in an enclosed container, and he extrapolated that covariance in two ways: (i) beyond the limits of pressure and temperature within which he made his observations, and (ii) by applying it to all gases, although his observations were confined to atmospheric air. This was an inductive generalization in Bacon's sense. There was no guarantee that the covariance observed by Boyle within narrow limits would still obtain outside those parameters, and there was even less certainty that it would apply in a similar way to all gases. However, even if the generalized conclusion were uncertain, it derived an obvious (limited) warrant from observations; for natural scientists who were committed to experimental methods, that was among the most secure evidence available. If counterexamples appeared in either extrapolation, the induction could be corrected by limiting its scope in the appropriate way.

There was a third type of reasoning which may be called 'retroductive', following Peirce's nomenclature introduced more than two centuries later. This is precisely the kind of reasoning with which Galileo, Descartes, Boyle, and others had grappled when they reflected on their scientific practice. It began with observations, and then postulated causes (often unobservable) of the observed phenomena. If the postulated or hypothetical causes satisfied the conditions listed by Boyle and Huygens, one then claimed that they were more or less probable because they explained the observed phenomena. Since this kind of reasoning could never achieve the truth-preserving features of deductive logic, it had to be classified also as inductive, although its logic differed significantly from what was called Baconian induction above.

If one reads Newton's very extensive work in mechanics and optics in the light of these three types of reasoning—deductive, Baconian inductive, and retroductive—it becomes clear that he struggled unsuccessfully to provide a description of his scientific method that both reflected his actual practice and guaranteed the certainty of his conclusions. The mathematical presentation of his theory in the *Principia* provided a superficial appearance of purely deductive inferences, on condition that the 'axioms' with which he began were as certain as mathematical axioms. Newton had claimed in the General Scholium, somewhat disingenuously, that 'in this experimental philosophy, propositions are deduced from the phenomena and are made general by induction' (*Principia* 943). This claim cannot be reconciled with the three axioms on which Newton's *Principia* relies. For example, the first axiom or law of nature is as follows: 'Every body perseveres in its state of being at rest or of moving uniformly straight forward, except insofar as it is compelled to change its state by forces impressed' (*Principia* 416). There are no observable bodies, in nature, on which no forces are impressed, and it was not possible for Newton to observe such phenomena. Even if they existed, however, there is no method by which any proposition could be 'deduced' from the bare phenomena. The gap between observation and proposition had to be filled by concepts, and these were not presented ready-made by his observations.

Even if one granted that the application to some bodies of apparently descriptive terms, such as 'hard', is based on experience, it would not justify their application to the imperceptible microscopic bodies of which observable bodies are composed. Newton addressed this issue in Rule III of the 'Rules of Reasoning in Philosophy' (which had been called 'hypotheses' in the first edition of the *Principia*). There he argued as follows: 'We know by experience that some bodies are hard. Moreover, because the hardness of the whole arises from the hardness of its parts, we justly infer from this not only the hardness of the undivided particles of bodies that are accessible to our senses, but also of all other bodies' (*Principia* 795). Apart from committing the fallacy of composition, this suspicious induction extends to all bodies a feature that is found by experience only in some. It also trades on frequent references to 'experiments', 'experience' and what is known 'by our senses' and compares the rigour of Newton's foundations with 'the dreams and vain fictions' of others. It would have been more accurate to acknowledge that, in this attempt to specify some of the universal properties of matter, the 'analogy of nature' on which Newton relied was not itself warranted by observation or experiment (McMullin 1978: 22–6; Shapiro 1993: 40).[5]

---

[5] Newton's description of his method contrasts with the acknowledged conjectural character (*conjicere*) of Descartes' description of the imperceptible causes (*caussae insensiles*) of observable effects, in Part Four of *Principia Philosophiae* (VIII-1 325–7).

What Newton actually did was to assume a contentious set of reciprocally defined concepts, such as absolute space, time, mass, and then use those concepts to describe bodies in motion in idealized conditions. Having made very significant assumptions about the concepts to be used in mechanics and the laws by which bodies move, Newton adopted nine 'hypotheses' to guide the development of mechanics (although, as mentioned above, these were renamed 'rules of reasoning' in later editions of the work). At best, having camouflaged the hypothetical character of his apparently axiomatic starting point, Newton developed mathematically a mechanics that was very much more successful, experimentally, than any previous theory. It is impossible to avoid the conclusion today that the warrant for his mechanics derived essentially from the experimental success that it enjoyed; for that reason, his mechanics was not deduced from an inductively warranted description of natural phenomena, as he claimed, but constituted a mathematical development of a small number of hypotheses that were indirectly warranted by their experimental success.

Newton's misrepresentation of his method was facilitated by the fact that one of the key explanatory factors on which his mechanics relied was gravity or, more generally, force. It was unclear whether gravity was an independent reality that explained causally why bodies move, or whether gravity merely named a dispositional feature of bodies that is defined in terms of their actual motions. Newton appreciated that the first option would have implied accepting the uncertainty of retroductive inferences, and he consistently rejected the suggestion that he was attempting to explain the cause of gravity. 'The cause of gravity is what I do not pretend to know' (Cohen and Schofield 1978: 298). This letter to Bentley confirmed the more general hesitation about forces that was explicit from the first edition of the *Principia* in which, according to Definition viii, the author claimed to provide only a mathematical concept of force, 'for I am not now considering the physical causes and sites of forces' (*Principia* 407).

While Newton was able to trade on the ambiguity of forces in the *Principia*, he was unable to avoid explicit retroductive inferences in the *Opticks*. The opening sentence tried to maintain the distinction that had camouflaged his use of hypotheses in the *Principia*: 'My design in this book is not to explain the properties of light by hypotheses, but to propose and prove them by reason and experiments' (Newton 1952: 1). However, Newton had been attempting to explain colour by using causal hypotheses for many years before publishing the *Opticks*. For example, when he made public 'An Hypothesis explaining the Properties of light, discoursed of in my several papers' in 1675 (Cohen and Schofield 1978: 178–90), it provoked the standard objection that had been familiar since the time of Copernicus, namely, that it may be possible to explain the same phenomena by different hypotheses. The French Jesuit, Ignace-Gaston Pardies, put this objection to Newton in 1672, to which he replied at length as follows:

...we should inquire diligently into the properties of things and establish them by experiments, and then more slowly pursue hypotheses for the explanation of them; for hypotheses ought to be accommodated only to explaining the properties of things, and not unlawfully assumed for defining them, except insofar as they may furnish experiments. For if solely from the possibility of hypotheses one conjectures about the truth of things, I see not how anything certain can be obtained in any science; since numerous hypotheses may always be devised, which shall seem to overcome new difficulties   (Cohen and Schofield 1978: 99, 106; Shapiro 1993: 18).

This temporary evasion failed to address the underlying issue of whether explanations, in optics, could be presented geometrically without making any assumptions about the nature of light or the realities that were represented geometrically as lines on a page. Newton tried to avoid this issue a second time, by classifying his causal hypotheses in the *Opticks* as 'queries' and by locating them in an appendix to the work. There he felt free to speculate that 'the rays of light are very small bodies emitted from shining substances', and that 'nothing more is requisite for putting the rays of light into fits of easy reflexion and easy transmission, than that they be small bodies which by their attractive powers, or some other force, stir up vibrations in what they act upon' (Newton 1952: 370, 372). The *Opticks* claimed that the assumptions made about light were not 'occult qualities' but 'general laws of nature, by which the things themselves are form'd; their truth appearing to us by phenomena, though their causes be not yet discover'd' (Newton 1952: 401).

Newton's consistent criticism of hypotheses and his efforts over a period of almost four decades to avoid them were, as Shapiro shows, 'a consequence of his equally long quest for certainty' (1993: 12). Nonetheless, he came close to acknowledging the logic and uncertainty of retroductive inferences in the final query to the *Opticks*. There he divided the method of natural philosophers into two phases, which he called analysis and composition. He claimed, as before, that the first phase was based exclusively on observation and induction:

This analysis consists in making experiments and observations, and in drawing general conclusions from them by induction, and admitting of no objections against the conclusions, but such as are taken from experiments, or other certain truths. For hypotheses are not to be regarded in experimental philosophy. And although the arguing from experiments and observations by induction be no demonstration of general conclusions; yet it is the best way of arguing which the nature of things admits of, and may be looked upon as so much the stronger, by how much the induction is more general.   (Newton 1952: 404)

This almost frank admission that inductive generalizations never amount to a deduction is tempered by claiming that this is the most one can hope to realize in natural philosophy. The second phase, which he calls alternatively 'the method of composition' or 'synthesis', disguises once more the hypothetical character of causal explanations. 'Synthesis consists in assuming the causes discover'd, and establish'd as principles, and by them explaining the phaenomena proceeding from them, and proving the explanations' (Newton 1952: 405). The inferences that are described by the terms 'discovered', 'established', and 'proving' remain as unclear to us and as intentionally veiled by Newton as his previous rejections of hypotheses required.

Apart from the underlying fear of uncertainty and his failure to acknowledge the role of probability in genuine knowledge, Newton had other more valid reasons for exercising due care concerning hypotheses. He repeated the objection that was frequently articulated by Descartes and made famous subsequently by Molière, that one explains nothing by inventing a new, specific occult quality to explain each natural phenomenon. 'To tell us that every species of things is endow'd with an occult specifick quality by which it acts and produces manifest effects, is to tell us nothing' (Newton 1952: 401). This is a restatement of the commonplace that one does not explain the effect of sleeping powder by attributing to it a 'soporific power'. In more general terms, Newton was intolerant of the profusion of guess-work that was associated, justifiably or otherwise, with Cartesians, and he was anxious to avoid relying on hypotheses that were 'assumed or supposed without any experimental proof'. He identified this kind of hypothesis in a draft letter to Cotes, as he prepared revisions for the second edition of the *Principia*:

Experimental philosophy reduces phaenomena to general rules & looks upon the rules to be general when they hold generally in phaenomena ... Hypothetical philosophy consists in imaginary explications of things & imaginary arguments for or against such explications, or against the arguments of experimental philosophers founded upon induction. The first sort of philosophy is followed by me, the latter too much by Cartes, Leibnitz & some others.    (Newton 1975: V, 398–9; see Shapiro 1993: 13)

These were legitimate reservations within Newton's almost obsessive efforts to avoid admitting that his natural philosophy necessarily used hypotheses. The phenomenal success of the *Principia*, and Newton's insistent description of his mechanics as not involving hypotheses, provided a misleading model for the natural sciences, according to which the certainty of mathematical inferences and the certainty of sensory observations compensated for the uncertainty that is necessarily involved in the confirmation of hypothetical explanations of natural phenomena.

In retrospect, it is difficult to understand the tenacity with which the ideal of demonstrative science survived when, as many natural philosophers pointed out, Aristotle's physics had never explained any phenomenon 'demonstratively' except in a trivial sense. While the early seventeenth century remained locked into this ideal of demonstration, many authors, such as Kepler, Galileo, and Descartes, claimed that their hypotheses were sufficiently warranted that they were almost 'demonstrated'. With the passing decades, however, the bankruptcy of the Aristotelian research programme, the comparative success of the new experimental sciences, the redefinition of what constitutes a scientific explanation, and the development of a concept of probability, made it possible for Huygens and others to claim, at the end of the century, that Aristotelian demonstration was irrelevant to the new sciences, and that probability was sufficient for hypotheses in natural philosophy.

However, the unwarranted demand for certainty was endorsed anew by some empiricists, initially by Locke and Berkeley, for whom sensory observations and inductive or deductive inferences provided the only secure foundations for knowledge. Their deep-seated suspicions of theoretical entities reflected the position articulated by Pascal many years earlier when he rejected his critic's hypotheses while failing to acknowledge his own: 'all things of that nature, the existence of which is not manifested to any of our senses, are as difficult to believe as they are easy to invent' (Pascal 1998: I, 380). This regressive positivism bartered the theoretical resources of the new sciences for a modified version of the traditional Aristotelian definition of knowledge.

## References

ARNAULD, A. and NICOLE, P. (1981). *La Logique ou l'Art de Penser*, ed. P. Clair and F. Girbal. Paris: Vrin [5th edn. 1683].

BERNOULLI, J. (1969). *Ars Conjectandi*, in *Die Werke von Jakob Bernoulli*. 3 vols. Basel: Birkhäuser Verlag, III, 107–259 [1st edn. 1713].

BLACKWELL, R. J. (1991). *Galileo, Bellarmine, and the Bible*. Notre Dame, IN: University of Notre Dame Press.

CLARKE, D. M. (1992). 'Descartes' Philosophy of Science and the Scientific Revolution', in J. Cottingham (ed.), *The Cambridge Companion to Descartes*. Cambridge: Cambridge University Press, 258–85.

COHEN, I. B. (1978). *Introduction to Newton's 'Principia'*. Cambridge, MA: Harvard University Press.

COHEN, I. B. and SCHOFIELD, R. E. (eds) (1978). *Isaac Newton's Papers & Letters on Natural Philosophy and Related Documents*. 2nd edn. Cambridge, MA and London: Harvard University Press.

COHEN, I. B. and SMITH, G. E. (eds) (2002). *The Cambridge Companion to Newton*. Cambridge: Cambridge University Press.

COPERNICUS, N. (1992). *On the Revolutions*. Trans. Edward Rosen. Baltimore and London: Johns Hopkins University Press [1st edn. 1543].

DASTON, L. (1998). 'Probability and Evidence', in D. Garber and M. Ayers (eds), *The Cambridge History of Seventeenth-Century Philosophy*. Cambridge: Cambridge University Press, II: 1108–44.

DRAKE, S. (ed.) (1957). *Discoveries and Opinions of Galileo*. New York: Doubleday.

DUHEM, P. (1969). *To Save the Phenomena: An Essay on the Idea of Physical Theory from Plato to Galileo*. Trans. E. Doland and C. Maschler. Chicago and London: University of Chicago Press [1st edn. 1908].

GALILEI, G. (1970). *Dialogo sopra i Due Massimi Sistemi del Mondo, Tolemaico e Copernicano*, ed. L. Sosio. Turin: Einaudi [1st edn. 1632].

GINGERICH, O. (2004). *The Book Nobody Read: Chasing the Revolutions of Nicolaus Copernicus*. London: Heineman.

HACKING, I. (1975). *The Emergence of Probability*. Cambridge: Cambridge University Press, 1975.

HANSON, N. R. (1970). 'Hypotheses Fingo', in R. Butts and J. Davis (eds), *The Methodological Heritage of Newton*. Oxford: Blackwell, 14–33.

HUNTER, M. (2009). *Boyle: Between God and Science*. New Haven and London: Yale University Press.

HUYGENS, C. (1962). *Treatise on Light*. Trans. S. P. Thomson. New York: Dover. [1st edn. 1690].

JANIAK, A. (ed.) (2004). *Isaac Newton: Philosophical Writings*. Cambridge: Cambridge University Press.

JANIAK, A. (2008). *Newton as Philosopher*. Cambridge: Cambridge University Press.

JARDINE, N. (1984). *The Birth of History and Philosophy of Science. Kepler's* A Defence of Tycho against Ursus. Cambridge: Cambridge University Press.

KEPLER, J. (1992). *New Astronomy*. Trans. William H. Donahue. Cambridge: Cambridge University Press [1st edn. 1609].

MCMULLIN, E. (1978). *Newton on Matter and Activity*. Notre Dame and London: University of Notre Dame Press.

MCMULLIN, E. (2001). 'The Impact of Newton's *Principia* on the Philosophy of Science'. *Philosophy of Science*, 28: 279–310.

MCMULLIN, E. (ed.) (2005). *The Church and Galileo*. Notre Dame, IN: University of Notre Dame Press.

MORIN, J.-B. (1631). *Famosi et antiqui problematis de telluris motu, vel quiete; hactenus optata solutio*. Paris.

NEWTON, I. (1952). *Opticks, or A Treatise of the Reflections, Refractions, Inflections & Colours of Light*. New York: Dover [4th edn. 1730].

NEWTON, I. (1975). *The Correspondence of Isaac Newton*. 7 vols. Volume 5 (1709–1713), ed. A. R. Hall and L. Tilling. Cambridge: Cambridge University Press.

PASCAL, B. (1967). *The Provincial Letters*, trans. A. J. Krailsheimer. Harmondsworth: Penguin [1st edn. 1656–57].

PASCAL, B. (1998). *Oeuvres complètes*, ed. Michel le Guern. 2 vols. Paris: Gallimard.

RÉGIS, P.-S. (1690). *Cours entier de philosophie ou Système Generale selon les Principes de M. Descartes, contenant la Logique, La Metaphysique, La Physique, et La Morale*. Paris.

SHAPIRO, A. E. (1993). *Fits, Passions, and Paroxysms*. Cambridge: Cambridge University Press.

SHAPIRO, B. J. (1983). *Probability and Certainty in Seventeenth-Century England*. Princeton, NJ: Princeton University Press.

WESTMAN, R. S. (1972). 'Kepler's Theory of Hypothesis and the "realist dilemma"'. *Studies in History and Philosophy of Science*, 3: 233–64.

# CHAPTER 13

......................................................................

# LANGUAGE AND
# SEMIOTICS

......................................................................

## JAAP MAAT

THE relationship between philosophy and the study of language underwent radical changes in early modern Europe. In medieval philosophy, metaphysical and ethical questions were deeply entangled with questions of linguistic meaning, which were discussed within a logical framework. In the post-medieval period the focus was shifted away from logic and metaphysics, and towards rhetoric and practical wisdom. The 'Age of Eloquence' cherished the humanist ideal of erudition and linguistic proficiency, and was sceptical about the value of abstract speculation. Although they were focused in entirely different ways, both medieval scholasticism and post-medieval humanism were closely connected with the study of language.

In the seventeenth century, the attitude towards language taken by philosophers became more diverse than in the preceding periods. Two major trends which are antagonistic to both scholasticism and humanism became prominent. First, leading philosophers, notably Descartes, tended to background language in approaching metaphysical and epistemological questions. On this view, conclusions about the structure of the world and the nature of thought could and should be reached without giving much consideration to the functions and the structure of language. The writings of Descartes' followers on language were aimed at showing how the structure of language reflected the structure of thought, assuming the latter to be prior to the former. The second trend was that a suspicion of language became widespread. Philosophers as different as Bacon, Hobbes, Spinoza, and Locke all pointed out various imperfections and abuses of words, or criticized language for exerting a pernicious influence on thinking.

Both trends can be seen as a reaction to the preoccupation with language that characterized earlier periods. In their effort to put all learning on a new footing and to scrutinize the foundations of knowledge afresh, the seventeenth-century reformers tended to downgrade the role played by language. However, there were important exceptions: both Hobbes and Leibniz assigned crucial significance to the nature and structure of language in their philosophy. Moreover, the attempt to turn away from language often failed. Typical in this regard is Locke's admission that he started out investigating the nature of human understanding without expecting to discuss language at all, but felt forced to do so once he realized how close a connection there is between words and ideas. He ended up devoting one of the four books of the *Essay* to '*Words or Language in general*', and identified 'semiotics or logic', that is, the study of language, as one of the three major fields into which all science can be divided.

This chapter sketches the context in which questions concerning language were approached in early modern Europe. First, it outlines some aspects of the disciplines traditionally concerned with language, which include logic, grammar, and rhetoric. Next, it describes two new developments in the study of language: the renewed attention to philosophical grammar, and the exploration of new symbolic systems which resulted in artificial languages. Finally, it discusses the views of language held by some of the most influential philosophers of the period: Bacon, Descartes, Hobbes, and Locke.

# I: THE ARTS OF DISCOURSE

Throughout the early modern period, the conceptual framework for the study of language was, for the most part, constituted by the three *artes sermocinales* or arts of discourse, which, since late Antiquity, had been grouped together in the trivium: grammar, rhetoric, and logic. A thorough training in each of these arts formed an essential and inescapable element of education, so that a familiarity with the main concepts and distinctions they contained was shared by all the learned, whether lawyers, scientists, or philosophers.

The study of grammar was mainly a subject in pre-university education. Schoolboys were expected to become acquainted with the details of Latin grammar, because a good command of Latin was an indispensable preliminary to theoretical studies of whatever sort. Consequently, the world of learning was inaccessible to most girls, who were not admitted to schools (pp. 456, 462). Most grammars were pedagogical in nature, and were aimed at teaching students how to master a language other than their own. Starting in the fourteenth century in Italy, a process of vernacularization was taking place, which however took centuries to be completed. Like all educated men, seventeenth-century philosophers could write Latin with ease. Most of them published works in the vernacular, but often alongside Latin versions.

Grammars of the vernacular languages were written from the sixteenth century onward, but Latin grammar retained a central position even in the seventeenth century, both in terms of its continuing importance in education and with respect to the theoretical framework it provided. The standard pattern of grammars had developed in Antiquity, and the most authoritative expression of this pattern was to be found in the *Institutiones Grammaticae* by Priscian (early sixth century AD). This work was divided into four parts, starting with the smallest components of speech, and progressing to more complex ones: letters, syllables, words, sentences. Numerous grammars followed the same pattern, although both medieval and post-medieval grammarians sometimes deviated considerably from this paradigm.

The majority of grammars devoted most of their attention to a discussion of the various parts of speech, most influentially described by Dionysius Thrax (*c.*100 BC), who himself represented a much older tradition. Thrax's *Technè* distinguished eight parts of speech: noun, verb, participle, article, pronoun, preposition, adverb, and conjunction. Roman grammarians omitted the article, as this was lacking in Latin, but added the interjection. The adjective, traditionally treated as a subtype of the noun, was not considered to be an independent word class until medieval times. Although many alternative systems of word classes were proposed in subsequent periods, they were mostly minor variations on the same traditional theme.

Rhetoric encompassed a corpus of precepts and rules for speaking and writing elegantly and persuasively, and was at the heart of an educational ideal inherited from Antiquity and revived by the humanists in the Renaissance. During the seventeenth century, rhetoric remained a central component of undergraduate studies, which were still very much humanistic in nature (Feingold 1997: 213). Instruction in rhetoric included the study of the ancient rules, but also practical exercises (such as the *progymnasmata*) in writing and declamation. Philosophers writing in this period, including those who were critical of rhetoric, were all familiar with rhetorical precepts and were well-trained in this tradition.

The most important classical sources for rhetoric were Aristotle's *Rhetoric*, the anonymous *Ad Herennium*, Cicero's *De Inventione*, *De Oratore* and other works, and Quintilian's *Institutio Oratoria*. In the sixteenth and seventeenth centuries, textbooks summarizing the basic principles of rhetoric were often written in the vernacular. A common pattern of organization followed Cicero's partition of the art of rhetoric into five arts or procedures: invention, arrangement, style, memory, and delivery. Ramus proposed a reform in the sixteenth century. With a view to creating clear boundaries between disciplines, he insisted that only style and delivery properly belonged to rhetoric. Some of the textbooks that appeared subsequently were in line with this proposal, and treated exclusively the tropes (metaphor, metonymy, synecdoche, and many more) and figures (such as amplification, definition, repetition), while other textbooks continued to cover the whole range of rhetorical arts. Another frequently produced type of book contained mostly or exclusively samples of good writing, or useful commonplaces, that is, quotations from outstanding authors to be used in composing texts or speeches.

Logic was a substantial part of undergraduate training at seventeenth-century universities. While Aristotle's works were studied in Latin translations, most tuition in logical theory relied on textbooks. Practical training was an integral part of logic teaching: students were required to participate in formal disputations in order to exercise their logical skills. Although logic was commonly defined as an art concerned with reason and with truth, it was primarily regarded as a linguistic discipline, closely associated, both institutionally and conceptually, with grammar and rhetoric.

There were few elements in standard logical theory as it was taught in the seventeenth century that were not directly derived from Aristotle's work. In Antiquity, substantial additions to logic were made by the Stoics, and in the scholastic period, the scope of logical investigations was considerably widened, which led to novel branches of logical theory. For these medieval developments, the influence of the humanists in the fifteenth and sixteenth centuries was devastating. The new *studia humanitatis* involved changes in the organization and the contents of the language arts, and the boundaries between logic and rhetoric were subjected to reforms. Thus Rudolf Agricola propounded a form of dialectic which merged rhetoric and logic on a model first created by Cicero, by dividing the art into invention and judgement. In the sixteenth century, Ramus propagated similar reforms, adding an emphasis on method, which was concerned with orderly arrangements of knowledge. In these humanist logics, the novelties created by the scholastics were discarded, and little attention was paid to the formal aspects of traditional logic. They treated syllogisms cursorily, and placed at the centre the finding of arguments for practical purposes by way of the 'topics of invention'. However, the majority of textbooks that appeared in the seventeenth century restored what the humanists had omitted, and returned to a pattern of exposition that could be directly associated with Aristotle's *Organon*. Some elements due to the Stoics, such as the treatment of hypothetical and disjunctive syllogisms, were also usually included, but the contributions of the schoolmen were discussed only occasionally and in diluted form.

Logic was less alive in the seventeenth century than it had been in previous periods. This is visible in the format in which it was described. Whereas most logical treatises in late Antiquity and the Middle Ages were commentaries on works by predecessors—most often by Aristotle—this format became increasingly rare. It was replaced by manuals and textbooks, which proliferated in the seventeenth century. The character of exposition thus changed from inquisitive and polemical to pedagogical and explanatory.

The most common division and arrangement of logical theory that was used in logic textbooks was into three parts, each of which represented a level of complexity such that the second presupposed the first, and the third presupposed the second. Many textbooks associated each level with items of two sorts: a linguistic entity and a psychological type of event, so that linguistic units, mental entities or operations, and parts of logical doctrine were brought into a threefold correspondence. The first part of logic treated terms or words, corresponding to the mental operation of conceiving or 'simple apprehension'. The second part treated propositions or sentences, the mental counterpart of which was judgement or 'composition and division'. The third part of logic expounded the theory of syllogisms. Syllogisms corresponded to discourse, consisting of several sentences, which were connected with the mental operation of reasoning. Thus, the common core of logical theory with which seventeenth-century philosophers were familiar consisted of what might be called the 'tripartite framework', containing three levels at which logic, language, and mind were closely interwoven.

Each part of logic was associated with one or more of works by Aristotle which constituted the *Organon*. Much of the material of the first part was provided by the *Categories*. The first part thus usually contained a discussion of each of the ten categories, or 'predicaments' as the Latin term read. The second part of logic discussed the subject matter of Aristotle's *On Interpretation*, which addressed, among other things, the quantity and quality of propositions. The third part of logic contained an exposition of the syllogism, which was based on Aristotle's *Prior Analytics*; this presented in more or less detail the various moods and figures of the categorical syllogism. The contents of Aristotle's *Posterior Analytics* was sometimes also included in the third part, but a number of textbooks included a fourth part on method, a remnant of Ramus's influence, in which various types of demonstration and topics such as definition and division were discussed. The subject matter of Aristotle's *Topics* and *Sophistical Refutations* was also commonly treated, usually in the third part or, if it existed, in the fourth.

At the beginning of the seventeenth century, the language arts came under attack by influential figures, such as Galileo and Bacon. Their criticisms were motivated by the assumption that knowledge of the natural world was the most useful of all, and that great progress was to be expected in this area if the right method were followed. These men were looking at the future with hopes of new discoveries. The language arts, by contrast, were informed by an attitude that looked for models in the past, and were linked with a body of learning that relied on the authority of classical authors, chiefly Aristotle.

Logic was a target of disparagement voiced by Bacon and Descartes. According to Bacon, 'the logic now in use does more harm than good'. His explanation of this claim depended significantly on the 'tripartite framework' discussed above, and on the assumption that logic was essentially a linguistic discipline: 'The syllogism consists of propositions, propositions consist of words, words are symbols of notions.

Therefore if the notions themselves (which is the root of the matter) are confused and over-hastily abstracted from the facts, there can be no firmness in the superstructure' (Bacon 1620: 48–9). Thus, Bacon viewed the tripartite framework as a building of which the lowest level, that is, words signifying notions, formed the foundation. Hence, the formal patterns were useless if the foundation on which they rested were unreliable. Furthermore, the appearance of stability created by the formal patterns could be misleading by masking the weakness of the foundation.

Descartes likewise argued that traditional logic was useless and potentially harmful. He observed that logic could never yield new knowledge, since logicians 'are unable to formulate a syllogism with a true conclusion unless they...have previous knowledge of the very truth deduced in the syllogism' (AT X 406; CSM I 36–7). Logic could also be dangerous, for logicians 'prescribe certain forms of reasoning in which the conclusions follow with such irresistible necessity that if our reason relies on them, even though it takes, as it were, a rest from considering a particular inference clearly and attentively, it can nevertheless draw a conclusion which is certain simply in virtue of the form' (AT X 405–6; CSM I 36). According to Descartes, such inferences are to be avoided at all times, as they occur while our reason is 'taking a holiday', whereas our primary concern should be to keep our minds alert. Leibniz later defended an opposite view of the mechanical character of logical inferences. In his view, what he called 'blind thought' was precisely a phenomenon that could be profitably exploited in enhancing the power of the human mind, provided that it was guided by a correct symbolism.

As a consequence of these and similar criticisms, the value of traditional logic became a matter of debate. Defenders of logic were not exclusively die-hard Aristotelians, as they included men like John Wallis, a co-founder of the Royal Society (Wallis 1687). Leibniz also defended logic against Locke's harsh censure of it as contributing to language abuse, and stimulating 'artificial Ignorance, and learned gibberish' (LRB 342; cf. *Essay* III. x. 6–9).

As far as the other arts of discourse are concerned, grammar was seldom condemned for inherent defects, but the vast amount of time and effort spent on language learning was increasingly felt as an unnecessary burden. This led to pedagogical reforms such as the one propagated by Comenius, which was meant to ensure that language learning was usefully combined with acquiring knowledge of the world. The problem of language learning was also one of the motivating forces behind the plans for artificial symbol systems and universal languages.

The repute of rhetoric, however, suffered severe blows in the course of the century. It was seen as a collection of precepts for concealment and deceit by its more vehement critics, or as an art which could be usefully applied in pleasing audiences for political purposes or for other matters which involved the 'passions', but which should be kept away strictly from all serious discourse of either a theological or scientific nature. Thus Thomas Sprat reported that the fellows of the Royal Society had decided 'to reject all the amplifications, digressions, and swellings of style', so as to avoid the danger that their design would be 'eaten out, by the luxury and redundance of *speech*' (Sprat 1667: 111–13). It was again Locke who was particularly scornful of rhetoric, 'that powerful instrument of error and deceit', whose precepts 'in all Discourses that pretend to inform or instruct' are 'wholly to be avoided' (*Essay* III. x. 34). Of course, the status of the discipline cannot be judged by the views of its critics alone, and Locke himself indicated that the charms of eloquence were not only ubiquitous, but were so attractive that one would argue in vain against them. A far less depreciatory stance towards rhetoric was taken by Hobbes, who identified metaphorical language as a possible source of error, but also stated that 'Reason and Eloquence, (though not perhaps in the Naturall Sciences, yet in the Morall) may stand very well together' (Hobbes 1996: 483–4). Hobbes himself devoted considerable efforts to studying rhetoric, and produced an abridged English translation of Aristotle's *Rhetoric*.

## II: THE STUDY OF LANGUAGE

Besides changes in the way the traditional language arts were viewed, there were also far-reaching internal changes in the early modern period: new objects of investigation were identified and new aims of linguistic study were formulated. Reports by missionaries on astonishing numbers of exotic languages increased sensitivity towards the diversity of languages. Acquaintance with Chinese script stimulated interest in writing systems, and subjects such as cryptography and sign systems for communication at a distance became popular. Shorthand systems were created, and attempts were made, sometimes successfully, to teach speech to the deaf. Articulatory phonetics was brought to high levels of sophistication. Two further developments, the emergence of 'philosophical grammar' and the invention of universal or philosophical languages, are discussed below.

In the course of the seventeenth century, a number of scholars discussed the structure of language in a way that was markedly different from the treatment found in ordinary, pedagogical grammars. They were concerned with what was alternatively called philosophical, natural, general, or rational grammar. For example, Campanella (1638) treated philosophical grammar as one of the five parts of rational philosophy, and Caramuel (1654) likewise discussed grammar 'philosophically'. Wilkins (1668) included a chapter on 'natural grammar' in his *Essay* on a philosophical language, and Leibniz worked for decades on a project which he often called 'rational grammar'. A common characteristic of these approaches to grammar was that they were not descriptions of a single language, but dealt with language in general. Most of those who were writing on the subject claimed that they were concerned with a science rather than an art. Further common features were the endeavour to specify links between language and human thinking, and a merging of elements taken from the logical and the grammatical traditions. Thus most of these grammars assumed, in accordance with the logical tradition, that the basic sentence structure is that of the categorical proposition, and that noun and verb, which together were sufficient to form such a proposition, are primary word classes, also called categorematic terms. All the other types of words were called syncategorematic terms. At the same time, most of these grammars also discussed the traditional parts of speech which were central to the grammatical tradition.

A final common trait is that these authors shared a method to which they often resorted without defining it, and which consequently is hard to describe in other than anachronistic terms. It consisted of the use of periphrasis in order to express a postulated underlying deep structure or logical form, which was supposed to be both equivalent to and more explicit than the paraphrased sentence or phrase. For example, the thesis that all verbs, at some level of analysis, consist of the verb 'to be' combined with an adjective or participle, already found in Aristotle's *Metaphysics* (AR 1606), formed a standard part of seventeenth-century philosophical grammars. Thus a sentence such as: 'A man walks' is assumed to be equivalent to the sentence 'A man is walking'. Since the latter expresses the copula or 'substantive verb' explicitly, and marks the connection between subject and predicate, it is closer to what in logic was considered to be the basic sentence structure.

Grammar of the philosophical type was no novelty in the seventeenth century. In fact, a theoretical approach to language aimed at investigating the relations between language and thought had been present in the Western linguistic tradition from the very beginning. It originated in the works of Plato and Aristotle and flourished briefly but spectacularly around 1300 in Modistic grammar, which linked parts of speech and grammatical categories with concepts in the human mind and with corresponding aspects of reality. The work of Scaliger and Sanctius in the sixteenth century can be seen as a revival of this type of grammar, although they each worked this out in completely different ways. The writings of some of the *Modistae* as well as those of Scaliger and Sanctius were known to the seventeenth-century authors working in this area, but the consensus was that philosophical grammar had been given relatively little attention in the past, and that it should be further developed (Bacon 1605: 400; Wilkins 1668: 297).

It should be noted however that the distinction between philosophical and ordinary grammar is not clear-cut, as both types of grammar were interrelated in multiple ways. Thus, most philosophical grammars took the traditional parts of speech for granted, and in many grammars that did not present themselves as philosophical the method of periphrasis was often used with a view to establishing equivalences between grammatical and logical forms. For example, equivalences such as 'verb = copula + participle' can be found in a number of sixteenth-century grammars (Padley 1976: 47, 1985: 238–9).

A particularly influential grammar of the philosophical type was the *Grammaire générale et raisonnée* (GGR), also known as the *Port Royal Grammar* (Lancelot and Arnauld 1660). This short book aims to show that all languages share a rational basis, which accounts for their universal characteristics. It discusses the technical apparatus of traditional grammar on the assumption that wherever languages are structurally similar, this is because these structural aspects correspond to properties of ideas that people have found convenient or necessary to make known to others. It is suggested that these ideas are prior to and independent of their expression: linguistic phenomena are often described as 'inventions', which can be explained by the need to mark aspects of what goes on in our mind. For example, the fact that languages have both proper names and common nouns is explained by observing that we have two sorts of ideas, one sort representing a single thing, the other representing several similar ones, and that people consequently needed different sorts of names (Lancelot and Arnauld 1660: 35).

In specifying the mental processes that underlie grammatical categories, the authors of the GGR had recourse to the standard distinctions of the tripartite framework that was so common in logic. They state that 'all philosophers teach that there are three operations of our mind: to conceive, to judge, to reason' (Lancelot and Arnauld 1660: 27). The traditional parts of speech are then connected with these operations: nouns are used to indicate the object of our thoughts and are thus connected with conceiving, the first operation of the mind. Verbs are used to indicate that the speaker is not only conceiving things, but judging them, and affirming the predicate of the subject, thus signifying the second operation of the mind. The third operation, reasoning, is defined in a way which reveals once more that it is taken from the logical context in which reasoning was linked with syllogisms: reasoning is 'using two judgments to make a third' (Lancelot and Arnauld 1660: 28). Since the third operation is an extension of the second, the authors explain, it plays no further role in their account of the rational foundation of the structure of language. The GGR also connects the traditional parts of speech with the logical tradition in another way: each part of speech is assigned to one of the two broad classes of 'material' or 'formal' words, a distinction which is parallel to the one traditionally known as that between categorematic and syncategorematic words.

A further characteristic of philosophical grammars is prominent in the GGR: the authors frequently assume that linguistic surface structure is systematically related to underlying forms that are not explicitly expressed but can be explicated by rephrasing or supplementing the surface expressions. The underlying forms are equated with elements of mental discourse. Examples of this procedure can be found throughout the book, and the usual analysis of the verb as consisting of the copula plus an adjective or participle is also stated (Lancelot and Arnauld 1660: 96).

Although the authors of the GGR were sympathetic to Cartesianism, there was little in the work of Descartes that could be used as a source for the contents of a book on language. However, the emphasis on the connection between rationality and language, and the clarity of style, may reasonably be ascribed to Cartesian influence. Both features may also account for the immediate success of the work. It was reprinted and translated many times, and formed the model and starting-point for a large number of writings on universal grammar well into the eighteenth century.

As mentioned, Leibniz was engaged in a project for a philosophical grammar, which he referred to as 'rational grammar'. If measured by its success, it stood in sharp contrast with the Port Royal grammar, as it went unnoticed in Leibniz's lifetime, and indeed has been given scant attention even by specialists until today. The main cause of this is that Leibniz never completed his project; what he wrote on the subject was either programmatic statements or tentative sketches. He produced dozens of papers dealing with grammar, many of which consisted of annotated lists of linguistic 'particles' such as prepositions and conjunctions. Most of this material remained unpublished until the 1990s, and some of it is still unpublished. Rational grammar was part of an even more ambitious project, the construction of a philosophical language.

Leibniz's rational grammar resembled other philosophical grammars in a number of respects, but there are important differences as well. A first and obvious likeness is that Leibniz's project is concerned with language in general, not with the grammar of particular languages. Further, Leibniz's primary focus was on the relation between language and thought. He also took the traditional parts of speech as a starting-point for his investigations, just like other philosophical grammars. Finally, he frequently used the method of rephrasing expressions so as to bring out the logical form underlying them.

A major difference between Leibniz and his contemporaries lay in his conception of what constitutes a logical language. Whereas his contemporaries used elements taken from traditional logic to explain aspects of existing languages, Leibniz envisaged work in the opposite direction. His primary aim, namely, the analysis of languages with a view to revealing the basic operations of human thought, was stated as part of a research programme, the outcome of which was unknown. The gentlemen of Port Royal already knew what the operations of the mind were, and proceeded to show how those were expressed in language. Leibniz, by contrast, observed that traditional logic did not sufficiently encompass all the inferential patterns that were in fact expressed in languages. The investigations of rational grammar were to show how logic should be enriched so as to capture those types of inferences. A related and equally fundamental difference is as follows: Leibniz was most interested in the operation of the mind that had traditionally been termed the third operation, namely ratiocination or logical inference. This was precisely what his contemporaries, as exemplified by the Port Royal grammarians, largely ignored.

There are also several aspects to Leibniz's rational grammar which could justify the traditional view that it was aimed at fitting language into the predetermined mould of syllogistic logic. He claimed in standard fashion that verbs are composed of 'to be + noun', and added some other reductionist principles: all substantives can be resolved into 'thing + adjective', and adverbs can also be reduced to adjectives. Further, Leibniz reduced sentences expressing relations, which are notoriously difficult to accommodate in syllogistic logic, to others that conformed better to the traditional subject–predicate structure. But this view overlooks the fact that Leibniz stated that 'very frequently' inferences are made 'which are to be proved not on the basis of logical principles, but on the basis of grammatical principles, that is, on the basis of the signification of inflections and particles' (A 6 4 344), and that most of the work that he carried out in the context of his rational grammar project centres on the latter principles (Schneider 1994; Maat 2004*b*).

Numerous projects for artificial symbol systems were proposed in the course of the seventeenth century. Most early schemes were intended to provide a writing system, which could serve as a 'universal character'. Some of these schemes used a numbering system to correlate items in dictionaries of different languages, so that written numbers could represent words of several languages at once. The schemes of Beck (1657), Becher (1661), and Kircher (1663) were of this type. Other writing systems were conceived as 'real characters', a concept requiring a brief explanation. The example of Chinese characters showed that it was possible to use a common script for mutually incomprehensible spoken languages and thus to overcome language barriers in writing. The possibility of this was further shown by Arabic numerals: the written sign '3' is pronounced differently as 'three', '*trois*', '*drei*' by speakers of diverse languages, but serves as a uniform notation for all these different spoken sounds. Astronomic signs, signs for minerals, and musical notes were perceived as language-independent in the same way. Symbols of this type were called real characters, because they did not represent speech sounds but things. The idea then was to invent signs of this sort for everything that one might want to talk about. The concept of such a real character was especially appealing to those who sought to reduce the time spent on language learning, and who shared the anti-linguistic sentiment summed up in the slogan that 'things are better than words' (Wilkins 1668: epistle dedicatory; Wilkins 1641: 56).

Schemes for a real character developed into more ambitious philosophical languages through various routes. One of these was via the implementation of the programmatic idea. This faced the problem of how to keep the number of signs required for a full-blown system of real characters within a manageable range. One solution was the use of a classification scheme, so that only categories of things would have to be designated by a distinct sign, and regular additions to such signs could indicate subcategories. But at this stage it became clear that devising a system of real characters involved a major scientific enterprise, namely the classification of 'all things and notions'. It was further noted that a system of written signs was inferior to a fully fledged language after all, so that the provision of both a 'character' and a spoken language seemed desirable.

In the 1660s, two artificial languages were published in England, each of which presented a different solution to this challenge. The first was Dalgarno's *Ars Signorum* (1661); the second was Wilkins's *Essay towards a Real Character, and a Philosophical Language* (1668). Dalgarno's little book was in Latin, and contained the description of a language that could be written and spoken, using the ordinary alphabet. This was because it had become clear to Dalgarno, on reflection, that it would be superfluous to provide two distinct symbol systems, since alphabetic writing could be used as both a free-standing script and as a notation of speech sounds. Wilkins's large volume, by contrast, retained the original plan, presenting a system of newly invented 'real characters', as well as a language consisting of speech sounds. A more fundamental difference between the two schemes was to be found in their solution to the problem of how to invent signs for 'all things and notions'. Dalgarno's language is built on a set of principles that could be characterized as logical atomism; Wilkins's language is the result of an encyclopedic, classificatory enterprise.

Dalgarno's professed aim was to construct a logical language, that is, a language the use of which coincided with a logical analysis of the thoughts expressed. This could be achieved in principle, Dalgarno believed, by inventing signs for primitive notions, out of which all concepts that are used in thinking are composed. Compound signs could then reflect the structure of complex concepts. Dalgarno did not explain how these primitive notions could be identified, nor did he give an example of such a notion. He went on to argue that a language strictly based on logical primitives would be impracticable, because most concepts, if completely analysed, become unrecognizable in the process, and words reflecting the analysis would grow to unwieldy lengths. An alternative way of constructing a language was to start from an overall classification scheme of the sort provided in logic textbooks, derived from Aristotle's categories or predicaments. But this approach was also problematic, in Dalgarno's view, for such a classification was arbitrary by nature and could not be established without giving rise to endless disputes. His solution was to take a middle course between these approaches: he drew up a classification scheme that was modelled on the predicaments, which was admittedly arbitrary and not wholly accurate, and which covered about one thousand words for things and notions. These words were called the radicals, and were meant to serve as primitives, out of which words for everything else were to be compounded. Thus, in many cases, users of Dalgarno's language would have to compose their own words as the occasion required. He claimed that this was an advantage because, as a consequence of this feature, the use of his language both required and furthered logical skills.

Dalgarno's attempt to create a logical language led him to work out a distinctive grammar. He asserted that logic and grammar are one and the same art, and noted that the logical part of speech resides mainly in the particles, that is, conjunctions, prepositions, and other syncategorematic words. Without the particles, speech is like a pile of bricks; it requires the cement of the particles to make it coherent. He further noted that the diverse functions performed by the particles should be expressed by radical words; after all, these were to be considered as the primitives out of which the entire building of speech, bricks as well as mortar, would have to be composed. For example, since the function of the verb 'to be', when used as a copula, is to indicate that the predicate is affirmed of the subject, the particle designating the copula should be expressed by a radical word meaning 'affirmation'. Likewise, the conjunction 'and' is expressed by a radical word meaning 'addition', and the adverb 'hardly' by a radical word meaning 'difficult'. Dalgarno thus started out on the assumption he shared with authors of philosophical grammars that all words are to be divided into two broad classes, termed 'radicals' and 'particles' in his case, but he ended up by abolishing the distinction. The guiding idea behind this was to make the surface structure of the philosophical language coincide with the logical form corresponding to the structure of thought. Philosophical grammar assumed an underlying form to which expressions of natural languages were implicitly related. This form is made fully explicit, or so Dalgarno intended, on the surface of what users of his philosophical language were saying (Maat 2004*a*: 101–25).

Wilkins's philosophical language, just like Dalgarno's, was meant to serve several purposes at once: to be a means of international communication, and to provide a language which was superior to existing languages. But whereas this superiority was sought by Dalgarno in a greater conformity between logic and speech, Wilkins claimed as the primary advantage of his scheme that a person learning his language would be instructed in the nature of things at the same time. This claim was supported by the fact that the words of his language reflected properties of the things designated by them. The lexicon of his language consisted of about four thousand radical words, the form of which was derived from extensive classificatory tables. The word for 'red', for example, was 'gida'. The syllable 'gi' indicated that red is a thing classified as a sensible quality, the letter 'd' indicated that it belonged to the subclass of 'colour' and 'a' that red was the second species of this class. The word for 'green' was 'gide', the colour enumerated as the third species under 'colour'. The classificatory tables were modelled on those found in the first part of logic textbooks, but adapted to the purposes of the philosophical language, which required much greater detail, but also a limit on the number of items categorized in each class.

The same method of forming radical words was used by Dalgarno, but in his scheme this method was less central, as it contained far fewer radical words. The reason why Dalgarno used it at all was that his scheme was a compromise between various approaches. In the 1650s, Dalgarno and Wilkins collaborated on the creation of a philosophical language, but because of differences of opinion concerning the value of the classificatory method they each pursued their own design. Dalgarno details the debate in an autobiographical treatise (Cram and Maat 2001: 351–90).

The grammar of Wilkins's language was based on what he called 'the true philosophy of speech', which resulted in a 'natural grammar' that was similar to other philosophical grammars in several respects. Thus Wilkins stated that there are two main word classes, integrals and particles, which he defined in a traditional way. He also maintained that the copula is a necessary part of every proposition, and that verbs should all be expressed by means of a particle designating the copula combined with a radical word designating a relevant adjective. In this way he incorporated some common tenets of philosophical grammar in his artificial language.

The languages of Dalgarno and Wilkins met with little success. The topic of a universal language had occupied many leading scholars in the middle of the century, but after publication of the English schemes this interest fizzled out. A notable exception to this trend was Leibniz, who worked on a grand project for a philosophical language all his life. He never managed to get beyond the preliminary stages of his project, to which he referred using various names, among which were '*lingua philosophica*' and '*characteristica universalis*'. There are numerous manuscripts dealing with aspects of it, ranging from short notes to long texts, which show that he considered various methods of implementing his scheme. However, the overall plan remained unaltered.

Leibniz claimed that the philosophical language he envisaged was unlike anything that had been proposed before him. Whereas Dalgarno and Wilkins had attempted to improve on existing languages by constructing artificial ones that putatively conformed better to the structure of thought or the nature of things, Leibniz believed that language itself could be a means to enhance thinking and improve knowledge. Much of the motivation for this belief came from mathematics. The great advantage of algebraic notation was that it could guide the mind to solutions that it would not easily reach without it. The very perfection of the notation guaranteed that the outcome was reliable. In Leibniz's view, a similar notation could be invented which included not only numbers in its range of application, but every thinkable subject. This would provide the means to accelerate the growth of knowledge spectacularly, and incidentally it would also be an instrument for deciding controversies by enabling disputants to calculate who was right. The Leibnizian notion of a perfect language thus hinges on an evaluation of mechanical proof procedures which is squarely opposed to Descartes'. Leibniz often called the use of such procedures 'blind thought'. Although it is plausible that he, just like Descartes, ranked insights based on intuition (in the sense of the clear and distinct perception of all the elements of one's own thought process) as superior to such blind thoughts, he was convinced that the latter were a prerequisite for most of the achievements of which the human mind was capable.

In Leibniz's view, the structure of the philosophical language was to be isomorphic to the structure of thought. He conceived the latter in a way roughly similar to what Dalgarno had suggested. All thinking consists of entertaining or manipulating concepts, and all concepts are ultimately analysable into primitive notions and combinations of them. If the philosophical language had a basic symbol for each of the primitive notions, all concepts could be expressed in terms of combinations of the basic symbols. The set of these basic symbols constituted what Leibniz called 'the alphabet of human thoughts'. Thanks to the isomorphism thus established between concepts and their linguistic expression, it would be possible to test and find truths by considering and manipulating the linguistic expressions alone. For example, assuming that a concept $A$ is composed of primitives designated by $a$, $b$, $c$, $d$, and that another concept $B$ is composed of $a$ and $b$, the truth of the proposition '$A$ is $B$' will be apparent. For the concept of the predicate can be seen to be included in that of the subject of the proposition as soon as both '$A$' and '$B$' are analysed in terms of the primitives that compose them (A 6 4 273). In this way, a mechanical decision procedure will be available that operates on the symbols rather than the concepts designated by them, and blind thoughts rather than conscious inspection of concepts will do the work.

Leibniz was well aware of the difficulties involved in this rather crude scheme, but he always believed these were not insuperable. There were two major difficulties he faced in his attempts to carry out this programme. First, he had to identify the primitive notions, and second, he had to show how all other concepts as well as the inferential relations between them could be accounted for, using combinatorics as the sole principle of complexity. He tackled these problems through linguistic investigations of two sorts: first, definitions of terms, of which he produced many long lists, analysing the meaning of each word into its components, and second, the exploration of rational grammar already discussed. This grammar was important to him because its results were essential to the success of the philosophical language. For example, the inference from '$A$ is with $B$' to '$B$ is with $A$' is sound. But in a natural language like English, this is not clear from the form of the expression, as it should be in the philosophical language. The soundness of the inference depends on the meaning of the preposition 'with'; hence the detailed analysis, in works on rational grammar such as 'The Analysis of Particles' (A 6 4 646–67), of prepositions and other particles, in which the soundness of inferences of this sort is recorded.

The second problem just mentioned could not be solved by linguistic enquiries alone. Another way of tackling it was through the creation of formal logical calculi. Leibniz's work in this field formed an unprecedented and seminal attempt to mathematize logic. Both his idea of a philosophical language and his related work in logic inspired Frege two centuries afterwards in creating his *Begriffschrift* (1879).

# III: LANGUAGE AND THOUGHT

The previous section has shown that philosophical grammars and artificial language projects were related to assumptions concerning the structure of thought in various ways. This final section sketches the views of Bacon, Descartes, Hobbes, and Locke on the relation between language and thought in general, and how they viewed the importance of the study of language for philosophy.

The writings of Francis Bacon were extremely influential for the study of language. His observations on the various sorts of semiotic systems inspired many of the activities that led to the construction of universal characters and philosophical languages later in the century. Also, his observation that philosophical grammar should be pursued much more thoroughly than had been the case thus far was put into practice. His attitude towards the language arts was not one of wholesale condemnation: as mentioned, he censured logic for being useless when it comes to the advancement of our knowledge of the natural world. But in other matters it could play a positive role, and this holds true even more for grammar and rhetoric. Nevertheless, he famously drew up a list of idols or false appearances which threatened the sound thinking that is required in the investigation of nature, as a counterpart to the fallacies identified by Aristotle. Of the four types of idol, those of the 'market-place' are the most troublesome; they derive from words which have been invented and are used for easy communication with common people; 'and thus a poor and unskilful code of words incredibly obstructs the understanding' (Bacon 2000: 42). A possible remedy would be to define one's terms as much as possible but, as Bacon indicates, this will not be sufficient, for definitions themselves consist of words, and words will exert a force on the understanding from which they originate: they 'shoot back upon the understanding of the wisest and . . . pervert the judgement' (1605: 396). Bacon thus suggested that the harmful influence of language on clear thinking was at least partly irremediable, and that it is impossible to separate thought and language altogether. However, he did not provide a further justification for this view.

Descartes wrote relatively little on language. This may be connected to his desire to discard the useless parts of traditional learning, much of which centred on language. It is also often assumed that Descartes assigned a secondary role to language, restricting it to a communicative function that mattered little to philosophy. Thought is wordless, the mind inspects its own clear and distinct ideas in language-independent ways. It is not until it comes to communicating these ideas to others that language enters the scene. Although this view of Descartes' position has recently been challenged (Clarke 2005: 158–80), there is little in what he wrote on language that contradicts it, and much that suggests that he in fact held it. But clearly, this issue cannot be resolved on the basis of these fragments alone. Two aspects of Descartes' remarks on language are most relevant in the present context:

first, his brief comments on a project for a universal language, and second, his thesis that language is a solid proof of rationality.

In 1629, Mersenne asked Descartes to comment on a brochure claiming, as was customary in such pamphlets, some sensational features of a newly invented universal language. Descartes' reply (AT I 80–1) was dismissive of most of these claims; he pointed out that the scheme could be rendered effective only by printing a large multilingual dictionary containing symbols indicating semantically equivalent words in different languages. These symbols could then serve as an international written code. Projects of this kind were in fact implemented by Beck, Becher, and Kircher several decades afterwards (as mentioned in Section II). Descartes went on, however, to sketch a much more useful invention: a language built on an orderly arrangement of all thoughts. If one could explicate the simple ideas out of which everything that is thought is composed, one could construct a universal language with all the usual benefits claimed for projects of this kind: it would be easy to learn, to pronounce, and to write. But more importantly, it would assist 'men's judgment, representing matters so clearly that it would be almost impossible to go wrong' (CSMK 13). He added that this language is possible, but noted that it depended on 'the true philosophy', without which an orderly arrangement as required could not be accomplished. Descartes was thus quite clear about what comes first, both logically and temporally: the true philosophy must be found, and must be accepted by everyone. After that, he would hope for a universal language. This suggests quite strongly that even the as yet imaginary universal language that could help protect the judgement against errors was itself of a secondary and derivative nature. Leibniz, of course, disagreed. He noted in his copy of this letter that this language did depend on the true philosophy, but not on its completion (Leibniz 1903: 28). Perfecting the language and perfecting philosophy could go hand in hand, in a process of mutual influence that Descartes did not consider.

Language, in Descartes' view, is of the utmost importance in at least one respect: it sets humans apart from animals. The use of language is intimately connected with rationality, and it is all and only humans who are capable of it. In the *Discourse on Method* (Part 5), this point is elaborated using a thought experiment which could be described as a reverse Turing test. Descartes maintains that it is possible to conceive of a machine that looks exactly like a human body and that utters words in response to physical actions such as touching it in a particular place. But, he adds, it is impossible to conceive of such a machine that could arrange words in different ways to reply to the meaning of everything that is said in its presence. The ability to use language requires a versatility and creativity that it is impossible to imitate by mechanical means. The use of language is essentially different from a mechanical, that is, a naturally caused response to a stimulus. As Descartes repeatedly explained to correspondents (AT IV 575; AT V 278), the capacity to use language thus marks an absolute divide between animals and humans: the cries and barks uttered by animals are *natural* signs of their passions, whereas the words uttered by humans are *conventional* signs which require intentions and rationality to be effectively used. Although these observations establish, or posit, a close connection between the capacity to use language and rationality, they do not specify the nature of this connection.

In contrast to Descartes, Hobbes propounded an explicit theory of the relation between language and thinking. His most extensive treatment is found in part 1 of *De Corpore* (1655), especially chapters 2, 3, and 4; but he also addressed the topic in *The Elements of Law* (1640), chapters 4, 5, and elsewhere, *Leviathan* (1651), part 1, chapter 4, and *De Homine* (1658), chapter 10. Hobbes's treatment in *De Corpore* follows the plan found in many logic textbooks. It discusses the elements of the tripartite framework in the usual order: names, propositions, and syllogisms, and associates each with a particular mental counterpart. Hobbes also borrowed most of the topics he discussed under each heading from what he found in logic manuals, but he selected only ones he found useful. Thus, he discussed the predicaments in the chapter on names, mentioned the traditional types of propositions in the next chapter, and explained some of the rules of the syllogism in the following one. But he also stated that most moods of syllogisms are superfluous, and left the detailed treatment of such issues to logicians. The first part of *De Corpore* (entitled *Computation, or Logic*) thus reads like an eclectic and idiosyncratic treatment of traditional logic. However, in these chapters Hobbes also presented an original account of how words and combinations of them function in various cognitive processes.

An important distinction in Hobbes's account is that between marks and signs, each of which designated one of the two principal roles that words can play. The first of these is to help the memory: without sensible marks, men's thought is inconstant. Recollection of previous thoughts is a necessary prerequisite to ratiocination, and to the possibility of going beyond the immediate present. Words thus primarily serve as marks, as mnemonic instruments for individual thinking, without which it is impossible to perceive the truth of universal propositions. The second role of words is to be signs of thoughts, which enable us to make them known to others. Both roles are fundamentally important for the growth and spread of knowledge, and the second is essential for society. But, Hobbes points out, words 'serve for marks before they be used as signs', because in order to be used as signs, words must be arranged in propositions. A word uttered in isolation cannot convey a thought to a hearer; it is only within the context of a proposition that a word can be meaningful to others.

In Hobbes's view, as in Descartes', there is a connection between the use of language and human rationality, but the conception both of this connection and of rationality differs widely. Hobbes maintained that the use of words as 'marks' is a prerequisite for ratiocination proper (HW I 14). He did not deny that wordless thought is possible, but did hold that such thinking is necessarily tied to the particular images that are available at a certain time and place. Without words, humans are in much the same position as animals, who have an ability to think, but one which is limited to the concrete situations in which they find themselves. It is only through the use of language that judgements become possible in which words acquire a universal application. In fact, everything that exists is particular, and the images or imaginations of which the train of thoughts consists are also particular; there is universality only in names.

Hobbes famously equated reasoning with computation. Propositions can be viewed as the addition of the subject and the predicate, and 'a syllogism is nothing but a collection of the sum of two propositions, joined together by . . . the *middle term*. And a proposition is the addition of two names, so syllogism is the adding together of three' (HW I 48). It is hard to see how on this account it will be possible to explain the validity of the various sorts of syllogisms. Hobbes wished to exclude from consideration in philosophy, as irrelevant, all syllogisms except the one known as Barbara (first figure; both premises and the conclusion universal and affirmative) (HW I 48). His thesis that reasoning is computation appealed to Leibniz, and has often been considered by modern commentators as a seminal insight. However, as Nuchelmans (1980: 168–9) has shown, the thesis was not original with Hobbes. It was probably first suggested by Ramus, and was found in a host of logic textbooks, among which was one written by Hobbes's friend Gassendi. If one is looking for original views in Hobbes's work, there are better candidates: his elaboration of the thesis that language is constitutive of higher cognitive functions, for example, or his articulation of a thesis reminiscent of Frege's context principle.

Locke's views of language have attracted more attention from modern scholars than those of any of his contemporaries. This is understandable in view of the lengthy treatment of words in the *Essay*, a book which became epoch-making soon after it appeared. Locke deviated from his original plan by inserting Book III, but found that 'it is impossible to speak clearly and distinctly of our Knowledge, which all consists in Propositions, without considering, first, the Nature, Use, and Signification of Language' (*Essay* II. xxxiii. 19). Locke first addressed the question 'to what it is that Names, in the use of Language, are immediately applied' (III. i. 6) and provided the famous answer: 'Words in their primary or immediate Signification, stand for nothing, but the *Ideas* in the Mind of him that uses them' (III. ii. 2). This statement has often been used in modern discussions of the philosophy of language to present Locke as the advocate of a naïve and obviously untenable semantic theory. For if words referred to ideas, how could they be used to refer to things in the world? And if words referred to individual ideas, admittedly hidden from others, how could one ever be understood?

Modern scholarship has sought to safeguard Locke's notion of signification from what was rightly seen as misdirected attacks of this sort. Thus, Lockean signification has been explained in terms of Fregean sense and reference, immediate signification being equivalent to sense, and mediate signification, through ideas, to reference (Kretzmann 1975). Ashworth (1981), rejecting Kretzmann's characterization of Locke's notion as a *semantic* theory, points out the scholastic background to Locke's views and argues that 'signification', as used by Locke, must be understood as making known and not as synonymous with 'meaning'. Hacking (1975) likewise denies that Locke intended to offer a theory of linguistic meaning. Lowe (2005: ch. 4) endorses this view, to the extent that 'signification' should not be confused with 'reference'. He argues that Locke propounded an ideational account of communication, and a successful one at that. According to Ott (2004) 'signification' is 'indication', in the sense given to this term by what he sees as a separate tradition to which Hobbes and the Port-Royalists also belonged, namely: to cause a significate to be available to the senses which without the sign would remain unperceivable. Losonsky (2007) argues that Locke's signification is indeed a theory of linguistic meaning after all, but one which mixes sense and reference, and which, if appropriately qualified, is far from absurd.

It is impossible to assess the merits of these views in the compass of this chapter. Two points may be noted, however. First, despite a lack of consensus among commentators on the import and scope of Locke's treatment of language, there is an overall agreement that it would be distortive uncritically to project post-Fregean, post-Wittgensteinean biases onto it, and that it should be understood on its own terms. Second, it seems that Locke's notion of signification, although undeniably pivotal, has occupied the debate a little too much. A too narrow focus on this notion may distract from the fact that Locke's investigations into the nature of language were driven by a suspicion of words, or at least by a desire to find a remedy against the misuse to which they are frequently put. His declared aim was 'to find the right use of Words; the natural Advantages and Defects of Language; and the remedies that ought to be used, to avoid the inconveniences of obscurity or uncertainty in the signification of Words' (*Essay* III. i. 6).

The theory was thus primarily intended to improve a linguistic situation that was felt to be problematic. Locke was taking Bacon's idols of the market-place seriously: words shoot back on the understanding and pervert the judgement! Theories of linguistic meaning are usually assessed by how well they succeed in describing and explaining how language works. Locke's investigations, by contrast, were informed by the realization that language often does *not* work. From this perspective, it would be a mistake to try and assess Locke's notion of signification as though it functioned as an answer to modern questions concerning the workings of language. It may be more faithful to Locke's intentions to regard the thesis that words signify, or make known (Ashworth), or express (Lowe), or indicate (Ott), the ideas of him who uses them as a starting-point which was obvious to him, and which next gave rise to the disconcerting observation that words are also used, and in a sense must be used, to refer to things. And *that* explains why language so often does not work. Ideally, our understanding should manage without words, but in fact, regrettably and unavoidably, it is infected by language. The theory next ventures to measure the damage done to the various kinds of ideas, and finds that simple ideas are least contaminated, but those of substance are worse off. Mixed modes, finally, are hopelessly bound up with words and hence most imperfect, constantly giving rise to misunderstanding. This picture is, of course, incomplete and rudimentary; it is sketched here to highlight a somewhat neglected but important aspect of Locke's theory of language (but see Guyer 1994: 115; Ott 2004: 87–9; Losonsky 2007: 296).

By the time Locke wrote his *Essay*, a particular remedy against the imperfections of language had been tried out with little success: Dalgarno's and Wilkins's artificial languages were no longer seen as a viable solution. It was very probably also Locke's view that projects of this sort did not address his concerns. He noted, possibly indirectly referring to artificial language projects (as suggested, for example, by Slaughter 1982: 199): 'I am not so vain to think, that any one can pretend to attempt the perfect *Reforming* the *Languages* of the world, no not so much as that of his own Country, without rendring himself ridiculous' (*Essay* III. xi. 2). The remedies that Locke recommended were all reducible to an appeal to use words with the utmost care, and to explain and define one's usage of terms wherever possible. This, he believed, was the only way to avoid the 'Obscurity, Doubtfulness, or Equivocation, to which Men's Words are naturally liable' (*Essay* III. xi. 3).

But Locke also called for the development of a more positive sort of linguistic investigation. This concerned the particles, a type of word that he distinguished from words that are names of ideas, following a long-standing tradition that influenced philosophical grammars and philosophical languages (Section II). Particles are not signs of ideas, but show actions of the mind relating to ideas at the time of utterance. Thus the particles 'is' and 'is not' show that the mind affirms or denies by connecting the parts of a proposition. Other particles serve to connect propositions to make a coherent discourse. The particles are thus essential for speech, which Locke (like so many of his contemporaries) described in terms of the tripartite framework of words, propositions, and discourse. Since the particles are marks of actions of the mind, it requires diligent study of these actions, of which there is a great variety, in order to understand the particles rightly. This, Locke claimed, was a much neglected part of grammar (*Essay* III. vii. 3).

Locke did not know that, when he wrote this, Leibniz was working on a project in which the analysis of the meaning of linguistic particles was central. This parallel concern may show that, by the end of the seventeenth century, the study of language was as important to major philosophers as ever before.

# REFERENCES

ASHWORTH, E. J. (1981). 'Do words signify ideas or things? The scholastic sources of Locke's theory of language'. *Journal of the History of Philosophy*, 19: 299–326.

BACON, F. (1605). 'The Advancement of Learning', in J. Spedding, R. L. Ellis, and D. D. Heath (eds), (1857–74), *The Works of Francis Bacon*, Vol. III. London.

BACON, F. (1620). 'Aphorisms concerning the Interpretation of Nature and the Kingdom of Man', in J. Spedding, R. L. Ellis, and D. D. Heath (eds), (1857–74), *The Works of Francis Bacon*, Philosophical Works. Vol. IV. London.

BACON, F. (2000). *The New Organon*. Ed. L. Jardine and M. Silverthorne. Cambridge: Cambridge University Press.

BECHER, J. J. (1661). *Character, pro Notitia Linguarum Universali*. Frankfurt.

BECK, C. (1657). *The Universal Character*. London.

CAMPANELLA, T. (1638). *Philosophiae Rationalis partes quinque, videlicet: Grammatica, Dialectica, Rhetorica, Poetica, Historiographia*. Paris.

CARAMUEL Y LOBKOWITZ, J. (1654). *Praecursor Logicus Complectens Grammaticam Audacem*. Frankfurt.

CLARKE, D. (2005). *Descartes's Theory of Mind*. Oxford: Clarendon Press.

CRAM, D. and MAAT, J. (2001). *George Dalgarno on Universal Language: The Art of Signs (1661), The Deaf and Dumb Man's Tutor (1680), and the Unpublished Papers*. Oxford: Oxford University Press.

DALGARNO, G. (1661). *Ars Signorum, vulgo character universalis et lingua philosophica*. London: J. Hayes. Text and English translation in Cram and Maat (2001).

FEINGOLD, M. (1997). 'The Humanities', in N. Tyacke (ed.), *The History of the University of Oxford*: Vol. IV. *Seventeenth-Century Oxford*. Oxford: Clarendon Press, 211–357.

FREGE, G. (1879). *Begriffsschrift, eine der Arithmetischen Nachgebildete Formelsprache des reinen Denkens*. Halle a/S: Louis Nerbert.

GUYER, P. (1994). 'Locke's Philosophy of Language', in V. Chappell (ed.), *The Cambridge Companion to Locke*. Cambridge: Cambridge University Press, 115–45.

HACKING, I. (1975). *Why Does Language Matter to Philosophy?* Cambridge: Cambridge University Press.

HOBBES, T. (1996). *Leviathan*. Ed. Richard Tuck. Cambridge: Cambridge University Press.

KIRCHER, A. (1663). *Polygraphia Nova et Universalis*. Rome.

KRETZMANN, N. (1975). 'The Main Thesis of Locke's Semantic Theory', in I. C. Tipton (ed.), *Locke on Human Understanding*. Oxford: Oxford University Press, 123–40.

LANCELOT, C. and ARNAULD, A. (1676 [1660]). *Grammaire générale et raisonnée*. Paris.

LEIBNIZ, G.W. (1903). *Opuscules et fragments inédits*. Ed. Louis Couturat. Paris: Alcan.

LOSONSKY, M. (2007). 'Language, Meaning, and Mind in Locke's Essay', in L. Newman (ed.), *The Cambridge Companion to Locke's Essay*. Cambridge: Cambridge University Press, 286–313.

LOWE, E. J. (2005). *Locke*. Abingdon, NY: Routledge.

MAAT, J. (2004a). *Philosophical Languages in the Seventeenth Century: Dalgarno, Wilkins, Leibniz*. Dordrecht: Kluwer.

MAAT, J. (2004b). 'Leibniz's texts on rational grammar'. In G. Haßler and G. Volkmann (eds), *History of Linguistics in Texts and Concepts*. Vol. II. Münster: Nodus, 517–26.

NUCHELMANS, G. (1980). *Late-Scholastic and Humanist Theories of the Proposition.* Amsterdam: North-Holland.

OTT, W. (2004). *Locke's Philosophy of Language.* Cambridge: Cambridge University Press.

PADLEY, G. A. (1976). *Grammatical Theory in Western Europe, 1500–1700. The Latin Tradition.* Cambridge: Cambridge University Press.

PADLEY, G. A. (1985). *Grammatical Theory in Western Europe, 1500–1700. Trends in Vernacular Grammar I.* Cambridge: Cambridge University Press.

SCHNEIDER, M. (1994). 'Leibniz' Konzeption der *Characteristica Universalis* zwischen 1677 und 1690'. *Revue Internationale de Philosophie,* 188 (2), 213–36.

SLAUGHTER, M. M. (1982). *Universal Languages and Scientific Taxonomy in the Seventeenth Century.* Cambridge: Cambridge University Press.

SPRAT, T. (1667). *The History of the Royal Society.* London.

WALLIS, J. (1687). *Institutio Logicae, ad communes usus accommodata.* Oxford: Leon. Lichfield.

WILKINS, J. (1641). *Mercury, or the Secret and Swift Messenger.* London: John Maynard & Timothy Wilkins. Facsimile edn of the third edition, 1708, with an introductory essay by B. Asbach-Schnitker; Amsterdam/Philadelphia: Benjamins, 1984.

WILKINS, J. (1668). *An Essay towards a Real Character and a Philosophical Language.* London: Samuel Gellibrand & John Martyn.

# CHAPTER 14

......................................................................

# FORM, REASON, AND METHOD

......................................................................

## MARY TILES

MANY philosophers in the early modern period claimed to have developed a new, universal method for acquiring knowledge of the natural world. As conceptions of the nature and goals of theoretical knowledge (*scientia*) were contested and modified, so too were the methods of reasoning that were appropriate for its acquisition and validation. Aristotelian syllogistic logic had been well adapted to Aristotelian conceptions of scientific knowledge of a world of individual substances organized by genera and species; it was knowledge of essences (or natures) qualitatively defined, and of causal explanations of phenomena in the form of syllogistic demonstrations that assumed such knowledge of essences as their premises. Accordingly, it explicitly denied scientific status to mathematical disciplines such as astronomy, optics, and music (while recognizing their practical utility), and had little to say about the role of reason in the process of acquiring knowledge of essences or natures. So-called 'modern science' could emerge, therefore, only on condition that the epistemological status of Aristotelian logic was demoted and the status and importance of mathematically formulated laws and mathematical methods were enhanced. This in turn could occur only against a backdrop of rapid advances in mathematical techniques and understanding, a process that was already under way in the sixteenth century.

The focus of this chapter is the unravelling of the link between scientific reason and logic, as this had been formulated in the Aristotelian tradition, and their reweaving in a pattern that integrated scientific reason with mathematics and the discovery of mathematically formulated relationships. During this transition,

Scholasticism came into disrepute and new tools (algebra, analytic geometry, calculus, symbolic logic, probability calculus, elementary statistics, and the theory of signs) became available to those advancing and seeking to justify claims concerning the scope and limits of human understanding. I shall focus here on one family of concepts—proportion (analogy, similitude), ratio (*logos*, reason), and measure (magnitude, quantity, extension)—and the way in which their transformations are implicated in the transition from natural magic to rational mechanics. This involves omitting discussion of other significant factors in this development, such as the rise of probability and statistics, for which readers might want to refer to Hacking (1975), Daston (1988) or Desrosières (1998), and novel contributions during this period to language, linguistic forms, and informal logic by people such as Comenius and Alsted (McArthur 1986; Ong 1958).

# I: FORMAL TECHNIQUES

Our current understanding of formal techniques or methods in mathematics and logic had no exact counterpart in the early modern period. What makes a system, language, or grammar formal in our sense is that its initial units are defined as mere marks or as letters that have no representational or other significance. It is a system of signs stripped of all signification beyond that implicitly conferred by the rules for their manipulation. There is another sense of 'formal', however, which implies the applicability of techniques or notations to a wide variety of subject matter, and thus as being concerned with 'form' as opposed to 'matter'. This sense of 'formal' had wide currency in the early modern period, although it varied with different conceptions of the contrast between form and matter. It is in this sense that Descartes, having dismissed the utility of all rules of reasoning, claimed that there must be a general science of order and measure, which is concerned with no particular subject matter but applies wherever a subject matter can be ordered and measured. Descartes considered reason to be an intuitive capacity required for understanding anything (including rules), so that 'other mental operations which dialectic claims to direct with the help of those already mentioned . . . are of no use here, or rather should be reckoned a positive hindrance, for nothing can be added to the clear light of reason which does not in some way dim it' (AT X 372–3; CSM I 16).

The term *clavis universalis* was used in the sixteenth and seventeenth centuries to designate a method or general science which would enable natural philosophers to see beyond the veil of phenomenal appearances, or the 'shadows of ideas', and grasp the ideal and essential structure of reality. Deciphering the alphabet of the world; reading the signs imprinted by the divine mind in the book of nature; discovering the correspondence between the original forms of the universe and the structure of human thought; constructing a perfect language capable of eliminating all equivocations and putting us in direct contact with things and essences rather than signs; the construction of total encyclopedias and ordered classifications which would be true 'mirrors' of cosmic harmony—these had been familiar themes among expositors of Lullism and artificial memory between the fourteenth and seventeenth centuries (Rossi 2000: xv). There are clear resonances here with the language in which Bacon, Descartes, and Leibniz later express their projects; Bacon announces a *novum organum*, Descartes talks of a *mathesis universalis*, and Leibniz dreams of a universal characteristic. The project of constructing a universal characteristic took two forms. One was the idea of creating a universal language—one that everyone would be able to understand, and where all terms would either be simple or be unambiguously defined (in a manner that is represented in the complexity of the written designator of the term). The other was that of trying to specify methods of reasoning that borrow notational techniques from algebra. When the two fuse, as in the case of Leibniz, the project is very similar to that of trying to construct an ideal logical language in the sense later proposed by Frege, Russell, or Carnap.

The underlying foundation of Lull's Art, as of other similar 'arts', is the worldview of Christian neo-Platonism, according to which the created world is a similitude or likeness of the divine perfections. Nicholas of Cusa summarized it as follows: 'The first foundation of the art is that everything God created and made, he created and made in the likeness of his dignities' (Bonner 1985: 51). This reflects the Augustinian view (incorporated in different ways in the philosophies of both Spinoza and Leibniz) that '*ordo et connexio idearum est ordo connexio rerum*' (Bonner 1985: 51). Lull's Art was thus based on an extreme realism. It assumes a particular kind of order in the universe, and that the task of the art is to make this order manifest. Moreover, since this order is the creative expression of ideas in the mind of God, the function of revelation is simultaneously religious and 'scientific'. The alleged infallibility of the art derives from the fact that it is based not merely on the actual structure of reality, but on an assurance that the human intellect is an imperfect reflection of God's intellect, and can find within itself an expression of his dignities.

This neo-Platonic framework underwrites the possibility of a universal method for acquiring knowledge by transfer through the various orders of being, because at each level similar structures and 'dignities' (active potentialities) will be in play. Each being and each order of being participates in, expresses, and reflects the one creator (the Analogy of Nature). Lull's schemes thus link to the conception of a Great Chain of Being (Lovejoy 1960), and of the correspondence between micro- and macrocosm. However, the Christian neo-Platonic vision will underwrite different methods or arts, depending on views regarding God and the nature of his intellect as it is reflected in the structure embodied throughout creation. This might be a Pythagorean, arithmetic structure expressing the harmony of the world, as in Kepler (1995) or in Newton's *Opticks* (1952: 122–8, 293–305); it might also be a traditionally conceived Aristotelian logical structure (Spinoza), or a structure expressible via the geometrical theory of proportions (Kepler, Descartes), or some combination of these (Leibniz).

Equally, for those who did not espouse a rational theology but adopted a more voluntarist, yet nonetheless benevolent God (Berkeley, Pascal), or those of a more nominalist and humanist bent (Hume), the claims of demonstrative method to be able to lead to substantive, certain knowledge of the world seem unfounded. For such thinkers, even though demonstrative methods (logic and mathematics) are incapable of yielding certainty or revealing necessary causal connections, humans may be able to discern the orderly, regular connections of natural signs with what they signify in the world, thereby learning the language in which a provident God speaks to Man, and may be able to put that knowledge to practical use. In this latter case, statistics, the study of signs, and a theory of probability all have a place.

For those espousing it, then, the broadly neo-Platonic Christian view was one whose details could vary as new ways of conceiving and representing structures were developed, particularly in the theory of proportions. Early Pythagorean views of harmony were based on simple arithmetical ratios that yield a musical scale. There were many intricate arithmetical elaborations of this theme, but the basic model was that the relationship between the various levels at which the intervals of the musical scale (and elaborations thereof) are realized is itself analogous to the relationship between different octaves, with harmonic resonances reverberating throughout the world (a model of causation based on sympathetic action at a distance). Thus the changing astrological relationship between planets, for example Mars and Venus, as well as their location relative to the signs of the Zodiac, may be assumed to have effects throughout the sublunary world based on the relationships at each level between things that are the counterparts of (or are governed by) Mars and Venus. It is notable that each of the three sixteenth-century editions of Euclid's *Elements* cited by Malet (2006)—those of Tartaglia (1543), Billingsley, with a famous preface by John Dee (1570), and Clavius (1574)—are all explicitly neo-Platonic in orientation.

# II: STRETCHING THE FABRIC OF THE ARISTOTELIAN FRAMEWORK

Neo-Platonic thinking destabilized the traditional Aristotelian conception of scientific knowledge as based on syllogistic demonstration from first principles, which was derived from Aristotle's *Posterior Analytics*. All authors of the period refer to the theory of the syllogism (*Prior Analytics*), which was assumed to be familiar since it was part of the standard university curriculum. The theory of the syllogism is a logic of subject and predicate; each sentence in a syllogism is one in which something is predicated of a subject (All A are B, No A are B, Some A are B, Some A are not B). It is natural then to treat each such sentence as expressing a relation between two terms. Those terms that can occur only in subject position refer to individual substances. Other terms, such as 'whale', might occur in either subject or predicate position. The possibility of being used either in a subject or predicate position allows connections to be made in valid syllogisms through a middle term. The clearest example of this is a first-figure syllogism, whose form (Barbara) is SaM, MaP, therefore SaP [where S = subject term, M = middle term, and P = predicate term]. Since assertions about an individual were treated as universal propositions, the following syllogism would be treated as having the form Barbara:

> Moby Dick was a whale.
> The whale is a mammal.
> So Moby Dick was a mammal.

Medieval scholastics had introduced further elaborations of this basic theory, many of them focused on refining logical theory to incorporate better the variety of linguistic forms encountered in disputation. Their concern was with the validity of argument, rather than with methods of acquiring new knowledge.

Aristotle's first requirement for a *demonstration* was that it be a valid syllogistic argument (or a series of such). However, a valid argument with true premises may serve only to establish *that* its conclusion is true; a demonstration has to show *why* it is true. Aristotle's example (78a23 ff.) was:

(1)  The planets do not twinkle.
     What does not twinkle is near.
     Therefore the planets are near.

(2)  The planets are near.
     What is near does not twinkle.
     Therefore the planets do not twinkle.

Argument (1) is not a demonstration, even though it is a valid argument, because it does not explain why the planets are near. They are not near because they do not twinkle. Argument (2), on the other hand, offers an explanation for the planets not twinkling, *viz.* that they are near. For Aristotle, only demonstrations in the sense of valid arguments constituting explanations increase understanding and therefore contribute to scientific knowledge.

In addition, Aristotle required scientific demonstrations to start from first principles, and these in turn had to be necessarily true, since they are accounts of essence for the kinds of things that a particular science is concerned with; they also had to be immediately known, that is, they may not be such as to require further demonstration. Here a distinction is drawn between the order of experience (things as we observe them) and the order of understanding; the latter is provided by demonstrative explanations from first principles. While Aristotle includes geometry as a science and frequently uses geometric examples, he does not count astronomy as a science because its mathematical demonstrations do not proceed from first principles regarding the nature or essence of heavenly bodies, but deal solely in relations between them.

In the work of those inspired by Lullian arts, it is not syllogistic demonstration that reveals causes; rather, causal connections are provided by the kind of analysis that uncovers fundamental components, their order, and the significant relationships within that order. Relationships of analogy or similitude are more causally significant that those revealed through syllogistic deduction. However, this whole method would not be counted as scientific by Aristotle because, like astronomy and optics, it focuses on the relationships between things and the application of methods of characterizing these relationships from one 'order of being' to another. The validity of syllogistic demonstrations is not disputed in this Lullian vision, but their epistemological value is much diminished.

However, given the official Thomist neo-Aristotelian position of the Catholic Church and the attractions of neo-Platonism (Feingold 2003; Rossi 2001), there were many influential intellectuals, among them many Jesuits such as Christopher Clavius and Athanasius Kircher, who were strongly motivated to forge a syncretic unity between neo-Platonic and neo-Aristotelian positions. There is also an analogy that can foster the illusion of unity around the search for links in an explanatory chain of reasons. The language used to discuss proportions can assimilate the task of finding a 'middle' term in a first-figure syllogism to that of linking two others in a relation of analogy (proportion), or similarity of ratios (reasons) A:X :: X:B. Here A is the antecedent (minor) term and B the consequent (major).

Before leaving the topic of the way in which Lull's 'logic' may have performed a kind of reset in thinking about logic and reasoning, it is worth mentioning the way in which his Art is focused on the formation of complex terms and how these were used to arrive at immediate assessments of the truth or falsity of propositions. Lull does not dismiss Aristotelian logic or the theory of the syllogism, and is not in direct conflict with it. Nonetheless, there is a shift of emphasis toward analysis, the definitions of terms, and an assessment of their relations of agreement/disagreement, identity/difference, or sympathy/antipathy. When Leibniz picks up the task of trying to develop an algebraic logical calculus, he similarly stresses the representation of terms on the basis of their composition from simples. Once this has been done, there is little need for much calculation. 'The laws of categorical syllogisms may best be proved by reduction to a consideration of the same and the different. For in a proposition or statement what we are doing is to state that two terms are the same as, or different from, one another' (Parkinson 1966: 95). Thus he frequently uses equations to represent propositions, and seeks to develop logic as an equation calculus.

> Analysis is of two kinds, either of mental concepts, without experience (except the reflective experience of the fact that we are conceiving in such and such a way), or of perceptions or experiences. The former does not need proof, nor does it presuppose a new proposition, and to this extent it is true that whatever I perceive clearly and distinctly is true; the latter presupposes the truth of experience. In God, only the analysis of his own concepts is required, and in him, the whole of this occurs at once. So he knows even contingent truths, whose complete proof transcends every finite intellect.    (Parkinson 1966: 77)

It should, however, also be stressed that Leibniz pushes the theory of forms of reasoning beyond Aristotelian syllogistic, in part because he is well aware that mathematical reasoning (even that of Euclidean geometry) cannot be constrained within those forms. He has ambitions to unite propositional with syllogistic logic, and to incorporate both intensional (modal) and extensional (existential) readings of terms. In short, he attempts to create a genuine universal logical language. 'If, as I hope, I can conceive all propositions as terms, and hypotheticals as categoricals, and if I can treat all propositions universally, this promises a wonderful ease in my symbolism and analysis of concepts, and will be a discovery of the greatest importance' (Parkinson 1966: 67). In pursuit of this goal, he introduces the use of variables to indicate quantifiers. Y means any one thing; Y with a line above means anything (Parkinson 1966: 67; Lenzen 2004).

Leibniz preserves a metaphysical place for subject–predicate logic (in the mind of God) even as he alters the character and epistemological significance of demonstration: it is only humans that need to go through it if they cannot see immediately, as they might be able to do if Leibniz could have developed the right notation. He seems to have a vision of allowing the interpreted notation to carry the cognitive burden through calculation-like moves. This is in contrast with Descartes, in *Rules for the Direction of the Mind* (Rule X; AT X 403), who insists that because the truth can well escape the fetters of formal reasoning, while the person relying on the rules remains trapped by those fetters, we need means of keeping our minds alert when engaged in chains of reasoning.

We should not forget that many of these neo-Platonic schemes were, in their own way, deterministic and that they attracted theological criticism on that count. Moral accountability, it was argued, required space for humans to exercise free will. One way of assuring this was to presume that, in God, the will could similarly triumph over the intellect and that the rational order prevailed only so long as God willed it (as was the case for Descartes' God as opposed to that of Leibniz or Spinoza). Since God could initiate departures from this order at any time, there could be no causal law known to reason that was absolutely universal and necessary. This counterargument equally subverts the Aristotelian conception of science, since now any order or regularity in the universe is both contingent and directly legislated by God as a Law of Nature. This has the effect of directing enquiry less into the quest for causes, and more into the quest for laws or regularities (Milton 1998).

We find this view explicitly spelled out by Isaac Barrow (1970), in the course of making the case that mathematics (geometry) is a science in the Aristotelian sense, and that it is the only such science because it is the only discipline in which there are demonstrations which are genuinely causal (they establish formal causes).

For every action of an efficient cause, as well as its consequent effect, depends upon the free will and power of an almighty God, who can hinder the influence and efficacy of any cause at his pleasure; neither is there any effect so confined to one cause, but it may be produced by perhaps innumerable others.   (Barrow 1970: 68)

An alternative result of the same emphasis on voluntarism is the occasionalist theory of causality that developed among Cartesians, especially Malebranche, and which is discussed in Chapter 2.


# III: Proportions: from the universal
## lyre to a science of extension

One threat to the schemes inspired by Lull, and to natural magic, astrology, and alchemy, came from developments in astronomy prompted by the work of Copernicus and Galileo. By removing the earth from the centre of the universe, Copernicus initiated a shift from a finite bounded cosmology to an infinite one, even though he retained a finite universe bounded by a sphere of fixed stars. If the order of such an unbounded universe were to be captured mathematically, it required the resources of geometry, with the infinite implicated both in the concept of the indefinite extension of a straight line and in the indefinite divisibility of any continuous magnitude. There had been early signs of this already in Cusanus (Koyré 1957; Cassirer 1963). Galileo, whose desire to emulate Archimedes inspired his work in mechanics, and whose use of the telescope enabled him to reveal changes and 'imperfections' in the heavenly bodies, destabilized the boundary between the corruptible, changeable sublunary world and the eternal, incorruptible celestial realm.

It was Galileo's work in mechanics, as much as his astronomy, that helped spur the mathematization of physics by overcoming a crucial conceptual obstacle, *viz.* the recognition of velocity as a state of a moving body which could thus be subject to change (acceleration or deceleration). The conceptual obstacle presented by Aristotelian physics was that change (*kinesis*) was defined by its endpoints, as a transition from one state of an object to another. This transition (which could be change of colour, change of shape, etc. as well as change of place) could occur more quickly (take less time to complete) or more slowly (take more time to complete), but could not itself be a state of the changing object, and thus could not itself be subject to change. In addition, Euclid stipulated that a ratio can exist only between magnitudes of the same kind. Thus there can be no ratio between a distance and a time, which is our usual measure of spatial velocity. In order to measure acceleration and use mathematics to formulate laws regarding velocity, therefore, the latter needed to be conceived as a state of a moving object and uniform (unchanging, constant) acceleration needed to be defined. Galileo, after toying with the idea that uniform acceleration should be defined as gaining equal increments of speed in equal distances travelled, settled on defining uniform acceleration as acquiring equal increments of speed (velocity) in equal intervals of time (i.e. as rate of change of velocity). With this he was able to formulate simple laws of motion for falling bodies and to characterize the path of a projectile as a parabola. However he lacked the mathematical instruments to take him very far, since he was relying almost entirely on traditional geometric methods, as found in Archimedes.

By bringing algebraic methods to bear on such geometric problems, while also working on the conceptual foundations of mechanics, Descartes was able to go further. In particular, in his geometry he emphasized methods for determining the gradient of the tangent to a curve at any given point. If this curve were, for example, the parabolic path of a projectile, the gradient of the tangent to the curve at a given point gives the velocity of the projectile at that point. It thus facilitates the mathematical conceptualization of (instantaneous) velocity as a state of a moving body, something that can be continuously changing. Motion (defined as the product of quantity of matter and velocity, which is more or less equivalent to momentum in modern terminology) then became a fundamental concept in Cartesian mechanics and cosmology. God at creation put a fixed quantity of motion into the universe, and this does not change. Thus, in all mechanical interactions, the quantity of motion must be preserved while being redistributed among the interacting objects.

However, Descartes did not yet see that this state of motion needed to include the direction of motion as well as its speed; in other words, he did not treat momentum as a vector quantity. It was Newton who recognized the importance of incorporating direction, and who worked out geometric methods for the composition and resolution of vector quantities. He uses the language of proportionality to express the connection between force and acceleration in his second law. 'A change of motion is proportional to the motive force impressed and takes place along the right line in which that force is impressed' (*Principia* 416). Newton also, most famously, developed (at roughly the same time as Leibniz) the methods of infinitesimal calculus which further advance the analytic treatment of motion and mechanics that Descartes had fostered. He thus provided the mathematical and conceptual tools necessary for developing dynamics as a mathematically formulated discipline, giving greater substantiation to the claim, made by Galileo, that mathematics is the language in which the Book of Nature is written.

Thus with the Renaissance revival of interest in the works of Archimedes, the extensive use of projective geometry by artists, with the geometric development of the theory of proportions as relationships between geometric magnitudes aided by the importation of algebraic methods, the language of proportions had become both much more sophisticated and much more important. Kepler, Galileo and Descartes, Leibniz and Newton, all use and further develop these tools in the context of creating a mathematically formulated dynamics linked to astronomical and cosmological theories. They thereby transgressed the medieval and Renaissance boundary, enshrined in the division of disciplines established by the Catholic Church, between mathematics and physics or natural philosophy (Baldini 2003; Rossi 2001: chs 3–9).

A mechanistic cosmology was then ready to displace or transform the notion of universal harmony without in one sense changing anything, but in another sense changing everything. God had now become an Analytic Geometer, not a Musician versed in arithmetic. Newton and other mechanists are still relying on the Analogy of Nature. The basic principles of mechanics, to be fully universal and applicable to all material bodies, have to be scale-invariant and apply in the same way at every order of magnitude, both to macroscopic and microscopic objects, on a terrestrial and an astronomical scale.

How do some of the above-mentioned transformations in the theory of proportions and the place it occupied occur? What developments in mathematical technique were required? Without attempting to expound the historical and conceptual development of the theory of proportions in detail, in Section V I will consider their impact via the views of the Cambridge mathematician Isaac Barrow, who in many ways set the stage for Newton on the one hand and, on the other, for Berkeley and a British tradition of geometrically grounded mathematical physics that was nominalist but not exactly empiricist.

# IV: NOTATION AND NEW NUMBERS

One notable feature of this history is the role of notation. Leibniz was very aware of the value of good notation, which makes it possible to see at a glance the way in which a designated entity is composed of (and hence related to) other simpler entities. He experiments not just with the use of letters as abbreviations, but also with the use of variables, both free and bound, as in his notation for infinitesimal calculus, in his *analysis situs* (early topology) as well as in his logic. The development of the theory of rational mechanics, and of algebraic methods to accompany it, to the point where it could be readily understood and used, depended on the development of good notation for dealing with ratios, proportions, equations, and functions. Once there is a notation that reflects arithmetic operations on magnitudes and the relations between them, it becomes natural to wonder whether every term permissibly formed actually designates a number. This is one route to the extension of the concept of number from integers, to negative as well as positive integers, to fractions (rational numbers) and to real and imaginary numbers. However, so long as number is conceived as the measure of some magnitude (whether discrete or continuous) these extensions are not unproblematic. How can there be a negative amount of something? The square root of an area is a line length (the side of a square with that area), but what is the square root of a line length?

Euclid's *Elements* contains two treatments of proportion. Book V deals with proportions of magnitudes in general (the theory often attributed to Eudoxus), whereas Book VII deals with proportions between numbers. Book X covers incommensurable magnitudes. All of these topics were thus traditionally positioned as belonging to the geometry of lines, planes, and solids (lengths, areas, and volumes) and for this reason it was traditionally presumed that no sense could be given to anything more than a magnitude raised to the third power (the cube of a line length yields a volume). Moreover, the fact that there seemed to be two treatments of proportion in the *Elements* generated confusion and sparked controversy from the Renaissance through the seventeenth century.

One can appreciate the importance of a transparent notation when trying to follow the reasoning of a famous Renaissance author, Cardano, whose *Great Art or the Rules of Algebra* was published in 1545. The work provides methods for solving cubic and biquadratic equations among other things, and Cardano was aware that there could be negative and irrational solutions and even solutions involving the square roots of negative quantities. However, he lacked a notation; his work is mainly conducted in words and geometric diagrams, with little use of symbols. For example:

When the highest power and the number are equal to a middle power, divide the coefficient of the middle power into two parts such that one times the root of the other raised to the nature of the middle power—[the root] being taken according to the nature of the power obtained by dividing the highest power by the middle—yields the constant of the equation. This root which was heretofore raised to the nature of the middle power is the value of *x*.    (Cardano 1968: 68)[1]

---

[1] In modern notation,

$$\text{if } x^n + N = ax^m \text{ (where } m < n), a = b + c, b\left({}^{n-m}\sqrt{c}\right)m = N, \text{ then } x = {}^{n-m}\sqrt{c}.$$

A systematic approach to algebra is introduced by François Viète (1540–1603) and subsequently by Simon Stevin (1548–1620), two of Descartes' predecessors. Viète calls his use of algebra (coupled with the geometric theory of proportions) to solve both arithmetic and geometric problems, the Analytic Art.

There is a certain way of searching for the truth in mathematics that Plato is said first to have discovered. Theon called it analysis, which he defined as assuming that which is sought as if it were admitted [and working through] the consequences [of that assumption] to what is admittedly true, as opposed to synthetics, which is assuming what is [already] admitted [and working] through the consequences [of that assumption] to arrive at and to understand that which is sought.   (Viète 2006: 11; cf. CSM I 116–22)

Descartes, in his *Geometry*, transforms this logical sense of analysis into a method for analytic geometry:

Thus if we wish to solve some problem, we should first of all consider it solved, and give names to all the lines—the unknown ones as well as the others—which seem necessary in order to construct it. Then without considering any difference between the known and the unknown lines, we should go through the problem in the order which most naturally shows the mutual dependency between these lines until we have found a means of expressing a single quantity in two ways. This will be called an equation.   (AT VI 372; Descartes 2001: 179)

Viète's best-known contribution is his introduction of letters of the alphabet to represent both the constant and variable terms in all equations (although he does not use an '=' sign in expressing what we would call equations). His notation is more complex than we would expect because he distinguishes eighteen kinds of magnitude: nine scalar and nine corresponding 'magnitudes of comparison' such as *length, plane, solid, plano-plane* (a plane multiplied by a plane), *plano-solid* (a plane multiplied by a solid), etc. Rules then have to be given for keeping track of all these different kinds of magnitudes and their behaviour under addition, subtraction, multiplication, and division. However, his notation has the advantage of making visible the operations that go into building up complex expressions, and he stresses the importance of this. Nonetheless, because his letters represent magnitudes rather than numbers, he has to worry about the dimensions of his terms. Viète insists that the failure to recognize this led to obscurity in older works on analysis, whereas he is scrupulous in trying to keep track with his superscripts (*plane, plano-plane,* etc.).

A further interesting feature of Viète's Analytic Art is that it blurs the boundary between Arithmetic and Geometry (or the use of numerical/algebraic methods with geometric methods). In discussing the functions of Rhetics (where one works on the basis of having set up an equation with a magnitude that is to be found), he illustrates that he is aiming to cover both purely numerical problems and geometric problems in which the Art is used as a supplement to geometrical reasoning. Rhetics performs its function

...with numbers, if the problem to be solved concerns a term that is to be extracted numerically, and with lengths, surfaces or bodies, if it is a matter of exhibiting a magnitude itself. In the latter case the analyst turns geometer by executing a true construction after having worked out a solution that is analogous to the true. In the former he becomes an arithmetician, solving numerically whatever powers, either pure or affected, are exhibited. He brings forth examples of his art, either arithmetic or geometric, in accordance with the terms of the equation that he has found or of the proportion properly derived from it.    (Viète 2006: 29)

This trend is found also in Stevin's more comprehensive works on arithmetic and geometry. Stevin is credited with having made further, decisive notational and conceptual improvements. He does use an '$=$' sign to express equations; he invented a decimal notation to replace the use of fractions, which was a notation very similar to ours. He uses numbers to express powers rather than Viète's elaborate dimensional naming systems. Moreover, he explicitly extends the concept of number to include irrationals, while treating numbers as measures of magnitudes. As Malet notes (2006: 77), numbers for Stevin 'abstract' the notion of measuring as an operation performed on an object; they are not abstracted directly from objects. Stevin's geometry is also remarkable in that (like that of Descartes forty years later) it does not follow the Euclidean 'synthetic' style of beginning with definitions and postulates, but rather appeals to the 'common way of conceptualizing'. Here he may well have been influenced by Ramist criticisms of what had been handed down as Euclid's *Elements*.

Peter Ramus had been an outspoken and influential Renaissance critic of the scholastics, and of the university curriculum which consisted of logic, rhetoric, and grammar. He presented himself, in typical Renaissance rhetoric, as advocating a return to a 'purer' Aristotelianism that was not corrupted by confusions and terminological complexities. One of his primary aims was 'to remove memory from the province of rhetoric, to which a secular tradition had assigned it, and to develop it as a constitutive element of dialectic or the new logic' (Rossi 2000: 98). He thought that logic should be expanded to include the theory of a redefined dialectic that included invention, disposition, and memory, in addition to syllogistic. Like Bacon, Ramus insisted that the only legitimate quest is for knowledge that has practical value. Moreover, he claimed that this was nowhere better illustrated than in mathematics, whose *raison d'être* was its practical use. But, unlike Bacon, Ramus drew no sharp distinction between the order in which we become acquainted with things and the order (reflecting reality) of understanding. This led to the critiques of Euclid mounted by Nicole and Arnauld in the *Port Royal Logic*, in which they argue that many of his proofs are obscure, unnecessary, and presented in the wrong order. In other words, the function of demonstration has shifted to establishing a human conceptual order, not one that reflects an external reality of Ideas.

These criticisms reflect the move noted above in connection with Lull, away from giving epistemological weight to Aristotelian demonstration towards relying on the achievement of clear, distinct, or adequate ideas. This was especially clear in mathematics, in which the field was freed up for completely new developments; authors like Stevin did not feel constrained by having to present everything in a strict Euclidean format of definitions, axioms, and successively proved lemmas and theorems, and recognized the importance of clarity in definitions, the distinction between simpler and more complex terms, and of orderly presentation. This allowed the kind of boundary crossing between algebra, arithmetic, and geometry that would otherwise have been hard to achieve.

# V: Geometry, the science of extension

The seventeenth and early eighteenth century remains a period in which foundational issues have not been resolved and various rival conceptions are still in play. One can get a real sense of this from Isaac Barrow's *The Usefulness of Mathematical Learning explained and demonstrated.* This work, published in English translation in 1734, contains the text of lectures read by Barrow at the University of Cambridge 1664–66, immediately after he became Lucasian Professor. (Newton, who succeeded him in this post, was then in the midst of his mathematically most creative period. His so-called *annus mirabilis*, 1666, was when he made major breakthroughs in his theory of gravitation and methods of infinitesimal calculus.) In these lectures Barrow ranges widely, and we see him responding to most of the important mathematical and philosophical currents of his day as he carves out his own empiricist mix of neo-Aristotelian and neo-Platonic doctrines. Barrow's position was influential since, as Pycior (1997) argues in more detail than can be provided here, he set the course of the geometric style of British mathematics in the eighteenth and nineteenth centuries, as distinct from the more formally algebraic and analytic style of French and German traditions.

Barrow disagreed decisively with his fellow countryman, John Wallis, by dismissing the claims of arithmetic and insisting to the contrary that the real subject matter of mathematics lies with geometry. For Barrow, the heart of geometry is the study of proportions and it is to this topic that he devotes his third lecture series. 'I have now reached nigh the very soul of the mathematics, *viz.* to proportionality, on which almost every Thing depends in mathematics which is wonderful and abstruse' (Barrow 1970: 293). Barrow's discussion makes it clear that, like Viète, he is not working with an abstract conception of the items with which the theory of proportions deals. Proportions, he says, are the comparisons of ratios between quantities, and quantities are quantities of some kind of entity. One cannot just treat the measures as numbers without generating nonsense. Thus, 'Who can understand what is the sum of two years added to three miles; or how much three ounces of weight exceeds two minutes of time; or what remains after the deduction of four degrees of velocity from three cylinders?' (Barrow 1970: 295). Barrow is very clear that a ratio ('reason' in its English translation) is a relation between two magnitudes, and that what is required is a definition that gives necessary and sufficient conditions for ratios to be said to be the same (proportional, analogous). This is not the same as giving a definition for a pre-existing kind of entity.

Barrow's nominalism is evident here in his flexible attitude toward definition—he acknowledges that, in general, mathematical terms can be defined in more than one way (but one should show the equivalence of the definitions). It is also evident in his refusal of any ontological status to abstract entities. This refusal of ontological status to relations needs also to be put in the context of Barrow's physical realism with regard to extended magnitudes; in other words, this is not merely an expression of empiricism, it is also integral to a view of the relationship between mathematics and the world that shares some features with neo-Platonic views. In his view every one of the objects of mathematics is at the same time both intelligible and sensible, and he argues for the universal applicability of mathematics on the ground that 'there is really no Quantity in nature different from what is called *Magnitude* or *continued Quantity*, and consequently . . . this alone ought to be accounted the Object of Mathematics; whose most general Properties it enquires into and demonstrates in the first Place' (Barrow 1970: 20). Later he says: '. . . Magnitude is the common Affection of all physical Things, it is interwoven in the Nature of Bodies, blended with all corporeal Accidents and well nigh bears the Principal Part in the Production of every natural Effect' (Barrow 1970: 21).

Here two important shifts have occurred marking a departure from classical Aristotelianism. First there is the denial, common in Renaissance and Early Modern authors, of any distinction between pure and applied mathematics. Second—and this represents a departure from medieval and Renaissance Thomist conceptions of the boundary between mathematics and physics—Barrrow claims that geometry, as the science of relationships between extended magnitudes, can serve to provide causal explanations in the classical Aristotelian sense of demonstrations of (formal) causes from first principles, and thus that the whole of physics is really applied geometry. Barrow is not the initiator of either of these shifts although he does bring them together in a manner that makes their impact quite clear. His position is very similar to that subsequently expressed by Berkeley, that mathematics does not deal with special abstract objects but with real physical objects (objects of experience, sensible magnitudes) and its results are about, for example, straight lines, wherever they occur. Indeed Barrow uses something very close to Berkeley's selective attention account of how a mathematical demonstration, seemingly about a particular line or triangle, can serve to establish a universal conclusion.

When Barrow presents his argument against the traditional distinction between pure and applied mathematics, he presents it as an argument against the position attributed by Proclus to Geminus. According to this view some parts of mathematics deal with things only perceptible to the understanding, and the others with things sensible. This Barrow says is 'a very weak and slippery foundation to rely upon' (Barrow 1970: 19). His nominalist inclinations lead him away from any reliance on innate ideas and to a very empiricist reading of Aristotle's view that there is nothing in the intellect that was not first in the senses. The fact that Barrow brings in a reference to Proclus at this point suggests that he is following the most influential geometry text of the period—that by Christopher Clavius (1574)—which was used in Jesuit colleges and elsewhere. In fact one can see the influence of Clavius throughout Barrow's discussions. Clavius' geometry, unlike Euclid's, includes practical applications after many of the theorems and it was standard to follow Proclus and portray geometry (or mathematics) as a middle term between practical earthly knowledge and abstract speculative knowledge.

In addition, as noted above, the attention given to the revival of Archimedes's works on statics and hydrostatics as well as his use of quasi-mechanical analogies in geometry (his barycentric method of 'weighing' areas), encouraged a fusion between mechanics and geometry. Galileo, Descartes and others were already using lines (one dimensional extended magnitudes) to represent times, speeds, and weights so extending the application of geometric methods but at the same time shifting the focus of geometric attention on to the theory of proportions, away from a focus on the characteristic properties of triangles, circles, etc. They were assuming that every ratio between physical magnitudes can be represented by (realized as) a ratio between line segments. Descartes asserts that any magnitude, whether it is called a root, square, or cube, can be represented by a line: 'the root, the square, the cube, etc. are nothing but magnitudes in continued proportion which, it is always supposed, are preceded by the arbitrary unit mentioned above' (CSM I 68). He defines dimension as 'simply a mode or aspect in respect of which some subject is considered to be measurable' (CSM I 62). Barrow asserts in turn that every ratio can be realized as a geometric ratio (1970: 327). This assumption is crucial if a geometric theory of ratios is to have the power of a real number system (see for example Bostock 1979: 211–70).

The remaining buttress supporting the fusion of geometry with rational mechanics is, following Descartes, realism with regard to extended magnitudes, and to spatial extension in the first instance. To be spatially extended is, on this view, to be a space-occupying (thus impenetrable) but movable material object. Matter is the substance whose essence is to be spatially extended. Thus geometry, far from being purely formal, becomes the science of matter in motion, while rest is now re-conceived as a state of zero motion.

But how, for a non-Platonist, can geometry yield any kind of certainty in relation to objects of experience? Barrow has eschewed reliance on innate ideas and insists that the magnitudes with which geometry deals are sensible. His argument is that mathematics (geometry) concerns what is possible and that sense perception, coupled with imagination, can serve to demonstrate the possibility of geometric figures, relationships, and hypotheses. And to those who say that we never encounter perfect mathematical objects he replies

[O]ne sensible Observation alone may sufficiently attest that every Magnitude treated of by Mathematicians is capable of a real Existence; and there is no need of a long Day to teach, but one only Discovery of Sense will abundantly evince, that all Mathematical Hypotheses are possible, that Magnitudes can be composed, divided and moved, fill Space, *etc.*   (Barrow 1970: 75)

Further, Barrow insists that

[A]ll imaginable Geometrical Figures are really inherent in every Particle of Matter . . . though not apparent to the Sense; just as the Effigies of *Caesar* lies hid under the unhewn Marble, and is no new Thing made by the Statuary, but is only discovered and brought to Sight by his workmanship.   (Barrow 1970: 76)

Here Barrow is very close to Kant's 'pure productive imagination' as the source of the signification of mathematical terms. However he looks back to find a precedent provided by Proclus, who attributed this idea (the use of imagination to justify magnitudes which are equal to the same thing are equal to one another) to Apollonius. It is worth noting in passing that, in this context, generative definitions are mentioned. Barrow does not insist on generative definitions, such 'as a circle is the locus of a point moving equidistant from a given point', but he does view them favourably. He is, however, clear that for him mathematics owes its demonstrative character to the clear, unambiguous definitions of its terms, and given that he takes these definitions to be the basis of 'causal' explanations, his view is essentially that expressed by Locke when he says that in mathematics real and nominal essence coincide. Barrow insists at the same time that geometry is a science meeting Aristotelian standards in that it does contain genuinely causal demonstrations (1970: 88). His claim is that mathematics (geometry) is the only discipline in which there can be such demonstrations. To argue this he has to claim that geometrical reasoning can be squeezed into a syllogistic form (which would be much harder if he included algebraic methods as part of the demonstrative apparatus), and he has to argue that the first principles of geometry can be known with certainty and are universal truths.

## VI: FORMAL CAUSES VERSUS FORMAL METHODS

In the context of the search for a method of discovery, disputes about the relationship between mathematical demonstration and causation have considerable significance. They are also debates about the causal status of the mathematically formulated laws of mechanics and over what is to be meant by 'cause'. It is clear that the more mathematics is assimilated to arithmetic or logistic and to 'mere' calculation (mindless manipulation of symbols according to rules) the less cognitive status it can be accorded. Conversely, the more it is assimilated to the science of extension the closer it comes to mathematical physics and a vehicle for revealing the underlying 'harmony' of creation, the world created in number, weight, and measure.

Newton famously gives his laws of mechanics, including the law of gravitational attraction, only descriptive status, and denies that they can provide causal explanations (because he seems to be looking for efficient mechanical causes grounded in the nature of each material object). He is still looking for attractive and repulsive forces to provide his causes. He also does not believe in complete determinism; his universe is one in which God continually needs to intervene by supplying additional creative energy to keep it going—it is an ongoing work of creation. Newton's God is coextensive with space and time (which are as it were his *sensorium*) so that geometry and mechanics, as descriptive of space–time relationships, are responsible to a metaphysical reality. However, Newton's space is not continuously filled with matter; there are empty regions of space (vacuua). So even if geometry is the science of space it is not thereby simply the science of matter.

For both Leibniz and Descartes matter and space are coextensive; there is no vacuum. This allows for an elision between the subject matter of geometry and mechanics (physics), and Leibniz allows that mathematically formulated laws of mechanics do give efficient and material causes, but not final or formal causes which belong to the metaphysical rather than the physical realm. His principle of pre-established harmony, however, assures him that there is a match between the logical conceptual order in the mind of God, and its manifestation to each human monad through its relational, mathematically describable, perception of the world consisting of other monads. Monads on the other hand are immaterial, have no interaction and so cannot affect one another, so there is no efficient or material causation at their level. The order of formal causation is logical, based on the relation between an individual substance (subject) and its attributes (predicates), whereas the order of physical (efficient and material) causation is mathematical. Notation is important, both in logic (ideal language) and mathematics because it can reveal, through the structure of the signs, the structure of the things signified (concepts or mathematical functions). Manipulation of signs by rules assured of preserving significance, can then be carried out automatically.

Barrow is clearly not convinced that computational rules can be specified that will ensure preservation of significance; he, like Viète, is worried about keeping track of the dimensions in his equations. He is thinking like a physicist rather than a pure mathematician because he sees no sharp divide between mathematics and mathematical physics. On the other hand Barrow's physics is not one in which efficient and material causal relations can be established with any certainty. Mathematics cannot demonstrate these; it can only reveal the necessary relationships between possible physical magnitudes. It is up to God to determine how exactly these possibilities are realized. In all cases, it is the assurance that both the universe and man are God's creation, and that the human intellect is an imperfect image of God's intellect, that underlies the assurance that humans are equipped to discern an order in the universe, the universe as ordered and conceived in the intellect of its creator. This confident realism underlying the way of ideas carries the transition from a Pythagorean order to the mechanistic vision of mathematical physics. But to the extent that God's will outstrips his reason the reach of mathematical demonstration is limited. It is Kant, who by taking God out of centre of the picture, provides a distinctively new depiction of the possibility of a mathematical physics—one able to float free of its Christian neo-Platonic foundations. It will be the realization of the paradoxes and pitfalls of attempting to use the methods of analytic geometry and infinitesimal calculus to go beyond the finite bounds of the old Pythagorean order that eventually forces a retreat from reliance on geometric intuition and a resort to more formal standards of rigor that, in the nineteenth century begin to revive the fortunes of symbolic logic with the move to seek security in rules that require no reliance on intuition, that is, on rules that can be treated as rules simply for (mechanical) notational manipulation.

# REFERENCES

BALDINI, U. (2003). 'The Academy of Mathematics of the *Collegio Romano* from 1553 to 1612', in M. Feingold (ed.), *Jesuit Science and the Republic of Letters*. Cambridge, MA: MIT Press, 47–98.

BARROW, I. (1970). *The Usefulness of Mathematical learning Explained and Demonstrated: being Mathematical lectures Read in the Public Schools at the University of Cambridge (1664–7)*. London: Frank Cass & Co. Ltd [1st edn. 1734].

BONNER, A. (1985). *Doctor Illuminatus: A Ramon Lull Reader*. Princeton, NJ: Princeton University Press.

BOSTOCK, D. (1979). *Logic and Arithmetic. Volume 2: Rational and Irrational Numbers*. Oxford: Clarendon Press.

CARDANO, G. (1968). *The Great Art or The Rules of Algebra*. Trans. T. R. Witmer. Cambridge, MA: MIT Press [1st edn. 1545: *Artis Magnae sive De Regulis Algebraicis*].

CASSIRER, E. (1963). *Individual and the Cosmos in Renaissance Philosophy*. Trans. M. Domandi. Oxford: Blackwell.

DASTON, L. (1988). *Classical Probability in the Enlightenment*. Princeton, NJ: Princeton University Press.

DESCARTES, R. (2001). *Discourse on Method, Optics, Geometry and Meteorology*. Trans. P. J Olscamp. Rev. edn. Indianapolis: Hackett [1st edn. 1637].

DESROSIÈRES, A. (1998). *The Politics of Large numbers: A History of Statistical Reasoning*. Trans. C. Naish. Cambridge, MA: Harvard University Press. [Originally published as *La politique des grands nombres: Histoire de la raison statistique*. Paris: Éditions La Découverte, 1993].

EUCLID (1956). *The Thirteen Books of Euclid's Elements*. Translated with a commentary by T. L. Heath. Vol. 2. New York: Dover.

FEINGOLD, M. (ed.) (2003). *Jesuit Science and the Republic of Letters*. Cambridge, MA: MIT Press.

HACKING, I. (1975). *The Emergence of Probability*. Cambridge and New York: Cambridge University Press.

KEPLER, J. (1995). *Epitome of Copernican Astronomy & Harmonies of the World*. Trans. C. G. Wallis. New York: Prometheus Books. [Originally published as *Harmonices Mundi* (1619), and *Epitome Astronomiae Copernicanae* (1618–21).]

KOYRÉ, A. (1957). *From the Closed World to the Infinite Universe*. Baltimore and London: Johns Hopkins University Press.

LENZEN, W. (2004). 'Leibniz' Logic', in D. M. Gabbay and J. Woods (eds), *Handbook of the History of Logic*, Vol. 3: *The Rise of Modern Logic: from Leibniz to Frege*. Amsterdam: Elsevier.

LOVEJOY, A. O. (1960). *The Great Chain of Being: A Study of the History of an Idea*. New York: Harper & Row.

MCARTHUR, T. (1986). *Worlds of Reference*. Cambridge: Cambridge University Press.

MALET, A. (2006). 'Renaissance notions of number and magnitude'. *Historia Mathematica*, 33/1: 63–81.

MILTON, J. (1998). 'Laws of Nature', in D. Garber and M. Ayers (eds), *The Cambridge History of Seventeenth-Century Philosophy*. Cambridge: Cambridge University Press, I: 680–701.

ONG, W. J. (1958). *Ramus: Method and the Decay of Dialogue*. Cambridge, MA: Harvard University Press.

NEWTON, I. (1952) *Opticks or A Treatise of the Reflections, Refractions, Inflections & Colours of Light*. New York: Dover Publications [4th edn. 1730].

PARKINSON, G. H. R. (ed.) (1966). *Leibniz: Logical Papers*. Oxford: Oxford University Press.

PYCIOR, H. (1997). *Symbols, Impossible Numbers, and Geometric Entanglements: British Algebra Through Commentaries on Newton's Universal Arithmetic*. Cambridge: Cambridge University Press.

ROSSI, P. (2000). *Logic and the Art of Memory: the Quest for a Universal Language*. Trans. with an introduction by S. Clucas. Chicago: University of Chicago Press.

ROSSI, P. (2001). *The Birth of Modern Science*. Trans. C. De Nardi Ipsen. Oxford: Blackwell Publishing.

STEVIN, S. (1958). *The Principal Works of Simon Stevin*. Vol II: *Mathematics*. Ed. D. J. Struik. Amsterdam: C. V. Swets & Zeitlinger.

VIÈTE, F. (1970). *Opera Mathematica*. Hildesheim & New York: Georg Olms Verlag [1st edn. 1646].

VIÈTE, F. (2006). *The Analytic Art: Nine Studies in Algebra, Geometry and Trigonometry from the Opus Restitutae Mathematicae Analyseos, seu Algebra Nova*. Trans. T. R. Witmer. Mineola, NY: Dover.

# CHAPTER 15

## INSTRUMENTS OF KNOWLEDGE

### JEAN-FRANÇOIS GAUVIN

THEORY and experiment, *theorica et practica*: these two sides of the scientific coin have for a long time shaped the study of science. Although instruments were usually included in the description and conceptualization of experiments, they were not granted a life of their own, as theory (always) and experiment (later) were (Hacking 1983; Radder 2003). Antiquarians, collectors, and instrument experts, however, recognized several decades ago the crucial role played by instruments throughout the evolution—and revolution(s)—of science. Historians, philosophers, and sociologists of science were slower in acknowledging the epistemic nature of instruments. Peter Galison (1988: 211) described what was, and perhaps still is, one of the most interesting and ambitious programmes of instrument research when he wrote:

We need a history of the material culture of science, but one that is not the dead collection of discarded instruments. In its place we need a history of the way that scientists deploy objects to meet experimental goals whether or not these were set by high theory; a history of instrument-construction linked to the history of technology; a history that encompasses the relation of instruments to forms of demonstration; a history of the laboratory that tracks the development of the organization of scientific work; and a history of the embodiment of theory in hardware.

When reviewing Galison's argument some years later, the editors of an *Osiris* issue on scientific instruments acknowledged that the 'philosophical debate over whether theory drives experiment or experiment drives theory has tended to obscure the independent role of instruments in science. Instruments come and go, but not necessarily in phase with the vicissitudes of experiment and theory. The traditional mix of experiment and theory needs a new ingredient—instruments. It is not just a matter of getting the quantities right; we need an entirely new recipe' (Van Helden and Hankins 1994: 6). Since then, academic chefs have prepared a variety of new scholarly dishes, giving to this *nouvelle cuisine* an instrument flavour for which we have slowly acquired a taste (Alder 2007; Baird 2004; Daston 2004; Pickering 1995).

Instruments were central to the early modern theory/practice discussion, whether one dealt with theoretical, mathematical, or so-called philosophical instruments. What is often left undiscussed, however, is the actual operation of an instrument— or *organum*, as it was commonly labelled. What did one need to know and do in order to use an instrument properly so that it generated knowledge? What kind of training did the body and/or the mind require? Behind each instrument of science was attached a special training, a particular practice or *habitus*, which involved either the mind and/or the body. Though instruments were essential to the practice of early modern science, these were useless if the required *habitus* was not properly carried out. *Organum* and *habitus*, I argue, are the most fitting (and historically appropriate) concepts available to us in discussing the role played by instruments and machines in relation to the theory and practice of early modern natural philosophy.

An early modern instrument is best described in terms of an *organum*, that is an abstract or material tool designed for the sake of an end. In the case of Descartes' *méthode* or Bacon's *novum organum*, these abstract (rational) instruments were truth-seeking methods formulated with one specific end: to acquire systematic truth. A material contraption such as Galileo's telescope, in contrast, was improved to look at the heavens and to see what had been hitherto invisible to the naked eye. Although the ends in these familiar examples are simply stated and well defined, the knowledge-claims they asserted were completely open-ended, not pre-determined. Truth-seeking methods, by definition, promised that one would discover something true, whatever it might be. Likewise, Galileo's telescope was meant to observe something that was never seen before, though precisely what it was remained undetermined. Hence, a seventeenth-century *organum* was not an instrument restricted to a *terminus ad quem*, in the strictest scholastic interpretation (the hammer in a blacksmith's hand was the most common example used). Instead, an *organum*, in the hands of an increasing number of natural philosophers, grew into an instrument guaranteeing a *terminus a quo*—a starting point, if used properly.[1]

---

[1] Though William Harvey had a materialistic and even mechanical account of the human body, comparing human physiology to hydraulic engineering, he did not acknowledge the open-endedness of instruments. To Harvey, instruments were embedded with the teleology of their ultimate user, God. Harvey's concept of instrumentalism was based on a world where all machines came from the Divine Being, *machina ex Deo* (Bates 2000; O'Rourke Boyle 2008).

(Al)chemical laboratories, apothecary shops, assaying shops, foundries, perfumeries, and such other experimental spaces, where distillation, combustion, smelting, and various related chemical operations were performed every day, have been historically described as sites where *theorica* and *practica* were bridged (Klein 2008). Mathematical instruments also bridged the scholastic chasm between theory and practice. It was certainly not a coincidence that Bacon likened his *novum organum* to a ruler or a compass. By the time he started writing about the reformation of knowledge, mathematical instrument-making had already developed into an important artisanal industry, especially in Nuremberg and London and, to a lesser extent, in Paris and the rest of Europe. It provided tools for such fields as surveying, navigation, horology, and clockmaking, ship building, drawing, map making, accounting, and the military. These instruments and their practitioners, according to Bennett (1986), transformed the practical mathematical sciences into legitimate natural philosophical knowledge. Bennett (2002: 214–30) also drew upon the notion of instrumental virtue to account for the relationship between an instrument, its operator, and the mathematical sciences in sixteenth-century Europe. Moral issues, Bennett claims, 'are relevant to both the instrument and the operator, while [the mathematical] forms of knowledge do not stand independent of action . . .' The dichotomy between things made and things done, or between making and doing, collapsed in the mathematical practices of the Renaissance. According to Bennett, early modern geometry was 'embodied' in instrument and operator. Virtue was not only found in the *scientia* of geometry, but also in the instrument and its operator. Both acquired and displayed virtue, and in the end they were as dependent on geometry's virtue as the latter was on the instrument's and operator's virtues.

This instrumental 'virtue' or habit, as will be discussed below, which encompassed *theorica* and *practica*, far exceeded the use of mathematical instruments in the seventeenth century. Galileo's understanding of the optics of his telescope, for instance, was squarely established on sixteenth-century practical optical knowledge and on his familiarity with the workshop procedures of spectacle makers. The significance of the Venice Arsenal as an epistemic space where theory and practical knowledge were intricately weaved also played a major role in Galileo's ways of knowing (Dupré 2005; Renn and Valleriani 2001). Blaise Pascal's arithmetical machine and Marin Mersenne's musical instruments were also described by their respective authors as instruments born from the indispensable combination of theory and practice. Pascal called it the '*légitime et nécessaire alliance de la théorie avec l'art*' (Pascal 1964–92: II, 340). Though a strict epistemic dichotomy existed between the savant who invented the arithmetical machine and the clockmaker who manufactured it, Pascal claimed, that without this partnership, only 'illegitimate little runts [*avortons*]' would be created (Gauvin 2008: ch. 3).

Recently, Dear has historicized the transformation of nature's study from a natural philosophical enterprise to a modern scientific one. This gradual shift started in the early seventeenth century when an emphasis on the 'instrumentality' of knowledge production, advocated initially by Francis Bacon, changed the fundamental character of natural philosophy. The latter discipline was no longer solely identified with *theorica*, or the speculative understanding and explaining of the natural world. Useful matter, *practica*, was slowly integrated into the practice of natural philosophy for the benefit of mankind. According to Dear, this shift 'resulted in the establishment of a new enterprise that took the old "natural philosophy" and articulated it in the quite alien terms of instrumentality—science was born a hybrid of two formerly distinct endeavors' (Dear 2006: 11). *Theorica* and *practica* became two essential components of natural philosophy during the so-called Scientific Revolution, with knowledge-producing instruments often bridging or unifying divergent branches of learning into *scientia*. This chapter examines the notion of instrumentality, not by providing a list of instruments and their typical functions, users, and makers, but rather by examining the notions of *instrument* and *practice* in early modern Europe.

# I: *QUID ORGANUM ERAT?* UNDERSTANDING THE CONCEPT OF EARLY MODERN INSTRUMENTS

What was an instrument in early modern Europe? To begin with, it was not 'scientific', as the common terminology has implied since the mid-nineteenth century (Warner 1990; Field 1988; van Helden 1983). Second, it was more diverse and wide-ranging than the telescope, microscope, thermometer, barometer, air pump, and pendulum clock, which are sometimes identified as 'philosophical' instruments. In *Thinking with Objects*, for instance, Bertoloni Meli gives a fascinating account of the wide variety of commonplace objects used by late Renaissance and seventeenth-century savants, engineers, and natural philosophers in their study of mechanics, such as pendulums, inclined planes, beams, projected balls, vibrating strings, and rolling spheres, which were 'just some notable examples of the engagement of scholars with the material world around them' (2006: 2). Bertoloni Meli, however, refrains from calling these things 'instruments' because that term conveys the idea of something more elaborate than the mundane tools and objects of everyday life. Yet, could they have been acknowledged as 'instruments' in the seventeenth century? Consider, for example, another such ordinary thing as the prism, which was chiefly used in the mid-1650s as a common decorative and entertainment object. In the hands of experimental practitioners, it was transformed into a genuine instrument of knowledge. Buchwald's (2008) reproduction of Descartes' experiments with prisms shows how important they were in developing the Cartesian model of colours, and Descartes' optical explanatory novelties were similar to those later proposed by Newton (Fig. 15.1). Robert Boyle also emphasized the status of the prism when he wrote, in his 1664 treatise on colour, that it was 'the usefullest Instrument Men have yet imploy'd about the Contemplation of Colours' (quoted in Schaffer 1989: 76).[2] By exploring the etymology of the word instrument—*instrumentum, organum*—I suggest that an early modern 'instrument' embraced not only the mundane and elaborate objects of craftsmanship, but also abstract instruments of knowledge, such as Bacon's famous *novum organum* or Descartes' *méthode*.[3]

Instrument, in English and French vernaculars, comes from the fourteenth-century *estrument* and, before that, from the Latin *instrumentum* (provision, apparatus, furniture, tool). This in turn was derived from *instruere*, that is to fit out, equip, or instruct. The primary definition of an instrument is 'that which is used by an agent in or for the performance of an action'. It is 'a thing with or through which something is done or effected'. An instrument, at its core, is thus 'anything that serves or contributes to the accomplishment of a purpose or end'. The 'thing' mentioned here is not only material, such as a craftsman's hammer, a natural philosopher's air pump, or a musician's viola da gamba, but it can be a person (as an instrument of God), an organ or body part, as well as a formal legal document in law or an authenticated record of a transaction drawn up by a notary-public.[4] It could also mean a religious or sacred text, such as Erasmus's *Novum instrumentum* (1516), which was an authoritative Latin translation of the Greek New Testament (Erasmus 1990). Etymologically, '*instrumentum*' is derived from the Greek ὄργανόν, or '*organum*' in Latin. Though the meaning of these two words was alike, as one can ascertain from contemporary dictionaries[5] or Thomas Aquinas's lexicon, distinctions existed.[6] '*Organum*', however, is more interesting

---

[2] On the importance of ordinary things in early modern Europe, see Roche (1997). Blaise Pascal's arithmetical machine is described in the *Lettre dédicatoire* to the chancelier Séguier as an '*instrument*' and '*machine*' indifferently, with few apparent distinctions between the two terms (Pascal 1964: ii).

[3] Cf. Biagioli's concept of 'instruments of credit' which he ascribed to Galileo. These instruments were not only the geometrical compasses or telescopes he designed and built, but also all the 'techniques he used to maximize the credit he could receive from readers, students, employers, and patrons' (Biagioli 2006a: 1–3).

[4] *OED, s.v.* instrument. The French definition for instrument is analogous; see *Trésor de la langue française informatisé*. Robert Estienne's *Dictionarium latinogallicum* (1552) also offers a very similar definition under '*instrumentum*'. For similar contemporary definitions, cf. the *Dictionnaire de l'Académie française* (1694), and Furetière, *Dictionnaire universel* (1690).

[5] Nicot's *Thresor de la langue françoyse* (1606) puts under the headword 'instrument' the Latin '*instrumentum*' and '*organum*'. 'Instrument' in Nicot's *Thresor de la langue françoyse* and '*organum*' in Estienne's *Dictionarium latinogallicum* (1552) have both the exact same definition: 'Instrument à faire quelque chose que ce soit.'

[6] See Ludwig Schütz, *Thomas-Lexikon: Sammlung, Übersetzung und Erklärung der in sämtlichen Werken des hl. Thomas von Aquin vorkommenden Kunstausdrücke und wissenschaftlichen Aussprüche*, at: www.corpusthomisticum.org/tl.html., last accessed 16 July 2010.

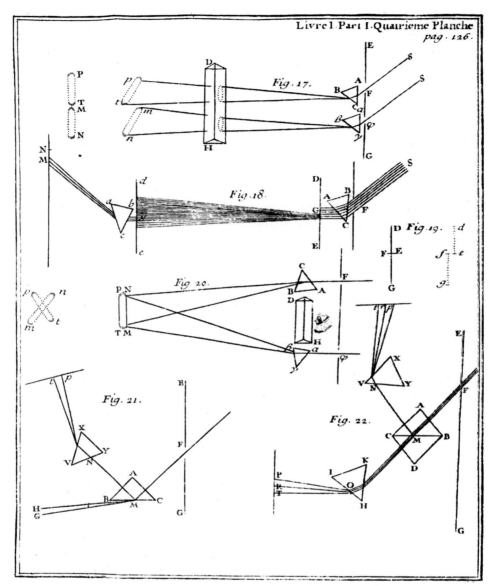

FIG. 15.1 Newton's experiments with prisms as depicted in his *Opticks*. This plate comes from the 1722 French translation by Pierre Coste. By then, these optical experiments were well established, thanks especially to Newton's and his followers' 'propaganda' from the Royal Society.

*Source*: © *Bibliothèque des livres rares et collections spéciales, Université de Montréal, 2009* as a word concept than '*instrumentum*' in the seventeenth century due to its clear association with Aristotle's *Organon* (or logic), and especially to Bacon's early modern criticism of it, the *Novum organum* (1620).

To Aristotle, an *organon* was anything that mediated between the doer and the deed. In his *Physics*, for instance, he explained that movement rested on three things: the moved (the deed), the mover (the doer), and the instrument of motion (what mediated between the two). The moved was in motion; the mover caused motion yet was unmoved; and finally the instrument of motion had to move something else and be itself in motion; 'it changes together with the moved, with which it is in contact and continuous, as is clear in the case of things that move other things locally, in which case the two things must up to a certain point be in contact' (AR I: 428). The instrument of motion was not therefore the cause of motion, in the same way the hand that throws a ball is not the cause of motion, but the instrument of motion. When trying to explain 'which part comes into being after which', in *Generation of Animals*, Aristotle complicated matters further by classifying instruments in two separate types: 'that which can generate, and that which serves as an instrument to what is generated.' Both, however, existed for the sake of the end' (AR I: 1151). Whether it was material (hammer, saw, lancet), immaterial (fire, breath) or living (bodily organ), an *organum*'s *raison d'être* was about the action leading toward a specific goal. Aristotle emphasized in his physics, physiology, and metaphysics the effectiveness of instruments, not their materiality or lifelessness. In his *Politics*, he described slaves and servants as property, and also as 'instruments' for maintaining life (AR II: 1989). For this reason Aristotle did not see a difference between the human body and any other natural or artificial instrument. Epistemically (not ontologically) speaking, anything that generated an action leading toward an end was an *organum*. Aristotelian logic was such an abstract instrument.

According to most early modern savants and scholars, logic was an art in the strict sense of the term. Since Antiquity, the notion of art was understood as knowledge for making things. 'Things' here should be understood not only as material objects, but also as productions of the mind. Art, more precisely, was acknowledged as a poietical or mechanical *habitus*, an organized and methodical disposition of body and mind toward the production of things and knowledge. Whether an art was defined as perfect or mediocre, it always entailed a system of principles (or actions) leading to an end. For our purpose, it is the second definition of '*ars*' that is especially interesting. Related to the idea of an end, logic (as a form of art) was said to be a *habitus organicus*, namely, an instrumental habit that uses the notion of *organum* and a disposition of the mind to achieve a predetermined goal (Goclenius 1613, *s.v. ars*). It was against this Logic, this end-producing and purely rational instrumental habit, at the foundation of medieval and Renaissance knowledge-claims, that Bacon offered his *Novum organum* (1620).

In his dedication to the English king, Lord Verulam pleaded for a regeneration or a renewal of the sciences that was long overdue. He compared James I to Solomon, and invited his sovereign to 'emulate that same king in another way, by taking steps to ensure that a Natural and Experimental History be built up and completed. . . . So that at last, after so many ages of the world, philosophy and the sciences may no longer float in the air, but rest upon the solid foundations of every kind of experience properly considered.' To achieve this goal, Bacon proclaimed that he had 'supplied the Instrument' (Bacon 2000: 4–5). Bacon likened his 'instrument' to a nautical compass of the mind, which could be used to 'sail to the more remote and secret places of nature' (2000: 10–11). He made full use of the material culture analogy of tools and machines from the mechanical arts in order to describe how best to renew the use of the human intellect. Aphorism two is famous in describing how one should think about this *novum organum*:

Neither the bare hand nor the unaided intellect has much power; the work is done by tools and assistance [*instrumentis et auxiliis res perficitur*], and the intellect needs them as much as the hand. As the hand's tools [*instrumenta manus*] either prompt or guide its motions, so the mind's tools [*instrumenta mentis*] either prompt or warn the intellect.   (Bacon 2000: 33)

In the preface, Bacon even went so far as to say that 'from the very start the mind should not be left to itself, but be constantly controlled; and the business done (if I may put it this way) by machines' (2000: 28). There is a constant reminder throughout the work of the importance of method and order, something evidently found in well-organized machines and skilled tool-using craftsmen. To reform *scientia*, according to Bacon's rhetoric, one ought to step into a workshop rather than a library to discover heuristic practices that would help in making a new instrument of knowledge (Bacon 2000: 70).

Bacon wanted his reader to understand how much the mechanical arts had contributed and would continue to contribute to human civilization, and that these were simply based on a few axioms and 'the patience and the subtle, ordered movement of hand and tool' (Bacon 2000: 69). To emphasize the point, Bacon also compared his *organum* to the most simple of mathematical instruments: 'In drawing a straight line or a perfect circle, a good deal depends on the steadiness and practice of the hand, but little or nothing if a ruler or a compass is used. Our method is exactly the same' (Bacon 2000: 50). Bacon's *organum* was meant as a new logic of practice and discovery, a new instrumental habit (i.e. logic, defined as a *habitus organicus*) elaborated to reform the old peripatetic one that was based on purely deductive and syllogistic arguments. Most importantly, this *new organon* was not created for the sake of generating predetermined (logical) end results, but was open-ended. The programmatic feature of Bacon's orderly method was strictly found in how individuals ought to train and use this instrument; it was not about the results it would generate. Acquiring Bacon's method or, for that matter, Descartes', which involved training oneself in order to operate this new instrument, was the key to knowledge-claims and useful discoveries. It was no different than someone trying to master the use of a telescope or an air pump to uncover nature's secrets. Material or not, an *organum* did not work on its own. It needed a user, and the latter had to participate in an intensive and ever more specialized training to become proficient with the instrument. Embedded in every rational or material *organum*, therefore, was a set of practices or habits that could produce, when correctly carried out, natural philosophical knowledge.

## II: THE INSTRUMENTALITY OF MATHEMATICS AND NATURAL PHILOSOPHY

Bacon's new knowledge-producing instrument represented a break from the scholastic concept of natural philosophy, an epistemic split already found in his earlier *Advancement of Learning* (1605). The numerous references to instruments and 'mechanicks' in the *New Organon* were compelling images of the innovative and methodical rhetoric aimed at bridging the 'inquiry of causes' with the 'productions of effects', namely, the study of natural causes by natural philosophers with the practices and utility purposes of artisans. Though original and 'aimed at providing detailed recipes suited for operational use', as Dear (2005: 396) puts it, Bacon's programmatic instrument did not 'rock the boat of established understandings of natural philosophy'. Furthermore, judging from Harkness's (2007: 246) recent study of Elizabethan London, Bacon 'disingenuously overlooked the instrumental mania that held London in its grip and ignored the instrument makers who were his neighbors in the parish of St. Dunstan in the West.' Bacon's own *organum* was essentially a rational tool, and its chief feature was orderliness. It had nothing to do with London's numerous workshop owners performing a very skilful yet seemingly disorganized hands-on 'artisanal epistemology' (Smith 2004), which was powerfully depicted in Hugh Plat's *Jewel House* (1594; Harkness 2007). Bacon's natural philosophical system was in fact epitomized by the fully organized Salomon's House described in his *New Atlantis* (1627), a metaphorical epistemic space where it was easier to confine, contain, and control experiments, suppressing all environmental conditions that might interfere with data gathering (Merchant 2008). Bacon's epistemic *instrument*, therefore, was meant 'to provide a respectable intellectual pedigree for operative knowledge'. In other words, usefulness and 'instrumentality had become attached to natural philosophy but had not usurped it' (Dear 2005: 396).

In England, late Renaissance mathematicians, starting with John Dee but especially later with Thomas Digges, William Bourne, and Robert Norman, played a significant role in fostering the transformation of mathematics from a theoretical, occult, and 'magical' discipline into a utilitarian, pragmatic, and somewhat pleasurable activity (Neal 1999). One major consequence of this emergent mathematical literacy was the growing development and use of instruments. Gradually, encouraged by specialized demands from seamen, surveyors, and artillerymen, London mathematical instrument-making turned into a formidable industry during the seventeenth century (Harkness 2007: 124–41; Johnston 1991; Turner 2000). In addition, the rising status of English bourgeois and gentlemen, seeking luxury items and requiring ever more skills and proficiency in mathematics to pursue careers in trade and government, provided instrument-makers with one of their primary clienteles (Turner 1973).

Mathematical practitioners such as surveyors, who had to perform calculations for a living, employed various types of dividers, sectors, surveying chains, compasses, theodolites, graphometers, and circumferentors, as well as plane tables and quadrants, all of which remained more or less standard in their use and manufacture throughout the sixteenth and seventeenth centuries (Bennett 1987). Yet a significant print market, consisting of a type of publication known as *usus et fabrica* books, existed in the late sixteenth and seventeenth centuries. It offered all sorts of inventions and their variation, showing the creative skills of their inventors and makers (Biagioli 2006a). Instruments such as *L'Henry-mètre* (Henry de Suberville Breton), the *Logocanon*, and the *Mécomètre* (Denis Henrion) or the *Pantagone* (Chapotot) are but a few examples of this original market. Other books, such as Edmund Gunter's *The storehouse of industrious devices benifitiall to all that delite in the mathematical sciences* (1620), depicted and advertised the vast array of mathematical tools available in London (Bryden 1992). This array of new instruments designed by and for mathematical practitioners required a specialized, often idiosyncratic training to put them into use, a training frequently acquired at the cost of abstract mathematical knowledge.

The collision between practice and theory generated epistemic tensions between mathematical practitioners. Gunter's original logarithmic scale, for example, published in his *De sectore et radio* (1623) and first adapted to a cross-staff, had a successful fortune and became known as 'line of proportion' in Edmund Wingate's *L'Usage de la reigle de proportion en l'arithmetique et geometrie* (1624), and as '*regle proportionnelle*' in Henrion's *Logocanon, ou regle proportionnelle* (1626). In 1630, Richard Delamain published a book describing a modified version of this mathematical instrument, which he called a 'mathematicall ring'. The invention was the focus of a bitter priority dispute between Delamain and William Oughtred. These circles of proportion were more than just Gunter's logarithmic scale rule or Wingate's line of proportion bent into a circle; each circle could be rotated separately on a central pivot so that this instrument was the ancestor of the slide rule, one of the most widely used mathematical instruments until the invention of the modern computer (Turner 1981). What is more interesting to note here is that during the acrimonious controversy between Delamain and Oughtred, William Forster, the translator of Oughtred's *The Circles of Proportion* (1632), wrote in the dedicatory epistle why the Cambridge-educated mathematician did not publish the description of his circles of proportion earlier, that is before Delamain. To Oughtred, Forster wrote,

the true way of Art is not by Instruments, but by Demonstration: and that it is a preposterous course of vulgar Teachers, to begin with Instruments, and not with the Sciences, and so instead of Artists, to make their Schollers only doers of tricks, and as it were Iuglers: to the despite of Art, losse of precious time, and betraying of willing and industrious wits, unto ignorance, and idelenesse. That the use of Instruments is indeed excellent, if a man be an Artist: but contemptible, being set and opposed to Art    (quoted in Hill 1998: 256–7).

Unlike Delamain, argued Oughtred, a deep knowledge of mathematics was a prerequisite to the use of an instrument, and to the education of a gentleman. Theory and practice went hand in hand; otherwise one turned into a mathematical 'Iugler' and mere 'doer of tricks'.

The so-called 'philosophical' instruments, such as the telescope, microscope, barometer, and air pump, were also constantly caught in the crossfire of theory versus practice discourses. In the *Sidereus nuncius*, Galileo does not describe the telescope (the *fabrica* part) because his experience told him that once you knew how to make a low-powered telescope, only a few more months of hands-on practice would allow one to make the high-powered instruments for which the later court philosopher became famous. What Galileo emphasized, however, was the use of his instrument. Training others how to use this *organum* (as he called it) was crucial to Galileo's authority as a natural philosopher, because he needed credible witnesses to validate his discoveries. The features of early telescopes, such as a narrow field of vision, double images, and colour fringes, made it difficult for the untrained eye to see the moons of Jupiter, for instance. Without such practical training—one could say habit here—'people who looked through a telescope for only a few minutes could legitimately believe that Galileo's claims were artifactual, as numerous spurious objects could be seen through a telescope's eyepiece at any given time' (Biagioli 2006b: 102). Galileo did not disclose craft practices; he kept a monopoly in place for a long time, but understood that to be taken seriously dignitaries, patrons, and natural philosophers had to acquire the habit of using the telescope in order to validate his observations. Practice, not theoretical assumptions, was at the core of Galileo's enterprise of self-fashioning.

Over the course of the seventeenth century, the telescope became an essential part of astronomical practices, and also in surveying and other mathematical practices involving levelling and the measurement of angles, distances, and altitudes. In Robert Hooke's eyes, good observational practices necessarily involved the use of telescopes. Hooke's stance, however, clashed with that of Johannes

Hevelius who, in the early 1670s, continued using sighting vanes on his astronomical instruments. According to Hooke, Hevelius

hath gone as far as it was possible for humane industry to go with Instruments of that kind, and [that] his Instruments were as exact, and compleat, and fit for use, as such Instruments with Common Sights could be made, and [that] he hath calculated them with all the skil and care imaginable, and deliver'd them with all the candor and integrity. But yet I would not have the World to look upon these as the bound or non ultra of humane industry, nor be perswaded from the use and improvement of Telescopical Sights, nor from contriving other ways of dividing, fixing, managing and using Instruments for celestial Observations, then what are here prescribed by Hevelius. For I can assure them, that I have my self thought of, and in small modules try'd some scores of ways, for perfecting Instruments for taking of Angles, Distances, Altitudes, Levels, and the like, very convenient and manageable, all of which may be used at Land, and some at Sea, and could describe 2 or 3 hundred sorts, each of which should be every whit as accurate as the largest of Hevelius here described, and some of them 40, 50, nay 60 times more accurate, and yet everyone differing one from another in some or other circumstantial and essential part    (Hooke 1674: 44).

The instrumental practices or habits, often required with a new set of instruments, are difficult to learn and acknowledge even when they have been proven worthy of acceptance and were becoming more and more popular.

Hooke's *Micrographia* (1665), in which he describes the use of a compound microscope, is another famous manifestation of the complexity involved in instrument-based knowledge. Microscopes were essentially of two types: simple (one lens, or glass bead) and compound (two or more lenses). Though the latter was in all probability invented first (closely tied to the invention of the telescope), it was the simple microscope that provided natural philosophers with the most astonishing anatomical discoveries in the last third of the seventeenth century. Individuals such as Marcello Malphighi, Nehemiah Grew, Jan Swammerdam, and especially Antoni van Leeuwenhoek, not only increased the body of knowledge of living things; they also perfected the microscope and the observational practices related to its use. Hooke recognized this fact with regard to the compound microscope, declaring that seeing with such an instrument required a 'sincere Hand and a faithful Eye, to examine, to record, the things themselves, as they appear'. One hand manipulated the microscope, while the other faithfully reproduced what was seen. In Catherine Wilson's words:

When Hooke speaks, for example, of the coordination of hand and eye, one remembers that hand and eye are *not* coordinated in microscopical work, that a new series of coordinated movements must be learned, with some difficulty. And involvement with 'things' turns out to involve not only delight and gratification, movement and progress, but the resistance offered by everything real, and the boredom, frustration, and even disgust associated with every manifestation of facticity. (Fig. 15.2)    (Wilson 1995: 102)

Such a 'disciplined seeing' (Dennis 1989: 323) was essential in order to communicate standard practices, and was necessary to validate data and expand the

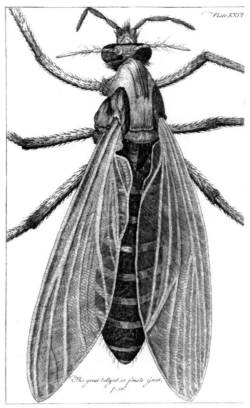

FIG. 15.2 'The Great-bellyed or Female Gnat', taken from the 1745 book reproducing and explaining Hooke's *Micrographia* plates. Accompanying the plate is the following description: 'Dr. Hooke permitted one of these Insects to penetrate the Skin of his Hand with its Proboscis, and suck out thence as much Blood as it could possibly contain, whereby it became red and transparent; and all this was done without his suffering any Pain, except while the Proboscis was making its Entrance; which the Doctor uses as an Argument to prove, that these Creatures do not wound the Skin and suck the Blood out of enmity and Revenge; but through mere Necessity, and to satisfy their Hunger.'

Source: © *Bibliothèque des livres rares et collections spéciales, Université de Montréal*, 2009.

community of practitioners. The instrumentality of natural philosophy, the new instrument-based knowledge of the Scientific Revolution, required practices that were not universal, but were targeted at specific classes of instruments or, most often, at one particular instrument. The epistemic, sociological, and technical problems associated with the experimental practices (and their replication) of Robert Boyle's air pump are among the best documented instances of the inherent savoir-faire embedded in machines and their use (Shapin and Schaffer 1985).

The organized institutions of knowledge, which were established in the second half of the seventeenth century, created epistemic spaces where the combination of theory and practice became the norm rather than the exception. The *Accademia del Cimento* in Florence, and the Royal Society of London, have frequently been described as the cradles of experimental science in early modern Europe, with their array of practitioners and arsenal of instruments. It would be a mistake to think otherwise with reference to the Parisian *Académie des sciences*. Reading the *Procès verbaux* of the Academy, one discovers how much instruments were integrated into the academicians' daily business and how numerous were the artisans in relation with the Academy. For mathematical and astronomical instruments, one could mention the armourers Sevin, Gosselin, Guerne, Tanguy, and Lagny. To these, one must add the mathematical instrument makers Ph. Le Bas, Migon, Butterfield, and Chapotot. For clocks and clock mechanisms in general Thuret was the chief service provider. Although the manufacture of lenses was often done by academicians themselves (Huygens, Auzout, Borel), instrument makers such as Pasquin, Le Bas, and Hartsoëker in France, Campani and Divini in Italy, were regularly employed. Specialized artisans and engineers were also hired for the construction and repair of mechanical models, found in the *chambre des machines*: Danglebert, Gayon, Potel, Buirette, Cosson, Langenach, and Colson (Stroup 1990: 250–1). The Academy's dealings with expert instrument makers and skilled *ouvriers* happened on a regular basis, if not daily. Aside from meetings focusing on pure mathematics, every facet of the Academy's life involved instruments, machines, and their inventors and makers. Moreover, the Academy became the foremost arbiter of inventions in France. In fact, a favourable endorsement was rapidly turning into a necessary condition for a royal privilege. Instruments and machines were simply everywhere in the *Académie des sciences*, and they were as well advertised in large numbers in the unofficial journal of the Academy, the *Journal des sçavans* (Gauvin 2008: ch. 4).

Instrument practices, whether to survey a field, observe the moons of Jupiter, perform logarithmic calculations, or generate new experiments under a controlled vacuum, all have something in common: they require coordinated movements, precise gestures (movements) that are difficult to characterize and ascertain. Such a bodily knowledge, impossible to articulate in plain spoken words or in writing, is often understood nowadays as tacit knowledge. Though this term is useful as a heuristic concept, it was certainly not in use in the early modern period. *Habitus*, however, is a concept that goes back to antiquity, and one that was still very much in the minds of natural philosophers, including Mersenne, Descartes, Pascal, and Hobbes. In the following section, I look at how the notion of habit was interpreted in the early modern period, how it was linked to 'instruments' and, finally, how it can be drawn upon in order to understand the *practica* facet of natural philosophy.

# III: *HABITUS* AND THE PRACTICE
## OF NATURAL PHILOSOPHY

Habit or *habitus*, according to the standard scholastic definition, was a quality of the first species associated with both the body and the mind. It was divided into two forms: the *habitus in corpore* was related to the body's health or medicine; the *habitus in anima* was linked to the passions (appetitive faculties), on the one hand, and to the intellect, on the other. The intellectual part of the *habitus in anima* was further divided into two types: (i) *speculativus* for the sciences; and (ii) *operativus* for the intellectual virtues (*practicus*, i.e. acting or things done) as well as the general notion of art (*poeticus seu factivus*, i.e. making or things made) (Goclenius 1980: *s.v. habitus*).

In his *Regulæ ad directionem ingenii*, Descartes criticized this conventional treatment of *habitus in anima* within the realm of *scientia*. He disapproved of the fact that the sciences had been connected to the uniqueness of *ars*; if one wished to acquire a specific knowledge, it demanded particular types of instruments and *habitus*, which led to a variety of training. Aristotle plainly expressed this condition when he wrote, for instance, that

science is an instrument of the intelligence (for it is useful to the intelligence just as flutes are useful to the flute-player), and many things in nature are instruments of the hands.... Now it is natural that where the instruments are prior, the faculties should also come into being in us first (for it is by using the instruments that we acquire a disposition); and the instrument of each faculty is related similarly to that faculty, and conversely, as the instruments are to one another, so are the faculties of which they are the instruments to one another   (AR II: 1503).

And as the Philosopher said in the *Politics*, 'for the exercise of any faculty or art a previous training and habituation are required' (AR II: 2121). Hence every intellectual faculty or art necessitated its own particular *organum* and *habitus*. Where Descartes saw a unity of *scientia*, an interconnectedness of knowledge commensurate with a universal wisdom, Aristotle and the scholastics discerned elements of science from the uniqueness of the instruments and dispositions that were needed to acquire them.

Descartes, however, could not discard the concept of habit that easily. Habit was an essential part of his method to discover the unity of *scientia*. In a 1645 letter to the princess Elisabeth, he wrote that in order to be prepared (*disposé*) always to judge well, one needed two things: knowledge of truth, and the habit (*l'habitude*) of remembering and recognizing this knowledge every time it was encountered. Such a habit was essential because, once a clear and distinct truth had been acquired, one could easily lose it by examining false manifestations, unless that truth had been turned into a habit by a long and repeated meditation. Meditation, which was turned into a habit of accepting clear and distinct ideas as true, was as important to Descartes' method as was the rational account describing how to achieve these truths. Furthermore, Descartes agreed with the scholastic view that habits were intellectual virtues (AT IV: 290–6). As will be explained in more detail below, a habit was not a natural power, but a quality based on effective actions and exercises. This definition helps explain why Descartes said of the *Discours de la méthode* that it consisted 'more in practice than theory' and why the four-rule method described in the same 1637 seminal work was not something that should be taught as much as something to be continually exercised (AT I: 349). The Cartesian method did not teach how to use *intuitus* and *deductio*, since both were natural powers. The method was rather created to instruct how the mastery of these powers could be achieved by developing a proper intellectual habit (Gauvin 2006: 188–92).

This is how John Wilkins explained habit in *An Essay towards a Real Character, and a Philosophical Language*. In it, we learn that habits—as in endowment, gift, talent—are '*superinduced Qualities*, whether infused or acquired, *whereby the natural Faculties are perfected*, and rend[e]red more ready and vigorous in the exercise of their several Acts, according to the *more* or *less* perfect Degrees of them' (1668: 200). A habit was not a natural faculty or power, but a technique or process for perfecting the latter. Once a habit was acquired, it was understood as fixed and virtually immutable, compelling the body or mind to move in a particular way.[7] In the *Regulæ*, Descartes adopted a similar definition to describe how the mental faculties of *perspicacitas* and *sagacitas*, which were understood as affections of intellectual virtues, that is as constituents of a more general description of habit (Wilkins 1668: 202), were to be exercised to uncover truths through the natural powers of *intuitus* and *deductio*. If *perspicacitas*, which aimed at 'attentively noting in all things that which is absolute in the highest degree', was truly the 'whole secret of the art', *sagacitas* was indispensable in figuring out the chain of inferences, the series from the most absolute to the most relative of things (AT X 382; CSM I 22). For such a series to become a clear and distinct idea or truth, one had to learn (by exercise) to go through each of the series' elements faster and faster until the whole series was perceived all at once. Acquiring such an *intuitus*, as Descartes described it, thus required a motion of the mind that was possible only through practice, that is the intellectual habit of *sagacitas*. Such 'mouvemens de l'esprit', as Nicolas Malebranche labelled *habitude* in *De la recherche de la vérité* (1674) was an 'automatic' motion not unlike the ones found in organic bodies.

---

[7] A disposition—as in propensity, proclivity, proneness, inclination, readiness, aptitude—played a similar role as habit, but was usually perceived as less perfect. For example, Philippe de La Canaye in his *L'Organe, c'est à dire l'instrument du discours* (1589: 59–60) says that 'l'Habitude est la perfection de la Disposition . . . Car [elle] n'est Habitude, que quand elle est hors de toute alteration, & qu'elle a atteinct le souuerain degré de sa perfection, soit que ceste qualité soit bonne ou mauuaise. Et ceste perfection de l'Habitude s'acquiert par exercice, accoustumance, meditation, & estude.'

The epistemic nature of the mind and body was acknowledged through the early modern concept of *habitus*. In his *Elements of Philosophy*, Hobbes perhaps best explained how habit and motion were linked together:

Habit... is a generation of motion, not of motion simply, but an easy conducting of the moved body in a certain and designed way. And seeing it is attained by the weakening of such endeavours as divert its motion, therefore such endeavours are to be weakened by little and little. But this cannot be done but by the long continuance of action, or by actions often repeated; and therefore custom begets that facility, which is commonly and rightly called *habit*; and it may be defined thus: HABIT *is motion made more easy and ready by custom; that is to say, by perpetual endeavour, or by iterated endeavours in a way differing from that in which the motion proceeded from the beginning, and opposing such endeavours as resist.*    (Hobbes 1995: IV, 348)

What Hobbes is describing here is evidently not limited to a *habitus in corpore*, namely, to bodily health and disposition as understood since Greek antiquity. It was related to bodily gestures, motions, and actions, whether one was learning to play the clavichord or crafting an object. When Hobbes says that habit was the result of 'perpetual endeavour' or 'iterated endeavours', he endowed habit with the notion of least effort. Endeavour had indeed a special meaning to Hobbes. He defined it as a '*Motion made in less Space and Time than can be given; that is, less than can be determined or assigned by Exposition or Number; that is, Motion made through the length of a Point*' (quoted in Osler 2001: 166–7). A habit was more than an automatic movement: it was a force. Through the repeated action of bodily organs (or of the mind, as we saw above with Descartes) habit became akin to a natural power or a second nature.[8] Hence, whether one dealt with logic as a *habitus organicus* or instrumental habit (virtue) of the mind, or a mathematical instrument as described earlier by Bennett, both mind and body received a special training in the form of *habitus* in order to use these instruments properly. The *habitus*, moreover, was specific to the *organum* that was deemed suitable for the accomplishment of the desired task.

To Hobbes, and to most early modern savants, including Pascal in his *Pensées*, habits or *coutume*, which was a similar notion but not identical to *habitude* (Ferreyrolles 1995: 17–19), were not about voluntary actions or free will.[9] As

---

[8] Hobbes (1995: IV, 348) also mentioned that habit was not restricted to living organisms (contrary to the Renaissance understanding of *habitus*, see Canaye (1589: 60)): 'Nor are habits to be observed in living creatures only, but also in bodies inanimate. For we find that when the lath of a cross-bow is strongly bent, and would if the impediment were removed return again with great force; if it remain a long time bent, it will get such a habit, that when it is loosed and left to its own freedom, it will not only not restore itself, but will require as much force for the bringing of it back to its first posture, as it did for the bending of it at the first.'

[9] Pascal (2000, S617): 'La machine arithmétique fait des effets qui approchent plus de la pensée que tout ce que font les animaux. Mais elle ne fait rien qui puisse faire dire qu'elle a de la volonté, comme les animaux.'

mentioned above, Hobbes contended that habits were 'attained by the weakening of such endeavours as divert its motion'. Habits were about constraining these 'endeavours' in order to compel the body or mind to carry out a specific undertaking. Whereas this constraining notion was made explicit in Pascal's writings on the arithmetical machine, Hobbes used musical instruments to explain the effect of habit. In the case of a 'man that playeth on an instrument with his hand'

it proveth only, that the habit maketh the motion of his hand more ready and quick; but it proveth not that it maketh it more voluntary, but rather less; because the rest of the motions follow the first by an easiness acquired from long custom; in which motion the will doth not accompany all the strokes of the hand, but gives a beginning to them only in the first    (Hobbes 1995: IX, 354).

The will, or reason, provides the first 'motion' to the hands; the subsequent motions are not voluntary, but 'acquired from long custom'. Two decades earlier, Mersenne had a somewhat similar approach when he designed a twenty-seven-key organ clavier, different from the customary ones and aimed at perfecting the harmony of the organ. He did not think organists ought to reject this new clavier, even if it meant learning anew how to play the organ:

Now it is certain that these keyboards ought to be preferred to the old ones, since they contain a greater number of consonances and other intervals in their justness....For it is of no importance that the difficulty of playing them is greater, inasmuch as it is not necessary to feel pity for the pains nor to avoid the work which leads to perfection. To this I add that they will be played as easily as the others when the hands become accustomed to them, because they follow the infallible rule of reason. And there is no need for working to hide their imperfection, as happens in ordinary keyboards since they do not have them . . .    (Mersenne 1957: 437; Mersenne 1963: III, 354).

Because this new clavier was organized by the rules of reason, Mersenne argued, an organist will learn how to play on it 'as easily as the others' once his 'hands become accustomed' to it. From these two examples of playing music, which since Aristotle was the most common illustration of *habitus*, it is obvious that bodily habits were not endowed with the power of creation that *ars* and *scientia* possessed in relation to the *habitus in anima*. However true this statement may be, bodily habits should also be viewed in the light of the nascent experimental science.

The gestures associated with the performance of instruments are now commonly referred to as tacit knowledge, a notion also closely linked to the conduct of experiments. In the early modern period, these gestures were constitutive of the 'Kinds of vertuous Habits' that were necessary in acquiring intellectual habits. As maintained by Wilkins (1668: 205), these virtuous habits 'may be gotten by Industry, and tend to the perfecting of the Mind or Understanding'. Building on the scholastic interpretation mentioned above, their object can be speculative, that is 'furnishing the mind with due Notions and conceptions concerning the Nature of things, their Causes, Differences, Relations and Dependencies', such as *science* (knowledge, skill, theory, learning, insight). Their object can also be active, that is 'denoting Skill in men and business, whereby we are inabled (*sic*) to judge what is fit and convenient, according to various cases and circumstances', such as *wisdom* (prudence, discretion, sapience, sage, politic) and *craft* (cunning, subtlety, shyness, policy, device, quirk, sleight, fetch, wile, trick, sly, shrewd, knave, shark). Finally, their object can be effective, that is 'implying Skill in those several Operations and Works which concern Human life', such as *art*. The manner of acquiring these intellectual habits (science, wisdom, craft, art) is by observation and repeated trials, such as *experience*, described as 'Practice, Exercise, Knowledge, conversant, versed, expert, Experiment, Empiric' and from the teaching of others, 'either *vivâ voce*, or *ex scriptis*'. What Wilkins is describing, in this section of the book, is the basis of Baconian natural philosophy: Practice, experiment, empiric, and exercise were manners of acquiring intellectual habits (science, wisdom, art). And these manners were themselves habits—'*customary*, and habitual *Actions* of men *considered as voluntary*' (Wilkins 1668: 206).

Habit is perhaps best understood nowadays as a *structure structurée et structurante*, following Pierre Bourdieu's (1980) definition, a restraining system of intellectual and bodily prescriptions that nonetheless allow for an open-ended and limitless set of outcomes. Descartes himself witnessed in weavers and embroiderers something akin to 'an infinite yet strictly limited generative capacity' emanating from calculated regularities; as an explicit sign of order, they conditioned the artisan's work habits. Artisans' know-how was to some extent organized because it followed a structured discipline moulded by regulated practices. Weaving and other simple arts, according to Descartes, 'present us in the most distinct way with innumerable instances of order, each one different from the other, yet all regular' (AT X 404; CSM I 35). An intellectual or bodily habit is therefore a structured discipline that generates knowledge. It is a discipline that requires a special kind of training, specific to each *organum*, and habitually idiosyncratic to an instrument: Otto von Guericke's air pump did not operate as Boyle's or as Huygens's air pumps, and thus caused numerous replication problems (Shapin and Schaffer 1985: ch. 6). (Fig. 15.3).

Instruments of knowledge, whether abstract or material, thus involved a variety of *habitus* that constrained the mind and/or the body to prescribed practices, from which original knowledge-claims could then be inferred. The instrumentality of seventeenth-century natural philosophy was not simply about the material instruments; it also concerned the redefinition of the concept of *organum* from a *terminus ad quem* to a *terminus a quo*. Hence, the early modern instrument of knowledge can be identified as both the mind and the body of the natural philosopher, the abstract method as well as the material and bodily modus operandi of the *organum*.

FIG. 15.3 Otto von Guericke's pump as depicted in a 1672 book published in Amsterdam. The author describes how to build it and how to make it work (an *usus et fabrica* book), with several experiments that can be conducted.

*Source*: © *Bibliothèque des livres rares et collections spéciales, Université de Montréal*, 2009.

## REFERENCES

ALDER, K. (ed.) (2007). 'Focus: thick things'. *Isis*, 98, 80–142.

BACON, F. (2000). *The New Organon*, ed. by L. Jardine and M. Silverthorne. Cambridge: Cambridge University Press [1st edn. 1620].

BAIRD, D. (2004). *Thing Knowledge: A Philosophy of Scientific Instruments*. Berkeley, CA: University of California Press.

BATES, D. (2000). '*Machina ex Deo*: William Harvey and the meaning of instrument'. *Journal of the History of Ideas*, 61: 577–93.

BENNETT, J. (1986). 'The mechanics' philosophy and the mechanical philosophy'. *History of Science*, 24: 1–28.

BENNETT, J. (1987). *The Divided Circle: A History of Instruments for Astronomy, Navigation and Surveying*. Oxford: Phaidon and Christie's.

BENNETT, J. (2002). 'Geometry in context in the sixteenth century: the view from the museum'. *Early Science and Medicine*, 7: 214–30.

BERTOLONI MELI, D. (2006). *Thinking with Objects: The Transformation of Mechanics in the Seventeenth Century*. Baltimore, MD: Johns Hopkins University Press.

BIAGIOLI, M. (2006a). 'From print to patents: living on instruments in early modern Europe'. *History of Science*, 44: 139–86.

BIAGIOLI, M. (2006b). *Galileo's Instrument of Credit: Telescopes, Images, Secrecy*. Chicago: The University of Chicago Press.

BOURDIEU, P. (1980). *Le Sens pratique*. Paris: Editions de Minuit.

BRYDEN, D. J. (1992). 'Evidence from advertising for mathematical instrument making in London, 1556–1714'. *Annals of Science*, 49: 301–36.

BUCHWALD, J. Z. (2008). 'Descartes's experimental journey past the prism and through the invisible world to the rainbow'. *Annals of Science*, 65(1): 1–46.

CANAYE, P. (1589). *L'Organe, c'est à dire l'instrument du discours*. Geneva: Jean de Tournes.

DASTON, L. (ed.) (2004). *Things that Talk: Object Lessons from Art and Science*. New York: Zone Books.

DEAR, P. (2005). 'What is the history of science the history *Of*? Early modern roots of the ideology of modern science'. *Isis*, 96: 390–406.

DEAR, P. (2006). *The Intelligibility of Nature: How Science Makes Sense of the World*. Chicago: The University of Chicago Press.

DENNIS, M. A. (1989). 'Graphic understanding: instruments and interpretation in Robert Hooke's *Micrographia*'. *Science in Context*, 3: 309–64.

DUPRÉ, S. (2005). 'Ausonio's mirrors and Galileo's lenses: the telescope and sixteenth-century practical optical knowledge'. *Galilaeana*, 2: 145–80.

ERASMUS, D. (1990). *Les Préfaces au Novum testamentum (1516)*. Ed. Y. Delègue, in collaboration with J. P. Gillet. Geneva: Labor et Fides.

FERREYROLLES, G. (1995). *Les Reines du monde. L'imagination et la coutume chez Pascal*. Paris: Honoré Champion.

FIELD, J. V. (1988). 'What is scientific about a scientific instrument?' *Nuncius*, 3: 3–26.

GALISON, P. (1988). 'History, philosophy, and the central metaphor'. *Science in Context*, 2: 197–212.

GAUVIN, J.-F. (2006). 'Artisans, machines, and Descartes's *organon*'. *History of Science*, 44: 187–216.

GAUVIN, J.-F. (2008). *Habits of Knowledge: Artisans, Savants and Mechanical Devices in Seventeenth-Century French Natural Philosophy*. Ph.D. dissertation (Harvard University).

GOCLENIUS, R. (1980). *Lexicon philosophicum*. New York: Georg Olms Verlag [1st edn. 1613].

GUERICKE, O. (1672). *Ottonis de Guericke experimenta nova (ut vocantur) magdeburgica de vacuo spatio primù à R. P. Gaspare Schotto . . . nunc verò ab ipso auctore perfectiùs edita, variisque aliis experimentis aucta . . .* Amsterdam: J. Janssonium à Waesberge.

HACKING, I. (1983). *Representing and Intervening: Introductory Topics in the Philosophy of Natural Science*. Cambridge: Cambridge University Press.

HARKNESS, D. E. (2007). *The Jewel House: Elizabethan London and the Scientific Revolution.* New Haven, CT: Yale University Press.

HELDEN, A. VAN. (1983). 'The birth of the modern scientific instrument, 1550–1700', in J. G. Burke (ed.), *The Uses of Science in the Age of Newton.* Berkeley, CA: University of California Press, 49–84.

HELDEN, A. VAN and HANKINS, T. L. (eds) (1994). *Instruments. Osiris,* 2nd series, 9: 1–250.

HILL, K. (1998). '"Juglers or Schollers?": Negotiating the role of a mathematical practitioner'. *British Journal for the History of Science,* 31: 253–74.

HOBBES, T. (1995). *The English Works of Thomas Hobbes* [electronic resource]. 16 vols. Charlottesville, VA: InteLex Corporation [Past Masters Collection].

HOOKE, R. (1674). *Animadversions on the first part of the Machina Coelestis of... Johannes Hevelius... Together with an explication of some instruments made by Robert Hooke...* London: T. R. for John Martyn.

HOOKE, R. (1745). *Micrographia restaurata, or, the copper-plates of Dr. Hooke's wonderful discoveries by the microscope, reprinted and fully explained...* London: J. Bowles.

JOHNSTON, S. (1991). 'Mathematical practitioners and instruments in Elizabethan England'. *Annals of Science,* 48: 319–44.

KLEIN, U. (2008). 'The laboratory challenge: some revisions of the standard view of early modern experimentation'. *Isis,* 99: 769–82.

MERCHANT, C. (2008). '"The violence of impediment": Francis Bacon and the origins of experimentation'. *Isis,* 99: 731–60.

MERSENNE, M. (1957). *Harmonie universelle: The Books on Instruments.* Trans. Roger E. Chapman. The Hague: Nijhoff.

MERSENNE, M. (1963). *Harmonie universelle, contenant la théorie et la pratique de la musique.* 3 vols. Paris: Centre national de la recherche scientifique [1st edn. 1636–37].

NEAL, K. (1999). 'The rhetoric of utility: avoiding occult associations for mathematics through profitability and pleasure'. *History of Science,* 37: 151–78.

NEWTON, I. (1722). *Traité d'optique: sur les reflexions, refractions, inflexions, et les couleurs de la lumiere.* Trans. Pierre Coste. 2nd edn. Paris: Montalant.

O'ROURKE BOYLE, M. (2008). 'Harvey in the sluice: from hydraulic engineering to human physiology'. *History and Technology,* 24(1): 1–22.

OSLER, M. J. (2001). 'Whose ends? teleology in early modern natural philosophy'. *Osiris,* 2nd series, 16: 151–68.

PASCAL, B. (1964–1992). *Oeuvres complètes.* Ed. Jean Mesnard. 4 vols. Paris: Desclée de Brouwer.

PASCAL, B. (2000). *Pensées.* Ed. Gérard Ferreyrolles. Paris: Le Livre de Poche.

PICKERING, A. (1995). *The Mangle of Practice: Time, Agency, and Science.* Chicago: The University of Chicago Press.

RADDER, H. (ed.) (2003). *The Philosophy of Scientific Experimentation.* Pittsburgh: University of Pittsburgh Press.

RENN, J. and VALLERIANI, M. (2001). 'Galileo and the challenge of the arsenal'. *Nuncius,* 16: 481–503.

ROCHE, D. (1997). *Histoires des choses banales. Naissances de la consommation, XVIIe–XIXe siècle.* Paris: Fayard.

SCHAFFER, S. (1989). 'Glass works: Newton's prisms and the uses of experiment', in D. Gooding, T. Pinch, and S. Schaffer (eds), *The Uses of Experiment. Studies in the Natural Sciences.* Cambridge: Cambridge University Press, 67–104.

SHAPIN, S. and SCHAFFER, S. (1985). *Leviathan and the Air-pump. Hobbes, Boyle, and the Experimental Life.* Princeton, NJ: Princeton University Press.

SMITH, P. H. (2004). *The Body of the Artisan: Art and Experience in the Scientific Revolution.* Chicago: University of Chicago Press.

STROUP, A. (1990). *A Company of Scientists: Botany, Patronage, and Community at the Seventeenth-century Parisian Royal Academy of Sciences.* Berkeley, CA: University of California Press.

TURNER, A. J. (1973). 'Mathematical instruments and the education of gentlemen'. *Annals of Science*, 30: 51–88.

TURNER, A. J. (1981). 'William Oughtred, Richard Delamain and the horizontal instrument in seventeenth-century England'. *Annali dell'Istituto e Museo di storia della scienza di Firenze*, 6(2): 99–125.

TURNER, G. L'E. (2000). *Elizabethan Instrument Makers: The Origins of the London Trade in Precision Instrument Making.* Oxford: Oxford University Press.

WARNER, D. J. (1990). 'What is a scientific instrument, when did it become one, and why?' *British Journal for the History of Science*, 23: 83–93.

WILKINS, J. (1668). *An Essay towards a Real Character, and a Philosophical Language.* London: Printed for Sa: Gellibrand, and for John Martyn, printer to the Royal Society.

WILSON, C. (1995). *The Invisible World: Early Modern Philosophy and the Invention of the Microscope.* Princeton, NJ: Princeton University Press.

# CHAPTER 16

# PICTURABILITY AND MATHEMATICAL IDEALS OF KNOWLEDGE

## STEPHEN GAUKROGER

DEMONSTRATION or proof is designed to compel belief in a conclusion, whether in mathematics, law, epistemology, or more generally any discipline that concerns itself with the justification of, or establishment of, beliefs. In the canonical case, this requires that the truth of the premisses be agreed to, that the argument be valid, and that the validity of the argument be evident. Nevertheless, there are qualifications in each of the three requirements: the premisses may be hypothetical or, in the case of a *reductio*, false; an argument may be considered valid but not formally valid, raising questions about just what validity consists in; and there may be dispute over just how evident the validity of a form of reasoning is.

I want to concentrate on the latter. In early-modern terms this question was often posed in terms of the 'clarity and distinctness' of a demonstration, and though there were a number of cognate terms, there was one core question that was always at issue: the perspicuity of a demonstration. In the early seventeenth century, this was thought, for example in Descartes, to lie in the transparency of the stages in the demonstration and in the transparency of the direction of the argument. It is in these terms that Descartes contrasts traditional geometrical demonstrations unfavourably with analysis or algebra. But with the development of infinitesimal calculus, transparency effectively comes to be abandoned by the advocates of calculus, notably Leibniz, as a conservative constraint that hinders progress in mathematics. One question at issue here is picturability. Leibniz was rejecting the picturability of geometrical demonstrations in favour of abstract demonstrations of calculus, and this goes in exactly the opposite direction to traditional defences of new methods in mathematics. Descartes' defence of algebra, for example, contrary to what one might expect, can be construed as a defence of superior picturability of algebraic procedures over geometrical ones.

I want to explore the role of picturability in mathematical demonstration in the seventeenth and eighteenth centuries, and to use this to draw attention to, and throw a little light on, the general question of the role that picturability places in cognitive grasp. Mathematical demonstration is particularly good in this regard, not because there is a clear distinction here between what is picturable and what is not, nor because the benefits of picturability are especially clear in this case, but rather because what it is that is considered problematic is something that can be identified with some precision.

# I: GEOMETRY VERSUS ANALYSIS

We can distinguish two ingredients in the requirement of transparency in demonstration generally: transparency of the stages in the demonstration, and transparency of the direction of the argument. What is at stake in the latter is a contrast between grasping how a conclusion is generated, and merely grasping that it follows from the premises. It is this issue, rather than the transparency of particular stages in the demonstration, that motivates sixteenth- and seventeenth-century doubts about geometrical demonstration. The issues go back to ancient mathematics. The Greek and Alexandrian mathematicians had employed various heuristic devices in their attempts to deal with mathematical problems, but had always sought to present their results in formal terms. In the course of the sixteenth and seventeenth centuries, some efforts were made to reconcile heuristic and formal methods, and various forms of demonstration had been singled out as problematic. In his 1557 edition of Euclid, for example, Peletier (1557: Proposition 1.4, note) questioned the use of proofs by contradiction, where we assume the opposite of the proposition to be demonstrated and show that it leads to a contradiction.[1] Closely connected with the latter was the exhaustion method, which involves a double *reductio*: unable to prove that A=B directly, we prove that A cannot be less than B and that A cannot be greater than B (Whiteside 1960: 331–48). The usefulness of this way of proceeding was not in doubt, but it was difficult to apply and the calculations were tedious. Moreover, although seventeenth-century mathematicians did not echo Peletier's concerns about the formal adequacy of proofs by *reductio*, there remained the question of whether it had the rigour or perspicacity required of formal geometrical proof. In particular, it did not show *how* the conclusion that A=B was generated, because the demonstration was indirect.

Directness of proof also motivated Descartes' attempt to devise a wholly perspicacious mathematics. Here, however, the matter is expanded beyond geometry proper. Consider two cases, that of the superiority of geometrical notation over arithmetical notation, and that of the superiority of algebraic proof over geometrical demonstration. These were among the basic questions to which Descartes' foundational work in mathematics in the late 1620s was directed. What was at issue was the question whether there is a means of representing mathematical operations in terms of operations so clear and vivid that one cannot fail but assent to them.

Consider first the arithmetical case. We cannot determine the truth of the statement that the sum of two numbers equals a third simply by inspecting the formula $2+3=5$, for we need to know about the representation of the numbers by digits in this way, the meaning of + and the meaning of =. Of course, in this case, we know the formula is true, but the issues are the same for any number, including very large ones. We would certainly not be able to recognize the truth of the formula immediately if it involved 100-digit numbers, for example. This prompts the question of whether there is a way of representing the operation, which shows us that the arithmetical statement is true. Descartes argues that if we represent numbers in terms of line-lengths, then we can recognize the truth of any arithmetical statement by manipulating the line lengths. In the case of the sum of two and three for example, we simply join two line lengths of two and three equal segments and we can see the sum formed before our eyes as it were. In Rule 18 of the *Regulae* (AT X 464–6; CSM I 73–4), he writes:

From these considerations it is easy to see how these two operations are all we need for the purpose of discovering whatever magnitudes we are required to deduce from others on the basis of some relation. Once we have understood these operations, the next thing to do is to explain how to present them to the imagination for examination, and how to display them visually, so later on we may explain their uses or applications. If addition or subtraction is to

---

[1] Hobbes was later to ask how on earth we could establish equality if not by superposition, which does seem a particularly compelling form of demonstration. On Peletier's conception of geometry see Cifoletti (2006: 398–410).

be used, we conceive the subject in the form of a line, or in the form of an extended magnitude in which length alone is to be considered. For if we add line *a* to line *b*,

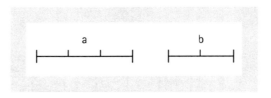

FIG. 16.1

we add the one to the other in the following way,

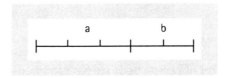

FIG. 16.2

and the result is *c*:

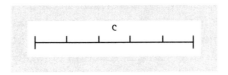

FIG. 16.3

And so on for subtraction, multiplication, and division:

Again, if we wish to multiply *ab* by *c*,

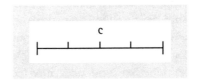

FIG. 16.4

we ought to conceive of *ab* as a line, *viz.*

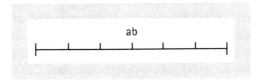

FIG. 16.5

in order to obtain for *abc* the following figure:

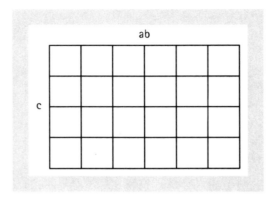

FIG. 16.6

As it turned out, this form of perspicuous representation did not meet the tasks for which Descartes designed it, for he had hoped to represent all mathematical operations in this way, thereby rendering even the most complex and arcane completely perspicuous, in such a way that the truth of such operations would be evident by simple inspection. But it is evident in the uncompleted Rules 19–21 of the *Regulae*, that, except in the simplest cases, we end up at best invoking complex geometrical constructions, and at worst being unable to provide any construction at all. It is precisely such latter cases, in the form of higher-order root extractions that arise in Rules 19–21, which is also the point at which he abandoned the *Regulae* (Gaukroger 1995: 178–81).

Our concern here is not with the failure of Descartes' specific project, however, but with the general problem of more or less perspicuous representations of mathematical operations. Note in this respect that manipulating line-lengths is not the same as manipulating lines, and Descartes is not reducing arithmetic to geometry. It is instructive that the case Descartes deals with can be treated in terms of points as well as line-lengths. That is, the operation can be represented by taking : and :. and bringing them together to form ::., which yields the result with the same clarity. It does not matter whether one uses line-lengths or points, and the manipulation of points in this way carries no suggestions of geometry.

This is reinforced in Descartes' explicit treatment of geometry, which he argued was representationally inferior to algebra. The notational case is peculiar in that discovery of the requisite notation seems to bring with it a demonstration (it is not surprising that Leibniz studied the unpublished manuscript of the *Regulae* closely), as if demonstration were simply a matter of displaying something in the right way; but when Descartes comes to urge the merits of analysis over geometry, it is not so much that the perspicuous mode of representation allows us to do something that modes of demonstration using different means do not allow us to do, but rather that use of this mode of representation is transparent: it allows us to follow the most direct route possible, and to see exactly what is going on in the demonstration.

The power of algebra, as Descartes construes it, is as a problem-solving technique which works by construing unknowns in terms of knowns, by providing a symbolism for them which enables them to be slotted into equations tying knowns and unknowns together in a systematic way. This procedure has immense advantages over the traditional geometrical proofs, and Descartes believes that an algebraic demonstration reveals the steps involved in solving the problem in a completely transparent way. Indeed it is the transparency of its operations, as much as its abstractness, that Descartes finds of the greatest value in his new algebra. As an example, compare a geometrical and an algebraic demonstration of the same theorem.[2] The theorem in question is set out in the *Elements*, II, 11 in these terms:

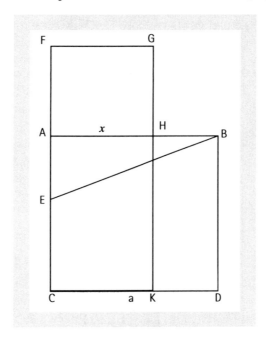

FIG. 16.7

Let AB be the given straight line; thus it is required to cut AB so that the rectangle contained by the whole and one of its segments is equal to the square on the remaining segment. Let ABCD be described on AB; let AC be bisected at point E and let BE be joined; let CA be drawn through to F, and let EF be made equal to BE; let the square FH be described on AF and let GH be drawn through to K. I say AB has been cut at H so as to make the rectangle contained by AB, BH equal to the square on AH. For since the straight line AC has been bisected at E and FA added to it, the rectangle contained by CF, FA together with the square

²  See the treatments of this question in Boyce Gibson (1898), and Schuster (1977: ii. 491–3).

on AE is equal to the square on EF [by Prop II.6]. Therefore the rectangle CF, FA together with the square on AE is equal to the square on EB. But the squares on BA, AE are equal to the square on EB, for the angle A is right [by Prop I.47]. Therefore the rectangle CF, FA together with the square on AE is equal to the sum of the squares on BA, AE. Let the square on AE be subtracted from each. Therefore the rectangle CF, FA which remains is equal to the square on AB. Now the rectangle CF, FA is FK, for AF is equal to FG, and the square on AB is AD. Let AK be subtracted from each; therefore FH which remains is equal to HD; and HD is the rectangle AB, BH for AB is equal to BD; and FH is the square on AH. Therefore the rectangle contained by AB, BH is equal to the square on HA. Therefore the given straight line has been cut at H so as to make the rectangle contained by AB, BH equal to the square on HA.

Now consider how we would solve the problem algebraically, along Descartes' own lines. First we assign symbols to knowns and unknowns, labelling AB as a, and AH, the unknown line, as x. The conditions of the problem are then translated into an equation:[3]

$$x^2 = (a - x)a$$

We can then deduce the solution in what Descartes calls 'an easy and direct' way:

$$x^2 + ax = a^2$$

$$x^2 + ax + \frac{1}{4}a^2 = a^2 + \frac{1}{4}a^2$$

$$(x + \frac{1}{2}a)^2 = a^2 + \frac{1}{4}a^2$$

$$(x + \frac{1}{2}a) = \sqrt{a^2 + \frac{1}{4}a^2}$$

$$x = \sqrt{a^2 + \frac{1}{4}a^2} - \frac{1}{2}a$$

The geometrical and algebraic demonstrations can be treated as equally picturable, in the sense that each is visual: we literally *see* what is going on in the demonstration. The contrast is not between a picturable form (geometry) and an abstract one (algebra). The difference lies rather in the fact that the algebraic notation records and makes it easy to grasp the chain of deduction involved in finding the solution, thereby making

---

[3] Euclid's proposition could also be expressed as AH×AB = (BH)², which translates as the equation ax = (a−x)²; there are thus two solutions.

it clear what has to be done to the known and unknown at each stage, whereas the geometrical solution does not reveal how the conclusion is generated.

## II: INFINITESIMAL ANALYSIS AND THE QUESTION OF DIRECT PROOF

Choosing between algebraic and geometrical demonstrations where the conclusion is secure is simply a means of deciding which demonstration is better at revealing how the conclusion is generated. It is a different matter from that in which a mode of demonstration that cannot be justified in its own terms yields a contentious result. Here we face a deeper conceptual problem, prompted by attempts to reconcile powerful heuristic techniques with the need for formal and genuinely revelatory demonstrations. It was common ground among seventeenth-century mathematicians that the ancient geometers had employed heuristic methods to discover various theorems which were quite different from the synthetic demonstrations by which they proved them. The exhaustion method is a case in point. In Proposition 8 of Book XII of Euclid's *Elements*, there is a straightforward proof that a prism with a triangular base can be divided into three equal pyramids with triangular bases, from which it follows directly that any pyramid is a third part of the prism which has the same base as it and is of equal height. But when, in Proposition 10, Euclid turns to what is in effect the parallel problem of showing that any cone is a third part of the cylinder which has the same base as it and is of equal height, the fact that we are dealing with curvilinear figures makes direct proof impossible, so we are supplied with an exhaustion proof, that is, a double *reductio*.

Cavalieri, in his *Geometria indivisibilibus* (1635), sought a method of demonstration of the cone/cylinder theorem which, unlike the method of exhaustion, provided a direct proof, one in which we can understand how the theorem emerges from the premises, rather than just being shown that the alternatives cannot hold. Among the procedures he used, the most powerful consisted of summing infinite aggregates of lines to measure areas, and infinite aggregates of planes to measure volumes. He employed this procedure in the demonstration that the volume of a cone is a third of that of a cylinder of the same height with which it shares a base. The method of summing was genuinely revelatory in a way that exhaustion procedures are not. In particular, Cavalieri was able to show why it is that a right triangle, whose sides are the base and height of a square and whose hypotenuse is the diagonal of the square, stand in the ratio of 1 to 2, yet when we rotate the triangle and the square around the height of the square, the cone and cylinder generated stand in the ratio 1 to 3.[4]

In short, not only does the method of indivisibles, by contrast with exhaustion methods, provide a direct demonstration, but this direct demonstration generates a ratio for the volumes of cones and cylinders which the exhaustion method is unable to do. Here transparency, in the form of a direct demonstration that proceeds via clear steps, seems to prove its mettle beyond dispute. The trouble was that the procedure also generated paradoxes. Galileo rejected Cavalieri's method using a *reductio* in which a Cavalieri-type indivisible demonstration is used to prove that the area of a cone and a bowl have equal areas, but where, in the limiting case of the last 'indivisibles', it turns out that the circumference of a circle, which contains infinitely many points, equals a single point (Galileo, 1974: 36–7). The case is one where $B = A + a_1$ and $B = A + a_2$ but where $a_1 \neq a_2$.

The ability of Cavalieri's procedure to generate paradoxes was more than matched, however, by its heuristic power, which was developed in a number of new areas by his younger contemporary Torricelli. The most brilliant and striking extension of the procedure was Torricelli's 1641 demonstration, using the method of indivisibles, that an acute hyperbolic solid of infinite length had the same volume as a cylinder of finite length (Torricelli 1644). That a figure of infinite length could be shown to have a finite volume was puzzling, for it was generally assumed, *contra* Cavalieri, that one could not establish ratios that involved infinite quantities. Yet what Torricelli had done was to establish a ratio between a finite quantity and an infinite one. Moreover, he was able to supplement his analytic demonstration using indivisibles with a synthetic one, although he made it clear which procedure had done the real work:

As for the method of demonstration, we shall prove a simple notable theorem in two ways, namely, with indivisibles and in the manner of the ancients. And this although, to tell the truth, it has been discovered with the geometry of indivisibles, which is a truly scientific method of demonstration which is direct and, so to say, natural. I feel pity for the ancient geometry which, not knowing or not allowing Indivisibles, discovered so few truths in the study of the measure of solids that a frightening paucity of ideas has continued until our times    (Torricelli 1644: Mancosu 1996: 131 (amended)).

Torricelli's demonstration opened up an intense discussion of the nature of indivisibles. He had employed a geometry of indivisibles which combined great heuristic power with a high degree of picturability, so that one could follow a direct, perspicuous route to the conclusion. This was an ideal combination, but, just as Descartes had found in his attempt to use the line-length reduction to ground his mathematics, heuristic power and generality, on the one hand, and perspicuity of demonstration, on the other, pull in opposite directions. These opposite directions

---

[4] See Mancosu (1996: 39–44), to which I am indebted here, and Andersen (1985).

are abstractness and picturability, and the discrepancies between the two come to a head in the dispute between Leibniz and Newton on infinitesimal calculus.

## III: Geometry versus calculus

The intensity of the dispute between Newton and Leibniz about who had invented the calculus (Hall, 1980) might lead one to expect that the disputants agreed at least about the merits of the discovery. However, with eighteenth-century British and continental mathematicians using the competing notations that Newton and Leibniz had devised (Guicciardini 1989), Newton's assessment of the legitimacy of calculus differed radically from that of Leibniz. The issues turned on two questions: analytical versus synthetic methods, and limit procedures versus differential equations. When, in the course of the 1740s, dissatisfaction with Newton's *Principia* was such that it began to be significantly revised, reworked, and rewritten, the dissatisfaction sprang from a perceived need to replace the synthetic mode of working through problems and the use of limit procedures with an analytic way of proceeding which used differential and integral calculus, employing the Leibnizian notation. Newton himself was aware that his geometrical presentation might be taken as outdated as early as 1710, when he wrote that

To the mathematicians of the present century, however, versed almost wholly in algebra as they are, this synthetic style of writing is less pleasing, whether because it may seem too prolix and too akin to the method of the ancients, or because it is less revealing of the manner of discovery   (Newton 1967–81: VIII, 451).

Nevertheless, if Newton believed that his work had been left behind, this was not, in his view, for good reasons. Having devised a differential and integral calculus in the early 1670s, he quickly came to reject this way of doing mathematics. To understand why, we need to consider first what proponents of calculus saw its strengths to be, before we turn to the question of what divides Leibniz and Newton over its legitimacy.

Leibniz's interest in mathematics dated from the mid-1660s, although his innovations began only with his stay in Paris in 1672, where Huygens offered him guidance on how to develop and refine his rudimentary mathematical skills (GM: V, 404). His interest at that time was in numerical series, for example in the demonstration that the sum of consecutive odd numbers can be expressed as the difference between two squares. As he tells us in his 1714 autobiographical note (written in the third person), 'the application of numerical truths to geometry, and the study of infinite series, was at that time unknown to our young friend, and he was content with the satisfaction of having observed such things in series of numbers' (GM: V, 398). Huygens set him the problem of finding the sum of the reciprocals of triangular numbers: $^1/_1 + {}^1/_3 + {}^1/_6 + {}^1/_{10} + {}^1/_{15} \ldots$ Writing each term as the sum of two fractions, he was able to show that the value of the terms is yielded by their order in the series of triangular numbers:

$$\frac{2}{t} - \frac{2}{t+1}$$

so that substituting the first $t$, 1, yields 1; the value of the second $t$, 2, yields $^1/_3$, and so on. Then he provides a formula for the sum of the terms, so that in the case of the sum up to $n$ we have:

$$\sum_{t=1}^{n} \frac{2}{t(t+1)} = 2 - \frac{2}{n+1}$$

As $n$ increases, $2/(n+1)$ becomes infinitely small or null, and hence the sum of the infinite series is 2. Examining other types of convergent and divergent infinite sequences, he developed the basis of a powerful and general method of summing.

On Huygens' advice, he also turned his attention to geometry, notably to Pascal's 1659 *Traité des sinus du quart de cercle* (Pascal 1963: 155–8). Traditional limit procedures had enabled one to determine tangents, for example, by the use of chords of decreasing size. If we take two points, P and Q, on the circumference of a circle and join them, then we determine a unique line, the chord PQ (Fig. 16.8). But there is no such unique line passing through a single point—there are infinitely many straight lines that pass through P alone—and the problem is to determine the unique one that is the tangent, that is the one that is at a right angle to the centre of the circle, or to the focus of a conic section. As Q approaches P, the chord PQ will provide a better and better approximation to the tangent at P. They cannot coincide, since then we would be back with the problem of determining a unique line from a single point, but if we make the distance infinitesimally small, we will generate the tangent from two points. Pascal associated with a point on the

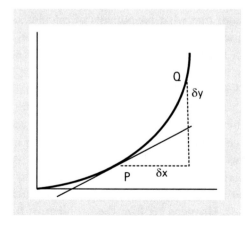

FIG. 16.8

circumference of a circle a triangle with infinitesimal sides, and translating this idea into Cartesian co-ordinate geometry, as Leibniz now did, he realized that the procedure could be applied to any curve, and proceeded to build up curves out of a polygonal figure having infinitely many sides. In short, he discovered that finding tangents to curves depended on the differences in the ordinates and abscissae, as these differences became infinitely small. At the same time, he realized that the problem of areas or quadratures was simply the inverse of this, so that the areas depended on the sum of the ordinates or infinitely thin rectangles making up the area. In other words, the techniques for dealing with the first question, which turned on the relationship between rates of change of continuously varying quantities, for which Leibniz provided rules for a differential calculus, were mirrored in an inverse set of techniques for dealing with the second, namely integral calculus.

These techniques take the form of simple rules, offered without demonstration, in Leibniz's 1684 paper, *Nova methodus pro maximis et minimis*, which was the first attempt to set out the rules governing infinitesimal procedures. The rules are introduced geometrically, translated into algebraic terms, and then redescribed in terms of differentials. This enables Leibniz to provide basic rules of addition, subtraction, multiplication, and division. Specifying rules for the manipulation of signs, depending on whether the ordinates increase or decrease, he moves to the behaviour of curves, leading him to introduce second-order differentials, and by these means he offers procedures for finding powers and taking roots. He concludes:

When one knows the *Algorithm*, if I may call it such, of this calculus, which I term *differential*, one can, by means of ordinary calculation, find all the other differential equations, and maxima and minima as well as tangents, without having to rid oneself of the fractions, irrationals, or the other peculiarities that have been a feature of methods used to date. . . . As a result, one can write the differential equation of any given equation simply by replacing each term . . . by a differential quantity. For each of the other quantities (which are not themselves terms but which contribute to forming one another), this differential quantity must be introduced in order to obtain the differential quantity of the term itself, not by means of a simple substitution, but following the algorithm that I have set out.   (GM: V, 222–3)

Nevertheless, it should be said that the programme advocated in *Nova methodus* was obscurely formulated, and the paper was so cautious in its presentation that it hardly mentioned infinitesimals at all (Bos 1974). The programme was quickly developed by the Bernoullis and others, however, and the first textbook, Guillaume de l'Hôpital's *Analyse des infiniment petits* (1696), written under the guidance of Johann Bernoulli, is far more explicit. The Preface to the *Analyse*, written by Fontenelle, was the manifesto of the group that devoted itself to the development of analytic methods, and drew the line between ancient and modern methods sharply:

What we have by the ancients on these matters, above all Archimedes, is certainly worthy of admiration. But apart from the fact that they deal with very few curves, and treat these somewhat superficially, the propositions are almost entirely particular and lack order, failing to communicate any regular and applied method.   (l'Hôpital 1696: iv–v)

The Leibnizian approach, developed so fruitfully by the Bernoullis and their followers, explicitly defends the idea of there being infinitesimal quantities whose addition to a given finite quantity does not change the value of the latter, so that two equal quantities remain equal when such a quantity is added to one of them but not the other: $A+a=A$.[5] It also depends crucially on the use of such infinitesimal quantities in resolving curves into polygons with an infinite number of infinitesimal sides, so that infinitesimal methods can be applied to curves. The geometrical interpretation provides a way to envisage in what sense differentiation and integration are the inverses of one another: determining tangents to curves (differentiation) and computing the area between the axis and the curve (integration).

Leibniz was not the only pioneer in general infinitesimal methods, however. Between 1670 and 1671 Newton composed a treatise on the use of infinitely small quantities, *De methodis serierum et fluxionum*,[6] in which the central idea is that of the 'fluxion'. Consider a point moving at a variable speed and generating a line (e.g. a planet moving at variable speed around the sun and generating an elliptical orbit, although Newton did not realize this application in 1671). The distance covered in a time *t* is called a 'fluent', the instantaneous speed is the 'fluxion', and the infinitely small speed acquired after an infinitely small increment of time is called the 'moment'. *De methodis* provides an algorithm for calculating fluxions, in which it is assumed that motion is uniform during equal intervals of time, and in which infinitesimals, once they have done their work, can be cancelled (following the principle $A+a=A$). The algorithm construes all quantities as continuous flows, and enables him to reduce a vast range of particularly intractable mathematical problems to two classes: given the space traversed, to find the speed at any time (corresponding to Leibnizian differentiation); and given the speed, to find the space traversed at any time (corresponding to Leibnizian integration). The problems of finding tangents, extremal points, and curvatures can be reduced to the first. The second, the class of 'inverse' problems, which includes the problem of determining the area under a curve, is more problematic, and Newton employed two procedures: either he changed the variable in order to reduce it to one of a catalogue of known fluents which he had built up, or he used series expansion techniques.

This part of the exercise comes under problem-solving, that is, under what was traditionally known as analysis. The demonstration of results from first principles, synthesis, was traditionally a different kind of exercise, and was resolutely

---

[5] 'I maintain that not only two quantities are equal whose difference is zero, but also that two quantities are equal whose difference is incomparably small.' *Responsio ad nonnullas difficultates a Dn. Bernardo Niewentiit circa methodum differentialem seu infinitesimalem motas* (GM: V, 322).

[6] The treatise was originally untitled: Newton (1967–81: III, 352–53). See Guicciardini (1999: ch. 2), to which I am indebted here.

geometrical. Proponents of the 'new analysis' such as Descartes and Leibniz were inclined to diminish the importance of synthesis, as an unnecessary and artificial process. Newton by contrast was committed to the virtues of the geometrical methods of the ancients as far as demonstration was concerned, and his model in mechanics was the rigorously geometrical *Horologium* of Huygens. It might seem, then, that Newtonian analysis, with its algorithm of fluxions, and Newtonian synthesis, with its rigorous geometrical demonstrations, are two complementary features of the Newtonian project, one a method of discovery, the other a method of presentation. As Newton himself put it in a draft preface to the second edition of the *Principia*, which has been published recently (*Principia* 49–50):

The ancient geometers investigated by analysis what was sought [i.e. found their solutions to problems by the method of analysis], demonstrating by synthesis what had been found, and published what had been demonstrated so that it might be received into geometry. What was resolved was not immediately received into geometry: a solution by means of the composition of demonstrations was required. For all the power and glory of geometry consisted in certainty of things, and certainty consisted in demonstration clearly composed [i.e. demonstrations according to the method of synthesis, or composition]. In this science, what counts is not so much brevity as certainty. And accordingly, in the following treatise I have demonstrated by synthesis the propositions found by analysis.[7]

But matters are not so straightforward, for Newton was in fact unable to accept two different canons of mathematical procedure. In contrast to Leibniz, who avoided geometrical demonstration, even though he was committed to the idea that his calculus required a geometrical grounding, Newton took the other direction. In the course of the 1670s, as Guicciardini (1999: 28) points out, he began to distance himself from his early mathematical researches, abandoning the calculus of fluxions in favour of a geometry of fluxions in which infinitesimal quantities were not employed. He began criticizing modern mathematical practices, and took Descartes to task, for example, for his algebraic solution to a problem that had defied the attempts of ancient geometers, that is Pappus' four-line locus problem. Newton showed that the algebraic solution did *not* demonstrate the unique power of analysis, as Descartes claimed, since it did in fact have a geometrical solution, which he went on to provide. What Newton appreciated in the ancient geometrical techniques (his model was Apollonius) was that they always had a definite interpretation in a geometrical construction. At no stage of a demonstration did they ever stop referring to anything. The techniques of the new analysis, by contrast, especially as developed by Leibniz and his followers, left the realm of the concrete once the problem had been presented, only to return to it at the solution, having proceeded via processes that eschewed all reference to the entities that the original problem (and the solution) dealt with.

---

[7] Cf. Newton 1967–81: VIII. 442–59 and *Principia*: 122–7.

# IV: Picturability and Human
## Cognitive Capacities

There were a number of basic questions on the nature of infinitesimals on which Leibniz and Newton were in agreement. They agreed that infinitesimals were useful fictions and did not actually exist; that they were best defined as varying quantities in a state of approaching zero; and that they can be completely avoided in favour of limit-based proofs, which provide them with a mathematically rigorous formulation (Guicciardini 1999: 159–63). There is one thing that is very distinctive about Leibniz's approach, however, and which separates him markedly from Newton on foundational questions. This is the importance he attaches to a mechanical algorithm. Although both Leibniz and Newton accept that it is limit-based proofs that provide the foundation for differential calculus, for Leibniz such proofs are a means of establishing legitimacy for procedures which differ significantly from standard mathematical operations, but such legitimation is not required on internal grounds, and one can proceed without constant reference to limit-based proofs. Indeed, it is distinctive of the Leibnizian programme that the algorithms that make up calculus be applied without reflecting on the steps: the procedure is secure and, as in the case of Leibnizian logic, it is a matter of supplying the premisses and letting the algorithm generate the conclusion by 'blind' reasoning. Once the general legitimacy of the procedure has been established by means of a theory of limits, the calculus takes on a life of its own, as it were. In September 1691, Leibniz writes to Huygens that 'what is better and more useful in my new calculus is that it yields truths by means of a kind of analysis, and without any effort of the imagination' (GM II: 104), and in December of the same year, that 'what I love most about my calculus is that it gives us the same advantages over the Ancients in the geometry of Archimedes that Viète and Descartes have given us in the geometry of Euclid or Apollonius, in freeing us from having to work with the imagination' (GM II: 123).

For Leibniz, the referential content of calculus has no bearing on the calculations that we are able to perform with it, and indeed it may operate with symbols devoid of reference, such as $\sqrt{-1}$, providing it is able to generate correct results.[8] For Newton, by contrast, limit-based proofs were the essence of differential calculus, and the employment of calculus hinged on one's ability to articulate it in terms of a

---

[8] We are perhaps not so worried about square roots of negative numbers appearing in the proof as seventeenth-century mathematicians were, but in our own times there have been parallel concerns about Feynman's use of negative probabilities in calculations (an idea originally proposed by Dirac), justified on the grounds that they allow otherwise intractable calculations and do not appear in the solution: Dirac (1942: 1–39), Feynman (1987: 235–248). At the other end of the chronological spectrum, similar concerns about negative integers appearing in the process of calculation were expressed in pre-modern mathematics: Klein (1968).

comprehensive theory of limits. Whereas Leibniz abandons geometrical interpretation once his calculus has proceeded past the legitimatory stage, and in fact
handles differential equations as algebraic objects, Newton never (at least after the
early 1670s) allows his calculus to transcend its original geometrical interpretation,
insisting that this is what provides it with reference and meaning.

Although the feature of calculus that its advocates stressed was its sheer power,
Leibniz's investment in the 'blind reasoning' that underpins its use is not a
pragmatic one: it goes to the heart of his understanding of what it means to be a
philosopher. As Matthew Jones has pointed out (2006: Parts 2 and 3), it is
important here to understand in what respect Leibniz's views emerge from a
reflection on Pascal. Pascal was obsessed with the fallen nature of human beings,
and with the limits that this placed on their capacity to understand. He believed
that it was irresponsible to ignore those limits, as he considered his contemporaries
were doing, particularly those active in natural philosophy and mathematics. The
human condition, he argued, was characterized by worthlessness and despair, not
egoism and optimism. The value of the true philosophy and the true religion lay in
their ability to teach us the remedies for our inabilities (*Pensées* frag. 149: 1963, 520).
The value of mathematics lay in its ability to reveal this to us clearly, especially
when the infinitely large and the infinitely small were considered.[9] In pursuing
mathematics in a serious way we are forced to recognize that infinities exist, Pascal
believes, but at the same time we also have to admit to our incomprehension of
such infinities, thereby forcing us to take stock of our limitations.

Newton's approach to infinitesimals, as I have indicated, was to insist that they
must remain anchored in limit procedures, and his preference was to replace
algorithms employing infinitesimals with geometrical demonstrations. Pascal, in
sharp contrast, takes infinitesimals at face value, stressing the combination of their
legitimacy and their lack of intelligibility, and drawing from this a general lesson
about the nature and limits of human knowledge. This lesson is one that bears
directly on the *persona* of the philosopher, in that recognition of our cognitive
limitations is an integral part of the morality of the philosopher, who must struggle
against optimism and egoism, along with various contrasting faults such as scepticism and relativism. Leibniz agreed with Pascal that our unaided faculties were
insufficient for the kind of knowledge to which we naturally aspire, although this in
itself was a widespread view motivated either by a sense of the fallen nature of
human beings, or because of the kind of systematic criticism of sense perception
that Descartes, and Cartesians such as Malebranche and Arnauld, among others,
had mounted. Unlike those accounts that saw limitations to knowledge as a result
of the Fall, the Cartesian approach had set out to undermine the reliability of
sensation only to replace it with the reliability of properly tutored reason, that is,

---

[9] See, in particular, his '*De l'esprit géométrique*' (Pascal 1963: 348–55).

reason that could issue in 'clear and distinct' judgements. Leibniz is very much in this latter tradition, and mathematics acts for him as a model of what knowledge could be, although he believes that it is mistaken to limit knowledge claims to what we grasp clearly and distinctly. Descartes had realized in 1629, in trying to reconcile his advanced algebraic techniques with his procedures for presenting mathematical operations clearly and distinctly, that the demands of the two pulled in different directions, but he left the matter unresolved. Leibniz bites the bullet: we must abandon clarity and distinctness. As he points out to Conring in a letter of 1678, there are symbolic operations which we cannot grasp clearly and distinctly but which nevertheless manifestly yield the kind of knowledge that mathematicians should be seeking (GM I: 199). This is clear from his attitude to one of his first discoveries, one that would be important in his subsequent invention of the calculus, namely his quadrature of the circle. What he discovered was a means of providing the area of a circle by means of an infinite series:

$$\frac{\pi}{4} = \frac{1}{1} - \frac{1}{3} + \frac{1}{5} - \frac{1}{7} \ldots$$

It is impossible, he points out to Conring, to express the ratio between a square and a circle by a single number, but we can express the ratio in an infinite series of numbers. As Jones notes (2006: 169–70), for Leibniz, series such as this offer 'the only exact knowledge of the quadrature of a circle available to embodied human beings without divine intervention'. They offer a way of transcending traditional limitations which restrict mathematical knowledge to quantities and geometrical constructions, so that 'a value can be expressed exactly, either by a quantity or by a progression of quantities whose nature and way of continuing are known' (GM: II, 96).

For Leibniz, our native abilities do not match our native capacities, and the way to realize our full capacities is through procedures that go beyond our unaided faculties. These procedures are, paradigmatically, algebraic analysis and infinitesimal algorithms, for these take us beyond the kind of pictorial geometrical representation on which our unaided faculties rely, to new and far more powerful forms of cognition, where this new power is manifested in a clear and explicit way in the novel and general results that they yield. On this view, then, it is not a question of appealing to unaided faculties to secure a legitimation of infinitesimals (Newton), or to use their inability to provide such a legitimation as a means of criticizing unaided faculties (Pascal), but rather of using them as an extension of our reason in much the same way that we might use a microscope or telescope as an extension of our vision. We don't use microscopes or telescopes to show that our natural vision is fundamentally lacking, nor do we insist that their use be limited to things we can see with unaided vision. Rather, we use them to take us beyond our natural faculties. Aristotle and the Aristotelian medieval tradition had held that we have the faculties and sense organs we do so that we might know the world: nature, or

God, has provided us with them for this purpose, and hence the idea that we might transcend them in any way is out of the question. This view was rejected by seventeenth-century thinkers, a rejection often motivated by notions of diminished capacities in the wake of the Fall. There had been a widely held view in the seventeenth century that the Fall had dulled Adam's senses, and that the use of artificial aids might effect the restoration of their prelapsarian acuity. But while there had also been a widespread view that reason too had been impaired in the Fall, this was diagnosed in terms of the passions triumphing over reason, the remedy being to control the passions. This was Malebranche's strategy, for example. The application of artificial aids in solving this problem was unprecedented,[10] but this is exactly what Leibniz seems to be doing. Whereas Descartes and Malebranche had focused on the inadequacy of our sense organs, Leibniz extends the criticism to our faculties. As far as the use of our faculties in mathematical reasoning is concerned, it is the fact that infinitesimal algorithms cannot be grounded in 'natural' mathematical reasoning that means that our use of them *must* be 'blind': it is they that guide us, we do not guide them.

## V: THE UNINTELLIGIBILITY OF CALCULUS

One extreme reaction to this kind of approach is that of Berkeley. Prior to *The Analyst* of 1734, Berkeley's arguments against the use of infinitesimals are similar to Newton's. Like Newton, but in contrast to Nieuwentijt for example, he has no doubt about the results achieved using infinitesimals; his concerns are rather with the legitimacy of the procedure used to generate these results, and he believes that they must be translated into geometrical terms. Moreover, what motivates this position in Berkeley is the question of our being able to represent the mathematical procedures to ourselves clearly and distinctly. But the flaw that Berkeley detects in the calculus is one of unintelligibility in its procedures, and the difficulty he isolates is one that must be traced back to his general theory of the impossibility of abstractive knowledge (Jesseph 1993: ch. 1).

In his *Essay*, Locke, discussing the abstract general idea of a triangle, struggles with the difficulty of forming such an abstraction in these terms:

---

[10] It is especially unprecedented in the case of mathematics where a more usual view was that the self-evident axioms of mathematics were an example of something that had been uniquely insulated from the corrupting effects of the Fall. Harrison (2007: 97–103) traces this position back to Luther and Melanchthon.

Does it not require some pains and skill to form the *general Idea* of a *Triangle*, (which is yet none of the most abstract, comprehensive, and difficult,) for it must be neither Oblique, nor Rectangle, neither Equilateral, Equicrural, nor Scalenon; but all and none of these at once. In effect, it is something imperfect, that cannot exist; an *Idea* wherein some parts of several different and non-existent *Ideas* are put together. (IV. vii. 9)

Berkeley's point is that if, as Locke shows, such a triangle is impossible, then it is inconceivable:

If any man has the faculty of framing in his mind such an idea of a triangle as is here described, it is in vain to pretend to dispute him out of it, nor would I go about it. All I desire is, that the reader would fully and certainly inform himself whether he has an idea or no. And this, methinks, can be no hard task for any one to perform. What more easy than for any one to look into his own thoughts, and there try whether he has, or can attain to have, an idea that shall correspond with the description that is here given of the general idea of a triangle, which is, *neither oblique, nor rectangle, equilateral, equicrural, nor scalenon, but all and none of these at once?*    (Berkeley 1710: § 15)

Since geometry cannot operate with entities that are inconceivable, some way of construing its subject matter other than as abstractions must be found, and Berkeley proposes that, to secure intelligibility and conceivability, we must construe them as objects of sense. To secure the generality of geometry, however, he devises a way of classifying particular geometrical figures in such a way that they are representative of all other lines and figures of any size. The basis of geometry then lies in the comparison of these and the ratios in which they stand to one another. This distinctive theory of what the legitimacy of geometrical operations consists in, which certainly reflects nothing in Newton, is then used to provide the grounds for a geometrical replacement for calculus, a replacement that is explicitly along Newtonian lines:

the supposition of quantitys infinitely small is not essential to the great improvements of the Modern Analysis. For Mr. Leibnitz acknowledges that his *Calculis differentialis* might be demonstrated *reductione ad absurdum* after the manner of the ancients; & Sir Isaac Newton in a late treatise informs us his method can be made out *a priori* without the supposition of quantitys infinitely small.[11]

There is a significant difference, however, between Berkeley's approach in these writings from the first decade of the eighteenth century, and the discussion in *The Analyst*, which contains his most extensive account of calculus.[12] In *The Analyst*, the epistemological criticisms of abstraction only come into play once he has set out independent arguments against calculus. These include the criticism that all proofs in calculus are fallacious, by standard logical criteria, and that the success of

---

[11] Berkeley, 'Of Infinities', Lecture to the Dublin Philosophical Society 19 November 1707 (BW: IV, 237).

[12] For the text and discussion see Jesseph (1992).

calculus is due to what he calls 'a compensation of errors' whereby infinitesimal differences are used in a calculation but dismissed from the result. Berkeley also attacks the Newtonian method of fluxions, however, on the grounds that it requires the postulation of infinitesimal quantities, despite what Newton himself and his followers claimed.

Berkeley's general criticisms of the calculus were dismissed, where they were noticed, by continental mathematicians, but since the *Analyst*, unlike Berkeley's earlier writings on the subject, was directed primarily against the Newtonian method of fluxions, it attracted a number of responses from British mathematicians. There was widespread agreement in Britain that the conceptual foundations of calculus were in dire need of clarification, and to this extent Berkeley's criticisms were not unprecedented. The problem was that mathematicians in general were increasingly convinced that calculus worked extremely well, to the extent of producing a powerful body of results that quite possibly could not be produced in some other way. That the phenomenal success of calculus was simply a question of 'compensation of errors' seemed unlikely at best. Berkeley himself made no effort to rewrite mathematics in his own favoured terms, and it was far from clear that it could be done. Moreover, some responses to Berkeley, notably those of Robins, Maclaurin, and Paman did succeed in providing a significant degree of clarification while meeting Berkeley's objections, and Maclaurin was deemed to have answered these objections decisively.[13]

# CONCLUSION: PICTURABILITY

The crowning achievement of late eighteenth-century mechanics, de Lagrange's 1788 *Mécanique analytique*, contains no geometrical diagrams. As de Lagrange boasts in the Preface to the first edition:

No figures will be found in this work. The methods I present require neither constructions nor geometrical or mechanical arguments, but solely algebraic operations subject to a regular and uniform procedure. Those who appreciate mathematical analysis will see with pleasure mechanics becoming a new branch of it.   (de Lagrange 1977: 7)

In the nineteenth century, the move against picturability took on a new dimension, as it was associated with individual variability that was paradigmatically manifested in sense experience, and sensory imagination generally. What was sought in

---

[13] Robins (1735); Maclaurin (1742); Paman (1745). Jesseph (1993: ch. 7) provides details of these and other responses.

those thinkers we associate with positivism, at least from Mach onwards, was a form of scientific knowledge that would survive translation, transmission, theory change, and differences among thinking beings due to such factors as physiology, psychology, history, culture, and language. Mid-nineteenth century research in history, anthropology, philology, psychology, and sensory physiology underscored how very differently humans reasoned, described, and believed (Daston and Gailson 2007: ch. 5).

In a context where objectivity was to be secured by removing interpretation, implicit or explicit, and seeking an unmediated representation of the world, the picturability versus abstraction question that had been pursued earlier in mathematics now emerged in a new context. Questions of objectivity do not arise in mathematics, at least in the context of the kinds of issue that I have been discussing. What was at stake was rather, ultimately, a question of the legitimacy of going beyond our ordinary conceptual resources, so that we could no longer represent demonstrations to ourselves in a way that made sure that we had a full grasp of every step, and in the knowledge that every step was secure in its own right. Yet, as I have indicated, Leibniz sees the 'imagination'—associated with geometrical picturability—as an obstacle to knowledge, tying what we can know about the world to contingent features of our psychological and physiological make-up. Leibniz was concerned to transcend the contingency of knowledge, the positivists to transcend what they perceived to be its subjectivity. Picturability is a target in both cases, for in both cases what is envisaged is a form of wholly abstract intellectual comprehension. But comprehension requires that one represent something to oneself, and the self that one is representing this to, even in the case of abstract mathematical operations, is not a pure intellect but something with a particular set of sensory and cognitive faculties. The means of representation have to be relative to what the representation is represented to, otherwise it is not a representation but more like what in medieval philosophy, and in the early-modern era in Malebranchean metaphysics, was the direct contemplation of universals. In such contemplation, we must take what we are contemplating at face value: unable to grasp it in a way that we can subject that grasp to critical appraisal, we have no means of assessing it. It is important to realize that supplementing our faculties—for example supplementing ordinary vision by the use of telescopes and microscopes—is indeed a supplementation, not a form of transcendence. Yet it is the latter that Leibniz is advocating: he is in effect substituting a contemplative understanding for a cognitive one. Contemplative understanding takes as given what cognitive understanding opens up for examination. The question that then arises is whether contemplative understanding is a legitimate substitute for cognitive understanding. Is Leibniz really offering something that extends our cognitive faculties, or is he attempting to substitute something that lies beyond our cognitive faculties? After all, while it is true that we do not trust microscopes and telescopes because we compare them with unaided vision, it remains the case that we trust them because the optics that guides them can be checked against unaided visual experience. If the optics told us that the angle of incidence equals the angle of reflection and we saw that this was not the case, we would reject the optics. Our trust in the telescope is not blind, as our trust in the calculus must ultimately be on Leibniz's account; and if this is the case, he has not provided a justification of the kind he is seeking. We are left with a pragmatic rationale: calculus delivers the results, though we are unable to understand how it does this.

## REFERENCES

ANDERSEN, K. (1985). 'Cavalieri's method of indivisibles'. *Archive for History of Exact Sciences*, 31: 291–367.

BERKELEY, G. (1710). *A Treatise concerning the Principles of Human Knowledge*. Dublin.

Bos, H. J. M. (1974). 'Differentials, higher-order differentials and the derivative in the Leibnizian calculus'. *Archive for History of Exact Sciences*, 14: 1–90.

BOYCE GIBSON, A. (1898). 'The Regulae of Descartes'. *Mind*, 7: 143–58.

CAVALIERI, B. (1635). *Geometria indivisibilibus continuorum nova quadam ratione promota*. Bologna.

CIFOLETTI, G. (2006). 'From Valla to Vièta: The rhetorical reform of logic and its use in the early modern logic'. *Early Science and Medicine*, 11: 390–423.

DASTON, L. and GAILSON, P. (2007). *Objectivity*. New York: Zone Books.

DE LAGRANGE, J. L. (1977). *Analytical Mechanics, translated from the Mécanique analytique, nouvelle édition of 1811*. Ed. and trans. A. Boissonnade and V. N. Vagliente. Dordrecht.

DE L'HÔPITAL, GUILLAUME (1696). *Analyse des infiniment petits pour l'intelligence des lignes courbes*. Paris.

DIRAC, P. (1942). 'The physical interpretation of quantum mechanics'. *Proceedings of the Royal Society of London*, A 180: 1–39.

FEYNMAN, R. P. (1987). 'Negative Probability', in F. D. Peat (ed.), *Quantum Implications: Essays in Honour of David Bohm*. London, 235–48.

GALILEI, G. (1974). *Two New Sciences: Including Centers of Gravity and Force of Percussion*. Trans. S. Drake. Madison, WI: University of Wisconsin Press.

GAUKROGER, S. (1995). *Descartes: An Intellectual Biography*. Oxford: Clarendon Press.

GUICCIARDINI, N. (1989). *The Development of Newtonian Calculus in Britain*. Cambridge: Cambridge University Press.

GUICCIARDINI, N. (1999). *Reading the Principia: The Debate on Newton's mathematical methods for Natural Philosophy from 1687–1736*. Cambridge: Cambridge University Press.

HALL, A. R. (1980). *Philosophers at War: The Quarrel between Newton and Leibniz*. Cambridge: Cambridge University Press.

HARRISON, P. (2007). *The Fall of Man and the Foundations of Science*. Cambridge: Cambridge University Press.

JESSEPH, D. (1992). *George Berkeley: De Motu and The Analyst: A Modern Edition, with Introductions and Commentary*. Dordrecht.

JESSEPH, D. (1993). *Berkeley's Philosophy of Mathematics*. Chicago: University of Chicago Press.

JONES, M. L. (2006). *The Good Life in the Scientific Revolution: Descartes, Pascal, Leibniz, and the Cultivation of Virtue*. Chicago: University of Chicago Press.

KLEIN, J. (1968). *Greek Mathematical Thought and the Origin of Algebra*. Cambridge, MA: MIT Press. Part II.

MACLAURIN, C. (1742). *Treatise on Fluxions*. 2 vols. Edinburgh.

MANCOSU, P. (1996). *Philosophy of Mathematics and Mathematical Practice in the Seventeenth Century*. New York: Oxford University Press.

NEWTON, I. (1967–81). *The Mathematical Papers of Isaac Newton*. Ed. D. T. Whiteside. 8 vols. Cambridge: Cambridge University Press.

PAMAN, R. (1745). *Harmony of the Ancient and Modern Geometry Asserted*. London.

PASCAL, B. (1963). *Oeuvres Complètes*. Ed. H. Gouhier and L. Lafuma. Paris: Editons du Seuil.

PELETIER, J. (1557). *In Euclidis Elementa Geometrica Demonstrationum Libri XV*. Basel.

ROBINS, B. (1735). *Discourse Concerning the Nature and Certainty of Sir Isaac Newton's Method of Fluxions*. London.

SCHUSTER, J. A. (1977). 'Descartes and the Scientific Revolution, 1618–34.' Unpub. Ph.D. diss. Princeton University (University Microfilms reprint: 2 vols.).

TORRICELLI, E. (1644). *Opera Geometrica*. Florence.

WHITESIDE, D. T. (1960). 'Patterns of mathematical thought in the later seventeenth century'. *Archive for History of Exact Sciences*, 1: 179–388.

# PART IV

# ETHICS AND POLITICAL PHILOSOPHY

# CHAPTER 17

........................................................................................

# VIRTUE AND VICE

........................................................................................

## P. J. E. KAIL

THE term 'virtue' in contemporary philosophy now plays a prominent role in the context of a particular approach to ethics, mainly (but not exclusively)[1] Aristotelian in its inspiration. Virtue ethics opposes consequentialist and deontological approaches by putting at its centre, not consequences or dutiful action, but human flourishing and excellence. Goodness is ultimately founded on human nature. Virtues themselves are character traits that both contribute to and constitute that excellence. These traits are dispositions that make one sensitive to, and appropriately responsive to, relevant situations, or as Christine Swanton puts it, 'a virtue is a good quality of character . . . a disposition to respond to, acknowledge, items within its field in an excellent or good enough way' (Swanton 2003: 19). As such, virtue ethicists emphasize the idea that ethical action is uncodifiable, and that moral knowledge is a quasi-perceptual sensitivity to the particularities of any given situation.

Although the hitherto popular idea that virtue was neglected during the early modern period is forcefully rejected by Jerome Schneewind in his classic paper 'The Misfortunes of Virtue' (1990), Aristotelian-inspired virtue ethics did not (for the most part) flourish in the minds of the thinkers with whom this chapter is concerned (though it continued in Thomistic guise in the universities). Why? As Schneewind argues, it cannot be so because teleology fell out of fashion; it might well have disappeared in physics, but in discussions of ethics appeal was often made to ends and purposes. One cause that contributed to virtue's misfortune was the dominant discourse of natural law, where notions of virtue were taken to be

---

[1] Hume and Nietzsche also figure in recent discussion of virtue ethics.

secondary to the law (Schneewind 1990: 48–50). A different contributory cause is of the kind implicit in Thomas Reid's claim that 'the ancients commonly arranged [morals] under the four cardinal virtues of prudence, temperance, fortitude and justice. Christian writers, I think, more properly, under the three heads of the duty we owe to God, to ourselves and to our neighbour' (1969: 376). In other words, Christianity was hostile to virtue-based ethics. There is some truth in this (Schneewind 1998: 287–8) but of course matters are far more complex, equivocal, and nuanced than Reid suggests.

First, the implied division between the ancients and moderns is misleading: the ancients were appropriated by moral philosophies that were explicitly Christian inasmuch as Stoic and Platonic, and sometimes Aristotelian, doctrines were tailored to fit early modern bodies of thought. Second, the notions of virtue and vice, as the presence or absence of dispositions of character, play an important role in what are explicitly Christian ethics, even if their presence doesn't amount to virtue ethics *per se*. Third—returning to the division between ancients and moderns—there were moderns whose ethics were not Christian. What is true is that a great many conceptions of moral philosophy stood in need of reconciliation with Christianity, and Aristotle's own view did not, for the most part, figure prominently in this project.

Nevertheless, virtue *qua* the moral dimensions of character did find a place in the moral philosophies of the period. In what follows I shall discuss, in an inevitably selective way, two movements in conceptions of virtue: first, the Cartesian tradition, wherein virtue is intimately related to the control of the passions, a control that is either directly attributable to the powers of reason alone or reason in co-operation with some other faculty. This idea is connected to perfection, which in turn is connected to our relation to God. Second, we cross the channel and see that some of these themes continue in Britain, though taking a more aesthetic, and less austere, turn.

# I: Cartesian virtue

Descartes' and Spinoza's conceptions of virtues each have elements traceable to Stoic moral philosophy. Indeed, it would be difficult to overestimate the role of Stoicism in the period, the popularization of which during the early part of the period owed itself to, among other works, Guillaume Du Vair's *Philosophie morale des Stoiques* (1585) and *De Constantia* (1584) by Justus Lipsius, both of which had the purpose of reconciling the Stoa with the Church. However, Stoicism was appropriated by many different people and transformed in many different ways.

In some cases, attempts were made to integrate Stoicism into Christianity, and into other systems that were anything but Christian. In Descartes and Spinoza, Stoicism manifests itself in a concern to control the passions and to explain happiness as consisting in a certain equanimity.

Descartes wrote no systematic ethical work, and so his views have to be pieced together from various works—in particular his final work, the *Passions of the Soul*—together with his correspondence. One of the earlier expressions of his ethical thought is his 'provisional ethics', which is given in Part III of the *Discourse on Method.* It is provisional because it is a code required for one who needs to 'live comfortably' once the metaphorical epistemic house has been razed to its foundations by Descartes' method of doubt. Its third maxim is to 'try always to master myself rather than fortune, and change my desires rather than the order of the world' (CSM I 123), and to make a 'virtue of necessity . . . [and] we shall not desire to be healthy when ill or free when imprisoned' (CSM I 124). This is quite clearly a Stoical view of the good. Goodness must depend solely on our power and cannot be hostage to worldly fortune. Since 'externals' such as natural goods and fortune are not entirely within our power, 'sovereign good' must be internal to our minds. Virtue cannot consist in knowledge *simpliciter*, since that is often beyond us. One thing, however, is in our power and that is the will: 'nothing truly belongs to him [a human being] but this freedom to dispose his volitions' (CSM I 384). This freedom furthers the aims of tranquillity by controlling our passions. Note that, unlike the Stoics, Descartes does not demand that the mind extirpate the passions, but instead that it control them.

However, virtue is not mere resignation but involves a perfectionist element in Descartes' account. For it is with respect to the freedom of our wills that we most resemble God, and so it is in its exercise we most resemble Him. Thus exercising the will provides a ground to esteem ourselves, for 'it renders us in a certain way like God by making us masters of ourselves' (CSM I 384). Such mastery involves a 'firm and constant resolution to carry out whatever reason recommends' (CSMK 257–8), for reason can 'consider without passion the value of all the perfections, both of the body and of the soul, which can be acquired by our conduct' (CSMK 265). In the *Passions of the Soul* this constant resolution becomes the key virtue of *générosité* (nobility) (CSM I 384). It has two components: the first is the point noted above that 'nothing belongs to him [a human being] but this freedom to dispose his volitions', and so 'he ought to be praised or blamed for no other reason than his using his freedom well or badly' (CSM I 384). The second consists in 'his feeling within himself a firm and constant resolution to use it well'. As I mentioned, Descartes does not demand extirpation of the passions, but their control. Passions can be useful to us inasmuch as they can indicate what is potentially good or bad for the mind–body composite. Nevertheless, they can disturb and mislead, and render one unstable and impetuous. The virtuous person, through this constant willing in line with reason, can correct the tendency to direct passions towards objects that lie outside the power of the will. This helps to check resentment or envy, and any remorse or regret concerning that which lies without our power need never be felt. The correct use of the will in line with reason is accompanied with an 'internal emotion of the soul' (CSM I 381), which is the source of happiness that virtue gives us, a form of intellectual pleasure. There is a certain joy that accompanies the awareness of our self-mastery, to the extent that apparent misfortunes and obstacles can actually increase this awareness and its accompanying joy: such 'troubles will serve rather to increase [the soul's] joy; for on seeing that it cannot be harmed by them, it becomes aware of its perfection' (CSM I 382).

Spinoza too has a conception of virtue indebted to Stoicism but, like Descartes, Spinoza transforms Stoic ideas. Greatly influenced by Descartes though he is, Spinoza differs sharply from him in a number of fundamental ways, not least in the fact that Spinoza's concerns are primarily social and ethical in a way which Descartes' aims are not. More narrowly, Spinoza's conception of freedom is radically different from Descartes', and he has a rather different conception of God (pp. 537–40). Every event is determined by an absolute necessity that stems from God's essence; and whilst Descartes maintains that God acts for purposes (though unknowable to us), the actions of Spinoza's God are purposeless. Human beings are themselves part of this God-or-nature, the single substance that comprehends all of our actions, and events that befall us are determined by this blind necessity. So too are our passions. Given this, the picture that Descartes sketches can have no place in the philosophy of Spinoza, and indeed Descartes is chided for going against naturalism by postulating human freedom as an 'empire within an empire' (Spinoza 2000: 163). It also entails a different view of what controls the passions, namely, that reason has powers of its own to control them and does not need the intermediate agency of a distinct will.

Our point of entry to this is Spinoza's view of *conatus*, a doctrine derived from Descartes' physics but transformed by Spinoza. *Conatus* is that 'by which each thing endeavours to persevere in its being' and thereby constitutes 'the actual essence of the thing' (*Ethics* 3p7; SC 499). The original notion might seem to originate in the Cartesian thesis that bodies will persist in motion, and Spinoza's naturalism encourages him to apply it universally. Each human being then is essentially *conatus*, a striving for persistence. It may, however, equally be thought to be an idea that echoes, perhaps, the Stoic notion of the 'primary impulse' of all creatures to self-preservation. *Conatus* sets the scene for Spinoza's definition of virtue, again redolent of his naturalism (*Ethics* 4D8): 'By virtue and power I understand the same; that is . . . virtue, in so far as it is related to man, is the very essence, i.e. the nature, of man, in so far as he has the power of doing certain things which can be understood through the laws of his nature alone' (Spinoza 2000: 228–9). To attain this virtue one must attain understanding, the highest form of which is knowledge of God: the 'highest good of the mind is the knowledge of God' (Spinoza 2000: 245), which in turn is related to a certain kind of 'blessedness', an 'intellectual love' which is a form of joy.

Let us attempt to understand a little better these somewhat rarefied thoughts by a very un-Spinozistic method, by moving backwards from their conclusion. The final idea concerning blessedness involves a number of difficult, bewildering indeed, ideas, including that of the human mind as eternal. One way to make some sense of this claim is that our highest possible level of understanding involves a grasp of the human mind in its proper relation to the single, eternal substance that is God-or-nature (Lloyd 1996). We understand the human mind as eternal inasmuch as it is a perfection in the mind of God, (as opposed to a temporally-bound striving to that perfection). Knowledge of this involves essentially intellectual love of God that is both a grasp of God's own 'love' of 'himself', and a love in which we participate insofar as we become aware that we too are subject to the same love since we are also modes of God.

Descending a little from these vertiginous levels, the connection between the knowledge of God as the mind's greatest good and that of virtue as power is forged through the idea that the difference between activity (or power) and passivity (and passion) lies in the transformative nature of reason. We are active to the extent to which the causation of any event involves 'adequate ideas', and we are passive when causation involves 'inadequate ideas'. In other words, we are active inasmuch as we grasp the causal determinants involved in the relevant action, and passive when we lack such understanding. Now, since knowledge of God implies knowledge through adequate ideas, knowledge of God increases our power or virtue, and we become closer to virtue to the extent to which we approximate such knowledge.

Given these connections between virtue, power, and knowledge, we can see why control of the passions and escape from 'human bondage' is a central concern of Spinoza, and Part IV of the *Ethics* is devoted to these issues. 'Human bondage' is defined as 'infirmity in moderating and checking the emotions'. Escape from bondage is an escape from that infirmity. However, in the long preface to Part IV, Spinoza reminds us that teleology and appeal to final causes have no place in philosophy (since there are none), and if virtue here means human excellence (which is equal to power), can we find any space of a teleology that the 'perfection of human excellence' insinuates? Put differently, what might be an end for humanity if there is no teleology? The key to this question lies in Spinoza's view that the goodness of something is determined by its being desired (rather than *vice versa*).

*Ethics* IV, as Edwin Curley puts it, 'is the construction of an idea of a model human being', which is the 'idea of a kind of person we necessarily desire to be' (Curley, 1988: 123). Ends come from desires, and Spinoza sketches what (he thinks) we necessarily desire to be. Among these aims are power and freedom, and it is the passions that are the obstacles to what we necessarily desire. For passions are responses to external causes that we do not understand, and so are not under our control since we lack such understanding. Such ill-understood responses issue in a range of attitudes: principally, these are desire (*cupiditas*), which fosters the pursuit of these either as a means of attaining joy (*laetitia*) or avoiding sadness (*tristitia*). Now, our ignorance of the causes of these passions means that any 'action' we take that is motivated by these attitudes is not free action at all. It is implicated in an illusion of freewill of a kind that is incompatible with Spinoza's thoroughgoing determinism, and, furthermore, not genuinely an action because of the ignorance involved. When one properly grasps that one is part of nature and understands the causal nexus in which one is situated, one can subsequently *identify* oneself with it and see actions as stemming from one's own nature. Like the Stoics, we come to realize that our nature is part of divine nature.

There are echoes of another Stoic doctrine in both Descartes and Spinoza. Descartes' *générosité* and Spinoza's virtue both seem at first blush to be solely self-regarding rather than other-regarding. But matters are more subtle than this suggests. For the Stoics, self-regard is paired with the idea that we extend interest beyond ourselves through 'appropriation' (*oikeios*) of the other. That is, we rightly recognize others as the same kind as us (they are 'appropriate' in nature) and that appropriation should extend beyond immediate, local ties and towards the whole *kosmos* of which we are a part. For Descartes, the analogue of this appropriation lies in his account of the extension of love. Our confused perceptions direct us first to the love of ourselves, but recognition of the worth of others can expand this love as a form of devotion. This further encourages one to view one's self and the loved one 'as a single whole of which one is but a part; and to transfer the care one previously took of oneself to the preservation of this whole' (CSMK 311). For Spinoza, the intellect expands our *conatus* for self-preservation to concern for the well-being of others through its recognition that one's power increases through co-operation. Rather than Hobbesian cynicism, Spinozistic desire for others' well-being is fostered by *conatus* motivating unity: nothing is 'more excellent for the preservation of their being than that all men should agree in everything in such a way that the minds and bodies of all should as it were constitute one mind and one body' (Spinoza 2000: 240).

Human excellence for both Spinoza and Descartes involves control of the passions and the perfection of nature, and involves further our affinity with God. Nicolas Malebranche, our third Cartesian, has a conception of virtue which in many ways differs profoundly from both Descartes' and Spinoza's, and is Augustinian in inspiration rather than Stoic. It is also far more explicit about its Christian character. Indeed, his whole philosophy can be seen as an attempt to fill in the Pauline doctrine that it is God in whom we live and have our being. One aspect of this intimate relation to God is a quasi-platonism wherein the ideas of our intellect are identical to the ideas in the Mind of God: another is the occasionalist doctrine that all causation is determined by the will of God, and hence He is the only true power. Since He is the only true power, it is He alone who is worthy of love. Within the mind of God, there is a universal Order, wherein the ideas stand in systematic relations of two kinds, those of *magnitude* and those of *perfection* (Malebranche 1993: I, I, 6). The former are the kinds of quantifiable relations that concern natural science, while the latter are normative moral relations (relations of the kind of which the sentimentalists of the eighteenth century would be very suspicious).

Virtue for Malebranche consists in a dominant and habitual love of this Order. The question then is how this is to be achieved. Malebranche's human beings are corrupted by Original Sin, and are moved by pleasures associated with worldly items. These pleasures are what he calls pleasures of 'concupiscence', and they produce a false love for those worldly items, which, as occasionalism reveals, are not the true causes of those pleasures. But the proper object of love is God, and more particularly the relations of perfection in the ideas of the mind of God. In one's struggle against concupiscence, one is aided by the Grace of Jesus Christ, a feeling that weighs in against sensual pleasures. But the will can have a role in virtue inasmuch as one can withhold assent to the natural judgements of the goodness of the objects of sensual pleasure and let one's love be directed towards order. But talk of willing here should not mislead: for Malebranche, the emphasis is on habituation and virtue in terms of habitual love, not simple acts of will by *fiat*. Our relation to Order can be understood through the 'light of reason' or through feeling. The former is rational perception of Order, but our reason is easily distracted by our senses, imagination and passions, which are the upshot of our embodiment. One must therefore develop what he calls 'strength of mind', a capacity to attend to Order without distraction. Habituation is involved in acquiring the capacity for attention. 'Freedom of the mind', on the other hand, is an acquired habit of suspending judgement in the manner mentioned above.

## II: FROM THE CAMBRIDGE PLATONISTS TO SHAFTESBURY

Malebranche's Christianized Platonism, and his emphasis on the centrality of love, have affinities with the group of thinkers known as the Cambridge Platonists. This movement, which emerged as a reaction against English Calvinism, centred on a Fellow of Emmanuel College, Benjamin Whichcote, and its famous names include Ralph Cudworth and Henry More. One platonic aspect of Cambridge Platonism was a staunch rejection of voluntarism, whereby the moral status of any particular item results from its being determined as such by God's will (a view which Descartes held, and which Malebranche strenuously resisted). Calvinism adhered to moral voluntarism, and, when combined with their view of predestination, issued in a view wherein moral goodness seems to play a marginal role. A second platonic element was the idea of, and indeed the very possibility of, virtue as the harmony of the soul. I say the 'very possibility of virtue' because the

Platonists had in their sights the Calvinist conception of human nature as inherently corrupt. Inspection of one's mind and conduct, which Calvinism demands, is supposed to issue in a vivid, coruscating, awareness of this corruption. Harmony of the soul is thus impossible.

For Whichcote, self-inspection reveals something different. Reason is that which relates us to God and its correct use makes us deiform or God-like. Moral knowledge and virtue is within the purview of reason, aided by a sense of rightness, and living in accordance with virtue increases our deiformity: nothing 'is the true improvement of our rational faculties but the exercise of the several virtues of sobriety . . . obedience to God, and charity to man' (Patrides 1969: 331, no. 541). To be virtuous is to live in heaven, inasmuch as Whichcote understands heaven as living in accordance with reason, a form of integrity involving 'humility, modesty, righteousness, temperance, reverence of deity and the like' (Patrides 1969: 329). Heaven is achievable on earth and the life of virtue is a life of happiness.

Whichcote never published anything in his lifetime, and his philosophy is contained primarily in sermons. Neither did he develop a metaphysics and epistemology to complement his views. That latter task was completed by Ralph Cudworth, who proposed subtle and complex views on metaphysics and epistemology, together with a trenchant rejection of voluntarism and a defence of freewill. It was Henry More, however, whose treatment of virtue and vice is of most interest. He published the only systematic ethics of the school during the seventeenth century, the *Encheiridion Ethicum* (1666). This was subsequently translated into English in 1690 as *An Account of Virtue*. Ironically the ethics presented here is the most Aristotelian of the period.

The work develops Whichcote's suggestion that ethical knowledge can attain the certainty of mathematics, but it also has an Aristotelian flavour (indeed, More's work is replete with quotations from Aristotle). Whilst rejecting the Aristotelian doctrine that the particular virtues aim at the mean (a view that had been criticized by the natural law theorists), he nevertheless held that virtue is the greatest good for humans. Hence, he defines 'ethics' as 'knowledge of happiness', and 'our acquisition of it' (More 1690: 3) and happiness as what the 'mind takes in from a sense of virtue' (1690: 4). The familiar theme of the control of the passions is repeated in his definition of virtue as 'an intellectual power of the soul, by which it over-rules the animal impressions of bodily passions; so as in every action it easily pursues what is absolutely and simply the best' (More 1690: 11). But what is 'the best'? Virtues aim at the right, or 'right reason', rather than the Aristotelian mean for More (1690: bk. II, ch. 9), and the virtuous person's knowledge of the right is facilitated by a 'boniform faculty'. This faculty is also our perfection since it is a form of sensitive love in virtue of which we most resemble God, and is in some sense analogous to the kind of affective and perceptual sensitivity of the virtuous agent of Aristotelianism.

Under the umbrella of virtue in general, More recognizes three kinds of 'primitive virtue', prudence, sincerity, and patience; these have a Stoical dimension insofar as they control the passions (More appeals to Marcus Aurelius in this context (1690: 95)), and allows the soul to 'have dominion over the passions' (1690: 98). In addition, there are the 'derived virtues' of justice (which comprises piety and probity), fortitude, and temperance, where 'derivative' means other-regarding. He also includes 'reductive virtues' such as magnificence, which may reduce to the six core ones. It is also interesting that More devotes most of the third book of his *Account* to theorems and practices for acquiring virtues. There is a general, meditative strategy, including such maxims as to 'meditate on our dissolution; the certain end of our frail body; and on the immortality of the soul' (More 1690: 119), and then particular instructions for each virtue. The Whichcote-inspired 'mathematical' aspect of *An Account* expresses itself in More's appeal to moral axioms or 'noemas', which he takes to be the self-evident basis for morality. Now these are important for the particular virtues inasmuch as they are supposed to provide guidance for controlling the passions. Few are guided by the boniform faculty, and are instead pulled by the strength of passions, and an intellectual grasp of moral truths can at least assist us in controlling passions.

Anthony Ashley Cooper, the third Earl of Shaftesbury, was both personally and intellectually affected by the Cambridge Platonists. One connection was through the friendship of his tutor, John Locke, while another was through Damaris Cudworth, daughter of Ralph and an accomplished philosopher in her own right. His first published piece was a preface to an edition of Whichcote's sermons. But Shaftesbury's account of virtue is also redolent of Roman Stoicism, which he traces to Socrates as its ultimate source. This philosophy, in Shaftesbury's writings, is opposed by 'epicureanism'. Epicureanism here is not used to describe that ancient school, but instead a portmanteau word for a disparate group who, in his mind, holds that 'there is no such thing in reality as virtue, no principle of order in things above or below' (Shaftesbury 1999: 43). Thomas Hobbes, quite obviously was a target of Shaftesbury, but then so too was possibly 'Gassendi's rehabilitation of Epicureanism' (Schneewind 1998: 264–9). Also in his sights were the natural law tradition, and the voluntarism of his tutor Locke, two views against which the Cambridge Platonists were set.

For them, as for Shaftesbury, the mistake of Hobbes, Locke, and others, was to tie moral goodness to obligatory acts, the motivation for which is based on reward or punishment. For Shaftesbury, moral goodness lies in the natural affections of humanity, and virtue in their disposition. But it is not merely abstract philosophical considerations that motivate Shaftesbury, however, but the political context in which his thought was forged. Mindful of the situation in France under Louis IV and in Post-Restoration England, his thought was set against absolute authority and toward republicanism. His grandfather, the first Earl, had been actively involved in the Exclusion Crisis, and was exiled for it. Shaftesbury's Whiggism extended to anti-clericalism, a view shared by John Toland and others, which viewed the established clerics as entirely interested in power in order to serve their own interests. 'Priestcraft' and monarchy were grouped together as sources of corruption in politics and civil society, and Shaftesbury was a supporter of Erastianism—the idea that the church should be under state control. The republicans looked back to, among others, James Harrington's vision of a republican utopia for England, penned in his *Oceana* (1656), and to the civics of ancient Rome and Greece. Shaftesbury's interest in virtue places itself in that context inasmuch as it is virtue, rather than law and authority, that he takes to be the basis of civil society.

Shaftesbury published his *Inquiry Concerning Virtue or Merit* in 1699, possibly through the agency of John Toland. He protested that the publication was against his wishes, but it is unclear whether this is true (Gill 2006: 83). His anti-clericalism and admiration for the marginal role of religion in Rome comes out in the opening part, where he divides forms of religious attitudes into pure theism, pure atheism, polytheism, and daemonism. This last attitude is one that views the gods not as necessarily good, but as arbitrary and capricious, and it is Shaftesbury's code for the voluntarism of Calvinism, the view he takes as the most pernicious. Provocatively, he argues that it is not impossible, though it is difficult, for an atheist to be virtuous. But what does Shaftesbury understand by virtue?

He conceives of every creature as a system within interlocking systems, the endpoint of which is the universe as a whole. A creature is well constituted when its elements function properly—when, that is, its 'parts' are conducive to the well-being of that creature. The natural goodness of any element, in other words, consists in it so functioning. In turn, the creature is also a part of a larger system, such as the species to which it belongs. The proper function of the particular creature—its natural goodness—consists in its being such as to contribute to the well-being of that species. Then 'if all the whole system of animals . . . be properly comprehended in one system of a globe or earth [and this itself have] a dependence on something still beyond . . . then [it is] in reality part only of some other system' (Shaftesbury 1999: 169). Hence each element of the universe functions properly when it is conducive to the good of the whole.

Let us, however, return to the terrestrial perspective. We can think of the natural good for some particular non-human creature in terms of biological function, since Shaftesbury thinks of the good in this context in terms of bodily well-being. He further holds that what is conducive to the well-being of any particular creature is also conducive to the well-being of the species, for the ends to which the particular creature's elements aim are the same as those for any other token member of the species. This sketch, however, is merely an account of natural goodness and does not yet constitute virtue. First, we need to narrow the focus on the proper functioning of which 'elements' are relevant to virtue. The concern here is with 'affections', which are evaluative attitudes directed towards particular objects and actions. Now affections involve the conception of their objects under the guise of the good, which marks a difference from mere biological function. Against Hobbes, Shaftesbury does not take all such states to be reducible to self-interest or 'private interest'. Shaftesbury instead takes our affections to be quite diverse, and a great number of them are other-regarding. But whether or not the affections have private or public interests as their aim, their natural goodness is still understood in terms of their conduciveness to the well-being of the whole. Thus the pursuit of private interest can be good if it contributes to the well-being of the whole, whereas some other-regarding passions can be deleterious to the whole (for example, over-indulgent love of one's children).

But again we have yet to arrive at virtue. The key here is a capacity of rational creatures to be reflectively aware of their affections. The mind 'is a spectator or auditor of other minds', including its own (Shaftesbury 1999: 172). Now, it is this reflective awareness that constitutes Shaftesbury's 'moral sense'. However, Shaftesbury is sparing in his use of the phrase, and imprecise in its definition. Sometimes it is thought of as a second-order affection, sometimes a 'sentiment', sometimes a 'judgement', and sometimes a 'sentiment or judgement' (Shaftesbury 1999: 173). This imprecision is perfectly understandable, since the term 'sentiment' had a variety of uses in the eighteenth-century (Jones 1983), and, despite this imprecision, it is clear that this reflective awareness is evaluative in character. This reflective capacity allows one to 'have the notion of a public interest and can attain the speculation or science of what is morally good and ill, admirable or blameable, right or wrong' (Shaftesbury 1999: 173). It is the capacity to be aware of one's affections and their aims, approve of them in this aesthetic character, and adjust them in light of this awareness: in effect, natural good and evil become moral good and evil when there is conscious awareness and approval of them.

This aesthetic approval is coupled with an emphasis on self-reflection as the basis of self-governance. Reflective awareness allows us to assess and control our first-order affections. This point reflects Shaftesbury's Stoic leanings, inspired by Epictetus's claim that we should concern ourselves most with that which lies within our power.[2] There is, furthermore, an intriguing suggestion scattered in Shaftesbury's writings that virtue, and its aesthetic appreciation, contribute to the very identity of the person. In his *Miscellany* IV, Shaftesbury considers the question: 'What constitutes the "we" or "I"?', and 'Whether the "I" of this instant be the same as that of any instant preceding or to come?' (Shaftesbury 1999: 420). His answer takes the perspective of a 'moralist' rather than the 'wonderfully refined speculations' of the 'metaphysician' (Shaftesbury 1999: 421). That is to say, rather than discussing the kinds of issues which are familiar to us now from discussions of personal identity, Shaftesbury considers how we can assess and regulate character dispositions and our future-regarding affections, and integrate them until 'at last a

---

[2] For a discussion, see Darwall (1995: 197–206), who suggests that the concern for self-governance may have a more immediate Cambridge Platonist providence (Darwall 1995: 191).

mind, by knowing itself and its own proper powers and virtues, becomes free and independent . . . the more it is its own master, the more it feels its own natural liberty and congratulates with itself on its own advancement and prosperity' (Shaftesbury 1999: 425). This integration, as Shaftesbury puts it elsewhere

keeps us the self-same person and so regulates our governing fancies, passions and humours as to make us comprehensible and knowable by other features than those of a bare countenance. For it is certainly not by virtue of our face merely that we are ourselves. It is not we who change when our complexion or shape changes. But there is that which, being wholly metamorphosed and converted, we are thereby in reality transformed and lost.    (Shaftesbury 1999: 127; see Winkler 2000)

This aesthetic appreciation is also an aesthetic appreciation of the order, design, and harmony of the universe and that of the particular systems within it. He also calls it an 'enthusiasm' that is 'rational' or 'reasonable'. The term 'enthusiasm' in eighteenth-century Britain was frequently coupled with 'superstition', and viewed as a species of false or corrupt religion. Enthusiasm was linked to excessive hope, giving false feelings of divine presence, and superstition to fear leading to abasement. Shaftesbury however works hard to carve out a space for an enthusiasm that he takes to be a genuine appreciation of the divine in nature, inasmuch as we finally come to appreciate that the order and harmony of the universe cannot but owe itself to design and intelligence.

Shaftesbury's theory is an intriguing form of naturalism. For, in determining whether one's second-order affection (a moral evaluation) is appropriate or not—a question explicitly addressed by him in the *Inquiry*—he appeals to facts about the proper functioning of the object of that affection. Thus 'to deserve the name of good or virtuous, a creature must have all his inclinations and affections, his dispositions of mind and temper, suitable and agreeing to his kind or of that system to which he is a part' (Shaftesbury 1999: 192). Among the affections natural to human beings are the other-regarding ones: no one 'will deny that [the] affection of a creature towards the good of the species is as proper and natural to him . . . as it is for the stomach to digest' (Shaftesbury 1999: 192). This suggests that natural teleology provides the norms for virtuous conduct (cf. Foot 2001). Shaftesbury also suggests that our own good and happiness consists in pursuing other-regarding conduct, and hence virtue and self-interest coincide. Therefore, Shaftesbury suggests, we have an obligation to virtue from self-interest, a suggestion of which his admirer Francis Hutcheson was critical, as we shall see. But Shaftesbury also suggests what Michael Gill has called 'a mental enjoyment account' of our reason to be virtuous (Gill 2006: 121–3; cf. Darwall 1995: 195–6). One aspect of this is Shaftesbury's claim that there is a certain kind of happiness that is only produced by virtue, a happiness that his comparison with pleasures of the body suggests has a certain hedonic quality. But more important is the idea that there is a certain contentment that comes with the self-integration that the virtuous life offers.

# III: Hutcheson and Butler

Shaftesbury's work was undeniably influential in eighteenth-century Britain, and continued to be such beyond the early modern period into Hume, and in what is perhaps the most interesting and subtle expression of the sentimentalist tradition, namely Adam Smith's *Theory of Moral Sentiments* of 1759. This influence took various forms, depending on which aspect of his thought captured the imagination. The notions of a self-authorizing moral sense and a natural teleology echo loudly in Butler's moral philosophy, and in Hutcheson's aestheticized moral sense. Neither philosopher was uncritical of Shaftesbury, of course, but Shaftesbury's appeal to a moral sense and his placement of other-regarding affections at the centre of human psychology and virtue took on a particular salience for Hutcheson because the early eighteenth century saw the emergence of a new *bête noir* to stand beside Thomas Hobbes. This was Bernard Mandeville's *The Fable of the Bees: Private Vices, Public Benefits*. Its origins lie in his 1705 verse work, *The Grumbling Hive; or Knaves Turn'd Honest*, to which he appended an extensive commentary in a second volume in 1714, both volumes comprising the *Fable of the Bees*.

This work had a huge impact throughout Europe, and gained a reputation as advocating a form of egoism and denying the reality of virtue (a position Shaftesbury would consider to be 'moral scepticism'; thus Shaftesbury explicitly falls under Mandeville's sights). What Mandeville's own views actually are, however, is difficult to determine. On the surface at least he subscribes to something called genuine virtue, and has a very austere and demanding conception of it. All passions are to be suppressed for the 'rational ambition' for the good of the whole, but the demandingness of genuine virtue is too much for ordinary humans. Our condition therefore is one of hypocrisy wherein we condemn self-interest and pursue it surreptitiously. Nevertheless, the pursuit of self-interest has the unintended, but welcome, consequence of producing society and its public benefits.

Whatever Mandeville may have intended by this, he was commonly taken to reduce all moral action and concepts to self-regarding prudential concerns that have but the thinnest moral veneer of mere words. This is certainly how Hutcheson understood it, and his *Inquiry into the Original of Our Ideas of Beauty and Virtue* (1725) advertises itself in its subtitle as a work in 'which the Principles of the Late Earl of Shaftesbury are Explain'd and Defended, against the Author of the *Fable of the Bees*'. The work is indeed set against the perceived view of Mandeville, but is no mere explication and defence of Shaftesbury. Although he was a far less graceful writer than Shaftesbury, Hutcheson was a more vigorous philosopher. The *Inquiry* comprises two treatises, the first on aesthetics, the second on morality. But the second is not independent of the former, since

Hutcheson's discussion of the sense of beauty in natural objects paves the way for the moral sense (Kail 2000, 2001). First, the realm of the aesthetic is important for Hutcheson because it provides an example of a distinct form of evaluative experience that cannot be reduced to self-interest. Second, he contends that aesthetic appreciation is sensitive to a particular formal property, namely 'uniformity amidst variety'. This feature is the mark of all good explanations, and by linking our aesthetic response to it we are thereby designed to contemplate the formal feature that will unlock the secrets of the universe. Hence, even without an explicit grasp of *what* feature one is tracking, or even *that* one is tracking it, one's aesthetic sentiments function to render salient to the subject a feature which one might subsequently reflect upon and come to grasp.

Now if we transfer this model into the moral realm, we get the following: first, Hutcheson postulates an irreducible moral response which is the source of the distinct content of moral discourse. The thought here is that once we recognize that there are aesthetic responses that cannot be adequately characterized in terms of other responses, such as desire or other interests, then we should be open to the idea that we have irreducible moral responses. Hutcheson sees this as superior to Hobbes and Mandeville, inasmuch as he takes them to lack the materials necessary to account for the conceptual distinctness of moral discourse, and Section I of his treatise on morals is devoted to establishing this point. Second, whilst aesthetic experience tracks uniformity amidst variety, the distinct moral experience is correlated with virtue, and virtue for Hutcheson reduces to benevolent character. What is important to stress here is that, though the inner sense of virtue that Hutcheson speaks of as the characteristic experience requires reflection on the particular character under consideration, the notion of a 'sense' is nevertheless appropriate. It is appropriate because although we can and do reflect on aspects of a particular person, such as her general disposition, the extent of her knowledge of relevant features of the situation, and for example her intentions, the feeling is designed to be sensitive to the fundamental character of benevolence, and one need not know either *that* the relevant features indicate benevolence *or* indeed to what that peculiar sentiment is so sensitive. One simply 'finds' the particular person amiable. Compare the aesthetic case: in the experience, for example, of some beautiful scene, Hutcheson claims that the response is sensitive to uniformity amidst variety. Nevertheless one need not know *that* it is this feature to which one is responding. To borrow a phrase from Hume, it is more properly felt than judged. Further reflection might make transparent that to which one is responding, and Hutcheson's identification of virtue with benevolence is, as it were, the end result of this reflection. His theory is a theory both of the response and an empirical discovery of what the response fundamentally tracks.

There is a further end that both virtue, and the sense of it, serves. On Hutcheson's view, our natural design is such that benevolence is conducive to the good of the whole, and so our approbation of it sustains and encourages the benevolence that promotes the well-being of humanity as a whole. This view may well mark an inheritance from Shaftesbury. But Hutcheson found Shaftesbury's teleological account of the motive to virtue to be wanting, and seemed more inclined to adopt a version of the mental enjoyment account. Reflection on our own virtue produces the highest form of pleasure. Thus he writes that 'Virtue is... called Amiable from its raising Good-will or Love in the Spectator... and not from the Agent perceiving the virtuous Temper to be advantageous to him... [but] every Spectator is persuaded that the reflex Acts of the virtuous Agent upon his own Temper will give him the highest Pleasures' (Hutcheson 2004: 222n.).

Nevertheless there is not the emphasis on self-reflection in Hutcheson as there is in Shaftesbury, and his account of virtue is sliding towards a form of virtue consequentialism which Shaftesbury would resist, as well as a rather reductive and monolithic view of the virtues. Indeed, it is Hutcheson who introduces mathematical calculation into ethics and the notion of the greatest good for the greatest number. It was Joseph Butler's own unique moral philosophy that placed self-reflection at the centre of virtue, and resisted the reductionism of Hutcheson's account. Butler's principal works comprise *Fifteen Sermons Preached at the Rolls Chapter* (1726), and *Analogy of Religion* (1736), which contains as one of its appendices the 'Dissertation on Virtue' (the other appendix being his famous discussion of personal identity). Similar to Shaftesbury, Butler emphasizes the role of system and our place in it, and a sense of naturalness in terms of the proper function of affections and passions in relation to their ends. He was also taken by the reflexive element in Shaftebury's account of virtue. But what troubled him was the lack in Shaftesbury's scheme of a genuine account of the normative *authority* of reflection. So, rather than talk of a moral sense and emphasize aesthetic appreciation as Shaftesbury did, Butler talks of *conscience*. Among the objects of conscience are of course actions, but also those 'principles from which men would act, if occasions and circumstances gave them power; and when fixed and habitual in any person, we call, his character' (Butler 2006: 310). Butler staunchly resists the reductive account of Hutcheson. Benevolence 'and the want of it, singly considered, are in no sort the whole of virtue and vice' (Butler 2006: 312). If it were, all sorts of vicious means to producing happiness, such as cheating or violence, would be justified by the ends they serve. Instead, he views virtue as comprising a range of dispositions that are related to restraint and control of one's first-order affections, and he makes a special effort to place prudence in a prominent position.

Butler subscribes to the dictum that virtue consists in following nature. But how are we to understand the role of conscience in this? In the *Sermons*, Butler distinguishes between three senses of 'natural'. The first is simply brute facts about our psychological endowment; desires are an aspect of our nature. Second, there is a sense of 'natural' that applies to motives for action, and their relative strengths. In this sense, it is natural for a greedy person to eat a lot or for the avaricious to seek more and more. The third and most pertinent sense of 'natural' is that we are so constituted to assess our own passions and actions. Conscience has a 'natural supremacy' whereby it 'passes judgment' on one's self and actions, and 'pronounces determinately some actions to be in themselves just, right, good, others to be in themselves evil, wrong and unjust' (Butler 2006: 58).

Butler's worry with Shaftsbury's account is that aesthetic approval of some feature of character does not by itself necessarily outweigh other grounds for approval (for example, the merely prudential). Nothing about aesthetic approval *per se* determines it as normatively authoritative over other possible sources. But what is the source of this 'natural supremacy'? There is interpretive disagreement here, divided into two main camps. The first camp emphasizes a proper function sense of 'natural', whereby conscience has authority because its proper function is, precisely, to control first-order affections. Hence the 'proper governour' (Butler 2006: 60) is proper simply because it is designed to be. A worry here is that if this line is pressed, any distinctive role for conscience may be swallowed up by the naturalism (Sturgeon 1976). For it seems that the content of conscience becomes mere approval of the implicit proper function of each first-order affection, which does not itself provide grounds for its being generally *authoritative* over other natural endowments or, indeed, allow us to adjudicate between them. Alternatively, and perhaps more promisingly, one might take 'constitution' in the sense that conscience constitutes a virtuous person in a political sense. Constitution implies a notion of authority and rights of enforcement. So, with Stephen Darwall, one might take it that just as one can only have a genuine constitution when there is legitimate authority, the normative authority of conscience should be viewed as a 'condition on the very possibility of an agent's having reasons to act at all' (Darwall 1995: 247). Butler is in effect heading towards Kant in an otherwise un-Kantian system.

# CONCLUSION

This survey is undoubtedly a highly selective one, and has focused primarily on the 'major figures' of the period. But this departure from how a proper history of the period should be written is not meant to be mitigated solely by the constraints of any handbook or companion piece. Instead, I hope that this survey shows that the very idea that virtue suffered from neglect (as opposed to misfortunes) during this period is extremely difficult to maintain, and that there are rich seams to be mined which are barely beneath the surface.

# REFERENCES

BUTLER, J. (2006). *The Works of Joseph Butler.* Ed. D. White. Rochester: Rochester University Press.

CURLEY, E. (1988). *Behind the Geometrical Method: A Reading of Spinoza's* Ethics. Princeton, NJ: Princeton University Press.

DARWALL, S. (1995). *The British Moralists and the Internal 'Ought': 1640–1740.* Cambridge: Cambridge University Press.

FOOT, P. (2001). *Natural Goodness.* Oxford: Clarendon Press.

GARRETT, D. (1996). 'Spinoza's Ethical Theory', in D. Garrett (ed.), *The Cambridge Companion to Spinoza.* Cambridge: Cambridge University Press, 267–314.

GILL, M. (2006). *The British Moralists on Human Nature and the Birth of Secular Ethics.* Cambridge: Cambridge University Press.

HUTCHESON, F. (2004). *An Inquiry into the Original of Our Ideas of Beauty and Virtue.* Ed. W. Leidhold. Indianapolis, IN: Liberty Press.

JAMES, S. (1997). *Passion and Action: The Emotions in Seventeenth–Century Philosophy.* Oxford: Oxford University Press.

JONES, P. (1983). *Hume's Sentiments: Their Ciceronian and French Context.* Edinburgh: Edinburgh University Press.

KAIL, P. J. E. (2000). 'Normativity and function in Hutcheson's aesthetic epistemology'. *British Journal for Aesthetics*, 40: 441–51.

KAIL, P. J. E. (2001). 'Hutcheson's moral sense: realism, skepticism, and secondary qualities'. *History of Philosophy Quarterly*, 18: 57–77.

LLOYD, G. (1996). *Spinoza and the Ethics.* London: Routledge.

LONG, A. A. (1986). *Hellenistic Philosophy.* 2nd edn. London: Duckworth.

MALEBRANCHE, N. (1993). *Treatise on Ethics.* Ed. Walton. Dordrecht: Kluwer.

MORE, H. (1690). *An Account of Virtue.* London.

PATRIDES, C. A. (ed.) (1969). *The Cambridge Platonists.* Cambridge: Cambridge University Press.

PENELHUM, T. (1985). *Butler.* London: Routledge & Kegan Paul.

REID, T. (1969). *Essays on the Active Powers of the Human Mind.* Ed. Brody. Cambridge, MA: MIT Press.

RUTHERFORD, D. (2004). 'On the Happy Life: Descartes vis-à-vis Seneca', in S. K. Strange and J. Zupko (eds), *Stoicism: Traditions and Transformations.* New York: Cambridge University Press, 177–97.

SCHNEEWIND, J. (1990). 'The misfortunes of virtue'. *Ethics*, 101: 42–63.

SCHNEEWIND, J. (1998). *The Invention of Autonomy: A History of Modern Moral Philosophy.* Cambridge: Cambridge University Press.

SHAFTESBURY, THIRD EARL OF (ANTHONY ASHLEY COOPER) (1999). *Characteristics of Men, Manners, Opinions, Times.* Ed. L. Klein. Cambridge: Cambridge University Press.

SORELL, T. (1993). 'Morals and Modernity in Descartes', in T. Sorell (ed.), *The Rise of Modern Philosophy.* Oxford: Oxford University Press, 273–89.

SPINOZA, B. DE (2000). *Ethics.* Ed. and trans. G. H. R. Parkinson. Oxford: Oxford University Press.

STURGEON, N. (1976). 'Nature and conscience in Butler's ethics'. *Philosophical Review*, 85: 316–56.

SWANTON, C. (2003). *Virtue Ethics: A Pluralist View.* Oxford: Oxford University Press.

WINKLER, K. (2000). '"All is revolution in us": Personal identity in Shaftesbury and Hume'. *Hume Studies*, 29: 125–41.

CHAPTER 18

................................................................

# EGOISM AND MORALITY

................................................................

## STEPHEN DARWALL

THE spectre of egoism in various different guises has haunted philosophical thinking about morality ever since the beginning of the modern period in the seventeenth and eighteenth centuries. Indeed, it is fair to say that modern ethical thought has defined itself, in contrast with ancient Greek ethics, by its concern with a specific ethical conception, *morality*, whose distinctness from eudaimonist prudential concerns is part of its very idea. The distinguishing mark of the moral, it has seemed, is its capacity to place us under *obligations* that bind irrespectively of whether complying with them is, in any particular instance, to the agent's advantage or not. If egoism of one sort or another were to prove correct, therefore, it would apparently follow either that we might be incapable of being moral or that morality itself might not even exist.

The great nineteenth-century systematizer of ethical theories, Henry Sidgwick, noted this difference between ancient and modern ethics when he wrote that

in Platonism and Stoicism, and in Greek moral philosophy generally, but one regulative and governing faculty is recognised under the name of Reason—however the regulation of Reason may be understood; in the modern ethical view, when it has worked itself clear, there are found to be two—Universal Reason and Egoistic Reason, or Conscience and Self-love.  (Sidgwick 1964: 198)

For ancient philosophers like Plato and Aristotle, there is a single fundamental object of ethical concern—the good—and one basic issue: how to live so as to realize the greatest good in one's life and so flourish and be happiest? For the

moderns, on the other hand, there are further questions that are no less fundamental: What ways of living are morally right or obligatory or, for that matter,
good *morally*? In their view, these latter questions can have answers only if there is a
source of ethical concern and normative reasons for acting other than the agent's
own good.[1] If there is not, then there might be no such thing as right and wrong,
moral good and evil.

## I: Egoism's challenge to morality

We can see this in a challenge that the philosopher who is sometimes seen as
originating modern ethical thought, Hugo Grotius, poses to the existence of a
natural (moral) law at the outset of his great work, *On the Law of War and Peace*
(1625), a challenge that will be echoed later by Hobbes's 'fool', Hume's 'sensible
knave', and Kant's worry that morality might be a 'chimerical idea without any
truth' (Schneewind 1998: 70–3). Who better to pose this challenge, Grotius says,
than the ancient sceptic Carneades, who held that '*Laws . . . were instituted by Men
for the sake of Interest*':

*As to that which is called* NATURAL RIGHT [or law], *it is a mere Chimera. Nature prompts all
Men . . . to seek their own particular Advantage: So that either there is no Justice at all, or if
there is any it is extreme Folly, because it engages us to procure the Good of others, to our own
Prejudice.*   (Grotius 2005: I, 79)[2]

---

[1] As I see it, what underlies these characteristics of the modern conception of morality is the idea
that we are responsible in the sense of *accountable* for certain elements of our conduct, to God and one
another. Hugo Grotius articulated a doctrine of fundamental rights that we all have standing to
demand of each, and early modern theological voluntarists, such as Pufendorf and Locke, argued that
morality itself derives from God's authoritative commands, although they also thought that forms of
accountability to one another follow from this. Hegel's characterization of the relation between
modern and ancient ethical thought is also relevant, since he thinks that the former is distinctively
marked by the idea of a 'right of subjective freedom' (Hegel 1991: 151). Any such autonomy right must
entail a correlative set of obligations that others not infringe it. The development of an ethical
conception that can accommodate the modern idea of human rights with a correlative notion of
moral obligation marks a genuine advance over ancient conceptions.

[2] Cf. Hobbes: 'The fool hath said in his heart, there is no such thing as justice; and sometimes also
with his tongue; seriously alleging, that every man's conservation, and contentment, being committed
to his own care, there could be no reason, why every man might not do what he thought conduced
thereunto: and therefore also to make, or not make; keep, or not keep covenants, was not against
reason, when it conduced to one's benefit' (L XV.4) And Hume: '[T]hough it is allowed, that, without
a regard to property, no society could subsist; yet, according to the imperfect way in which human
affairs are conducted, a sensible knave, in particular incidents, may think, that an act of iniquity or
infidelity will make a considerable addition to his fortune, without causing any considerable breach in
the social union and confederacy. That *honesty is the best policy*, may be a good general rule; but is

Carneades holds that there is only one source of reasons for acting, the agent's own interest, and hence that there could not be any reason for anyone to follow any law that might conflict with it. If that were true, however, there could be no such thing as the moral law, since it purports to obligate us to do things whether or not it is in our interest to do them.

A similar, but crucially different, challenge was familiar to the ancients. After all, a central task of Plato's *Republic* is to respond to Glaucon's claim that there is no intrinsic reason to be just, since though it is to everyone's advantage for a system of justice to exist, *acting* justly is not necessarily advantageous. Each benefits most if he can act unjustly toward others while benefiting from their just acts toward him. Socrates's (and so Plato's) response is that there is indeed always a reason to be just since, even if injustice may be instrumentally beneficial, just conduct is nonetheless beneficial intrinsically, since it realizes harmony in the soul. Aristotle and Stoic writers take a similar tack when they hold that acting ethically (and justly) realizes the just person's nature as a rational human being and so benefits him intrinsically.

For most moderns who followed Grotius, however, this ancient strategy does not respond to a Carneadean challenge to morality as they conceive it, that is, to an obligating moral law as opposed to an intrinsically beneficial ethical ideal (even one that includes justice). H. A. Prichard famously argued, at the beginning of the twentieth century, that a defence of this kind makes 'moral philosophy rest on a mistake' (Prichard 2002). That an action benefits us, whether intrinsically or extrinsically, is one thing; whether morality requires the action is quite another. Moreover, no fact of the former kind can adequately support a claim of the latter sort. This would certainly be Kant's view in the late eighteenth century, but so also was it that of early modern writers like Locke, Butler, Hutcheson, and even, as we shall see, Hobbes.[3] As these philosophers saw it, if Carneadean egoism were true,

---

liable to many exceptions: And he, it may, perhaps, be thought, conducts himself with most wisdom, who observes the general rule, and takes advantage of all the exceptions' (Hume 1985: 256). The passage from Kant is from the *Groundwork* (Kant 1996: 445).

[3] T. H. Irwin argues that Grotius's own view should be understood as being squarely within the ancient tradition he variously calls Stoic or Aristotelian Naturalism. See Irwin (2003, 2007, 2008). However, this makes it hard to see how Grotius's contemporaries and followers could have understood his project as being so fundamentally different from the ancients. I cannot argue the point properly here, but Irwin's interpretation fails to appreciate Grotius's doctrine that genuinely obligating (moral) law involves 'command' rather than 'counsel' and that considerations of the good, taken in themselves, can establish only counsels and not justified demands and, therefore, obligations. Grotius himself explicitly points out that ancient conceptions of right and law lack any conceptual connection to obligation and legitimate demand. Thus Grotius contrasts the Aristotelian conception of distributive justice that 'ancients' and even some 'moderns' include under the concept of right with right 'properly speaking', since the latter includes doing for others 'what in Strictness they may demand' (2005: 88–9). And Grotius ties the broadest sense of right (*ius*) he is concerned with to obligation in a juridical sense. Unlike 'Counsels' and other 'reasonable' 'Precepts', he says, law and right 'lay us under . . . Obligation' (2005: 148).

then morality might prove no more than 'a chimerical idea without any truth', as Kant would later say (Kant 1996: 445).

Egoism of the kind we have just been discussing is usually called *rational egoism*. Since it concerns normative reasons for acting, however, a better name might be *normative egoism*. Morality is threatened by normative egoism in a way that ancient ethical conceptions are not. Aristotle's *Nicomachean Ethics*, for example, begins with the claim that the agent's happiness or eudaimonia is the 'chief good', that is, what agents should most fundamentally seek. But if all normative reasons for acting derive from the agent's good, then there would appear to be no such thing as what the moderns conceive moral obligation to be. Not every early modern thinker accepted this consequence, however, as we shall see. John Locke was notable, for example, for defending a conception of morality and moral obligation while nonetheless accepting normative egoism.

Normative egoism was not the only form of egoism prominently discussed in the early modern period. Two others were similarly concerned with motives and agency, but whereas normative egoism was a claim about what *should* (or rationally would) motivate, egoism of these other kinds concerned what *can* motivate human beings, either as a matter of contingent psychological fact (*psychological egoism*) or owing to the very nature of agency and the will (*agency egoism*). Psychological egoism holds that it is a contingent fact of human psychology, confirmable by empirical methods, that human beings are motivated only by self-concern, that is, by motives that relate in some way or other to their own welfare or happiness. Agency egoists hold that only egoistic motivation is consistent with the nature of human agency and will. The line between these two views is naturally blurry. The main difference is that the former position results from actual observation of human behaviour, whereas the latter is the conclusion of philosophical or moral psychological reflection on the form that any recognizably human action must take.

Whereas normative egoism seemed to threaten the very existence of morality, psychological and agency egoism put in doubt not this, but whether human beings can actually measure up to morality's standards. The issue was not whether it is possible for human agents to perform the specific acts that morality requires, since in any given case this might be done for self-interested reasons, perhaps because of socially or legally created incentives. The question was whether it is possible for people to comply with moral obligations *for the very reasons* that made the relevant acts morally obligatory. Is action *on moral reasons* possible, either as a matter of contingent psychological fact or given the nature of human agency? In other words, is it possible for human beings to be morally good or virtuous?

Here again, modern conceptions of moral virtue seemed vulnerable in ways that ancient conceptions of virtue were not. Neither Plato nor Aristotle saw any tension in the doctrines that, in Aristotle's formulation, the happiest human agents choose virtuous activity for its own sake as noble, on the one hand, and, on the other, that human agents necessarily aim most fundamentally at their own happiness. As most early moderns understood things, however, *moral* virtue is not simply an excellence whose realization intrinsically enhances the value and happiness of the virtuous person's own life. Early modern moral philosophers tended to agree with Francis Hutcheson that genuinely moral motivation is necessarily *disinterested*. However, if either psychological or agency egoism is true, then all human motives are ultimately self-interested; and if that is so, then moral virtue seems simply unattainable for human beings.

Hutcheson was, as we shall see, a central figure in the early modern defence of morality and moral virtue against egoism of different kinds; indeed, he argued against all three of normative, psychological, and agency egoism. But egoism also took a further form that Hutcheson thought potentially more damaging to the cause of virtue even than those already mentioned. Hutcheson actually agreed with Locke, though for very different reasons, that the existence of morality, moral obligation, and moral virtue would not be imperilled if the only normative or motivating reasons agents have for acting are restricted to their own good. Both Locke and Hutcheson were *morality/reasons externalists*, since they held that it is possible to be morally obligated without having normative reason to act as morally required (Darwall 1997a: 306–10). So even if normative egoism were true, morality could still exist and obligate. Still, Hutcheson did hold that the truth of either psychological or agency egoism would make it impossible for human beings to be morally virtuous, and so he argued against these doctrines.

Although none of normative, psychological, or agency egoism, as we have defined these, directly threaten the validity of moral categories, in Hutcheson's view, only their instantiation, egoism took yet a different form in Bernard Mandeville's writings that Hutcheson thought would imperil morality, should it prove true.[4] Hutcheson believed that the source of moral ideas is no form of motivation, nor reason, but a distinctive disinterested sentiment, which Hutcheson called the moral sense, that we have when we contemplate agents' motives as observers. If we lacked this disinterested sentiment, Hutcheson held, we could neither frame moral ideas nor make moral judgements. As Hutcheson understood him, however, Mandeville denied that human beings ever have genuinely disinterested attitudes of any kind. However we might like them to be, human attitudes as we actually find them are always ultimately self-serving. We can call egoism of this form, *attitude egoism*. Although psychological egoism is normally understood as a claim about motivation, attitude egoism holds that all human attitudes are fundamentally

---

[4] For this reason, Hutcheson appended the following on the title page of the first edition of his *Inquiry Concerning the Original of Our Ideas of Beauty and Virtue*: 'In Which the Principles of the Late Earl of Shaftesbury are Defended Against the Author of the Fable of the Bees' (2004: 10). Shaftesbury had also advanced the idea that moral distinctions are tied to a disinterested contemplative response, which he also sometimes called a 'moral sense' (Shaftesbury 2001: ii, 24–7).

self-interested, whether they are motivating or not. As Hutcheson saw things, if attitude egoism were true, human beings would lack moral sense and so morality and moral judgement would not exist.

We can now see why ethical philosophers of the early modern period had to contend with egoism in the various guises we have distinguished, and we shall explore in more detail below exactly how they attempted to do this. But this raises a second set of issues: What *non*-egoistic psychic features did early modern thinkers think are necessary for moral conduct and virtue? What is the psychology of the moral agent as the early moderns conceived it?

If egoism hypothesizes self-interested motivation, and moral conduct is defined by contrast with that, then a natural thought would be that distinctively moral motivation is *other*-interested, that is, that it is some form of *benevolence*. Certainly, this was Hutcheson's view. Hutcheson held that any morally virtuous motive involves some desire for others' pleasure or happiness, whether some individual's, as a parent's love for her child, or everyone's happiness, as is the object of the universal benevolence that Hutcheson believed morally best. No early modern thinker denied that benevolence is among the moral virtues; however, there was a lively debate about whether it exhausts them. Some, like Leibniz, agreed that it did, holding that God's benevolence for His creatures is an exemplar of moral virtue. Others, notably Bishop Butler and early intuitionists like Samuel Clarke, argued that benevolence is but one of the virtues, and that others—most conspicuously, reciprocity or justice—were no less central to virtuous character. What was as issue was nothing less than the nature of moral agency, and the differences on this question during the early modern period provided a basis for contrasting systematic theories of right conduct of a later period. It is significant that we find in Leibniz and Hutcheson the first formulations of the greatest happiness principle that will be the core of the utilitarian moral theories of Bentham and Mill in the late eighteenth and nineteenth centuries, and, as well, that late-eighteenth-century deontological theories, like Kant's and Richard Price's, can be seen to be rooted in accounts of moral autonomy, integrity, and conscientious conduct of the kind found in Bishop Butler.

In what follows, we shall examine these early modern debates and discussions. How, more precisely, did egoism of the different forms we have identified threaten early modern moral theories, and how exactly did moral philosophers of the seventeenth and early eighteenth centuries seek to defend their theories against them? To what extent did they try to disprove these forms of egoism, and if so, how effective were they? And to what extent were they prepared to concede egoism in one or another form, and attempt to defend a conception of morality even so? More positively, what forms of non-egoistic motivation were thought to be essential to moral conduct and virtue and what was most deeply at issue between philosophers who disagreed about this?

# II: Egoism with Natural Law?

We should begin with two seventeenth-century thinkers who were both widely associated with forms of egoism, but who attempted to defend conceptions of morality nonetheless: Thomas Hobbes and John Locke. Both are notable since the egoistic aspects of their respective philosophical views were thought by many who followed them to undermine morality despite their defences. For philosophers like Shaftesbury, whose views on virtue and sentiment inspired Hutcheson, Hobbes's and Locke's egoism made morality 'unnatural' and virtue impossible. Shaftesbury actually thought Locke the more dangerous thinker, since Hobbes's absolutist, 'slavish principles' made his views unpopular. In Shaftesbury's view, it was Locke who 'struck the home blow' against morality and virtue (Rand 1900: 403).

There is no doubt, however, that egoism was more widely associated with Hobbes than with Locke during the period. Partly this is due to their different strategies in political philosophy. Both Hobbes and Locke were central figures in the social contract tradition, which attempts to justify political authority from the starting point of a 'state of nature' in which no such authority is recognized. Both argue that political authority is the upshot of an agreement or contract between individuals in the state of nature. Here, however, the similarities end. Locke assumes that there are certain basic rights—to life, liberty, and property—even in a state of nature, and that individuals in such a state would sensibly enter into an authority-creating agreement in order to protect these. But Hobbes recognizes no such natural rights. He argues that individuals enter into a mutual contract out of self-interest, mostly because of their dominant interest in self-preservation.

It is somewhat ironic, therefore, that Hobbes's fundamental normative and psychological views are actually less obviously egoist than those of Locke. Locke's normative and psychological egoism are clear and prominent aspects of his overall view, as we shall see. Hobbes's views have certainly *seemed* pretty unambiguously egoistic to his readers, however. He appears to assert agency egoism when he writes: 'of the voluntary acts of every man, the object is some *good to himself*' (L XIV.8). And normative egoism of some kind can seem implicit in Hobbes's reply to the 'fool', who claims that breaking covenants, and so violating the (third) law of nature 'is not against reason, when it conduce[s] to one's benefit', since 'reason . . . dictateth to every man his own good' (L XV.4). In reply, Hobbes argues primarily against 'act egoist' views that reckon normative reasons by the actual benefits of the act in question; just because something turns out well does not 'make it reasonably or wisely done' (L XV.5). It is possible to interpret Hobbes's reply, as Gregory Kavka does, as nonetheless involving a kind of 'rule egoism', namely, as arguing that it is more sensible to follow a policy or rule of always keeping covenant, even when one thinks one would do better by not doing so, and that the most sensible act follows from the most sensible policy (Kavka 1995).[5]

However egoistic they may be, there are aspects of Hobbes's views that blunt any threat to morality, at least as Hobbes saw it. First, it is not even clear that Hobbes really is a psychological or an agency egoist. Because he says that 'whatsoever is the object of any man's appetite or desire that is it which he for his part calleth *good*' (L VI.7), it used to be common to interpret Hobbes as a metaethical subjectivist (Gauthier 1967: 7; Hampton 1986: 29; Kavka 1986: 47). Commentators tended to read Hobbes as holding that what it is for something to be good (for someone), or what someone means when she says something is good, is that she desires it. If this were true, it would tie the fact or concept of value to facts about the person's desires, and so perhaps to her interests, in a straightforward way. But that is not what Hobbes says. He does not say that, in calling something good, a person says that she desires that thing. He says, rather, that what a person desires she calls good. There is nothing subjectivist about this claim. To the contrary, I have argued elsewhere that Hobbes is best read as saying that when someone says something is good she *expresses* her desire for it rather than says that she desires it. This is no more subjectivist than would be a comparable claim about belief. 'Whatsoever is the object of any man's belief', we might say, 'that is it which he for his part calleth true.'

The best way to read Hobbes, I have claimed, is as an expressivist projectivist who holds that in desiring something, we see it as good and project onto it a property, value or goodness, that it does not in fact actually have (Darwall 2000). Hobbes quite explicitly compares the case of value to that of colour, thereby introducing an analogy that will run through sentimentalist writers like Hutcheson and Hume (L VI.9). And Hobbes takes a projectivist, Galilean view of colours, holding that in sensory experience we project onto objects colour properties they don't actually have (L I.4). Thus although Hobbes does not think that, metaphysically, there is anything more to value than being desired, just as he thinks there is nothing more to colour than colour experience or its material underpinnings, this commits him to none of metaethical subjectivism, normative egoism, or psychological or agency egoism. Whether he held any form of egoism must turn on what he thought about the *content* of human desires. What then about Hobbes's saying that an agent always aims at some 'good to himself' (L VI.7)? What could be a clearer statement of agency egoism than that? As I read him, however, Hobbes is saying no more here than that agents always aim at things they *hold good*, and so that are goods to them in this sense. There is nothing egoistic about that, since

---

[5] For a very different, and to my mind more plausible interpretation, see Lloyd (2009). Lloyd argues that what underlies Hobbes's natural laws is not egoism, but a 'reciprocity theorem', *viz.*, that individuals be prepared to act towards others as they would have (in the sense of expect) others to act toward them.

someone might hold only, say, the welfare of others to be good, caring not a fig for himself.

Even so, Hobbes might still end up being a psychological egoist, depending on his view about the contents of human desires, and he certainly says things that can sound egoistic even here. Thus he writes that a person feels pity 'from the imagination that the like calamity may befall himself' (L VI.46). And the desires that he holds put us into 'competition' in the state of nature, leading to a state of war of all against all, are also clearly self-regarding (L XIII). Despite all this, many scholars today argue that Hobbes was not a psychological egoist (e.g. Gert 1967).

In any case, it is clear that Hobbes agrees with the early modern conception of morality as aiming to direct agents to discharge obligations irrespective of whether doing so will benefit them in the case at hand. In order that 'all men' be, as he says, 'inexcusable', the moral law can be rendered into a fairly simple formulation: 'do not that to an other, which thou wouldst not have done to thyself' (L XV. 35). Everyone is always obligated by this principle, at least *in foro interno* ('to a desire they should take place'), and when there is sufficient security that others will comply, *in foro externo* ('putting them in act'), regardless of whether the obligated act will benefit the agent or not (L XV. 36).

However we should view Hobbes, there can be no doubt that Locke held all three of normative, agency, and psychological egoism. More specifically, Locke is an egoistic hedonist. He believes that human agents are capable of being moved, and that they have reason to be moved only by thoughts of their own pleasure. God, Locke writes in the *Essay Concerning Human Understanding*, 'has been pleased to join to several thoughts, and several sensations, a perception of delight', and 'if this were wholly separated from all our outward sensations and inward thoughts, we should have no reason to prefer one thought or action to another; negligence to attention, or motion to rest. And so we should neither stir our bodies, nor employ our minds' (*Essay* II. vii. 3). There is, however, an important ambiguity in these remarks, one that Locke attempts to clarify in the *Essay*'s later editions. When we talk about 'reasons', either normative reasons or an agent's reason for acting, we typically have in mind some *consideration*, a proposition, if you like, which, if true, counts in favour of an action or, in the case of an agent's reason, which the agent held true and that she counted in favour of an action. So considered, Locke would be claiming that only *thoughts of pleasure* can motivate, or that human agents can only take such thought to be reasons for acting and act on. Alternatively, we might focus on the hedonic quality of the motivational state, regardless of its content. We might think that being moved to realize some possible state of affairs consists in being (pleasurably) attracted by it or in finding its non-realization painful to contemplate. And this could be so regardless of the contents of the contemplated states. Theoretically, anyway, one might be pleasurably attracted by thoughts of one's own future pain or find painful the thought of experiencing pleasure in the future.

Beginning with the second edition of the *Essay*, Locke both clarifies the distinction between these different lines of thought and tries to combine them. In the first edition, he had held not just that only considerations regarding the agent's pleasure give her normative reasons to act (*normative egoistic hedonism*) but also that agents always act to bring about their own greatest good (maximizing *psychological egoistic hedonism*). '[T]he preference of the Mind [is] always determined by the appearance of Good, greater Good' (*Essay*, 256n.). In the second edition, however, Locke changed his view.

> [W]hat is it that determines the Will in regard to our Actions? And that upon second thoughts I am apt to imagine is not, as is generally supposed, the greater good in view: But some (and for the most part the most pressing) *uneasiness* a Man is at present under. This is that which successively determines the Will, and sets us upon those Actions, we perform. This *Uneasiness* we may call, as it is, *Desire*, as it is an uneasiness of the Mind for want of some absent Good    (*Essay* II. xxi. 31).

Locke does not give up normative egoistic hedonism. He still thinks that only considerations of good (that is, pleasure) or evil (pain) to the agent give her any normative reason to act (as he had put it before, 'to prefer one Thought or Action, to another' (*Essay* II. vii. 3). What has changed is his view about what is necessary actually to motivate action. Thoughts of pleasure or pain that an action would bring about may not motivate us, since such thoughts can leave us cold. To motivate, Locke now holds, the thoughts must involve some 'uneasiness'; desire must have a prick.

We shall return to Locke's theory of desire presently, since Hutcheson makes an important objection to it that is central to his criticism of psychological egoism and his defence of benevolent, other-regarding motivation. But we should note first how Locke's egoism, both psychological and normative, interacts with his theory of morality. Locke is clear, first, that considerations of moral right and wrong are incapable of motivating agents.

> The pleasure that a man takes in any action or expects as a consequence of it is indeed a Good in it self able & proper to move the will. But the Moral Rectitude of it considered barely in it self is not good or evill nor in any way moves the will but as pleasure & pain either accompanies the action it self or is looked on to be a consequence of it.[6]

This does not, however, imperil the existence of moral right and wrong, in Locke's view. The reason is to be found in Locke's theological voluntarism, his doctrine that moral obligation consists in morality's being God's law, which He commands us to follow. It is because God has superior authority over us that we are obligated to do as He commands. That is just what moral obligation is, and any such command would seem to exist independently of our motives for complying with it.

---

[6] From an entry titled '*Voluntas*' in Locke's Commonplace Book (quoted in Colman 1983: 48–9).

Things are not quite so simple, however. Locke also believes that God's commands would have been 'vain' (as they could not possibly have been), if He hadn't also made it possible for his creatures to follow His commands. So we can assume that God has also given us adequate motives to follow them. And Locke criticizes ancient ethics, like Aristotle's, as providing no more than 'names' for virtues that are but 'empty sounds', since the ancients don't connect them to the distinctive practical 'force' of divine law (King 1830: 2, 129–30). By 'force', Locke here means motives created by the 'rewards and punishments' that God 'annexe[s]' to His law.

The resulting picture is as follows. Locke agrees with Hobbes, and other early moderns like Grotius, that human beings would be worse off if all were independently to follow self-interest. We humans face what has come to be called a 'collective action problem', to which morality provides the solution by giving us reasons to act against independent self-interest, in our common interest. God benevolently gives us this solution by addressing commands to us, thereby creating the moral law. And He makes it possible, given our egoistic nature, to follow this law, and so take advantage of this solution, by giving us the incentives of divine sanctions. Without God's commandments and His sanctioning incentives, we would be stuck, if not in a war of all against all, then in something only marginally less unpleasant.

Hobbes and Locke are both representatives of the early modern natural law tradition begun by Grotius, which includes, most prominently, Samuel Pufendorf, but also Bishop Richard Cumberland and others. A central element of this tradition is the connection it stressed between moral obligation and responsibility. What we are morally obligated to do is what we are morally responsible or accountable for doing—as the early modern natural lawyers saw it, to God whose superior authority stands behind and makes His commands binding on us.

The natural lawyers generally agreed that this conceptual connection to accountability creates moral psychological constraints on any intelligible conception of moral obligation. Roughly speaking, someone can be subject to a moral obligation only if he can intelligibly be held responsible for complying with it. And someone can intelligibly be held responsible for complying with an obligation only if he can be expected to know what he is obligated to do *and*, having acquired this knowledge, to be able to act on it.

These ideas were clearly in the background of the changes Locke made in the chapter 'Of Liberty' in the second edition of the *Essay* (II. xxi). He links the very concept of a person to responsibility and the capacity to be obligated and held accountable. 'Person,' he writes, is a 'forensick term appropriating actions and their merit; and so belongs only to intelligent agents capable of a law.' And the identity of a person over time, he says, 'whereby [a person] becomes . . . *accountable*', entails that an agent be able to 'ow[n] or imput[e] to it *self* past actions' on the same grounds 'that it does the present' (*Essay* II. xxvii. 26). Any intelligible concept of moral obligation, in Locke's view, must be linked to that of responsibility.

It must be the case that violations can be 'imputed to [the agent's] election' (*Essay* II. xxi. 56).

Locke then faced two problems. One was to explain how, if psychological egoism is true, agents can be held responsible for doing what is morally right. After all, Locke thought, 'moral rectitude . . . considered barely in itself' does not 'mov[e] the will'; only considerations of the agent's pleasure and happiness do. The solution to this problem, again, is God's eternal sanctions and our knowledge of them. But this raises a second problem, since what actually determines human action, in Locke's view, is not agents' judgements of their long-term happiness and pleasure, but rather their currently strongest desire or 'greatest present uneasiness'. What solves this second problem is the new view of freedom that Locke presents in chapter 21 of the second edition of the *Essay*. Human agents are not simply stuck with their current desires; they are 'at liberty to consider the objects of them, examine them on all sides, and weigh them with others' (II. xxi. 47). By being able to step back from current desires and vividly consider their objects, human beings are able to bring the strength of their current desires, their uneasinesses, into line with their judgements of long-term pleasure in a way that, given God's benevolently designed sanctions, enable us to take responsibility for complying with His commands (Darwall 1995: 156–71; Yaffe: 2000). Through free deliberation, we are able to form desires whose strengths are appropriately in line with long-term good or evil, pleasure or pain, that we have in view.

## III: MORAL DEMANDS AND THE WILL

In this way, Locke tried to link up an egoistic moral psychology with a natural law conception of morality. Though he was a morality/reasons externalist, he nonetheless felt the need to develop a theory of free moral agency that could explain how moral agents can reasonably be held responsible for complying with moral law. In the event, this conception of moral agency proved too externalist still for many of his critics, most obviously, for philosophers outside the natural law tradition, like Cudworth, Leibniz, and Shaftesbury, but also for some within it, like Pufendorf. Shaftesbury objected that in 'refer[ring] all to reward', Hobbes and Locke make virtue 'unnatural' (Whichcote 1698: Preface; Shaftesbury 2001: 15). He thought they conceived the virtuous person to be like a trained animal who goes through his paces for fear of the whip. Cudworth, Leibniz, and Shaftesbury argue that true virtue, by contrast, springs from a form of love that is natural to human beings and intrinsic to moral agency, but which finds no place in Hobbes's and Locke's moral psychology. Moreover, Leibniz, Shaftesbury, and Hutcheson (whose more systematic development of this idea we shall examine presently) oppose their love-based ethics to any based on a conception of law. Cudworth is more equivocal. 'Love', he says, 'is at once a Freedome from all Law, a State of purest Liberty, and yet a Law too, of the most constraining and indispensable Necessity' (Cudworth 1969: 125).

More to the point at this juncture, however, is Cudworth's distinction between two fundamentally distinct kinds of freedom of the will, 'animal free will' and 'moral free will', and his claim that the former is insufficient for moral agency and therefore for moral obligation (Darwall 1995: 144–7). By animal free will, Cudworth means the sort of Lockean freedom just discussed: the capacity to step back from current desires and make a practical judgement of overall good or happiness on which the agent can then effectively act. There is no doubt, Cudworth says, that beings endowed with animal but not moral free will 'might have societies, polities and laws . . . enforced with punishments and rewards to good purpose, in order to the advantage of the private persons and the safety of the whole, which is the very constitution of *Leviathan*' (quoted in Darwall 1995: 145). However, if the only way in which agents can act on the law is to avoid sanctions, then 'this utterly destroys all morality'. A law of this kind is impotent to establish an 'obligation truly moral' (quoted in Darwall 1995: 145). Morality is possible, in other words, only if agency egoism is false.

Samuel Pufendorf makes a similar criticism from within the natural law tradition. Law and obligation properly so-called, Pufendorf says, 'differ in a special way from coercion' (Pufendorf 1934: 91). Non-moral goods and evils like those involved in sanctions 'bear down the will as by some natural weight'. Obligation, however, 'affects the will morally', so that it 'is forced of itself to weigh its own actions, and to judge itself worthy of some censure unless it conforms to a prescribed rule' (1934: 91). So long as an agent can have only self-interested reasons of the sort involved in sanctions for complying with a rule or standard, she cannot see herself as *accountable* for compliance and so cannot take responsibility for conforming to the standard. And if that is so, then she cannot actually be genuinely obligated. Moral obligation requires that the obligated agent be able to take responsibility for compliance by being motivated by her own judgement of blameworthiness or self-blame. It is insufficient even that an agent be capable of judging that God would be in a position to complain were she not to comply, since that could leave *her* cold. What seems to be required is that she be able to be moved by her own (imaginative prospective) blame of herself from a standpoint that she and God (or anyone) can implicitly share (Darwall 2006: 111–14).

I have dealt at some length with these natural law aspects of Hobbes and Locke so that we could see how their conceptions of morality interacted with the forms of egoism they espoused. Many subsequent early modern philosophers shared their desire to account for morality, though not necessarily within a law-based conception of obligation, but these later thinkers generally held that this required rejecting egoism of the various forms we have distinguished (with some notable exceptions;

for example, John Gay and Bishop Berkeley). And they held this by and large for the same reasons. Since moral action and virtue involves action on moral as opposed to self-interested reasons, if agency or psychological egoism were true, moral virtue would be impossible. And if normative egoism were true, moral considerations would not even provide normative reasons for acting at all.

Although, however, later philosophers generally agreed on this, there was nonetheless substantial disagreement about the form that non-egoistic, moral motivation takes. Leibniz, Hutcheson, and to some extent, Shaftesbury and Cudworth, held that moral virtue consists in forms of love and benevolence. Butler, and to some extent Cudworth and Shaftesbury, maintained that it involved moral self-direction that consists in the agent's acting on her own conscientious judgement, including, Butler added, by seconding motives that are potentially at odds with benevolence, like justice. And intuitionists like Samuel Clarke held that action on moral reasons involves motivation through rational insight into universal moral truths. We turn now to considering the arguments these philosophers gave against egoism in its various forms and in favour of the forms of moral motivation they respectively championed.

## IV: The critique of egoism and the case for moral motivation and sentiment

Certainly the philosopher who took on psychological egoism most directly and systematically was Bishop Butler. It is fair to say, in fact, that Butler is widely credited now with having refuted the doctrine. He argued, first, that although there is a virtually tautologous sense in which every action we perform is something we want to do, nothing egoistic follows from that, since 'every particular affection, even the love of our neighbour, is as really our own affection, as self-love' (Butler 1983: 4.7).[7] What matters, again, is the content of our desires or motivating attitudes, and nothing about this content can follow from the fact that we never act except on one of our own desires.

Second, Butler points out that it is simply impossible that every desire could have the agent's pleasure or happiness as its object since pleasure itself typically has an object towards which the agent has a direct positive attitude, we might call it 'liking', and that this is what desire itself also involves.

That all particular appetites and passions are towards external things themselves, distinct from the pleasure arising from them, is manifested from hence; that there could not be this

---

[7] Butler references are to the sermon and paragraph number in the Darwall (1983) edition.

pleasure, were it not for that prior suitableness between the object and the passion: there could be no enjoyment or delight from one thing more than another, from eating food more than from swallowing a stone, if there were not an affection or appetite to one thing more than another.    (Butler 1983: 4.6)

'External' here means external to desire. A desire's object, say to eat food rather than a stone, may be for some experience. The point is that, to get pleasure or enjoyment from an experience, one must like the experience *itself* and not just something further that the experience might cause. Moreover, liking the experience itself in prospect is just what the desire to eat is; the desire's object is not some *further* experience of pleasure that is consequent upon the experience of eating.

Without moving one iota in the direction of psychological egoism or hedonism, therefore, we might grant not just that every action is motivated by some desire of ours, but also that we never act without some aim that is capable of pleasing us (like eating some particular food). It would not follow from this that our real aim is our own pleasure (being pleased), since we can be pleased by something only if we like *it*, and if that is so we will already have a tendency to aim at the thing that gives us pleasure directly. To drive the point home, we might simply imagine an agent who has but one desire, which is some form of benevolence, say, to make others as happy as possible. If that were so, then he would have to be such as to be pleased by others' happiness. But that would not, and in fact could not, mean that the real object of his desire or aim was his own pleasure (taken in the happiness of others).

Butler makes a parallel point about self-interest and self-love. 'The very idea of an interested pursuit', Butler writes, 'necessarily presupposes particular passions or appetites, since the very idea of interest or happiness consists in this, that an appetite or affection enjoys its object.... Take away these affections, and you leave self-love absolutely nothing at all to employ itself about...' (1983: Preface, 37). Since self-love cannot explain our desires for particular objects, psychological hedonism and egoism must be false.

Despite the force of these abstract philosophical arguments against agency and psychological egoism, nothing follows from them directly about whether we are capable of benevolently desiring the good of others for its, or their, own sake. It is consistent with what we have said that every particular desire or passion has as its object some experience or mental state of the desirer. But Butler is surely right to think that the main sources of support for psychological and agency egoism, at least when these do not spring from self-serving cynicism, have historically been abstract philosophical arguments and theories of action that are apt to involve confusions of the kind just discussed. Whether we are capable of benevolence, however, is an empirical question, 'a mere question of fact or natural history'. The evidence here seems fairly clear. Butler concludes: 'that there is some degree of benevolence amongst men, may be as strongly and plainly proved in all these ways, as it could possibly be proved, supposing there was this affection in our nature' (1983: 1.6n.).

If less well-known to readers of succeeding centuries, Francis Hutcheson's arguments against psychological egoism and in favour of benevolent desires as natural in human beings, are no less trenchant. Hutcheson diagnoses the major source of resistance to belief in 'disinterested desires' as the failure to see that desires are basic psychic items that cannot be defined in terms of pleasant or painful sensations. He specifically cites Locke's definition of desire, as 'an uneasy Sensation in the absence of Good', as an instance of this error (Hutcheson 2002: 28). 'Desire is as distinct from any Sensation, as the *Will* is from the *Understanding* or *Senses*.' To convince oneself of this, Hutcheson writes, one need only recall that when one feels such an uneasy sensation, one may in addition '*desir[e] to remove [the] Uneasiness or Pain*' (Hutcheson 2002: 28). Desire is a fundamentally different psychic state from any pleasant or painful sensation. As philosophers these days would put Hutcheson's point, if a desire has some object, say, that I eat some food, then it involves some disposition to bring that object about, say, the state consisting in my eating some food.

Once we see this, we can appreciate that there is no reason *owing to the nature of desire* to think that the objects of desires must be restricted to states of oneself or, *a fortiori*, to one's own pleasure or well-being. Disinterested desires are no less intelligible; we can have an 'ultimate Desire of the Happiness of others' no less than for our own happiness (Hutcheson 2002: 6). Benevolent desires are ultimate in the sense of not being able to be derived from self-interest nor from any other desire. Just as we cannot be 'bribed' to have an intrinsic desire for something that it is not in our nature to desire (e.g. to eat a saucer of mud), so neither could we acquire benevolent desires by learning that it might be in our interest to have them (Hutcheson 2004: 210). The most such a self-interested reflection can give us is the desire to have that desire. It might cause us to 'turn our Attention' to 'Qualitys in the Object' of the desire we want to have, but for us to acquire the desire itself, we must come to want the object (in virtue of its qualities) for its own sake (Hutcheson 2004: 210).

Both Hutcheson's *Inquiry into the Original of Our Ideas of Beauty and Virtue* (1725) and his *Essay on the Nature and Conduct of the Passions and Affections* (1728) are replete with arguments against agency and psychological egoism, and in favour of disinterested benevolent desires. The latter work also contains a powerful argument against normative egoism. Hutcheson argues that benevolence, especially, indeed, universal benevolence, is no less rational or, as Hutcheson puts it, 'calm', a desire than is self-love. Both self-love and benevolence are to be contrasted with appetites and 'passions' that arise in us without any prior thought of their objects and, consequently, without any conception of their objects' *value*. Desires or affections, by contrast, 'arise in our Mind, from the Frame of our Nature, upon Apprehension of Good or Evil in Objects' (Hutcheson 2002: 18). Hutcheson takes it to be a basic truth of human nature *both* that reflection on our own happiness leads to a desire for it (from, as it were, a first-person point of view) *and* that disinterested (third-person) reflection on the happiness of individuals considered independently of their relation to us, leads no less to a desire for that also.

Hutcheson's idea anticipates almost exactly Sidgwick's famous 'duality of practical reason' in *The Methods of Ethics* (1967: Preface). Calm rational deliberation from a first-person standpoint invariably leads us to prefer our own greater to our lesser happiness, and when we contemplate things disinterestedly, we invariably prefer greater rather than lesser *aggregate* happiness, considering everyone's happiness equally. Any variance from these preferences, Hutcheson believes, can be explained by failures of clear thought, either narrowness of perspective or the perturbing influence of passion and appetite. Moreover, much like Sidgwick, Hutcheson takes the view that there is no way of weighing self-love against universal benevolence. Each is a fully rational ultimate desire.[8]

# V: MORAL VIRTUE AS BENEVOLENCE

This entails, as against normative egoism, that benevolence and beneficent conduct are no less rational than self-love and self-interested conduct. But Hutcheson also argues that benevolence, especially universal benevolence, is uniquely *morally* good. This requires him to challenge egoism of a different form, namely, the attitude egoism that he finds in Mandeville. According to Hutcheson, the very existence of morality and moral goodness depends upon a disinterested mental state, although in this case a sentiment or 'Sensation' rather than any motivation or desire, which Hutcheson calls 'moral sense'. Hutcheson's *Inquiry* begins with a definition of 'moral goodness' as a 'Quality apprehended in Actions, which procures Approbation' (2004: 85). 'Approbation' here refers to a disinterested, distinctively moral response that Hutcheson treats, along with 'Condemnation', as the two irreducible 'simple ideas' that together serve as the basic building blocks of all moral ideas (Hutcheson 2004: 214). There are certain motives (all, Hutcheson maintains, forms of benevolence) that are such that, when we contemplate them disinterestedly, we feel approbation, and there are others (malevolence and negligent lack of benevolence) that give rise to disinterested condemnation.

As Hutcheson understands him, Mandeville holds that no such disinterested response exists in human beings, and that human approvals and disapprovals are always self-interested at some level. This is a form of attitude egoism, as we have defined it. Against this position, Hutcheson deploys arguments of the same form he uses to defeat psychological egoism and to support the existence of disinterested desires. The thought that it would benefit me to feel approval or condemnation can

---

[8] For a discussion of this aspect of Hutcheson's views, and its consistency with his doctrine that reason can neither motivate nor criticize ultimate ends, see Darwall (1997b).

cause a desire in me to feel these sentiments, but it cannot give rise to the sentiments themselves, any more than reflection on the benefits of being benevolently motivated can give rise to benevolence. When we 'consul[t] our own breasts', it is as clear as it possibly could be that we naturally feel the disinterested responses of approbation and condemnation.

Just as calm reflection on the prospect of happiness and unhappiness gives rise to a desire for the greatest happiness of all, so likewise, Hutcheson believes, does reflection on benevolence give rise to approbation, with the greatest approbation arising when we contemplate universal benevolence. It follows that benevolence is morally good and universal benevolence is morally best. There is thus a happy (Hutcheson believes, divinely ordained) coincidence between the normative or rational priority of universal benevolence (in its disinterested sphere) and its moral superiority. Moreover, because Hutcheson believes that universal benevolence aims at the greatest happiness of all, he draws the conclusion that moral sense recommends actions to 'our Election' in proportion to their overall happiness. So 'that Action is best which procures the greatest Happiness for the greatest Numbers' (Hutcheson 2004: 125).

Although Hutcheson's formulation of the greatest happiness principle is the first in English, there is good reason to believe that he took it from Leibniz (Hruschka 1991). Leibniz's ethics also give prominence to benevolence or love as an ideal of ethical character or motivation, emphasizing God's universal benevolence as an exemplary standard. Like other critics of voluntarist natural law, such as Cudworth and Shaftesbury, Leibniz stresses an internal source of moral action, a core 'inclination of the soul', over 'external acts', and also like them, places love in this central role (Leibniz 1988a: 72–5). He also anticipates Hutcheson in holding that all the virtues, including justice, can be summed into benevolence. Justice, he says, is 'the charity of the wise man' (Leibniz 1988b: 171). The result, in both writers, is a principle they bequeath to the utilitarian tradition to come, in Leibniz's formulation: 'To act in accordance with supreme reason is to act in such a manner that the greatest quantity of good available is obtained for the greatest multitude possible and that as much felicity is diffused as the reason of things can bear' (quoted in Hruschka 1991: 172).

# VI: MORAL VIRTUE, AUTONOMY, AND PRACTICAL REASON

To this point, we have considered the debate between early modern philosophers, like Locke and Hobbes, who combined some variety of egoism with a law-based conception of morality, on the one hand, and, critics, like Shaftesbury, Leibniz,

Hutcheson, and, to a lesser extent, Cudworth, who combine their rejection of egoism with a dismissal of the modern natural law tradition, substituting for it an ethics of love. To conclude, we should note some reactions against the Hobbes/ Locke combination of egoism and natural law that nonetheless retain a conception of morality as embodying an obligating law, and that deny that moral virtue can be identified with benevolence.

Though they agree with them in rejecting egoism, Butler and rational intuitionists like John Balguy and Samuel Clarke disagree with Leibniz and Hutcheson on three central issues. First, they neither reject the notions of moral obligation, right, and wrong, nor make them subsidiary to an ethics of virtue. Second, they hold that the virtues are various, being neither all forms of nor derivable from benevolence, and that some, like justice and honesty, depend upon independent, obligating moral norms. Third, they hold that moral agency involves a form of self-directing motivation, like Butler's 'conscience' or Clarke and Balguy's 'reason', which differs essentially from any desire like benevolence.

We have already considered Butler's explicit critique of psychological egoism. But there is also a powerful critique of agency and normative egoism that is implicit in his moral psychology. Rational and moral agency, Butler argues, require more complex psychic capacities than self-love can provide. An agent must be capable of stepping back from her various desires, including from self-love and benevolence, and making her own normative *judgements* concerning which she should act on, on which she can then act. In Butler's terms, we do this is through the 'principle of reflection' or 'conscience'. 'It is by this faculty, natural to man, that he is a moral agent, that he is a law to himself' (Butler 1983: 2.8). Acting on our own reflective normative judgements is what genuine autonomy is. The autonomous moral agent is not stuck, as is Hutcheson's, without any perspective from which to assess the competing demands of self-love and benevolence.

No desire is self-authenticating, not even benevolence or self-love. These are simply desires for one's own greatest happiness and the happiness of all, respectively, and one could act on either without doing so because there is any normative *reason* to do so. The latter requires that one be able to step back from either desire, and form an informed, dispassionate, and disinterested attitude toward it on which one can then act. The capacity to form such attitudes is what Butler means by conscience or the principle of reflection. There can be reason to act for one's own good only to the extent that that is approvable by reflection or conscience. Moreover, Butler holds that genuine virtue must involve self-direction by conscience also. Benevolence unguided by moral judgement is not sufficient.

It follows equally that there can be reason to act benevolently for the good of others only if and to the extent that conscience approves of that also. Butler argues that as important as others' welfare and happiness is, moreover, there are numerous instances in which conscience's approvals conflict with acting for the greater good. In his *Dissertation upon the Nature of Virtue*, Butler lists several examples that will provide familiar objections that later deontological writers, like W. D. Ross in the twentieth century, make to utilitarianism. For example, we disapprove of injustice and being false with others even when this would produce more happiness overall (Butler 1983: Diss.8). A virtuous person, consequently, is not simply benevolent; he also has a sense of justice and integrity, among other virtues, with conscience playing a 'superintendent' role.

Rational intuitionists pressed many of these same points against Hutcheson, but with greater stress on the metaphysical independence and necessity of fundamental moral truths—as Clarke put it, 'eternal distinction[s] of Right and Wrong'—and claimed 'natural and necessary difference between Good and Evil antecedent to all arbitrary and positive constitution whatsoever' (Clarke 1897: 496, 495). With the latter, Clarke had an empirical sensibility like Hutcheson's moral sense most clearly in his sights, but there is no reason that the criticism could not apply as equally to a Butlerian conscience if, as Butler sometimes supposed, its content is settled, not by the very nature of morality and moral agency, but by God's election (Butler 1983: Diss.8). In any case, Clarke and the intuitionists were agreed that morality requires sources of distinctively moral motivation that are additional to, and sometimes at odds with, benevolence. Cudworth, Shaftesbury, Leibniz, and Hutcheson were agreed, as against Locke and Hobbes, that morality, as the early moderns conceived it, required a source of motivation additional to self-interest.

## REFERENCES

BUTLER, J. (1983). *Five Sermons*. Ed. Stephen Darwall. Indianapolis, IN: Hackett Publishing Co.

CLARKE, S. (1897). From *Discourse upon Natural Religion*, in *The British Moralists*. Ed. L. A. Selby-Bigge. Oxford: Clarendon Press.

COLMAN, J. (1983). *John Locke's Moral Philosophy*. Edinburgh: Edinburgh University Press.

CUDWORTH, R. (1969). 'A Sermon Preached Before the House of Commons', in C. A. Patrides (ed.), *The Cambridge Platonists*. Cambridge: Cambridge University Press, 90–127.

DARWALL, S. (1995). *The British Moralists and the Internal 'Ought': 1640–1740*. Cambridge: Cambridge University Press.

DARWALL, S. (1997*a*). 'Reasons, Motives, and the Demands of Morality: an Introduction', in S. Darwall, A. Gibbard, and P. Railton (eds), *Moral Discourse and Practice*. New York: Oxford University Press.

DARWALL, S. (1997*b*). 'Hutcheson on practical reason'. *Hume Studies*, 23: 73–89.

DARWALL, S. (2000). 'Normativity and projection in Hobbes's *Leviathan*'. *The Philosophical Review*, 109: 313–47.

DARWALL, S. (2006). *The Second-Person Standpoint*. Cambridge, MA: Harvard University Press.

GAUTHIER, D. (1967). *The Logic of Leviathan: The Moral and Political Theory of Thomas Hobbes*. Oxford: Oxford University Press.

GERT, B. (1967). 'Hobbes and psychological egoism'. *Journal of the History of Ideas*, 28: 503–20.

GROTIUS, H. (2005). *The Rights of War and Peace*. Ed. with an intro. by Richard Tuck. 3 vols. Indianapolis, IN: Liberty Fund.

HAMPTON, J. (1986). *Hobbes and the Social Contract Tradition*. Cambridge: Cambridge University Press.

HEGEL, G. W. F. (1991). *Elements of the Philosophy of Right*. Ed. Allen W. Wood, trans. H. B. Nisbett. Cambridge: Cambridge University Press.

HRUSCHKA, J. (1991). 'The greatest happiness principle and other early German anticipations of utilitarian theory'. *Utilitas*, 3: 165–77.

HUME, D. (1985). *An Enquiry Concerning the Principles of Morals*, in *Enquiries Concerning Human Understanding and Concerning the Principles of Morals*. Ed. L. A. Selby-Bigge, 3rd. ed., rev. P. H. Nidditch. Oxford: Clarendon Press.

HUTCHESON, F. (2002). *An Essay on the Nature and Conduct of the Passions and Affections, with Illustrations on the Moral Sense*. Ed. with an introd. by Aaron Garrett. Indianapolis, IN: Liberty Fund.

HUTCHESON, F. (2004). *An Inquiry Concerning the Original of Our Ideas of Beauty and Virtue*. Ed. with an introd. by W. Leidhold. Indianapolis, IN: Liberty Fund.

IRWIN, T. H. (2003). 'Stoic Naturalism and Its Critics', in B. Inwood (ed.), *The Cambridge Companion to the Stoics*. Cambridge: Cambridge University Press, 345–64.

IRWIN, T. H. (2007). *The Development of Ethics: A Historical and Critical Study*. Vol. I. Oxford: Oxford University Press.

IRWIN, T. H. (2008). *The Development of Ethics: A Historical and Critical Study*. Vol. II. Oxford: Oxford University Press.

KANT, I. (1996). *Practical Philosophy*. Trans. and ed. Mary J. Gregor. Cambridge: Cambridge University Press. References are to page numbers of the Preussische Akademie edition.

KAVKA, G. S. (1986). *Hobbesian Moral and Political Theory*. Princeton, NJ: Princeton University Press.

KAVKA, G. S. (1995). 'The rationality of rule-following: Hobbes' dispute with the Foole'. *Law and Philosophy*, 14: 5–34.

KING, P. (1830). *The Life of John Locke, with Extracts from His Correspondence, Journals, and Common-Place Books*. 2 vols. London: Henry Colburn & Richard Bentley.

LEIBNIZ, G. W. (1988a). 'Opinion on the principles of Pufendorf', in *Political Writings*, 2nd ed. 64–76.

LEIBNIZ, G. W. (1988b). *Political Writings*. Ed. P. Riley. 2nd edn. Cambridge: Cambridge University Press.

LLOYD, S. A. (2009). *Morality in the Philosophy of Thomas Hobbes: Cases in the Law of Nature*. Cambridge: Cambridge University Press.

PRICHARD, H. A. (2002). 'Does Moral Philosophy Rest on a Mistake?' in J. McAdam (ed.), *Moral Writings*. Oxford: Oxford University Press.

PUFENDORF, S. (1934). *On the Law of Nature and Nations*. Trans. C. H. Oldfather and W. A. Oldfather. Oxford: Clarendon Press.

RAND, B. (1900). *The Life, Unpublished Letters, and Philosophical Regimen of Anthony, Earl of Shaftesbury*. London: Swan Sonnenschein.

SCHNEEWIND, J. B. (1998). *The Invention of Autonomy*. Cambridge: Cambridge University Press.

SHAFTESBURY, Earl of (Anthony Ashley Cooper) (2001). *Characteristicks of Men, Manners, Opinions, Times.* Ed. D. den Uyl. 3 vols. Indianapolis: Liberty Fund.

SIDGWICK, H. (1964). *Outlines of the History of Ethics for English Readers.* 6th edn. Boston, MA: Beacon Press.

SIDGWICK, H. (1967). *The Methods of Ethics.* 7th edn. London: Macmillan.

WHICHCOTE, B. (1698). *Select Sermons of Dr. Whichcot.* Ed. A. A. Cooper, 3rd Earl of Shaftesbury. London: A. & J. Churchill.

YAFFE, G. (2000). *Liberty Worth the Name.* Princeton, NJ: Princeton University Press.

# CHAPTER 19

# REALISM AND RELATIVISM IN ETHICS

## CATHERINE WILSON

As philosophers of the early modern period began to reconsider the problems of error, superstition, and illusion, to question traditional authorities, and to devote attention to scientific methodology and the logic of discovery, the problem of the nature and foundations of moral rightness and moral obligation became visible to them as it had not been earlier. The invention of the printing press, identified by Elizabeth Eisenstein as an important 'agent of change' (Eisenstein 1980), extended European intellectual horizons in ways that affected the theory and substance of religion and morality. In the temporal dimension, readers rediscovered the literature of the ancients, especially Stoicism and Epicureanism, thanks to new editions, translations, and commentaries. Plato, too, was recognized as a moralist, and the expansive discussions of Cicero and Plutarch showed how it was possible to think about morality outside of a Christian framework. In the geographical dimension, the exploration of the New World and the Near and Far East furnished readers with written accounts of Mexico, Peru, Turkey, and India. In England, the censorship of books and pamphlets was relaxed in the anarchic conditions of the Civil War and the Interregnum, during the 1640s and 1650s. Visionaries claimed that an inner light or God Himself had revealed to them the truth of strange or disturbing doctrines, and they broadcast their views widely, though not with impunity.

Libertines and antinomians claimed that what was conventionally deemed sinful was in accordance with nature or even pure Christian living.

Michel de Montaigne, at the start of the early modern period, declared that 'there is no constant Existence, neither of the Objects Being, nor our own. Both we, and our Judgements, and all mortal things, are evermore incessantly running and rowling, and consequently, nothing certain can be establish'd from the one to the other, both the judging and the judged being in a continual Motion and Mutation' (Montaigne 1685: 429). This typically humanist scepticism reflected a wide acquaintance with human customs and moral texts, and the absence of confidence-inspiring examples of recent knowledge acquisition. The variety of opinions and practices looked like a permanent disposition, and one's own might appear quite arbitrary. The Cartesian interpretation of 'secondary' qualities, as ideas that constitute a subjective response to an external stimulus, would soon put additional pressure on the notions of objective good and evil. According to Hobbes,

Whatsoever is the object of any mans Appetite or Desire; that is it, which he for his part calleth *Good*: And the object of his Hate, and Aversion, *Evill*; And of his Contempt, *Vile* and *Inconsiderable*...For these words of Good, Evill, and Contemptible, are ever used with relation to the person that useth them: There being nothing simply and absolutely so; nor any common Rule of Good and Evill, to be taken from the nature of the objects themselves...    (Hobbes 1996: 39).

In the vast catalogue of actual and possible human practices and conventions, were there right and wrong ways to structure human relations, and, if so, how could they be determined? As patterns of classification of good and evil are idiosyncratic, Hobbes saw no basis for awarding superiority to one person's scheme over another's 'insomuch that while every man differeth from other in constitution, they differ also one from another concerning the common distinction of good and evil' (Hobbes 1994: 44). Spinoza agreed: 'As far as good and evil are concerned, they also indicate nothing positive in things, considered in themselves, nor are they anything other than modes of thinking, *or* notions we form because we compare things to one another' (SC 545: *Ethics* IV: Preface). We deem what is useful to us 'good' and what prevents us attaining our desires 'evil'.

Philosophers and clerics wondered how to draw the line between 'indifferent things' that might surprise or arouse negative feelings but that could not be matters of moral obligation or prohibition and practices that ought to be required or proscribed. Ongoing religious strife prompted analogous questions about rites and rituals; were they expressive choices that might seem peculiar but harmed no one, or were they deeply symbolic and provocative acts of aggression? Individual early modern philosophers did not try to adjudicate between realism and relativism, which they did not recognize explicitly as distinct philosophical positions or families of positions. But they raised questions about religious epistemology and the foundations of morals, and attempted to steer a course between what they saw as the prejudices and intellectual laziness of untutored people and the harshness and rigidity of the theologians. Although there was no single *telos* to the writings of early modern philosophers, the underlying issues may be interpreted retrospectively in terms of some familiar categories of moral epistemology.

For the medievals, the source of moral obligation resided in the vertical relationship of authority between the Creator and his Creation, and the Creator's power of reward and punishment. The Thomist position in ethics was and remains that morality is God-given, and that 'reason cannot find or invent a new order' (Hochstrasser and Schroder 2003: 7), and the epistemology of divine command was uncomplicated, if somewhat circular. The Word of God, as revealed in Scripture, constituted moral truth, and the provision of so many evident moral truths in Scripture confirmed both its status as a book of divinely-inspired morals and the status of the traditional prohibitions and obligations that it commanded. Theological writers of the seventeenth century continued to avail themselves of every possible adjective of petrification to emphasize the ineluctability of morals. Even for the gentle Cambridge Platonist Benjamin Whichcote, morality was eternal, immutable, and appreciated by reason: '[In] the Measures of Vertue and Vice; the Grand Instances of Morality; there can be no Allowance, no Variation; because they are Matters unalterable, unchangeable, indispensible . . .' (Whichcote 1698: 81).

While the humanist scholars of the Renaissance who were familiar with the moral writings of the ancient pagans had questioned divine command theory as a basis for ethics, they had not formulated coherent and widely acceptable alternatives. To deny that ethics is founded in God's commands implied, to many early modern philosophers as it had to their ancestors, that there could be neither moral knowledge nor moral propriety. The atheist depicted in the apocryphal, often-quoted Book of Wisdom of 'Solomon', has a superficial knowledge of Epicureanism. 'Let us enjoy the good things that are present', this amoralist with no fear of hell says, 'and let us speedily use the creatures as in youth. . . . Let us oppress the poor just man, and not spare the widow, nor honour the ancient grey hairs of the aged' (*Book of Wisdom*, King James Version 2:10). The identification of selfish indifference, untrustworthiness, and predation with atheism was typical in late as well as early seventeenth-century polemics. Carneades, who appears as the author's foil in the Prolegomena to Hugo Grotius's *On the Law of War and Peace*, asserts that men, like animals, seek only the satisfaction of their own interests, that law and custom are transitory and designed for expediency, and that justice does not exist or is best ignored by the powerful.

Nevertheless, beginning with Grotius himself, philosophers began to propose and defend foundations for ethics that reversed the traditional order of reasons. God has ordained the rules of morality, they proposed, because, given human nature, these rules are conducive to human happiness in the temporal dimension. They recognized that morality was not an established code of duties and prohibitions, but a subject for open-ended theoretical inquiry, and they conceded the difficulty of securing foundations for moral knowledge and establishing a method of demonstration for moral truths as secure as those being explored for mathematics and natural science. Joseph Butler emphasized the controversial nature of his enquiry by referring to 'Morals, considered as a Science, concerning which speculative Difficulties are daily raised' (Butler 1749: iii). The subject, he thought, required 'a very peculiar Attention'.

By the mid-eighteenth century, secular foundations for morality were widely assumed, and philosophers discovered, articulated, and defended new grounds for obligation and new incentives for conformity. These developments paralleled the shifting epistemology of the natural sciences, in which the discovery of novelties and the provision of new explanations took precedence over the formalization of the already known. These grounds and reasons reflected an increased understanding of the horizontal relations between human beings, and the impediments to the realization of human aims. On the emerging view, the objectivity of moral norms depended neither on the human theological situation, nor on the heart's or the faculty of reason's access to universal propositions, but on needs and propensities, on the need for co-operation and trust in human relations if the benefits of social life were to be realized, and the mixture of malice, greed, sociability, and altruism that was supposed to characterize human beings. As Grotius had put it earlier, '[C]are for society in accordance with the human intellect' gives rise to '[justice] properly so called', and the obligations to refrain from theft, keep promises, and compensate for damages would exist 'even if we were to suppose (what we cannot suppose without the greatest wickedness) that there is no God, or that human affairs are of no concern to him' (Grotius 2005: III, 1747–8).[1]

# I: ANCIENTS AND MODERNS

Ancient moral philosophy had been organized into sects or schools, comprising Cynics, Epicureans, Stoics, Academicians, Peripatetics, and others. These schools contested one another's positions in ontology, defending or rejecting atomism,

---

[1] Several historians give a *telos* to moral philosophy in the early modern period, or identify in it a basic dialectic. Stephen Darwall (1995) sees British moral philosophy between Hobbes and Hume as an ongoing discussion of the source of moral obligation—whether it is internal and spontaneous, or external and coercive. J. B. Schneewind (1998) describes the progress of moral philosophy from Montaigne to Kant as a gradual 'invention of autonomy', which implied the rejection of a morality of obedience to an external, usually divine, legislator. Schneewind further contrasts the pragmatism of the natural law theorists who, following Grotius, saw human conflict as inevitable and unending with the perfectionism of philosophers like Malebranche, whom he regards as a significant influence on later moralists (Schneewind 1998: 225 ff).

final causes, providence, and so on, as well as debating the nature of human happiness and moral goodness and their relationship to pleasure. Even if each school considered itself to be in possession of the unique truth and the others wrong or mostly so, the student was in principle free to choose amongst them, lending an elective and so relativistic aspect to moral theory. The philosophically engaged continued to make choices in the early modern period as they had in antiquity, thanks to the publication of new editions of classical texts. Cicero's works began to appear in print in the last quarter of the fifteenth century, and Seneca's in the early sixteenth. A neo-Stoical strand was evident in French drama, in the novel, and in philosophy by the end of the sixteenth century (Moreau 1999), and Cicero's letters and treatises, especially *On Duties*, *On Ends*, and the *Tusculan Disputations*, were cited throughout the seventeenth and eighteenth centuries; Locke and the Cambridge Platonists drew on him equally, despite their differences. Cicero sharply distinguished duty from interest and the ethical from the pleasure-enhancing. The exercise of the virtues could entail the loss of external goods, pain and distress; this was seen as in no way detracting from the obligatoriness of the virtues or their contribution to a morally good life.

A neo-Epicurean strand, somewhat less confident and robust, also became evident as the texts of Epicurus and his follower, the poet Lucretius, were translated and read. As 'honesty', moral right, and natural sociability were characteristically Ciceronian moral concepts, pleasure, human agreement or convention, and human welfare or utility were characteristically Epicurean. For the Epicureans, the enjoyment of pleasure and the avoidance of pain were the natural aim of every animal and, accordingly, the ground of ethics and political concord. Under different conditions of life, and for different agents, the painful and pleasurable consequences of actions varied, bringing a relativistic dimension into their ethics. The Epicurean agent's ability to imagine the future consequences of various actions, including the wrathful retaliation of others for antisocial actions, gave him or her access to moral knowledge on the latter scheme. Moral ignorance and moral failure, on this latter view, arose from the inability to perceive correctly one's long-term hedonic interests and to appreciate the requisites of securing them. This basically egoistic form of consequentialism, married however to the presumption of divine retribution and reward, resurfaces in Locke.

In France, the leading moralists of the late seventeenth and early eighteenth centuries, including La Rochefoucauld, La Fontaine, and Molière, were literary figures rather than academic philosophers (Rattner and Danzer 2006). Alternative realities were used for moral suasion or simply for escapism in a characteristically French format: utopian treatises that mimicked the popular travel literature of the period. Thomas More had furnished the model in his *Utopia* of 1516, which described an imaginary society whose attitudes and practices with respect to labour, recreation, religious observance, equality, and sex and gender, were more 'reasonable' and humane than they were in the real world. Representative works, which include Gabriel de Foigny: *La Terre australe connue* (1676), Daniel Veiras: *L'Histoire des Severambes* (1677–9) and Claude Gilbert: *Histoire de Calejava* (1700), provide information about how their authors judged their existing societies (Leibacher-Ouvrard 1989).

The absence of a strong line of theoretical development in academic moral philosophy in France in the early modern period is perhaps to be explained by both external and internal considerations. From the external perspective, French atheism and libertinism perturbed the orthodox, but censorship was more effective than in the English context, and these clandestine movements did not produce overt polarization and so open intellectual debate. Only Gassendi, who moved in libertine circles, was able to articulate a form of Epicurean moral and political theory (Gassendi 1699). By contrast, the splintering of the Anglican Church into numerous Protestant sects in England, and the role played by the radical sects and their opponents in the politics of the Interregnum, had given questions of truth and epistemic authority a particular urgency in England.

The dominance of Cartesianism in French academic philosophy was an internal factor limiting development. While Descartes' personal ethical views as expressed in his letters are characteristically thoughtful, original, and interesting, it cannot be said that Descartes advanced moral epistemology, and there is no authentically Cartesian tradition that might link Cartesian epistemology and philosophy of science to moral knowledge. Cartesian anthropology, unlike Hobbesian anthropology, was concerned with the health and illness of the human body, not with the health and illness of society. When faced with a sick soul in the person of the Princess Elizabeth, Descartes had little idea what to say. He announced repeatedly that he did not like writing on ethics (AT V 86–7; CSMK I 326). He defended a pragmatic conception of morals: one ought to conform to the customs of one's country, whatever they are, so as to fit in and be able to live unmolested (AT VI 22–7; CSM I 122–4), while maintaining grandly that God was the cause of 'all order, every law, and every reason for anything's being good or true' (AT VII 435; CSM II 293). By contrast, for Leibniz and Malebranche, the perfections of God imply not only a permission to human beings to perfect their knowledge but a duty to seek personal and social moral advancement. Malebranche believes that there exists an infinity of moral truths, only some of which are currently known to us. He distinguishes between 'morality', which is conventional and 'changes according to places and times' (he cites hard drinking as German morality, and duelling as old French (Malebranche 1699: 15–16) and the duties known by universal reason that accord with immutable order, though he confesses that the immutable order is 'not easie to be found' (Malebranche 1699: 17). For Leibniz, the highest purpose of morality is to spread 'the greatest possible happiness' in the terrestrial sphere that constitutes the 'noblest part of the universe' (LL 327; GP IV 462).

A distinct strand of epistemological and moral pessimism, meanwhile, emerged from the confrontation with casuistry. Casuistry, associated especially with Jesuit authors, was a necessary but contested method applied to the resolution of concrete moral dilemmas. It involved attempts to give precise definitions to moral terms such as 'lying' and 'chastity' that appeared in blanket prohibitions and obligations and the collection of arguments for and against particular courses of action, with justification proceeding either from the weight of learned opinion ('probabilism') or, more controversially, from the mere existence of some specimen of learned opinion on one side or the other.[2] Pascal's *Lettres Provinciales*, composed in 1656–7, ridiculed and excoriated the Jesuits as apologists for corruption and laxity, but his arguments were aimed more broadly against any systematic approach to morals that did not recognize essential human depravity. As he laments in his *Pensées*, from concupiscence 'we have established and developed . . . admirable rules of polity, ethics, and justice, but at its root, the evil root of man, this evil stuff of which we are made is only concealed, it is not pulled up' (Pascal 1966: 211).

Pierre Bayle reversed Pascal's stance to argue that the absolute requirements for subscription and compliance of both religion and morality were incompatible with human nature, that, for every human being, 'the reigning Passion of his Soul, the Biass of his Constitution, the Force of inveterate Habits, and his Taste and Tenderness for some Objects more than others' will always make obedience to moral and religious authority impossible (Bayle 1708: I, 272). Both Pascal and Bayle drew comparisons between the unfathomability, infinite depth, or opacity of nature and our epistemological helplessness in the face of it, and the moral helplessness of individual human beings. This position contrasts with the optimism of Locke and Butler, for whom our minds are well adapted to moral knowledge and for whom our motivational structure is in principle adequate for correct behaviour.

The capacity of all human beings to read and understand Scripture by themselves and the 'Priesthood of Believers' are fundamental articles of Protestantism. The doctrines that access to moral truth is obtained with the help of the 'candle of the lord' and that the godly can do no wrong were meanwhile developed to new extremes in the Interregnum period of the English Civil War when censorship was temporarily suspended and effective policing became difficult. Members of dissident religious groups, including Seekers, Levellers, Muggletonians, Diggers, Ranters, and Quakers claimed intuitive or personally revealed theological and moral knowledge of a heterodox form.[3] According to Ranter moral logic, sin was impossible for God's creatures; either it did not really exist except in men's estimation, or it was good to engage in base actions insofar as they were liberating

---

[2] Casuistry was also deeply mistrusted by many English moralists (Sampson 1988).

[3] Friedman describes the methodology of one such visionary, the Ranter George Foster. 'The visions . . . took two forms. At times, God would speak directly to Foster and impart some truth in direct conversation. More often, however, God would show Foster an image and ask him what he saw. Foster would then describe the images in detail and God would then explain their meanings. The two formats were used interchangeably . . .' (Friedman 1987: 128).

to individuals and subversive of the social order. While some Ranters merely flaunted convention and Puritan prescription with merry disinhibited behaviour—singing, dancing, and whistling—others thought it possible for human beings to be laws unto themselves. If they 'were acted & guided by that inward law of righteousnesse within', said Bauthumley, 'there need be no laws of men, to compell or restrain men . . .' (quoted in Smith 1983: 260).

The epistemic authority of inspired prophets, ancient and contemporary, was strenuously contested by several early modern philosophers. The question how to separate truth from error and how to frame sound hypotheses concerning invisible entities concerned them in the moral and theological sciences as well as in the natural sciences. Genuine moral and political understanding was to be distinguished not only from the pronouncements of the ancients, but also from the work of the imagination and fancy (Wilson 1993). Hobbes decisively rejected conscience, associated as it was with rebellious sentiments, as a source of valid political opinion. As far as he was concerned, appeals to illumination and inner conviction were divisive and dangerous. While no one could prevent anyone from believing what they liked, justice and injustice were to be defined and justice upheld by the Sovereign and his deputies. Spinoza too explicitly rejected prophetic utterances as a source of social direction. Prophecy, according to Spinoza, is 'certain knowledge about something revealed to men by God' (Spinoza 2007: 13), and 'although we clearly understand that God can communicate with men directly, nevertheless, for a person to know things which are not contained in the first foundations of our knowledge and cannot be deduced from them, his mind would necessarily have to be vastly superior, far surpassing the human mind' (Spinoza 2007: 19). Apart from Christ, he claimed, no human being has received direct illumination from God, except through their imagination.

## II: The moral law of nature

Legal theory, as it was derived from Roman jurisprudence and incorporated into scholastic philosophy in the medieval period, posited an immutable order in the moral law of nature (pp. 475 ff.). Richard Hooker's eloquent *Laws of Ecclesiastical Polity*, first published in 1593, emphasized an important and influential Thomistic distinction between, on one hand, the laws that direct individuals 'in the means whereby they tend to their own perfection' and, on the other, the laws that touch them 'as they are sociable parts united into one Body', which oblige them to prefer the communal good to their individual good (Hooker 1666: 7). The law of nature, whose existence was said to be denied by Epicureans and Sceptics, old and new, was argued by its proponents to be evident from the *consensus gentium*, the agreement of all or nearly all nations and tribes; from the phenomena of conscience and self-reproach, to which all, or nearly all are subject; from the lawfulness observed in corporeal nature; from the need for such a law if human society was to exist; and because, as Locke put it, 'without natural law there would be neither virtue nor vice... there is no fault, no guilt, where there is no law' (Locke 1997: 88). James Tyrell, in his epitome of Cumberland's *De legibus naturae*, declared that

we are both sufficiently agreed what we understand by this Term, since we both thereby mean certain Principles of immutable Truth and Certainty, which direct our voluntary Actions concerning the election of good, and the avoiding of evil Things, and so lay an Obligation, as to our external Actions, even in the state of Nature, and out of a Civil Society, or Common-weal. That such eternal Truths are necessarily and unavoidably presented to, and perceived by Men's Minds, and retained in their Memories, for the due ordering or governing of their Actions, is what is here by us affirmed, and by them as confidently denied.   (Tyrrell 1692: 2–3)

The law of nature was said by Christian writers to be 'written in our hearts, prompting us to worship... God; to be just in our Dealings; to honour our Parents, and the like' (Morland 1695: 105–6). It stood above, and so either justified or superseded legal custom and the conventions that characterized different regions and regimes, 'the Customs observ'd by Princes and States among themselves' (Lloyd 1691: 50), so that violations of the law of nature could in principle justify resistance to authority.

As the prominence of the debates over casuistry indicate, what the concept of a moral law of nature won with respect to intuitive acceptability and universal acknowledgement, it lost with respect to useful applicability. Rarely did writers attempt to specify the laws of nature, beyond a few prohibitions on unnatural sexual and familial relations and basic familial duties of maintenance and the political duty of obedience, though Grotius argued influentially and morally for the appropriateness of international regulations that would make wars less cruel and barbarous. The notion of natural law lent itself nevertheless to creative reinterpretation, and Hobbes's and Cumberland's correctives to and development of Grotius's line of argument are significant in this regard. Locke's views will be discussed later.

Hobbes had no use for the law of nature construed as a *supra*-civic source of authority that could justify disobedience to an established regime on the grounds of the conscience of the individual. He maintained, however, that the law of nature directed individuals to their own self-preservation, and that concern for the self was the true basis of human society. In his *Leviathan*, he declared that moral and civil philosophy were the 'Science of what is *Good* and *Evill*, in the conversation, and Society of Man-Kind', and he left their objectivity in no doubt (1996: 110). He contrasted his own scientific approach with the subjectivity of the ancient philosophers, who, he thought, had elevated their preferences into dogma. It was pointless to argue over whether the good for human life consisted in pleasure, happiness, or the exercise of virtue, and equally pointless to argue over the necessity or dispensability of external goods. 'There is no such *Finis ultimus* . . . nor *Summum Bonum* . . . as is spoken of in the Books of the old Morall Philosophers' (Hobbes 1996: 70). Human beings were driven by their various needs and wants, and the tranquillity of the sage was psychologically impossible to achieve.

Hobbes described manners as 'small morals', which one sympathizer, the anti-Platonic philosopher Samuel Parker, glossed as 'skill in all the Arts of behaviour and conversation' (Parker 1666: 27). Hobbes might as well have described morals as 'grand manners', for he produced a catalogue of nineteen social rules, which he denominated the laws of nature, including the imperatives to show respect for the persons, characters, and lives of others, to accept an equal division of goods, to use impartial judges, and to be forgiving and complaisant (Hobbes 1996: 91–109). These laws differ from traditional laws of nature in a number of ways. First, they are not addressed to biological relationships, such as that obtaining between parent and child, nor do they proscribe any sex acts; nor are they concerned with hierarchical relationships. Rather, they concern civic and social relations between and amongst equals. Second, they are by no means engraved on every heart; indeed they are 'too subtile . . . to be taken notice of by all men; whereof the most part are too busie in getting food, and the rest too negligent to understand' (Hobbes 1996: 109). They are simply true—acknowledged or not. Third, unlike the traditional laws of nature, Hobbes's laws are said to 'oblige in conscience', but they are not obligatory under all circumstances. '(H)e that should be modest, and tractable, and performe all he promises, in such time, and place, where no man els should do so, should but make himself a prey to others, and procure his own certain ruine, contrary to the ground of all Lawes of Nature, which tend to Natures preservation' (Hobbes 1996: 110).

While Hobbes declared that there was no *summum bonum*, he meant this only in the sense the ancients attached to the term. All reasonable men, in his view, whatever else they desired and pursued, and however fractious they showed themselves to be, desired peace and the benefits of civilization in the form of the products of human industry and safe travel and were averse to war and the loss of their lives and possessions. Obedience to the laws of nature was the essential precondition of their success in achieving their desires. Moral ignorance reflected nothing more than a lack of insight into cause and effect relationships. What was salient for his critics, however, was Hobbes's notion that moral properties arose from a contract or agreement, and that there were no antecedent obligations that could be enforced before contracts (Hobbes 1996: 101). The terms 'just' and 'unjust', he declared provocatively, have no application until there is a coercive power in place (Hobbes 1996: 101), and the doctrine that it is sinful to act against one's conscience was 'repugnant to Civill Society' (Hobbes 1996: 223). To Hobbes, the need for a supreme authority whose peacemaking decrees could be fully enforced was an inevitable deduction from anthropology and history; and so pressing was the need, in his eyes, for such a ruler that he closed his eyes for the most part to the objection—better supported than his own conjecture by anthropology and history—that any temporal ruler holding absolute power is unlikely to limit themselves to the role assigned to them of furthering peace, human development, and civilization. It was not only republicans who took issue with Hobbes; his views were regarded by theologians as cynical, demeaning, and demoralizing. Bishop Bramhall commented that 'If men had sprung up from the earth in a night like mushromes or excrescences, without all sense of honour, justice, conscience, or gratitude he could not have vilified the human nature more than he doth' (Bramhall, 1657: 465–6). Hobbes's contractualist interpretation of obedience and obligation was said to be appropriate for an alternative world in which men lived without natural authority or religion, but to fail to reflect the hierarchically-organized world into which humans as a matter of fact are born.

Richard Cumberland's treatise, *De legibus naturae* (1672), was one of the most important moral treatises of the late seventeenth century. Conveniently abbreviated, edited, and translated by James Tyrrell, it is a complex and deep treatment that is in many respects critical of Hobbes. Cumberland denied that all men had a right to all things in the state of nature; he ascribed to human beings a divinely-implanted motive of benevolence and a desire for the common good, and he attributed free will to humans as distinct from animals. He further maintained that the laws of nature obligated only insofar as they represented divine impositions backed by the power of punishment and reward. In other respects, however, Cumberland rehabilitated the Hobbesian programme that had laboured under such opprobrium. He too proposed to consider man as 'a natural Body, as an Animal, and also as a rational Creature . . . subject to the same Laws of Matter and Motion with other things' (Tyrell 1692: f3). He agreed that the purpose of morals was, broadly speaking, to make human beings happy in their temporal lives and to alleviate their miseries, rather than to bring them closer to God.

# III: Relativism and the role
## of travel literature

Montaigne had thrown down the gauntlet in his essay 'On the Cannibals', and declared that 'we have no other level of Truth and Reason, than the Example and Idea of the Opinions and Customs of the place wherein we Live' (Montaigne 1685: 366). La Mothe Le Vayer offered many examples of moral diversity in his pseudonymous dialogue of 1630–1, which purported to show the impossibility of justification as opposed to mere submission (pp. 232–2). Yet these sceptics had no followers who were willing explicitly to affirm and develop the idea that opinion and custom were the standard of truth in morality, or that there was no such thing as moral truth.

On the fringes of the learned world, however, some libertine and antinomian sects maintained that no actions were obligatory, and that as noted there could be no sin because God is the author of all actions; 'all is permitted'. These sects constituted a small, if disturbing minority, but many more writers were impressed by the variety and strangeness of human moral and legal codes, which left them unsettled and wondering. In some regions in which Christianity was unknown or barely known, indigenous civilizations had developed advanced political and economic structures with their own legal and moral codes. In other regions, human beings appeared to observers to be living in a morally rudderless state of nature. Arguments for the truth of moral and theological principles drawn from the *consensus gentium* (the agreement of all) inevitably lost credibility as the true variety of human beliefs and customs became evident. Thomas Blount, following Montaigne, remarked on 'the great diversity of Laws and Customs in the World'. He cited the killing of aged parents, the boiling and mashing of the dead for food, brutality to women, the nakedness of virgins, and the unchastity of their married counterparts. There is a country where 'whenever the King spits, the greatest Ladies of his Court put out their hands to receive it' (Blount 1692: 68). Blount decided that 'there is no Opinion or Imagination so idle or ridiculous, which is not established by Laws and Customs, in some place or other', and that 'we are civil or uncivil, good or bad, foolish or wise, or any thing else according to Custom'. Blount seemed undecided whether the existence of these practices and our spontaneous reaction to them implied that there was no valid epistemological perspective from which to view one's own customs, or whether it implied that we can judge authoritatively of the absurdity or wrongness of other people's customs, or indeed whether both are the case. Tolerance and cool, objective consideration were in any case recommended. A wise man, he concluded, 'ought to suspend his Judgement, and not to be over-forward in Censuring and Condemning the Practices and Customs of other Nations' (Blount 1692: 74).

To be sure, European philosophers saw a relationship between what appeared callous and cruel in the practices of savages and their ignorance of other branches of knowledge such as architecture, mathematics, and science. Leibniz argued that Europeans had every right to suppose that they had more good sense than savages since they subdued them 'almost as easily as they do the beasts' (LRB 98). But he allowed that the savages' morality might be superior insofar as 'they have neither greed for the accumulation of goods nor ambition to dominate', and he observed that that 'intercourse with Christianity has made them worse in many respects' (LRB 99). Many Christian authors took an uncompromising attitude towards the heathen. Samuel Clarke, whose contempt extended to 'Mahometens' and Jews, argued that a divine revelation was necessary for true morality, although those barbarous tribes that had not received it could manage 'in performing the functions of the Animal Life, and directing themselves wholly by the Inclinations of Sense' (Clarke 1732: 319).

Tolerance expressed towards strange and disturbing practices might imply the adoption of a critical stance towards the mores of one's own society. John Dunton suspected that 'it has bin the fatal...happiness, or rather Crime of most other *Ramblers*, Real or Feign'd, who have committed their Observations and Adventures to Writing, to *encourage Vice* by their Examples, even while they pretend to reprove it in their words' (Dunton 1691: 4–5). Many examples of moral otherness concerned sexual morality and the treatment of women; this dimension of human life garnered more attention than the morality of gift-giving, labour, wealth, and other human activities, revealing some uneasiness in European Christians who had their own official ideals and experienced some discomfort with what they could not fail to recognize as hypocrisy.

Moralists who posited innate moral knowledge were necessarily concerned to stress that there was little real underlying disagreement about right and wrong. Butler, who conceded 'the Appearance...of some small Diversity amongst Mankind with respect to...their natural Sense of moral Good and Evil' (Butler 1749: 26), minimized it. If, he maintained, we understand what we mean by the shape of the human body, we can understand what we mean by the moral standard to be applied to human life; all that is required is that we show 'men to themselves... what Course of Life and Behaviour their real Nature points out' (Butler 1749: 27). Locke had earlier put this real nature into question. He began his philosophical career as a rather critical natural law theorist. In Essay V of his youthful *Essays on the Law of Nature*, he argues that there is a law of nature that establishes the standard of right and wrong, but that the standard 'cannot be known from [the] general consent of men'. Nor is it represented in positive consent arising from relationships founded on common interests and convenience—'instinctual compacts'. This is shown by the ubiquity of vices, wicked conventions, and evil traditions. Most nations, he noted, revel in 'plunder, deceit, oppression, assault, and in gaining as many possessions as they can by force of arms: all this is regarded as true glory and the height of generalship' (Locke 1997: 111). There is no vice, infringement of moral law or moral wrong so horrifying and contrary to human nature that 'anyone who consults the history of the world and observes the affairs of men will not readily perceive to have been not only privately committed somewhere on earth, but also approved by public authority and custom. Nor has there been anything so shameful in its nature that it has not been either sanctified by religion, or put in the place of virtue and abundantly rewarded with praise' (Locke 1997: 109).

This litany of moral outrages continues in the early pages of his *Essay Concerning Human Understanding*. Here Locke presented his own frightful catalogue of the moral practices of savages, including patricide, infanticide, the discarding of female progeny, bestiality, and multiple sex partners for women. These examples were drawn from Isaac Vossius, Jean de Thévenot, Garcilaso de la Vega, and John Lery, to show that neither care for children, nor reverence for human life, nor respect for women is a universal principle. Locke then took on a conceptually difficult task: to determine the origin of our moral notions in the causal relations that obtain between the mind and the world, while at the same time defending the notion of universally binding obligations willed by God.

# IV: LOCKE AND THE OBJECTIVITY
## OF MORAL TRUTH

Locke wrote the *Essay* with aims that he presented as modest but which were in fact ambitious. 'Our Business here is not to know all things', he declared in the Introduction, 'but those which concern our Conduct.' 'If', he thought, 'we can find out those Measures, whereby a rational Creature put in that State, which Man is in, in this World, may, and ought to govern his Opinions, and Actions depending thereon, we need not be troubled, that some other things escape our Knowledge' (*Essay* I. i. 6). The difficulty of acquiring knowledge of corporeal nature was contrasted by Locke with the ease of knowing morality, a theme later elaborated by Butler in his sermon on human ignorance (1749: 314).

To Locke, it seemed that moral knowledge ought in principle to be more easily obtained than knowledge of substances such as 'Gold' or 'Opium', insofar as their inner essences were forever hidden from the inquirer, and their powers could be determined only by laborious trial and error. By contrast, morally relevant terms such as 'Murder' and 'Justice' were 'mixed modes' made by the mind, and their referents could not be obscure in the same way. Locke's moral epistemology is notoriously tangled, but he deserves credit for suggesting that moral inquiry is an open-ended process in which, provided the inquiry is carried out carefully and impartially, improvement in beliefs is virtually guaranteed (Wilson 2003). So he implies a parallel between natural science and morals even while arguing that moral inquiry alone is 'suited to our natural Capacities', and indeed is the 'proper Science and Business of Mankind in general' (*Essay* IV. xxi. 11).

The savages, according to Locke, were ignorant and misguided. Morality, no more than advanced mathematics, could be what Whichcote termed 'Things of Natural Knowledge, or of first Inscription in the Heart of Man by God . . . known to be true as soon as ever they are proposed' (Whichcote 1698: 8). Instead, everywhere people take their own 'reverenced Propositions', as principles for judging of 'Truth and Falsehood, Right and Wrong...' (*Essay* I. iii. 24). Acquiring correct moral views was hard work; it required 'Reasoning and Discourse, and some Exercise of the Mind, to discover the certainty of their Truth' (*Essay* I. iii. 1). Yet while Locke suggested in this manner that moral inquiry was open-ended and productive of new and certain knowledge, his fallback position was that a proper education in one's youth based on the New Testament and the writings of Cicero would supply all the truly obligatory elements of morality. This was no misfortune in Locke's mind, for, even while he argued for a universal standard of morality that might be unknown to certain peoples but was nevertheless binding on them, he believed that this standard applied only to a limited number of moral items. Much of human practice concerned 'indifferent things'. Locke followed Hobbes in denying that there was a *summum bonum*, and ridiculed the ancient philosophers who, he said, 'might have as reasonably disputed, whether the best Relish were to be found in Apples, Plumbs, or Nuts; and have divided themselves into Sects upon it' (*Essay* II. xxi. 55). A good deal could be left to the individual, and we need not 'clog every action of our lives, even the minutest of them . . . with infinite Consideration before we began it and unavoidable perplexity and doubt when it is donne' (Locke 1976: I, 559).

In Chapter XIX of the fourth book of his *Essay*, Locke in his turn addressed the problem of 'Enthusiasm' in predictably negative terms. He declared that all acceptable propositions are either irresistibly self-evident, or demonstrated, or probable insofar as the arguments upon which they rest are persuasive. God can, Locke owns, 'enlighten the Understanding by a Ray darted into the Mind immediately from the Fountain of Light' (*Essay* IV. xix. 5), but disturbed minds are often roused to 'odd Opinions and extravagant Actions . . . (T)hey feel the Hand of GOD moving them within, and the impulses of the Spirit, and cannot be mistaken in what they feel' (*Essay* IV. xix. 8). All propositions, including those purporting to be of supernatural origin, must therefore be examined by the natural light or derived directly from Scripture. The Old Testament prophets, to whom Locke is more sympathetic than Spinoza, had outward signs—a burning bush, the miracle of the rod and serpent—which modern prophets lack (*Essay* IV. xix. 15). Locke's rejection of truth by illumination, his insistence that normative truth be either rationally demonstrable or drawn directly from the Christian and Stoic traditions, was connected with his strong defences of private property—the preservation of which was, he thought, the main task of a theory of justice—and of monogamy, and his rather punitive attitude towards the poor.

Where ineluctable duties were concerned, Locke referred even in the *Essay* to 'the unchangeable Rule of Right and Wrong, which the Law of God hath established . . .' (*Essay* II. xxvii. 11). The idea of God played a crucial role in his moral psychology, which depended heavily on a theological cost–benefit analysis that would-be profligates were urged to undertake, weighing the joys of heaven and the torments of hell against the temptation of the moment. However, his insistence in the *Essay* on the sensory or experiential basis of all knowledge through the formation, comparison, and manipulation of personal ideas, together with certain hints of linguistic and social conventionalism, marked Locke as a Hobbist in the eyes of some of his critics. In Book II, in a passage subsequently modified to emphasize that he was referring to the common usage of terms rather than to the basis of good and evil, he observed that

The measure of what is every where called and esteemed *Vertue* and *Vice* is this approbation or dislike, praise or blame, which by a secret and tacit consent establishes it self in the several Societies, Tribes, and Clubs of Men in the World; whereby several actions come to find Credit or Disgrace amongst them, according to the Judgement, Maxims, or Fashions of that place.... And by this approbation and dislike they establish amongst themselves, what they will call *Vertue* and *Vice*' (*Essay* II. xxviii. 10).

These views outraged John Edwards, who, in his *Eternal and Instrinsick Reasons of Good and Evil*, declared that 'The Reasons of Good and Evil are Eternal and Unchangeable ... there are such things as Right and Wrong, without any Positive Law of Constitution ... these had the start of all human Contracts and Customs ... Religion and Virtue are engrafted into our very nature, and are every waies suited to the frame of Rational Creatures' (Edwards 1699: 2).

Edwards carried on in this vein at length. The rules of righteousness, he thundered, 'are no imaginary and precarious things, nor do they depend upon humane Institution and Arbitrement; but they are Real and True in themselves, they are Solid and Substantial, there being an Intrinsick Goodness and Excellency in them' (Edwards 1699: 2). In arguing that the reproaches of conscience and secrecy, and fear of punishment indicated that human beings *did* know the moral law, Edwards seemed to miss Locke's point that savages committed blatantly cruel acts in an enthusiastic or casual way. However, he points out that eating the dead and dispatching their 'old sick Parents out of the world' might be looked on as kindnesses. 'We are not concerned', Edwards drew himself up to say, 'for the Brasilians or Caribes, no nor for the Soldanians and Hotentots, with the noise of whom our Ears are mightily grated of late. The strange behaviour of these People is no real reproach to Human Nature, nor any impeachment of the General Laws of Morality' (Edwards 1699: 18).

Edwards denied that moral rules are derived, like spinning and weaving, from tradition, and he rejected Cumberland's proposal to allow 'Experimental Observation' a role in the formation of moral codes. To suppose that the senses supply us with moral knowledge, he says,

makes all morality contingent and uncertain, for all Natural and Bodily Motion (on which he holds it depends) is so ... External and Corporeal Causes are shifting and fickle; Objects work on us differently, yea the operations of the same Objects are not always the same; and therefore Moral Goodness, which is founded on these, is no fix'd thing, but is unsteady and floating: we know not where to have it ...    (Edwards 1699: 25).

Perhaps the most doctrinaire moral realist of the early modern period was Samuel Clarke, whose *Discourse concerning the Being and Attributes of God* was compiled from sermons of the early 1700s and went through many editions. Clarke continues to be cited in modern times for his view that there exist 'eternal and unalterable *Relations, Respects,* or *Proportions* of things', a 'natural and necessary difference between Good and Evil antecedent to all arbitrary and positive constitution whatsoever' (Clarke 1732: 185, 194). Bad practices on the part of the morally ignorant afford 'no just Objection against the *Certainty* of any Truth' (Clarke 1732: 198), and Clarke appears to deny that any proposition of morality is undecidable: '[T]he natural and essential difference between Good and Evil, Right and Wrong ... must be ... essential and unalterable in all even the smallest and nicest and most intricate Cases, though it be not so easy to be discerned and accurately distinguished' (Clarke 1732: 185).

# CONCLUSIONS

There are many ways to interpret and present the main points of epistemological contention in early modern moral philosophy. There is a broad spectrum of opinion on the source of moral authority, with individual conscience or personal perception accepted by some, the judgements of one's peers or one's political superiors advanced by others, and God alone assumed to be the sole source of moral direction by still others. There is disagreement as to whether good and evil are projections of human desires and interests or reside in actions, events, and persons themselves, and as to whether there is any rational ground for condemning foreign or savage practices outright. It is safe, nevertheless, to say that a distinct line of philosophical argument emerges and amasses strength, despite stern resistance. Philosophical opinion shifts from the position that moral rules are commands of God, which express *his* preferences for our conduct and were revealed in Scripture and to which we are motivated by our obligation to obey him, to the position that moral rules are formulas for the harmonious social life that *we* prefer, that are supported by the emotions of sympathy and motivated by a purely human desire for security and the general good.

Not only does human welfare emerge as important to secure in this world, and as able to be assured through the construction and maintenance of laws and institutions, rather than deferred to the hereafter and acquired through grace or merit, but the role of God is importantly detachable. 'Nature', just as well as God, may be seen as the source of our benevolent motives, and the force of moral obligation can be said to derive from the interest a psychologically normal and reasonable person takes in the welfare of others, an interest that distinguishes him or her from the morally deficient. Moral rules are increasingly conceived as what Hobbes calls 'convenient Articles of Peace, upon which men may be drawn to agreement', following from 'Feare of Death; Desire of such things as are necessary to commodious living; and a Hope by their Industry to obtain them' (Hobbes 1996: 90). Shaftesbury expresses the point even more positively. Personal virtue, he declares, 'upholds Societies, maintains Union, Friendship, and Correspondence among men.' It is 'that by which Countries, as well as privat Families, flourish and are happy' (Shaftesbury 1699: 199). Although he conceded that theism offered 'securities and advantages to Virtue' through the depiction of an all-seeing judge and the promise of reward for virtue unrewarded in terrestrial life, Shaftesbury boldly insisted on a firm separation between morality and theology. He pointedly invoked the Stoic formula of life according to nature, and made affection for the self and for society the two pillars of morality.

The evolution described above drew for its language and concepts on a rediscovered ancient philosophy. Both the Stoic concepts of honourable behaviour and natural sociability and the Epicurean concepts of welfare and convention were recruited to probe more deeply into the problems of moral belief and moral knowledge. Confidence in human reason and perception—indeed, in the moral emotions—was recovered, and suspicion of priestly authority and scriptural revelation deepened. Progress in moral theory was further fuelled by the expansion of trade and the rise of capitalistic institutions that depended upon the maintenance of social order and co-operation, trust, and the moderation of the more reactive social emotions. This was not to say, however, that the early moderns succeeded in solving the deep problems of social injustice that permeated their societies.

This development was not irreversible: Kant, for one, sought to halt it.[4] There was meanwhile a good deal of free play in these opposed starting points, and room for incursion of one into the other, or ambivalent or inconsistent self-positioning. Divine command theorists could note that God's rules were not arbitrary; that obedience to them generated human happiness. Perfect objectivity, and what one anti-Hobbes writer and critic of Locke called 'reasons fetch'd from the Constitution of the Universe' (Lowde 1694: 73) could equally be claimed by philosophers who sought a grounding for morals in human nature and those who sought it in the common desires and capabilities of humankind. Samuel Clarke, who refers to 'the Fitnesses and Unfitnesses of things', that are 'eternal and in themselves absolutely

---

[4] As Schneewind observes, Kant revived a morality of obedience but posited a subject-internal source of authority (1998: 659).

unalterable' (Clarke 1732: 246), noted that because the 'bare Light of Nature' was insufficient to reveal men's moral duties to them, and because they were corrupt and degenerate, social life would be the nasty and brutish mêlée Hobbes had posited had God not seen fit to reveal ethics to them (Clarke 1732: 317–19).

Epistemic confidence in moral judgements co-existed, as it still does, with a recognition of the fragility of moral knowledge claims. A form of moral pyrrhonism is exemplified by Bernard Mandeville, who, in his *Fable of the Bees, or Private Vices, Publick Benefits*, developed the analogy between the moral sense and aesthetic judgement to show that morality resembled fashion and that relativism was inevitable.

In the Works of Nature, Worth and Excellency are as uncertain (as the comparative value of paintings): and even in Humane Creatures what is beautiful in one Country is not so in another. How whimsical is the Florist in his Choice! Sometimes the Tulip, sometimes the Auricula, and at other times the Carnation shall engross his Esteem, and every Year a new Flower in his Judgement beats all the old ones. . . . The many ways of laying out a Garden Judiciously are almost Innumerable, and what is called Beautiful in them varies according to the different Tastes of Nations and Ages. In Grass Plats, Knots and Parterre's a great diversity of Forms is generally agreeable; but a Round may be as pleasing to the Eye as a Square . . . and the preeminence an Octagon has over an Hexagon is no greater in Figures, than at Hazard Eight has above Six among the Chances. . . . In Morals there is no greater Certainty.    (Mandeville 1732: I, 327–30).

Mandeville expressed deep scepticism about the existence of at least some of the standard virtues. He attacked Shaftesbury, deeming the pursuit of the *pulchrum* a 'Wild-Goose-Chase' (Mandeville 1732: I, 331). 'Honour', he maintained, ' . . . is a Chimera without Truth or Being, an invention of Moralists and Politicians' (Mandeville 1732: I, 216). Yet the position that private vice produces social utility, leaving all members of the society better off than they would be in a virtuous commonwealth, was not merely clever paradox-making in a basically libertine literary framework; the suave Mandeville, like the itinerant preachers of the Interregnum, was distressed by moral hypocrisy and by the blindness to truths about their society prevalent amongst the intelligentsia. In his *Enquiry into the Causes of the Recent Executions at Tyburn*, in which he denounces capital punishment for trivial offences, Mandeville describes anger, pride, and envy as 'evil in themselves', and refers to 'evil customs, mismanagements, and perverse opinions' (Mandeville 1725: 67). A social construction account of morality co-existing with deeply felt convictions about right and wrong reflects a stance that characterizes revisionary philosophers who, like Hobbes, took humans as they were and demanded reform of their institutions, rather than, like Pascal, a total overhaul of the human character.

## REFERENCES

BAYLE, P. (1708). *Miscellaneous Reflections, Occasion'd by the Comet which appeared in December 1680.* London.

BLOUNT, T. P. (1692). *Essays on several subjects written by Sir Tho. Pope Blount.* London.

BRAMHALL, J. (1657). *Castigations of Mr. Hobbes his last animadversions in the case concerning liberty and universal necessity.* London.

BUTLER, J. (1749). *Fifteen sermons preached at the Rolls Chapel... To which are added, six sermons preached upon publick occasions.* London.

CLARKE, S. (1732). *A Discourse concerning the being and attributes of God, the obligations of natural religion, and the truth and certainty of the Christian revelation.* London. [Comprising *A Demonstration of the Being and Attributes of God* (1705) and *The Unchangeable Obligations of Natural Religion and the Truth and certainty of the Christian Revelation* (1706)].

CUMBERLAND, RICHARD (1672). *De legibus naturae, disquisitio philosophica in qua earum forma, summa capita, ordo, promulgatio, & obligatio è rerum natura investigantur: quinetiam elementa philosophiae Hobbianae, cum moralis tum civilis, considerantur & refutantur...* London.

DARWALL, S. (1995). *The British Moralists and the Internal Ought 1640–1730.* Cambridge: Cambridge University Press.

DE LA VEGA, G. (1688). *The royal commentaries of Peru in two parts... rendred into English by Sir Paul Rycaut...* London.

DUNTON, J. (1691). *A voyage round the world, or, A pocket-library divided into several volumes...: the whole work intermixt with essays, historical, moral, and divine, and all other kinds of learning.* London.

EDWARDS, J. (1699). *The Eternal and Intrinsick Reasons of Good and Evil.* Cambridge.

EISENSTEIN, E. L. (1980). *The Printing Press as an Agent of Change.* Cambridge: Cambridge University Press.

FRIEDMAN, J. (1987). *Blasphemy, Immorality, and Anarchy: The Ranters and the English Revolution.* Athens, OH, and London: Ohio University Press.

GASSENDI, P. (1699). *Three Discourses of Happiness, Virtue and Liberty.* Trans. and ed. F. Bernier. London [1st edn. 1680].

GROTIUS, H. (2005). *The Rights of War and Peace.* 3 vols. Ed. R. Tuck. Indianapolis: Liberty Fund [1st edn. 1625].

HOBBES, T. (1994). *The Elements of Law Natural and Political.* Ed. J. C. A. Gaskin. Oxford: Oxford University Press [1st edn. 1650].

HOBBES, T. (1996). *Leviathan.* Ed. R. Tuck. Cambridge: Cambridge University Press [1st edn. 1651].

HOCHSTRASER, T. J. and SCHROEDER, P. (2003). *Early Modern Natural Law Theories: Contexts and Strategies of the Early Enlightenment.* Dordrecht: Kluwer.

HOOKER, R. (1666). *Of the lawes of ecclesiastical politie eight bookes, by Richard Hooker.* London.

LEIBACHER-OUVRARD, L. (1989). *Libertinage et Utopies sous le Règne de Louis XIV.* Geneva: Droz.

LEITES, E. (ed.) (1988). *Conscience and Casuistry in Early Modern Europe.* Cambridge: Cambridge University Press.

LLOYD, W. (1691). *A discourse of God's ways of disposing of kingdoms*. London.

LOCKE, J. (1976). *Correspondence of John Locke*. Ed. E. S. De Beer. 10 vols. Oxford: Clarendon Press.

LOCKE, J. (1997). *Essay Upon the Law of Nature*, in *Locke, Political Essays*. Ed. M. Goldie. Cambridge: Cambridge University Press [1st edn. 1663].

LOWDE, J. (1694). *A discourse concerning the nature of man both in his natural and political capacity, both as he is a rational creature and member of a civil society*. London.

MALEBRANCHE, N. (1699). *A treatise of morality in two parts . . . translated into English, by James Shipton, M.A.* London [1st edn. 1684].

MANDEVILLE, B. (1725). *Enquiry into the Causes of the recent Executions at Tyburn*. London.

MANDEVILLE, B. (1732). *The Fable of the Bees or Private Vices, Publick Benefits*. 2 vols. London.

MONTAIGNE, M. DE (1685). *Essays of Michael, seigneur de Montaigne in three books, with marginal notes and quotations of the cited authors, and an account of the author's life . . . new rendered into English by Charles Cotton, Esq.* London.

MOREAU, J. P. (ed.) (1999). *Le stoïcisme au XVIe et au XVIIe siècle*. Paris: Albin Michel.

MORLAND, S. (1695). *The Urim of conscience to which the author has had recourse for plain answers, in his own particular case*. London.

PASCAL, B. (1966). *Pensées*. Trans. A. J. Krailsheimer. London [1st edn. 1670].

PARKER, S. (1666). *A Free and Impartial Censure of the Platonick Philosophers*. Oxford.

RATTNER, J. and DANZER, G. (2006). *Europaische Moralistik in Frankreich von 1600 bis 1950*. Wuerzburg: Loeingshausen and Neumann.

SAMPSON, M. (1988). 'Laxity and Liberty in Seventeenth-century English Political Thought', in E. Leites, *Conscience and Casuistry in Early Modern Europe*. Cambridge: Cambridge University Press, 72–118.

SCHNEEWIND, J. B. (1998). *The Invention of Autonomy: A History of Modern Moral Philosophy*. Cambridge: Cambridge University Press.

SHAFTESBURY, THIRD EARL (ANTHONY ASHLEY COOPER) (1699). *An Inquiry Concerning Virtue*. London.

SMITH, N. (ed.) (1983). *A Collection of Ranter Writings from the 17TH Century*. London: Junction Books.

SOMERVILLE, J. (1988). 'The "New Art of Lying": Equivocation, Mental Reservation and Casuistry', in E. Leites, *Conscience and Casuistry in Early Modern Europe*. Cambridge: Cambridge University Press, 159–84.

SPINOZA, B. DE (2007). *Tractatus Theologico-Politicus*. Ed. J. Israel, trans. M. Silverthorne and J. Israel. Cambridge: Cambridge University Press.

TYRRELL, J. (1692). *A brief disquisition of the law of nature according to the principles and method laid down in the Reverend Dr. Cumberland's . . . Latin treatise on that subject: as also his confutations of Mr. Hobb's principles put into another method*. London.

WHICHCOTE, B. (1698). *Select sermons of Dr. Whichcot (sic) in two parts*. London.

WILSON, C. (1993). 'Enthusiasm and its critics: historical and contemporary perspectives'. *History of European Ideas*, 17: 461–78.

WILSON, C. (2003). 'The Moral Epistemology of Locke's Essay', in L. Newman (ed.), *The Cambridge Companion to Locke's Essay*. Cambridge: Cambridge University Press, 381–405.

CHAPTER 20

# THE FREE WILL PROBLEM

## PAUL RUSSELL

*I acknowledge this liberty, that I can do if I will; but to say I can will if I will,
I take to be an absurd speech.*

Thomas Hobbes, *Of Liberty and Necessity*

Thomas Hobbes changed the face of moral philosophy in ways that still structure and resonate within the contemporary debate. It was Hobbes's central aim, particularly as expressed in the *Leviathan,* to make moral philosophy genuinely 'scientific', where this term is understood as science had developed and evolved in the first half of the seventeenth century. Specifically, it was Hobbes's aim to provide a thoroughly naturalistic description of human beings in terms of the basic categories and laws of matter and motion. By analysing the individual and society in these terms, Hobbes proposed to identify and describe a set of moral laws that are eternal and immutable, and can be known to all those who are capable of reason and science (L 15.40). Even more ambitiously, it was Hobbes's further hope that these 'theorems of moral doctrine' would be put into practical use by public authorities with a view to maintaining a peaceful, stable social order (L 31.41).

My concern in this chapter is not so much Hobbes's larger project but the free will problem as it arises within his naturalistic science of morals. There can be no doubt that Hobbes's specific contributions on the subject 'Of Liberty and Necessity' shaped our modern understanding and interpretation of the free will problem. The particular arguments that Hobbes advanced on this topic served to establish a number of the core features of modern compatibilism—an influence that has lasted for well over three centuries. However, while Hobbes is generally credited with being the founding figure of modern compatibilism, thereby laying down the tracks for others who followed, such as Hume, Mill, Schlick, and Ayer, his particular arguments on this topic are widely dismissed, even by compatibilists, as being too crude and simplistic to be credible. In particular, Hobbes's understanding of the nature of 'liberty' is said to be far too thin and insubstantial a foundation on which to rest the edifice of morality, and his entire project of a naturalistic science of morality consequently judged as not credible.

I address this general criticism of Hobbes's compatibilism by taking a closer look at the role of liberty as it relates to the foundations of his project of a scientific understanding of morality. I argue that Hobbes's understanding of the role of liberty in the foundations of morals, and the particular way in which moral agents become subject to law and liable to punishment, has been misunderstood in important respects, not least by his influential contemporary critic, John Bramhall. Hobbes's views are more subtle and complex than the form of 'simple compatibilism' that Bramhall and others have generally attributed to him, and there are significant lessons to be learned from Hobbes's compatibilist arguments when they are properly understood.

# I: AGAINST FREE WILL: HOBBES ON BRAMHALL'S *TRUE LIBERTY*

Until the seventeenth century the primary focus of the free will debate as it had evolved in Western philosophy was on theological issues. The major issue was how divine foreknowledge and predestination could be reconciled with human freedom and moral responsibility, and with rewards and punishments in a future state (LN: Introduction). Related to this, although moving in the other direction, was the concern with the problem of evil and the worry that God was in some way the source of sin in the world, something that would clearly compromise the divine moral attributes. In the seventeenth century, although these issues remained very much alive, the focus shifted to a different set of concerns, *viz.* how the concepts and categories of the natural sciences relate to our self-image as free and moral beings who are accountable to each other as well as to God. Concerns about necessity and determinism appear in this context, not in the form of a transcendent intelligent agent who controls and governs all that we do, but in the form of a natural order, devoid of any intelligent purpose, that conditions and limits all that we may think and do. While issues of explaining and interpreting the nature and

possibility of human freedom persist, the character of these issues and philosophical challenges to our self-image is evidently different. The significance of Hobbes's
writings on this subject is that they serve as the clearest and most influential
statement of this shift of focus, in the free will debate, from theological worries
to concern about the implications of scientific naturalism for moral life.

Hobbes developed and fine-tuned his views on liberty in large measure in
response to criticisms presented against his necessitation and compatibilist doctrines by John Bramhall, who was Bishop of Derry (Jackson 2007). Bramhall's
metaphysical and moral commitments manifest an allegiance to the notions and
jargon of a scholastic Aristotelianism that Hobbes routinely castigates and ridi-
cules, most prominently in the last part of the *Leviathan* (Pink 2004). Bramhall's
account of the nature of 'liberty' presupposes a moral psychology that is committed to powers and faculties of the (human) soul that cannot be analysed in
terms of bodies and motion. Human moral agents are capable of governing
themselves by exercising rational powers that make them subject to eternal laws
of justice that express the will of God (LN 50) and, at the same time, release them
from the determination of natural causes (LN 46, 48–9, 56, 63). On Bramhall's
scheme, therefore, genuine moral agents are capable of rational self-government in
such a manner that they are subject to (prescriptive) moral law. Unlike animals,
moral agents are not moved by whatever desires may fall upon them and, unlike
mere inanimate bodies, they are not necessitated by antecedent motions of bodies
in an endless causal series. Moral agents are neither animals nor mere machines.
They are persons with rational powers of a kind that make them subject to the laws
of God and, as such, they enjoy a liberty and freedom which serves as a foundation
of all moral life.

There are two distinctions with regard to liberty that are essential to Bramhall's
position: (i) between *voluntary* acts and *free* acts, and (ii) between *liberty* and
*necessity*. According to the first distinction, although children, fools, and madmen
are capable of voluntary or spontaneous action, they are not capable of free action.
Free action is deliberate and involves a 'power of election' or rational choice.
According to Bramhall, 'true liberty' depends on deliberation, which must be
understood in terms of two faculties of the soul, the will and the understanding
(LN 45–7). Free action or true liberty requires that the will have 'power over itself'
(LN 44).

the question is plainly this, whether all agents and all events, natural, evil, moral . . . be
predetermined extrinsically and inevitably without their own concurrence in the determination; so as all actions and events, which either are or shall be, cannot but be, nor can be
otherwise, after any other manner, or in any other place, time, number, measure, order, nor
to any other end, than they are . . .    (LN 45; cf. 72).

How, then, can the will have power over itself? The will, as a distinct faculty of the
soul, must engage the understanding 'to consult and deliberate what means are

convenient for attaining some end'. The understanding is, therefore, commanded by the will and serves as its 'counselor' (LN 46). As such, any 'obligation the understanding does put to the will, is by the consent of the will, and derived from the power of the will, which was not necessitated to move the understanding to consult' (LN 46). Insofar as the will is moved by the understanding, it is 'not as by an efficient, having a causal influence into the effect, but only by proposing and representing the object'. The understanding determines the will, therefore, 'not naturally but morally' (LN 46; cf. 48). With this distinction between moral and natural efficacy in place, Bramhall concludes that he has established a crucial distinction between 'true liberty', which involves moral determination through the use of reason, and necessity, whereby an act consists in 'an antecedent determination to one' (LN 43, 47, 56, 63). When an action is 'done by an extrinsical cause, without the concurrence of the will', it is compelled and therefore unfree (LN 54–8, 62).

Bramhall rejects the criticism made by Hobbes that his account of free actions involves 'something beginning from itself' (LN 61, 65; cf. 38). He argues that, although 'nothing can begin without a cause... many things may begin, and do begin without a necessary cause' (LN 65). To understand how this is possible, one must distinguish the *faculty* of will from *acts* of will or election (LN 59). The power of willing found in a reasonable being 'takes not beginning from itself but from God', whereas the act of willing 'takes not beginning from itself but from the faculty or from the power of willing which is in the soul' (LN 61, 62). 'The general power to act is from God', says Bramhall, 'but the specification of this general and good power to murder, or to any particular evil, is not from God but from the free will of man' (LN 50). It is these powers of the rational soul that make it possible for the free agent to act otherwise, which would not be possible where actions are determined by antecedent, external causes (LN 45, 59). Without 'true liberty' of the kind enjoyed by a rational soul there remains only a 'brutish liberty: that can serve the purposes of neither religion nor morality' (LN 44, 47–8; cf. 4). The essence of sin 'consists in this, that one commits that which he might avoid. If there be no liberty to produce sin, there is no such thing as sin in this world' (LN 6). In sum, the reality of sin proves the existence of true liberty, which is a precondition of sin or moral evil in this world.

The vision of human moral agency that Bramhall advances is well captured by Spinoza as follows: 'They seem to conceive man in nature as a dominion within a dominion. For they believe that man disturbs, rather than follows, the order of nature, that he has absolute power over his actions, and that he is determined only by himself' (SC 491). Bramhall holds that moral agents, including human agents, are capable of following laws of reason and justice as established by God. 'The rule of justice then is the same both in God and in us; but it is in God as in him who does regulate and measure, in us as in those who are regulated and measured' (LN 50). Rational agents are capable of deliberation and choice, and are not governed or necessitated to act according to external, antecedent causes. On this view of things, humans participate with God in a community of beings (which also included angels and evil spirits) governed by laws of reason *as opposed to* laws that govern physical (material) nature. It is a condition of the possibility of moral life that human agents cannot be understood as simply part of the natural order of things whereby they are subject to the same causal forces and principles that direct the movements of animals and inanimate bodies. Moral evaluation presupposes a moral law that we are capable of obeying, and that is itself wholly distinct from any scientific laws that may describe the necessary motions of bodies. It is this alternative, anti-naturalistic self-image of man that Hobbes set out to demolish.

Hobbes's objections to Bramhall's scheme are both general and specific in nature. At the more general level, Hobbes rejects the entire set of metaphysical and epistemological assumptions with which Bramhall operates, most of which he dismisses as the unintelligible jargon of the 'schoolmen'. Early in the *Leviathan* he simply dismisses the term 'free will' as entirely meaningless and absurd speech, something he closely associates with the use of other insignificant terms such as 'incorporeal substance', 'spirits', etc. (L 5.5, 8.9, 12.7, 34.2, 46.15; cf. LN 16). His philosophical task is, therefore, to provide an alternative set of real and true definitions of the terms involved in this context, such as will, deliberation, understanding, passion, and so on, in light of his own purely materialistic metaphysical commitments (L 46.15; cf. 4.14). Hobbes also raised specific objections to Bramhall's metaphysical scheme, the most important of which is a rejection of any 'third way' between chance and necessity (LN 70). The key instrument that Bramhall uses to find a way between necessity and chance is the distinction between moral and physical efficacy. Hobbes simply states that he does not know what this means (LN 20). According to Hobbes, there is *one* kind of causation, which must be understood in terms of the antecedent motions of matter or body (Hobbes 1966a: I, 121–7). To suggest that an effect is produced by a cause which is not sufficient for the effect to be produced is, Hobbes maintains, contradictory and incoherent (LN 38–9). We cannot even 'imagine anything to begin without a [sufficient] cause' (LN 39). Similarly, 'nothing takes beginning from itself, but from some other immediate agent without itself' (LN 38). On this view of things, it is no less absurd to say that 'to will is an act of it according to that power' than to say that 'to dance is an act allowed or drawn by fair means out of the ability to dance' (LN 33; cf. 82). While an agent may be free to do what he will, Hobbes denies that we can make any sense of the suggestion that 'the will can determine itself' (LN 16, 72, 73, 82). It is no more the will that wills than it is the understanding that understands. The fundamental source of confusion here is to suppose that the power of willing is distinct from acts of willing (LN 75, 82, 85). In short, on the key question of whether the will can determine itself, Hobbes's answer is clear: there is no such power, ability, or capacity, because the very notion involved is absurd and without meaning.

# II: LIBERTY, LAW, AND THE BASIC OBJECTIONS

Hobbes's critique of the doctrine of free will has provided the materials for much of the writings of later generations of compatibilists against libertarian metaphysics (Ayer 1954: for a compatibilist account of free will, rather than free action, see Frankfurt 1971). The challenge for libertarianism, in face of these criticisms, has been to decide which elements of Bramhall's scheme can be salvaged or revised and which need to be jettisoned or repudiated.[1] For our purposes, however, it is the other side of the debate that is of particular interest and importance, namely: how Hobbes can provide an alternative account of 'liberty' that serves the ends of morality and religion. As already noted, Hobbes must do this within the confines of his materialist philosophical anthropology. The *Leviathan* presents an analysis of human nature that serves as the foundation for this 'scientific' moral philosophy. On Hobbes's account, (in)famously, man is nothing more than an arrangement of bodies with a particular structure and motions. Human thought, sensation, understanding, passions, and the will are all defined and described in terms of relevant motions of body. The processes involved in human thought and action are entirely mechanical in character. External objects cause motions, which in turn give rise to pleasure or pain and the various particular passions; these in turn generate some appetite or aversion towards the object as it has been presented to us (cf. L, ch. 6). According to Hobbes, deliberation is nothing more than an alteration or succession of appetites and aversions that may come upon us concerning some act or object. What we call the will is simply 'the last appetite or aversion' that moves us to act (L 6.53). These are all activities that are strictly, philosophically, defined in terms of particular motions within the human body as it responds to its environment (i.e. the motions of external bodies upon it).

In this way, Hobbes's materialist account of human nature is combined with a conception of philosophical and scientific method that is evidently mechanical in character. In *De Cive* Hobbes uses the metaphor of a watch to explain his approach:

Concerning my method... everything is best understood by its constitutive causes. For as in a watch, or some such small engine, the matter, figure, and motion of the wheels cannot be well known, except it be taken insunder and viewed in parts; so to make a more curious search into the rights of states and duties of subjects, it is necessary, I say, not to take them insunder, but yet that they be so considered as if they were dissolved; that is, that we rightly understand that the quality of human nature is, in what matters it is, in what not, fit to

---

[1] Bramhall's distinction between moral and physical causation, and its relation to the exercise of rational powers, remains a significant feature of some prominent eighteenth-century libertarian systems, such as those of Clarke (1998), Reid (1969), and Kant (1873). While remaining committed to the need for alternative possibilities, libertarians are widely divided about most other issues relating to causation and the nature of the self that is the source of (moral) action.

make up a civil government, and how men must be agreed amongst themselves that intend to grow up into a well-grounded state . . .    (Hobbes 1972: 98–9).

Granted this 'clockwork' conception of human nature, how is any recognizable form of liberty possible? Hobbes makes matters more complicated by offering more than one definition of liberty (Skinner 2008). In the first place, he is committed to the following definition: 'Liberty, or Freedom, signifieth (properly) the absence of opposition; (by opposition, I mean external impediments of motion;) and may be applied no less to irrational, and inanimate creatures, than to rational' (L 21.1—cf. L 14.2; LN 38, 39). Evidently, this general definition of liberty, as Bramhall had been quick to point out several years before the publication of the *Leviathan*, not only fails to distinguish humans from animals; it does not even distinguish humans from inanimate creatures. Rivers, stones, and tennis balls, no less than the actions of human beings, can be said to be free in this sense.

Perhaps with this objection in mind, Hobbes further refines his definition as follows: 'A Free-Man, is he, that in those things which by his strength and wit he is able to do is not hindered to do what he has a will to' (L 21.2). From this definition it follows that it is man and not the will that may or may not be free (LN 16, 89) and that, when we are speaking of a man in this context, we are concerned with the freedom of a body that is moved by the internal motions that constitute the will (L 21.2; 6.49–54). With respect to a liberty of this kind, 'it cannot be conceived that there is any liberty greater than a man to do what he will. . . . He that can do what he wills has all liberty possible, and he that cannot has none at all' (LN 31). Liberty, thus considered, is something that the agent has or does not have; it does not come in degrees (although the extent of our liberty may vary greatly). Most importantly, as Hobbes acknowledges, a liberty of this kind does not distinguish humans from animals, or man from beast (LN 83; and cf. 18–19; also L 6.1, 6.49–53). Animals, no less than humans, are capable of deliberation and voluntariness. The same is true of the actions of fools, madmen, and children (LN 17–19). Whatever boundary is to be drawn between moral and non-moral agents, therefore, this distinction does not rest with the presence or absence of *liberty*, since this is something that moral and non-moral agents alike may enjoy.[2]

As if this road were not challenging enough, Hobbes further expands this conception of liberty to include actions that may be performed or done out of fear (L 21.3; and cf. 14.27, 20.2). He cites Aristotle's famous example of sailors throwing their cargo overboard to save themselves, but observes that while this action may be necessitated, it is no more necessitated than actions done from other motives and is, moreover, still voluntary (L 21.3; LN 18, 30) (Aristotle 1925: III,

---

[2] In the *Leviathan* Hobbes confuses matters by speaking of agents as being at liberty until deliberation puts an end to the oscillation we experience between appetite and aversion, i.e. when the will is set in motion (L 6.50). This may be described as a kind of liberty of the *will* in the agent and it is a suggestion that Locke subsequently develops (*Essay* II. xxi. 47).

1 [1110a]). Although many of Hobbes's followers have found this claim difficult to accept, it is, nevertheless, a view that is integral to his entire moral system.[3] This view is so because it is a fundamental claim of Hobbes that a person motivated by fear (of death) may freely give his consent whereby he makes himself a *subject* who has recognized and accepted sovereign authority over him, either by covenanting with others or by directly covenanting with the sovereign (L 14.27, 20.2). Covenants in these circumstances, though they are motivated by fear and so compelled, are still valid and voluntarily and freely undertaken. In this way, it is crucial to Hobbes's system that *individuals make themselves subjects through their free acts of consent* even if they are motivated by fear and in this sense compelled to undertake these actions.

Bramhall's criticism of Hobbes's account of liberty is motivated as much by issues of religion as by those of morality, although for Bramhall these issues can hardly be separated. For Bramhall it is crucial to provide an account of liberty that not only does not compromise human moral standing in relation to God and a future state (i.e. Heaven and Hell), but also does not compromise the integrity of God's basic moral attributes, especially divine justice. With regard to the latter issue, Bramhall raises what may be called the dual-law objection: it would clearly be unjust 'for the same person to *command* one thing and yet to *necessitate* him that is commanded to do another thing' (LN 3; my emphasis). A law must be deemed 'unjust and tyrannical which commands a man to do that which is impossible for him to do' (LN 51). Accordingly, God cannot possibly command us to avoid some action which God or secondary causes necessitate us to do. It follows that 'God's chiding proves man's liberty', which is understood as 'true liberty from necessity' (LN 3).[4] This objection is especially effective against Hobbes. It was a particular concern of Hobbes throughout the *Leviathan*, as in his other writings, that no kingdom, no society, can survive where there are 'two masters' or 'two sovereigns' making divergent laws (L 18.16, 19.3, 20.4, 26.41, 29.8, 29.15, 39.5, 43.1). As he says, more than once, 'a kingdom divided against itself cannot stand' (L 18.16, 29.15). Where any person is subject to two distinct systems of law, which require divergent and inconsistent things of them, only chaos and anarchy can follow. Bramhall's dual-law objection provides a variation on Hobbes's own theme with respect to the free will issue. If there is a *moral* law that commands our obedience, then we cannot also be subject to a *physical* law that makes obedience impossible. This would not

---

[3] Hobart (1934), Schlick (1939), Ayer (1954), wish to allow some forms of freedom-defeating *internal* compulsion. The difficulty then becomes how we can draw a principled line that allows that some voluntary actions, willed by the agent, to be nevertheless unfree. Frankfurt (1971) is an influential effort to deal with this difficulty. Hobbes rejects this possibility.

[4] Thomas Reid expressed the same general objection against the necessitarian view: 'That the moral laws of nature are often transgressed by man, is undeniable. If the physical laws of nature make his obedience to the moral laws to be impossible, then he is, in the literal sense, *born under one law, bound unto another*, which contradicts every notion of a righteous government of the world' (Reid 1969: 337).

only compromise God's justice; it would also erode the essential foundations of morality insofar as it presupposes the accountability of man.

Closely related to this line of objection is Bramhall's general objection to Hobbes's account of liberty in terms of the absence of external impediments or, more narrowly, in terms of mere voluntariness. As Bramhall notes, if liberty is understood in terms of nothing more than the absence of external impediments, then even 'inanimate creatures' have a liberty of this kind (LN 44, 65; cf. LN 38).[5] Nor will it help to fall back on Hobbes's narrower view of a free agent defined as 'he that can do if he will and forbear if he will' (LN 39; cf. 31; and also L 21.2). While definition along these lines makes the required reference to a will, a freedom of this kind also belongs to animals, fools, madmen, and children. This is, as Bramhall sees it, a 'brutish liberty' that cannot serve the required purpose of distinguishing between moral and non-moral agents (LN 44).

On Bramhall's account, Hobbes compounds this mistake by giving a utilitarian or pragmatic justification for punishing actions that are done even though they are necessitated. It is certainly true that Hobbes maintains that the aim of punishment is to deter those who might otherwise break the law; he also argues that when the aim is only to 'grieve the delinquent for that which is past and not to be undone', it is not strictly punishment at all but an 'an act of hostility' (LN 25; L 28.7). To this Hobbes adds that excessive punishment is also an act of hostility, since 'the aim of punishment is not revenge but terror' (L 28.10; cf. L 44.26). In opposition to these views Bramhall argues that it 'is not lawful to do evil that good may come of it' and that punishment cannot be justified with reference only to its deterrent effects (LN 52). At the same time, he also argues that punishment may be justified solely on the basis of retributive considerations, with a view to satisfying the requirements of law by giving each what they are due (LN 52). Without true liberty, however, punishments are 'as vain as they are undeserved' (LN 4). The utilitarian perspective on punishment that Hobbes seems to endorse conflates training a dog with punishing a moral agent for wrong-doing; this is a criticism that subsequent generations of incompatibilist critics would echo (Campbell 1951: 114–17).

There is an intimate connection between the dual-law objection and the failings that Bramhall finds in Hobbes's conception of liberty, which I will refer to as the *liberty objection*. The liberty objection holds that (true) liberty cannot simply be a matter of voluntariness because, apart from anything else, this does not serve to distinguish moral and non-moral agents. The dual-law objection holds that no agent can be subject to both moral and physical laws, as this would undermine desert, which is the basis of all justified reward and punishment. If liberty were simply a matter of voluntariness or being able to do what we will without external impediment, then it is not clear how an agent who is necessitated to break the

---

[5] Many incompatibilists have pointed out that a liberty of this kind is consistent with speaking of the motions of a clock as being free (e.g. Clarke 1998: 133, 136; Kant 1873: 189).

moral law could in fact have kept it, given that he could not have willed otherwise than he did. Mere voluntariness, therefore, cannot serve as the relevant foundation for our ability to obey or disobey the moral law. That requires 'true liberty' or 'free will'. In this way, any agent who is properly subject to praise or blame, or to rewards or punishment, for obeying or disobeying the moral law cannot at the same time be subject to physical laws that necessitate their conduct. It follows that any agent who is subject to moral law must have free will (true liberty) and, therefore, cannot be necessitated to act. These two closely related objections concerning liberty and the dual-law problem may be called the *basic objections*.

The basic objections turn on a particular interpretation of Hobbes's position that is encouraged if one reads Hobbes's views on this subject primarily in the context of his controversy with Bramhall, and if one makes little reference to his overall moral system as presented in *Leviathan*. This interpretation may be described as the *simple compatibilist* interpretation. There are three important and related elements to the simple compatibilist position.

1. Liberty, understood directly in terms of voluntariness or an agent doing as he will unimpeded by external constraints, serves as a full and proper account of *moral* agency, whereby we may distinguish moral from non-moral agents (e.g. agents who are or are not liable to rewards and punishments, etc.). Call this the *voluntariness* claim.
2. Rewards and punishments may be justified directly in terms of their desirable social effects, especially as this relates to securing obedience to the law. Call this the *utility* claim.
3. The distinction between humans and animals, or between normal adults and children, fools, and madmen, lacks any deep significance for morality or moral agency (except as it may concern the effectiveness of rewards and punishments). Individuals of all these kinds are capable of acting freely and may, to a greater or lesser extent, be influenced by the impositions of rewards and punishments. Call this the *shallow morality* claim.

Bramhall attributes all these claims to Hobbes (e.g., LN 65). Furthermore, many of Hobbes's most influential followers in the classical compatibilist tradition may be read as taking views that are consistent with the three simple compatibilist doctrines described above. Subject to some qualifications, this includes prominent figures in the twentieth century, such as Schlick (1939), Hobart (1934), Ayer (1954), and Smart (1961).

Simple compatibilism thus understood gives substantial credibility to both of the basic objections. If liberty is conceived simply in terms of voluntariness, then it seems impossible to draw an appropriate distinction between moral and non-moral agents. Similarly, if we accept that punishment is justified directly in terms of its influence over the will of the agent, then we may have an answer for the dual-law objection but not one that can explain the basis of such practices in terms of desert or justice. Considerations of desert and justice require that agents be blamed or punished for what they could have avoided. The fact that punishment may have the desirable effect of changing the future behaviour of agents in no way shows that this condition has been satisfied (LN 6, 52–3). If Hobbes is indeed committed to simple compatibilism, then he is plainly vulnerable to both of the basic objections.

In the next section, however, I argue that a closer reading of Hobbes's views on liberty (and necessity) in light of the details of his moral system in *Leviathan* shows that he rejects all three of the key claims of simple compatibilism. When read in this light, he has the resources to provide more sophisticated and convincing replies to the basic objections than the simple compatibilist reading makes possible.

## III: Liberty, consent and the foundation of morals

If liberty consists of voluntariness, it suggests that animals, fools, and children should be regarded as moral agents who are subject to law and its associated sanctions (LN 65). Hobbes does indeed take the view that liberty is voluntariness, or the absence of external obstacles to what we will to do, and that fools, madmen, children, and animals have a liberty of this kind. He adds, furthermore, that individuals of these kinds deliberate before acting no less than their normal, adult human counterparts. With respect to liberty and deliberation, therefore, no relevant distinction can be drawn between these classes of individual. Does this imply that Hobbes regards animals, fools, children, etc. as fully fledged moral agents?

This would be correct only if he assumed, with Bramhall, that liberty is sufficient to make an individual a moral agent. It is Bramhall's view that 'true liberty' is both *necessary and sufficient* for moral agency, and that this is what distinguishes moral agents from non-moral agents since, evidently, animals, fools, children, etc. lack true liberty. Hobbes claims, however, that it is a mistake to suppose that the relevant distinction between moral and non-moral agents rests with any kind of liberty. Since fools and madmen clearly enjoy liberty in the form of voluntariness, but are *not* moral agents, he cannot accept the more general assumption that the distinction between moral and non-moral agents rests on some relevant account of liberty or freedom. Call this mistaken view the *liberty assumption*. Hobbes argues that, while liberty is required for an agent to become subject to law, its role is very different from Bramhall's account of the matter.

According to Hobbes, each individual in a state of nature, antecedent to any established sovereign authority with the right and power to make and enforce laws, is at liberty to preserve his own life as he may judge necessary. Being at liberty in this sense is not properly understood in terms of voluntariness or the absence of external impediments. Rather, it is a liberty constituted by the 'right of nature', something that every person has unless he has divested himself of this (natural) right (L 14.1). This is done by renouncing or transferring this right, whereby a person becomes obliged or bound by *law* (L 14.3). A liberty of this kind must be understood in terms of the absence of a particular kind of obstacle or external impediment to action, namely, the impediments and constraints of *obligation* and *law.* Where obligation and law begin, natural liberty comes to an end.[6] There is only one way, therefore, in which a person's natural right or liberty may be limited, and that involves the agent's exercise of his own (voluntary) consent. Specifically, it is through the 'laying down' of our right to all things, on condition that others do likewise, that serves to make us obliged and bound not to use our voluntary actions in a manner that violates these constraints (L 14.7). This mutual transferring of right is what Hobbes calls a contract, and it serves as the foundation of legitimate political authority, whereby a sovereign is authorized to represent our own will. The making of contracts of this kind, which requires language or the power of speech, is the basis of justice and injustice (L 14.13, 15.2). Justice is to perform our contracted duties and injustice is to violate them.

Thus, being an agent who acts according to his will (i.e. is not obstructed by external impediments) does not make an individual a moral agent who is subject to law (and thus liable to punishment when it is violated). On the contrary, a liberty of this kind is indeed to be found in animals, fools, children, and madmen and other such voluntary agents who are clearly not moral agents. To become a moral agent, subject to law and its associated obligations and sanctions, an agent must *voluntarily consent* by means of some relevant form of *speech*, which is a free act of his own (L 21.10). The act of consent is a *particular kind of free act* performed by an individual who must have the power of speech. Simply being able to do what one wills unobstructed by external impediments (i.e. acting voluntarily) does not make an agent a *moral* agent who is subject to law. We may conclude, in light of this, that Hobbes rejects the first claim of simple compatibilism (i.e. the voluntariness claim).

The second claim of simple compatibilism, that rewards and punishments can be justified in terms of beneficial social effects such as deterrence, certainly plays some role in Hobbes's moral system. Although our contractual obligations and duties are established through speech or words, Hobbes makes clear that 'mere words' are too weak to constrain and ensure compliance. We therefore require a

---

[6] Hobbes's multiple use of the term 'liberty' in this context requires care. While an agent may voluntarily (and in that sense freely) break the law, an agent who is obliged to obey the law has no *right* to do so (and in that sense is not free to break the law). For a discussion of these two senses of freedom, see Pettit (2005).

system of sanctions to enforce them (L 14.7, 14.18, 14.31, 17.2, 21.6). By freely placing ourselves in a commonwealth under the authority of a sovereign, we thereby limit our natural liberty and make ourselves subject to 'the artificial chains called civil laws' (L 21.5). Punishment is defined by Hobbes as 'an evil inflicted by a public authority on him that hath done or omitted that which is judged by the same authority to be a transgression of the law, to the end that the will of men may thereby the better be disposed to obedience' (L 28.1). It is clear from this definition that punishment can be imposed only by a sovereign or public authority on an individual who is *subject to law* (L 28.13) and that individuals who have not consented to authority are not liable to punishment. Such individuals, who remain in a state of nature, may be 'declared enemies' and may be destroyed or killed because they are considered 'noxious'; but they are not punished or liable to punishment of any kind.

Hobbes thus rejects the utility claim. He argues instead that agents who have not consented to become subjects of sovereign authority are not liable to punishment of any kind, because the law has no application to them and they have no duty to obey it (i.e. they retain their natural liberty). These considerations apply to all individuals who cannot give consent, including animals, children, fools, and madmen. Even if these individuals are capable of deliberation and voluntary action, and may have their wills and future conduct influenced by harsh treatment (HW: V, 195–7), this does not make them moral agents liable to punishment. Those who may be judged to deserve punishment are necessarily individuals who have freely *consented* to make themselves subjects to law. We may conclude that, on Hobbes's account, individuals cannot be liable to punishment simply because they act freely (voluntarily) or because their will and future conduct can be influenced in socially desirable ways by means of harsh treatment. To represent Hobbes's doctrine as having commitments of this kind is to overlook entirely key features of his contractualist moral system.

The third claim of simple compatibilism, that is the shallow morality claim, suggests that there is no deep significance for morality or moral agency in respect of the difference between humans and animals or between normal adults and fools, children, and madmen. This is a natural corollary of the first two claims. Since Hobbes is not committed to either the first or the second claims of simple compatibilism, there is no reason to assume that he is committed to the shallow morality claim on either of these grounds. Hobbes denies that the correct basis for drawing the distinction between moral and non-moral agents is the possession or absence of free will—something that he holds is incoherent and meaningless. The relevant basis for this fundamental distinction is whether or not an agent has freely consented to become a subject to law and, thereby, to be liable to punishment if the agent violates that law. It is, therefore, the *particular free or voluntary act* (i.e. consenting through speech) and not the more general fact that an agent acts freely, as such, that makes an agent a moral agent (Pettit 2008). Animals, children, fools, and madmen may act freely but they cannot consent by use of speech and thereby make themselves moral agents. It follows that, for Hobbes, the distinctions mentioned do indeed have deep moral significance. What Hobbes denies is that the basis of these distinctions can be understood simply in terms of liberty *of any kind*, since what matters is consent, which is itself a free act of which not all (free) agents are capable.[7]

Having established that Hobbes rejects all three of the claims of simple compatibilism, we may now return to the two basic objections. The liberty objection holds that Hobbes's account of liberty in terms of the absence of any external constraint on action (e.g. chains, etc.) cannot be accepted since it fails to distinguish moral from non-moral agents. The relevant reply on behalf of Hobbes has two parts. First, Hobbes may grant that his account of 'liberty' fails to distinguish moral from non-moral agents because it is a mistake, in his view, to rest this distinction on any account of liberty (i.e. as per the liberty assumption). This would include not only a meaningless and illusory conception of liberty based on free will but also Hobbes's own preferred account of liberty in terms of voluntariness. Second, it is not the case that Hobbes is unable to draw any relevant distinction here. The relevant distinction rests with the role of speech and consent. An agent becomes a moral agent who is subject to law if and only if he can and does freely renounce his natural right to all things. This requirement excludes all animals, fools, children, and madmen, since they plainly cannot give the consent whereby they may become subjects who are moral agents liable to punishments.

What, then, of the other basic objection, the dual-law objection, that a moral agent cannot be subject to both moral and physical laws, as this would erode the basis of desert and make all punishment unjust? The essentials of Hobbes's reply to this objection are now clear. It is not Hobbes's view that mere voluntariness or the efficaciousness of punishment serves as a basis for moral desert or retributive practices. On the contrary, only a moral agent who has freely consented to accept and recognize sovereign authority can be said to *deserve* moral praise or blame or the sanctions associated with it. Contrary to Bramhall, it is not free will that serves to ground these practices and the attitudes associated with them, but rather the agent's status as a subject in a system of law. This is something that only the agent can bring about through his own free act of consent. We may conclude, therefore, that we are not required to rest the foundations of morality on an illusory and incoherent doctrine of free will, because mere voluntariness and social utility

[7] It is true, of course, that Hobbes's incompatibilist critics, such as Bramhall, would object that an act of consent is itself free in the relevant sense only if it is not necessitated. From Hobbes's perspective, however, this objection is groundless because it presupposes a meaningless and incoherent form of liberty or freedom that is unavailable to us. That is to say, according to Hobbes, it is precisely because no alternative form of liberty understood in terms of 'free will' is available to us that we must resist the temptation to rest the notion of consent on a general requirement of this kind.

cannot, by themselves, play this role. The entire edifice of the *Leviathan*, notably Parts I and II, is devoted to showing that this is not our predicament.


# IV: THE ETERNAL MORAL LAW AND
## THE DUAL-LAW OBJECTION

The reply outlined above explains how, on Hobbes's view, agents may be subject to both moral and physical laws without any inconsistency or conflict. The reconciliation depends not on agents possessing free will of a kind that releases them from the realm of physical laws but rather on the role of consent, involving speech, whereby a person may voluntarily make himself subject to the rule of a sovereign who represents his own will and has the authority to command his obedience (L, ch. 16; and also L 18.10, 26.1–3, 26.12). However, critics may argue that this reply is, at best, incomplete insofar as it is relevant only to the case of civil laws. Civil laws are 'those rules, which the commonwealth has commanded [the subject] . . . to make use of, for the distinction of right and wrong, that is to say, of what is contrary, and what is not contrary to the rule' (L 26.3; also 18.10). Although civil laws may be valid or apply to subjects only in virtue of their prior consent, this is evidently not the case with the 'laws of nature' or eternal, immutable moral laws. The latter are clearly distinct from civil laws that depend entirely on the will of the sovereign and the prior consent of the subject. The eternal laws of nature, which I will refer to as the *eternal moral law* hereafter (to avoid confusion with physical and civil laws), are valid for and apply to all human beings. This is true, moreover, whether they have consented to become subjects to a commonwealth or not. It cannot be the case, therefore, that the dual-law objection, insofar as it concerns the relationship between the eternal moral law and the physical law, can be answered by reference to the role of consent in subjecting an agent to law.

How can Hobbes explain the way in which an agent may be subject to both the physical laws of nature and the eternal moral law? The physical laws of nature may necessitate an agent to act contrary to the eternal moral law. In these circumstances the agent would be obliged by one law to do what another law makes impossible, and could hardly deserve blame or punishment for failing to obey the eternal moral law. Hobbes's reply to this version of the dual-law objection requires a careful account of his understanding of the *nature* of the eternal moral law. Although we may use the language of law in this context, Hobbes is clear that the eternal moral law has a complex relationship with civil law. All laws, strictly speaking, must be commands of a sovereign authority (L 26.3, 26.12) Although eternal moral law may be regarded as commanded by God, this is highly problematic since God's word must be known through revelation and prophecy (L 31.3). The opening chapters of the third part of *Leviathan* make clear how unreliable and problematic this form of moral knowledge must be (L chs 32 and 33; esp. 29.8, 32.5, 36.9–14, 43.1, 47.2–4). With this in mind, we may consider God's word in respect of the 'dictates of natural reason' (L 31.3). 'These dictates of reason men use to call by the name of laws, but improperly: for they are but conclusions or theorems concerning what conduceth to the conservation and defence of themselves, whereas law properly is the word of him that by right hath command over others . . . ' (L 15.41). The eternal moral law is thus prior to and distinct from the civil law. This, indeed, must be true given that Hobbes makes clear that the sovereign authority is not subject to civil law (L 26.6) but is subject to eternal moral law (L 30.15; cf. 29.9). Although the civil law and eternal moral law 'contain each other' insofar as the commonwealth may establish eternal moral law as civil law and, in the opposite direction, the eternal moral law requires obedience to the civil law (L 26.8), the two forms of 'law' must still be distinguished. Most importantly, Hobbes emphasizes the point that the eternal moral law, which it is the point and purpose of his *Leviathan* to identify and describe, is not itself strictly 'law' *until the Commonwealth makes it so.*

That which I have written in this Treatise, concerning the moral virtues, and of their necessity, for the proving and maintaining peace, though it be evident truth, *is not therefore presently Law*; but because in all Commonwealths in the world, it is part of the civil law: For though it be naturally reasonable; yet it is by the sovereign power that it is Law . . .    (L 26.22: emphasis added)

It is important not only to understand the intimate relationship between the eternal moral law and civil law (i.e. law in the strict sense of the commands of sovereign authority) but to keep in mind the way they are nevertheless distinct and independent of each other.

Hobbes holds that the eternal moral law is best understood in terms of 'theorems' or 'conclusions' about which actions are conducive to peace and happiness and which actions lead to war and death (L 14.3, 15.34, 26.22). Insofar as all men agree that peace is good, they must also agree that the means to peace are also good (L 15.40). Moral philosophy is, therefore, conceived by Hobbes as the science of good and evil in respect of what conserves peaceful society (L 15.34–40). It is a particular kind of scientific investigation, which aims at the discovery of particular kinds of 'law'. The laws that are identified describe the motions of certain kinds of body, human beings, and the consequences that diverse motions will have by way of maintaining or destroying the social body that they form when united together. Thus the eternal moral law is a *physical* law or scientific claim that has a particular content or object of study. These laws of nature are no more prescriptive than any other scientific law which we may or may not put into use for our own ends. Granted that we know these laws (based on 'science'), and that we have certain ends (i.e. peace and preserving our lives), these 'laws' provide practical guidance about what actions we should or should not undertake. The practical value of the science of morals is certainly of central concern to Hobbes (L Intro 1–4, 31.41, 46.40–2, Rev. 16–17). With respect to the science of morals, we may remain ignorant of these truths or we may simply ignore them. If this is the case, then we either lack moral knowledge or make no use of it, and we will suffer the (natural) consequences accordingly. However, these natural consequences of acting contrary to the eternal moral law are not strictly punishments at all (e.g. the sovereign is not punished when he fails to follow the eternal moral law but will surely suffer harm nevertheless; L 28.8).

With these observations we may now address the dual-law objection as it concerns the relationship between eternal moral law and physical laws of nature. It is evidently Hobbes's view that there is no conflict or inconsistency here of any kind insofar as the eternal moral law is properly conceived as 'theorems' describing the motions of bodies and their consequences. As such, the eternal moral law is a particular kind of physical law. These theorems describe actions that may be undertaken or avoided with a view to creating and preserving society or destroying it. The actions required to create and maintain society presuppose individuals who can consent to authority and obey (civil) law. This rules out animals, fools, children, and madmen, since actions of this kind are not possible for them. Moreover, the individuals whose actions are the object of investigation are themselves able to use their reason (based on their powers of language, proper definitions, and so on) to acquire knowledge of these laws by means of the methods of *science*. We have, therefore, on Hobbes's account, the ability to discover and learn these laws and put them to practical use. By 'knowing ourselves' scientifically, we may guide our actions in ways that secure our common end, viz. a peaceful life in society. Many individuals may remain ignorant of these laws or choose to ignore them. As in other walks of human life, they will bear the natural and inevitable consequences or costs of doing this. There exists, however, no conflict at all between 'moral' and 'physical' law, since the former is, on Hobbes's analysis, simply a particular mode or form of the latter. The dual-law objection is, accordingly, groundless.

# V: Gods, clocks, and the
## LIBERTY ASSUMPTION

The basic objections advanced by Bramhall presuppose a reading of Hobbes along the lines of simple compatibilism. On this reading, the core disagreement between Hobbes and Bramhall rests on this issue:

1.  What conception of liberty is the relevant basis on which to distinguish moral from non-moral agents?

According to the liberty objection, voluntariness or the absence of external obstacles to what is willed cannot possibly serve as an adequate account of this distinction, since non-moral agents who are not subject to law or liable to punishment have a liberty of this kind. For this reason Bramhall insists that we need a form of liberty, understood in terms of free will, that can serve to make these distinctions. However, this criticism wholly misrepresents the relevant issue for Hobbes.

The right question to ask, according to Hobbes's account, is this:

2.  Does *any form of liberty* serve as the relevant basis for distinguishing moral from non-moral agents?

Hobbes answers this question firmly in the negative. Liberty is to be understood in terms of voluntariness and the absence of external impediments to action, but it does not serve as the relevant basis for distinguishing moral from non-moral agents. To accomplish this task we must turn to the details of Hobbes's moral system and his account of the origin of (civil) law and sovereign authority in the (free) consent of subjects who are capable of speech and reason. The interesting and important point that is being made is that the whole free will controversy, conceived in terms of the first question, rests on a mistake: namely, the *liberty assumption*. Even if Hobbes's general position on this subject is vulnerable to the objection that he places too much emphasis on the role of speech and consent in distinguishing moral from non-moral agents, he may still be correct in holding that this distinction is not to be located in some special or unique form of liberty that moral agents must possess. This is an approach that plainly deflates the significance of liberty when it comes to understanding and describing the foundations of moral life.

While Hobbes's aim was to deflate the significance of liberty in his own account of the foundations of moral life it should be clear, nevertheless, that it is not his view that liberty is *irrelevant* to the foundations of moral life or to drawing the distinction between moral and non-moral agents. On the contrary, liberty, properly understood in terms of voluntariness, is necessary for morality. On Hobbes's account, no agent can become subject to law and, through this, liable to punishment, unless he has freely consented to make himself subject to sovereign authority. This said, it remains true that the freedom involved in such acts of consent is not of a distinct or unique kind that differentiates (human) moral agents from non-moral agents. The source or root of this distinction must be found elsewhere and it is the task of Hobbes's contractarian theory to identify and describe the relevant source of this distinction. The threat posed by the liberty assumption is that, not only does it take our attention away from the relevant contractarian foundations of morals, it also encourages us to search for an illusory account of *moral* freedom (e.g. free will) that can serve to fill the void generated by the assumption that some distinct form

of freedom is required of moral agents. The relevant cure for the free will controversy, therefore, rests not so much with Hobbes's views about liberty and necessity,
as with the specifics of his contractarian moral theory.

It is important to consider the wider significance of the divide between Hobbes
and Bramhall as this continued to influence the free will problem throughout the
early modern period. Bramhall's free will position turns, crucially, on the liberty
assumption, and takes for granted that Hobbes accepts the liberty assumption.
Within the compatibilist tradition, as it evolved after Hobbes, there have been
many who have accepted the same liberty assumption. When compatibilists travel
down this track, they divide between those who believe that Hobbes's account of
liberty in terms of voluntariness is more or less correct (e.g. as simple compatibilists hold), and those who believe that this account requires some substantial
revision or amendment (i.e. a theory of freedom that can play the role required
by the liberty assumption). Insofar as the parties on both sides of the free will
debate (i.e. compatibilists and incompatibilists) are committed to the liberty
assumption, it has generated a philosophical dynamic that takes the form of a
familiar, apparently intractable, dilemma. On one hand we may, with Bramhall and
other libertarians, aim to provide an account of liberty that attributes to moral
agents a God-like capacity or power to transcend the operations of nature and the
physical laws that govern it. Unlike other (natural) agents in the world, moral
agents are, on this account, able to govern their conduct in such a way that their
powers of reason and will provide open alternatives which the agent alone decides
or determines. Whatever path is taken, it is not merely a function of antecedent
conditions over which the agent had no control. The obvious difficulty with this
account, as Hobbes observes, is that the attempt to secure God-like powers for
moral agents comes at a high cost: it detaches moral agents from the fabric of the
natural order and the physical laws that govern it; hence the force of Spinoza's
remarks cited above, about a 'dominion within a dominion'. It is a perennial
challenge for libertarian metaphysics to try and restore some plausible 'fit' between
the moral and the natural realms consistent with these metaphysical ambitions.
Perhaps the most dramatic version of this difficulty that libertarians face can be
found in the schism between Kant's noumenal and phenomenal being, insofar as
human agents must somehow reconcile this dichotomy within their own experience and self-interpretations.

Compatibilists are plainly unwilling to pay the price of an anti-naturalistic
metaphysics of the kind that Bramhall advocates. However, insofar as compatibilists continue to adhere to the liberty assumption, they face a different challenge.
The model of freedom to which the compatibilist is committed is, as we have
noted, vulnerable to the charge that it remains mechanical in character. Simple
compatibilism, with its view of liberty understood in terms of mere voluntariness,
is evidently vulnerable to this objection (*pace* the liberty objection). Those compatibilists who aim to provide a 'deeper' account of liberty face the objection that,

no matter how much complexity they give to alternative compatibilist theories, they can never escape from the spectre of 'mechanism' (Frankfurt 1971: Dennett 1984). A freedom that fails to transcend the causal laws of nature cannot successfully or categorically distinguish human agents from other agents in the world who are plainly incapable of moral conduct. In this way, a commitment to the liberty assumption appears to trap us between two unattractive models or ideals: (i) a God-like freedom that is incoherent and impossible, and (ii) a clockwork freedom that is inadequate to the demand of distinguishing moral from non-moral agents. Neither of the two rival models looks like a plausible (or attractive) metaphysical foundation for moral life.

The irony of Hobbes's legacy on this subject is that he is generally understood as falling squarely on one side of this dilemma, alongside the simple compatibilist. Much of the contemporary debate, which has been considerably influenced by the Hobbes–Bramhall exchange, has taken for granted the liberty assumption and reads Hobbes this way as well (Berlin 1969: xv; Davidson 1973: 63; Kane 1996: 10–12) It is evident, nevertheless, that Hobbes challenges the liberty assumption and, to this extent, aims to find a way around the dilemma that it has generated. Granted that no account of liberty or freedom serves as the relevant basis on which to distinguish moral from non-moral agents or explains the basis on which an agent becomes subject to law and liable to punishment, the correct compatibilist strategy rests, on Hobbes's account, with a proper appreciation and description of the *contractualist* features that shape and structure the moral community. From this perspective human agents may indeed use their liberty to make themselves moral agents. In doing this, however, they are not employing a distinct kind of liberty but rather using a liberty that they share with animals and other non-moral agents to perform a distinct kind of act (i.e. consent) whereby they become moral agents subject to law and any punishments that are required to enforce it. Hobbes's effort to reorient the free will debate along these lines is easily lost sight of unless his rejection of the liberty assumption is properly recognized and acknowledged. Whether one finds this strategy promising or not, it is clear that it is a key part of Hobbes's attempt to deflate the free will issue and puts considerable distance between his own views and those of simple compatibilism of a kind that Bramhall and others have attributed to him.

## REFERENCES

ARISTOTLE (1925). *Ethica Nicomachea*. Trans. by W. D. Ross. Oxford: Oxford University Press.

AYER, A. J. (1954). 'Freedom and Necessity'. Reprinted in G. Watson (ed.), *Free Will*. Oxford: Oxford University Press, 15–23.

BERLIN, I. (1969). *Four Essays on Liberty.* Oxford: Oxford University Press.

CAMPBELL, C. A. (1951). 'Is "Freewill" a Pseudo-Problem?' Reprinted in B. Berofsky (ed.), *Free Will and Determinism.* New York: Harper & Row, 112–35.

CHISHOLM, R. (1964). 'Human Freedom and the Self'. Reprinted in G. Watson (ed.), *Free Will.* Oxford: Oxford University Press, 26–37.

CLARKE, S. (1998). *A Demonstration of the Being and Attributes of God and Other Writings.* Ed. E. Vailati. Cambridge: Cambridge University Press.

DAVIDSON, D. (1973). 'Freedom to Act'. Reprinted in D. Davidson, *Essays on Actions and Events.* Oxford: Clarendon Press.

DENNETT, D. (1984). *Elbow Room: The Varieties of Free Will Worth Wanting.* Oxford: Clarendon Press.

FISCHER, J. and RAVIZZA, M. (1998). *Responsibility and Control: A Theory of Moral Responsibility.* Cambridge: Cambridge University Press.

FRANKFURT, H. (1971). 'Freedom of the Will and the Concept of a Person'. Reprinted in G. Watson (ed.), *Free Will.* Oxford: Oxford University Press, 322–36.

HOBART, R. E. (1934). 'Free Will as Involving Determinism and Inconceivable Without It'. Reprinted in B. Berofsky (ed.), *Free Will and Determinism.* New York: Harper & Row, 63–95.

HOBBES, T. (1966a). *Elements of Philosophy: The First Section Concerning Body.* Reprinted in HW, Vol. 1.

HOBBES, T. (1966b). *The Questions Concerning of Liberty, Necessity and Chance.* Reprinted in HW, Vol. 5.

HOBBES, T. (1972). *Man and Citizen.* Ed. with an introduction by B. Gert. Brighton: Harvester.

JACKSON, N. D. (2007). *Hobbes, Bramhall and the Politics of Liberty and Necessity: A Quarrel of the Civil Wars and Interregnum.* Cambridge: Cambridge University Press.

KANE, R. (1996). *The Significance of Free Will.* Oxford: Oxford University Press.

KANT, I. (1873). *Critique of Practical Reason and other Works.* Trans. T. K. Abbott. London and New York: Longmans, Green & Co.

PETTIT, P. (2005). 'Liberty and Leviathan'. *Philosophy, Politics and Economics,* 4: 131–51.

PETTIT, P. (2008). *Made with Words: Hobbes on Language, Mind and Politics.* Princeton, NJ: Princeton University Press.

PINK, T. (2004). 'Suarez, Hobbes and the Scholastic Tradition in Action Theory', in T. Pink and M. W. F. Stone (eds), *The Will and Human Action.* London: Routledge, 127–53.

REID, T. (1969). *Essays on the Active Powers of the Human Mind.* Ed. B. Brody. Cambridge, MA: MIT Press.

SCHLICK, M. (1939). 'When is a Man Responsible?' Reprinted in B. Berofsky (ed.), *Free Will and Determinism.* New York: Harper & Row, 54–63.

SKINNER, Q. (2008). *Hobbes and Republican Liberty.* Cambridge: Cambridge University Press.

SMART, J. J. C. (1961). 'Free Will, Praise and Blame.' Reprinted in G. Watson (ed.), *Free Will.* 2nd edn. Oxford: Oxford University Press, 58–71.

WALLACE, R. J. (1994). *Responsibility and the Moral Sentiments.* Cambridge, MA: Harvard University Press.

WATSON, G. (ed.) (1982). *Free Will.* Oxford: Oxford University Press.

# CHAPTER 21

# THE EQUALITY OF MEN AND WOMEN

## EILEEN O'NEILL

In the late medieval period and the Renaissance, numerous texts appeared in Europe on the topic of the relative merits of men and women, especially with respect to the moral and intellectual virtues. While defences of women's virtue were frequently influenced by the courtly love tradition and by popularized versions of Platonism, these were countered by satirical attacks on woman's nature and marriage, and by diatribes on women's natural imperfection and moral failings. Beginning around 1400 and continuing into the eighteenth century, a distinctive genre provided arguments for women's fitness for education, for political authority, and for more active roles in society. The confluence of these literary traditions gave rise to the genre known as the *Querelle des femmes* [Quarrel about Women] (Richardson 1929; Jordan 1990). Formal characteristics of the genre include argumentation; appeals to the authority of scripture, Early Church Fathers, and great philosophers of the past; and examples of illustrious women. The arguments of many *Querelle* texts were often so unconvincing that the genre has sometimes been characterized as a literary one that was meant more to amuse rather than convince its readers (Maclean 1977: 25); however, feminist interpretations take it more seriously (Kelly 1984; King and Rabil 2002).

Among the earliest examples of this genre are Jean de Meun's attacks on woman's nature and courtly love in his contribution to the *Romance of the Rose* (*c.*1270), Matholeus' thirteenth-century misogynist poem, *Lamentations*, and Christine de Pizan's defence of women in, among other works, her *Book of the City of Ladies* (*c.*1405) (Richardson 1929; Bornstein 1981; Willard 1984; Quilligan 1991; Brabant

1992; Richards, *et al.* 1992; Green 1995; Forhan 2002; Green and Mews 2005; Broad and Green 2007). Christine defends women's capacity for governing themselves and others, and women's capacity for the intellectual and moral virtues not only by appealing to experience and examples, but also on scriptural premises. In response to the reading of 1 Corinthians 11:7 that assumes that the 'image of God' refers to bodily features and thus that women, with their female bodies, are not made in God's image, Christine draws on Genesis 1:27 ('God created man in his own image, in the image of God he created him; male and female he created them') and argues (Pizan 1997: 132):

1. The image of God is nothing corporeal, but rather an immortal, intellectual soul.
2. When God created man and woman he 'put completely equal souls, one as good and noble as the other, into the female and male bodies'.
3. Therefore, woman was formed by God in his image.
4. Therefore, woman's soul is not less noble, but rather equal in value, to the soul of man.

This argument becomes a staple of early modern discussions of the equality of men and women.

Another argument—in response to the Aristotelian charge that woman's body is a defective male body, and a cause for shame—shows, however, that Christine does not argue for the equality of men and women in all respects (Pizan 1997: 132). It implies that women's bodies are not only *not* defective; they are superior in a number of ways, for example, with respect to their material cause.

1. Woman's body was made by the supreme craftsman, God.
2. God creates nothing defective. (unstated assumption)
3. God was not ashamed of his creation of the body of woman.
4. Therefore, woman's body is neither defective nor a cause of shame.
5. The matter from which God formed man's body was a lowly matter, clay; the matter from which God formed woman's body was the noblest matter God had ever created, the body of man.
6. The place of the creation of man's body was a field in an ordinary earthly city, Damascus; the place of the creation of woman's body was the most noble on earth, terrestrial paradise.
7. Therefore, in terms of its creator, matter, and the place of its creation, woman's body is not less perfect than man's.

Henricus Cornelius Agrippa, in his *Declamation on the Nobility and Preeminence of the Female Sex* (1529), argues along similar lines for the equal 'nobility' of men and women (1996: 43). But Agrippa further claims that 'setting aside the divine essence of the soul in humans, in everything else that constitutes human being the illustrious feminine stock is almost infinitely superior to the ill-bred masculine race' (1996: 44). To support this conclusion, Agrippa uses premises (5) and (6) of

Christine's argument against the Aristotelian view that woman's body is a defective version of man's (1996: 48–50). He further argues that 'since beauty itself is nothing other than the refulgence of the divine countenance', and since women 'were much more lavishly endowed and furnished with beauty than man', 'the beauty of women merits for them an increase in esteem and honor, not only in the eyes of humans, but also in the eyes of God' (1996: 50, 54) (Nauert 1965; Maclean 1980; Jordan 1990; King 1991).

The claim that physical beauty merits women greater honour than men is transformed by Lucrezia Marinella, in *The Nobility and Excellence of Women and the Defects and Vices of Men* (1600), in light of her commitment to neoplatonic metaphysics (Labalme 1981; Panizza 1999; Kolsky 2001; Broad and Green 2009). Here Marinella argues that precisely because women are physically more beautiful than men, 'the souls of women possess an excellence which men's do not', since 'the nobility of the soul can be judged from the excellence of the body' (1999: 56–7). Thus, she rejects the argument for the equality of men's and women's souls, which Christine and Agrippa advanced (1999: 57). Marinella also rejects Moderata Fonte's argument in *Floridoro* (1581) for the equality of men's and women's souls, *viz.* since men and women are members of the same species, they must have the same substantial form, which is the human soul (Marinella 1999: 55). 'It is not impossible that within the same species there should be souls that are from birth nobler and more excellent than others, as is written by the Master of Sentences, Peter Lombard. Given this fact, I would say that women's souls were created nobler than men's, as can be seen from the effect they have and from the beauty of their bodies' (Marinella 1999: 55).

The *Querelle* argument that women and men are equal because they are made in God's image and are endowed with the same immortal soul became a mainstay of philosophical defences of the equality of men and women in the early modern period and, subsequently, in the nineteenth-century fight for women's suffrage (Stanton 1972: 15–16). Notwithstanding this argument, the texts typically concluded either the general superiority of men or of women, as exemplified by Marinella, or the superiority of one of sexes in some respects, as in Christine, Agrippa, and Fonte. One explanation for this phenomenon is that those authors who wrote within an Aristotelian framework, and who therefore accepted Aristotle's norm/defect theory of gender difference, held that equality requires sameness.

According to the norm/defect theory, male bodies are the norm and are produced under paradigmatic conditions; female bodies, which are produced under non-optimal conditions, are defective ones that fall short of the norm. This difference between a perfect (i.e. male) and a defective (i.e. female) body results in differences in the humours of males and females, which lead to differences in temperament and disposition. Thus women, who are by nature cold and wet, are disposed to acting imprudently and to letting their passions rule them. Nonetheless, male and female humans are members of the same species and because, according to Aristotle, each species is determined by a unique form, male and female humans are equal with respect to their form. Within the Aristotelian framework, then, while the constellation of women's qualities are inferior to those of men, in the one respect in which men and women are the same, namely in relation to their form, they are equal (Matthews 1986).

Christians who worked within this Aristotelian framework took the soul to be the substantial form of humans and concluded that, in the one respect in which men and women are the same, namely in relation to their soul being made in God's image, they are equal. Some philosophers argued that women are men's equals in more respects than just their human form/soul. These authors either neglected or rejected his norm/defect theory of gender difference.[1] However, in the early modern period, authors increasingly began to theorize equality not in terms of sameness, but with sexual/gender differences in mind. This chapter will focus on the *explicit* affirmations of the equality of men and women by Marie le Jars de Gournay, François Poullain de la Barre, and Gabrielle Suchon, and the *implicit* defence of equality by Anne Thérèse de Lambert. These four theorists of gender difference show in striking relief how metaphysical and epistemic systems as diverse as Pyrrhonian scepticism, Aristotelianism, and Cartesianism were the backdrop to discussions of the equality of the sexes. They also reveal how the complementarity theory of gender difference, later endorsed by Rousseau and used to maintain women's limited access to education and other social freedoms, had been used in the early modern period to argue for better education for women and for their greater participation in society.

# I: MARIE DE GOURNAY (1565–1645)

It is often claimed that Marie de Gournay's *Equality of Men and Women* (1622) was the first work to argue for women's equality (as opposed to superiority or inferiority) with respect to men (Ilsley 1963: 205; Broad and Green 2009: 125).[2] But at least

---

[1] For example, Baldesar Castiglione's *The Book of the Courtier* rejects Aristotle's norm/defect theory of gender difference and suggests instead a complementarity theory; according to this, the qualities typically displayed by women are different from those of men but equally necessary for human flourishing (1967: 219–20).

[2] On Gournay's *Egalité*, see also Devincenzo (2002); Fogel (2004); Franchetti (2006). Maclean (1977) argues that Olivier's *Alphabet of the Imperfection and Malice of Women* (1617) spawned numerous *Querelle* texts, possibly including Gournay's *Equality*. A comparable pamphlet war on the woman question also raged in England in this period. In response to Joseph Swetnam's *The Araignment of Lewde, Idle, Froward and unconstant Women* (1615), numerous defences of women appeared (e.g., Speght 1617; Sowernam 1617; Munda 1617). See Kelly (1984); Ferguson (1985).

as early as 1501, defences of the equality thesis were being written, such as Mario Equicola's *On Women* (Fahy 1956; Kolsky 1991). In order to determine what is philosophically original in Gournay's text, it will be worth surveying four main lines of reasoning in Equicola's short treatise. He begins by reading Genesis 1: 27 as Christine de Pizan had done: the 'image of God' is the rational soul, which God bestowed equally upon male and female humans (2004: 22, 24). But he is not simply grounding the equality of men and women in biblical revelation. For Equicola, Moses (who, he assumes, is the author of Genesis), along with Hermes Trismegistus and Plato, contributed to 'the *pia philosophia* which, in turn, constituted an element of the Neoplatonic corpus' (Kolsky 1991: 73). Second, Equicola argues that God fashioned the bodies of men and women out of a single material, which implies that the soul and body of man and woman have the same 'origin and principle' (2004: 24).

Third, in response to natural philosophers who had based differences between men's and women's bodies on contrary qualities of the elements (e.g. that women are colder and more humid than men), Equicola raises sceptical doubts about which animals are hot and which are cold (2004: 28). Sometimes, he appears to be a Renaissance sceptic: 'Who, indeed, except he who came from heaven, could demonstrate or declare without a doubt, by means of native mental ability (*ingenio*) or reflection (*cogitatione*), the causes and reasons for heavenly and natural things?' (2004: 28).[3] Even when he notes that some doubts are resolved, since the senses and the necessities of life reveal the truth to us, he still might be expressing a sceptical view: the mere appearances and customs of everyday life are insulated from sceptical doubt, for we do not believe that appearances reveal any truths about the true natures of things. However, Equicola also makes claims that are difficult to read as evidence of a genuinely sceptical stance: 'We make our way by means of more evident things, since it appears clearer than light that woman is composed of the same elements as man is. Indeed her body is born out of the same semen, is nourished, grows up, gets old and dies. She receives the same spirit; she aims for the same goal of happiness. She reasons with the same opinion, understanding and speech, since rational mortal creatures have a single nature and all have an equal innate liberty' (2004: 30).[4]

Equicola's fourth line of reasoning advances inferences drawn from experience and practical life, as well as from history and sociology, for the conclusion with which 'all the naturalists agree': 'many differences in bodies, characters, and native ability' derive, not from our nature, but from 'diverse habits of education and

---

[3] The University of Massachusetts Center for Translation made available an English translation of an Italian translation of Equicola's text (Equicola 2004) against which I checked my own translation of the Latin original. I have used the latter in this chapter.

[4] On the important, but neglected, issue of the relation of Renaissance and early modern scepticism to the woman question, see Wilkin (2008).

training' (2004: 30). Equicola considers the social and political roles appropriate for women, since mental and physical traits do not befall us by a necessity of nature. He reminds the reader that, in the *Laws* and the *Republic*, Plato thought that women's bodies were fit for physical training and that their nobility of mind made them suited for education in leading an army. In short, it is 'custom, not nature, that prohibits women from political life and from warfare' (2004: 34).

Like Equicola, Gournay argues that the differences between men's and women's accomplishments—given women's lack of education and experience in the world— may simply be due to these deprivations, rather than to any irremediable differences in their natures (O'Neill 2007: 25–7). She also presents an argument that women are, equally with men, made in God's image. But she uses these arguments for purposes quite different from those of Equicola. Finally, the role of scepticism in Gournay's text undercuts any claim that she is arguing for the equality of men and women. All this requires some explicit comments on her method.

Gournay has baffled commentators by appearing to provide arguments for the equality thesis and offering examples of intelligent and prudent women, and yet by stating: 'while I think very highly of both the dignity and ability of the ladies, I do not claim, at this time, to be able to prove this by means of reasoning since the opinionated can always dispute this; nor by examples, since they are too common; thus only by the authority of God himself, of the pillars of his Church, and of the great men who have served as the guiding light of the World' (Schiff 1910: 63).[5] Some commentators have maintained that, despite her explicit claim, Gournay's arguments were intended to justify the equality thesis, and that the arguments are therefore internally inconsistent (Rowan 1980: 276; Bijvoet 1989: 10). Douglas Lewis has argued that Gournay's own experience and her knowledge of women's accomplishments provide the principal evidence for her thesis (Lewis 1999: 64). However Gournay is best understood, following the lead of her mentor Montaigne, as a Pyrrhonian fideist (O'Neill 2007).

As a Pyrrhonian sceptic, Gournay holds that reason has not (at least yet) revealed to us the true natures of things that lie beyond appearances, and thus that the dogmatic philosophers' arrogant use of reason to determine woman's nature has been to no purpose. Like Montaigne, she consistently finds equipollent arguments both for and against philosophical claims; the function of her arguments, in this treatise, is to apply scepticism therapeutically to expose the hubris of dogmatic misogynists. Non-theoretical judgements of ordinary life, such as 'It is raining today', are insulated from scepticism, and the sceptic can therefore live her life in accordance with appearances, while escaping from the vanity of dogmatizing about the true natures of things. But surely the equality of men and women with respect

---

[5] All translations of Marie de Gournay's *Égalité des hommes et des femmes* (1622) are my own. The copy text is included in Schiff (1910).

to their moral and intellectual abilities is not an appearance, but a theoretical claim. How, as a Pyrrhonian, can Gournay hold this thesis?

Gournay and Montaigne differ from the ancient Pyrrhonists because there is a second set of propositions that is insulated from scepticism, namely, the articles of faith that God has revealed in Scripture, preserved in the Catholic faith, and sometimes made known to the great pagan philosophers in the time before Christ. As a fideist, Gournay holds that faith requires no justification from reason and is known with greater certitude than anything else, for our only access to truth is through God's revelation. Further, as a *Catholic* fideistic sceptic, Gournay and Montaigne appear to hold that by abandoning the vanity of reason which has given rise to all of the theological disputes and fissures within Christianity, and by embracing the tradition of the Catholic faith, as pagan sceptics submit to the appearances and customs of ordinary life, fideistic sceptics attain something comparable, but superior, to the Pyrrhonians' state of tranquillity (O'Neill 2007: 24; Popkin 2003; Penelhum 1983).

From this perspective we can reevaluate Gournay's remarks about her method, which initially appeared inconsistent. When she declines to prove her thesis of equality 'by means of reasoning, since the opinionated can always dispute this', this refers to the Pyrrhonian experience that there are always equipollent arguments available. Her arguments, then, are mere counters to those of the misogynists and are meant to show only that reason alone should lead us to a sceptical conclusion about the equality of the sexes. When she says that she will prove her thesis 'only by the authority of God himself', 'the pillars of his Church', and the 'glorious witnesses' of the ancient world, she is expressing her Catholic fideism: our knowledge of woman's true nature can be known only through divine revelation, as given in Scripture and as preserved by the Catholic faith, or as directly intuited by the great minds that God illuminates.

An analysis of one of Gournay's arguments will illustrate how this Pyrrhonian/ fideistic reading sheds light on the originality of her contribution to the *Querelle* literature.

[T]he human animal is neither man nor woman, the sexes having been created not as ends in themselves but *secundum quid*, as the School says, that is, solely for the purpose of propagation. The unique form and *differentia* [defining characteristic] of this animal, consists only in the human soul. And if we are permitted to jest in passing, a little joke that teaches us will not be inappropriate: nothing resembles a male cat on the window ledge more than a female cat. . . . Man was created male and female, the Scriptures say, reckoning the two as only one. . . . Thus, the great Saint Basil later said: 'Virtue in man and in woman is the same, since God has bestowed upon them the same creation and the same honour; *masculum et foeminam fecit eos*'. Now in those who have the same Nature, their actions are likewise the same, and whenever their works are the same, they will be esteemed and valued the same in consequence. That, then, is the opinion of this powerful pillar and venerable witness of the Church. Concerning this point, it is timely to remember that certain ancient quibblers went so far with their foolish arrogance as to contest that the female sex, as opposed to the male sex, is made in the image of God, which image they must have taken to be in the beard, according to my understanding.   (Schiff 1910: 70–1)

This is not a positive argument for the equality of men and women on the basis of both sexes having been made in the image of God.[6] Rather, she presents an equipollent argument in response to the 'ancient quibblers' who had argued that women are not made in God's image (Horowitz 1979; Maclean 1977, 1980):

1. Forms/souls of creatures specify the properties essential to being a member of a particular species. (Teaching of the schools, which the opponents hold)
2. Gender-specific properties are only essential for procreation; they are not essential for being a member of a species, and so are not specified by the forms/souls. (Teaching of the schools, which the opponents hold)
3. God created human males and females in a single act of creation, endowing them with the human form/soul. (View of St Basil and the traditional view of the Catholic Church)
4. Therefore, human males and females have the same human form/soul. (By 3)
5. Therefore, human males and females are members of the same species. (By 1 and 4)
6. The 'image of God' refers to the human form/soul. (Traditional view of the Catholic Church)
7. Therefore, human males and females are both made in the image of God. (By 4 and 6)

In response to the ancient quibblers' rejection of (7), Gournay raises a sceptical worry about what the 'image of God' could be, if it is not the human form/soul, by making the ironic remark that it must 'be in the beard'. She thereby lays bare the astonishing implication of her opponents' views: To deny that women are made in God's image, is (as Aquinas held) to deny that women share the same form/soul as men, and this, for any Aristotelian scholastic, is to deny that women are human—at which even the ancient quibblers will recoil. (The opponent had aimed at showing that not all *members of the human species* are equally made in the image of God.)

Unlike Christine and Equicola, Gournay has not used rational argument to prove that women are made in God's image and share in the human Form. She believes that on faith. The aim of her argument is sceptical and therapeutic: to show her interlocutors their hubris in rejecting the Church Fathers' divinely-inspired glosses on the account of woman's creation in Genesis I, and in using their paltry reason to interpret St Paul to prove that women's souls are inferior to men's.

---

[6] Deslauriers (forthcoming) thinks *only some* of Gournay's arguments in *Egalité* are equipollent, sceptical ones and that this is a positive, original argument, which draws on Aristotle's *Categories*. Deslauriers thinks this argument is not a response to the view that women are not made in God's image. On Gournay's scepticism, see also Broad and Green (2009: 131).

Rebecca Wilkin notes that 'Gournay applied the sceptical notion of equipollence to articulate the first philosophical—that is non-theological—theory of equality as it concerned men and women' (2008: 182). Gournay's treatise certainly is a philosophical treatment of the equality of the sexes, precisely because of the sceptical arguments. However, to claim that it is non-theological fails to see the crucial role that fideism plays in *Equality*.

# II: François Poullain de la Barre (1647–1723)

In Europe in the second half of the seventeenth century, although Aristotelianism continued to be a framework within which philosophers addressed the issue of the equality of men and women, some theorists began to adopt modern metaphysical and epistemological frameworks. Poullain de la Barre emerges as a paradigmatic Cartesian theorist of the equality of the sexes, since (i) he is firmly committed to a wide range of Cartesian doctrines, and (ii) among those with Cartesian leanings, he theorizes explicitly the broadest range of respects in which men and women are equal. In 1673–75, Poullain published three books defending the equality thesis and arguing for the social reforms that the thesis implied. This defence comes as a surprise, when seen against the backdrop of much of the literature on the woman question in the same period. Some treatments of the issue (Decrues 1687; Vertron 1699), as in earlier *Querelle des femmes* texts, appear to be merely exercises of wit and displays of learning (Richards 1914), while many others argue either for the inferiority of women (Olivier 1617; Rolet (L.S.R.) 1623) or for their superiority (L.S.D.L.L. 1643; Du Soucy 1646; Gilbert 1650; Guillaume 1665; Noel 1698).[7] In contrast, this section highlights the main lines of argumentation in Poullain's *On the Equality of the Two Sexes*, discusses their originality and philosophical importance, and indicates the role of Cartesianism in shaping and grounding them.

Poullain begins *Equality* by noting that those who support the equality thesis have to 'refute two adversaries': (i) the common people, whose refutation will constitute Part One of the treatise, and (ii) most of the scholars, whose refutation will take place in Part Two. The former adversaries 'are limited to the hackneyed, old arguments about how things have always been this way' (Poullain de la Barre

---

[7] Numerous texts on the woman question were devoted to the virtues that befit women, e.g., Du Bosc (1632/1634/1636) and Grenaille (1639/1640). The *femmes fortes* texts were a subset of a literary genre that emerged in France (1630–50), which praised famous women for their moral strength and heroic deeds, e.g., Le Moyne (1647); Scudéry (1642/1644). See Maclean (1977); Clarke (1990).

2002: 50). Their most powerful argument for the inferiority of women runs something like this (2002: 54):

1. If women were fit for learning, governing, and holding public offices, then they would be enjoying these benefits and roles.
2. But women are not enjoying these benefits and roles.
3. Therefore, women were never fit for learning, governing and holding public office.

Poullain challenges the soundness of this reasoning by charging that premise (1) derives from the false 'opinion we have of the fair-mindedness of our (the male) sex'—since popular opinion is grounded in self-interest—and in 'a false idea we have of custom: if something is well established, we think it must be right' (2002: 54). Rather than accept the dictates of custom or habit uncritically, he argues that we must 'reject everything we have accepted from second-hand information without examining it further' (2002: 53). If people 'seek out the truth for themselves . . . they quickly come to realize that we are full of prejudices and that we have to make a real effort to get rid of them before we can hope to come to a clear and distinct understanding' (2002: 49). Clarity and distinctness are needed, since Poullain takes them to be the criteria for truth (2002: 50).

Poullain uses Cartesian method to shake the reader's confidence in what custom teaches about the nature of women. This method is not the sceptical doubt of the *Meditations*. Poullain offers no sceptical scenarios explaining how women came to be and to behave as they now appear to us—scenarios later to be overthrown once we have eliminated our ungrounded prejudices about women. Daniel Garber (1992: 55) has argued that 'in the *Discourse* it is experience in the very most general sense that is supposed to free us from prejudice; travel and study of the book of nature is supposed to loosen the bias of youth and education'. This would seem to be the Cartesian method that Poullain is using. He rejects what custom and scholastic education have led people to believe about the great differences between the minds and bodies of the two sexes, since experience reveals that in childhood women are quicker at learning than boys; as adults they are more eloquent and more learned about the passions than men; and their imagination knows no bounds (2002: 61–2). In fact, experience reveals that 'as far as the two sexes are concerned, there is as much aptitude in one as in the other' (2002: 61). Given this, how can we explain women's inferior status?

It would be un-Cartesian if Poullain simply accepted what his senses reported to him about women. Descartes had argued against both the common person and the scholarly Aristotelian that they were unjustified in judging that, simply because they had a sensory perception of X, X exists in the external world and is exactly similar to their sense experience. He held that reason and imagination are needed to construct theories that could explain the nature of body and the physiological process involved in sense perception. And these scientific explanations were always hypothetical. The logic of hypothetical explanations was adapted from problems in physics to other disciplines, including history. Thus if a Cartesian wished to explain the present inferior condition of women in society, it is perfectly in keeping with Cartesian method to formulate an historical hypothesis, an invented reconstruction of past events, which might causally result in current historical realities.... Poulain's explanation of the inferior status of women should be read as a typical Cartesian hypothesis designed to explain rationally an observed social phenomenon    (Clarke 1990: 11).

Poullain's 'historic conjecture' is a hypothetical explanation of women's subordination to men. He suggests that, at the dawn of history, society was approximately egalitarian and women 'contributed equally to the tasks of tilling and hunting'. But since men 'were the stronger and physically superior sex' and 'since women's strength was sapped for a time by the indisposition of pregnancy and its aftermath', wives came to depend on their husbands. As families and clans grew, women's dependence on men became 'more widespread and hence more perceptible'. Poullain hypothesizes how societies were formed according to a 'might makes right' principle and discusses the role of warfare in extending the rule of the stronger. Within this social context, the status of women, who were physically weaker than men and who were frequently part of the booty of war, plummeted dramatically, to the point where they were thought to contribute nothing more to society than their reproductive powers (2002: 56–8). Poullain concludes that this historical conjecture 'makes it quite clear that it is exclusively through their superior physical strength that they [men] have kept for themselves all external advantages, from which women are excluded', including the sciences and public positions (2002: 60). This hypothesis may have influenced other seventeenth-century theorists. In *An Essay in Defence of the Female Sex* (1696), published anonymously but attributed to Judith Drake, we find an explanation of women's subordination that bears a strong resemblance to Poullain's (1696: 38–9; Smith 1982: 117).

In Part Two of *Equality*, Poullain argues that 'women considered according to the principles of sound philosophy are as capable as men of all manner of studies' (2002: 82), where the 'sound philosophy' is Cartesianism. Many commentators have taken Poullain's thesis of sexual equality to be merely an 'equality of the mind' (Fraisse 1994: 181). Erica Harth has claimed that Cartesian dualism implies (i) that mind 'is freed from bodily and therefore sexual impediments' (1991: 149; 1992: 81), and (ii) that the thinking subject is drained 'of all feeling and emotion connected to the body' (1991: 150; 1992: 82).[8] On this reading, this dualism 'lent philosophical

---

[8] Harth's understanding of Cartesian dualism is misguided because, although Descartes believes that the mind can exist separated from the body (in the sense that there is nothing inconceivable about such a separation), he also believes that while we are alive our soul is in union with, and thus not separated from, the body. It is because of this union that the thinking subject is not drained of all feeling and emotion. For Descartes, thought includes understanding, willing, affirming and denying, but also sensing, feeling, and imagining (O'Neill 1999: 240–1). Steinbrügge (1995: 11–12) has a similarly misguided understanding of Cartesian dualism and of its role in Poullain's arguments.

weight to the commonplace' namely, 'the mind has no sex'. 'Poullain de la Barre used it as the linchpin of his Cartesian arguments in support of women' (Harth 1991: 149; 1992: 81). No doubt Harth, Fraisse, and other commentators are laying a great deal of stress on Poullain's remark, which has the marginal annotation: 'the mind has no sex': 'It is easy to see that the difference between the two sexes is limited to the body since that is the only part used in the reproduction of humankind. Since the mind merely gives its consent, and does so in exactly the same way in everyone, we can conclude that it has no sex' (2002: 82).

But Poullain further argues that 'it is rather the constitution of the body, but particularly education, religious observance, and the effects of environment which are the natural and perceptible causes of all the many differences between people' (2002: 82). He then attempts to demonstrate that there is no significant anatomical difference between men and women. The brain and the sense organs, which are in union with the mind, function in more or less the same way in both men and women. He is not employing Harth's reading of Descartes' dualism as the linchpin of an argument for the equality of men and women's minds. Rather, he argues that 'women are equal to men in mind *and body*; it is merely custom and habit that account for the prejudice of the inferiority of women' (O'Neill 1999: 242; Clarke 1990; Stuurman 2004).[9] Much of Part Two of Poullain's treatise is devoted to lending support to his nurture-rather-than-nature explanation of the differences between the sexes. He argues that if women were given the same training and opportunities as men to develop their physical power, they might acquire a comparable strength. Further, he maintains that whatever defects in character or virtue the women of his time display, they are due to custom and tradition, which can be changed, and to lack of education, which can be remedied.

Poullain also provides an argument for the radical claim that women, as well as men, have a right to study the sciences, since they equally have a right to clear and distinct knowledge:

1. Everyone seeks happiness.
2. Only knowledge of clear and distinct truths, which are acquired through study, can bring true happiness in this life.
3. Everyone has a right to all the means for achieving the true happiness in this life of which they are capable.
4. Therefore, women, as well as men, have a right to knowledge of clear and distinct truths, which are acquired through study. (Poullain 2002: 91–2)

Poullain notes that the happiness that consists in knowledge of clear and distinct truths has virtue as an essential component (2002: 92), since (i) minds can only be truly happy if they have knowledge of clear and distinct truths about themselves,

---

[9] Compare Anon. [Drake] (1696: 32 ff.).

for example, knowledge that they are leading a virtuous life; (ii) minds can lead a virtuous life only if their attempts to will what is right are caused by knowledge of clear and distinct truths about themselves and the good, for example, knowledge of how to moderate desires and to regulate passions, and knowledge of the world and our duties. It follows that, if women were allowed to study and thus to come to know a range of clear and distinct truths and thereby increase their capacity for virtue, they would also be capable of various offices in civil society; they would make good teachers, ministers, civil rulers, civil servants, military strategists, judges and lawyers (2002: 95–9).

Poullain's arguments represent a significant development compared to earlier arguments that were grounded in Scripture, and to Gournay's arguments, which aimed at revealing the futility of reason's attempts to discover the true nature of woman and her capacities. Poullain remarks in the Postface of his treatise: 'The Bible makes no mention of inequality, and as its sole purpose is to provide us with a rule of conduct consistent with its ideas of justice, it leaves to individuals the freedom to judge as best they can the true and natural state of things' (2002: 121). Rather than claim that human reason is a frail instrument, which is unable to attain truth, Poullain asserts an Enlightenment view about the autonomy and value of reason: 'Since every man possesses his own reason and his own understanding, he should use them to govern himself independently of others when he reaches the age of discernment'. He should use reason and understanding 'to judge things according to truth and justice' (2002: 183–4).

Given Poullain's feminism, his radical social egalitarianism (which included not only gender, but also, racial equality), and his Enlightenment rejection of custom and authority in favour of autonomous reason, Siep Stuurman has persuasively argued that he emerges as a leading figure of the early 'Radical Enlightenment' and that his works are among the most radically egalitarian European texts to appear prior to the French Revolution. Yet Stuurman perceptively notes that 'most feminist authors built their argument on subtle combinations of "equality" and "difference", and we will see that Poullain's feminism, despite its forceful emphasis on equality, also contains a subtext on female virtue and difference' (Stuurman 2004: 20). He acknowledges certain differences between women's physiology and men's, and the social consequences that result from these. These elements of 'difference feminism' help to shed light on Lambert's views, which are discussed below.

Poullain, in a section of his treatise devoted to showing in detail how women's brains are such that women 'have an advantageous disposition for the sciences', appears to claim that there are physiological differences between men and women, which causally influence women's minds (given mind–body union) to operate somewhat differently, and better, than men's minds. Poullain had also argued that there are no gendered minds. But is he now suggesting that there are gendered mind–body unions?

[W]e find that all women have a great deal of verve and imagination as well as good memories. All this means that their brain is constituted in such a way as to receive even faint and almost imperceptible impressions of objects that escape people of a different disposition, and it is easily able to retain these impressions and recall them to mind whenever they are needed.... From this it follows that those who have a great deal of imagination and can look at things more efficiently and from more vantage points are ingenious and inventive, and find out more after a single glance than others after long contemplation.... Their speech is fluent and graceful and expresses their thoughts to best advantage    (Poullain 2002: 100–1).

Poullain realizes that women can 'get carried away by the superabundance of their ideas'. However, with practice and effort, they can acquire the discernment and accuracy needed 'to avoid the errors and mistakes to which one is susceptible if one flits from one thing to another' (2002: 101). All this 'is sufficient evidence to show that, as far as the head alone is concerned, the two sexes are equal' (2002: 101–2).

Poullain is no doubt drawing on the opening section of Part One of the *Discourse on the Method*, where Descartes states that 'the power of judging well and of distinguishing the true from the false—which is what we properly call "good sense" or "reason"—is naturally equal in all men, and consequently the diversity of our opinions does not arise because some of us are more reasonable than others but solely because we direct our thoughts along different paths and do not attend to the same things. For it is not enough to have a good mind; the main thing is to apply it well' (CSM I 111). The Cartesian position, then, is that there is egalitarianism with respect to rational ability; however, what Poullain has called 'discernment and accuracy' are also needed to attain truth, and these can easily be acquired by the use of Descartes' simple rules of method. It is also instructive to see what Descartes has to say here about verve or wit, imagination and memory:

I have often wished to have as quick a wit, or as sharp and distinct an imagination, or as simple or prompt a memory as some others. Apart from these, I know of no other qualities which serve to perfect the mind: for as regards reason or sense ... I am inclined to believe that it exists whole and complete in each of us. Here I follow the common opinion of the philosophers, who say there are differences of degree only between the *accidents*, and not between the *forms* (or natures) of *individuals* of the same *species*    (CSM I 111–12).

On the Cartesian view, then, reason is an all or nothing affair; all humans have it. Only the accidental features, what Descartes calls 'modes', such as the mental modes of sensation, imagination and memory, come in degrees. That women have sensations with more vivacity, a bolder imagination, and a keener memory does not show that they have a different kind or form of mind than men do. It shows rather that, when the human mind is united to a woman's body, this mind–body union experiences some heightened accidental mental features. While Poullain might have claimed that women's mind–body union is superior to that of men in terms of accidental mental features, he chose instead to underline the equality of men's and women's minds and bodies.

In stark contrast to Poullain's position, Nicolas Malebranche's views about the influence of women's bodies on their mental capacities may threaten orthodox Cartesian egalitarianism. In the *Search After Truth*, Malebranche states:

This delicacy of the brain fibers is usually found in women, and this is what gives them great understanding of everything that strikes the senses. It is for women to set fashions, judge language, discern elegance and good manners. They have more knowledge, skill, and finesse than men in these matters. Everything that depends upon taste is within their area of competence, but normally they are incapable of penetrating to truths that are slightly difficult to discover. Everything abstract is incomprehensible to them. They cannot use their imagination for working out complex and tangled questions. They consider only the surface of things, and their imagination has insufficient strength and insight to pierce it to the heart, comparing all the parts, without being distracted.... [B]ecause insignificant things produce great motions in the delicate fibers of their brains, these things necessarily excite great and vivid feelings in their souls, completely occupying it.   (MLO 130–1)

Although Malebranche agrees with Poullain about women's vivacity of sense and feeling, and their eloquence, he does not grant them greater powers of memory, and he maintains that they are so lacking in discernment and accuracy, and so unable to concentrate, that they are largely incapable of using their imagination to solve a problem—as Cartesians do when they study geometry. Still, memory and imagination are mere accidental features of the human mind, stemming from its union with a body. Further, Malebranche notes that all men and women 'differ from each other only in degree with regard to the delicacy of the brain fibers' and 'we need not posit essential differences where we do not find perfect *identity*' (MLO 131). So, perhaps Malebranche would agree with Poullain that while women's minds are essentially identical to men's, differences in degree in the bodies of the two sexes bring about different *accidental* mental features in the male and female mind–body unions: for Poullain, these are favourable to women, while for Malebranche the males have the advantage.

The problem with this reading is that it does not take into account Malebranche's claims that normally women 'are incapable of penetrating to truths that are slightly difficult to discover' and that 'everything abstract is incomprehensible to them'. This suggests that Malebranchean female bodies may disrupt the mind's capacity for performing deductions and for grasping first truths. If so, they are thereby threatening the very rationality that Descartes thought was so equally apportioned to humans.

# III: Gabrielle Suchon (1631–1703)

In the Preface to *A Treatise on Ethics and Politics* (1693), Gabrielle Suchon claims that women are 'denied freedom, knowledge and authority' (2010: 73). Because 'the majority of women imagine that constraint [lack of freedom], ignorance [lack of knowledge], and subjugation [lack of authority] are so natural to their sex that their suffering can never be remedied', Suchon sets out to prove that women's privation of these three things is 'based on custom rather than on a natural inability to study, govern, or act freely' (2010: 73, 74). Her hope is that her book will inspire a nobility of spirit and magnanimity in women 'so that they can protect themselves against servile constraint, stupid ignorance, and base and degrading dependence'. In so doing, 'they will not have to revolt against men or shake off the yoke of their obedience, as the Amazons did long ago'. Women could be Christian Amazons of sorts, who, through their moral strength and magnanimity, continue to pay men the deference they owe them, and allow the men to exercise all their privileges, while putting to good use some privileges that women cannot be denied 'without great injustice' (2010: 84, 85). In this eclectic text, Suchon boldly argues for claims reminiscent of those of Poullain (whom she mentions numerous times), such as the sameness and equality of men's and women's minds, women's equal capacity to govern, as well as the view that men have usurped their power over women by force rather than by right or reason. However, unlike Poullain, she does not think her arguments warrant an overhaul of social practices that were based on prejudice and mere custom. Rather, she tries to exact small social concessions in the wake of the sheer weight of the case she makes against women's subordinate status. Suchon's method is also eclectic. She mounts her case by relying on the *Querelle* arsenal of arguments, citations of authorities, and examples of women who displayed freedom, knowledge and authority; yet she also makes use of natural law and natural rights that are grounded, not in human nature or reason, but in divine decrees (Hoffman 1978; Le Doeuff 1998; Broad and Green 2009; Stanton and Wilkin 2010).

In Part I of her treatise, 'On Freedom', Suchon claims that 'freedom is in man a natural right, which emanates from the power of the Sovereign', namely God (2010: 100). This is based on her reading of Genesis 1:26, from which she concludes: 'Man's intelligence and immortality attest to the grandeur of God's principle; He fashioned man's soul to be free and independent in order to resemble Him more closely. The principle of an intellectual substance is to operate and move freely without constraint, after understanding has made things manifest. Man bears within him the character of his sovereign, which is none other than freedom and the free disposition of all his movements' (2010: 93). Suchon reads 'man' in this quotation as referring to all human beings, regardless of sex. Thus, she remarks that reasonable minds should not condemn the view that women are capable of freedom, since 'the creator is no less generous to women than to men' (2010: 75). In short, both men and women equally have a natural right to freedom, grounded in God's decree.

Among the various pre-conditions for complete freedom that Suchon discusses is 'man's freedom to choose his estate and vocation', which she thinks is 'as natural to him as it is for fire to burn' (2010: 101). However, she also holds that 'as soon as man suffers violence and constraint, it ceases to be a right and becomes tyranny' (2010: 101). The Church forbids rulers and heads of families to force their subjects and children to marry against their will, and civil law requires the consent of both parties for a marriage to be legitimate. Similarly, canon and civil laws 'forbid constraining as well as soliciting people to enter the cloister against their will' (2010: 101)—an argument that had been developed at length by Arcangela Tarabotti in the Renaissance text, *Paternal Tyranny* (2004).

Suchon argues that women, equally with men, 'possess the ability and qualities necessary to gain knowledge successfully', drawing once again on Genesis 1:26–27. While her argument shows that neither women's minds nor their bodies are relevantly different from men's, it does not assume a Cartesian, mechanical conception of body. Rather Suchon relies on the *Querelle*'s scripture-based account of the origin of man's and woman's bodies, which was used by Equicola:

To locate the differences between the sexes in their soul as well as in the body is not only to contradict reason, but also to oppose Catholic belief, since God creates souls equally and fashions them in His image and likeness.... That the body of the common mother of mankind was drawn from Adam's side is beyond dispute; she was a part of him. Who could then doubt the competence and ability of the sex, whose bodies and souls have the same origin as those of men? Equal to men in their inherent dignity, women have as much right to cultivate the finer areas of understanding as the first sex.    (2010: 157)

Suchon also claims that 'God created nothing useless: that is an established truth. He destined the least of His creatures for specific uses and appropriate ends.... Indeed, in keeping with natural law, all intelligent creatures pursue their innate desire for goodness and truth' (2010: 157). Given the teleology of the Aristotelian scholastic framework within which Suchon is writing, each individual creature, in virtue of its essence or nature, flourishes only to the extent that it exercises its powers in actions and operations in such a way as to achieve its goal or purpose. Thus, women, as rational creatures, 'would not exist in perfection of being if they were kept from acting in accordance with their intelligent and spiritual natures' (2010: 158), and there is 'no justification for prohibiting them from studying the human sciences' (2010: 158). Suchon's argument is comparable to that of New Spain's Sor Juana Inés de la Cruz, who had also argued, in *The Reply* (1691), from within an Aristotelian scholastic framework for the appropriateness of her scholarship and writing (Paz 1988; Merrim 1991; Arenal and Powell 1994).

In addition to the Aristotelian argument in support of women engaging in study, Suchon has a theological and moral one. She claims that: 'All men are required to know the principal truths that are the foundation of the Christian religion and to understand their individual duty, each according to his estate' (2010: 144). Suchon argues that 'to strive to understand holy and divine truths is an absolute necessity for us. This is a precept which, if left unfulfilled, precludes us from salvation'

(2010: 143). Therefore, women must not limit their 'contemplation to perishable things and never lift our sights to those that are eternal' and men, therefore, must not bar women from studying (2010: 145). Similar arguments for women's education, grounded in the need for women to understand scripture and to grasp fully the grounds of religious doctrine and moral precepts, also appeared in Anna Maria van Schurman's *A Practical Problem: Whether a Christian Woman is Fit to Study Letters* (1641), in Damaris Masham's *Occasional Thoughts in Reference to a Vertuous or Christian Life* (1705) and in Mary Astell's *The Christian Religion, As Professs'd by a Daughter of the Church of England* (1705).[10]

Despite her arguments about women's capacity and need for education, and their natural right to it, Suchon adopted the conservative assumption that women 'cannot rebel against men's orders; women must thus abstain from public study' (2010: 186–7). She concludes that women should have their own private 'colleges, universities, and academies in which to study languages, rhetoric, philosophy and other sublime fields of knowledge . . . ' (2010: 185–6). Astell also argues for women's academies in *A Serious Proposal to the Ladies* (1694).

In the last part of her treatise, Suchon argues that Genesis 1:26–27 shows that at the creation God also equally granted women, as well as men, political authority:

Part of the power men exert over women is usurped more often than it is legitimate, since custom has more force than justice in the way in which we are treated. For God formed man and woman in His image and likeness; He gave them power and dominion conjointly over the animals of the earth, the fish of the sea, and over all that is under the heavens. He made them both masters in equal measure, and His commandment to populate the earth and subjugate it was for Eve as well as for Adam, to whom the Lord gave her as a companion and an associate, not a servant or slave' (Suchon 2010: 198–9).

Since God included women in the direction and supervision of the universe, he granted them intelligence, prudence, judgement, and reason. These qualities, which 'determine the proper order of state, provinces, and cities, are as natural to women as they are to men'. Thus, she concludes, 'I see no reason why persons of the sex should have no role in government' (2010: 221). However, since 'good sense demands that we submit to customs as much as we can and are obliged to', she reasons that 'women today will never undertake to dispossess men of their power and authority: it would be a mental aberration to aim for such morally impossible goals' (2010: 192).

---

[10] Anna Maria van Schurman, however, cautions that while women's fitness for study is a *means* to perfect themselves in this life, and to promote their love of God and their eternal salvation, strictly it is not necessary for their eternal salvation or happiness (1998: 27). On Schurman see Birch (1909); Baar *et al.* (1996); Irwin (1977, 1989). On Masham, see Hutton (1993); Weinberg (1998); Broad (2002); Penaluna (2007). On Astell, see Perry (1985, 1986, 1990); Springborg (2005); Broad (2002); Kolbrener and Michelson (2007); Sowaal (2007).

Suchon maintains that the Church's exclusion of women from ecclesiastical offices cannot be due to women's incapacity, since experience shows that women have successfully served as abbesses of large Church-approved religious orders, where men and women submitted to their authority in all things, except the administering of sacraments. But Suchon's deference to the Church compels her to draw yet another politically conservative conclusion; although 'the exclusion of women from offices and ecclesiastic dignities is based on their sex and should not be taken as a sign of incompetence... providence has disposed of their destiny otherwise, and custom has always opposed their elevation: for the sake of propriety, women must not deviate from well-worn paths' (2010: 220). On this issue, a quite different position was taken by Margaret Fell, who not only argued in defence of women's preaching in *Women's Speaking Justified, Proved and Allowed of by the Scriptures* (1666), but also intended these arguments to support women's preaching (Ross 1949; Kunze 1994; Leucke 1997; Broad and Green 2009).

Despite Suchon's portrayal of marriage in her time as 'a course that few girls would choose, if they could fathom the disgraces and misfortunes involved' (2010: 124), she nonetheless agrees with most of her seventeenth-century counterparts in following the doctrine of St Peter, 'who teaches us to be submissive to any man who has power over us' (2010: 192). Peter 3:1 ('Likewise you wives, be submissive to your husbands') leads Suchon to argue, in *On the Celibate Life Freely Chosen, or Life without Commitments* (1700), for the importance of a third option of 'estate and vocation' for women, other than marriage or the convent, in both of which women lack authority and suffer many forms of constraint, and in both of which a life of scholarship for a woman is close to impossible (Bertolini 2000). She develops the notion of a 'neutralist'—one who voluntarily chooses to live a secular celibate life free from the commitments of marriage and the convent, and who devotes herself to study, moral improvement and contemplation of divine things, as well as charitable actions for the benefit of others.

Suchon's feminist yet politically conservative view about the irremediable subordination of women in marriage bears comparison with Astell's similar position in *Some Reflections Upon Marriage* (1700) (1996). In contrast, Poullain is quite remarkable in the depth and scope of his Cartesian egalitarianism. He maintains that: 'Between people of more or less the same age there should exist only a subordination based on reason, in which case those with less instruction would submit voluntarily to those with more' and 'women have as much good sense as—and often more than—their husbands'. He concludes that, 'since the will of the one is not the rule of the other, if a woman has to do what her husband wants her to, then no less must he in his turn do what she tells him to [do]' (Poullain 2002: 78).

# IV: ANNE THÉRÈSE DE LAMBERT
# (1647–1733)

In *New Reflections on Women* (1727), Anne Thérèse de Lambert echoed many of the views that we have seen expressed in the works of Poullain and Suchon; for example: 'Men have usurped their authority over women through force rather than by natural right' (1995: 35). She notes that in the previous century there were salons 'where conversation and reflection were encouraged', 'where people acquired polish and refinement', and where women were not made to feel ashamed of engaging in learned and witty conversation (1995: 36). But from the moment Molière's play *Les Femmes savantes* [The Learned Ladies] appeared, 'women were made to feel as ashamed of their knowledge as they were of the most reprehensible vices' (1995: 34). Consequently, they came to believe that their physical attractiveness and sexual allure were the only features with which they could gain some leverage in a world in which men had usurped all the power. In response to the 'tyranny of men, who are determined that we should make no use of our faculties' and who 'control our emotions' (1995: 36), Lambert suggests that 'women can redress the balance, and themselves exert power only through beauty and virtue'. But she warns that beauty is 'a tyranny of short duration' and urges women to rely on their 'intrinsic qualities'—the part of women 'worthy of respect, and which lasts' (1995: 35). Thus, while she does not speak of the equality of the sexes in just those terms, she is concerned with women gaining greater social equality with respect to men, and the means by which they will do so.

Lambert's strategy is (i) to review those cognitive features with respect to which women surpass men, according to the philosophers; (ii) to show how education and training are all that women need, given their natural cognitive abilities, to be able to make judgements as sound and as accurate as those of men; (iii) to show how the cognitive abilities in which women excel make them suited to be excellent judges of moral matters, and not just fine arbiters of taste and etiquette; and (iv) to provide a new 'philosophy of love', according to which women—now trained to make sound and accurate judgements, and praised by men for their contributions to culture—will no longer use their physical attractiveness to gain power over men, and will instead seek romantic relationships with men based on mutual respect and love. Lambert believes that education is needed to become virtuous for the same reasons Poullain did, and thus she thinks that by accomplishing (i)–(iii) she will have shown how to achieve a more egalitarian balance of social power between men and women. This will lead to a new, more egalitarian paradigm of heterosexual romantic love (iv), which will constitute a revision of moral behaviour. The remainder of this chapter focuses on (i)–(iii).

Lambert notes that 'an author of considerable repute has accorded the female sex all the charms of the imagination. In matters of taste, he says, they are supreme. They are also the best judges of the perfection of the language—all of which, it seems to me, is no small advantage!' (1995: 38). Commentators typically identify the 'author' here as Malebranche (Hine 1995: 58, fn. 4; Barth-Cao Dahn 2002: 66; Beasley 2006: 36). We have seen that while Malebranche attributes to women superiority in matters of taste and eloquence, he also charges that they are incapable of concentration and are easily distracted, with the result that they typically cannot use their imagination to pierce through the givens of sense to 'truths that are slightly difficult to discover'. Women's vivid sensations stored in memory, as well as their feelings and emotions, completely occupy their mind's attention. Perhaps, then, Lambert also has Malebranche in mind when she states: 'Those who attack women have alleged that when the mind considers something, it works less well in women, since they are hampered by emotion [*sentiment*], which overrides everything' (1995: 40). Her own view is closer to that of Poullain, Suchon, and the Abbé de Bellegarde, who hold that women can discover more from a single sensory intuition than men can after considerable study (Poullain 2002: 101; Suchon 2010: 26; Bellegarde 1705: 129–30).[11] She also endorses Bellegarde's (1705: 138) and Claude Buffier's (1704: 342–3) claim that vivid imagination and strong feelings—far from blocking women from understanding the arts and sciences—are an advantage, in that they make for delicacy of discernment, and a penetrating and subtle mind: 'I agree that, for ideas to impinge on the mind, for light to dawn, as it were, attention is essential. However, in the case of women, ideas arise spontaneously and arrange themselves in a particular order intuitively, rather than as a result of reflection. . . . In my opinion, feeling does not vitiate understanding' (Lambert 1995: 40).[12]

Recall that Malebranche takes women to be superior to men in matters of taste, since such matters as fashion, elegance, and etiquette are a function of sensory appearances and not of the clear and distinct ideas that penetrate 'to truths that are slightly difficult to discover'. Lambert agrees with Malebranche to the extent that she views taste as requiring sensation and feeling. For her it is a union of feeling (*sentiment*) and mind/intelligence (*esprit*), in opposition to her friend Mme. Dacier's view that taste is a harmony between mind/intelligence (*esprit*) and reason (*raison*) (1995: 38–9). But Lambert disagrees with Malebranche in holding that taste depends not only on 'delicate feelings in the heart' but also on 'a soundness of judgment' (1995: 40). Thus, taste can enable the mind to 'penetrate to the heart of

---

[11] Scholars are divided about whether Lambert read any of Poullain's feminist treatises. Stuurman (2004: 280–1) argues that she did; Fasssiotto (1984: 55) argues that this is not clear. See also Hine (1973*a*). On the relation of Lambert's views to Charles Perrault's, see DeJean (1997); Beasley (2006). On Lambert's intellectual milieu, see Stock (1961), Hine (1973*b*) and Marchal (1991).

[12] On the relation of Lambert to Buffier and Bellegarde, see Hine (1995).

things' (1995: 39). Furthermore, taste is not just a matter of aesthetics and etiquette; the sensibility involved in sound taste is such that 'without it, we shall never find humanity or generosity' and rather than being a drawback, it 'is an asset to the mind and is in the service of virtue' (1995: 40–1). With Lambert, then, we are progressing toward a theory of moral sentiments that will culminate in the views of Hume and Adam Smith.

If good taste is 'the gift of nature' such that it 'cannot be deliberately acquired' or taught according to 'hard and fast rules' to one who lacks this innate gift, and if this taste enables the mind 'to penetrate to the heart of things', then why do women need to be educated? Poullain holds that for women to add 'discernment and correct thinking' to their native cognitive talents, they must 'remain sedentary and spend some time thinking of a given thing' in order to avoid the errors that an overabundant imagination generates; acquiring this concentration and discipline requires training in accordance with the rules of Descartes' method. Lambert agrees that 'it is only in solitude that we learn to recognize the true value of things which our imagination has overrated' (1995: 36). According to Faith Beasley, the type of education Lambert thinks women need is not 'book learning' or even training in Descartes' rules of method, but 'social education' that is acquired 'through contact with worldly society'. Beasley quotes Lambert from the latter's *Reflections on Taste*: 'Nature gives it [taste]; it cannot be acquired; the civilized world simply perfects it' and she claims that 'according to Lambert, taste once made perfect by worldly society can assume its primary function, that of determining value and guiding judgment' (2006: 34). Beasley concludes that 'in the worldly salon milieu, taste is developed according to a worldly sense of reasoning. In a broader sense, the salon milieu was offering a new way to reason and to construct value and knowledge' (2006: 39).

It is not obvious, however, that Lambert holds that women (or men) of the salons have a 'different way of knowing'. For example, it is far from clear that, when she describes the exemplary salon figure, Henrietta of England, as superior 'through her reasoning powers' [*par sa raison*] Lambert is making use of a worldly notion of reason alternative to that of Descartes and Poullain. Further, when she claims that 'feeling does not vitiate understanding', it is not clear she intends readers to supply an alternative, worldly sense to 'understanding' (1995: 40). She does contrast women's native intelligence and wit, which is infused with feelings, with the tiresome pedantry of some of the male scholars, but she can hold this view without having to give up a roughly Cartesian account of good sense or reason.

However, some of the rhetoric in Lambert's essay, which intensifies the inegalitarian strain we have seen in Poullain, is suggestive of Beasley's reading. For example, Lambert states that feeling 'produces different kinds of minds, which are capable of throwing a brighter light on ideas and presenting them in a livelier, sharper, and clearer focus' (1995: 40). This could be read as suggesting a contrast between the feminine and masculine mind. A similar reading applies to Lambert's characterization of Mme de la Sablière, the paradigm of the woman of '*sensibilité*' ('She has never spent her time thinking—only feeling'), as well as for the claim that Sablière's passions 'ruled her imagination and her reason' (1995: 41).

Thus, while Lambert continued to support Poullain's thesis of equality, she had also already begun 'to make gender-specific differentiations within this concept'. On the other hand, 'sentiment, newly attributed to women, was not yet regarded as opposed to reason. More sensitivity did not (yet) mean less reason' (Steinbrügge 1995: 18, 20). Within the context of Cartesianism, this is surely correct. Descartes thinks that all humans have reason; while women may have more vivacious sensations and feelings and a bolder imagination, this does not mean that they have a different kind or form of mind/reason than men do. Lambert is therefore an equivocal figure: she both 'accorded women a new characteristic, but it was precisely this well-meaning addition that facilitated women's reduction to that selfsame characteristic. . . . Madame de Lambert is important to the extent that she showed the way to a definition of human nature divided along gender lines' (Steinbrügge 1995: 20).

A more accurate way of situating Lambert within the history of the philosophy of sexual difference and equality may be this: while Malebranche accorded women a Cartesian mind, he saw the influence of the female body on women's mind–body unions as a source of difference and inferiority with respect to women's ability to grasp clear and distinct concepts and perform deductions. This jeopardized Malebranche's very attribution of a *Cartesian* mind to women. Similarly, Lambert's rhetoric of women's heightened feelings that yield a different kind of mind from men's—minds in which passions dominate reason—puts Lambert on the threshold of the complementarity view of gender differences that Rousseau will later develop in his inegalitarian theory.

On the other hand, Lambert may be anticipating the later, radical break with the Cartesian conception of the scope and power of reason that culminates in Hume. She may be suggesting that the sphere in which the feminine mind–body union excels goes far beyond aesthetics and morals; sense, imagination, and the passions may also provide us with our best accounts of the natural world. Perhaps sentiment is more effective at revealing matters of fact than reason is. After all, she states: 'I would argue that we are just as certain of reaching the truth by strong intuitive convictions as we are by the breadth and accuracy of rational arguments. Besides, we always reach our goal faster by this means' (1995: 40). We might, therefore, read Lambert as intimating that the achievements of the pure understanding are not as epistemically valuable as Cartesians had thought, and that the sphere in which the masculine mind–body union excels may be far narrower than they had believed. Lambert's feminine mind–body union may be a stage on the high road to the Humean mind. She may think that most of our claims to knowledge in everyday life, natural science, metaphysics, and morals are grounded in sentiment and custom; the role of rational deduction is limited, for example, to sciences such as mathematics. In that case, we could trace a philosophical progress of sentiment theory from Lambert to Hume.[13]

## References

AGRIPPA, H. C. (1996). *Declamation on the Nobility and Preeminence of the Female Sex*. Ed. and trans. by A. Rabil. Chicago/London: University of Chicago Press.

ANONYMOUS [DRAKE, J.]. (1696). *An Essay in Defence of the Female Sex. Written by a Lady*. London: A. Roper and E. Wilkinson.

ARENAL, E. and POWELL, A. (1994). 'Introduction', in S. Juana Inés de la Cruz, *The Answer/ La Respuesta, Including a Selection of Poems*. New York: The Feminist Press at the City University of New York.

ASTELL, M. (1705). *The Christian Religion, As Profess'd by a Daughter of the Church of England. In a Letter to the Right Honourable T. L., C. I.* London: R. Wilkin.

ASTELL, M. (1996). *Astell: Political Writings*. Ed. by P. Springborg. Cambridge: Cambridge University Press.

ASTELL, M. (1997). *A Serious Proposal to the Ladies, Parts I and II*. Ed. by P. Springborg. London: Pickering and Chatto.

BAAR, M. DE, *et al*. (eds) (1996). *Choosing the Better Part: Anna Maria van Schurman (1607–1678)*. Dordrecht/Boston/London: Kluwer.

BARTH-CAO DANH, M. (2002). *La Philosophie cognitive et morale d'Anne Thérèse de Lambert (1647–1733): la volonté d'être*. New York: Peter Lang.

BEASLEY, F. E. (1992). 'Anne Thérèse de Lambert and the Politics of Taste'. *Papers on French Seventeenth-Century Literature*, XIX/37: 337–44.

BEASLEY, F. E. (2006). *Salons, History, and the Creation of Seventeenth-Century France: Mastering Memory*. Aldershot: Ashgate.

BELLEGARDE, ABBÉ DE (1705). *The Letters of Monsieur l'Abbé de Bellegarde To A Lady of the Court France, On Some Curious and Usefull Subjects*. London: Geo. Strahan.

BERTOLINI, S. (2000). 'Gabrielle Suchon: une vie sans engagement?' *Australian Journal of French Studies*, 37/3: 289–308.

BIJVOET, M. (1989). 'Marie de Gournay: Editor of Montaigne', in K. M. Wilson and F. J. Warnke (eds), *Women Writers of the Seventeenth Century*. Athens/London: University of Georgia Press, 3–29.

BIRCH, U. [C. Pope-Hennessy]. (1909). *Anna van Schurman: Artist, Scholar, Saint*. London/ Bombay/Calcutta: Longmans, Green and Co.

BORNSTEIN, D. (1981). *Ideals for Women in the Works of Christine de Pizan*. Detroit: Michigan Consortium for Medieval and Early Modern Studies.

BRABANT, M. (ed.) (1992). *Politics, Gender, and Genre: The Political Thought of Christine de Pizan*. Boulder: Westview.

BROAD, J. (2002). *Women Philosophers of the Seventeenth Century*. Cambridge: Cambridge University Press.

[13] I would like to thank Desmond Clarke for valuable, detailed comments on earlier drafts of this chapter. I dedicate this chapter to the memory of Sue Weinberg (1924–2010).

BROAD, J. and GREEN K. (eds) (2007). *Virtue, Liberty, and Toleration: Political Ideas of European Women, 1400–1800.* Dordrecht: Springer.

BROAD, J. and GREEN K. (eds) (2009). *A History of Women's Political Thought in Europe, 1400–1700.* Cambridge: Cambridge University Press.

BUFFIER, C. (1704). *Examen de préjugés vulgaires pour disposer l'esprit à juger sainement de tout* in *Oeuvres philosophiques du Pére Buffier.* Paris: Adolphe Delahays [collected edn 1843].

CASTIGLIONE, B. (1967). *The Book of the Courtier.* Trans. by G. Bull. Harmondsworth: Penguin.

CLARKE, D. M. (1990). 'Introduction', in F. P. de la Barre, *The Equality of the Sexes.* Trans. and annotated by D. M. Clarke. Manchester and New York: Manchester University Press, 1–39.

DECRUES, J. B. (1687). *Les Entretiens de Théandre et d'Isménie.* Paris.

DeJEAN, J. (1997). *Ancients Against Moderns: Culture Wars and the Making of a Fin de Siècle.* Chicago/London: University of Chicago Press.

DESLAURIERS, M. (forthcoming). 'Marie de Gournay and Aristotle on the Unity of the Sexes,' in E. O'Neill and M. Lascano (eds), *Feminist History of Philosophy: The Recovery and Evaluation of Women's Philosophical Thought.* Dordrecht: Springer.

DEVINCENZO, G. (2002). *Marie de Gournay: Un cas littéraire.* Fasano: Schena Editore/ Paris: Presses de l'Université de Paris-Sorbonne.

DU BOSC, J. (1632). *L'honneste femme.* Paris: Pierre Billaine. (1634). Second part. Paris: André Soubron. [1636]. Third and last part. Paris: Augustin Courbé.

DU SOUCY, F. (1646). *Le Triomphe des Dames.* Paris: Chez l'autheur.

EQUICOLA, M. (2004). *De mulieribus/Delle donne.* Trans. by G. Lucchesini and P. Totaro. Pisa/Roma: Istituti Editoriali e Poligrafici Internazionali.

FAHY, C. (1956). 'Three Early Renaissance Treatises on Women'. *Italian Studies: An Annual Review,* XI: 30–55.

FASSIOTTO, M.-J. (1984). *Madame de Lambert (1647–1733) ou le féminisme moral.* New York: Peter Lang.

FELL [Fox], M. (1666). *Womens Speaking Justified, Proved and Allowed of by the Scriptures.* London.

FERGUSON, M. (1985). 'Introduction' in M. Ferguson (ed.), *First Feminists: British Women Writers 1578–1799.* Bloomington, IN: Indiana University Press/Old Westbury, NY: The Feminist Press, 1–50.

FOGEL, M. (2004). *Marie de Gournay: itinéraires d'une femme savante.* Paris: Fayard.

FONTE, M. (1581). *Tredici canti di Floridoro.* Venice.

FONTE, M. (1997). *The Worth of Women, Wherein Is Clearly Revealed Their Nobility and Their Superiority to Men.* Ed. and trans. by V. Cox. Chicago/London: University of Chicago Press.

FORHAN, K. L. (2002). *The Political Theory of Christine de Pizan.* Aldershot: Ashgate.

FRANCHETTI, A. L. (2006). *L'ombre discourante de Marie de Gournay.* Paris: Honoré Champion.

FRAISSE, G. (1994). *Reason's Muse: Sexual Difference and the Birth of Democracy.* Trans. J. M. Todd. Chicago/London: University of Chicago Press.

GARBER, D. (1992). *Descartes' Metaphysical Physics.* Chicago/London: University of Chicago Press.

GILBERT, G. (1650). *Panegyrique des dames.* Paris: Augustin Courbé.

GOURNAY, M. DE (2002*a*). *Oeuvres complètes.* Ed. by J.-C. Arnould *et al.* 2 vols. Paris: Honoré Champion.

GOURNAY, M. DE (2002*b*). *Apology for the Woman Writing and Other Works.* Ed. and trans. by R. Hillman and E. Quesnel. Chicago/London: University of Chicago Press.

GREEN, K. (1995). *The Woman of Reason.* Cambridge: Polity.

GREEN, K. and MEWS, C. J. (eds) (2005). *Healing the Body Politic: The Political Thought of Christine de Pizan.* Turnhout: Brepols.

GRENAILLE, F. DE. (1639). *L'honneste fille, premiere partie.* Paris: Jean Paslé; (1640) Second part. Paris: Toussainct Quinet; (1640) Third part. Paris: Antoine de Sommavile & Toussainct Quinet.

GUILLAUME, J. (1665). *Les Dames illustres ou par bonnes et fortes raisons, il se prouve, que le Sexe feminin surpasse en toutes sortes de genres le Sexe masculin.* Paris: Thomas Jolly.

HARTH, E. (1991). 'Cartesian Women'. *Yale French Studies,* 80: 146–64.

HARTH, E. (1992). *Cartesian Women: Versions and Subversions of Rational Discourse in the Old Regime.* Ithaca: Cornell University Press.

HINE, E. M. (1973*a*). 'The woman question in early eighteenth-century literature: the influence of François Poulain de La Barre'. *Studies on Voltaire and the Eighteenth Century,* CXVI/5: 65–79.

HINE, E. M. (1973*b*). 'Madame de Lambert, her sources and her circle: on the threshold of a new age'. *Studies on Voltaire and the Eighteenth Century,* CII: 173–91.

HINE, E. M. (1995). 'Introduction', in E. M. Hine (tr.), *New Reflection on Women by the Marchioness de Lambert.* New York: Peter Lang, 1–32.

HOFFMAN, P. (1978). '*Le féminisme spirituel de Gabrielle Suchon*', *XVIIe siècle,* 121: 269–77.

HOROWITZ, M. C. (1979). 'The image of God in man—is woman included?' *Harvard Theological Review,* 72/2–3: 175–206.

HUTTON, S. (1993). 'Damaris Cudworth, Lady Masham: between Platonism and Enlightenment'. *British Journal for the History of Philosophy,* 1/1: 29–54.

ILSLEY, M. H. (1963). *A Daughter of the Renaissance, Marie le Jars de Gournay: Her Life and Works.* The Hague: Mouton.

IRWIN, J. (1977). 'Anna Maria van Schurman: From Feminism to Pietism'. *Church History,* 46: 48–62.

IRWIN, J. (1989). 'Anna Maria van Schurman: The Learned Maid of Utrecht', in K. M. Wilson and F. J. Warnke (eds), *Women Writers of the Seventeenth Century.* Athens: University of Georgia Press, 164–85.

JORDAN, C. (1990). *Renaissance Feminism: Literary Texts and Political Models.* Ithaca, NY: Cornell University Press.

JUANA INÉS DE LA CRUZ, SOR (1994). *The Answer/La Respuesta, Including a Selection of Poems.* Ed. and trans. by E. Arenal and A. Powell. New York: The Feminist Press at the City University of New York.

KELLY, J. (1984). *Women, History and Theory: The Essays of Joan Kelly.* Chicago/London: University of Chicago Press.

KING, M. (1991). *Women of the Renaissance.* Chicago/London: University of Chicago Press.

KING, M. and RABIL, A. (2002). 'The Other Voice in Early Modern Europe: Introduction to the Series', in M. Le Jars de Gournay, *Apology for the Woman Writing and Other Works.* Ed. and trans. by R. Hillman and C. Quesnel. Chicago/London: University of Chicago Press, vii–xxv.

KOLBRENER, W. and MICHELSON, M. (eds) (2007). *Mary Astell: Reason, Gender, Faith.* Aldershot: Ashgate.

KOLSKY, S. (1991). *Mario Equicola: The Real Courtier.* Geneva: Librairie Droz.

KOLSKY, S. (1999). 'Moderata Fonte's *Tredici canti del Floridoro*: women in a man's genre'. *Revista di Studi Italiana*, 17: 165–84.

KOLSKY, S. (2001). 'Moderata Fonte, Lucrezia Marinella, Giuseppi Passi: an early seventeenth-century feminist controversy'. *The Modern Language Review*, 96: 973–89.

KUNZE, B. Y. (1994). *Margaret Fell and the Rise of Quakerism.* New York: Macmillan.

LABALME, P. H. (1980). 'Women's Roles in Early Modern Venice: An Exceptional Case', in P. H. Labalme (ed.), *Beyond their Sex: Learned Women of the European Past.* New York: New York University Press, 129–52.

LABALME, P. H. (1981). 'Venetian women on women: three early modern feminists'. *Archivo Veneto*, 5: 81–108.

LAMBERT, MADAME DE (1990). *Oeuvres.* Ed. by Robert Granderout. Paris: Honoré Champion.

LAMBERT, MADAME DE (1995). *New Reflections on Women* by the Marchioness de Lambert. Trans. by E. M. Hine. New York: Peter Lang.

LE DOEUFF, M. (1998). 'Suchon, Gabrielle', in E. Craig (ed.), *Routledge Encyclopedia of Philosophy.* Vol. 9. London: Routledge.

LE MOYNE, P. (1647). *La gallerie des femmes fortes.* Paris: Antoine de Sommaville.

LEUCKE, M. S. (1997). '"God Hath Made No Difference Such as Men Would": Margaret Fell and the politics of women's speech'. *Bunyan Studies*, 7: 73–95.

LEWIS, D. (1999). 'Marie de Gournay and the engendering of equality'. *Teaching Philosophy* 22/1: 53–76.

L.S.D.L.L. (1643). *La Femme genereuse.* Paris.

L.S.R. [ROLET, L. S.] (1623). *Tableau historique des ruses et subtilitez des femmes.* Paris: Rolet Boutonne.

MACLEAN, I. (1977). *Woman Triumphant: Feminism in French Literature, 1610–1652.* Oxford: Clarendon Press.

MACLEAN, I. (1980). *The Renaissance Notion of Woman: A study in the fortunes of scholasticism and medical science in European intellectual life.* Cambridge: Cambridge University Press.

MARCHAL, R. (1991). *Madame de Lambert et son milieu. Studies on Voltaire and the Eighteenth Century*, 289. Oxford: Voltaire Foundation.

MARINELLA, L. (1999). *The Nobility and Excellence of Women and the Defects and Vices of Men.* Ed. and trans. by A. Dunhill. Chicago/London: University of Chicago Press.

MASHAM, D. (2004). *The Philosophical Works of Damaris, Lady Masham.* Introd. by J. G. Buickerood. Bristol: Thoemmes Continuum.

MATTHEWS, G. (1986). 'Gender and essence in Aristotle'. *Australasian Journal of Philosophy*, supplement to 64: 16–25.

MERRIM, S. ed. (1991). *Feminist Perspectives on Sor Juana Inés de la Cruz.* Detroit: Wayne State University Press.

MUNDA, C. (pseudo.) (1617). *The Worming of a mad Dogge.* London: Laurence Hayes.

NAUERT, C. G. (1965). *Agrippa and the Crisis of Renaissance Thought.* Urbana: University of Illinois Press.

NOEL, C. M. D. (1698). *Les Avantages du Sexe.* Anvers.

OLIVIER, J. [TROUSSET, A.] (1617) *Alphabet de l'imperfection et malice des femmes.* Paris: Jean Petit-Pas.

O'NEILL, E. (1999). 'Women Cartesians, "Feminine Philosophy", and Historical Exclusion', in S. Bordo (ed.), *Feminist Interpretations of René Descartes*. University Park, PA: Pennsylvania State University Press, 434–57.

O'NEILL, E. (2007). 'Justifying the Inclusion of Women in Our Histories of Philosophy: The Case of Marie de Gournay', in L. Alcoff and E. Kittay (eds), *The Blackwell Guide to Feminist Philosophy*. Malden, MA; Oxford: Blackwell, 17–42.

PANIZZA, L (1999). 'Introduction to the Translation', in Lucrezia Marinella, *The Nobility and Excellence of Women*. Ed. and trans. by A. Dunhill. Chicago/London: The University of Chicago Press, 1–34.

PAZ, OCTAVIO (1988). *Sor Juana or, The Traps of Faith*. Trans. by M. S. Peden. Cambridge, MA: Harvard University Press.

PENALUNA, R. (2007). 'The Social and Political Thought of Damaris Cudworth Masham', in J. Broad and K. Green (eds), *Virtue, Liberty, and Toleration: Political Ideas of European Women, 1400–1800*. Dordrecht: Springer, 111–22.

PENELHUM, T. (1983). *God and Scepticism: A Study in Scepticism and Fideism*. Dordrecht: Reidel.

PERRY, R. (1985). 'Radical doubt and the liberation of women'. *Eighteenth-Century Studies*, 18/4: 472–93.

PERRY, R. (1986). *The Celebrated Mary Astell: An Early English Feminist*. Cambridge: Cambridge University Press.

PERRY, R. (1990). 'Mary Astell and the Feminist Critique of Possessive Individualism'. *Eighteenth-Century Studies*, 23/4: 444–57.

PIZAN, C. DE (1997). *The Book of the City of Ladies*, in R. Blumenfeld-Kosinski and K. Brownlee (eds and trans.), *The Selected Writings of Christine de Pizan*. New York/London: Norton.

POPKIN, R. H. (2003). *The History of Scepticism: From Savonarola to Bayle*. Oxford/New York: Oxford University Press.

POULLAIN DE LA BARRE, F. (1675). *De l'Excellence des hommes, contre l'egalité des sexes*. Paris: Du Puis.

POULLAIN DE LA BARRE, F. (1983). *De l'Education des dames pour la conduite de l'esprit dans les sciences et dans les moeurs*. Facsimile reprint of Paris: Antoine Dezalier, 1679. Ed. by B. Magné. Toulouse: Université de Toulouse le Mirail.

POULLAIN DE LA BARRE, F. (1984). *De l'Egalité des deux sexes*. Paris: Fayard.

POULLAIN DE LA BARRE, F. (2002). *Three Cartesian Feminist Treatises*. Introd. and annotations by M. M. Welch; trans. by V. Bosley. Chicago/London: University of Chicago Press.

QUILLIGAN, M. (1991). *The Allegory of Female Authority: Christine de Pizan's Cité des Dames*. Ithaca, NY: Cornell University Press.

RICHARDS, E. J., *et al.* (eds) (1992). *Reinterpreting Christine de Pizan*. Athens, GA: University of Georgia Press.

RICHARDS, S. A. (1914). *Feminist Writers of the XVIIth Century, With Special Reference to François Poulain de la Barre*. London: D. Nutt.

RICHARDSON, L. M. (1929). *The Forerunners of Feminism in French Literature of the Renaissance from Christine of Pisa to Marie de Gournay*. Baltimore: Johns Hopkins University Press, Paris: Presses Universitaires de France.

ROSS, I. (1949). *Margaret Fell: Mother of Quakerism*. London: Routledge and Kegan Paul.

ROWAN, M. M. (1980). 'Seventeenth-century French feminism: two opposing attitudes'. *International Journal of Women's Studies*, 3/3: 273–91.

SCHIFF, M. (1910). *La fille d'alliance de Montaigne, Marie de Gournay*. Paris: Honoré Champion.

SCHURMAN, A. M. VAN (1641). *Nobiliss. Virginis Annae Mariae a Schurman Dissertatio De Ingenii Muliebris ad Doctrinam, & meliores Litteras aptitudine. Accedunt Quaedam Epistolae eiusdem Argumenti*. Leiden: [Elsevier].

SCHURMAN, A. M. VAN (1998). *Whether A Christian Woman Should Be Educated and Other Writings from Her Intellectual Circle*. Ed. and trans. J. L. Irwin. Chicago/London: University of Chicago Press.

SCUDÉRY, G. [MADELEINE] DE (1642). *Les femmes illustres, ou les harangues heroïques, avec les veritables portraits de ces heroines, tirez des medailles antiques*. Paris: Sommaville & Courbé; (1644). Second part. Paris: Toussainct Quinet & Nicholas de Sercy.

SEIDEL, M. A. (1974). 'Poulain de la Barre's *The Woman as Good as the Man*'. *Journal of the History of Ideas*, 35/3: 499–508.

SMITH, H. L. (1982). *Reason's Disciples: Seventeenth-Century English Feminists*. Urbana/Chicago: University of Illinois Press.

SOWAAL, A. (2007). 'Mary Astell's serious proposal: mind, method, and custom'. *Philosophy Compass*, 2/2: 227–43.

SOWERNAM, E. (pseud.) (1617). *Ester hath hang'd Haman: or an Answere to a lewd Pamphlet, entituled, The Arraignment of Women*. London: Nicholas Bourne.

SPEGHT, R. (1617). *A Mouzell for Melastomus*. London: Thomas Archer.

SPRINGBORG, P. (2005). *Mary Astell: Theorist of Freedom from Domination*. Cambridge: Cambridge University Press.

STANTON, E. C. (1972). *The Woman's Bible*, Parts I and II. New York: Arno Press.

STANTON, D. and WILKIN, R. (2010). 'Introduction', in G. Suchon, *A Woman Who Defends All the Persons of Her Sex: Selected Philosophical and Moral Writings*. Chicago/London: University of Chicago Press.

STEINBRÜGGE, L. (1995). *The Moral Sex: Woman's Nature in the French Enlightenment*. Trans. P. E. Selwyn. New York: Oxford University Press.

STOCK, M.-L. (1961). *Poullain de la Barre: A Seventeenth-Century Feminist*. Ph.D. dissertation, Columbia University.

STUURMAN, S. (2004). *François Poulain de la Barre and the Invention of Modern Equality*. Cambridge, MA: Harvard University Press.

SUCHON, G. (1693). *Traité de la morale et de la politique divisé en trois parties: Sçavoir la liberté, la science, et l'autorité, où l'on voit que les personnes du sexe pour en être privees, ne lasisent pas d'avoir une capacité naturelle, qui les en peut rendre participantes*. Lyon: B. Vignieu [Author given as Aristophile, G. S.]

SUCHON, G. (1700). *Du celibat volontaire, ou La vie sans engagement*. 2 vols. Paris: Jean & Michel Guignard.

SUCHON, G. (2010). *A Woman Who Defends All the Persons of Her Sex: Selected Philosophical and Moral Writings*. Ed. and trans. by D. C. Stanton and R. M. Wilkin. Chicago/London: University of Chicago Press.

SWETNAM, J. (1615). *The Araignment of Lewde, idle, froward and unconstant women: or the vanitie of them, choose you whether*. London: T. Archer.

TAILLEMONT, C. DE (1553). *Discours des champs faëz: A l'honneur et exaltation de l'amour et des dames*. Lyons.

TARABOTTI, A. (2004). *Paternal Tyranny*. Ed. and trans. by Letizia Panizza. Chicago/London: University of Chicago Press.

VERTRON, G. DE (1699). *Conversations sur l'excellence du beau sexe, La Nouvelle Pandora.* Paris.

VINCENT OF BEAUVAIS (1495–96). *Miroir historial.* Trans. by J. de Vignay. Paris: Verard.

WEINBERG, S. (1998). 'Damaris Cudworth Masham: A Learned Lady of the Seventeenth Century', in J. G. Haber and M. S. Halfon (eds), *Essays on the Work of Virginia Held: Norms and Values.* Lanham: Rowman and Littlefield, 233–50.

WILKIN, R. M. (2008). *Women, Imagination and the Search for Truth in Early Modern France.* Aldershot: Ashgate.

WILLARD, C. C. (1984). *Christine de Pisan: Her Life and Works.* New York: Persea.

# CHAPTER 22

# NATURAL LAW AS POLITICAL PHILOSOPHY

## IAN HUNTER

NATURAL law is generically understood in terms of norms of conduct present in human nature, or derived from reflection on it, and hence foundational for 'positive' law and politics. Such notions of natural law break surface today as the tips of several discursive icebergs whose intellectual vagaries, coupled with their historical depth and doctrinal bulk, make them difficult to fathom and dangerous to navigate. In charting the course taken by some key natural-law discourses in seventeenth-century England and Germany, this chapter aims to elucidate their massive yet largely submerged importance for the history of political thought.

Natural law formed part of Europe's pagan heritage. It was transmitted in Stoic (Ciceronian) ethical philosophy as the idea of a natural cosmic order to which man should attune himself (Wilson 2008: 15–20). In Roman law it was present in the form of natural drives for self-preservation and procreation that man shares with the animals and that form the basis for certain legal rights (Justinian 1913: I.2). What was decisive for the history of natural law in early modern philosophy was not these pagan ideas themselves but the manner in which they were transmuted when combined with other conceptions of law in late-medieval Christian monastic and university contexts. From the thirteenth century onwards these contexts constituted a matrix for the disciplines of theology, jurisprudence, and moral and political philosophy in which various constructions of natural law took place. Through its formulation of a law of conduct embedded in man's nature by divine providence, but known by reason and capable of issuing in civil laws, natural law provided a means of configuring the relations between religious, civil, and moral law (Stolleis 2008). It thus formed a uniquely powerful political 'language' for programming the relation between ecclesial and civil authority in early modern Europe.

The different disciplinary cultures of theology, jurisprudence, and philosophy nonetheless supported different conceptions of law, including law as divine reason, civil command, moral imperative, biblical law, and natural ordering. They also supported a variety of overlapping conceptions of human nature, drawing on moral anthropologies in which man was viewed as rationally self-governing, naturally sociable, dangerously fractious, requiring a superior, and so on. This meant that the 'law of nature' could be ceaselessly formulated and reformulated depending on how 'law' and 'nature' were understood. 'Consequently', as Stolleis puts it, 'there is no such thing as "the" natural law; instead, in the course of some 150 years, the success of natural law was based on a wide variety of religious, theoretical and political approaches and motifs' (2008: 51).

This was particularly the case during the sixteenth and seventeenth centuries. Here the fracturing of the Catholic church into rival confessional churches, coupled with the emergence of territorial states imbued with rival confessional establishments, called forth mutually inimical forms of natural law as the 'theory-programs' for opposed religious and political orders (Hochstrasser and Schröder 2002). For this reason, natural law is best understood, not as a philosophical doctrine, but as an intellectual genre or language in which a wide variety of conflicting doctrines were formulated (Haakonssen 2004).

Rather than a history of seventeenth-century natural law, then, this chapter offers an outline of several different contextual uses of the language of natural law, as it was deployed in formulating the intellectual architecture for rival constructions of political and religious authority. Since Thomas Aquinas (1225–74) not only provided an authoritative model for the natural law writers of the sixteenth-century 'second scholasticism' but also set the scene for their anti-scholastic opponents of the following century, it is necessary to begin with a brief review of his account of natural law.

# I: SCHOLASTIC NATURAL LAW

Aquinas elaborated his construction of natural law as a part of a complete system of metaphysical theology in the *Summa theologiae*. At the centre of Aquinas's theology one finds a metaphysical conception of God as the divine mind or reason from whose creative intellection emanate the essences or 'natures' of all things (creatures), thereby constituting the *lex aeterna* or eternal law of the cosmos (ST I-II, q. 93). Human nature is included here because it shares the rational nature of God, albeit only in the diminished form of a divine image, and is able to 'participate' in God's intellection of the nature of things. That is how man comes to understand the law of his own nature, or the natural law (ST I-II, q. 94).

Through his intellection of the natures of things, God imbues them with the law of the 'perfection' or completion of their own nascent essences or 'goods'. Thus, the entire universe of creatures is understood as governed by the law of God's rational intellection of it (Brett 1997: 88–122). Natural law results from divine law, as man's mode of grasping the 'goods' or purposive tendencies of his own nature from within the limits of his natural reason. This permits to him to understand, for example, that self-preservation and sexual procreation are goods in accordance with the natural law, because they are acts necessary for the realization of his nature and hence are objectively right. Similarly, human nature is inclined by the law of its perfection to know the truth about God and to live in society, which means that these too are objectively right (ST I-II q. 94, a. 2). Human law (both civil or positive law) is located at the bottom of this theo-juridical hierarchy, where it is understood as the form in which natural law is enacted in the laws of ecclesial and civil authorities. Aquinas thus regards the justice of positive civil law as conditional on whether it embodies the 'right' embodied in natural law—hence 'natural right'—for otherwise it is a 'perversion of law' (ST I-II, q. 95, a.2). Aquinas's natural law was designed, therefore, as the form in which the law of divine reason is grasped within the limits of man's own rational nature and then mediated to the civil law. The entire array of laws, theological, civil and common, is thus united under a metaphysical-theological normativity in which all government shares the end of perfecting man's rational nature (Schwab 2006).

Thomist natural law also drew heavily on Greek political philosophy, especially the conception of the *polis* (the city or state) that was elaborated in Aristotle's *Politics* and *Nichomachean Ethics*. According to Aristotle's moral anthropology, man is a political animal whose 'rational and sociable' nature can be completed or perfected only in the *polis*, which permits him to realize the virtues of benevolence, charity, and mercy, culminating in the summatory virtue of justice (Aristotle 1996: 11–14). Aristotle thus supplied Aquinas with a conception of the civil state as a natural political association within which man could achieve 'happiness', understood as the satisfaction that results from the perfection of his sociable nature in a virtuous conduct of life. Since Aquinas viewed human nature as participating in divine intellection, Thomists extended the virtues and happiness that man realizes in the *polis* to include the eternal spiritual beatitude that man obtains through contemplative union with God (Lucca and Aquinas 1997: I.9, 81–4). This had profound consequences for the way in which Thomist natural law conceived of church and state and the relation between them. On the one hand, it meant that the church was itself understood as a kind of *polis* or state, into which men entered to perfect their rational and sociable nature and through whose laws they could achieve this end. On the other hand, it meant that the civil state was imbued with religious ends, as the temporal happiness it secured was a means to spiritual happiness, just as the civil virtues were a means to the contemplation of God (Lucca and Aquinas 1997: I.15, 97–101). Consequently, civil laws should embody the natural law through which man accedes to the perfection of his sociable and rational nature, culminating in the perfection of his spiritual nature.

In the context of the protracted struggle between the Catholic Church and the Holy Roman Empire, Thomist natural law was a theocratic theory-programme for the supremacy of the authority of the papal church over that of its civil imperial rival. The final end for which man entered society, the contemplation of God, could not be achieved without divine assistance mediated through Christ's earthly officials, the 'regal priesthood', at the head of which sat the pope as Christ's representative on earth (Lucca and Aquinas 1997: I.15, 100). Just as the temporal happiness obtained through the state is subordinate to the spiritual happiness realized through the church, so too must earthly princes be subordinate to the pope. Their role is to function as the 'secular arm' of the divine law mediated by the church, for example, by using their civil laws to punish schismatics and heretics (ST II-II, q. 39, a. 4). This meant that it was possible for the pope to abrogate the duty of subjects to obey their king should the latter himself commit heresy or apostasy (ST II-II, q.12, a. 2).

With the splintering of the church into rival Catholic and Protestant confessions in the sixteenth century, and the associated rise of mutually hostile confessionalized states, these theocratic dimensions of Thomist natural law took on a new historical significance. These were revived in the political theology of the 'second scholasticism' via such theologians as Francisco Vitoria, Domingo de Soto, and Francisco Suárez (Brett 1997; Skinner 1978: 135–72). For example Suárez, in his *Defensio fidei catholicae* (1613), could justify the pope's dethroning and regicide of a 'schismatic and heretical' prince: specifically, the Protestant James I of England (r.1603–25). His justification was based on the premise that it is the duty of the prince to secure not just the temporal welfare of his subjects but also their eternal spiritual happiness, which gives the pope jurisdiction over the secular prince himself (Suárez 1944: 685–702). When James required his subjects to swear an oath that included fealty to the Protestant religion, he attempted to assert the temporal king's supremacy in spiritual or ecclesial affairs, in direct transgression of the natural law which awards this supremacy to the pope as Christ's earthly representative, thus justifying the pope's authorization of James's dethronement and possibly his assassination (Suárez 1944: 705–25). When scholastic natural law was thus deployed in the counter-Reformation battle against Protestant churches and states, it provided the context in which the anti-scholastic natural law constructions of the seventeenth century emerged.

## II: THE LANGUAGE OF NATURAL LAW IN GROTIUS, HOBBES, AND LOCKE

The Dutch jurist Hugo Grotius (1583–1645) is often regarded as having inaugurated post-scholastic or 'modern' natural law with the publication of his widely-disseminated *The Rights of War and Peace* (*De jure belli ac pacis*) of 1625 (Tuck 1987). There is much in Grotius's work that supports this view of it, although his work also displays significant indebtedness to scholastic natural law. This indebtedness can be seen in the Prolegomena and Chapter 1 of the first book. Here Grotius seeks to provide universal moral-philosophical foundations for natural law and justice against the sceptics who, he claims, would reduce justice to a matter of custom founded in interest. It is here that he constructs natural law in the scholastic manner as the rule for conduct that accords with man's sociable nature and that is acceded to via his natural reason (Grotius 1925: 9–13, 34–40). It is true that, even here, Grotius departs from scholastic constructions by claiming in a famous formulation that the natural law would be valid even were God not to exist (Grotius 1925: 13). In doing so Grotius was turning sociability into a self-sufficient moral principle such that natural law would not be viewed as man's mode of acceding to the divine *lex aeterna* and human law would not be seen as the devolved form of this religious law. At the same time, though, in treating sociability as a universal human essence acceded to by reason, this dimension of Grotius's work could be and was used by Christian natural jurists as a bulwark against even more radically secular forms of natural law, in which sociability would be treated as a conduct to be imposed on man, rather than a nature to be realized (Schneider 1967).

Perhaps the more consequentially anti-scholastic dimension of Grotius's work arises from the fact that although he appeals to man's rational and sociable nature to provide the moral foundation of natural law, he does not deploy this as the foundation of the sovereign authority of the civil state. Rather than treating civil sovereignty as grounded in rights to self-defence and property inherent in man's sociable nature, Grotius offers a functional characterization of sovereignty. He thus views it in terms of the unchallengeable exercise of legislative, judicial, and financial powers that have been bestowed on the state by households in search of 'public tranquillity' (Grotius 1925: 101–11). Seen from the perspective of its future receptions, there is thus an ambivalence in Grotius's construction of natural law, with Grotian sociability seeming to oscillate between the human nature on which justice is founded, and the conduct that is required of man by a state founded in public tranquillity. This is what permitted Grotius to be cited on both sides of the argument between the Christian natural jurists and their anti-scholastic opponents.

The most uncompromising repudiation of scholastic natural law, and the most profound reworking of the language of natural law for the purposes of political philosophy, was that undertaken by Thomas Hobbes (1588–1679). By the time Hobbes came to write his major works in the 1640s and 1650s, the European religious and political conflicts had broken out in England in the form of the English Civil War (1641–1651). This was fought between a predominantly Anglican royalist faction and a predominantly Calvinist (Presbyterian) parliamentary faction, and consumed the kingship and finally the life of James's son, Charles I (r.1625–49). Thomistic Aristotelian natural law continued to play an important role in shaping factional religious and political programmes in this context, in part through the continuing Catholic resistance to the state supremacism of the English crown. Of more immediate importance though was a Protestant scholastic version of this natural law designed to support the religious supremacism of the Anglican church (Goldie 1983; 1991), and an opposed Calvinist form of natural law that focused not on the communal perfection of man in the polis but on man as an isolated individual seeking protection in the 'state of nature' (Skinner 1978: 318–38).

Despite his own support for the royalist cause, Hobbes's reconstruction of the language of natural law was designed to lay waste to both the Aristotelian-metaphysical natural law of the Anglican scholastics and the Calvinist natural rights idiom of the parliamentary Presbyterians or their more radical republican splinter groups. Hobbes argued that, by making the authority of the sovereign's civil laws conditional on a higher form of right or justice, both the scholastic and Calvinist constructions undermined the rationale of civil sovereignty—the provision of social peace—which necessitated a form of natural law that was internal to this rationale. That is what Hobbes set out to supply.

In his masterwork, *Leviathan*, Hobbes launched a frontal assault on the fundamentals of scholastic natural law by deploying a new moral anthropology (Malcolm 1991). According to Hobbes's quasi-Epicurean anthropology, man does not act through desires grounded in rational access to objective goods divinely implanted in his nature. He does so, rather, on the basis of desires arising from the manner in which sense-impressions give rise to pleasurable or painful movements of his bodily nerve-fibres (Hobbes 1991: 37–9). The scholastic conception of objective right was the first casualty of this new anthropology; for Hobbes, right and wrong, good and evil are understood only in terms of desire and aversion. It is on this basis that Hobbes introduces a radically new understanding of natural law. Since all men will seek life and shun death in order to satisfy their pleasure-seeking desire, they will share a common desire for self-preservation. As this desire can be satisfied only through the establishment of peaceable relations or 'society' among men, the basic natural law governing human conduct is: '*That every man, ought to endeavour Peace, as farre as he has hope of obtaining it; and when he cannot obtain it, that he may seek, and use, all helps, and advantages of Warre*' (Hobbes 1991: 92). It is in seeking peaceable society that men will cultivate the virtues of benevolence, mercy, and charity, not because they are exercises of natural virtues or goods, and not because they lead upwards towards the rational contemplation of God—which requires priestly mediation—but because it is in everyone's self-interest to practise such sociable virtues in order to secure peaceful relations among men (Hobbes 1991: 110–11).

On this basis Hobbes was able to effect a fundamental reconstruction of the language of natural law. On the one hand, he was able to divorce natural law from the scholastics' divine law. For Hobbes, natural law is no longer the form in which man rationally accedes to the objective goods of his 'rational and sociable nature', but is the minimalist command to 'seek peace' that flows from his desire for self-preservation. On the other hand, this also enabled him to divorce natural law from natural right. A jural right capable of imposing obligation on others no longer flows from the peace-seeking norm of natural law because, in the state of nature when 'men live without a common Power to keep them all in awe', this norm is incapable of generating obligation (Hobbes 1991: 88). Rather than being a realization of natural law in juridical relations, Hobbesian natural right is symptomatic of the transgression of natural law (Malcolm 1991: 536). It arises in the state of nature where men encounter the violent depredations of other men and, in accordance with their desire for self-preservation, exercise a right to do or take forcefully whatever they please. This issues in Hobbes's famous characterization of the state of nature as the state of war of 'every man against every man', where men are in 'continuall feare, and danger of violent death', and where life is 'solitary, poore, nasty, brutish, and short' (Hobbes 1991: 88–9). Unlike his Calvinist opponents, Hobbes did not regard individual natural rights as the foundation of political society but as its chief obstacle, and he should not be regarded as the progenitor of a liberal theory of society grounded in subjective rights (Skinner 1996).

The conception of political authority and the state that emerged from this reconstructed language of natural law differed radically from that of the scholastic political theologians, no less than from that of the Calvinist natural rights theorists. Hobbes repudiated the Aristotelian conception of the state as a natural institution required for the perfection of human nature as sociable; he treats the state instead as a wholly artificial institution into which men enter to provide themselves with the sociability that they lack by nature (Hobbes 1991: 117–21). Hobbes also rejected the Calvinist conception of the state as the political trustee for individual subjective rights. He viewed it instead as the institution of a sovereign power for the purpose of achieving social peace (Hobbes 1991: 121–9).

Men enter the Hobbesian state not because their nature inclines them to sociability but because it leads them to war. Further, they do not enter the state because their individual judgements lead them to agree that the appointment of a sovereign is the best way to achieve peace. They do so because their ineradicably conflicting judgements produce permanent hostility among them, leading to the 'warre of every man against every man'. It is the mutual fear endemic in this condition that drives their agreement to appoint a sovereign who will judge for them in this matter. Hobbes's state is thus envisaged as arising from a fear-driven agreement among individuals to subject themselves to a sovereign power that is unitary in the sense of constituting a single locus of political decision and legislative agency, and absolute in the sense that its commands or laws are not accountable to any other law or judgement (Hobbes 1991: 121–7). Despite the fact that Hobbes expressed a pragmatic preference for monarchy as the best governmental means of exercising this sovereign power, he acknowledges that it may also be properly exercised by both aristocratic and democratic forms of government (Hobbes 1991: 129–30).

The radical reconstruction of the relation between church and state that flowed from this new conception of political authority may be regarded as the culmination of Hobbes's reinvention of the language of natural law, since this relation had proved incendiary for the European religious wars, including the English Civil War. Hobbes moved against the Thomistic subordination of state to church and the Anglican doctrine of a shared civil-ecclesial authority on two fronts simultaneously. First, he denied the existence of a universal church possessing the moral capacity to subordinate civil sovereigns to 'higher' natural- or divine-law norms mediated by the priesthood (Hobbes 1991: 268–9, 320–2). As there is only one earthly society, that is the civil society that men enter through the appointment of a sovereign power to 'keep them in awe', political and spiritual authority, state and church, must be united in the civil sovereign (Hobbes 1991: 377–8). Second, as a result of his excoriating attack on Aristotelian metaphysics, Hobbes repudiated academic metaphysical claims to accede to the essences or natures that are supposedly intelligized by God, and the associated claims to exercise ecclesial and civil authority on the basis of this 'higher' knowledge (Hobbes 1991: 269–79, 458–74; Serjeantson 2006). Heresy *qua* erroneous belief could not, therefore, be accepted as a crime in civil law, because theological claims to accede to true metaphysical knowledge of the Christian mysteries were unfounded. Only the sovereign could make civil law, and heresy could be understood only as a cover for the clergy's attempt to exercise civil power under false pretenses (Condren 2005).

Since the only evidence for Christ's existence and teachings is the historical evidence contained in the Bible, and since rival theological interpretations of this evidence had proved to be a major source of civil conflict, it was the sovereign's right to provide an authoritative interpretation of biblical doctrine for the purposes of public religion (Hobbes 1991: 297–300, 306, 320–2). Needless to say, in denying the primacy of both the corporate church and the individual conscience in the determination of public faith, Hobbes's theology and ecclesiology were anathema to the Anglican and Calvinist factions. Nonetheless, in denying that external conduct was governed by inner theological truth or religious belief, Hobbes was able to open a significant space for religious toleration (Burgess 1996; Ryan 1988; Tuck 1990), which is discussed in Chapter 26. For if this (anti-metaphysical) denial meant that external religious worship could be regarded as 'indifferent' with regard to salvation and hence as amenable to determination by a 'Christian souveraigne', it also meant that it was both impossible and beyond his office for the sovereign to attempt to coerce his subject's inner beliefs (Hobbes 1991: 323, 471–2).

John Locke (1632–1704) lived through the same factionalized and violent times as Hobbes: the English Civil War and regicide (1641–51), the tumultuous period of the republican Commonwealth (1649–60), the restoration of the (crypto-Catholic) Stuart monarchy (1660), and finally its overthrow by the armies of the Dutch Protestant William of Orange (1688). In using the language of natural law to provide a political theory suited to these times, however, Locke's articulation of this idiom differed in almost every regard from that of his notorious predecessor, and drew on the more traditional form associated with Calvinist natural rights doctrine (Tully 1991). Locke appealed to reason to re-establish the continuity between natural law and natural right, making use of a non-Thomist variant of scholasticism in order to invest natural rights in individuals who could hold the state accountable for their realization. Locke belonged to a political faction opposed to Hobbes. He was secretary and adviser to Anthony Ashley Cooper, the first Earl of Shaftesbury (1621–83), one of England's powerful anti-royalist and anti-Anglican Protestant houses, while Hobbes was secretary to the royalist magnate William Cavendish, the first Duke of Newcastle (1592–1676). It was in his capacity as adviser to a dissident political and religious faction that Locke reworked the political potentialities of natural law, principally in his *Two Treatises of Government*, but also in a series of related essays on religious toleration.

In attacking absolutist tyranny in the *Two Treatises*, however, it was not Hobbes whom Locke had in his sights—Locke scarcely mentions him—but twin enemies of a different kind. The First Treatise was written as a refutation of Robert Filmer's *Patriaracha* of 1680 (Laslett 1960: 67–79). Filmer justified absolutist monarchy not on Hobbesian grounds but on the patriarchalist grounds that God had bestowed kings with a divine right to paternal rule over their subjects, similar to the natural authority of fathers over children and masters over slaves. More broadly, though, the *Two Treatises* and the essays on toleration were written to undermine the political-theological programme of Anglican royalism. This programme claimed supreme spiritual authority for the Anglican episcopacy in determining true religion and morals for the English nation, and viewed the king as a mere member of the church who exercised a co-ordinate civil authority for the enforcement of this religion on dissenters in a theocratic manner (Goldie 1983). Thus, despite the fact that the *Two Treatises* were published in 1690, both the First Treatise and the more fundamental Second Treatise were not composed in justification of William of Orange's 1688 overthrow of James II; they were written nearly a decade earlier under quite different circumstances (Laslett 1960: 45–66). At that time, following Charles II's alignment with a now Anglican-royalist parliament and the passing of measures restricting the religious and civil rights of dissenting Protestants, Locke was deeply involved in Shaftesbury's plot to overthrow the government, should parliament fail to pass a bill excluding Charles's professedly Catholic brother James from succession to the throne. In this highly charged religious and political context, Locke wrote the *Two Treatises*, with its natural law defence of revolutionary resistance to a government in breach of natural rights.

Locke begins the Second Treatise by stipulating that man is the collective inheritor of a law of nature that God formed in Adam and that is identical with the 'law of Reason' (Locke 1960: 305). It is because he possesses the innate capacity to govern his conduct in accordance with a law prescribed by his own reason that Locke's man can be regarded as born free, equal, and rationally self-governing: 'The *Freedom* then of Man and Liberty of acting according to his own Will is *grounded on* his having *Reason*, which is able to instruct him in that Law he is to govern himself by, and make him know how far he is left to the freedom of his own will' (Locke 1960: 309).

Locke's insouciance regarding the need to justify his rationalist anthropology philosophically should not be counted against him, however. Where such justifications were provided, as with the Thomists and Hobbes, they were equally subordinate to the religious and political purposes for which the divergent anthropologies were elaborated. From the historian's viewpoint, then, none of the anthropologies should be regarded as any closer to the truth than the others. In Locke's case, the point of identifying natural law with an innate capacity for rational self-governance was to permit a series of 'natural powers'—for self-preservation, the acquisition of property, social co-operation, and the punishment of malefactors—to be treated as natural rights. Locke regards these as jural rights that exist in the state of nature without giving rise to Hobbes's state of war, because they are expressions of man's capacity for rational self-governance (Locke 1960: 280–1).

The fact that Locke grounds his conception of property in man's possession of himself by virtue of his capacity for rational self-governance is central to his construction of natural law and natural rights. Not only does this make individuals the source and arbiters of natural rights, but it expands the notion of property rights to include 'Lives, Liberties and Estates' (Locke 1960: 350). This could even make religious liberty into something like a property right that is capable of being defended by individuals against those who would infringe the natural right to its free exercise. If Locke's rationalist anthropology permitted him to ignore Hobbes's vision of the state of nature as a state of war, it also permitted him to reject Filmer's posit of a divinely appointed patriarchal royal authority, and the Anglican conception of spiritual authority flowing from the apostolic succession through the episcopal hierarchy of a corporate national church.

This reworking of natural law was designed to support Locke's distinctive construction of political authority and the civil state. If individuals already possess the capacity to govern their freedom for the common good in accordance with natural law in the state of nature, and if they already possess a wide array of natural 'property' rights on this basis, then the only reason that they have for appointing a common authority over themselves and entering the civil state is better to exercise this rational self-governance and protect the rights flowing from it (Locke 1960: 350–1). The appointment of a magistrate or public authority as a common judge will thus obviate the disagreements between individuals over their rights in the state of nature. Similarly, by delegating their natural rights of self-defence and punishment to the state, individuals will create a political authority with an unparalleled capacity to protect their natural property rights in the broad sense and which will function as the corporate representative of individuals' powers of rational self-governance.

Locke thus conceives of political society or the state on the model of a fiduciary trust whose authority is grounded in the rational consent of its individual members. This is formed first by individuals agreeing among themselves to delegate their rights of property and judgement to a common authority (the 'social compact'), and second by consenting to the appointment of a governmental authority as a trustee whose authority is conditional on its representative exercise of their judgement and protection of their rights. By basing his conception of the commonwealth on the individual's putative capacity for rational self-governance of his own liberty and rights, Locke produced a natural-law architecture for political authority that is diametrically opposed to that of Hobbes. Since the governance of their liberties and rights in the state of nature is only delegated to the government in civil society, Lockean individuals can always reassume this governance, should they decide that civil authority is not governing them as they would themselves:

Though in a Constituted Commonwealth, standing upon its own Basis, and acting according to its own Nature, that is, acting for the preservation of the Community, there can be but *one Supream Power*, which is the *Legislative*, to which all the rest are and must be subordinate, yet the Legislative being only a Fiduciary Power to act for certain ends, there remains still *in the People a Supream Power* to remove or *alter the Legislative*, when they find the *Legislative* act contrary to the trust reposed in them.   (Locke 1960: 366–7)

Unlike the Thomists' Aristotelian *polis*, Locke's state is not a natural order in which the goods of man's rational and sociable nature are realized; it is an artificial arrangement through which individuals consent to have their natural rights protected by the corporate representative of their self-governing reason. Unlike the Hobbesian Leviathan, though, Locke's artificial state is not one that individuals enter through mutual fear, exchanging obedience for protection in accordance with the minimal command to seek peace. Rather, it is one that they enter rationally and conditionally, in order better to exercise rights of judgement and property that they already possess through their reason in the state of nature. Like the scholastic political theologians, then, Locke subordinates the state's civil laws to natural-law rights, making the latter available as a moral-philosophical means of delegitimating the former. However, natural-law rights are no longer declared by ecclesial theologians on behalf of a church, but by philosophical intellectuals on behalf of an ideological faction, albeit one intent on defending a particular kind of church.

In relation to the religious and political struggles of 1670–88, Locke's reworking of natural law provided him with a political theory-programme that justified revolutionary resistance to any government that acted without right—for example, by seeking to govern a religious liberty that had not been entrusted to it—or that acted against right, by failing to protect the 'Lives, Liberties and Estates' that had been entrusted to it (Tully 1991). It was a direct result of Locke's fundamental vestment of political authority in the rational self-governance of individuals— 'popular sovereignty'—that he should make individuals themselves into the final judges of whether a government was governing without or against right. This justified Shaftesbury's insurrectionary activities of the 1670s, but also forced Locke to acknowledge that when individuals disagreed about this crucial issue, then it became a matter for the 'judgement of heaven'.

Locke's important doctrine of religious toleration was deeply embedded in his natural-law political theory, and is discussed in Chapter 26.

# III: Pufendorf and natural law in the German Empire

The massive reconstruction of the language of natural law undertaken by Samuel Pufendorf (1632–94) was motivated by the distinctive religious, political, and juridical circumstances of the Holy Roman German Empire. Unlike the unified territorial kingdom of England, the German Empire consisted of seven electoral states whose princes ('Electors') elected the (Habsburg) emperor, and a complex array of smaller principalities and estates: imperial cities, bishoprics, nobilities, and knights' circles. These overlapping jurisdictions were ordered not by a monarchy but by the institutions of imperial public law, at the pinnacle of which stood the *Reichskammergericht* (Imperial Chamber Court) and the *Reichshofrat* (Imperial Aulic Court) (Friedeburg and Seidler 2008: 102–28). The religious fracturing of the Empire during the second half of the sixteenth century by successive waves of confessionalization or 'reformations'—Lutheran, Catholic, and Calvinist—had witnessed the emergence of mutually hostile confessional states, a protracted period of religious civil war, and the reshaping of the imperial constitution via two momentous public-law religious peace treaties (Schilling 1995). The Religious Peace of Augsburg (1555) recognized two imperial religions, Tridentine Catholicism and Augsburg Protestantism, and the right of Protestant princes to reform their territorial churches (the *jus reformandi*). Nearly a century later the Treaties of Westphalia (1648) ended the Thirty Years War by recognizing three religions, Catholic, Lutheran, and Calvinist, albeit under a complex web of imperial regulation that permitted the maintenance of dominant religions within particular territories, accompanied by rights of private worship and emigration for religious minorities (Heckel 1989*b*).

The highly juridified character of the imperial political order, together with the nexus of religious reform and territorial state-building that characterized the emergence of confessional states, led to a proliferation of natural-law discourses in the early modern German Empire (Hochstrasser and Schröder 2002; Scattola 2001). This was in keeping with the basic role of the language of natural law in articulating theology, jurisprudence, and political philosophy for the purposes of particular religious and political programmes and interests (Stolleis 1988: 268–97). In addition, one of the central uses of German natural-law discourses in this setting was to provide a reception-context for the main forms of positive law—Romano-canon law, imperial public law, and vestigial common law—in accordance with the theological and political imperatives of rapidly centralizing confessional-state jurisdictions (Haakonssen 2006).

During the high tide of confessionalization (1550–1700), state-building princes and reforming theologians satisfied their voracious need for juridical and theological expertise through an unprecedented programme of university-building, resulting in the mushrooming of rival religious universities across the Empire (Schindling 1988). This meant that German natural law was the work of university professors. Unlike the scholastics who had elaborated their theocratic natural law as the members of religious orders, and unlike Hobbes and Locke who had articulated natural-law political theories in the service of rival ideological faction-leaders, seventeenth-century German natural-law thinkers belonged to the stratum of *gelehrte Räte*. They were academic advisers to governments who combined university teaching with the elaboration of natural-law theories for the states and princely courts in whose universities they worked (Hammerstein 1996; Schnur 1986).

The array of natural law discourses that emerged in this setting can be broadly divided into two rival kinds. 'Christian natural law' was elaborated by theologians and theological jurists who drew on the sixteenth-century 'second scholasticism' in order to supply an intellectual architecture for the harmonization of spiritual and civil authority in emerging confessional states (Schneider 2001). In contrast, secular or anti-scholastic natural law was developed by political philosophers and political jurists who drew on several cognate sources—Bodin's doctrine of state sovereignty, Grotius's political humanism, Conring's historicization of law, and

Hobbes's secular absolutism—in order to provide rationales for the subordination of religious to civil authority in projected secularized states (Dreitzel 2001; Tuck 1987).

Catholic forms of Christian natural law were particularly concerned to forestall the pluralization of the Empire's religious constitution portended by the Peace of Augsburg, and to attack the separation of spiritual and civil authority which Catholic political theologians associated with the 'two kingdoms' doctrine of the Lutheran heresy. Andreas Erstenberger (d. 1584), secretary to the Imperial Aulic Court, thus argued that the attempt to achieve temporal peace through the legal recognition of a plurality of religions contradicted the spiritual unity commanded by the natural law and the cognate laws of the old and new testaments. This threatened the supremacy of the church and opened the floodgates of disobedience and heresy (Erstenberger 1586: 108–95; Heckel 1989a: 3–11). Closer to the peak of the counter-Reformation the Jesuit political theologian Adam Contzen (1573–1635), who combined academic (Thomistic) theology and philosophy with his role as spiritual adviser to Elector Maximilian I of Bavaria, drew on the full force of Suárez and the second scholasticism to attack the Lutheran separation of ecclesial and civil authority. Contzen reactivated the Thomist model according to which natural law is man's way of acceding to divine law, which implies that the prince's civil law must be subordinate to natural law and that the pope provides the authoritative explication of divine law as Christ's earthly representative (Contzen 1629: 332–43). Accordingly, heretical princes could be deposed by the pope, as Suárez had argued.

Protestant forms of Christian natural law initially took their lead from Philip Melanchthon's less metaphysical construction (Kusukawa 1992). In Melanchthon (1497–1560), the norms of natural law are supplied not through participation in divine intellection but by the 'spiritual sword' of the Ten Commandments and Christ's ethic of fraternal love, which were understood as supplying the model of an ideal moral community. The Christian magistrate is empowered to punish fallen man's deviations from these norms with the sword of the civil law (Melanchthon 1965: 122–9). The mix of theological, juridical, and political purposes served by Melanchthon's natural law is reflected in the three uses that were assigned to it by Lutheran philosophical theologians: as a norm for disciplining sinners, heretics, and infidels (*usus politicus*); as a means for discerning sin and revealing God's judgement (*usus paedagogicus*); and as a norm of conduct for the religiously reborn (*usus in renatis*) (Dreitzel 2001: 840). The proclamation in 1577 of Lutheran orthodoxy's intensely metaphysical confessional statement, the Formula of Concord, ushered the return of a full-blooded metaphysics to Lutheran universities, exemplified in the works of Christoph Scheibler and Balthasar Meisner (Sparn 1976, 2001). In developing a metaphysics of spiritual substance to defend the Lutheran view of how Christ's two natures were united in his person and thence made present in the Eucharistic host, Scheibler and Meisner restored the thematics of the divine mind's creative intellection of the forms of things, and the human mind's capacity for participation in this intellection, as the image of God. They thereby supplied core texts for a distinctively Protestant metaphysical scholasticism, not only to German universities but also to *ante-bellum* Oxford and Cambridge, where their works epitomized the 'vain philosophy' of the universities attacked by Hobbes in Chapter 47 of *Leviathan* (Serjeantson 2006).

The doctrine of natural law that Meisner elaborated was one in which man's capacity for rational participation in the divine law tracks the hierarchical path of laws—human, natural, divine—at the pinnacle of which we find, not the pope, but the Lutheran episcopacy and the Protestant prince in his dual Augsburg persona as highest bishop and supreme magistrate (Meisner 1616). This kind of natural law in turn provided the context for assimilating Romano-canon law, imperial public law, and common law in the centralizing legal codes of Protestant confessional states (Landau 2000; Lück 2000). In the most important of these codes, Benedict Carpzov's *Practica nova imperialis saxonica rerum criminalium* (New Imperial Saxon Practice of Criminal Law) of 1635, which was compiled for Electoral Saxony, the prince is thus treated as God's earthly viceroy, framing civil laws in accordance with natural law and divine law. This permitted civil infractions to be treated as instances of sinful conduct, and religious heterodoxy to be punished as the civil crime of heresy (Carpzov 1635: 1–7).

Finally, Protestant metaphysical natural law was resurgent in the last third of the seventeenth century in the work of Valentin Veltheim (University of Jena), Johann Joachim Zentgrav (Strasbourg University), and Valentin Alberti (University of Leipzig) (Schneider 2001: 824–30). These philosophers and theologians argued that, in accordance with the *usus in renatis*, certain men could accede to natural-law norms through their reborn reason, the *imago Dei* (Alberti 1676). This allowed them to identify the state of nature with man's prelapsarian state of innocence (*status integritatis*) and to model civil society as an ideal moral community, as opposed to Hobbes's warlike state of nature and subjected political community (Ahnert 2006: 83–93). By the 1680s, however, these Protestant scholastics were engaged in a desperate rearguard action against Pufendorf's root-and-branch rejection of the rationalist anthropology underlying Christian natural law and the theocratic subordination of civil authority that it supported: a rejection that they accurately characterized by using a despised adjective, 'Hobbesian'.

The reception that Hobbes's political thought found in this bitterly divided cultural and political context varied in accordance with the rival schools of German natural law and the opposed religious and political programmes that they articulated (Dreitzel 2003). Hobbes was excoriated by the metaphysical Christian natural jurists for his 'atheist and indifferentist' derivation of natural law from human peace-seeking and his political subordination of the church (Schneider 1967). This was largely because they were reacting to Pufendorf's incorporation of Hobbes into his formidable campaign to expel religious and metaphysical norms from the foundations of political authority, and to replace them with norms of a natural law whose minimal command to seek peace could be assimilated to the secularized commands of an absolute civil sovereign (Döring 1993).

Against an earlier view that Pufendorf remained indebted to a Grotian (neo-Aristotelian) conception of man's natural sociability, Palladini shows that Pufendorf fully accepted Hobbes's key anti-scholastic construction. Following in Hobbes's footsteps and departing from the path of Grotius and the scholastics, Pufendorf treats sociability not as a nature or essence that is realized in the civil state, but as a mode of behaviour to be obtained through the artifice of civil discipline (Palladini 2008: 27–31). This was Hobbes's Copernican revolution in natural-law thought that Pufendorf exploited in a different religious and political context, as a key weapon in his campaign against rationalist metaphysical natural law and the German confessional state. Here its articulation by an honoured adviser to the Swedish and Brandenburg courts would help to rescue Hobbesian natural-law political theory from the marginalization that it suffered in England, even if this meant adapting it to different religious and political circumstances.

Pufendorf begins the reconstruction of natural law in *De jure naturae et gentium* (1672) with his own version of Hobbes's Epicurean moral anthropology (Pufendorf 1717 (DJN)). Man is a creature whose natural weakness means that he should co-operate with his fellows to survive, but whose divided mind and fractious passions, coupled with his depraved inclination for limitless mutual harm, threaten the sociability that he requires to survive and flourish (DJN II.3.xiv, 135–36). The natural law that Pufendorf derives from this anthropology—'This then will appear a Fundamental Law of Nature, *Every man ought, as far as in him lies, to promote and preserve a peaceful Sociableness with others, agreeable to the main End and Disposition of human Race in general*' (DJN II.3.xv, 137)—coheres closely with Hobbes's formulation: '*That every man, ought to endeavour Peace, as farre as he has hope of obtaining it; and when he cannot obtain it, that he may seek, and use, all helps, and advantages of Warre*' (Hobbes 1991: 92). Moreover, in using this minimalist formulation of the end of natural law to divorce it from both the higher (theological) end of realizing man's intellectual nature, and from the notion of natural rights grounded in a capacity of rational self-governance, Pufendorf was orienting his natural law to the same end as Hobbes's. Like Hobbes he sought to provide the intellectual architecture for a form of civil authority restricted to the maintenance of social peace, but unchallengeable by those claiming to speak in the name of higher theological purposes or more fundamental natural rights.

In a significant departure from his English mentor, however, Pufendorf did not ground this anthropology in Hobbes's materialist physiology. Instead, Pufendorf provided the anti-rationalist anthropology with a different kind of doctrinal basis, in his theory of 'moral entities' (*entia moralia*) (Hunter 2001: 163–8). According to this doctrine, norms and virtues do not flow from a rational or moral nature that man shares with God. Rather they are attached to comportments, to *entia moralia*, *personae morales*, which have been 'imposed' or instituted 'by understanding

Beings, chiefly for the guiding and tempering of the Freedom of voluntary Actions, and for the procuring of a decent Regularity in the Method of Life' (DJN I.1.iii, 3). Analogous to the manner in which physical entities occupy physical space, moral entities or personae occupy moral space—that is, a space of moral action constituted by convention or institution—which is how Pufendorf understands the notion of 'status' or condition (DJN I.1.vi, 4). The Hobbesian–Epicurean anthropology from which Pufendorf derives the natural law thus delineates the moral persona that man has by occupying the 'natural status' (*status naturalis*), which is to be understood as the status or condition imposed or instituted by God so that man will govern his conduct in accordance with the natural law. All other statuses, such as marital and family statuses, commercial and professional statuses, ecclesial and sacerdotal statuses, and especially the status of political subjection associated with membership of the civil state (*status civilis*), are 'adventitious' or artificial statuses that man himself has instituted for the governance of his conduct (DJN I.1. vii, 4–5).

This treatment of the Epicurean anthropology as man's divinely imposed *status naturalis* provided Pufendorf with a powerful weapon against all metaphysical forms of natural law, especially the versions formulated by his enemies Veltheim, Alberti, and Strimesius. This treatment requires that moral norms be derived immanently, from within the needy and vicious persona that has been imposed as man's *status naturalis*, rather than transcendentally, from a rational nature through which he might participate in God's divine law and thence partially restore the ideal moral community of his lost state of innocence (*status integritatis*) (Hunter 2001: 169–80). At the same time, however, the conventionalist or institutionalist character of the *entia moralia* doctrine also meant that Pufendorf established a certain distance from the physicalistic anthropology of his English ally, tracking Hobbes's path towards de-transcendentalizing civil authority at a slight but significant remove.

Pufendorf's double strategy, of deploying Hobbesian weaponry against his Christian natural law opponents while keeping a certain distance from Hobbes, can be seen in his crucial discussion of moral obligation. After dismissing the possibility that men might obligate themselves (or be rationally self-governing) as incompatible with man's driving passions and flighty mind, Pufendorf deploys his dual strategy to delineate the character of the 'superior' who is required to impose obligation on man's will from without (DJN I.6.vii, 62). Given man's fractious and self-interested nature, if the superior's commands or laws are to obligate the will, then the superior must combine the capacity to coerce the disobedient with a 'just Reason' for so commanding; for, without the former, laws will not be obeyed and, without the latter, they will not be felt as obligations (DJN I.6.ix, 63). Hobbes, Pufendorf argues, treats the sovereign's right to command as arising when the equality of physical strength of those at loggerheads in the state of nature compels them to appoint a supreme authority for mutual defence. This means that the

Englishman grounds the sovereign's right to rule in his power to compel the disobedient, but fails to ground it in the obligation that subjects feel not to disobey the sovereign's commands (DJN I.6.x, 63–5).

As a result of his *entia moralia* doctrine, however, Pufendorf treats the agreement to appoint a sovereign as something more than the transfer of natural power and right to a supreme authority. By agreeing to subject themselves to one who can protect them, Pufendorf's mutually fearful individuals transform the moral space or status in which their conduct acquires moral valency; this is the transition from the *status naturalis* to the *status civilis*. Through the political pact they institute the new persona of the political subject defined by the obligation to obey the one who protects, thereby constituting the 'just Reason' for the sovereign's command (DJN I.6.x, 63–5). For Pufendorf, however, the anti-Hobbesian scholastics and Christian natural jurists are far less able to comprehend the source of the right to rule. In locating superiority in the intellectual excellence of man's rational nature, these thinkers forget that, in the absence of coercive power, there is no reason for strong-willed men to heed such an excellent nature, as the Epicureans realized in their image of disinterested gods lacking all effective governance of human affairs (DJN I.6.xi, 66–7).

In a similar manner Pufendorf is critical of Hobbes's argument that, as a result of man's conflicting desires and his capacity to inflict harm, the state of nature is equivalent to the state of universal war (DJN II.2.v–vi, 109–11). The state of nature is indeed the condition that man is in prior to all human acts and institutions, particularly the institution of civil sovereignty. Yet it remains a status or institution, imposed by God, from which man can deduce the natural law that governs his conduct in this condition (DJN II.2.ix, 113–14). Through consideration of his natural weakness and his need to be sociable, man is thus capable of treating his neighbours as friends in the state of nature, just as independent monarchs are capable of treating each other as friends in the state of nature that exists between them in the absence of a superior. At the same time, though, Pufendorf acknowledges that the viciousness of man's nature means that 'this natural peace is but too weak and uncertain', that the friendship among men is 'unreliable', so that men should be perpetually prepared for war, which is close to what Hobbes means by the 'condition of war' (DJN II.2.xii, 116–17). In fact, Pufendorf is far more concerned to rebut the teaching of the Protestant scholastics, that the state of nature is a state of peaceable society among men modelled on their society with God, to which they can accede by virtue of their reason, understood as the *imago Dei* that allows man to participate in holiness (DJN II.3.v–vi, 122–4). Such a doctrine, Pufendorf argues, completely misunderstands the role of the state of nature in natural law; it is not that of a status through which man accedes to the rational law of divine society, but one through which he accedes to knowledge of the imposed law that governs his earthly society through the ordering of peaceable relations (DJN II.3.xiii, 132–5).

Pufendorf's conception of the sovereignty pact as an act of institution that imposes a new moral status and persona imbues his construction of civil society or the political state with a subtlety that is easily overlooked. On the one hand, deploying copious citations from Hobbes's *De cive*, Pufendorf follows Hobbes's rejection of the Aristotelian conception of man as the political animal and the state as the natural expression of man's inborn sociability. Despite man's need for sociability, his vicious passions and ambitions, coupled with his infantile incapacity to see that the state serves his own long-term interest in security, mean that, far from being natural, the capacity to be a good citizen or 'political creature' is itself the product of social discipline within the civil state: 'So far it is therefore from true, that Man is by Nature a *political creature*, or by Birth is fitted for the Discharge of *civil Duties*; that 'tis as much as can be done, to train up some few, by long Discipline, to a tolerable Behaviour in this Respect' (DJN VII.1.iv, 627). This means that the state cannot be understood as a natural outgrowth of the sociability commanded by the natural law, as man's limitless ambition and driving self-interest means that he is incapable of voluntarily banding together in a civil state on the basis of his rational understanding of the law of nature (DJN VII.1.ix–xi, 632–4). Rather than natural sociability and reason, it is mutual fear that drives men into the compact to form a civil state: 'Therefore the true and leading Cause, why the Fathers of Families would consent to resign up their natural Liberty, and to form a Commonwealth, was thereby to guard themselves against those Injuries, which one Man was in Danger of sustaining from another. . . . And this account is seconded by those who deduce the Original of Commonwealths from *Fear*' (DJN VII.1.vii, 629–30). This means that the state is an artificial institution driven by the need for security, and designed to impose the discipline through which individuals acquire the sociable comportment of the citizen.

At the same time, however, Pufendorf's *entia moralia* doctrine leads to a certain distancing from Hobbes's account of how the civil state is established. By treating the political pact as the instituting of a new moral status and personae, Pufendorf rejects all accounts of the origins of sovereignty in terms of the transfer of pre-existing rights, powers, and freedoms from the natural to the civil state, or from God or the people to the sovereign. This applies to Hobbes's account of the political pact, according to which the multitude transfers its natural powers and rights of government to the sovereign (Hobbes 1991: 120–1). In treating the obligation of the subject and the authority of the sovereign as internal to the pact that creates these new civil personae, Pufendorf seeks to avoid the recognition of a people possessing natural rights and freedoms, even just for the momentary purpose of transferring them to the Hobbesian sovereign (Seidler 2002).

If subject and sovereign are twin moral entities imposed through the fear-driven political pact, then sovereignty cannot be understood in terms of the representation of an antecedent will, judgement, or rights. The will of the sovereign to command subjects in all matters pertaining to their security and peace is internal to the artificial personae and the new moral space of the civil state (*status civilis*) instituted by the pact. Of course, if Pufendorf's version of the political pact had the effect of extinguishing the last glimmer of popular sovereignty in Hobbes's political doctrine, then it was utterly inimical to natural-rights based conceptions of popular sovereignty of the kind elaborated by Locke. Pufendorf expunged the possibility of holding the sovereign accountable to rights or virtues supposedly present in a state of nature; for example, the rights and virtues that the Christian natural jurists purported to derive via man's rational participation in the divine law and the ideal moral community of man's condition of innocence.

The strategic flexibility that Pufendorf's construction of multiple moral personae delivered to his political thought can be seen in his discussion of whether the sovereign has the right to command the moral judgement of his subjects. According to Pufendorf, to the extent that Hobbes argues that justice and injustice depend on the civil law and its commander, then he goes too far, as individuals possess the capacity to judge conduct according to natural law, and the sovereign's right to command extends only to that conduct of subjects pertaining to their common peace and security (DJN VIII.1.v, 751–2). At the same time, however, only the sovereign can judge the measures suited to realizing peace and security, as this is a capacity instituted for the persona of the sovereign within the moral space of the *status civilis*. Hobbes is right then to treat as seditious the attempt to make obedience to the sovereign's commands conditional on the subject's knowledge of good and evil. If the sovereign's commands do not stretch to cover the moral judgements of 'men' in the state of nature, then subjects in the civil state have no moral capacity to make their obedience to sovereign command conditional on their moral judgements as men (or Christians). In each case duties and rights are specific to particular moral entities or personae and the purposes for which they have been instituted, such that individuals as citizens in the *status civilis* lack the capacity to know whether the sovereign's governmental measures agree with the natural law that they know as men in the *status naturalis*:

In *another Sense* indeed, what Mr. *Hobbes* saith, may be safely enough admitted; that is, supposing that by *good* and *evil* we understand no more than the *advantage*, or *disadvantage* of the Commonwealth. For then it really will appear to be a *seditious Doctrine*, that *every private Person is Judge of good and evil* . . . and that, in Consequence, every Man's Obligation to Obedience may depend upon that Judgment. For it is necessary that Subjects . . . *should be ignorant of some things as well as know others. For if every one should have the Liberty to dispute what he was commanded, Obedience and Authority would soon sink together.* (DJN VIII.1.v, 752).

Finally, the capacity of Pufendorf's natural law to pluralize moral personae in relation to diversely instituted moral spaces or statuses provided a powerful instrument for the disarticulation of church and state and the articulation of religious toleration (Seidler 2003). In his *De habitu religionis christianae ad vitam civilem* (On the relation of the Christian religion to civil life) of 1687, which was written in the aftermath of the revocation of the Edict of Nantes in 1685 and the renewed persecution of French Protestants, Pufendorf constructed church and state as discrete moral spaces or statuses occupied by discrepant moral personae. The church is a voluntary association formed for the purpose of divine worship and eternal salvation whose personae are the auditor and the teacher joined by the non-coercive bonds of love and emulation (Pufendorf 2002: 32–7, 69–73). The state though is a compulsive association entered for the purpose of mutual security and whose personae are the subject and the sovereign, joined by coercive enforcement of the obedience that the former owes for the protection of the latter (Pufendorf 2002: 56–9). Even when occupied by the same individual the different personae are morally intransitive. The sovereign is only an auditor or teacher in the church, hence incapable of exercising civil power in his Christian persona or combining the personae of ruler and bishop. For his part the individual is only a subject in the state, hence incapable of making his civil obedience contingent on the religious or moral beliefs that he holds in his persona as a Christian or 'man' (Pufendorf 2002: 91–4). Pufendorf's doctrine of multiple moral personae thus provided him with a powerful intellectual weapon for use against Christian natural law and the confessional state, but also against Calvinist resistance theory and the notion of natural religious rights, both of which unified diverse civil personae—man and subject, Christian and citizen—on the basis of rationalist moral anthropologies.

This weapon was wielded to great effect by Pufendorf's most important German follower, the academic political jurist Christian Thomasius (1655–1728), who used it to attack the civil enforcement of Lutheranism in the Saxon confessional state in particular and in 'papalist' jurisdictions more broadly (Hunter 2007). In his *adiaphora* disputation of 1695, Thomasius argued that, because the sovereign's right to rule is conditional on the exercise of coercive power for the maintenance of external civil peace, this right does not extend to the religious and moral beliefs of his subjects, unless these threaten external peace and thus become policeable civil conduct. At the same time, though, because the Christian community is an 'invisible church', held together only by bonds of fraternal love, all of its public forms of worship, from baptism to the Eucharist and the hymnal, are indifferent with regard to salvation (*adiaphora*) (Thomasius 2007). This makes such forms of worship both incapable of being forcibly imposed on fellow Christians, but also incapable of forming the basis of a civil right against the sovereign should he determine that their practice constitutes a threat to civil peace. For, unlike Locke's state, Thomasius's Pufendorfian state is not inhabited by a Christian citizen bearing rights and freedoms that derive from the state of nature, but only by a political subject bearing the obedience that he owes to the state that guarantees social peace. The right of toleration is thus not a right of religious freedom possessed by individuals against the state, but a right of religious governance possessed by the state, to be granted to all religions to the extent that their forms of worship do not threaten civil peace. Against the grain of modern expectations, in the context of multi-confessional Brandenburg-Prussia, Thomasius's Pufendorfian doctrine could support an expansive form of religious toleration, inclusive of Catholics and atheists (Thomasius 1740: 349–51). Somewhat unexpectedly, by removing natural rights grounded in rational self-governance from the basis of the civil state, it became possible to accept as full citizens cultural groups whose imputed failure to practise rational self-governance might otherwise disqualify them from civil rights. The Lockean future was thus only one of several to be projected by the diverse forms of natural-law thought.

## REFERENCES

AHNERT, T. (2006). *Religion and the Origins of the German Enlightenment: Faith and the Reform of Learning in the Thought of Christian Thomasius.* Rochester: University of Rochester Press.

ALBERTI, V. (1676). *Compendium Juris Naturae, orthodoxae Theologiae conformatum.* Leipzig.

ARISTOTLE (1996). *The Politics and The Constitution of Athens.* Cambridge: Cambridge University Press.

BRETT, A. S. (1997). *Liberty, Right and Nature: Individual Rights in Later Scholastic Thought.* Cambridge: Cambridge University Press.

BURGESS, G. (1996). 'Thomas Hobbes: Religious Toleration or Religious Indifference', in C. J. Nederman and J. C. Laursen (eds), *Difference & Dissent: Theories of Tolerance in Medieval and Early Modern Europe.* London: Rowman & Littlefield, 139–62.

CARPZOV, B. (1635). *Practica nova imperialis saxonica rerum criminalium.* Frankfurt.

CONDREN, C. (2005). 'Curtailing the Office of the Priest: Two Seventeenth-Century Views of the Causes and Functions of Heresy', in I. Hunter, J. C. Laursen, and C. J. Nederman (eds), *Heresy in Transition: Transforming Ideas of Heresy in Medieval and Early Modern Europe.* Aldershot: Ashgate, 115–28.

CONTZEN, A. (1629). *Politicorum Libri Decem.* Cologne.

DÖRING, D. (1993). 'Säkularisierung und Moraltheologie bei Samuel von Pufendorf'. *Zeitschrift für Theologie und Kirche,* 90: 156–74.

DREITZEL, H. (2001). 'Naturrecht als politische Philosophie', in H. Holzhey and W. Schmidt-Biggemann (eds), *Die Philosophie des 17. Jahrhunderts, Band 4: Das heilige Römische Reich deutscher Nation, Nord- und Ostmitteleuropa.* Basel: Schwabe, 836–48.

DREITZEL, H. (2003). 'The reception of Hobbes in the political philosophy of the early German Enlightenment'. *History of European Ideas,* 29: 255–89.

ERSTENBERGER, A. (1586). *De Autonomia, das ist, von Freystellung mehrelay Religion und Glauben.* Munich.

FRIEDEBURG, R. V. and SEIDLER, M. J. (2008). 'The Holy Roman Empire of the German Nation', in H. A. Lloyd, G. Burgess, and S. Hodson (eds), *European Political Thought 1450–1700: Religion, Law and Philosophy.* New Haven and London: Yale University Press, 102–72.

GOLDIE, M. (1983). 'John Locke and Anglican Royalism'. *Political Studies,* 31: 61–85.

GOLDIE, M. (1991). 'The Political Thought of the Anglican Revolution', in R. Beddard (ed.), *The Revolutions of 1688*. Oxford: Clarendon Press, 102–36.

GROTIUS, H. (1925). *De jure belli ac pacis libri tres/The Rights of War and Peace in Three Books*. Oxford: Clarendon Press.

HAAKONSSEN, K. (2004). 'Protestant Natural-Law Theory: A General Interpretation', in N. Brender and L. Krasnoff (eds), *New Essays on the History of Autonomy: A Collection Honoring J. B. Schneewind*. Cambridge: Cambridge University Press, 92–109.

HAAKONSSEN, K. (2006). 'German Natural Law', in M. Goldie and R. Wokler (eds), *The Cambridge History of Eighteenth-Century Political Thought*. Cambridge: Cambridge University Press, 251–90.

HAMMERSTEIN, N. (1996). 'Relations with Authority', in H. D. Ridder-Symoens (ed.), *A History of the University in Europe: Volume II, Universities in Early Modern Europe (1500–1800)*. Cambridge: Cambridge University Press, 114–54.

HECKEL, M. (1989a). 'Autonomia und Pacis Compositio: Der Augsburger Religionsfriede in der Deutung der Gegenreformation', in K. Schlaich (ed.), *Martin Heckel: Gesammelte Schriften. Staat, Kirche, Recht, Geschichte*. Tübingen: J.C.B. Mohr, 1–81.

HECKEL, M. (1989b). 'Zur Historiographie des Westfälischen Friedens', in K. Schlaich (ed.), *Martin Heckel Gesammelte Schriften: Staat, Kirche, Recht, Geschichte*. Tübingen: J. C. B. Mohr, 484–500.

HOBBES, T. (1991). *Leviathan*. Cambridge: Cambridge University Press.

HOCHSTRASSER, T. J. and SCHRÖDER, P. (eds) (2002). *Early Modern Natural Law Theories: Contexts and Strategies in the Early Enlightenment*. Dordrecht: Kluwer.

HUNTER, I. (2001). *Rival Enlightenments: Civil and Metaphysical Philosophy in Early Modern Germany*. Cambridge: Cambridge University Press.

HUNTER, I. (2007). *The Secularisation of the Confessional State: The Political Thought of Christian Thomasius*. Cambridge: Cambridge University Press.

JUSTINIAN, C. F. (1913). *The Institutes of Justinian*. London.

KUSUKAWA, S. (1992). 'Law and gospel: the importance of philosophy at Reformation Wittenberg'. *History of Universities*, 11: 33–58.

LANDAU, P. (2000). 'Carpzov, das Protestantische Kirchenrecht und die frühneuzeitliche Gesellschaft', in G. Jerouschek, W. Schild, and W. Gropp (eds), *Benedict Carpzov: Neue Perspektiven zu einem umstrittenen sächsischen Juristen*. Tübingen: Diskord, 227–56.

LASLETT, P. (1960). Introduction, in P. Laslett (ed.), *John Locke: Two Treatises of Government*. Cambridge: Cambridge University Press, 3–127.

LOCKE, J. (1960). *Two Treatises of Government*. Cambridge: Cambridge University Press.

LOCKE, J. (1997). *Political Essays*. Cambridge: Cambridge University Press.

LUCCA, P. and AQUINAS, T. (1997). *On the Government of Rulers: De regimine principum*. Trans. J. M. Blythe. Philadelphia: University of Philadelphia Press.

LÜCK, H. (2000). 'Benedict Carpzov (1595–1666) und der Leipziger Schöffenstuhl', in G. Jerouschek, W. Schild, and W. Gropp (eds), *Benedict Carpzov: Neue Perspektiven zu einem umstrittenen sächsischen Juristen*. Tübingen: Diskord, 55–72.

MALCOLM, N. (1991). 'Hobbes and Spinoza', in J. H. Burns and M. Goldie (eds), *The Cambridge History of Political Thought 1450–1700*. Cambridge: Cambridge University Press, 530–57.

MEISNER, B. (1616). *Dissertatio de legibus in quatuor libellos distributa*. Wittenberg.

MELANCHTHON, P. (1965). *Melanchthon on Christian Doctrine: Loci Communes 1555*. New York: Oxford University Press.

PADOA-SCHIOPPA, A. (1997). 'Hierarchy and Jurisdiction: Models in Medieval Canon Law', in A. Padoa-Schioppa (ed.), *Legislation and Justice*. Oxford: Oxford University Press, 1–15.

PALLADINI, F. (2008). 'Pufendorf disciple of Hobbes: the nature of man and the state of nature: the doctrine of *socialitas*'. *History of European Ideas*, 34: 26–60.

PUFENDORF, S. (2002). *Of the Nature and Qualification of Religion in Reference to Civil Society*. Indianapolis, IN: Liberty Fund.

RYAN, A. (1988). 'A More Tolerant Hobbes', in S. Mendus (ed.), *Justifying Toleration: Conceptual and Historical Perspectives*. Cambridge: Cambridge University Press, 37–60.

SCATTOLA, M. (2001). 'Models in History of Natural Law', in D. Simon and M. Stolleis (eds), *Ius Commune XXVIII*. Frankfurt a. M. Klostermann, 91–160.

SCHILLING, H. (1995). 'Confessional Europe', in T. A. J. Brady, H. A. Oberman, and J. D. Tracy (eds), *Handbook of European History 1400–1600: Latin Middle Ages, Renaissance and Reformation. Volume II: Visions, Programs and Outcomes*. Leiden: E. J. Brill, 641–82.

SCHINDLING, A. (1988). 'Schulen und Universitäten im 16. und 17. Jahrhundert. Zehn Thesen zu Bildungsexpansion, Laienbildung und Konfessionalisierung nach Reformation', in W. Brandmüller, H. Immenkötter, and E. Iserloh (eds), *Ecclesia Militans. Studia zur Konzilien- und Reformationsgeschichte Remigius Bäumer zum 70. Geburtstag gewidmet*. Paderborn: Ferdinand Schöningh, 561–70.

SCHNEIDER, H.-P. (1967). *Justitia Universalis. Quellenstudien zur Geschichte des Christlichen Naturrechts bei Gottfried Wilhelm Leibniz*. Frankfurt a. M. Klostermann.

SCHNEIDER, H.-P. (2001). 'Christliches Naturrecht', in H. Holzhey and W. Schmidt-Biggemann (eds), *Die Philosophie des 17. Jahrhunderts, Band 4: Das heilige Römische Reich deutscher Nation, Nord- und Ostmitteleuropa*. Basle: Schwabe, 813–35.

SCHNUR, R. (ed.) (1986). *Die Rolle der Juristen bei der Enstehung des modernen Staates*. Berlin: Duncker & Humblot.

SCHWAB, D. (2006). 'Der Staat im Naturrecht der Scholastik', in D. Klippel and E. Müller-Luckner (eds), *Naturrecht und Staat: Politische Funktionen des europäischen Naturrechts (17.–19. Jahrhundert)*. Munich: Oldenbourg, 1–18.

SEIDLER, M. J. (2002). 'Pufendorf and the Politics of Recognition', in I. Hunter and D. Saunders (eds), *Natural Law and Civil Sovereignty: Moral Right and State Authority in Early Modern Political Thought*. Basingstoke: Palgrave, 235–51.

SEIDLER, M. J. (2003). 'The Politics of Self-Preservation: Toleration and Identity in Pufendorf and Locke', in T. J. Hochstrasser and P. Schröder (eds), *Early Modern Natural Law Theories: Contexts and Strategies in the Early Enlightenment*. Dordrecht: Kluwer, 227–55.

SERJEANTSON, R. W. (2006). 'Hobbes, the Universities, and the History of Philosophy', in C. Condren, S. Gaukroger, and I. Hunter (eds), *The Philosopher in Early Modern Europe: The Nature of a Contested Identity*. Cambridge: Cambridge University Press, 113–39.

SKINNER, Q. (1978). *The Foundations of Modern Political Thought: Volume Two, The Age of Reformation*. Cambridge: Cambridge University Press.

SKINNER, Q. (1996). 'Thomas Hobbes's Antiliberal Theory of Liberty', in B. Yack (ed.), *Liberalism without Illusions: Essays on Liberal Theory and the Political Vision of Judith N. Shklar*. Chicago: University of Chicago Press, 149–72.

SPARN, W. (1976). *Wiederkehr der Metaphysik: Die ontologische Frage in der lutherischen Theologie des frühen 17. Jahrhunderts*. Stuttgart: Calwer Verlag.

SPARN, W. (2001). 'Die Schulphilosophie in den lutherischen Territorien', in H. Holzhey and W. Schmidt-Biggemann (eds), *Die Philosophie des 17. Jahrhunderts, Band 4: Das heilige Römische Reich deutscher Nation, Nord- und Ostmitteleuropa*. Basle: Schwabe, 475–97.

STOLLEIS, M. (1988). *Geschichte des öffentlichen Rechts in Deutschland. Erster Band: Reichspublizistik und Policeywissenschaft 1600–1800.* Munich: C. H. Beck.

STOLLEIS, M. (2008). 'The Legitimation of Law through God, Tradition, Will, Nature and Constitution', in L. Daston and M. Stolleis (eds), *Natural Law and Laws of Nature in Early Modern Europe: Jurisprudence, Theology, Moral and Natural Philosophy.* Farnham: Ashgate, 45–56.

SUÁREZ, F. (1944). *Selections from Three Works.* Oxford: Clarendon Press.

THOMASIUS, C. (1740). *Vollständige Erläuterung der Kirchenrechts-Gelahrtheit.* Frankfurt and Leipzig.

THOMASIUS, C. (2007). 'The Right of Protestant Princes regarding Indifferent Matters or Adiaphora', in I. Hunter, T. Ahnert, and F. Grunert (ed. and trans.), *Christian Thomasius: Essays on Church, State, and Politics.* Indianapolis, IN: Liberty Fund, 49–127.

TUCK, R. (1987). 'The "Modern" Theory of Natural Law', in A. Pagden (ed.), *The Languages of Political Theory in Early-Modern Europe.* Cambridge: Cambridge University Press, 99–122.

TUCK, R. (1990). 'Hobbes and Locke on Toleration', in M. G. Dietz (ed.), *Thomas Hobbes and Political Theory.* Lawrence: University of Kansas Press, 153–71.

TULLY, J. (1991). 'Locke', in J. H. Burns and M. Goldie (eds), *The Cambridge History of Political Thought 1450–1700.* Cambridge: Cambridge University Press, 616–53.

WILSON, C. (2008). 'From Limits to Laws: The Construction of the Nomological Image of Nature in Early Modern Philosophy', in L. Daston and M. Stolleis (eds), *Natural Law and Laws of Nature in Early Modern Europe: Jurisprudence, Theology, Moral and Natural Philosophy.* Aldershot: Ashgate, 13–28.

CHAPTER 23

....................................................

# SOVEREIGNTY AND OBEDIENCE

....................................................

## URSULA GOLDENBAUM

THE concepts of sovereignty and obedience do not enjoy a good press today. Sovereignty is often considered simply as state power, as that which deprives citizens of their own power and excludes them from political participation and forces them to obey. It is understood as the essence of any state whatsoever. However, the concept of sovereignty is quite recent, and was coined as late as 1576 by the French lawyer Jean Bodin (1962: 84). Although it was indeed meant as an exclusive concept, it was supposed to exclude other competing state powers rather than single citizens, especially the estates, that is social and occupational classes, who were then claiming equal power with the ruler.

In this chapter, I will first explore conflicting conceptions of the people's right of resistance to the king as they developed in the political upheavals following the Reformation, especially at the hands of Lutheran, Calvinist, and Catholic monarchomachs or regicides, that is, the opponents of sovereign or absolute power. A second section will focus on Hobbes and Spinoza, on their more differentiated and coherent concept of sovereignty, as well as on their discussion of civil rights. The last section will survey the understanding of sovereignty and obedience that was developed by three thinkers who absorbed the lessons of Hobbes and Spinoza but softened their radical ideas: Samuel Pufendorf, John Locke, and Christian Wolff. By adapting the radical ideas of their infamous forerunners, the work of these three theorists became highly influential in legal theory and political philosophy until the middle of the eighteenth century and beyond. As a result, John Locke is today considered almost as a contemporary theorist, especially in the Anglo-American world.

# I: THE PEOPLE'S RIGHT OF RESISTANCE: WHO ARE 'THE PEOPLE'?

The estates' claim to power had been supported by the theory that posited a contract between the ruler and *the people*. As the ruler was considered to owe his or her power to the people, then by mutual contract he or she had obligations to the people. If the contract were not fulfilled, the people had the right of resistance. This theory had been first developed in the city republics of Northern Italy during the fourteenth century; it was based on Aristotle's views on tyranny (Skinner 1992: I, 49–53), and on the Roman law dealing with kingship (Hinsley 1986: 83–8, 92). It was subsequently taken up by Marsilius of Padua, a citizen of the city republic of Venice (Skinner 1992: I, 63–5), in order to assert the independence of the Emperor from the Pope on the grounds that he owed his power to the people. As a result, however, the Emperor was supposed to be indebted to the people.

This theoretical position seems already to point to the concepts of popular sovereignty and constitutionalism, and it has frequently been interpreted that way. This requires a brief comment on the use of the term 'constitutionalism', which has been used to refer to theoretical approaches as diverse as that of the Republican defenders of Italian city republics, both Protestant and Catholic monarchomachic authors, Locke, and modern democratic theory. This vague and extended use of the term is anachronistic and may be confusing. One can agree with Howell Lloyd's claim that 'it entails no anachronism to describe as "constitutionalist" contemporary ideas to the effect that power ought to be exercised within institutionally determined limits. Such ideas may be expected to have flourished in the age of Renaissance and the Reformation, of humanist learning, of critical and historical reappraisal of the Roman texts' (Lloyd 1991: 255). Skinner also uses the term 'constitutional' in this wide scope (Skinner 1992: II, 158), and Julius Franklin entitles his edition of monarchomachic authors as *Constitutionalism and Resistance* (Constitutionalism 1969). The same anachronistic habit can be seen in the widespread historical evaluation of the *Magna Carta libertatum* (1225), which resulted from a conflict between the barons and the king of England. Since it arose from the struggles between competing supreme powers within the state, it had nothing to do with popular sovereignty or the human rights of individual subjects as we understand them today. It is still widely celebrated, though, as a major step in the history of human rights, as restricting the absolute power of the king against 'his subjects', although it guaranteed nothing else than the liberties and privileges of a small noble class. However the 'shocking view that the [Great] Charter merely sprang from the private ambition of a few selfish barons' (Skinner 2002: 262) remained unnoticed until recently because of the 'whiggish myth' of an almost uninterrupted tradition of so-called constitutional rights in

English history. Thus, although Marsilius's theory may appear modern, agreeable, and almost Lockean, the meaning of 'the people' makes it a quite different political theory. The people for Marsilius and other partisans of this theory were understood as 'its prevailing part' (Marsilius 2005: III, 2, 6); in the case of the Holy Roman Empire, the people were the few Electoral Princes who would elect the Emperor. When it was adopted by Calvinist, Lutheran, and Catholic theologians and lawyers during the sixteenth century, 'the people' meant the estates, considered as a collective unity, or the parliament. Individual citizens and other residents of states and provinces were not considered as political subjects at all. When the partisans of this version of contract theory in France called for disobedience and for resistance against the king in the years of civil war, Bodin was led to produce his new concept of sovereignty that gave all power in state affairs to the king.

Whereas Bodin still argued within the traditional contract theory and considered the people as a legal person, the modern political theory of individual citizens with individual rights was developed by theoreticians who are seldom given credit for their theoretical achievement. Often, Hobbes and Spinoza are even seen as having dismissed human rights and liberties altogether because of their eagerness to strengthen sovereign power. However, only the Hobbesian fiction of the state as constituted by the covenanting of single individuals paved the way for individual political rights of the citizens, which are guaranteed by an indivisible sovereign power.

In the seventeenth century and after, the development of the contract theory into a theory of the people's right of resistance was often credited to the Protestants and, more specifically, to the Calvinists, since it was used by Protestant theorists to legitimize various political revolutions—for example in England in 1649 and 1688, or in the Dutch revolt against Spain (Grunert 2004: 119–74; Wenzel 1997: 33–46). Luther, however, and Calvin, had argued in favour of the strict obedience of the subjects to their ruler, as taught by the Bible; they referred especially to 1 Samuel 8, 9–20, and demanded submission even to tyrants. The shocking recent experience of the Peasant Wars in the southern German territories of the Empire in 1524/5, and the notoriously violent reign of Anabaptism in the German city of Münster in 1534/5, were still in their minds (Constitutionalism 1969: 156). However, each reformer reluctantly changed his views: Luther, when it came to conflict between the Protestant princes and the Emperor Charles V, and Calvin, when it came to conflict between the estates or princes of particular Protestant territories and the king of France (Skinner 1992: II, 189–224). Facing a military conflict with their supreme ruler, the question arose whether the Protestant princes and estates, who were lower political authorities and protectors of Protestant subjects and represented the people, were permitted to stand up against the supreme power (Skinner 1992: II, 194–206).

In Scotland and in the Netherlands, the Calvinists sought to justify their resistance against their Catholic rulers. The Scottish Calvinist and humanist George Buchanan built his argument on contract theory, Roman law, and history; he asked that the liberties and rights of the people be observed and that the king be obliged to obey the law (Skinner 1992: II, 339–45; Pečar 2007: 304–5). The Calvinist theologian John Knox, on the other hand, based his argument for an active right of resistance almost exclusively on the Bible, putting himself into the position of a prophet and citing the Theocracy of Israel as a model for a state according to the order of God. Knox appealed to 2 Kings 14, 2 Kings 9–10, and 2 Kings 21, 1–18, all of which concerned God's punishment of kings or queens who had disobeyed God's orders. Thus he asked Queen Mary Stuart to obey the divine law, by considering her above all as God's subject; by doing so, he followed the prophet Jeremiah, who admonished the people as well as the queen to obey the law of God (Knox 1966: 425–55). But Knox's radical position about the people's resistance was approved neither by Calvin nor by his Swiss and French partisans, who at this time were still trying to mediate and negotiate with the French court.

In France, civil strife and military battles between the Huguenots and the Catholic League shook the kingdom for the last four decades of the sixteenth century. It was not, however, until the massacre of the Huguenots on the bloody night of St Bartholomew in 1572 that the theory of an active right to resist tyrants was taken up by the leaders of Calvinism in France and Switzerland. From then on, writings and pamphlets against the French tyranny, which employed both legal and biblical arguments that had been developed by French, German, Dutch, and Scottish lawyers and theologians (Skinner 1992: II, 210), were disseminated to other parts of Europe. Suddenly, there was no longer any doubt, in spite of all the earlier warnings of Calvin and Luther, that the people had a right of resistance.

Within a decade of the night of St Bartholomew, Jean Bodin, who had long been sympathetic with the Huguenots during their negotiations with the French court, published *Les six livres de la république*, which took a clear stand against the right of resistance by providing for the first time a clear definition of Sovereignty: 'Maiestie or Soueraigntie is the most high, absolute, and perpetuall power ouer the citizens and subiects in a commonweale' (Bodin 1962: 84). Bodin gave all power unequivocally to the king, making his rule absolute. However, this was neither simply a defence of the institution of the French king's absolute power, nor simply directed against the Huguenots. It also stood against the threat of a direct or indirect intervention of the Catholic Church into French politics. In addition, Bodin retained the theoretical model of traditional contract theory, that is, he still considered the people to be the source of the king's power and a legal person itself. He thus argued within the same theoretical framework as the Huguenot monarchomachic theorists, by seeing the people as a holy, organic, and immortal unity constituted by the particular bodies of the estates and the parliament (Gierke 1950: 59).

At that point, it seemed to be an odd move when James VI/I, king of Scotland and England, turned back to the old-fashioned theory of divine right of kings. But at a second look, this move of the learned king is less surprising: not only was James challenged by Calvinist monarchomachs who supported John Knox in Scotland; he was even more challenged by the Catholic Church, which questioned his rule and began to raise doubts about his succession on the English throne even before Elizabeth's death (Doleman [Parson] 1595; Lake 2004: 243–60). In 1605, two years after he assumed power, the gunpowder plot came to light; it had been organized by Catholics, and intended to blow up the king and the parliament. This aggressive political move of the Catholic camp, intended to regain Scotland and England, had been backed by a theory of the people's right of resistance. During the sixteenth century, large parts of the Empire had been lost to Protestant rulers, although the battle still continued until the Peace of Westphalia and further. England had been cut off from the Catholic Church by Henry VIII in 1532/3, and had turned to Protestantism (although with several interruptions). Scotland had turned to Calvinism by decree of the parliament in 1560. The Dutch Revolt in 1581 had turned the assets of the Spanish Empire into a Protestant and independent country. The Catholic Church and its allies, especially Spain, tried everything possible to change the situation and to get the lost territories back under their influence, and they were not shy to interfere openly in other states. The Catholic theologians and lawyers, especially in Spain, adopted the allegedly constitutional theory of the right of resistance, and adapted it to their own political purposes.

The new theory had already been adopted by Francisco Vitoria (1991: 14, 32, 40). It was further developed by his followers, including Domingo de Soto, Diego de Covarruvias, and Fernando de Vasquez at the University in Salamanca. Although it was initially put on the *Index librorum prohibitorum* by the Pope in 1590, the Catholic version of the 'constitutional' theory of social contract, which permitted the people to resist tyranny, provided a perfect theoretical framework to defend the supreme power of the Pope over kings. According to Suárez, sovereignty was no longer exclusively given by God to the Pope or the emperor (Suárez 1944: 672–82). Suárez discusses explicitly the right of resistance of the people and distinguishes two ways of being a tyrant: there are tyrants who have usurped power and lack a legal title, and tyrants who have become such by ruling unjustly (Suárez 1944: 705, 854). He vindicates a right of resistance on the part of the entire state [*republica*] against a tyrant without a legal title to rule. In the case of tyrants who have turned into tyrants while exercising a legal title, everyone could still defend himself or herself. But no dependent state or province, and certainly no private person, had the right of resistance. However, 'the state as a whole is superior to the king' (Suárez 1944: 855) and the *republica* would thus be justified in deposing the king. In addition, a legal king who was not a tyrant could justly go to war against any province within his state if it revolted against him (Suárez 1944: 855), as for example the Spanish king during the Dutch revolt.

Using this new theoretical approach, Suárez argued directly against James VI/I of Scotland and England, and answered the latter's infamous claim of divine right. State affairs had to be settled in favour of the spiritual well-being of subjects, even if the *raison d'Etat* called for a different policy (Suárez 1944: 667–82). Therefore, the Pope could ask the state [*respublica*] as a whole to depose the king if he disobeyed, in order to avoid heresy and schism. Still, Suárez did not give the right of resistance to private men, but asked for 'accordance with the public and general deliberations of its communities and leading men' (Suárez 1944: 718). If the ruler was excommunicated by the Pope, the state as a whole was permitted to ask other rulers for support, even by invading the country. The Pope himself was also licensed to engage another ruler to intervene (Suárez 1944: 701–2).

Although the Catholic theorists' argument for deposing a tyrant clearly resembles that of the Protestant monarchomachs, it was intended neither to restrict political power in favour of the subjects nor to strengthen human rights, although one sometimes reads that it did (Soder 1973: 11–13). It strove rather to restrict the king's power in favour of that of the Pope. The so-called constitutional theory of contract was therefore not exclusively designed to become a theory of Republican rights and liberties, as is often said (Skinner 1992: II, 345–8). It served fundamentalist Calvinists as well as the authoritarian Catholic Church. Its deployment at any given moment depended on the definition of 'the people'.

The general notion of 'the people', as it appears in all Protestant and Catholic monarchomachic writings during the sixteenth and early seventeenth centuries, is that of an organic and immortal unity, constituted by the estates and independent of the state. Whereas kings would die, *the people*, 'like a corporate body', would never die (Constitutionalism 1969: 79, 168). Three classes within the people were distinguished: the common people without any office, who had no right of resistance as single individuals, although they did have the right of self-defence. They were asked to be patient, to pray, or in the worst case to leave the territory— exactly as it was taught by Luther and Calvin. Second, there were subjects with a lower-level office, called lower magistrates or Ephori. Examples were mayors, senators, members of a city council, dukes, barons, etc. They were supposed to serve according to their office, reporting not to the ruler as a person but to his office. Finally, there were higher magistrates who were close to the king. If the king turned into a tyrant and the higher magistrates did not fulfil their admonishing function, the lower authorities had the duty to warn the higher authorities first and then to take action by themselves. They were even justified to take up arms and to resist the tyrannical ruler in order to protect those subjects who depended on them. Most important for practical politics, they were justified in asking foreign allies for support (Constitutionalism 1969: 108–15; Suárez 1944: 701–2).

It was not left to the discretion of the individual subjects, to any Dick, Tom, or Harry, to make judgements about these preconditions of legitimate resistance or to stand up against authority.[1] *The people*, as addressed in these allegedly constitutional doctrines, are not the multitude of single individuals in the state but the organic and immortal whole represented by their estates:

When we speak of the people collectively, we mean those who receive authority from the people, that is, the magistrates below the king who have been elected by the people or established in some other way. These take the place of the people assembled as a whole and are ephors to kings and associates in their rule. And we also mean the Assembly of the Estates.   (Constitutionalism 1969: 149; see Suárez 1944: 718)

The emphasis of this organic character of the people is expressed most clearly by Duplessis-Mornay's metaphor of a ship not being constituted by the 'planks, nails, and pegs' but by its 'prow, deck, and rudder', and that of a house not being a whole due to single 'stones, beams, and mortar' but by the 'roof, walls, and foundation' (Constitutionalism 1969: 152). Whereas the people were considered as an immortal unity,[2] the multitude [*la populasse*], on the contrary, is despised as the 'many-headed monster' (149). Thus, when we read the sentence of great pathos: 'the people as a whole is greater than the king' (161), it is a far cry from our modern understanding of popular sovereignty as the participation of all individual *citizens* in state power (cf. Walzer 1966: 18).

# II: HOBBES AND SPINOZA

Hobbes proudly dated the beginning of political philosophy at the publication of his *De cive* (HW I, ix). There he initiated his discussion with a thought-experiment in which he dissolves the state (HW II, xiv). This thought-experiment already questions the traditional natural law by the very metaphors employed. In contrast with Duplessis-Mornay, who had compared 'the people' with a ship, built of the 'prow, deck, and rudder', Hobbes does not see any 'people' remaining after the dissolution of the state. If all political bonds were removed, nothing would remain but single human individuals, the multitude, just as the dissolution of a clock would leave nothing but single screws and wheels. Spinoza will formulate it explicitly: 'Nature forms individuals, not people' (Spinoza 2004a: 232). This new individualistic approach is indeed a revolution in political and natural law theory.

---

[1] Although the Spanish Jesuit Juan de Mariana is considered as giving the right of resistance to individuals, his referring to the *vox populi* points beyond individual decision-making (Mariana 1599: 665–9; Reinhardt 2007: 286–92).

[2] Johann Althusius, currently experiencing a re-evaluation as a 'constitutionalist' (Bonfatti, *et al.* 2002; Friedeburg, 2006) clearly considers 'a representational person' as representing 'men collectively and not individually' (Althusius 1964: 35).

As a result of this approach, the nature of these human beings (the elements of the state) has to be explored to find out how they are to be connected in a stable, that is peaceful, way. Neither Hobbes nor Spinoza ever gets tired of emphasizing how we humans are led by passions rather than by reason. Thus, anthropology and psychology become parts of political science. When striving for self-preservation, human beings have to compete with each other. Given that the power of human beings to get what they want and need is limited, and given that they are equally and mutually dangerous to each other, they need a state to guarantee their safety and property. Spinoza emphasizes more than Hobbes the need to co-operate in order to satisfy human needs (Spinoza 2004a: 202–3).

What is needed to protect human beings in their struggle for self-preservation is a guarantor of contracts, constraining the contractual parties to keep their promises as well as protecting them against others. Such a guarantor does not exist by nature and thus has to be created by humans as an artifact, like a machine. In order to be able to enforce the law, that is, to protect life and property within the state, it needs enforcement power. Thus every single individual, including women (L ch. 20 [4–7]), needs to promise to everyone to give up his/her own power and transfer it to a sovereign, so that the latter becomes the most powerful. The prospective subjects need to authorize the sovereign in the most general way, by giving him (or them) general power to act in their name and thus creating the artificial person, the Leviathan or the commonwealth. They will thereby be the authors of *all* actions that the sovereign will take in order to keep the state and its subjects safe and to give them as much liberty as possible to work for their self-preservation. It is this idea of the state as constituted by the mutual agreement of its prospective subjects or citizens (i.e. *individual* human beings), thus becoming the guarantor of their rights and duties, which is the modern idea of the state. Thus Thomas Hobbes, in spite of his bad reputation, was right to see himself as the very starting point of political science. 'Hobbes closes one chapter in the history of the modern theory of the state and opens another and more familiar one. Arguably he is the earliest political writer to maintain with complete self-consciousness that the legal person lying at the heart of politics is neither the person of the sovereign nor the person constituted by the *universitas* of the people, but is rather the artificial person of the state' (Skinner 2002: 14).

Having presented the model for the generation of a state by covenanting individuals, Hobbes shows that every functioning state can be considered *as if* everyone had covenanted with everyone and thereby authorized the sovereign, even in case of patrimonial or conquered states. The conquered individuals, who were no longer a people, needed to submit as individuals and promise obedience under the condition of being protected in order to become the subjects instead of slaves of the sovereign. Thus the rights and consequences of such a paternal and even despotic dominion are the same as those of a sovereign by institution, and for the very same reasons (L ch. 20, [14]). It is already clear that in neither case can there be any right of resistance for the people against the sovereign, because the people are only the result of covenanting. Thus the sovereign cannot break any contract with the people, since the sovereign did not make a contract in either case.

Once general power has been given to the sovereign, there is no way out except by the destruction of the state, at no small cost. The sovereign is authorized by the covenanters in order to protect them, not just their mere life, but with 'all ... contentment of life' (L ch. 30, [1]). It is in order to meet this expectation that the sovereign needs to be the supreme arbiter regarding all means of peace and defence, the supreme commander of the army, the supreme arbiter about inner discord and hostility, the supreme judge of crimes, the supreme guarantor of property, the supreme censor of all books and public speeches insofar as they could threaten the state, the supreme legislator, and the supreme governor. All these rights of the sovereign are mostly identical with the definition given by Bodin (1962: I, ch. 8). But Hobbes does not take them from experience; rather, he deduces them strictly from the very definition of sovereignty. He considers the division of sovereignty as meaningless speech, since it is a contradiction in itself. As soon as the sovereign cannot rely on the obedience of everyone, *his* or *their* power to guarantee safety, peace, law, and liberty to *his* or *their* subjects would vanish and so would the state (L ch. 18). The knowledge of the people about their obligation to obey the sovereign seems so urgent to Hobbes that he even asks to set aside some labour time to instruct the people about the sovereign and their obligation (L ch. 30, [10]).

Hobbes points explicitly to the monarchomachic argument mentioned above, according to which the people as single subjects were beneath the king, but were above the king if considered as the entire people. The nominalist Hobbes soberly states:

This great authority being indivisible, and inseparably annexed to sovereignty, there is little ground for the opinion of them, that say of sovereign kings, though they be *singulis majores*, of greater power than every one of their subjects, yet they be *universis minores*, of less power than them all together. For if by all together, they mean not their collective body as one person, then all together, and every one, signify the same; and the speech is absurd. But if by all together, they understand them as one person, which person the sovereign bears, then the power of all together, is the same with the sovereign's power; and so again the speech is absurd: which absurdity they see well enough, when the sovereignty is in an assembly of the people; but in a monarchy they see it not and yet the power of sovereignty *is the same* in whomsoever it be placed.    (L ch. 18, [18]; my emphasis)

This strict understanding of sovereignty is the same for all three possible forms of state—democracy, monarchy, and aristocracy (L ch. 19, [1–2]).[3] Hobbes uses the

---

[3] Of course, mixed state forms are, by definition, impossible because a sovereign can be only one individual, all individuals, or a few individuals, leading to either monarchy, or democracy, or aristocracy. Tyranny, oligarchy, and anarchy are dismissed as mere slander of the only possible state forms (L ch. 19, [1]).

example of the Roman democracy to show this sameness of the need for obedience in all state types and at the same time the absurdity of the right-of-resistance theory: If '*the people of Rome*' had made a 'covenant with the Romans', to hold the sovereignty under certain conditions, and the covenant were not performed by *the people of Rome* according to these conditions, 'the Romans might lawfully depose the *Roman people*' (L ch. 18, [4]; my emphasis). Although Hobbes is clear about his personal preference for monarchy, he is not at all passionate about it. Monarchy seems to have the advantage that the interest of the king is almost identical with the interest of the whole commonwealth: 'For no king can be rich, nor glorious, nor secure, whose subjects are either poor, or contemptible, or too weak' (L ch. 19, [4]). But Hobbes not only discusses the disadvantages of the monarchy; he also acknowledges the great advantage of a democracy which does not have to struggle with the crucial problem of succession, which is the Achilles heel of every monarchy in terms of security.

In addition, Hobbes speaks continuously, throughout the *Leviathan*, of *the sovereign* or of *the sovereign assembly*, thus not acknowledging any difference in their relation to the subjects. His only concern is the sufficient power of the sovereign to guarantee the safety of all subjects and their liberties no matter which state-form it is. Against the mainstream opinion of his own time, Hobbes does not admit that tyrannical rulers arose from monarchy alone. One thing that provoked his sarcastic comments was the monarchomachic call for a right of the people to resist using the 'specious name' (L ch. 21, [9]) of the liberty of the people. He especially mocked the then-popular idea that free states were appropriate to free men, while monarchies produced obedient subjects, or indeed slaves:

There is written on the turrets of the city of Lucca in great characters at this day, the word LIBERTAS; yet no man can thence infer, that a particular man has more liberty, or immunity from the service of the commonwealth there, then in Constantinople. Whether a commonwealth be monarchical, or popular, the freedom is still the same.    (L ch. 21, [8])

But given that nobody ever asked more bluntly for unconditioned obedience of the subjects, how can Hobbes speak about freedom at all?[4] He answers that human liberties simply originate from the sovereign who alone can guarantee them. Paradoxically, liberties are related to obedience. Hobbes states that 'in the act of our *submission*, consisteth both our *obligation* and our *liberty*; which must

---

[4] Hobbes's infamous definition of liberty or freedom as the absence of external impediments of motion, which is explicitly seen as applicable to irrational and inanimate things (L ch. 21, [1]) such as water freely flowing, is certainly meant to provoke the defenders of 'the liberty of the people'. But it also allows him to find a new approach to a concept of freedom beyond free will, which he denies. Compare the interesting recent and extended discussion of Hobbes on freedom by Skinner (2008). Confronting Hobbes with his Republican opponents calling for 'liberty', Skinner sees Hobbes as the winner of the battle, although he seems not to be happy about this (Skinner 2008: 216) when he asks whether Hobbes also won the argument. But given the bad reputation of Hobbes, what else could have brought the victory if not his crystal-clear argument? See above, Chapter 20.

therefore be inferred by arguments taken from thence' (L ch. 21, [10]). It is from the cause of the state and the sovereign, that we can deduce the limits of our due obedience as well as of our liberties in the state: 'it is manifest, that every subject has liberty in all those things, *the right whereof cannot by covenant be transferred*' (L ch. 21, [11]; my emphasis). It is from this limited ability to covenant that Hobbes can infer to what are literally inalienable rights of individual subjects to resist any order to kill, wound, or maim oneself, or to resist those that would require one to abstain from the use of food, air, medicine, or any other thing without which one cannot live. Therefore nobody is bound to confess a crime or to accuse himself. Nobody is obliged to kill another man except if our refusal 'frustrates the end for which the sovereignty was ordained' (L ch. 21, [15]). Above all, it is due to this natural limit of covenanting that we cannot be obliged to think or to feel according to an order because our thoughts are not in the scope of our will. In addition to these liberties or limits of obligation, which can be deduced from the very nature of human beings and their limited ability to covenant, the 'liberty of a subject, lieth . . . only in those things, which in regulating their actions, the sovereign hath pretermitted; such as the liberty to buy, and sell, and otherwise contract with one another; to choose their own abode, their own diet, their own trade of life, and institute their children as they themselves think fit' (L ch. 21, [6]). These liberties can therefore vary from one state to another according to positive law. Of course, our duty to obey clearly ends if the sovereign lacks the power to protect us and the commonwealth falls apart (L ch. 21, [21]).

Hobbes's sober talk about liberty reflects his passion against its abuse by the mighty people in the Parliament. These men, who were able to pay their own army and persuade the common people by their popularity and demagogic speech, had caused the civil war. It was not the common people, Hobbes argued, who had complained about the lack of liberty or who were unable to understand the need for obedience to the sovereign. It was the mighty people, who were ambitious and longing for even more power within the state, as well as the learned men who were afraid to admit their errors (L ch. 30, [6]). Against the mighty, who pretended to fight for liberty while requesting their own privileges, Hobbes stressed the equality of all subjects before the sovereign and before the law and argued against tax exemptions for the privileged. All the possible liberties of the people, the security of a civil life, the equality of the subjects before the law, the denial of privileges to certain classes, the guaranteeing of the products of one's labour and the property of each single subject, independently of his/her social state, against even the mightiest of other subjects, could be granted only by the even mightier sovereign.

Hobbes's deep worry about the mighty within the state seems to be the true reason he named his political masterwork after the biblical Leviathan. While the frontispiece cites only the first line 'out of the two last verses of the one-and-fortieth of *Job*': 'There is nothing, saith he, on earth, to be compared with him', Hobbes quotes the full passage within the book, thereby clearly pointing to the mighty whom the sovereign had to be strong enough to resist: 'God having set forth the great power of *Leviathan*, calleth him king of the proud. *He is made so as not to be afraid. He seeth every high thing below him; and is king of all the children of pride*' (L ch. 28, [27]; my emphasis). Also, in contrast to the monarchomachic tradition, Hobbes uses the metaphor of the many-headed Hydra to characterize the mighty (L ch. 30, [24]), whereas Duplessis-Mornay had used it earlier to describe the multitude (Constitutionalism 1969: 149).

Hobbes openly admits the possibility that the natural person or persons of the sovereign could abuse his or their power and indeed had done so in the past, although not only in monarchies. However, 'the consequences of the want of it, which is perpetual war of every man against his neighbour, are much worse' (L ch. 20, [18]). Besides this problem, Hobbes leaves another difficulty unsolved, *viz.* freedom of speech. Since he himself was one of the most outspoken authors in history, he clearly is in favour of freedom of thought. Nevertheless, he consistently ascribes the right of censorship to the sovereign. Moreover, consistently with his political approach to sovereignty, religion has to be administrated by the sovereign, since it is of the greatest influence on the opinions of the subjects (L ch. 23, [6]). But although Hobbes asks for one unique form of public worship in the common-wealth, he admits 'a private worship' (L ch. 31, [11–12]). This is due to the fact that we cannot be forced to believe anything on command: 'for men's belief, and interior cogitations, are not subject to the commands, but only to the operation of God, ordinary, or extraordinary. Faith of supernatural law, is not a fulfilling, but only an assenting to the same; and not a duty that we exhibit to God, but a gift which God freely giveth to whom he pleaseth' (L ch. 26, [41]). This creates a 'private sphere' wherein no sovereign can reach. This private sphere, though, is free only 'in secret' because 'in the sight of the multitude, it is never without some restraint, either from the laws, or from the opinion of men; which is contrary to the nature of liberty' (L ch. 31, [12]). It is here that Hobbes struggles with the concept of freedom of speech; he is ready to adhere to freedom of thought, but hesitates in fear of disobedience to the sovereign.

Spinoza is often contrasted with Hobbes (Negri 2004: 58, fn. 37; 115), but it is he who first embraced Hobbes's doctrine without reservation: the constitution of the commonwealth by the multitude (i.e. by the many single individuals instead of by the people); the concept of indivisible sovereignty; the demand for obedience; individual inalienable rights and the rejection of the right of resistance. However, the Dutch philosopher took up two great problems that had been addressed but not solved by Hobbes. Surprisingly, Spinoza did so within the theoretical frame-work of Hobbes's naturalistic and mechanical approach. Hobbes's commonwealth, once constituted by covenant, would either work or fall apart, depending on the obedience of the people and the competent policy of the sovereign. Spinoza developed a flexible model. First, he used Hobbes's often neglected reservation that our thoughts cannot be subject to the covenant because they do not depend on our will. But he extends this argument: nothing that we are not capable of doing, not even in order to avoid punishment or to obtain rewards, can be required of us (Spinoza 2004b: ch. 3, sect. 8). No one can become wise at the behest of the sovereign and nobody can change his/her own nature on command. Spinoza argues that this is true not only for thinking but also for speaking out loud or for expressing one's feelings, for example, of respect or contempt. In addition, the persecution of free speech would have a destabilizing impact on the state, by undermining the morals of the subjects/citizens by forcing them to lie. A suppression of free speech would rather lead to persecution of those sincere subjects or citizens who care about the commonwealth and worry about its future, rather than those who don't care or who are ready to lie (2004a: 261–2). It could not be in the interest of the sovereign to punish the state's most supportive subjects or citizens for expressing their opinions and thoughts, so long as they do not question the sovereign power as such.

In contrast to Hobbes's inflexible model, Spinoza understood the relation between the sovereign and the subjects/citizens as a balance of power. The power of the sovereign depends on the transferred power of the united subjects or citizens, but the amount of that power is not constant over time. As human beings cannot transfer *all* their power to the sovereign once and forever, as Hobbes had acknowledged in the case of the power of thinking, Spinoza argues that this is true more generally (Spinoza 2004a: 214). The more the subjects favour their government and its policies, the more they will obey, for example by paying taxes, instilling patriotism in their children, or volunteering for military service. Obedience means much more than simply not resisting the power of the sovereign; it can include a broad spectrum of behaviour from the sacrifice of one's own life for the commonwealth at the one end, through passive acceptance and protest, up to outright revolt against the government at the other. Of course, the sovereign can simply enforce some demands. However, it will never get as much support from its subjects/citizens as it could get through the spirit of patriotism and love of the sovereign. The crucial factor for the stability of the commonwealth is power over minds (Spinoza 2004a: 252–3). Thus, Spinoza makes the process of the constitution of the state in some way permanent (Spinoza 2004b: ch. 2, sect. 16). As the agreement of the subjects or citizens cannot be won by suppression of their opinions, but only by engaging in a free discourse between the subjects/citizens and the sovereign, freedom of speech is clearly a precondition for the higher stability of the state and the greater obedience of the subjects/citizens to the sovereign. This is clear from the subtitle of the *Theologico-Political Treatise*.

In his *Theologico-Political Treatise*, Spinoza bluntly declares that democracy is the most natural state-form, because it leaves everyone equal and free, as in the state of nature, and open to expressive discourse (Spinoza 2004a: 205–7). Another feature that especially recommends democracy to Spinoza is that this state-form is open to procedural change, in contrast to Hobbes's inflexible model. Nobody has to give up power once and for all; he or she remains further involved in the procedure of shaping the commonwealth and its policies. Nevertheless, Spinoza is not too passionately concerned about the form of the state, so long as the freedom of the people within the state (and thus the state's stability) can be guaranteed. In his *Political Treatise* (Spinoza 2004*b*), he provides the institutional apparatus for peaceful political changes and the productive input of the opinions of the many into the political decision-making process, by attempting to work it out for all three state-forms, though he could not finish the section on democracy. Last, but not least, Spinoza provides the means for the different institutions of the state to check each other in order mutually to control each other's power. This does not mean, though, that sovereignty should be divided (Spinoza 2004*b*: ch. 2).

As Spinoza says, the only difference between him and Hobbes is that he does not see the civil state as cut off from the state of nature (Spinoza 2002: 891–2). Individuals necessarily strive for self-preservation, whether in the state of nature or in the commonwealth. They get into conflict with the sovereign every time the latter's policy restricts them in their striving. The sovereign, acquiring its power from the individuals, can lose some of it when the consent of the people is shrinking. They do not even have to disobey by means of overtly aggressive actions against the state; they can weaken it dramatically by being less supportive, by cheating on their taxes, by avoiding military service, etc. As the frequent popularity polls for political leaders today suggest, the balance between the power of the people and the power of the sovereign can be considered as continuously swinging, depending on the degree of their agreement.

Given Spinoza's general agreement with Hobbes, despite his constructive differences, it does not come as a surprise that they both fought against the same opponents. The Dutch philosopher is less concerned with the Catholic enemies than Hobbes (L III, ch. xlii),[5] although he takes a clear stand against their claims for political power too. But the whole first part of Spinoza's *Theologico-Political Treatise*, often neglected by political philosophers because of its biblical and theological focus, was a direct refutation of the Calvinist (and Catholic) appeals to the Hebrew state and the special role of the High Priest as the adviser of the king. Spinoza shows that the High Priest did not possess sovereign power in the first Hebrew state, and when the Priest acquired such power, it led to the decline of the Hebrew state. As was the case for Hobbes, it was Spinoza's main goal to exclude the church from the rule of the state and from sovereignty (Spinoza 2004*a*: ch. 19). And here Spinoza, although emphatically calling for freedom of speech, is as ready as

---

[5] Jeffrey Collins emphasizes this rather underestimated concern of Hobbes—'that it was precisely these clerical opponents (and, by the same token, anticlerical proponents) who fully grasped the partisan implications of Hobbes's political writings within the context of the English Revolution. Their primary concern, moreover, was neither Hobbes's theory of obligation, nor his theological heterodoxy as such, but his radically Erastian ecclesiology: his project to reduce Christian church, its clergy and doctrine, to an arm of the state' (Collins 2005: 4–5).

Hobbes to have the sovereign ban all speeches and books questioning the sovereign and its essential rights. They cannot be seen as an argument but as an action against the state and, as such, they must be banned and punished (Spinoza 2004a: 303).

# III: 'Taming the Leviathan': Samuel Pufendorf, John Locke, and Christian Wolff

As is well-known, the new conception of natural right, as developed by Hobbes and Spinoza, was considered as an outburst of radical thinking leading to atheism, libertinism, and 'Machiavellism'.[6] But although they were either refuted or not mentioned at all in standard academic literature at the time, the principles of their revolutionary new approach to political philosophy were immediately adopted by Pufendorf, Locke, and Wolff, who would dominate the discussion within political philosophy for the first half of the eighteenth century and beyond, in the Holy Roman Empire, in Britain, and the United States. Jean Barbeyrac's translation of Pufendorf into French made a strong impact in the Francophone world until Rousseau. The Latin translations of Pufendorf and Wolff made their way to Italy, Spain, and East Europe.

In order to ease acceptance of their general ideas, these three philosophers avoided acknowledging their deep debt to their widely abhorred forerunners. But to the extent that they mention Hobbes or Spinoza, they discussed them rather seriously and fairly. Obviously, they did not share all the radical philosophical conclusions of Hobbes and Spinoza. In addition, whereas the two radicals had lived rather private lives, Pufendorf, Locke, and Wolff held public offices and needed to adapt to the legal reality in their countries, and neither equality nor freedom, nor inalienable rights, were as yet acknowledged there, not even in post-revolutionary Britain. The situation was comparable in the Empire, where even the feudal institution of serfdom still required a justification. Indeed both Pufendorf and Wolff did offer such a justification, although reluctantly, while Locke is infamous for having defended slavery in the interests of the Lords Proprietors of Carolina.

However, in clear contrast with traditional natural law, which included a social contract between the people and the ruler, and the right of resistance, all of these three philosophers embraced the modern individualistic approach of Hobbes and Spinoza, which included the following:

---

[6] The subtitle of this section is adopted from Parkin 2003.

1. The state as constituted by a voluntary agreement of single, equal, and free individuals (Pufendorf 2003: book II, ch. 6, v, vi; Pufendorf 1994: book VII, ch. 2, 1; Locke 1988: §§ 4, 15; Wolff 1975: ch. 1, esp. § 2; Wolff, 1968: I, Prol., §§ 3ff., § 81);
2. The concept of indivisible sovereignty as the very idea of the modern state (Pufendorf 1994: book VII, ch. 4, 11, ch. 6 and 7: Pufendorf 2003: book II, ch. 7, ix; Locke 1988: 148; Wolff 1975, 441–51; Wolff 1968: VIII, §44);
3. their formulation of inalienable *individual* rights (Pufendorf 2003: book II, ch. 13, xi–xiv; Pufendorf 2002: sect. 6; Locke 1988: §§ 35, ch. 11, and § 190; Wolff 1975, § 356). However, the question whether these rights were conceived as individual rights is still under discussion (Klippel 1976).

Their work was of the greatest influence on the academic development of political and legal theory, because they soon became acknowledged authorities to whom one could easily refer. Moreover, Pufendorf and Wolff both taught at universities.

Given their different political and legal environments, it does not come as a surprise that they differed considerably on the details in spite of their agreement with Hobbes and Spinoza, and with each other, about the three fundamental ideas mentioned above. Pufendorf had to deal with the specific situation of the Empire. He is famous for his critique of the 'irregularity' of its constitution in his *De statu Imperii Germanici*, which was published anonymously in 1667. This book shows Pufendorf's inclination to strengthen the sovereignty of the single states within the Empire. John Locke started publishing his political writings in 1689, the year after the Glorious Revolution, clearly legitimating its political results[7]—that is the restriction of the king's power and the *de facto* sovereignty of the parliament (Locke 1988: §§ 149–50).

Correspondingly, it is especially in their different evaluations of state-forms that the three thinkers differ from each other. It is interesting how closely Pufendorf and Wolff follow Hobbes and Spinoza in their discussion of the covenant as an exchange of equal burdens—that is of safety for obedience—whereas Locke does not discuss this explicitly (Pufendorf 2003: book II, ch. v–x; Locke 1988: § 123; Wolff 1975: §§ 433–5). Pufendorf is even less concerned about the state-forms than Hobbes, almost literally agreeing with the latter's refutation of any other than three possible regular forms (Pufendorf 2003: book II, ch. 8). Locke, on the other hand, is keen to argue in favour of the special British post-revolutionary state-form of the king in parliament as the best means to avoid absolute monarchy. His chapter on state-forms has two paragraphs, declaring that it is simply at the

---

[7] As the glorious revolution was the result of the political activities of a political faction associated with Locke's mentor Shaftesbury since at least the early 1680s, it is not surprising that Locke started his work as early as these activities had started, about 1680. Therefore, I do not see any contradiction between the claim that Locke's *Second Treatise* justifies the result of the revolution and the fact that he began to work on this text as early as 1679 (as Laslett convincingly argued). For this whole discussion about the origin of the *Two Treatises*, see Laslett 1988: 45–66.

discretion of the covenanting people to establish any form they want (Locke 1988: §132). It is Christian Wolff who pays more attention to the discussion of the pros and cons of the various state forms, trying to get a grip on the difficult relations of the Empire and the single states within, as well as the subjects or citizens and their governments (Wolff 1975, §§229–69 and §§ 436–8). Interestingly enough, Wolff sees enormous advantages in democracy, calling it, with Aristotle, 'Politie', after the model of the Greek Polis (Wolff 1975: § 236; Aristotle 1997: III, ch. 7 [1279b–1280a]).

The greatest difference among the three thinkers is their position on the right of resistance. Pufendorf bluntly denies it, in full agreement with Hobbes and Spinoza (Pufendorf 1994: book VII, ch. 8). Locke openly admits such a right, although with large caveats. His advice to the people to appeal to heaven as the last way out from tyranny refers to Judges 11: 27, that is, he suggests the right to go to war (Locke 1988: §§ 20–1). He uses the monarchomachic vocabulary throughout his *Second Treatise of Government* (Locke 1988: §§ 90, 138, 151, 155, 163, 192), and he ascribes to the people a right of resistance even in advance—as it was needed in order to justify the state putsch in 1688, called the Glorious Revolution.[8] Wolff is reluctant to admit a right of resistance, and suggests passive disobedience and a moderate critique instead (1975: §§ 408–14, § 433–34; 1968: VIII, § 1060). He allows for active resistance only if the tyrant turns hostile to his people, and points to Nero as an example (Wolff 1975: § 434; Wolff 1968: VIII, § 1060). However, a right of resistance could be established by the people when designing their state-form, after having covenanted with each other (Wolff 1975: §§ 436–7; Wolff 1968: §§ 37–44, 66, 77).

Notwithstanding their diverse views on the right of resistance, all three thinkers are again in agreement when it comes to the limits of the sovereign's power (Pufendorf 2003: book I, ch. 1, xxiii; Locke 1988: §§ 204–10, and ch. 19; Wolff 1975: §§ 356, 434; Wolff 1969: § 40). They all restrict state power to the *external* actions of subjects and reserve a *private* sphere for freedom of conscience, in general agreement with Hobbes and (in Wolff's case) even with Spinoza. Wolff explicitly extends this freedom of conscience to all thoughts, that is beyond religion (Wolff 1975: §§ 356, 359–62). But they all clearly argue in favour of tolerance and freedom of speech, even if limited (cf. Zurbuchen 1996: 163–84).

Their philosophical differences reflect not only their political intentions but also their religious convictions. Pufendorf writes as a rather strict Lutheran, and separates natural law focused on temporal affairs from moral philosophy as treated by theology in accordance with the Bible. When talking about the nature of human beings, he is not shy to address their God-given special dignity on the one hand

---

[8] Compare Hobbes's interesting comment concerning the legitimacy of forcing a king to exclude his heir from the succession because of an anticipated deviation by the prospective heir from his duty. Hobbes wrote his comment at the request of William Cavendish in 1679, which was obviously related to the activities of Shaftesbury and Locke to hinder a Catholic succession (Skinner 2002: 33–5).

(Pufendorf 2003: book II, ch. 1, iii, viii) and their corruption and weakness due to the Fall on the other hand (Pufendorf 2003: book II, ch. 6, i). Locke also refers to specific Christian patterns when he discusses the natural state, its God-given rules, and the nature and duties of men (Locke 1988: § 6, footnote to § 135, § 172). Wolff is considerably more secular; he is neutral to the denominations and restricts himself to rational natural theology. He lays down his groundwork for Natural Law, starting from single individuals striving by nature for their perfection rather than by appealing to any additional God-given gifts such as their dignity or sociability. Wolff's striving for perfection (Wolff 1975: § 1), which is sometimes misunderstood as a return to scholasticism (Bachmann 1983: 161; Haakonssen 2006: 269, 275), clearly adapts Spinoza's notion of striving for self-preservation (leading in fact to perfection).

Pufendorf's religiously inspired strict separation between moral philosophy (backed by the letter of the Bible) and natural law was criticized by Leibniz (Leibniz 1988: 65–75) and led to an ongoing opposition of the eighteenth-century Wolffians against the school of Pufendorf and his disciple Thomasius (Haakonssen 2002; Grunert 2002). The latter followed Hobbes's voluntaristic approach even more strictly than Hobbes himself, by constructing the state, the law, and therefore justice entirely on the will of the sovereign. The Wolffians, on the other hand, in agreement with Leibniz, insisted on an objective, that is, a true concept of justice and natural law, independent of the powerful will not only of the ruler but even of God. In agreement with Grotius' notorious saying about the continuing validity of natural law even (were it possible) in the absence of God (Grotius 2005: Pr. Disc., XI), natural right and law were considered as valid not only in the state of nature but within the civil state, thus binding on the sovereigns. As a result, philosophy of morals, religion, and law had to be consistent and could not be separated. This discussion has continued in German philosophy of law since then under the labels of Historicism versus Natural Law theory, and Legal Positivism (*Rechtspositivismus*) versus Natural Law. These discussions took a new turn after the Second World War, after the absolute will of the sovereign during the Nazi time had turned out to be insufficient to guarantee a just legal system.

# CONCLUSION

It is common and even plausible to favour historical theories of liberty, popular sovereignty, and the people's right of resistance over those theories which stress the absolute power of a sovereign and demand obedience from the people. Constitutionalism is often celebrated, especially in the Anglo-American literature, as leading to our modern understanding of democracy and human rights. It is, however, a fundamental misunderstanding to see our modern concepts of popular sovereignty, democracy, and human rights as due to so-called constitutionalist theories, which are in fact monarchomachic theories (Protestant or Catholic), while dismissing the great theoretical achievement of Hobbes and Spinoza. The theoretical (and political) battles over the social contract and the rights of the people certainly contributed to understanding the modern state that was just developing. But, paradoxically, it was the sober naturalistic and individualistic approach of Hobbes and Spinoza and their later partisans, along with their coherent conception of the interconnectedness of sovereignty and obedience, which paved the way for individual human rights. Thus Quentin Skinner rightly emphasizes that if 'we were to try...to trace the roots of English liberalism, we should hardly look for them in this whig attitude to political life. The insistence of Hobbes on human equality as the necessary point of departure, the insistence of the levelers on a theory of natural rights as the appropriate political inference, the insistence of all the writers on sovereignty I have examined on some principle of utility as the proper measure of a government's value—these, the more systematically rationalist attitudes, are also the more recognisably liberal in temper' (Skinner 2002: 263; cf. Skinner 1965: 151–78). Hobbes's and Spinoza's approach paved the way for our modern understanding of the state as an artificial construction based on the fiction of mutually covenanting individuals, and which allows for liberty and individual rights by guaranteeing the law through sovereign power.

## References

ALTHUSIUS, J. (1964). *The Politics of Johannes Althusius*. Trans. and abridged with an introduction by F. S. Carney. Boston: Beacon Press.

ARISTOTLE (1997). *The Politics*. Trans. and ed. by Peter Philipps Simpson. Chapel Hill, NC: University of North Carolina Press.

BACHMANN, H.-M. (1977). *Die naturrechtliche Staatslehre Christian Wolffs* (=Schriften zur Verfassungsgeschichte, 27). Berlin.

BEZA, T. (1574). *Du Droit des Magistrats sur levrs svbjets* [The Right of the Magistrates], [Heidelberg?]. See Constitutionalism.

BODIN, J. (1962). *The Six Books of a Commonweal*. Trans. R. Knolles, introd. by K. D. McRae. Cambridge, MA: Harvard University Press.

BONFATTI, E., DUSO, G., and SCATTOLA, M. (eds) (2002). *Politische Begriffe und historisches Umfeld in der Politica methodice digesta des Johannes Althusius* (=Wolffenbütteler Forschungen, 100). Wiesbaden: Harassowitz.

COLLINS, J. R. (2005). *The Allegiance of Thomas Hobbes*. Oxford and New York: Oxford University Press.

Constitutionalism (1969). *Constitutionalism and Resistance in the Sixteenth Century. Three Treatises by Hotman, Beza, & Mornay*. Trans. and ed. J. Franklin. New York: Pegasus.

DOLEMAN, R. [ROBERT PARSONS] (1595). *A conference about the next succession to the crowne of Ingland.* [Antwerp].

DUPLESSIS-MORNAY, P. (1579). *Vindiciae contra tyrannos* [Defence of Liberty against Tyrants]. See Constitutionalism.

FRIEDEBURG, R. VON (2006): 'Persona and office: Althusius on the formation of magistrates and councilors', in C. Condren, S. Gaukroger, and I. Hunter (eds), *The Philosopher in Early Modern Europe. The Nature of a Contested Identity.* Cambridge: Cambridge University Press, 160–81.

GIERKE, O. (1950). *Natural Law and the Theory of Society 1500–1800.* Trans. with an Introd. by E. Barker. 2 vols. Cambridge: Cambridge University Press.

GROTIUS, H. (2005). *The Rights of War and Peace.* Ed. with an introd. by R. Tuck. Indianapolis: Liberty Fund.

GRUNERT, F. (2002). 'Sovereignty and Resistance: The Development of the Right of Resistance in German Natural Law', in I. Hunter and D. Saunders (eds), *Natural Law and Civil Sovereignty: Moral Right and State Authority in Early Modern Political Thought.* New York: Palgrave Macmillan, 123–38.

GRUNERT, F. (2003). 'The Reception of Hugo Grotius's De Jure Belli ac Pacis in the early German Enlightenment', in T. J. Hochstrasser and P. Schröder (eds), *Early Modern Natural Law Theories: Contexts and Strategies in the Early Enlightenment.* Dordrecht: Kluwer, 89–105.

GRUNERT, F. (2004). '"Händel mit Herrn Hector Gottfried Masio". Zur Pragmatik des Streits in den Kontroversen mit dem Kopenhagener Hofprediger', in U. Goldenbaum, et al. (eds), *Appell an das Publikum. Die öffentliche Debatte in der deutschen Aufklärung 1687–1796.* Akademie Verlag, 119–74.

HAAKONSSEN, K. (ed.) (1999). *Grotius, Pufendorf and Modern Natural Law.* Aldershot: Ashgate.

HAAKONSSEN, K. (2002). 'The Moral Conservatism of Natural Rights', in I. Hunter and D. Saunders (eds), *Natural Law and Civil Sovereignty: Moral Right and State Authority in Early Modern Political Thought.* New York: Palgrave Macmillan, 27–42.

HAAKONSSEN, K. (2006). 'German natural law', in M. Goldie and R. Wokler (eds), *The Cambridge History of Eighteenth-Century Political Thought.* Cambridge: Cambridge University Press, 251–90.

HINSLEY, F. H. (1986). *Sovereignty.* Cambridge: Cambridge University Press.

KLIPPEL, D. (1976): *Politische Freiheit und Freiheitsrechte im deutschen Naturrecht des 18. Jahrhunderts* (=Rechts- und staatswissenschaftliche Veröffentlichungen der Görresgesellschaft, N.F. 23). Paderborn.

KNOX, J. (1559). *The Blast of the Trumpet against the Monstruous Regiment of Women.* Geneva.

KNOX, J. (1966). 'The History of the Reformation in Scotland', in D. Laing (ed.), *The Works of John Knox.* 6 vols. Edinburgh, 1895; Reprint New York.

LAKE, P. (2004). 'The King (the Queen) and the Jesuit: James Stuart's *True Law of Free Monarchies* in Context/s', in *Transactions of the Royal Historical Society,* 6th Series, 14, 243–60.

LASLETT, P. (1988). 'Introduction' to *John Locke: Two Treatises of Government.* Cambridge: Cambridge University Press, 3–126.

LEIBNIZ, G. W. (1988). 'Opinion on the Principles of Pufendorf (1706)', in P. Riley (ed.), *Leibniz: Political Writings.* Cambridge: Cambridge University Press, 64–75.

LLOYD, H. A. (1991). 'Constitutionalism', in J. H. Burns and M. Goldie (eds), *The Cambridge History of Political Thought 1450–1700*. Cambridge: Cambridge University Press, 254–97.

LOCKE, J. (1988). *Two Treatises of Government*. Ed. with an Introd. by P. Laslett. Cambridge: Cambridge University Press.

LOCKE, J. (2003). 'A Letter concerning Toleration', in J. Locke: *Two Treatises of Government, and A Letter concerning Toleration*, ed. and with an Introduction by I. Shapiro. New Haven and London: Yale University Press, 211–54.

MARIANA, J. DE (1599). *De rege et Regis Institutione Libri III*. Toledo: Pedro Rodriguez.

MARSILIUS OF PADUA (2005). *The Defender of Peace*. Cambridge: Cambridge University Press.

NEGRI, A. (2004). *Subversive Spinoza: Uncontemporary Variations*. Ed. T. S. Murphy. Manchester and New York: Manchester University Press.

PARKIN, J. (2003). 'Taming the Leviathan—Reading Hobbes in Seventeenth-Century Europe', in T. J. Hochstrasser and P. Schröder (eds), *Early Modern Natural Law Theories: Contexts and Strategies in the Early Enlightenment*. Dordrecht: Kluwer, 31–52.

PEČAR, A. (2007). 'Auf der Suche nach den Ursprüngen des Divine Right of Kings. Herrschaftskritik und Herrschaftslegitimation in Schottland unter Jacob VI.', in A. Pečar and K. Trampelbach (eds), *Die Bibel als Politisches Argument. Voraussetzungen und Folgen biblizistischer Herrschaftslegitimation in der Vormoderne*. Munich: Oldenbourg, 295–314.

PUFENDORF, S. [Monzambano] (1667). *De statu imperii Germanici liber unus*. Geneva [Amsterdam].

PUFENDORF, S. (1994). *The Political Writings*. Trans. by M. J. Seidler, ed. by C. L. Carr. Oxford: Oxford University Press.

PUFENDORF, S. (2002). *Of the Nature and Qualification of Religion in Reference to Civil Society*. Trans. by J. Crull, ed. and with an Introd. by S. Zurbuchen. Indianapolis, IN: Liberty Fund.

PUFENDORF, S. (2003). *The Whole Duty of Man, According to the Law of Nature*. Trans. by A. Tooke, ed. with an introd. by I. Hunter and D. Saunders. Indianapolis, IN: Liberty Fund.

REINHARDT, N. (2007). 'Juan de Mariana: Bibelexegese und Tyrannenmord', in A. Pečar and K. Trampedach (eds), *Die Bibel als politisches Argument. Voraussetzungen und Folgen biblizistischer Herrschaftslegitimation in der Vormoderne*. Munich: Oldenbourg, 273–94.

SKINNER, Q. (1965). 'History and ideology in the English Revolution'. *The Historical Journal*, 8: 151–78.

SKINNER, Q. (1992). *The Foundations of Modern Political Thought*. 2 vols. Cambridge: Cambridge University Press.

SKINNER, Q. (2002). *Visions of Politics*, vol. III: *Hobbes and Civil Science*. Cambridge: Cambridge University Press.

SKINNER, Q. (2008). *Hobbes and Republican Liberty*. Cambridge: Cambridge University Press.

SODER, J. (1973). *Francisco Suárez und das Völkerrecht. Grundgedanken zu Staat, Recht und internationalen Beziehungen*. Frankfurt/M.: Alfred Metzner Verlag.

SPINOZA, B. DE (2002). *Complete Works*. Trans. S. Shirley, ed. M. L. Morgan. Indianapolis, IN: Hackett.

SPINOZA, B. DE (2004a). 'A Theologico-Political Treatise', in *A Political Theologico-Treatise and A Political Treatise*. Trans. and ed. by R. H. M. Elwes. Mineola, NY: Dover.

SPINOZA, B. DE (2004b). 'A Political Treatise', in: *A Theologico-Political Treatise and A Political Treatise*. Trans. and ed. by R. H. M. Elwes. Mineola, NY: Dover.

SUÁREZ, F. (1944). *Selections from Three Works: De legibus, ac Deo Legislatore (1612), Defensio fidei Catholici (1613), De triplici virtute Catholica: Fide, Spe, et Caritate (1621)*. Vol. 2. Trans. by G. L. Williams, A. Brown, and J. Waldron. Oxford: Clarendon Press.

TUCK, R. (1999). 'Grotius, Carneades and Hobbes', in K. Haakonssen (ed.), *Grotius, Pufendorf and Modern Natural Law*. Aldershot: Ashgate, 43–104.

VITORIA, F. DE (1991): *Political Writings*. Ed. A. Pagden and J. Lawrance. Cambridge: Cambridge University Press.

WALZER, M. (1966). *The Revolution of the Saints*. London: Weidenfeld & Nicholson.

WENZEL, D. (1997). 'Les fondements du pouvoir légitime. Une controverse politico-confessionelle à la fin du 17ième siècle', in A. Schober (ed.), *Le christianisme dans les Pays de langue allemande*. Limoges, 33–46.

WOLFF, C. (1968). 'Jus naturae', in C. Wolff, *Gesammelte Werke*, vol. II, 17–24 (=Book I-VIII). Hildesheim, New York: Olms.

WOLFF, C. (1969). *Institutiones*, in C. Wolff: *Gesammelte Werke*, vol. II, 26, Hildesheim, New York: Olms.

WOLFF, C. (1975). 'Vernünfftige Gedancken von dem gesellschaftlichen Leben der Menschen und insonderheit dem gemeinen Wesen', ed. by H. W. Arndt, in C. Wolff: *Gesammelte Werke*. Hildesheim, New York: Olms, vol. I. 5 (=German Politics).

ZURBUCHEN, S. (1996). 'Samuel Pufendorf's Concept of Tolerance', in C. J. Nederman and J. C. Laursen (eds), *Difference and Dissent. Theories of Tolerance in Medieval and Early Modern Europe*. Lanham, 163–84.

# PART V

# RELIGION

# CHAPTER 24

......................................................

# CONCEPTIONS
# OF GOD

......................................................

## STEVEN NADLER

FOR a long time, textbook histories of philosophy in the seventeenth century usually divided thinkers into two camps: rationalists and empiricists. To the former belonged Descartes, Spinoza, and Leibniz, and to the latter belonged Locke, Berkeley, and Hume. The division was made on an alleged difference in epistemology. Rationalists were said to believe that human knowledge was primarily an affair of reason, with science often proceeding in an *a priori* manner, while empiricists gave priority to sense experience and experimental method.

Fortunately, we now work with a more sophisticated, albeit complicated, picture of early modern theory of knowledge and philosophy of science. But a distinction between rationalism and some anti-rationalist alternative is not necessarily without value, particularly if it is regarded not as a rigid, exclusive, and exhaustive division between general types of philosophy or two precise groups of individual philosophers but rather as a difference in approach to specific philosophical issues.

In the domain of philosophical theology, in fact, there is a very useful distinction to be made between rationalism and anti-rationalism in the seventeenth century. The terms capture an important set of differences in the way in which certain early modern philosophers conceived of God. More specifically, the terms pick out two different models of thinking about the structure of God's being and the nature of divine agency, of His *modus operandi*. The rationalist conception of God regards God as analogous to a rational agent endowed with will and understanding and acting, very much as we act, on the basis of practical reasoning. According to the anti-rationalist, or voluntarist, conception, God's understanding is not distinct from His will, and in the very structure of His being and agency God transcends practical rationality altogether. On the first conception, God always acts for good reasons; on the second, God's will is absolute and completely unmotivated by (logically) independent reasons. Moreover, both of these approaches need to be contrasted with a third, *sui generis* view, one which every mainstream philosopher and theologian in the period regarded with fear and trembling: the God of Spinoza.

# I: THE RATIONALIST GOD

These three major philosophical conceptions of God in the seventeenth century—the rationalist God, the voluntarist God, and the God of Spinoza—have much in common. All attribute to God some common essential characteristics: eternity, necessity, and infinitude, as well as being the ultimate causal power behind all things. What is distinctive about the rationalist conception of God—which is not necessarily the God adopted by all the thinkers traditionally labelled 'the rationalists' or even by all thinkers who opt for rationalist approaches to other philosophical topics—are three primary features: the functional (but not ontological) distinction between will and understanding in God; the claim that God's will is guided in its choices by His understanding; and the claim that such guidance is not merely descriptive (with the understanding simply laying out the different options available) but also normative, and comes in the form of wisdom providing objectively compelling or motivating reasons.

Odd as it may seem, those who differ radically about God's causal agency, such as a concurrentist like Leibniz and an occasionalist like Malebranche, can share a conception of God. Both Leibniz and Malebranche are committed to the view that God is a rational being who does things for intelligible and objective purposes, whose choices are informed by the dictates of a logically independent wisdom.

Rational beings are those for whom reasons matter. Such agents are motivated teleologically by aims; they act for the sake of achieving something. And they strive to achieve their aims because they believe them to be good, they perceive them as desirable in their own right. Moreover, such rationality is instrumental: agents select means toward their desired goals because they believe, with justification, that those means are the most efficient way to them. To pursue ends that one does not believe to be good, or to follow a path toward one's end that one knows not to efficiently lead there, is to act irrationally.

Now consider Leibniz's God. He contemplates an infinite number of possible worlds and recognizes that one of them (the one that contains the simplest laws and the greatest amount of perfection) is, in absolute terms, the best of all. His desire is to produce as much perfection as possible, and so He brings that best of all possible worlds into existence. The optimality of that world provides Him with a compelling reason to create it; and had there been no such compelling reason, Leibniz's God would not have created a world at all. The principle of sufficient reason is binding even upon God. As Leibniz says, '[God] does nothing without acting in accordance with supreme reason' (*Theodicy* §8; GP VI.107; Leibniz 1985: 128). This is true for all of God's choices, large and small. It is beautifully reflected in Leibniz's argument for his famous law of the identity of indiscernibles, which says that 'there is no such thing as two individuals indiscernible from each other'. The reason why there cannot be two distinct things in nature that are absolutely identical in all intrinsic respects—two leaves, or two snowflakes, 'without any difference within themselves'—is because, in the complete absence of any differences between the two, God would have no compelling reason to put one of them in one place and the other in another place, rather than vice versa. Consequently, God, 'who never does anything without wisdom', will not create such things.[1]

God, then, on Leibniz's view, is never indeterminate; He never acts without knowledge of what He is doing and without being determined by reasons to do it. 'His will is always decided, and it can be decided only by the best.' God can never have what Leibniz calls a 'primitive particular will', that is, an *ad hoc* volition that is independent of any law or principle. 'Such a thing would be unreasonable. [God] cannot determine upon Adam, Peter, Judas, or any individual without the existence of a reason for this determination; and this reason leads of necessity to some general enunciation. The wise mind always acts according to principles, always according to rules, and never according to exceptions' (*Theodicy*, §337, GP VI 315; Leibniz 1985: 328).

Leibniz recognizes that this amounts to a kind of constraint on God, but insists that it is no more than the kind of determination that reasons ordinarily bring to bear on rational choices. His critics, less sanguine about the consequences of putting restrictions on God than Leibniz was, were concerned that if these reasons lead God 'of necessity', then God loses His freedom of choice. Pierre Bayle argued that Leibniz subjects God to a kind of fate: 'There is therefore no freedom in God; He is compelled by His wisdom to create, and then to create precisely such a work, and finally to create it precisely in such ways. These are three servitudes that form a more than Stoic *fatum*, and that render impossible all that is not within their sphere' (quoted by Leibniz at *Theodicy*, §227, GP VI 253; Leibniz 1985: 268).

---

[1] See Leibniz's fourth letter to Samuel Clarke (GP VII 372: LL 687). This is only one of many occasions where Leibniz employs this argument for his law. See also Leibniz's Fifth Paper (for Clarke): 'I infer from [the principle of sufficient reason] . . . that there are not in nature two real, absolute beings, indiscernible from each other, because if there were, God and nature would act without reason in treating the one otherwise than the other; and that therefore God does not produce two pieces of matter perfectly equal and alike' (GP VII 393: LL 699 [translation modified]).

But the necessity that binds God, Leibniz says, is 'a happy necessity', because it has its source in God's own nature. 'This so-called *fatum*, which binds even the Divinity, is nothing but God's own nature, his own understanding, which furnishes the rules for his wisdom and his goodness' (*Theodicy*, §191, GP VI 230; Leibniz 1985: 246–7). The determination of God's choice is characterized only by what Leibniz describes as a *moral* (as opposed to a logical, metaphysical, or absolute) necessity, that is, the necessity of reasons that compel choice in a rational being—a being who, because of His goodness and wisdom, is moved infallibly to choose the best. 'There is always a prevailing reason that prompts the will to its choice.... The choice is free and independent of [absolute] necessity because it is made between several possibles, and the will is determined only by the preponlering goodness of the object' (*Theodicy*, §45; GP 1127–8; Leibniz 1985: 148).

In his early works, Malebranche often seems more interested in defending the sheer power of God's will than its wisdom and rationality. 'God is a being whose will is power and infinite power', he wrote in the *Christian Conversations* in 1677 (OCM IV 30–1). But even in the *Search After Truth* (1674–5) and especially in the *Treatise on Nature and Grace* (TNG 1680) it is clear that Malebranche's God, like Leibniz's God, does not act arbitrarily. This is true in the ordinary course of nature (and grace), where God's ubiquitous causal activity is guided by laws. But the fact that, as Malebranche insists, God must choose the most simple laws for the world He creates, and then seek to produce as just and perfect a world as possible relative to those laws, shows that there is a higher authority than His will alone. God, Malebranche says, 'cannot act against Himself, against His own wisdom and light'. He may be indifferent as to whether or not anything other than Himself exists, that is, indifferent about whether or not to create at all. But having decided to create, '[God] is not indifferent, although perfectly free, in the way in which He does it; He always acts in the wisest and most perfect way possible. He always follows the immutable and necessary order' (*Search After Truth*, Elucidation 8, OCM III 85–6; MLO 586–7).

God's power is in itself infinite and incomprehensible. However, once Malebranche's God does decide to act 'external to Himself', that power is subordinated to His wisdom, and especially to what Malebranche calls 'Order'. Order consists in the eternal, immutable verities that stand above all things. These are pure logical and mathematical truths, absolutely true with the highest necessity, but also moral and metaphysical principles about what Malebranche calls 'relations of perfection'. They determine the relative value of various kinds of being, and even of God's own attributes. Order shows that a soul is more noble than a body, and a human being more worthy than a dog; and it proclaims that, as important as God's mercy is, the simplicity and generality of His ways are even more important, and thus cannot be violated even to save a good person from drowning or damnation. Order is 'the exemplar of all God's works', and his volitions must conform to its principles. The dictates of Order serve God as universal reasons for everything He does. Even if, on some rare occasion, God must act by what Malebranche calls a 'particular volition' and violate the laws of nature or grace to perform a miracle, this will be only because Order demands it (TNG, II.45; OCM V 106).

Thus, when Malebranche's God, considering the infinite possibilities in His understanding, chooses to create a world, Order sets one of His attributes (simplicity) above the others, which in turn determines which laws He will establish for the world, and then how, given those laws, He can thereby accomplish as much perfection as possible in the relationship of the physical to the moral, that is, of the relationship between the pain of punishment or the pleasures of reward, on the one hand, and, on the other hand, sin or virtue.[2] God's wisdom, the dwelling place of Order, stands above his will and guides it. 'In Himself', Malebranche says, 'God has good reasons for everything He does' (*Dialogues on Metaphysics*, IX.3; OCM XII 201; MS 152).

Like Leibniz, Malebranche is concerned that his account of divine rationality might be seen as compromising God's freedom. He even concedes that, in a manner of speaking, it does. 'The wisdom of God renders Him impotent in the following sense, that it does not allow Him to will certain things, nor to act in certain ways.... God is impotent in the sense that he cannot choose ways of acting unworthy of his wisdom, or that do not bear the character of his goodness, of his immutability, or of his other attributes' (TNG, Third Elucidation; OCM V 180). But, once again, this is only the impotence of a perfectly rational being to act contrary to unassailable reasons. God's choices are compelled or determined; there are standards that God is bound to observe. However, these standards lie in God's wisdom, and the obligation to obey them comes from His nature alone.

## II: The voluntarist God

In contrast to the rationalist God, who operates by a familiar form of agency just because it is *our* form of agency, the voluntarist God is a deity whose will is absolute, unguided, and unmotivated by any independent reasons or considerations of truth, goodness, or beauty. This is essentially the conception offered by Euthyphro in response to Socrates' questions in the dialogue that bears his name.

---

[2] 'Assuming that God wants to act, I contend that he will always do it in the most wise manner possible, or in the manner which most bears the character of his attributes. I insist that this is never an arbitrary or indifferent matter for Him.... Immutable Order, which consists in the necessary relationship that exists between the divine perfections, is the inviolable law and the rule of all His volitions' (Reply to Arnauld's *Philosophical and Theological Reflections on the New System of Nature and Grace*, OCM VIII 752–3).

Euthyphro suggests that something is pious (or right or good) simply because the gods favour it, thereby implying that had the gods favoured something else instead, then that would have been pious (or right or good). This conception of God, which implies a kind of agency radically different from that which characterizes human rational agency, finds its clearest expression in the seventeenth century with the Cartesian doctrine of the creation of the eternal truths.

Readers of Descartes' first publication, the *Discourse on Method* and its accompanying scientific essays, as well as the six chapters of his popular *Meditations* of 1641, may not have noticed that their author departs from the standard view on divine power. The *Meditations* is devoted to showing that human beings can acquire true knowledge of things, as long as they use their rational faculties properly and give their assent only to what they clearly and distinctly perceive with the intellect rather than relying on the misleading testimony of the senses. This, Descartes argues, is because those faculties have been provided by God, an all-powerful, all-perfect being who is incapable of malevolent behaviour. Such a God would never give His creatures a cognitive faculty that is systematically deceptive and conducive to falsehoods. As long as that faculty is used correctly, it will provide true and reliable beliefs. On this account, God's moral character apparently prevents Him from the mere possibility of having bad intentions. 'It is impossible that God should ever deceive me. For in every case of trickery or deception some imperfection is to be found; and although the ability to deceive appears to be an indication of cleverness or power, the will to deceive is undoubtedly evidence of malice or weakness, and so cannot apply to God' (Fourth Meditation, AT VII 53: CSM II 37).

Nonetheless, some years before composing the *Meditations*, Descartes had arrived at a much more extreme understanding of divine power. In a series of letters to Mersenne in the spring of 1630, he reveals to the Minim friar an opinion that he fears will be a disturbing vision to many.

The mathematical truths that you call eternal have been laid down by God and depend on Him entirely no less than the rest of His creatures. Indeed, to say that these truths are independent of God is to talk of Him as if He were Jupiter or Saturn and to subject him to the Styx and the Fates.    (To Mersenne, 15 April 1630; AT I 145: CSMK 23)

God created the visible universe (including the principles that govern it, such as the laws of physics) and the souls over which He stands in judgement; on this, Descartes and his predecessors were in agreement. As for the 'eternal verities', the earlier philosophers for whom they are independent of and binding upon God regarded them as uncreated. Descartes, however, rejects such a distinction between the created world and uncreated truths. He insists that these truths, too, are created things. For Descartes, even necessary and unchanging truths are ultimately, like empirical truths, contingent upon an act of the divine will. God made it true that one plus one equals two, but He could just as well have made it true instead that one plus one equals three. Similarly, '[God] was free to make it not true that all the radii of the circle are equal—just as free as He was not to create the world' (To Mersenne, 27 May 1630; AT I 152; CSMK 25).

Descartes does not deny that these are a special class of truths, different from empirical truths about bodies and minds that actually exist in the world. He says that mathematical truths, although established by God, nonetheless remain eternal and necessary because of the eternity and immutability of the will that creates and sustains them. 'It will be said that if God had established these truths He could change them as a king changes his laws. To this the answer is: Yes He can, if His will can change. "But I understand them to be eternal and unchangeable." I make the same judgment about God' (To Mersenne, 15 April 1630; AT I 145–6; CSMK 23). Descartes apparently wants to maintain a distinction between necessary and contingent truths. But, contrary to the traditional view, the eternity and necessity of the eternal truths is not something that belongs to them intrinsically, independently of what God (eternally) decides.

What Descartes says to Mersenne about mathematical truths applies to all the so-called eternal truths, including metaphysical and moral principles, to all values whatsoever. It applies even to the laws of logic.

Our mind is finite and so created as to be able to conceive as possible the things that God has wished in fact to be possible, but not be able to conceive as possible things which God could have made possible, but which He has nevertheless wished to make impossible.... [This] shows us that God cannot have been determined to make it true that contradictories cannot be true together, and therefore that He could have done the opposite....I agree that are contradictions which are so evident that we cannot put them before our minds without judging them entirely impossible...But if we would know the immensity of His power we should not put these thoughts before our minds.   (To Mesland, 2 May 1644; AT IV 118–19; CSMK 235)

God can make a mountain without a valley, a plane triangle whose interior angles are more or less than 180 degrees, and an extended space without body (a metaphysical impossibility for Descartes, for whom extension is the essence of matter). God can even make two logically inconsistent propositions (such as 'Descartes is French' and 'Descartes is not French') true at the same time and thus violate the law of non-contradiction; or make one and the same proposition both true and false at the same time and thus violate the law of excluded middle. As Descartes puts it, '[God] could have made it false that...contradictories could not be true together' (AT IV 118; CSMK 235).[3]

The upshot is that whatever is true is true only because God has made it so, and—as Euthyphro would agree—nothing is good unless God makes it good. 'It is

---

[3] There is a good deal of controversy in the scholarly literature over whether or not the principles of logic are included in the doctrine of the created truths; compare, for example, Funkenstein (1980) and Frankfurt (1977).

impossible to imagine that anything is thought of in the divine intellect as good or true, or worthy of belief or action or omission, prior to the decision of the divine will to make it so' (Sixth Replies; AT VII 432; CSM II 291). If God knows that something is true or good, it is because He wills it to be true or good; He does not believe it because He sees that it is true, nor does he will it because He sees that it is good. Absolutely nothing is true or good independently of His will.

God did not will the creation of the world in time because He saw it would be better this way than if He had created it from eternity; nor did He will that the three angles of a triangle should be equal to two right angles because He recognized that it could not be otherwise, and so on. On the contrary, it is because He willed to create the world in time that it is better this way than if He had created it from eternity; and it is because He willed that the three angles of a triangle should necessarily equal two right angles that this is true.... If some reason for something's being good had existed prior to His preordination, this would have determined God to prefer those things that it was best to do. But on the contrary, just because He resolved to prefer those things that are now to be done, for this very reason, in the words of Genesis, 'they are very good'; in other words, the reason for their goodness depends on the fact that He exercised His will to make them so.    (Sixth Replies; AT VII 432, 435–6; CSM II 291, 294)

Descartes sees this doctrine as the natural consequence of a proper understanding of the divine nature. God's simplicity means that there is no real distinction between His attributes. In particular, God's understanding is not separate from His will. 'In God willing and knowing are a single thing in such a way that by the very fact of willing something He knows it and it is only for this reason that such a thing is true' (To Mersenne, 6 May 1630; AT I 149; CSMK 24). God's will cannot be directed by His wisdom, by what He knows and judges, because this would imply a distinction between two faculties and a priority of one over the other. For God to know that one plus one equals two is identical with God willing that one plus one equal two. To Mersenne, he wrote that 'you ask what God did in order to produce [these truths]. I reply that from all eternity He willed and understood them to be, and by that very fact He created them. Or, if you would reserve the word "created" for the existence of things, then He established them and made them. In God, willing, understanding and creating are all the same thing without one being prior to the other even conceptually' (To Mersenne, 27 May 1630; AT I 152–3; CSMK 25–6).

Descartes also regards the creation of the eternal truths as the only position that is consistent with God's omnipotence and greatness. 'The power of God', he insists, 'cannot have any limits': not epistemic or moral limits, and—what his medieval predecessors were not willing to concede—no even logical limits.

I do not think that we should ever say of anything that it cannot be brought about by God. For since every basis of truth and goodness depends on his omnipotence, I would not dare say that God cannot make a mountain without a valley, or bring it about that 1 and 2 are not 3. I merely say that He has given me such a mind that I cannot conceive a mountain without a valley, or a sum of 1 and 2 that is not 3; such things involve a contradiction in my conception.    (For Arnauld, 29 July 1648; AT V 224; CSMK 358–9)

For Descartes, then, divine omnipotence requires not only that God enjoy complete independence of being and power, but also the total dependence of everything else upon Him. This means that He is the cause not only of the existence of things but also of their essences. This, in fact, is precisely how God creates the eternal truths. By establishing the essential nature of the triangle to be what it is—and He could have made it different from how it in fact is, although we cannot possibly conceive it otherwise than having the properties it does—He thereby causes there to be certain truths about triangles, even if it should happen that no triangles ever actually exist. Replying to Mersenne, he writes: 'You ask me by what kind of causality God established the eternal truths. I reply: by the same kind of causality as He created all things, that is to say, as their efficient and total cause. For it is certain that He is the author of the essence of created things no less than of their existence; and this essence is nothing other than the eternal truths' (To Mersenne, 27 May 1630; AT I 151–2; CSMK 25).

It follows from all this that Descartes' God must be an absolutely free and arbitrary God, guided or limited by no laws, principles, standards, or values that are independent of His will or causal power.[4] The Cartesian God is bound by no objective canons of rationality or morality. When God creates the truths, He does so 'freely and indifferently' (To Mesland, 2 May 1644; AT IV 118; CSMK 235). It is, Descartes writes, 'self-contradictory to suppose that the will of God was not indifferent from eternity with respect to everything that has happened or will ever happen' (Sixth Replies; AT VII 431–2; CSM II 291). Such a God is not rationally determined to make the choices He makes. He does not do what He does for objective reasons, because all such reasons—moral, metaphysical, and logical—are the effect of His will. In this respect, God's mode of activity is completely different from human action (and from the agency of the rationalist God) which operates on the basis of practical reasoning in conformity with independent values and standards. 'The supreme indifference to be found in God is the supreme indication of His omnipotence,' Descartes says, whereas human beings rarely act out of indifference but rather tend to pursue those things that they, through the understanding, perceive to be good (Sixth Replies; AT VII 432–3; CSM II 292).

Descartes was well aware of the originality, even the audacity, of his position. He encouraged Mersenne 'not to hesitate to assert and proclaim everywhere that it is

---

[4] Marion (1981: 282–6) rightly cautions against using the label 'voluntarism' for Descartes' position, insofar as it suggests a continued distinction between divine faculties, except now with will having priority over understanding—which is incompatible with Descartes' insistence that there is no such distinction in God. However, the term, while misleading in this way, does serve well to highlight the fact that for Descartes, the eternal truths are dependent on God's causal power, even if His willing those truths is identical with His understanding them.

God who has laid down these laws in nature just as a king lays down laws in his kingdom', but he also asked that Mersenne 'not mention my name' (To Mersenne, 15 April 1630; AT I 145; CSMK 23). While he eventually softened this cautious stance and explained the doctrine in letters to others and even in some of his published writings, his hesitations were justified. The doctrine became so controversial in the second half of the seventeenth century that even his most devoted followers hesitated to accept it (Schmaltz 2007).

One Cartesian philosopher who *did* find the doctrine not only acceptable but also useful for his own polemic purposes was the Jansenist theologian Antoine Arnauld. He devoted many years of his life to attacking Malebranche's system, and especially the Oratorian's account of divine providence in the *Treatise on Nature and Grace*. The voluntarist conception of God served his theological onslaught well.

To be sure, Arnauld's approach and language in his monumental critique of Malebranche's *Treatise*, the *Philosophical and Theological Reflections on the New System of Nature and Grace* (1685), sometimes suggests that he too, no less than Malebranche, is committed to a rationalist picture of God's ways. Part of what bothers Arnauld about Malebranche's philosophy is the central assumption of the latter's doctrine of the Vision in God, namely, that the eternal ideas in the divine understanding play an essential role in human knowledge as well, and thus are revealed to human beings on a regular basis in the ordinary course of nature. This, he believes, gives Malebranche the temerity to make bold judgements about the quality of God's creation and especially about its conformity to the principles of Order, as well as to speculate about the reasons that guide God in the realms of nature and grace. This picture of a God whose wisdom is accessible to human knowledge and whose reasons are transparent to finite minds is, to Arnauld, intolerable. 'We believe that God's providence extends to all things; this is one of the primary truths of the Christian religion. But to know how this happens and in what way everything that happens in the world is directed, regulated, and governed by the secret orders of this infinite providence is something that infinitely surpasses our intelligence' (To Mersenne, 15 April 1630; AT I 145; CSMK 23).

Throughout the *Reflections*, Arnauld insists on the 'inscrutability' and 'incomprehensibility' of God's judgements. 'What could be more bold and more presumptuous of blind human beings, full of shadows, and so little capable of discovering on their own what is hidden in God, than to try to judge for certain, solely by the idea of the perfect being, without the aid of any divine revelation, what is more or less worthy of His wisdom' (AO XXXIX 595). It exceeds the natural cognitive capacities of human beings to assess God's ways of acting on the basis of His attributes. This applies to God's behaviour both in the realm of nature and in the realm of grace. Why, contrary to what Malebranche claims, does not God will to save all individual human beings? And why does God not always give to a person who receives grace an amount sufficient to overcome his concupiscence? In these and all other cases, Arnauld seems to say that God has His reasons, but that they must remain hidden, *cachées*, in his 'incomprehensible designs' (AO XXXIX 631). Arnauld thus sometimes proceeds as though his God is no less rational an agent than Malebranche's (or Leibniz's) deity. 'God does not act capriciously,' he insists. 'It is not at all true that God acts without an end or design' (AO XXXIX 631).

And yet, as troubling as it is to Arnauld to see Malebranche try to 'provide reasons for the impenetrable judgments of God' and so casually plumb the depths of His infinite wisdom, his objections to the 'new system of nature and grace' run deeper than a worry about divine transparency. Arnauld is fond of quoting St Augustine on 'the profound abyss of God's judgments' (AO XXXIX 491). But what he has in mind is something more radical even than what his fellow Port-Royalist Pascal, writing in the *Pensées*, called 'man's nothingness' and 'unworthiness' to know God. For Arnauld, the incomprehensibility of God's action is not merely due to the infinite chasm between human wretchedness and divine eternity. It is explained by the nature of God itself.

Arnauld ultimately wants to defeat Malebranche's whole way of conceiving the relationship between will and wisdom in God. For Arnauld, God does not 'consult His wisdom', as Malebranche would say. This is a false and thoroughly improper way to think of the relationship among God's attributes and the nature of God's activity.

Did he [Malebranche] really think that this was an expression perfectly conforming to the idea of the perfect being, to say of God that He consults His wisdom? One consults only when one is in doubt; and one consults about how to accomplish one's desires only when there may be some difficulty in achieving what one desires. Neither the one nor the other can be said about the perfect being, whose knowledge is infinite and whose will is all-powerful.    (AO XXXIX 449)

Part of Malebranche's problem, according to Arnauld, is that to distinguish wisdom from will in God and have His wisdom guide His will by providing compelling reasons for its choices is to undermine divine freedom. Malebranche repeatedly says that 'God's wisdom renders Him, in a sense, impotent' by determining Him to choose one world rather than another.[5] Malebranche takes comfort in the 'in a sense' qualification, as well as in God's original indifference as to whether or not to create a world in the first place, and so is not particularly troubled by the implications of this for His freedom. Arnauld, however, is. He conceives of God's freedom as consisting in an absolute 'liberty of indifference,' thoroughly undetermined in the creation and governance of things. God's will is not guided by anything whatsoever external to it, not even by the dictates of His own wisdom.

By following Malebranche in the manner in which he conceives God, I do not see how He can be indifferent to creating or not creating something outside Himself, if He was not indifferent to choosing among several works and among several ways of producing them. For God . . .

---

[5] In addition to the passage cited above, see *TNG*; OCM V 180, 185.

according to [Malebranche], having consulted His wisdom, is necessarily determined to produce the work that it [wisdom] has shown him to be the most perfect, and to choose the means that it has shown Him also to be the most worthy of Him.   (AO XXXIX 600)[6]

Malebranche's God, Arnauld claims, cannot possibly satisfy what he sees as Aquinas's authoritative demand that the will of God remain perfectly self-determining, never willing anything external to itself necessarily (AO XXXIX 598–9).

To be fair, Malebranche, despite his deterministic language, strives to preserve the ultimate contingency of God's creative act. But (and this is Arnauld's point) Malebranche's account fails miserably; he ends up subjecting God to 'a more than stoical necessity' (AO XXXIX 599).[7] In fact, Arnauld appears to be saying, how could it be otherwise? In a perfectly rational being, in whom there are no passions exercising a contrary influence, reasons must determine and necessitate the will and render it 'impotent' to choose otherwise. When His wisdom dictates the creation of one world over all the others, Malebranche's God must obey; He *must* create that world, Arnauld insists, and Malebranche apparently agrees. Not even miracles are freely ordained by Malebranche's God. In the name of divine freedom, Arnauld therefore rejects the thesis of the *priority* of divine understanding over divine will. In Arnauld's God, wisdom (*sagesse*) does not rule over the will (*volonté*).

Even more fundamental than the idea that wisdom must not exercise a determining influence on God's will, however, is Arnauld's radical refusal—like Descartes before him—to distinguish between will and wisdom in God in the first place. One should not, he warns, speak of God 'consulting His wisdom' before He wills, 'as if His will is not His wisdom, as if everything that He wills is not essentially wise as soon as He wills it' (AO XXXIX 578). Arnauld once again cites approvingly the words of Aquinas: 'God's will is God Himself', adding the following gloss: 'Note that he does not say that it is the wisdom of God that determines His will . . . but that it is the divine will that determines itself, freely and indifferently, toward all things to which it does not bear a necessary relation, that is, to all things that are not God' (AO XXXIX 599).[8]

Malebranche's distinction between wisdom and will in God and his rationalistic depiction of God's behaviour, Arnauld warns, constitute an anthropomorphization of God's nature and of His ways. It portrays God as if He, like human beings, has a mind constituted by different faculties, with a will that is able to select only from among the options that the understanding presents to it (one can will only what one

---

[6] According to Arnauld, it also generates a problem of consistency for Malebranche because Malebranche does want to say that God *is* indifferent in the initial choice to create a world outside Himself.

[7] As Sleigh points out (1990: 45–7), this concern (worded in almost exactly the same way) reappears less than two years later in his criticisms of Leibniz.

[8] As Carraud suggests (1996: 99–100), however, it is 'a strangely Cartesian' Aquinas that Arnauld is framing here.

knows) and that is guided in its choice by the dictates of reason: '[Malebranche] speaks about [God] as if he were speaking about a human, in making Him consult His wisdom on everything He would like to do... as if His will, in order to will nothing other than what is good, had need of being regulated by something other than itself' (AO XXXIX 599–600). Arnauld sees God as a being in whom will and wisdom are one and the same, and thus for whom the will is a law unto itself. This God indifferently creates reasons through its volitions. It does not, like Malebranche's God, have a will that takes its lead from wisdom's antecedent reasons:

If we are asked why God has created the world, we should reply only that it is because He wanted to; and... if we are asked again why He wanted to, we should not say, as [Malebranche] does, that 'He wanted to obtain an honour worthy of Himself'. The idea of God does not allow us to accept Malebranche's proposition. We ought rather to say that He wanted to because He wanted to, that is, that we ought not to seek a cause of that which cannot have one.    (AO XXXIX 433)[9]

Arnauld's God is a deity who does not act for reasons at all. It is a God who, in the very structure of His being, transcends practical rationality altogether.

Unlike Descartes' account, Arnauld's conception of God and His arbitrary will is not motivated primarily by philosophical considerations, but by religious and theological ones. It is also intimately connected to the Jansenist view of the nature of grace and its distribution. If, as Jansenist doctrine claims, God's grace is not to be given to individuals because of anything they may have done to deserve it, if it must be an entirely gratuitous gift, unrelated to merit, then it would seem that there cannot be any reasons for God to provide a person with grace at all. Why, then, does God give grace to a person? There is no response to this question by Arnauld's logic other than that God acts with infinite and unmotivated mercy.

# III: The God of Spinoza

For the third, highly singular conception of God, there is no alternative but to name it after the individual who conceived it. The God of Spinoza—or, more accurately, 'God or Nature' (*Deus sive Natura*)—does not choose the best of all possible worlds. Spinoza's God, in fact, does not choose anything whatsoever. Spinoza's identification of God with the eternal, infinite, necessarily existing

---

[9] Carraud (1996) notes that this is Arnauld's refusal 'to submit God to causality, that is, to submit His will to rationality in the form of a principle of reason'. Lennon (1978: 186) recognizes that, contrary to Malebranche's 'rationally constrained' God, for Arnauld 'divine self-determination [is] utterly unconstrained and thus mysterious'.

substance of Nature itself—with the most general natures of things (Thought and Extension) and the universal causal principles and laws embedded in these—means that whatever exists within Nature (and this is everything possible) 'follows from' or is caused by God or Nature with an absolute, inevitable necessity. Nothing whatsoever could possibly have been otherwise: not the universe itself, nor any individual thing or event within it. 'All things, I say, are in God, and all things that happen, happen only through the laws of God's infinite nature and follow . . . from the necessity of his essence' (*Ethics* IP15S [VI]; SO II 60; SC 424).

The metaphysics of God in the *Ethics*, motivated as it is by an extreme anti-anthropomorphism, rules out any depiction of God that involves Him considering alternative possibilities, acting for purposes, making choices based on reasons, and assessing outcomes. 'There are those who feign God, like man, consisting of a body and a mind, and subject to passions. But how far they wander from the true knowledge of God, is sufficiently established by what has already been demon-strated' (*Ethics* IP15S [I]; SO II 57; SC 421). All talk of God's purposes, intentions, goals, preferences, or aims is just a fiction propagated by manipulative ecclesiastics. 'All the prejudices I here undertake to expose depend on this one: that men commonly suppose that all natural things act, as men do, on account of an end; indeed, they maintain as certain that God himself directs all things to some certain end, for they say that God has made all things for man, and man that he might worship God' (*Ethics* I, Appendix; SO II 78; SC 439–40).

God is not some goal-oriented planner who then judges things by how well they conform to his purposes. Things happen only because of Nature and its laws. 'Nature has no end set before it . . . All things proceed by a certain eternal necessity of nature.' To believe otherwise is to fall prey to the same superstitions that lie at the heart of organized religions.

[People] find—both in themselves and outside themselves—many means that are very helpful in seeking their own advantage, e.g., eyes for seeing, teeth for chewing, plants and animals for food, the sun for light, the sea for supporting fish. . . . Hence, they consider all natural things as means to their own advantage. And knowing that they had found these means, not provided them for themselves, they had reason to believe that there was someone else who had prepared those means for their use. For after they considered things as means, they could not believe that the things had made themselves; but from the means they were accustomed to prepare for themselves, they had to infer that there was a ruler, or a number of rulers of nature, endowed with human freedom, who had taken care of all things for them, and made all things for their use. And because they had never heard anything about the temperament of these rulers, they had to judge it from their own. Hence, they maintained that the gods direct all things for the use of men in order to bind men to them and be held by men in the highest honor. So it has happened that each of them has thought up from his own temperament different ways of worshipping God, so that God might love them above all the rest, and direct the whole of Nature according to the needs of their blind desire and insatiable greed. Thus this prejudice was changed into superstition, and struck deep roots in their minds.   (*Ethics* I, Appendix; SO II 78–9; SC 440–1)

In a letter to one of his more troublesome correspondents, the merchant Willem van Blijenburgh, Spinoza emphasizes the absurdity of conceiving God in this way. The language of traditional theology, he says, represents God 'as a perfect man' and claims that 'God desires something, that God is displeased with the deeds of the impious and pleased with those of the pious'. In all philosophical rigour, however, 'we clearly understand that to ascribe to God those attributes that make a man perfect would be as wrong as to ascribe to a man the attributes that make perfect an elephant or an ass' (Ep. 23; SO IV 148; Spinoza 1995: 166). Some years later, in a letter to the Dutchman Hugo Boxel, Spinoza resorts to sarcasm to make his point:

When you say that you do not see what sort of God I have if I deny him the actions of seeing, hearing, attending, willing, etc. and that he possesses those faculties in an eminent degree, I suspect that you believe that there is no greater perfection than can be explicated by the aforementioned attributes. I am not surprised, for I believe that a triangle, if it could speak, would likewise say that God is eminently triangular, and a circle that God's nature is eminently circular.    (Ep. 56; SO IV 260; Spinoza 1995: 277)

A judging God who has plans and acts purposively is a God to be obeyed and placated. Opportunistic preachers are then able to play on our hopes and fears in the face of such a God. They prescribe ways of acting that are calculated to avoid being punished by that deity and earn His rewards. But, Spinoza insists, to see God or Nature as acting for the sake of ends—to find purpose in Nature—is to misconstrue Nature, to 'turn it upside down' by putting the effect (the end result) before the true cause. In Spinoza's view, the traditional religious conception of God leads only to superstition, not enlightenment. Like the belief in miracles, the projection of purposiveness and practical reason onto God or Nature is due only to ignorance of the true causes of phenomena.

If a stone has fallen from a room onto someone's head and killed him, they will show, in the following way, that the stone fell in order to kill the man. For if it did not fall to that end, God willing it, how could so many circumstances have concurred by chance (for often many circumstances do concur at once)? Perhaps you will answer that it happened because the wind was blowing hard and the man was walking that way. But they will persist: why was the wind blowing hard at that time? why was the man walking that way at that time? If you answer again that the wind arose then because on the preceding day, while the weather was still calm, the sea began to toss, and that the man had been invited by a friend, they will press on—for there is no end to the questions that can be asked: but why was the sea tossing? why was the man invited at just that time? And so they will not stop asking for the causes of causes until you take refuge in the will of God, i.e., the sanctuary of ignorance.    (*Ethics* I, Appendix; SO II 80–1; SC 443)

God as Nature is not endowed with will, much less with freedom of the will. God may be the cause of all things, even the free cause of all things, but this is only because whatever is, is in Nature and is therefore brought about by Nature; and because Nature is all there is, there is nothing outside Nature to constrain it to do one thing rather than another.

There can be nothing outside [God] by which He is determined or compelled to act. Therefore, God acts from the laws of His nature alone, and is compelled by no one.... From this it follows, first, that there is no cause, either extrinsically or intrinsically, which prompts God to action, except the perfection of His nature.... It follows, secondly, that God alone is a free cause. For God alone exists only from the necessity of His nature ... and acts from the necessity of His nature.   (*Ethics* IP17; SO II 61; SC 425)

For this reason, Spinoza makes it clear that while neither option is acceptable, if he were forced to choose he would favour the voluntarist God rather than the traditional rationalist one. 'I confess that this opinion, which subjects all things to a certain indifferent will of God, and makes all things depend on His good pleasure, is nearer the truth than that of those who maintain that God does all things for the sake of the good. For they seem to place something outside God, which does not depend on God, to which God attends, as a model, in what He does, and at which He aims, as at a certain goal. This is simply to subject God to fate. Nothing more absurd can be maintained about God, whom we have shown to be the first and only free cause' (*Ethics* IP33S2; SO II 76; SC 438–9).

 In the end, though, Spinoza's God is neither an arbitrary nor a rational deity. The existence of God or Nature itself is absolutely necessary—it cannot not exist; and whatever happens in nature—everything that has been or will be—is caused by God or Nature, not by choice but by necessity, and thus comes about through natural principles with a geometric inevitability.

I think I have shown clearly enough ... that from God's supreme power, or infinite nature, infinitely many things in infinitely many modes, i.e., all things, have necessarily flowed, or always followed, by the same necessity and in the same way as from the nature of a triangle it follows, from eternity to eternity, that its three angles are equal to two right angles.   (*Ethics* IP17S1; SO II 62; SC 426)

To say that the things that follow from God's nature might not have been, or could have been otherwise, is to say that God's nature itself might have been different, which, Spinoza insists, is absurd, because God or Nature necessarily exists as it is. 'Things could have been produced by God in no other way, and in no other order than they have been produced' (*Ethics* IP33; SO II 73; SC 436).

 For Spinoza, this is not the best of all possible worlds; it is the only possible world.

# IV: TENSIONS

In response to the criticisms by Bayle and Arnauld of what they regarded as a threat to God's absolute freedom, Leibniz and Malebranche both criticized the voluntarist conception of God in the name of defending divine wisdom, goodness, and justice.

They insisted that if God is as Descartes says He is, then claims about God's wisdom and justice are trivial or meaningless.

Leibniz was a lifelong foe of divine voluntarism. In his mind, the flaws of Descartes' doctrine run deep. Not only does it offer a false picture of God's nature and of the way in which He operates, he thought, but it threatens religious piety and even everyday morality. To claim, as Descartes does, that 'the principles of goodness and beauty are arbitrary' is, Leibniz argues, ultimately to deprive the works of God of any true goodness or beauty. These qualities would be nothing but an extrinsic, merely accidental feature of God's work, derived only from the fact that God has brought them about; such value-properties could just as well have belonged to some other works, had God chosen to create them instead.

Leibniz insists that the view that 'the eternal truths of metaphysics and geometry, and consequently the principles of goodness, of justice, and of perfection are effects only of the will of God' undermines the necessity and objectivity of all epistemic, moral, and aesthetic standards and judgements. What is good and right and true and just and beautiful could just as well have been otherwise, and there would be no compelling reason why God did not in fact make them otherwise.

More troubling, the moral character of God Himself is threatened by the voluntarist position. 'In saying, therefore, that things are not good according to any standard of goodness, but simply by the will of God, it seems to me that one destroys, without realizing it, all the love of God and all His glory; for why praise Him for what He has done if He would be equally praiseworthy in doing the contrary? Where will be His justice and His wisdom if He has only a certain despotic power, if arbitrary will takes the place of reasonableness, and if in accord with the definition of tyrants, justice consists in that which is pleasing to the most powerful?' (*Discourse on Metaphysics* §2; GP IV 427–8; Leibniz 1980: 4–5).[10] Almost twenty years later, in his 'Reflections on the Common Conception of Justice', Leibniz reaffirms his position with a resounding rejection of Euthyphro's view:

It is generally agreed that whatever God wills is good and just. But there remains the question whether it is good and just because God wills it or whether God wills it because it is good and just; in other words, whether justice and goodness are arbitrary or whether they belong to the necessary and eternal truths about the nature of things, as do numbers and proportions.... As a matter of fact, [the arbitrary view] would destroy the justice of God. For why praise Him for acting justly if the concept of justice adds nothing to His act. And to say *stat pro ratione voluntas*—'Let my will stand for the reason'—is definitely the motto of a tyrant. ('Reflections on the Common Concept of Justice'; LL 562)

Unlike Descartes' 'despotic' God, Leibniz's rational God chooses nothing from caprice or indifference; rather, He does things only for reasons. And the reasons

---

[10] Marion (1985) argues that in formulating his critique of Descartes' doctrine, Leibniz wilfully misreads it to introduce a priority of will and understanding in God.

that move God are objective and independent of His will. 'Every act of willing', Leibniz says, 'presupposes some reason for the willing, and this reason, of course, must precede the act.'

Leibniz's fear is that the Cartesian position on the eternal truths makes it impossible to offer a theodicean justification of God's ways that provides a coherent and satisfactory solution to the problem of evil. If whatever God does is good just because God does it, then a defence of God's justice and goodness is meaningless. 'Indifference with regard to good and evil would indicate a lack of goodness or of wisdom. . . . If justice was established arbitrarily and without any cause, if God came upon it by a kind of hazard, as when one draws lots, His goodness and His wisdom are not manifested in it, and there is nothing at all to attach Him to it' ( *Theodicy*, §175-6; GP VI 218–19; Leibniz 1985: 236–7). It would make no more sense to ask why God does what is good than to ask why the Devil does what is evil, since whatever the Devil does is, by the fact of his doing it, evil.

Despite his unquestionable Cartesian credentials, Malebranche unequivocally departed from his philosophical mentor's views on the eternal truths and the concomitant conception of God that informs them. His critique of Descartes on this issue is, essentially, the same as Leibniz's.

If eternal laws and truths depended on God, if they had been established by a free volition of the Creator, in short, if the Reason we consult [according to the Vision in God doctrine] were not necessary and independent, it seems evident to me that there would no longer be any true science and that we might be mistaken in claiming that the arithmetic or geometry of the Chinese is like our own. For in the final analysis, if it were not absolutely necessary that twice four be eight, or that the three angles of a triangle be equal to two right angles, what assurance would we have that these kinds of truths are not like those that are found only in certain universities, or that last only for a certain time? (*Search After Truth*, Elucidation 10; OCM III 132; MLO 615)

Again, the concern is not just with mathematics. Piety is what it is, regardless of what anyone (including God) wants it to be. Goodness, beauty, and other universal norms are independent of the desires, preferences, and inclinations of all agents, human and divine. God cannot make what is unjust into what is just, nor can He, through His will alone, reverse all of the values that inform our judgements about what is true and false and good and bad. In the *Dialogues on Metaphysics*, Malebranche's spokesman Theodore, fearful of the ethical consequences of the Cartesian doctrine, sounds the alarm: 'Everything is inverted if we claim that God is above Reason and has no rule in His plans other than His mere will. This false principle spreads such blanket darkness that it confounds the good with the evil, the true with the false, and creates out of everything a chaos in which the mind no longer knows anything.' There are moments when this character's concerns, while expressed in more picturesque terms, echo those of Leibniz. If Descartes is right, then claims about God's moral nature are empty and there is no point in praising God for what He has done, because He would be equally praiseworthy had He done just the opposite.

According to this principle, the universe is perfect because God willed it. Monsters are works as perfect as others according to the plans of God. It is good to have eyes in our head, but they would have been as wisely placed anywhere else, had God so placed them. However we invert the world, whatever chaos we make out of it, it will always be equally admirable, since its entire beauty consists in its conformity with the divine will, which is not obliged to conform to order.... All the beauty of the universe must therefore disappear in view of that great principle that God is above the Reason that enlightens all minds, and that His wholly arbitrary will is the sole rule of His actions    (*Dialogues on Metaphysics* IX.13; OCM XII 220–1; MS 168–9).

There was, however, one point on which all hands agreed—whether they were partisans of the rationalist God or partisans of the voluntarist God. It was that if there was anything to be avoided, it was the God of Spinoza.

The case of Leibniz is especially instructive in this regard. Leibniz recognized and even flirted with the potential dangers in his own views. Writing to the legal scholar Magnus Wedderkopf in 1671, Leibniz explains that 'the ultimate reason' for the divine will is the divine intellect, 'for God wills the things He understands to be the best and most harmonious and selects them, as it were, from an infinite number of all possibilities.' He concedes that 'because God is the most perfect mind it is impossible for Him not to be affected by the most perfect harmony, and thus to be necessitated to do the best by the very ideality of things' (A II: 1.117; LL 146).[11]

The question is whether it is logically conceivable that God, an absolutely perfect being, would not pursue the most perfect course and will the existence of the best of all possible worlds? Could God, given what He essentially and necessarily is, possibly choose otherwise? In 1671, Leibniz is certain that the answer to this question is no; moreover, this is a position he maintains throughout his later writings on the topic.[12] But then it appears that the existence of the best of all possible worlds and everything in it is no less necessary than the existence of Spinoza's nature. Creation must ultimately be the result not of God's choice but of God's being, so there really are no other possible worlds.

Leibniz expended much intellectual energy throughout the rest of his philo-sophical career to find some way to avoid this shocking Spinozistic dénouement. During at least one of his meetings with Spinoza in The Hague in 1676, Leibniz seems to have turned the discussion to the question of whether there are any

---

[11] Leibniz may be trying to pull back at the last minute when, in the next line, he says that 'this in no way detracts from freedom. For it is the highest freedom to be impelled to the best by a right reason.' The door to necessitarianism has been opened, however, and it is not clear whether Leibniz can close it simply by substituting reasons that 'impel' rather than necessitate.

[12] In his comments on some letters from Spinoza to Oldenburg (which Oldenburg allowed Leibniz to see when he was in London on the way to The Hague), Leibniz singles out as standing in need of explanation Spinoza's claim that 'all things follow from the nature of God with an inevitable necessity'. He provides the following gloss: 'The world could not have been produced in any other way, since God is not able not to act in the most perfect manner. For since He is perfectly wise, he chooses the best' (A VI: 3.364). For a more extensive discussion of Leibniz's views on this, see Adams (1994, ch. 1).

possible worlds not actually created by God.[13] Spinoza would have immediately explained that there are not. Gaping at the yawning metaphysical chasm opening up before him, Leibniz very soon thereafter came upon what would become an essential part of his response to the charge that, according to his own principles, the existence of the world is absolutely necessary. It appears in the notes he made while reading the *Ethics* a year later, just after its publication. Commenting on Spinoza's proposition that 'the world could not have been produced in any other way than it has been produced, for it follows from the immutable nature of God', Leibniz replies that 'on the hypothesis that the divine will chooses the best or works in the most perfect way, certainly only this world could have been produced, but if the nature of the world is considered in itself, a different world could have been produced' (A VI: 4b.1776; LL 204). Relative to God's nature and will, no other world is possible. God must choose the best, this particular world is the best, and so God cannot but choose it.[14] However, this does not mean that there is not an infinity of other conceivable worlds that, taken on their own terms, are possible in themselves insofar as there is nothing internally inconsistent about them. God, because of what He is, might not be able to choose them, but that does not keep them from being worlds that are logically possible in their own right.

Leibniz admits that 'when I found myself very close to the opinions of those who hold everything to be absolutely necessary'—that is, Spinoza—this solution is what 'pulled me back from the precipice' ('On Freedom'; LL 263). The presence of alternative possibilities, while none of them is compatible with God's nature, is nonetheless sufficient, at least to Leibniz, for preserving the reality of God's choice. He says that this means that God's willing the best of all possible worlds is not metaphysically or logically necessary but only morally necessary, even if God could not conceivably choose otherwise. God's creation of the best avoids the geometric determinism of Spinoza's philosophy because Leibniz's God is an agent who does what He does because it is the one alternative among many that He ought to do according to reason, according to a choice that is influenced by a judgement of what is good. The choice may be infallible and inevitable, it may be a 'moral absurdity' to think that a perfectly good and wise God might do otherwise, but it nonetheless remains a choice.

Perhaps emboldened by the ingenuity of this approach, Leibniz sometimes seems to want to retreat even from the idea that God cannot possibly choose anything but the best. He speaks of 'reasons that impel' or 'prompt' or 'incline without necessitating', and he compares the rational considerations that morally move the divine will

---

[13] The issue appears in the notes that Leibniz prepared before their meeting (Leibniz 1961: 529–30; LL 168–9).

[14] Another strategy adopted by Leibniz is to claim that while the world chosen by God is the best of all possible worlds, it is not necessarily the best of all possible worlds. Therefore, the claim that God chooses this world is not absolutely necessary. See, for example, Leibniz (1948: II 493).

with weights that, by causing an imbalance, physically move bodies. God's choosing the best may not, he occasionally suggests, be necessary at all. 'God does not fail to choose the best, but He is not constrained to do so: nay, more, there is no necessity in the object of God's choice, for another sequence of things is equally possible. For that very reason the choice is free and independent of necessity, because it is made between several possibles, and the will is determined only by the prepondering goodness of the object' (*Theodicy* §45: GP VI 128; Leibniz 1985: 148).

Leibniz insists, in fact, that it is the Cartesian God, Arnauld's God, whose will is independent of all determining reasons, that most closely resembles the Spinozist deity. It is an odd claim, because Spinoza's God wills nothing at all. But writing to Gerhard Wolter Molanus around 1679, Leibniz offers his standard criticism that 'Descartes's God, or perfect being, is not a God like the one we imagine or hope for, that is, a God just and wise, doing everything possible for the good of creatures.' He adds that 'Descartes's God is something approaching the God of Spinoza . . . Descartes's God has neither will nor understanding, since according to Descartes He does not have the good as the object of the will, nor the true as the object of the understanding' (GP IV 299; LAG 242). Leibniz means that Descartes, by eliminating rational choice in God, essentially eliminates divine choice altogether. A God who does not will for the sake of reasons and to achieve what is good is not really endowed with intellect and will at all, just like the God of the *Ethics*.

The fear of God—of Spinoza's God—has clearly possessed him. Leibniz cannot allow that God might be anything but a person, an agent who acts as we act. Soon after his conversations over the *Ethics* with Tschirnhaus, Leibniz notes that 'God is not as some represent him—something metaphysical, imaginary, incapable of thought, will, or action, so that it would be the same as if you were to say that God is nature, fate, fortune, necessity, the world. Rather, God is a certain substance, a person, a mind' (A VI: 3.474–5). Thirty-five years later, near the end of his life, Leibniz wrote in the *Theodicy* that, according to Spinoza, 'all things exist through the necessity of the divine nature, without any act of choice by God', adding that 'we will not waste time here in refuting an opinion so bad, and indeed so inexplicable' (*Theodicy* §173; GP VI 217; Leibniz 1985: 234). A bad and inexplicable opinion, perhaps, but one that Leibniz went to a great deal of trouble to avoid.


# V: THE CONCEIVABILITY OF GOD

Underlying the differences among these philosophers on God's *modus operandi* is a more fundamental disagreement, one that evokes medieval debates over whether terms that describe creatures are applicable, either univocally or at least by analogy, to God. The God of Leibniz and Malebranche is essentially an accessible, intelligible God, one whose ways are familiar to us. His nature and faculties can be understood by human reason and his way of acting conceived in terms very similar to those that capture our own way of acting. True, the rationalist God is, unlike human beings, omnipotent, endowed with infinite power. But there are well-defined limits to that power. These two philosophers, like so many before them, agree that God certainly cannot do what involves a logical contradiction. But they also agree that neither can He make the values of things different from what they, in fact, are. The rationalist God's will is bounded by uncreated logical, mathematical, metaphysical, and moral truths; these are truths that He cannot violate or change, not even in theory. Put another way, this God operates just as human beings operate: through practical reason, confronted with objective values that are not of His making and that normatively serve Him in making the choices that He makes. God's wisdom may be inscrutable to human beings, surpassing our finite understandings—although Malebranche, with his doctrine of the Vision in God, appears to deny this—but we can nonetheless understand God's rational nature.

Spinoza, as we have seen, has great contempt for this representation of God. Like Maimonides before him, Spinoza employs a philosophical theology calculated to undermine the anthropomorphization of God. He mocks our attempts to depict God in human terms, insisting that 'a triangle, if it could speak, would likewise say that God is eminently triangular, and a circle that God's nature is eminently circular. In this way each would ascribe to God its own attributes, assuming itself to be like God . . . ' (Ep. 56; SO IV 260; Spinoza 1995: 277). On the other hand, because Spinoza identifies God with Nature, and because the attributes of God or Nature (or at least two of them: Thought and Extension) are perfectly knowable—we conceive them through adequate ideas—he also concludes that God's (Nature's) essence can be adequately known by human beings. Spinoza's God is thoroughly conceivable, but only because of his reductive naturalization of God and refusal to model God's power on human agency.

Descartes' (and Arnauld's) God, by contrast, is, in the deepest sense, unintelligible. The voluntarist God, in whom there is no distinction between will and understanding (except perhaps by a 'distinction of reason'), is opaque to human understanding. Such a God cannot be conceived in any terms that might be used to depict human nature, not even by analogy. In the Cartesian scheme, God's knowledge, His relationship to truths and values, is radically different from ours. We perceive truths—objective and independent truths—through the understanding, and then give our assent to them through the will, a separate faculty of the mind. Nothing remotely like this pertains to the voluntarist God. Indeed, we can have no conception at all of what it is for God to know/will something. We cannot form an idea of God's nature and action that is adequate to their reality. As one scholar has shown, what Descartes rejects is the Scholastic (Suárezian) doctrine of univocity (or analogy) applied to the divine understanding and human understanding, whereby terms employed to conceive the human can also be used to conceive the divine (Marion 1981). For Descartes, 'no essence can belong univocally to both God and His creatures' (Sixth Replies: AT VII 433; CSM II 292). With the divine rationalism of Leibniz and Malebranche, there is a commensurability between the human and the divine; with the divine voluntarism of Descartes, we cannot even conceive of what the divine is like.

# REFERENCES

ADAMS, R. M. (1994). *Leibniz: Determinist, Theist, Idealist.* Oxford: Oxford University Press.

CARRAUD, V. (1996). 'Arnauld: A Cartesian Theologian? Omnipotence, Freedom of Indifference, and the Creation of the Eternal Truths', in E. Kremer (ed.), *Interpreting Arnauld.* Toronto: University of Toronto Press, 91–110.

FRANKFURT, H. (1977). 'Descartes on the creation of the eternal truths'. *The Philosophical Review,* 86: 36–57.

FUNKENSTEIN, A. (1980). 'Descartes, Eternal Truths, and the Divine Omnipotence', in S. Gaukroger (ed.), *Descartes: Philosophy, Mathematics and Physics.* Sussex: Harvester Press, 181–95.

LEIBNIZ, G. W. (1948). *Textes inédits d'après les manuscrits de la bibliothèque provinciale de Hanovre.* Ed. G. Grua, 2 vols. Paris: Presses universitaires de France.

LEIBNIZ, G. W. (1961). *Opuscules et fragments inédits de Leibniz.* Ed. L. Couturat. Paris: Presses universitaires de France, 1903; reprinted Hildesheim: Georg Olms.

LEIBNIZ, G. W. (1980). *Discourse on Metaphysics/Correspondence with Arnauld/Monadology.* Ed. and trans. G. Montgomery. La Salle, IL: Open Court.

LEIBNIZ, G. W. (1985). *Theodicy: Essays on the Goodness of God, the Freedom of Man, and the Origin of Evil.* Ed. A. Farrar; tr. E. M. Huggard. La Salle, IL: Open Court.

LENNON, T. (1978). 'Occasionalism, Jansenism, and Skepticism: Divine Providence and the Order of Grace'. *Irish Theological Quarterly,* 45: 185–90.

MARION, J.-L. (1981). *Sur la théologie blanche de Descartes.* Paris: Presses universitaires de France.

MARION, J.-L. (1985). 'De la création des vérités éternelles au principe de la raison. Remarques sur l'anti-cartésianisme de Spinoza, Malebranche, Leibniz'. *XVIIe siècle* 37: 143–64.

NADLER, S. (2008). *The Best of All Possible Worlds: A Story of Philosophers, God, and Evil.* New York: Farrar, Straus & Giroux.

SCHMALTZ, T. (2007). *Radical Cartesianism.* Oxford: Clarendon Press.

SLEIGH, JR., R. C. (1990). *Leibniz and Arnauld: A Commentary on Their Correspondence.* New Haven, CT: Yale University Press.

SPINOZA, B. (1995). *The Letters.* Tr. Samuel Shirley. Indianapolis: Hackett.

# CHAPTER 25

......................................................................................................

# THE
# EPISTEMOLOGY OF
# RELIGIOUS BELIEF

......................................................................................................

## DESMOND M. CLARKE

'*Reason* must be our last Judge and Guide in every Thing.'
(*Essay* IV. xix. 14)

The first decades of the early modern period witnessed the deaths of three reformers whose interpretations of the Christian tradition subsequently inspired a number of distinct churches: Martin Luther (1483–1546), Philip Melanchthon (1497–1560), and Jean Calvin (1509–64). At almost the same time, the Council of Trent (1545–63) redefined the religious teaching of the Catholic Church in response to those reformers. The disparate theological doctrines that emerged from these events in the mid-sixteenth century had significant repercussions well beyond the churches that endorsed them. The wars that erupted frequently in Europe, including the Thirty Years war (1618–48), while not primarily religious, assumed distinctly religious dimensions when the warring kingdoms gave official and exclusive recognition to particular churches (Wilson 2009: 25–48). During this period of intense competition between different Christian churches, both within and between kingdoms, the fate of those who belonged to the Jewish tradition became even more precarious than it had been previously, and the Inquisition acquired the reputation for which it became infamous.

When contemporary philosophers reflected on religious beliefs, their primary challenge was to account for the apparent certainty with which members of different churches believed propositions that were manifestly incompatible, and to clarify the evidence that allegedly supported such beliefs. Evidently, it was also possible to understand religious beliefs as not making objective claims—as being, in some sense, poetic expressions of traditional lifestyles—or for believers to resort to fideism by simply accepting their beliefs uncritically, living their lives accordingly, and never entertaining questions about the veracity or otherwise of their faith. However, when religious beliefs were understood as making claims about a transcendent God or expressing views about the reality and nature of an afterlife, it was a matter of logic that inconsistent beliefs could not all be true and, as Leibniz pointed out, that the 'inner' conviction of religious believers alone could not confirm their claims (LRB 507). Thus the need to reflect on the epistemology of religious belief resulted from the realist or objective interpretations of such claims that were adopted in most of the Christian churches. It was also reinforced by an intellectual climate in which familiar beliefs, in politics and natural philosophy, were vigorously challenged by political crises and new discoveries, and by a renewed interest in a form of scepticism that challenged all traditional doctrines (Popkin 1960).

The confluence of these religious, political, and philosophical developments focused attention on the nature of religious faith, the kinds of evidence that supports religious beliefs, and the degree of certainty that could justifiably be claimed by religious believers for their disparate creeds. Although such questions arise with respect to all religious traditions, their application in this chapter is limited to Christianity, as the dominant religious tradition in early modern Europe.

# I: Religious belief and knowledge

There was no single model available of what constitutes 'knowledge' by reference to which one could address questions such as: is religious belief a form of knowledge, and is it legitimate to apply to it the same epistemological questions that are appropriate to other kinds of knowledge? One such model, which was in the process of being replaced by a hypothetical and probabilistic alternative in natural philosophy (Chapter 12), defined knowledge in terms of (i) first principles that were known by intuition to be certain, and (ii) other truths that are deduced from such principles. When this model was applied, it seemed clear to Locke that religious faith cannot be a form of knowledge (*Essay* IV. xviii. 2; LW III: 146).

Nonetheless, Malebranche, Locke, and Berkeley, among others, argued that it is possible to 'demonstrate' that God exists and thus that at least one proposition that is also subject to religious faith can be known. Descartes concluded in the *Meditations*: 'it is possible to have true knowledge of the existence of God' (AT VII 443; CSM II 299), and Locke claimed in the *Essay* that there is no truth 'which a man may more evidently make out to himself, than the existence of a God' (I. iv. 22). He argued: 'Our reason leads us to the knowledge of this certain and evident truth, that *there is an eternal, most powerful, and most knowing Being . . .* we have a more certain knowledge of the existence of God, than of any thing our senses have not immediately discovered to us . . . equal to mathematical certainty' (*Essay* IV. x. 6). Berkeley—for whom, notoriously, knowledge of even familiar external realities became problematic—concluded that 'the existence of God is far more evidently perceived than the existence of men' (BW II 108).

Thus, for those for whom God's existence was demonstrated by philosophical argument, it was redundant to invoke faith as the basis of that particular belief. However, the vast majority of Christians in the early modern period could not read or write (Ariès *et al.* 1986: III, 76), and they were incapable of performing the inferences required for a demonstration of God's existence. They *believed* that God existed, that He had communicated various doctrines to mankind, and that the churches to which they belonged reported truthfully about God's communications. The validity of thus relying completely on religious belief without any 'proofs' of God's existence was disputed within and between various Christian churches.

Pascal and Malebranche, though members of the same church, supported alternative positions. Malebranche argued that all religious faith presupposes knowledge of God's existence: 'Knowledge . . . of the existence of a God is absolutely necessary, since even the certainty of the faith depends on the knowledge that reason gives of the existence of a God' (OCM II 52; MLO 291). Since religious faith, for Christians, is based on God's communication through Scriptures, it must presuppose a God who communicates with us and does not deceive. Malebranche concluded: 'if you are not convinced by reason that there is a God, how will you be convinced that he speaks? Could you know that he spoke, without knowing that he exists?' (OCM IV: 14).

However, for many theologians of the period, the failure of repeated attempts to prove God's existence had the opposite effect to what was intended by their proponents. Such unconvincing arguments exposed the frailty of the foundations on which religious belief was said to depend or, possibly, it revealed the cryptic atheism of philosophers who merely pretended to prove God's existence. This at least was the public reaction of Dutch Calvinists to Descartes' *Meditations*, in a book commissioned by the theologian Gisbertus Voetius and written by Martin Schoock (1643). Schoock argued, with a subtle comparison with the serpent that deceived Adam, that while Descartes was 'giving the impression of combating atheists with his invincible arguments, he injects the venom of atheism delicately and secretly in those who, because of their feeble minds, never notice the serpent that hides in the grass' (Schoock 1643: Preface). According to Schoock, Descartes' real objective was to undermine proofs of God's existence by offering demonstrations that failed to convince. One of Berkeley's critics, John Hervey, stopped short of similarly impugning the Irish bishop's motives; however, his evaluation of the merits of Berkeley's argument was equivalent: 'he is likelier (by telling people his are the best arguments to prove a God) to make, than to convert Atheists' (Hervey 1732: 63).

Pascal rejected completely the assumptions underlying the apologetic strategy proposed by Malebranche or Berkeley. This famous supporter of Port-Royal and Jansenism argued that 'the metaphysical proofs of God are so far removed from man's reasoning, and so complicated, that they have little force' (Pascal 1995: 63; 2000: ii, 605). The gap between the limited capacity of human intelligence and the infinite reality of God was such, he argued, that the very first step towards religious belief must be a leap of faith rather than a philosophical argument. In one of the most famous passages of the *Pensées*, he argued:

If there is a God, he is infinitely beyond our comprehension, since, having neither parts nor limits, he bears no relation to ourselves. We are therefore incapable of knowing either what he is, or if he is. That being so, who will dare to undertake a resolution of this question? It cannot be us, who bear no relationship to him. Who will then blame Christians for being unable to provide a rational basis for their belief . . .    (Pascal 1995: 153; 2000: ii, 677)

The argument that followed this passage in the *Pensées*, which has since become known as Pascal's wager, was not therefore proposed as a novel proof of God's existence, but as a retrospective defence by a religious believer of the rationality of his faith or, perhaps, as an argument to show that it is reasonable to take steps to become a believer. The disorganized condition of Pascal's scribbled notes that were published posthumously as the *Pensées* made it difficult to distinguish various wager arguments in the text, or to decide if they provide a valid support for whatever conclusion(s) he intended (Hájek 2008). However, any plausible interpretation of the relevant fragments seems to provide an equally sound basis for any religious believer to wager successfully for their own convictions, on condition only that they assign (i) an infinite value to God's existence, and (ii) a higher than zero probability to the proposition that God exists. Thus, if the wager worked for Pascal, it would work equally for members of every church, and could not serve to identify which (if any) religious beliefs are true.

Although few other religious beliefs, apart from God's existence, were ever said to be demonstrable, it was commonplace to claim that religious beliefs were even more certain than ordinary knowledge-claims. This attitude was reflected in the concluding paragraph of Descartes' *Principles of Philosophy* (Part I): 'whatever God has revealed to us must be accepted as more certain than anything else. And although the light of reason may, with the utmost clarity and evidence, appear to suggest something different, we must still put our entire faith in divine authority rather than in our own judgment' (AT VIII-1 39; CSM I 221). One reason for this conviction was that, if God revealed something, it must be true. However, that failed to address the question of how one decides if something was actually revealed by God, and whether it is reasonable to *believe* a proposition because one believes that God revealed it (Jolley 2007: 443–4).

# II: DIVINE REVELATION

The ultimate source of evidence to which all the Christian churches appealed was the life and teaching of Jesus Christ as reported in the New Testament. They claimed that God had *revealed* certain 'truths' to mankind, that Christ's disciples had recorded them accurately, and that these beliefs were transmitted reliably through the churches to believers of later generations. In the seventeenth century, that kind of 'revealed' evidence became the focus of the first important contributions to biblical criticism, which helped to remove the protective veil that had previously put the scriptures beyond the reach of historical and literary analysis.

The standard account of how revelation provided reliable evidence assumed a comparison with what happens when we believe a report from a trustworthy witness. According to this analogy, if we have reason to trust someone as a truthful witness, and if they tell us about something that they witnessed and are capable of understanding, then it is reasonable to believe their report despite the fact that we have no first-hand experience of the reality in question. The reasonableness of our trust and consequent belief is proportionate to the trustworthiness of the witness. If God is the witness, then, our trust should be unconditional. The logic of this analogy was outlined by many authors, including Boyle in the *Christian Virtuoso*, Part I (B xi: 313). Hobbes summarized it thus in the *Leviathan*.

When a mans Discourse . . . beginneth at some saying of another, of whose ability to know the truth, and of whose honesty in not deceiving, he doubteth not . . . the Discourse is not so much concerning the Thing, as the Person; and the Resolution is called BELEEFE, and FAITH; *Faith*, in the man; *Beleefe*, both *of* the man, and *of* the truth of what he sayes. So that in Beleefe are two opinions; one of the saying of the man; the other of his virtue.    (Hobbes 1991: 48)

However, few Christians claimed to have had direct reports from God; they relied, rather, on indirect reports from human witnesses of what they had interpreted as communications from God. Hobbes concluded accordingly: 'it is evident, that whatsoever we believe, upon no other reason, then what is drawn from authority of men onely, and their writings; whether they be sent from God or not, is Faith in men onely' (Hobbes 1991: 49).

With the exception, therefore, of those who claimed to have had a direct communication from God (and whose reports were generally distrusted), religious belief in the time of Hobbes was based on (i) reports about religious matters that were contained in various written documents; (ii) claims that those documents were authentic rather than apocryphal; (iii) claims about how the documents should be interpreted; and (iv) the fundamental assumption that the credibility of these documents was warranted by the veracity of God who 'inspired' them in some sense. The line of transmission, as Hobbes said, evidently relied on faith 'in men only'. Any defect in the human transmission would therefore compromise the authenticity of the transmitted message; more seriously, if the original link between the scriptures and God through 'inspiration' was not adequately explained and defended, the very basis of the alleged certainty of religious doctrines found in such writings would be undermined.

All these difficulties were ignored by the Roman Catholic Church in the Council of Trent, when it assigned to itself the exclusive authority to interpret the scriptures:

no one, relying on his personal judgment in matters of faith and morals . . . shall dare to interpret the sacred scriptures either by twisting its text to his individual meaning in opposition to that which has been and is held by holy mother church, whose function is to pass judgment on the true meaning and interpretation of the sacred scriptures; or by giving it meanings contrary to the unanimous consent of the fathers . . .    (Tanner 1990: ii, 664)

This claim to have exclusive authority to interpret the Scriptures was circular, because it depended on the Church's interpretation of biblical texts in which Christ had allegedly given that authority to the successors of the apostles. If Trent had misread the Bible, as the reformers claimed, the Church could not defend its misinterpretation by appealing to its own Bible-based authority. Locke identified a comparable circularity in the beliefs of so-called enthusiasts: '*It is a Revelation, because they firmly believe it, and they believe it, because it is a Revelation*' (*Essay* IV. xix. 10). Despite these objections, the Tridentine text later became the focus of attention in the Galileo affair (discussed below), in which the interpretation of Scripture assumed a central role.

Trent's refusal to engage with genuine problems in biblical interpretation became more apparent when theologians began to examine the languages in which the original documents were written. Since the original writings were not available for examination, it was inevitable that readers in the early modern period had to rely on tradition—that is, the passing from one generation to another of copies of documents—to support claims about their accuracy and authenticity. Although different Christian churches disputed the status of some books of both the Old and

New Testaments, there was wide agreement about the canonical status of the four gospels. Even that degree of consensus, however, did not resolve disputes about the meaning of the gospels, nor did it guarantee that their teaching was revealed by God.

The interpretation of ancient texts in cultural contexts that differ significantly from those of their original composition was already problematic in the early centuries of the Christian era. Augustine had addressed some of the underlying issues about biblical interpretation in *De Genesi ad litteram* (1982). His immediate objective was to make sense of the six 'days' of creation, as described in the opening chapters of the Book of Genesis, where God was said to have created light on the first day, although the sun and moon were created only three days later. In more general terms, Augustine needed to interpret in some non-literal sense the account of creation in which God is portrayed as working like an artisan and resting on the seventh day; Christians did not believe that God could get tired, or that his creative action was remotely similar to human labour.

In response to those issues, Augustine proposed a number of hermeneutic principles (McMullin 2005): (i) the Scriptures are concerned primarily with human salvation, rather than the provision of natural knowledge; (ii) their teaching is expressed in a language that is adapted to their audience; and (iii) a correct interpretation of the Scriptures cannot conflict with what is known by reason and experience. However, Augustine set a very high threshold for deciding when to prefer knowledge based on reason and experience to a literal reading of the bible; he claimed that Christians should always accept the latter unless it conflicts with some item of natural knowledge that is 'demonstrated'.

Augustine also warned against linking the church's reading of scriptures with what was known in the fourth century, lest subsequent developments in knowledge force Christians to reject their earlier interpretations. It seems beyond doubt that this advice was not followed in the early centuries of the Christian era. Theologians interpreted the Scriptures in light of selective applications of Greek philosophy and, when inevitable disputes arose about the validity of these interpretations, Councils of the Church resolved them in favour of one or other disputed interpretation. Thus, during the early centuries of the Christian era, church councils issued official doctrines about two natures in Christ, three persons in God, the compatibility of grace and free will, the existence of heaven and hell, etc. When this process gathered pace in the Middle Ages and the Renaissance, it was not surprising that Reformers in the early modern period challenged the whole edifice of Christian teaching that was inextricably bound up with various borrowed philosophical theories.

The manifest difficulties involved in linking Christian beliefs, through the scriptures, to divine revelation were obliquely acknowledged in the first edition of the Jesuits' syllabus of studies, the *Ratio Studiorum* (Anon 1596). 'It is more probable that the first copies and uncorrupted sources were all dictated individually by the Holy Spirit with regard to their substance, in different ways however according to the different conditions of the instruments' (1596: 323). This modest concession was deleted from all subsequent editions of the syllabus, but not before it had raised the question of whether only texts in the original languages were 'inspired', and whether only core doctrines (if such could be identified) rather than the details of their presentation are matters of religious faith. It was almost a century before Richard Simon (1638–1712), an Oratorian priest, began to address issues in biblical criticism (Steinmann 1960). Simon conceded that only the original texts, rather than translations (including the Latin edition used by his own Church) were 'inspired' (Simon 1687: 14). He also argued that not every word of the Scripture had been dictated by God (Simon 1689: 61). God's inspiration was in some sense global, rather than specifically applied to each sentence in the scriptures, and writers such as Christ's disciples who recorded religious doctrines did not cease to be normal human beings in the manner in which they wrote. Simon concluded that it would be an obvious mistake to assume, when translating a biblical text, that individual words were inspired by God or that their meaning is unambiguous. He added, critically, that most of those who claimed to teach the bible authoritatively did not know the original languages well enough to provide reliable interpretations (Simon 1687: 12).

Jean Le Clerc (1657–1736) provided an Arminian response to Simon's work. Le Clerc understood Simon's detailed biblical scholarship as undermining the competence of individual Christians to interpret the scriptures and providing a justification for the Catholic Church's claim to be a unique authoritative interpreter of the Bible. However, he also agreed with Simon on a number of issues.

people believe commonly two things which seem to me groundless: . . . they believe, first, that the sacred historians were inspir'd with the things themselves; and next, that they were inspir'd also with the terms in which they have express'd them. In a word, that the holy history was dictated word for word by the Holy Spirit, and that the authors, whose names it bears, were no other than secretaries of that Spirit, who wrote exactly as it dictated.    (Le Clerc 1690: 30)

Le Clerc proposed that the scriptures be read as one reads any other ancient book, and that the reliability of their transmission to us is no greater (nor less) than that of other ancient books. It follows that Christian belief is based 'only on human reasons'; however, he was satisfied with those reasons because, he wrote: 'I am a man, and not an angel' (Le Clerc 1685: 336, 337). One such reason was borrowed from Grotius, who argued that minor differences in accounts of the same events that are found in the gospels confirm, rather than undermine, the truthfulness of the witnesses. 'It is the constant practice of *false* witnesses to concur, by previous agreement, so exactly in their several depositions, that there may not exist, even in appearance, the faintest colour of a difference' (Grotius 1814: 99). In other words, the slightly different reports of the same events that are found in gospels written by different evangelists provide a reason for believing that they did not conspire together to produce false accounts of the life of Jesus.

The scale of the problems involved in the interpretation of the Bible is starkly demonstrated by the diversity of radically different readings that were adopted by various Christian churches. Poulain de la Barre adopted a position similar to that of Le Clerc (Poulain 1720: 267, 274–5); accordingly, he found no biblical basis for denying women full access to the Christian ministry (Poulain 1990: 106), although that interpretation continues to be rejected by most Christian churches today. If the texts of the New Testament are so opaque that one cannot determine their teaching even about the admission of women to the ministry, it seems proportionately less plausible to claim that they could determine unique doctrines about the Trinity or other so-called 'mysteries'.

In light of irresolvable uncertainties about the accuracy, authenticity, and interpretation of biblical texts, many turned to 'reason' to establish independent limits for Christian beliefs.

# III: FAITH AND REASON

The meaning and scope of 'reason' as a criterion for deciding what to believe on faith is illustrated by two of the most contentious theological issues that arose in the early modern period: the theology of the Eucharist, and the Galileo affair. Both involved fundamental disputes about how to interpret the scriptures, and about the extent to which one may use knowledge acquired from experience to delimit what is proposed for acceptance on faith.

Christians had been widely agreed for centuries that the Eucharist was a celebration, in some sense, of the last supper celebrated by Christ (Matthew 26; Mark 14; Luke 22). According to the gospel accounts, when Jesus shared bread and wine with his disciples, he told them: 'This is my body', 'this is my blood', and invited them to celebrate in a similar manner in his memory. Subsequent generations of Christians believed that Christ was in some sense 'present' at such Eucharistic celebrations. However, it seemed apparent to reformed churches that this presence was spiritual, sacramental, or symbolic; however it was described, it was a type of presence that was distinct from the physical presence involved when human beings sit down to dine together.

In contrast, the Council of Trent adapted a scholastic theory of substances and appearances, and invented a neologism, 'transubstantiation', to define the way in which Christ is present in the Eucharist. According to Trent, 'transubstantiation' meant 'the change of the whole substance of the bread into the substance of the body of Christ Our Lord, and of the whole substance of the wine into the substance of his blood' (Tanner 1990: ii, 695); as a result, 'Our Lord Jesus Christ, true God and true man, is truly, really and substantially contained in the propitious sacrament of the holy eucharist under the appearances of those things that are perceptible to the senses' (Tanner 1990: ii, 693). This was subject to the objection that Christ is bodily present in many different locations simultaneously, although Christians also believed that Christ had been assumed bodily into heaven after his resurrection from the dead. Trent rejected that objection explicitly:

Nor are the two assertions incompatible, that our Saviour is ever seated in heaven at the right hand of the Father in his natural mode of existing, and that he is nevertheless sacramentally present to us by his substance in many other places in a mode of existing which, *though we can hardly express it in words*, we can grasp with minds enlightened by the faith as possible to God . . .    (Tanner 1990: ii, 693–4; emphasis added)

Even sympathetic readers of Trent, such as Descartes, were concerned that a defective philosophical theory of substance had been used to define the meaning of a religious belief, and that objections to the former could undermine the credibility of the latter (Armogathe 1977). On a philosophical level, Descartes could not understand how any substance could be separated from the qualities by which it is recognized, nor how the observable properties of bread and wine—which, all agreed, continue after the consecration of the Eucharist—could exist independently of the substance of which they are the usual natural appearances.

Critics of this doctrine claimed that transubstantiation was inconsistent with what we know by experience or can conclude reliably from perception. Calvinists in particular claimed that the dogma defied reason. Moise Amyraut, a Remonstrant professor at Saumur, provided a standard expression of this objection. He distinguished between (i) religious teachings that are accessible to reason, and (ii) those which cannot be understood (*comprises*) by reason. While the latter included some truths 'which are simply beyond reason but at the same time do not destroy reason'—such as the mysteries of the Trinity or the Incarnation (Amyraut 1641: 59)—they also included propositions that are 'contrary to reason' (Amyraut 1641: 76), if 'the subject matter falls within the scope of things that we understand adequately'. Amyraut included the doctrine of transubstantiation among those that conflict with 'arguments which are so strong and so evidently correct that, in order not to follow reason, one must renounce nature itself' (1641: 76–7).

While Amyraut's argument relied ultimately on the clear evidence of our senses, and on the failure even of those who accepted the disputed doctrine to provide supportive reasons, others argued that the Tridentine teaching involved a logical contradiction. For example, the Cartesian natural philosopher, Jacques Rohault (1618–72), defended Trent as follows: 'One can entrust things to the power of God in two ways; one, by knowing positively that they are possible, and the other, by merely not knowing positively that they are impossible, even though they are inconceivable to us' (Rohault 1978: 118). Since we cannot know that transubstanti-ation is impossible for God, we should conclude that it is possible. In reply, the anonymous author [Élie?] of *Reflexions physiques sur la Transubstantiation* con-ceded that the question whether one body can be changed into another is a question of physics and, since our knowledge of physics is imperfect, one cannot conclude that such a change is impossible. However, the Calvinist objection was not that transubstantiation is impossible because it conflicts with what is known in physics, but that it implies a contradiction:

The axioms on which I rely to show that transubstantiation is a dogma which implies a contradiction are not the simple principles of physics; but they are axioms of eternal truth which one cannot doubt without quenching all the light of reason. For example, when I say that a round and flat host cannot be the body of a man, which is neither round nor flat . . . I rely on this axiom: that a thing cannot both be and not be at the same time.    (Élie[?] 1675: 33–4)

Locke's version of this objection in the *Essay* occurs in the context of discussing how people adopt principles uncritically and then reject anything, no matter how clearly proved, that is inconsistent with them. He described as 'false and absurd' the belief of Roman Catholics that something is 'really the Body of Christ, which another man calls Bread' (*Essay* IV. xx. 10).

Berkeley was equally critical of the doctrine of transubstantiation (BW II 98; III 309) because he rejected the theory of a material substance on which it was based. However, Berkeley's objection relied, as Trent had done, on a disputed philosophical account of substance, and was therefore only as persuasive as the arguments in favour of the latter. All those involved in the dispute agreed that, following the Eucharistic consecration, the normal appearances of bread and wine remained unchanged. Their disagreement, therefore, was not about reporting uncontentious observable facts; it focused on the intelligibility or otherwise of introducing the concept of a substance to describe an invisible alleged change in bread and wine. It is clear from Trent's confession of faith that those who endorsed transubstantiation acknowledged that they did not understand how this was possible. This was the appropriate point at which to appeal to mysteries, to which I return in the next section. Before doing so, it is necessary to mention some of the issues concerning faith and reason that emerged during the Galileo affair.

When Galileo published the *Dialogue Concerning the Two Chief World Systems* in 1632, he precipitated the most lengthy and famous intellectual conflict between science and religion in the history of ideas. The dispute originated when Galileo strayed into biblical interpretation in his *Letter to Cristina* (1615) and explicitly invoked the authority of Augustine's *De Genesi ad litteram* to support a non-literal interpretation of the Bible. In that *Letter*, Galileo set out his scientific conviction about Copernicanism: 'I hold the sun to be situated motionless in the center of the revolution of the celestial orbs while the earth rotates on its axis and revolves about the sun' (Drake 1957: 177). However, Copernicanism seemed to conflict with Joshua

10:12, in which the sun was commanded to stand still. This lured Galileo into claiming that many biblical passages are obscure, and that some should be understood in a metaphorical or 'spiritual' way.

nobody will deny that it [the Bible] is often very abstruse, and may say things which are quite different from what its bare words signify. Hence in expounding the Bible if one were always to confine oneself to the unadorned grammatical meaning, one might fall into error... it would be necessary to assign to God feet, hands, and eyes, as well as corporeal and human affections, such as anger, repentance, hatred.... These propositions uttered by the Holy Ghost were set down in that manner by the sacred scribes in order to accommodate them to the capacities of the common people, who are rude and unlearned.   (Drake 1957: 181)

Galileo took his cue from Augustine to argue that, since 'the Bible...was not written to teach us astronomy', no scientific theory, such as Copernicanism, could be heretical if it has 'no concern with the salvation of souls' (Drake 1957: 212, 186).

The following year, 1616, the Roman curia rebuked Galileo for what it perceived as his inexpert and unauthorized dabbling in biblical interpretation. Since it interpreted the text of Joshua as implying that, apart from miracles, the sun normally moves, it forbade members of the Church 'to hold, teach, or defend... in any way, either verbally or in writing' that the sun is immobile (Blackwell 1991: 128). This was presented by Rome as merely implementing Trent's decision that the authoritative interpretation of the Scriptures was reserved exclusively to the pope and the bishops. Galileo's subsequent publication of the *Dialogue* in 1632 was both an implicit challenge to the Church's authority to interpret the Bible and an explicit breach of the 1616 injunction not to teach that the sun is immobile. The rest of the familiar story was almost inevitable.

In this controversy, Rome relied on a traditional Aristotelian understanding of *knowledge* —as propositions that are demonstrated from first principles (p. 299)— to reject Galileo's claim that he *knew* that the Sun was immobile. When measured by this standard of knowledge, Galileo's claim was merely an astronomical hypothesis, and did not provide a legitimate basis for rejecting a literal interpretation of the Bible. According to Rome, therefore, Galileo exceeded the warrant of his own discipline in two ways; he was merely proposing an hypothesis or theory, which was not certain; and he purported to interpret the Scriptures although this exceeded the scope of his disciplinary competence.

Neither transubstantiation nor the Galileo affair provided examples of an unambiguous conflict between so-called 'demonstrated knowledge' and religious belief. In each case, it was open to defenders of the religious belief to argue that the opposing view was not definitively established by reason. During the course of the seventeenth century, however, it became less plausible to demand that scientific knowledge must satisfy the requirements of Aristotelian demonstrations, and it became correspondingly implausible to defend religious beliefs simply because they were not shown to be inconsistent with demonstrations.

This became especially clear to writers, such as Boyle, who understood the hypothetical and uncertain character of most knowledge-claims. Boyle argued in *Advices in Judging of Things said to Transcend Reason* (1681), that 'there are many Truths, such as Historical and Political ones, that by the nature of the things are not capable of Mathematical or Metaphysical Demonstrations, and yet being really Truths, have a just Title to our Assent' (B IX: 398). Once the demand for demonstration is relaxed, one may ask what evidence, if any, is required to make a belief reasonable. Boyle replied to that question: ''tis not reasonable to give assent to any thing as a Truth but upon a sufficient Reason of that Assent' (B IX: 397), although he did not explain what was meant by 'sufficient'. However, his extended writing on this issue helped to clarify the position that is summarized in Locke's discussion in the *Essay.*

If there are truths that are known by the use of our natural cognitive faculties, it is impossible for a revealed truth to conflict with them; therefore, an apparent conflict is a clear sign that we have misinterpreted an apparent revelation. However, assuming that an alleged revelation is consistent with what is otherwise known, even if 'known' is redefined as 'believed on the basis of probable reasons', the question remains about whether one has sufficiently probable reasons to accept that God had revealed what was subsequently attributed to him. Those who supported Locke's position claimed that one first required persuasive reasons to accept that something was revealed (and therefore worthy of religious faith). Those who dissented accepted that it was reasonable (i) merely to believe that some proposition had been revealed, and then (ii) to believe the proposition itself on the basis of what is believed to have been its inspired origin. Evidently, this is no longer a case of believing someone whom one *knows* is a credible witness, which is what was assumed in the analogy used by Hobbes; it involves *believing* that there was a credible witness whose credentials cannot be examined, and that there has been a long line of credible transmitters of a doctrine, who also escape any critical examination by the believer.

However, even this further relaxation of the epistemic demands on faith assumed that any proposition proposed for belief must be intelligible. The latter issue arose especially in respect of so-called mysteries.

# IV: Mysteries

When Descartes claimed that it was possible to have true knowledge of the existence of God, he added immediately: 'we lack knowledge of the Persons of the Holy Trinity, since the latter can be perceived only by a mind which faith has illuminated' (AT VII 443; CSM II 299). In other words, 'some things [that] are believed through faith alone—such as the mystery of the Incarnation, the Trinity, and the like' (AT VIII-2 353; CSM I 300). The question raised by critics such as John Toland, in *Christianity not Mysterious* (1696), was whether it is even possible to believe a proposition that is not understood at all, and whether 'mystery' should therefore be redefined within Christianity so as to exclude propositions or doctrines that are conceptually beyond our grasp. The initial problem, then, both for critics and defenders of religious mysteries, was to define more clearly the scope of the term 'mystery'.

Bayle had astutely remarked, in his *Dictionary*, that Catholic and Protestant theologians agreed about the transcendence of religious mysteries: 'The Roman Catholics and Protestants fight it out upon abundance of articles of religion, but they perfectly agree on this point, that the mysteries of the Gospel transcend reason . . . The conclusion from this is, that the mysteries of the Gospel . . . neither can nor ought to be submitted to the rules of natural reason' (Bayle 1710: I, lvi). Bayle acknowledged that mysteries could transcend our reason either by being inconsistent with it (which was discussed in Section III) or simply by being incomprehensible. The focus in this section is on the epistemic status of so-called mysteries in the second sense, that is as propositions that cannot be understood.

Boyle had also addressed this issue in *A Discourse of things above Reason* (1681), in which he was careful to distinguish various kinds of 'things' that we cannot understand (B IX: 366–7, 386–7). Boyle's list of what he called the *Incomprehensible*, the *Inexplicable*, and the *Unsociable* included realities that we fail to understand—though we are certain of their existence—or conclusions we infer validly from known propositions but cannot reconcile with others that are known. None of these were comparable to the epistemic objections to so-called mysteries; in the latter cases, it was not simply a matter of failing to understand some phenomenon, which was and remains a familiar experience for natural philosophers, but of being invited to assent to a proposition that is not (adequately) understood.

Descartes addressed this question in the context of proving God's existence, when he argued: 'If one has no idea, that is no perception which corresponds to the meaning of the word "God", it is no use saying that one believes that *God* exists. One might as well say that one believes that *nothing* exists, thus remaining in the abyss of impiety and the depths of ignorance' (AT IX-1 210; CSM II 273). At the same time, Descartes repeated a traditional thesis about the limited ability of human intellects to comprehend God, which anticipated the point made later by Boyle about the limited scope of human reason.

I know that my intellect is finite and God's power is infinite, and so I set no limits to it; I consider only what I am capable of perceiving, and what not, and I take great pains that my judgment should accord with my perception. And so I boldly assert that God can do everything which I perceive to be possible, but I am not so bold as to assert the converse, namely, that he cannot do what conflicts with my conception of things—I merely say that it involves a contradiction.   (AT V 272; CSMK 363)

Any consistent reading of these texts implies that a limited understanding of its meaning is a precondition of assenting to any proposition, and that it is impossible to assent to judgements that express what seem impossible to us. Much of the debate about mysteries was concerned, therefore, with setting the minimum degree of understanding required to express a credible proposition.

Toland borrowed substantially from Locke's theory of meaning in the *Essay*, according to which words are meaningful only for language-users who have the corresponding ideas (Ott 2004). This set an appropriately low threshold for the degree of understanding required for belief. Toland acknowledged that we cannot fully understand the nature even of material things. Hence, 'nothing can be said to be a mystery, because we have not an adequate idea of it' (Toland 1978: 75), since even in the case of physical bodies we know 'nothing of bodies but their properties' (Toland 1978: 76); an inadequate understanding of things would be sufficient to make belief or judgement possible. Without specifying the threshold where belief becomes impossible, Toland argued that, if we have no concept at all of what we are invited to believe, then belief is impossible.

Now since by revelation men are not endu'd with any new faculties, it follows that God should lose his end in speaking to them, if what he said did not agree with their common notions. Could that person justly value himself upon being wiser than his neighbours, who having infallible assurance that something called *Blictri* had a being in nature, in the mean time knew not what this *Blictri* was?   (Toland 1978: 133)

Thus, if God were to propose to us, directly or indirectly, something to be accepted on faith, he would have to communicate it in terms that we understand, that is by using words that correspond to our ideas. This does not set limits to God's nature or to what may be the case in creation, but to what is possible for human beings to believe.

Without such an understanding, the only option is that discussed by Hobbes in *De Cive*, when he distinguished between (i) believing some proposition (which includes internal assent to its truth, and therefore presupposes understanding) and (ii) merely expressing publicly that a given proposition is true, which he calls 'profession'. 'By what hath been said the difference appears, first, between *faith* and profession; for that is always joined with inward assent; this not always. That is an inward persuasion of the mind, this an outward obedience' (HW II, 305). Mere profession without inward assent may be motivated by fear, obedience, or respect (HW II, 203). It need not involve understanding what is professed (Hobbes 1991: 49); nor does it imply accepting the truth of what is professed, as in the case of Jansenists who were forced publicly to abjure their theology of grace. This kind of profession is such, therefore, that it need not raise any questions for the professing person of consistency or otherwise with their other beliefs. It raises the possibility that one could profess belief even in meaningless propositions.

John Cameron, one of Amyraut's colleagues at the college of Saumur, objected to the suggestion that religious faith might be understood in that way. Cameron developed a theory about the metaphorical or spiritual interpretation of St John's gospel (VI: 53), in which Christ is reported as teaching that those who eat his body and drink his blood would be rewarded with eternal life. Cameron argued that this text required Christians, not simply to profess blind belief in some proposition, but to do certain things such as 'eating his body' in some sense. Cameron accepts that we do not understand how God created the world; however, that does not compromise our salvation because we are not expected to create anything. Nor are we required to understand the Trinity (Cameron 1663: 91–2). However, we do need to know what is required by the command to 'eat' the body of Christ, since it is impossible to obey a command without understanding it, and the kind of 'eating' involved must be spiritual, since the nourishment required for a life in union with God is also spiritual (1663: 74). The conclusion is that Christian beliefs that require corresponding actions must be understood sufficiently to determine the required action.

The apparent mystery in many Christian beliefs, according to Toland, derived from the scholastic language in which they were expressed rather than from the original teaching of the Scriptures: 'the grossest mistakes and whimsies of the Fathers... have been occasioned by the several systems of philosophy they read before their conversion' to Christianity. He claimed that the 'uncorrupted doctrines of Christianity' are not above the comprehension of ordinary believers, who fail to understand 'the gibberish of your divinity schools' (Toland 1978: 126, 147). One response to this diagnosis, therefore, was to simplify the content of what Christians were required to believe and to filter out unintelligible doctrines that originate in philosophical or theological systems.

Hobbes had given a clear lead in this direction in *Leviathan*: 'The... Onely Article of Faith, which the Scripture maketh simply Necessary to Salvation, is this, that JESUS IS THE CHRIST' (Hobbes 1991: 407). Locke, in *The Reasonableness of Christianity*, argued for similar reasons that the fundamental articles of Christianity had been preached originally to an uneducated people, and that the core beliefs of Christianity should therefore be understood in the language and context in which they were originally taught. The Scriptures were

a Collection of Writings designed by God for the Instruction of the illiterate bulk of Mankind in the way to Salvation; and therefore generally and in necessary points to be understood in the plain direct meaning of the words and phrases, such as they may be supposed to have had in the mouths of the Speakers, who used them according to the Language of that Time and Country wherein they lived, without such learned, artificial, and forced senses of them, as are sought out, and put upon them in most of the Systems of Divinity... (Locke 1999: 6).

Locke also restricted his search for what he called 'the Fundamental Articles of the Faith' (Locke 2002: 215) to the gospels and the Acts, because the Epistles sent to various churches in the first century AD were intended for people who were already Christians and were therefore already in possession of the core beliefs of the church. His analysis concluded that there is only one core Christian belief, which is very similar to that identified by Hobbes: 'all that is to be believed for Justification, was no more but this single Proposition: that *Jesus of* Nazareth *was the Christ, or the Messiah*' (Locke 1999: 33; Nuovo 2003: 132–7).

This approach to the mysteries of Christianity was widely understood by critics as a reduction of religious faith to a purely natural religion, and its proponents were called variously Socinians, Unitarians, or even atheists. Defenders of more comprehensive creeds, which included belief in the Incarnation and the Trinity, required a correspondingly inclusive account of the intelligibility of the language in which they expressed their beliefs.

# V: Speaking of God

Berkeley addressed this issue, in a controversy with other bishops of the Church of Ireland. The Bishop of Cloyne argued that we do not have an 'idea' of ourselves as mental substances because ideas are the passive objects of perception, whereas our minds are the active subjects that perceive them; nonetheless, we have an awareness of our thinking that may be called a 'notion'. All the terms that refer to this active thinking agent, such as 'I', acquired their meaning simply by denoting that reality, as names of a perceiving subject. However, Berkeley quickly converted this 'notion' of an inner, active experience to a concept of an immaterial substance, although this apparently smooth transition faced a number of objections.

One objection is that Berkeley could have used any conventional symbol he wished to designate the experience of thinking. For example, he could have borrowed a word from the local people to whom he ministered in Cloyne and called it a '*smaoineamh*'. Evidently, for those who do not speak this language, such a name would have no conceptual relations with other familiar words in English; it would function merely to denote, as a rigid designator, the experience of thinking. If Berkeley were subsequently to go beyond a simple naming ceremony along these lines, by exploiting words that are already equipped with a rich conceptual history and many implicit connotations, he would beg the fundamental question about the kind of reality to which his self-reflection provided access. In other words, Berkeley was not entitled to name his experience 'the activity of an immaterial substance' until the latter terms had acquired a meaning, as names, in the only way available to his nominalist theory of language.

To address that issue, he could have classified various properties as 'material' because they are found to co-exist with experiences that he had named material, and he could have then defined 'immaterial' in contrast with 'material'. However, this risked incurring the objection raised by one of Descartes' Jesuit critics, Pierre Bourdin. Bourdin objected that one cannot legitimately classify some property as immaterial unless (i) one knows all the properties of material things, and (ii) knows that a given property is not one of those. Otherwise one argues like a peasant who is familiar with only four kinds of animal and, when presented with a novel animal, concludes: 'It is not an ox, or a horse, or a goat, or a donkey. And so . . . it is not an animal; and hence it is a non-animal' (AT VII 497; CSM II 337). Berkeley could have concluded validly that the experience of thinking displays properties that are not found in other familiar material things, such as (in his taxonomy) ideas of flowers, trees, clouds, etc. and, in that sense only, it is not similar to many material things.

However, even this solution raised another objection that had been raised by Boyle in the *Christian Virtuoso* Part II, where he argued that 'immaterial' is not a name of something with which we are acquainted, but of something that, by definition or otherwise, we do not know.

For though superficial considerers take up with the vulgar definition, that a *spirit is an immaterial substance*, yet that leaves us exceedingly to seek, if we aim at satisfaction in particular inquiries. For it declares rather what the thing is *not*, than what it is; and is as little instructive a definition, as it would be to say, that a *curve line is not a strait line*, which sure will never teach us what is an ellipse, a parabola, an hyperbola, a circle, or a spiral line, *etc.* (B: xii, 474)

These objections from Boyle and Bourdin imply that, while we know some of the properties of material things, we cannot conclude that a phenomenon that fails to display all those properties is immaterial. Second, even if we could do so, we would still know nothing of the reality in question apart from what properties it does *not* have. Hobbes drew the conclusion that, by speaking in this way, we fail to make any sense. 'And therefore if a man should talk to me of . . . *Immateriall Substances* . . . I should not say he were in an Errour; but that his words were without meaning; that is to say. Absurd' (Hobbes 1991: 34).

Despite the objections to which this kind of nominalism is subject, Berkeley adopted such a theory of meaning as his default account in his early works. Since we have no direct experience of God, in the way in which we have perceptions of colours, shapes, etc., he had to extend the capacity of language if he wished to accommodate the realities that Christians talked about. Having assumed that we have a 'notion' of ourselves as a thinking agent and, counterfactually, that no questions were begged by describing the subject of such thinking activities as an immaterial substance, Berkeley argued that we can acquire a notion of God as an infinite immaterial substance simply by denying the limitations that characterize human thinking. 'For all the notion I have of God is obtained by reflection on my own soul, heightening its powers, and removing its imperfections. I have therefore, though not an inactive idea, yet in myself some sort of an active thinking image of the Deity' (BW II: 231–32).

He furthermore claimed that, in this transition from naming our experience of thinking to talking about God, words are applied literally and univocally to God and to the subject of human thinking. This was an attempt to protect traditional Christian teachings against Toland, who argued that religious propositions were meaningful only if they signified ideas that are already available to us from experience, and against two of Berkeley's contemporary bishops in the Church of Ireland, William King and Peter Browne, whom Berkeley accused of emasculating religious language by relying on a theory of analogy.

King had defended a familiar version of the scholastic view that human concepts are inadequate to comprehend the infinite reality of God, and that we can talk meaningfully about God only by using analogically concepts that acquire their primary meaning when applied to realities that fall within the scope of our under-standing. 'The nature of God considered in it self, is in effect agreed on all hands to be incomprehensible by humane understanding; and not only his nature, but likewise his powers and faculties . . . are so far beyond our reach, that we are utterly incapable of framing exact and adequate notions of them' (King 1727: 33). For example, King assumed as obvious that we cannot attribute human passions literally to God (1727: 36), and that God 'is the object of none of our senses, whereby we receive all our direct and immediate perception of things' (1727: 41). He concluded: 'This *analogical knowledge* of God's nature and attributes is all we are capable of at present, and we must either be contented to know him thus, or sit down with an intire ignorance and neglect of God, and finally despair of future happiness' (King 1727: 48).

In response to this view, Berkeley expanded his theory of language, in *Alciphron*, and proposed a supplementary account of how talk about mysteries could be meaningful. He continued to defend the application to God in a literal sense of predicates that are usually applied to human agents; otherwise, our talk of God would be in danger of becoming empty, like talk about a material substance of which nothing is known or can be said:

for he who comes to God . . . must first believe that there is a God in some intelligible sense, and not only that there is something in general, without any proper notion, though never so inadequate, of any of its qualities or attributes. . . . Nor will it avail to say there is something in this unknown being analogous to knowledge and goodness . . . For this is in fact to give up the point in dispute between theists and atheists . . .    (BW III 164–5)

In addition to applying some terms literally to God, Berkeley claimed that Chris-tian language about mysteries may also be meaningful without signifying corresponding ideas in the mind, merely by cultivating dispositions in listeners or by motivating them to certain kinds of action:

having granted that those signs may be significant, though they should not suggest ideas represented by them, provided they serve to regulate and influence our wills, passions, or conduct, you have consequently granted that the mind of man may assent to propositions containing such terms, when it is so directed or affected by them, notwithstanding it should not perceive distinct ideas marked by those terms. Whence it seems to follow that a man may believe the doctrine of the Trinity...although he doth not frame in his mind any abstract or distinct ideas of trinity, substance, or personality;...    (BW III 296–7)

It is difficult to avoid the conclusion that Berkeley misunderstood the scholastic language of analogy, and that he equated it too readily with the ruse of free-thinkers who emptied familiar words of all meaning before using them in religious propositions. Browne commented: 'How little this author understands the doctrine of divine analogy, which he is all along not confuting but reviling' (Browne 1733: 399). However, it is equally difficult to understand how hearing the word 'Trinity' could inspire a Christian to any appropriate act or disposition if it communicated no specific ideas at all. In other words, religious terms may carry an emotive meaning, in Berkeley's sense, only if they also had some prior cognitive meaning. Bishop Browne expressed this objection forcefully in his response to *Alciphron*:

You may profess indeed to believe in *Father*, *Son*, and *Spirit*; in the *Grace* of God; and in the *Mediation* and *Intercession* of Christ; but yet it is not always *necessary* or *possible* for you to acquire, or exhibit to your mind, any *ideas*, conceptions or notions of the things marked out by those words; tho' by this rule you may as well be said to have faith in the noise of sounding brass or a tinkling cymbal. Nay your believing a God would be very useful; tho' upon his scheme it may be no more than faith in a monosyllable....The *end* of assent indeed is not the imparting or acquiring ideas, conceptions or notions; but surely some of these must necessarily be acquired or exhibited to the mind for the *object* of our assent; otherwise it would be just such another useful assent as one *parrot* may yield to another. (Browne 1733: 539–40)

As King and Browne urged, the meaningfulness or otherwise of all the core beliefs of Christianity depends on one's account of talk about God. If the latter fails, it is difficult to speak meaningfully about grace and salvation, and even to explain the meaning of the Hobbesian profession that 'Jesus is the Messiah'.

# CONCLUSION

When Christians were presented with sets of propositions, in the form of creeds, they were expected not simply to 'profess' them, in Hobbes's sense of that term, but to assent to them as true. These creeds included doctrines that were believed to have been taught in person by Jesus of Nazareth to his disciples and to have been 'divinely inspired'; they were recorded in documents that were passed on from one generation to the next. The alleged divinity of Jesus was supported by miracles, an issue that is not discussed here. Some of the related issues that were debated in the early modern period included: (i) whether an individual's belief results from a free decision, or whether it is a spontaneous response to the evidence presented, almost as we believe facts that we experience without deciding to assent to them (Passmore 2000); and (ii) whether assenting to proposed beliefs is subject to moral or ethical constraints, including an obligation not to believe what is otherwise unsupported by evidence (Wolsterstorff 1994).

However, the most prominent feature of Christian creeds in the early modern period was their plurality and mutual inconsistency. Efforts to address this issue focused on the capacity of our natural cognitive faculties to limit the scope of faith and to establish the authenticity and meaning of documents that were said to have been 'inspired' by God. Critics of religious mysteries challenged the very possibility of giving an internal assent to propositions that are inadequately understood.

Despite these challenges, many commentators repeated the commonplace that the certainty of religious beliefs exceeds the certainty provided by other kinds of evidence, because the authority and trustworthiness of the source (God) is indubitable. However, as Locke pointed out, any doubt about the authenticity or interpretation of what is proposed for belief undermines the apparent indubitability of its source. Since the testimony of 'God himself . . . carries with it Assurance beyond Doubt, Evidence beyond Exception' we may as well doubt our own existence as doubt whether 'any Revelation from GOD be true'; nonetheless 'our Assent can be rationally no higher than the Evidence of its being a Revelation, and that this is the meaning of the Expressions it is delivered in' (*Essay* IV. xvii. 14). In other words, the probability of any religious belief depends on the probability that it was revealed by God, and that it has been correctly interpreted. The proliferation of inconsistent creeds by a wide range of churches, each of which was 'Orthodox to it self' (Locke 1983: 32), provided many reasons to doubt both the source and the interpretation of doctrines that were presented as if they were indubitable. These issues remain equally unresolved today.

# REFERENCES

AMYRAUT, M. (1641). *De l'élévation de la foy et l'abaissement de la raison en la créance des mystères de la Religion.* Saumur: Jean Lesnier.

ANON. (Six Jesuit Fathers) (1596). *Ratio atque Institutio Studiorum.* Rome.

ANSTEY, P. R. (2003). *The Philosophy of John Locke.* London and New York: Routledge.

ARIÈS, P., et al. (1986). *Histoire de la vie privée*. 3 vols. Paris: Editions de Seuil.

ARMOGATHE, J.-R. (1977). *Theologia cartesiana: l'explication physique de l'Eucharistie chez Descartes et Dom Desgabets*. The Hague: Nijhoff.

Augustine of Hippo (1894). *De genesi ad litteram libri duodecim*. Ed. J. Zycha. *Corpus Scriptorum Ecclesiasticorum*, vol. xxviii (Section iii, Part 1). Prague/Leipzig.

Augustine of Hippo (1982). *De Genesi ad litteram*. Trans. J. J. Taylor. New York: Newman House.

AYERS, M. (1991). *Locke: Epistemology and Ontology*. London and New York: Routledge.

BAYLE, P. (1710). *An Historical and Critical Dictionary by Monsieur Bayle, trans. into English, with many additions and corrections, made by the author himself, that are not in the French editions*. 4 vols. London.

BLACKWELL, R. J. (1991). *Galileo, Bellarmine, and the Bible*. Notre Dame, IN and London: University of Notre Dame Press.

BROWNE, P. (1733). *Things Divine and Supernatural Conceived by Analogy with Things Natural and Human*. London. Reprt. New York and London: Garland (1976).

CAMERON, J. (1663). *Sept sermons sur le VI chap. de l'évangile selon S. Jean*. Geneva.

DRAKE, S. (ed. and trans.) (1957). *Discoveries and Opinions of Galileo*. New York: Doubleday.

ÉLIE, R. [?] (1675). *Reflexions physiques sur la Transubstantiation & sur ce que Mr. Rohault en a écrit dans ses Entretiens*. La Rochelle.

FITZPATRICK, E. A. (1933). *St Ignatius and the Ratio Studiorum*. New York and London: McGraw-Hill.

GALILEI, G. (1967). *Dialogue Concerning the Two Chief World Systems—Ptolemaic & Copernican*, trans. Stillman Drake. 2nd edn. Berkeley and Los Angeles: University of California Press.

GROTIUS, H. (1814). *Six Books of Hugo Grotius on the Truth of Christianity and of the Two Supplementary books of Mr. Le Clerc*. Trans. S. Madam. London.

HÁJEK, A. (2008). 'Pascal's Wager'. *The Stanford Encyclopedia of Philosophy* (Fall 2008 Edition), E. N. Zalta (ed.), <http://plato.stanford.edu/archives/fall2008/entries/pascal-wager/>.

HERVEY, J. (1732). *Some Remarks on the Minute Philosopher*. London: J. Robinson.

HOBBES, T. (1991). *Leviathan* Ed. R. Tuck. Cambridge: Cambridge University Press.

HUNTER, M. and WOOTTON, D. (eds) (1992). *Atheism from the Reformation to the Enlightenment*. Oxford: Clarendon Press.

JOLLEY, N. (2003). 'Reason's dim Candle: Locke's critique of enthusiasm', in P. R. Anstey (ed.), *The Philosophy of John Locke*. London and New York: Routledge, 179–91.

JOLLEY, N. (2007). 'Locke on Faith and Reason', in L. Newman (ed.), *The Cambridge Companion to Locke's 'Essay Concerning Human Understanding'*. Cambridge: Cambridge University Press, 2007, 436–55.

KING, W. (1727). *Divine Predestination and Fore-Knowledge, consistent with the Freedom of Man's Will*. 3rd edn. Dublin: Gowan [1st edn. 1702].

LE CLERC, J. (1685). *Sentimens de quelques théologiens de Hollande sur l'Histoire critique du Vieux Testament*. Amsterdam: Henri Desbordes.

LE CLERC, J. (1690). *Five Letters Concerning the Inspiration of the Holy Scriptures*. London.

LOCKE, J. (1983). *A Letter Concerning Toleration*, ed. James H. Tully. Indianapolis, IN: Hackett [1st edn. 1689].

LOCKE, J. (1999). *The Reasonableness of Christianity as delivered in the Scriptures*. Ed. J. C. Higgins-Biddle. Oxford: Clarendon Press [1st edn. 1695].

LOCKE, J. (2002). *Writings on Religion.* Ed. V. Nuovo. Oxford: Clarendon Press.

McMULLIN, E. (ed.) (2005). *The Church and Galileo.* Notre Dame, IN: University of Notre Dame Press.

NUOVO, V. (2003). 'Locke's Christology as a key to understanding his philosophy', in P. R. Anstey (ed.), *The Philosophy of John Locke.* London and New York: Routledge, 129–53.

OTT, W. R. (2004). *Locke's Philosophy of Language.* Cambridge: Cambridge University Press.

PASCAL, B. (1995). *Pensées and Other Writings.* Trans. H. Levi. Oxford and NY: Oxford University Press.

PASCAL, B. (2000). *Oeuvres complètes.* Ed. M. le Guern. Paris: Gallimard.

PASSMORE, J. (2000). 'Locke and the Ethics of Belief', in G. Fuller, R. Stecker, and John P. Wright (eds), *John Locke: An Essay Concerning Human Understanding in Focus.* London and New York: Routledge, 187–209.

POPKIN, R. H. (1960). *The History of Scepticism from Erasmus to Descartes.* Rev. edn. Assen: Van Gorcum.

POPKIN, R. H. (1992). 'Jewish anti-Christian Arguments as a Source of Irreligion from the Seventeenth to the Early Nineteenth Century', in M. Hunter and D. Wootton (eds), *Atheism from the Reformation to the Enlightenment.* Oxford: Clarendon Press, 159–81.

POULAIN DE LA BARRE, F. (1720). *Le Doctrine des Protestants sur la liberté de lire l'Ecriture Sainte, le service divin en langue entendue, l'invocation des saints, le sacrement de l'eucharistie. Justifiée par le Misssel Romain & par des Réfléxions sur chaque point. Avec un commentaire philosophique sur ces paroles de Jesus-Christ, Ceci est mon Corps; Ceci est mon Sang, Matth. Chap xxvi, v. 26.* Geneva: Fabri & Barrillot.

POULAIN DE LA BARRE, F. (1990). *The Equality of the Sexes.* Trans. D. M. Clarke. Manchester: Manchester University Press.

ROHAULT, J. (1978). *Entretiens sur la philosophie,* ed. P. Clair. Paris: Centre national de la recherche scientifique.

SCHOOCK, M. (1643). *Admiranda Methodus Novae Philosophiae Renati Des Cartes.* Utrecht: J. van Waesberge.

SIMON, R. (1687). *De l'Inspiration des Livres Sacrés: avec une Réponse au livre intitulé, Défense des Sentimens de quelques théologiens de Hollande sur l'Histoire Critique du Vieux Testament.* Rotterdam: Reinier Leers.

SIMON, R. (1689). *A Critical History of the Text of the New Testament: A Critical History of the Versions of the New Testament.* London: Taylor.

STEINMANN, J. (1960). *Richard Simon et les origines de l'exégèse biblique.* Paris: Declée de Brouwer.

TANNER, N. P. (ed.) (1990). *Decrees of the Ecumenical Councils.* 2 vols. London and Washington, DC: Sheed and Ward/ Georgetown University Press.

TOLAND, J. (1978). *Christianity not Mysterious: or, A Treatise shewing, That there is nothing in the Gospel Contrary to Reason, nor above it; And that no Christian Doctrine can be properly call'd a Mystery.* New York: Garland [1st edn. 1696].

WILSON, P. H. (2009). *Europe's Tragedy: A History of the Thirty Years War.* London: Allen Lane.

WOLTERSTORFF, N. (1994). 'Locke's Philosophy of Religion', in V. Chappell (ed.), *The Cambridge Companion to Locke.* Cambridge: Cambridge University Press, 172–98.

WOLSTERSTORFF, N. (1996). *John Locke and the Ethics of Belief.* Cambridge: Cambridge University Press.

# CHAPTER 26

## RELIGIOUS TOLERATION

### PHILIP MILTON

EARLY modern Europe saw a slow growth in religious toleration, though the process was uneven, fitful, and very far from complete. The reasons for this were complex, and it seems likely that philosophical arguments played a relatively small part, at least in the shorter term. In the longer term they may have proved more influential, and it is therefore worth examining some of them in more detail. Four important philosophers will be considered here: Hobbes, Spinoza, Locke, and Bayle.

## I: HOBBES AND SPINOZA

On the face of it Hobbes may seem an unlikely proponent of religious toleration. In his earlier writings he left a vestige of ecclesiastical independence, but in *Leviathan* he demanded a complete and unconditional subordination of ecclesiastical authority to the civil power. All churches must be authorized by the civil power, and any assembly meeting without such warrant is unlawful (*Lev* 248; Hobbes 1682: 71). In all commonwealths the sovereign is the supreme pastor and has the right to administer the sacraments, consecrate churches, ordain the clergy, determine the canon and the interpretation of scripture, and so on (*Lev* 199, 205–6, 295–9, 300, 323).

The sovereign may, of course, delegate these rights to the clergy, but if he does so they act on his authority, not on their own.

Hobbes made it quite clear that these rights are not the special preserve of Christian rulers. It is the law of nature, not the Bible, that makes every sovereign the supreme pastor (*Lev* 248, 295, 299, 323). Similarly, it is a principle of natural reason that there should be one uniform public worship (*Lev* 192). This applies in all cases, even where the sovereign is not a Christian and seeks to impose non-Christian forms of worship on Christian subjects. Hobbes knew this would be unacceptable, but he tried to justify his stance by appealing to the biblical story of Naaman, who accompanied his master to the house of Rimmon even though he himself acknowledged no God but the God of Israel (2 Kings 5: 15–19). Christian subjects of an infidel sovereign are similarly placed: 'They have the licence that Naaman had, and need not put themselves into danger for it' (*Lev* 271, 331; Hobbes 1682: 48).

It is evident from this and from other remarks that Hobbes had no qualms about requiring people to conform publicly to a religion they did not inwardly believe. 'A private man', he wrote, 'has alwaies the liberty, (because thought is free,) to beleeve, or not beleeve in his heart, those acts that have been given out for Miracles. . . . But when it comes to the confession of that faith, the Private Reason must submit to the Publique' (*Lev* 238). He did, however, limit this submission to external actions, because 'internall Faith is in its own nature invisible, and consequently exempted from all humane jurisdiction' (*Lev* 285).

One reason why Hobbes insisted so strongly on this was that his own beliefs were far removed from Christian orthodoxy. He regarded religion in general as a purely natural phenomenon, the product of ignorance and fear of invisible powers (*Lev* 52–4), and he made it quite clear that the difference between it and superstition was political: '*Feare* of power invisible, feigned by the mind, or imagined from tales publiquely allowed, Religion; not allowed, Superstition' (*Lev* 26). Although he may perhaps have retained some kind of belief in God, his insistence that God, like everything else, is corporeal (Hobbes 1682: 31, 40, 69, 130–1) leaves one wondering what kind of deity he could have had in mind. So too does his statement that 'because the Universe is All, that which is no part of it, is *Nothing*, and consequently *no where*' (*Lev* 371). This means, he subsequently explained, that God is 'either the whole Universe, or part of it' (Hobbes 1682: 86), though he did not indicate which of these he had in mind.

What is clear is that he thought that very little could be known or truthfully said about God. In his unpublished critique of Thomas White he stated that all that can be known about God is that he exists and that 'Everything else . . . pertains not to the explanation of philosophical truth, but to proclaiming the states of mind that govern our wish to praise, magnify and honour God . . . [and] are rather oblations than propositions' (Hobbes 1976: 434). A similar account can be found in *Leviathan*: 'the Attributes which we give to God, we are not to consider the signification of Philosophicall Truth; but the signification of pious Intention' (*Lev* 191).

This essentially non-cognitive view of religion leads to a complete separation between it and philosophy. On this Hobbes was explicit. In the dedication to *De Corpore* he explained that it was essential 'to distinguish between the Rules of Religion, that is, the Rules of Honoring God, which we have from the Laws, and the Rules of Philosophy, that is, the Opinions of private men; and to yeild what is due to Religion to the Holy Scripture, and what is due to Philosophy to Natural Reason' (Hobbes 1656: sig. B2). Where Holy Scripture was concerned, he left attentive readers in little doubt that he was himself unpersuaded by claims that it was divinely inspired. It is, he wrote, 'evidently impossible' to see 'how a man can be assured of the Revelation of another, without a Revelation particularly to himselfe': the most we can have is 'a firmer, or a weaker belief' (*Lev* 148, 149). Such beliefs, he thought, were very weak indeed: 'if a man pretend to me, that God hath spoken to him supernaturally, and immediately, and I make doubt of it, I cannot easily perceive what argument he can produce, to oblige me to beleeve it. It is true, that if he be my Soveraign, he may oblige me to obedience, so, as not by act or word to declare I beleeve him not; but not to think any otherwise then my reason perswades me' (*Lev* 196).

Much of the second half of *Leviathan* was taken up with constructing a revised version of Christianity that would, Hobbes thought, be conducive to the maintenance of civil peace and order—always for him the primary consideration. This meant discarding divisive and contentious doctrines, and Hobbes sought to reduce Christianity to one single article: 'The (*Unum Necessarium*) Onely Article of Faith, which the Scripture maketh simply Necessary to Salvation, is this, that JESUS IS THE CHRIST' (*Lev* 324). Since no Christian ruler was likely to require his subjects to deny this, they could obey him in all other matters without placing their salvation in jeopardy. Christian subjects of non-Christian rulers could either follow the practice of Naaman, as Hobbes recommended, or 'expect their reward in Heaven' (*Lev* 331; cf. *Lev* 362).

When it came to church government, Hobbes was pulled in different directions. In the final chapter of *Leviathan* he described with evident satisfaction how after the Reformation the power of the clergy had been dismantled stage by stage, so that 'we are reduced to the Independency of the Primitive Christians to follow Paul, or Cephas, or Apollos, every man as he liketh best: Which, if it be without contention . . . is perhaps the best' (*Lev* 385). This should not be taken as an endorsement of Independency or religious toleration. Although Hobbes greatly preferred the Independents to the Presbyterians, whose clergy he regarded (along with the Catholics) as the authors of the Kingdom of Darkness (*Lev* 382), it is hard to find in his writings any support for their fundamental tenet—the right of individual congregations to choose ministers and determine forms of worship for themselves. It is even harder to see him attending conventicles or joining in extempore prayer with those claiming immediate inspiration from the Holy Spirit. Despite his undoubted anticlericalism and probable unbelief, there is little reason to doubt his remark, made when he thought he was on his death-bed, that 'he liked the religion of the church of England best of all other' (Aubrey 1898: i. 353). After his return to England in 1651 he found, according to his prose autobiography, 'that the Church, as governed by the Assembly, was full of sedition' and he described how he sought and eventually found a church 'where the pastor was a good and learned man, who administered the Lord's Supper in accordance with the rites of the Church [of England]' (Hobbes 1994: 249).

One reason why Hobbes was anxious to make such claims was that in the late 1660s he became convinced that the bishops were planning to have him burnt as a heretic. There was little if any likelihood of this—very few heretics had been burned in Protestant England, the last in 1612—but Hobbes, who was always inclined to believe the worst of the clergy, was sufficiently alarmed to write a number of works arguing that the offence of heresy had been abolished, and that in any case his writings, *Leviathan* especially, were not heretical. These works shed considerable light on his religious views, but they were not concerned with the general question of religious toleration. On this his opinion remained as before: people should conform outwardly to whatever form of religion was required by the civil authorities but should be allowed to keep their private opinions to themselves.

Hobbes is not an easy writer to assess, mainly because he could not afford to be entirely candid, especially on matters to do with religion. One of his French friends, J.-B. Lantin, mentioned how 'He used to say that he sometimes made openings, but could not reveal his thoughts more than half-way; he said he imitated people who open the window for a few moments, but then close it again immediately for fear of the storm' (quoted Malcolm 2002: 542). When, as a very old man, he read Spinoza's *Tractatus Theologico-Politicus*, he told Aubrey that Spinoza 'had out throwne him a barres length, for he durst not write so boldly' (Bodleian Library, MS Aubrey 9, fo. 7). This was a shrewd judgement: if Hobbes wrote boldly, Spinoza did so more boldly still.

In a letter written in 1665, shortly after he began working on the *Tractatus Theologico-Politicus*, Spinoza explained that he was writing to combat the prejudices of the theologians, to rebut the complaints of the common people, who had accused him of atheism, and to vindicate the freedom of philosophizing (Spinoza 1928: 206). By the prejudices of the theologians he meant any kind of supernatural religion, any religion in which God is conceived of as a creator separate from his creation. His primary aim was to defend the freedom to philosophize, and he sought to create the kind of society which would allow him and other like-minded persons to discuss and express their philosophical opinions without being hindered by the civil or ecclesiastical authorities, especially the latter.

Spinoza sought to achieve this not by subordinating faith to philosophy but by making a complete separation between them (Spinoza 2007: 179, 188, 190, 194). This was possible, he explained, because they have wholly different aims: 'the aim of philosophy is nothing but truth, but the aim of faith . . . is simply obedience and piety' (Spinoza 2007: 184). Like Hobbes, but more explicitly, he adopted an essentially non-cognitive view of religion, in which faith is of purely instrumental value. He was quite open about this: 'faith requires not so much true as pious dogmas, that is, such tenets as move the mind to obedience, even though many of these may not have a shadow of truth in them. What matters is that the person who embraces them does not realize that they are false' (Spinoza 2007: 181).

In some respects these pious dogmas resemble the Noble Lies in Plato's *Republic*, though with one very important difference. Plato required, in the interest of maintaining social unity, that the Guardians should believe their own stories. Spinoza did not. The free man, his ideal, must clear his mind of falsehood and illusion and see things as they really are. Among the errors to be discarded is any belief in providence or the miraculous, or in God as 'omniscient, compassionate, wise, etc.' (SC 89). Spinoza's God was exceedingly unlike the God of Abraham, Isaac, and Jacob. 'God', he wrote, 'is described as a legislator or a prince, and as just, merciful etc., only because of the limited understanding of the common people and their lack of knowledge' (Spinoza 2007: 64–5). It was for the common people that the scriptures had originally been written, and Spinoza candidly explained that believing in the biblical narratives was 'supremely necessary to ordinary people whose minds are not competent to perceive things clearly and distinctly' (Spinoza 2007: 77).

This disdain for the common people is a recurrent feature of the *Tractatus Theologico-Politicus* (Spinoza 2007: 3, 5, 7, 10, 13, 23, 78, 81, 82, 93, 97, 177, 210, 256). They were, Spinoza thought, obstinately credulous and superstitious, and since he considered it impossible to rid them of these vices, he hoped they would not even try to read his book as they would be sure to misunderstand it (Spinoza 2007: 12). Women, it may be noted, came even lower in his estimation. He poured scorn on those who implored divine assistance with 'womanish tears' (Spinoza 2007: 4), and his last remarks in the *Tractatus Politicus*, left unfinished at his death, were an explanation of how women were by nature 'necessarily inferior' to men and should be ruled by them (Spinoza 1958: 445).

Spinoza's own political preference was for some kind of republicanism. In the Dutch politics of his day he aligned himself with the De Witt brothers and the States party, and he was appalled when they were lynched by an Orangist mob in 1672. Nevertheless, his account of the state is quite as absolutist as anything to be found in Hobbes. In the *Tractatus Theologico-Politicus* he stated quite unambiguously that 'the sovereign power is bound by no law and everyone is bound to obey it in all things', that 'we are obliged to carry out absolutely all the commands of the sovereign power, however absurd they may be', and that 'No offence can be committed against subjects by sovereigns, since they are of right permitted to do all things' (Spinoza 2007: 200, 203). In the *Tractatus Politicus* he added that a citizen has 'no right to decide what is fair or unfair, moral or immoral', and that 'the will of the commonwealth must be taken for the will of all' (Spinoza 1958: 287). As in

Hobbes, the sovereign authorities must have complete control over all aspects of religion: 'No one has the right and power without their authority or consent, to administer sacred matters or choose ministers, or decide and establish the foundations and doctrines of a church, nor may they give judgements about morality and observance of piety, or excommunicate or receive anyone into the church, or care for the poor' (Spinoza 2007: 245).

What this might mean in practice can be seen from Spinoza's description of a model aristocratic commonwealth in the *Tractatus Politicus* (Spinoza 1958: 411). He insisted that all the patricians, the governing class, should adhere to the simple universal faith previously outlined in the *Tractatus Theologico-Politicus* (Spinoza 2007: 182–3). Given that the first principle of this was that 'God . . . is supremely just and merciful'—something which Spinoza did not himself believe—it is clear that this was a religion intended for others. The churches (*templa*) belonging to the state religion should, he explained, be large and magnificent, with only patricians or senators being permitted to officiate. It all sounds rather like Robespierre's cult of the Supreme Being. Anyone wishing to worship elsewhere—and this would include any form of Christian (or Jewish) worship—would find themselves being treated very differently. Although such believers would, at least in theory, be entitled to build as many churches as they wished, Spinoza insisted that these should be 'small, of fixed dimensions, and situated some distance apart'. Congregations would also be limited in size, and large ones forbidden. All this is reminiscent of the situation of Christians and Jews in traditional Islamic societies: they are tolerated provided they are sufficiently subservient and acknowledge their second-class status.

There is no room within Spinoza's system for religious believers (or anyone else) to claim that their rights have been violated by the sovereign power. He did not see a right as a liberty, as Hobbes had done, or as a claim entailing correlative obligations, but as a power: 'the natural right of each individual, extends as far as its power . . . and he has as much right against other things in nature as he has power and strength' (Spinoza 1958: 269). This means that the more power something has the more right it has, so that, to use his own example, when big fish eat smaller ones they do so by 'sovereign natural right' (Spinoza 2007: 195). Similar considerations apply to human relations with animals (*Ethics*, 4p37s1: SC 566). The same is true in politics. Because the right of the commonwealth is equated with its power, 'the more the commonwealth exceeds a citizen or subject in power, the less right he has' (Spinoza 1958: 285). Those who are completely powerless therefore have no right at all.

Spinoza occupies an ambiguous place in the history of religious toleration. What he valued most of all was *libertas philosophandi*, what Mill later called the liberty of thought and discussion. This was especially needed in matters to do with religion, where freedom was most under threat: 'the supreme right of thinking freely, about religion . . . belongs to each and every individual . . . [and] every individual will also possess the supreme right and authority to judge freely about religion and to explain it and interpret it for himself' (Spinoza 2007: 116). This freedom was not confined, as in Hobbes, to private thoughts. The individual, Spinoza wrote, 'may say and teach what he thinks without infringing the right and authority of the sovereign power, that is, without disturbing the stability of the state' (Spinoza 2007: 253). When it came to religious practice, including religious worship, he was far more restrictive. His fundamental principle was that 'religious worship and pious conduct must be accommodated to the peace and interests of the state and consequently must be determined by the sovereign authorities alone' (Spinoza 2007: 238). It is no injustice to say that what he valued most was not the freedom to practise religion so much as the freedom to think, say, write, and publish what one likes about it.

# II: LOCKE

Locke was a contemporary of Spinoza, though they never met or corresponded. Although he owned copies of both the *Tractatus Theologico-Politicus* and the *Opera Posthuma*, there is little if anything in his works to suggest they had much influence. In one of his replies to Stillingfleet he described Hobbes and Spinoza as 'justly decried Names' and claimed, probably truthfully, that he was 'not so well read' in either (Locke 1699: 422). He certainly differed profoundly from them in philosophy, politics, and (most of all) religion.

Even in 1660, when Locke still allowed the magistrate to impose forms of religious worship, he thought toleration was desirable in principle. 'I know not', he asked,

how much it might conduce to the peace and security of mankind if religion were banished the camp and forbid to take arms . . . if the believer and unbeliever could be content as Paul advises to live together, and use no other weapons to conquer each other's opinions but pity and persuasion, if men would suffer one another to go to heaven every one his one [own?] way, and not out of a fond conceit of themselves pretend to a greater knowledge and care of another's soul and eternal concernments than he himself.   (Locke 1967*b*: 161)

When he wrote this Locke was very doubtful whether such an ideal was practicable, but within a few years he came to think it was. The fundamental principle underlying all of his arguments for toleration from the 1667 *Essay concerning Toleration* onwards was clearly stated at the beginning of the *Epistola de Tolerantia*: 'I regard it as *necessary above all* to distinguish between the business of civil government and that of religion, and to mark the true bounds between the church and the commonwealth' (Locke 1968: 65, italics added; Locke 1997: 248).

Locke began by explaining what he took to be the proper business of civil government. Sometimes he wrote as if government was only needed to protect people from fraud and violence (Locke 2006: 269; Locke 1692: 62). On other occasions he described its aim in more general terms as providing 'preservation and peace', 'quiet and comfortable liveing', or 'civil peace and prosperity' (Locke 2006: 281–2, 304, 333). One such formulation can be found in the *Epistola*, where he stated that the government exists only for the preservation of civil goods, namely 'life, liberty, bodily health and freedom from pain, and the possession of outward things' (Locke 1968: 67). The essential thing is that these are all things to be enjoyed in this world.

Locke regarded civil government as essential because disputes will inevitably arise, and if these are not settled there will be a downward spiral of violence leading ultimately to something very much like the Hobbesian state of nature. The only way to avoid this, he explained, was 'by setting up a Judge on Earth, with Authority to determine all . . . Controversies' (Locke 1967a: 343). Hobbes would entirely have agreed, though he thought that this judge, the sovereign, must have authority to settle *all* controversies, including religious ones. Locke did not. He was, of course, perfectly well aware that seventeenth-century Europe was riven by bitter and intractable religious disputes—for which, like Hobbes, he was inclined to blame the clergy—but he did not think that it was necessary, or indeed legitimate, to create a judge to resolve them. God has not done so, and it is not for us to create a Hobbesian mortal god to act in his absence.

Locke was able to argue along these lines because he saw religion in general, and religious worship in particular, as an essentially private matter, a matter for each individual believer and the god he worships. '[T]he place time and manner of worshipping my god', he wrote, 'is a thing wholy between god and me' (Locke 2006: 272). 'Noe man', he noted in one of his commonplace books, 'has power to prescribe to an other what he should beleive or doe in order to the saveing his own soule, because it is only his owne private interest and concerns not another man' (Locke 2006: 388–9). This includes the magistrate, who has no authority to interfere in matters of religion which remain the private concern of individual believers (Locke 2006: 281, 304, 311–12, 389; Locke 1968: 67; Locke 1690: 17).

Locke did, of course, accept that individual believers will usually wish to join together to form churches or other religious societies, but he insisted that these are purely voluntary associations which everyone should be left free to join or leave as they wished. 'It is', he wrote in 1681 in his critique of Stillingfleet, 'part of my liberty as a Christian and as a man to choose of what Church or religious society I will be of, as most conducing to the salvation of my soul, of which I alone am judge, and over which the magistrate has no power at all' (King 1829: 356). No one is born a member of any church, and churches have no coercive powers over their own members, let alone over anyone else. Their only legitimate sanction is expulsion, and anyone is free to leave without suffering any penalty (Locke 1968: 73, 77, 81; Locke 2002: 75; Locke 2006: 328, 331, 389–90).

The inevitable consequence of this is a multiplicity of churches and other religious societies. This was a development Locke welcomed, so long as these societies were prepared to live in peace with one another. His 1688 paper 'Pacifick Christians' contains a set of principles for one such society (Locke 1997: 304–6), and one of his notebooks contains comments on what looks like an earlier venture along similar lines (Locke 2006: 403). Conversely, there is little if any room for an established church—certainly not for one which sought to maintain a monopoly by coercion. Although Locke remained, at least nominally, a member of the Church of England, his critique of Stillingfleet contains a very hostile account of established churches (Locke 2002: 75–8), and there is another disparaging reference to 'establish'd Sects under the specious Names of National Churches' in the *Third Letter for Toleration* (Locke 1692: 84). He also strongly objected to the use of religious tests for civil office, something he regarded as a prostitution of religion (Locke 1690: 11; Locke 1692: 174).

For Locke Christianity itself required the separation of church and state—an expression he did not himself use but which accurately reflects his intentions. He acknowledged that in the Old Testament there was a complete fusion of civil and religious authority, but he insisted that this was a special dispensation which applied to the Jews and to them alone. There is, he stated in the *Epistola*, 'absolutely no such thing under the Gospel as a Christian commonwealth (*respublica Christiana*)'. Christ, he added, 'introduced no new form of government, peculiar to his own people, nor did he arm any magistrate with a sword with which to force men into the faith or worship he prescribed for his people, or prevent them from practising another religion' (Locke 1968: 117).

Although Locke's arguments for toleration were not based on religious scepticism or religious indifference, he did place considerable stress on the limitations of the human understanding, especially in matters of religion. The existence of God was, he thought, demonstrable by natural reason (*Essay* IV. x. 1–6), but the particular tenets of the Christian (or any other) religion could only rest on faith—that is on a belief that God has revealed himself to particular persons (*Essay* IV. xviii. 2). Such beliefs may be true, but they cannot be certain and do not count as knowledge: 'For whatever is not capable of Demonstration (as such remote Matters of Fact are not) is not, unless it be self-evident, capable to produce Knowledg, how well-grounded and great soever the Assurance of Faith may be wherewith it is received; but Faith it is still and not Knowledg; Perswasion, and not Certainty' (Locke 1692: 3).

Locke readily acknowledged that in 'popular ways of talking' faith and knowledge were often muddled together, but he thought it essential that they should not be (Locke 1692: 3; Locke 1706: 250). He did so because he was convinced that those who overestimated the certainty of their own opinions were unduly inclined to impose them on others, something they would become less likely to do if they were better instructed (*Essay*: IV. xvi. 4; IV. xix. 2). It is therefore essential that people should learn to apportion their beliefs to the evidence for them, by 'not entertaining any Proposition with greater assurance than the Proofs it is built upon will warrant' (*Essay*: IV. xix. 1). In the *Conduct of the Understanding* Locke recommended that 'we should keep a perfect indifferency for all Opinions...and imbrace them according as Evidence, and that alone gives the attestation of Truth' (§33, Locke 1706: 101). This indifferency is, however, only possible if belief is to some extent voluntary. Locke thought it was. In Draft A of the *Essay concerning Human Understanding* he stated that 'Assent, Suspense, or dissent are often voluntary actions and doe depend on the will' (Locke 1990: 73), and he repeated this almost word-for-word in the published version (*Essay* IV. xx. 15). He did not, however, regard assent as purely voluntary: we cannot choose to believe anything we like. Knowledge, he wrote, is '*neither wholly necessary, nor wholly voluntary...* all that is *voluntary* in our Knowledge, is the *employing*, or with-holding any of *our Faculties*' (*Essay* IV. xiii. 1–2). The same is true of belief.

In his writings on toleration Locke placed rather more stress on the involuntary aspects of belief. In the *Essay concerning Toleration* he argued that the magistrate cannot have a power to impose belief because no one can legitimately demand the impossible, and 'a man cannot command his owne understanding...which can no more apprehend things otherwise then they appear to it, then the eye see other colours then it doth in the rainbow' (Locke 2006: 272). Belief is treated here as an involuntary response, akin to perception. Similar remarks appear in his later writings. In a commonplace book entry dated 1679 he remarked that 'noe compulsion can make a man beleive against his present light and perswasion' (Locke 2006: 389), and in the *Epistola* he stated simply that 'To believe this or that to be true is not within the scope of our will' (Locke 1968: 121). Coercion is not merely morally objectionable: it does not even work.

This argument was treated by Locke's opponent Jonas Proast and by some modern writers (e.g. Waldron 1988) as his main argument, something he firmly denied (Locke 1690: 6). It also establishes less than might at first sight appear. It would not trouble those like Hobbes (or Locke himself in the early 1660s) who were primarily concerned to maintain public order and who were therefore satisfied with outward conformity. Moreover, although one cannot simply decide by an act of will to believe something, this does not mean that coercion applied by others is incapable of inducing belief, even true belief. Everything depends on whether coercion is accompanied by adequate reasons or is merely a substitute for them.

Proast was willing to concede that coercion cannot directly induce sincere belief, but he maintained that it can sometimes do so indirectly by forcing people to consider arguments and examine evidence that they might otherwise have ignored. Locke was not persuaded. He was prepared to concede, at least for the sake of the argument, that coercion might perhaps be justified if it were used merely to make the negligent and inattentive examine matters properly, and that if having done so they were then allowed to adhere to the conclusions that seemed right to them, but he did not think there was any likelihood of this happening (Locke 1692: 204–5). Proast, he complained, was being disingenuous. As everyone knew, coercion was never used merely to make people examine: in reality it was invariably used to impose conformity, and those who duly examined arguments but remained unpersuaded soon found that they had not done what was required (Locke 1690: 35, 38, 63–4; Locke 1692: 39, 214–15, 227).

Locke's fundamental contention was not so much that belief is involuntary but that coercion, whether direct or indirect, is all too likely to induce false beliefs. In his controversies with Proast he repeatedly insisted that if magistrates were, as Proast maintained, under a duty to enforce the true religion, they would inevitably enforce the religion they *believed* to be true (Locke 1690: 14; Locke 1692: 3–5, 36, 59, 61, 201; Locke 1706: 246, 256–7, 258, 266, 269, 277). Since magistrates are in the same position as the rest of mankind, they cannot possibly *know* that the doctrines they propose to enforce are true: at most they can *believe* that they are, and the assurance with which such beliefs are held provides no guarantee whatever of their truth. Proast, he thought, was badly mistaken in ignoring this (Locke 1706: 258–9). All too often the opposite was true: 'those often who believe on the weakest Grounds, have the strongest Confidence: and thus all Magistrates who believe their Religion to be true, will be obliged to use Force to promote it, as if it were the true' (Locke 1692: 225–6). Any religion enforced in this fashion was, Locke thought, much more likely to be false than true. In the *Third Letter for Toleration* he said it would be at least twenty times more likely to do harm (Locke 1692: 204) and in the *Fourth Letter for Toleration* he went further, suggesting that there were 'five hundred Magistrates of the false Religion for one that is of the true' (Locke 1706: 265).

One reason why rulers were so often mistaken, Locke thought, was because they were usually surrounded by flattery and rarely subjected to criticism. 'The only difference between Princes and other Men', he wrote, 'is this, that Princes are usually more positive in matters of religion, but less instructed' (Locke 1706: 260). Furthermore, they could not overcome their fallibility by appealing to an infallible authority—even assuming there was one—because it was for them to judge where this was to be located, and their judgement must inevitably be fallible (Locke 1968: 95–9). Moreover, although Locke regarded the Bible itself as 'infallibly true' he insisted that the 'natural obscurities and difficulties incident to Words' would mean that any interpretation of it would inevitably be 'very fallible' (*Essay* III. ix. 23). Catholics, of course, appealed to an infallible church, but Locke rejected this: there was no infallible interpreter on earth and had not been one since the time of the Apostles (Locke 1997: 206). Established churches were no better placed: 'experience shews us that national Churches or great numbers of Christians united into one Church are no more priviledged from Errour then great congregations.

And where they assume to themselves an absolute power of imposeing are generaly lesse apt to be in the right' (Locke 2002: 78).

At the beginning of the *Essay concerning Toleration* Locke referred to 'the Question of liberty of conscience' (Locke 2006: 269), but neither there nor in his later writings did he base his arguments on any duty to respect the consciences of others. Indeed he dismissed the whole idea, remarking that 'the conscience, or persuasion of the subject, cannot possibly be a measure by which the magistrate can, or ought to frame his laws . . . there being noe thing soe indifferent which the consciences of some or other, doe not check at, a toleration of men in all that which they pretend out of conscience they cannot submit to, will wholy take away all the civil laws' (Locke 2006: 276). For Locke conscience was very far from being an infallible inner light or the voice of God. In 1660 he described it as 'nothing but an opinion of the truth of any practical position' (Locke 1967*b*: 138), and a similar view can be found in Draft B (Locke 1990: 110). In the *Essay concerning Human Understanding* he dismissed it as 'nothing else, but our own Opinion or Judgment of the Moral Rectitude or Pravity of our own Actions' (*Essay* I. iii. 8). It is simply moral belief and nothing more.

Although Locke advocated a very wide degree of toleration, including the toleration of non-Christian religions (Locke 1968: 145), he did not think it should be universal. In the *Essay concerning Toleration* he denied that it could be extended to those who 'mix with their religious worship, and speculative opinions, other doctrines absolutely destructive to the society wherein they live' (Locke 2006: 284). The worst offenders, he thought, were the Catholics, whom he described as 'irreconcileable enemys' who owed 'a blinde obedience to an infalible pope, who has the keys of their consciences tied to his girdle' (Locke 2006: 291). His remarks in the *Epistola* were more cautious, perhaps because a Catholic was now on the throne in England, but he made it clear that toleration should not be granted to those who maintained that faith need not be kept with heretics or that excommunicated kings must forfeit their kingdoms. He also added that a 'church can have no right to be tolerated by the magistrate which is so constituted that all who enter it *ipso facto* pass into the allegiance and service of another prince' (Locke 1968: 133). He was a very cautious man and the example he gave was a Muslim who 'owes a blind obedience to the Mufti of Constantinople, who himself is entirely subservient to the Ottoman Emperor' (Locke 1968: 135), but there can be little doubt that he thought there were other instances closer to home.

Locke also thought that toleration should not be extended to those who were themselves unwilling to practise it, and here too he had Catholics in mind (Locke 2006: 290). In the *Epistola* he stated that those

who attribute to the faithful, religious, and orthodox, that is to themselves, any privilege or power above other mortals, in civil affairs; or who on the plea of religion claim any authority over men who do not belong to their ecclesiastical communion, or who are in any way separated from it—these have no right to be tolerated by the magistrate: as neither have those who refuse to teach that dissenters from their own religion should be tolerated (Locke 1968: 133).

Indeed he thought that if a law was passed granting toleration, 'all churches [should be] obliged to teach, and lay down as the foundation of their own liberty, the principle of toleration for others' (Locke 1968: 135). Churches which were not prepared to do this would, presumably, be proscribed.

Locke also refused to extend toleration to atheists. They were not mentioned in the original version of the *Essay concerning Toleration*, but in an addition made some years later (it is not possible to say exactly when, but it would certainly have been before he left England in 1683) he noted that although speculative opinions were normally to be tolerated, atheism was not to be included among these because 'beleif of a deitie' was 'the foundation of all morality'. Anyone who denied God was 'to be counted noe other then one of the most dangerous sorts of wild beasts and soe uncapeable of all societie' (Locke 2006: 308). This is the kind of extreme language Locke applied to absolute monarchs, who were also regarded as 'dangerous and noxious Creatures' because they were 'not under the ties of the Common Law of Reason' (Locke 1967a: 297). The same uncompromising rejection of atheism can be found in the *Epistola*, though in somewhat milder language: 'those who deny the existence of the Deity (*qui numen esse negant*) are not to be tolerated at all. Promises, covenants, and oaths, which are the bonds of human society, can have no hold upon or sanctity for an atheist; for the taking away of God, even only in thought, dissolves all' (Locke 1968: 135).

In saying this Locke was not concerned with the fate of atheists in the hereafter: that was strictly their business and theirs alone. He was, however, firmly convinced that obligation is dependent on law, and that law requires a law-maker who is able to enforce it with the appropriate rewards and punishments (*Essay* II. xxviii. 6; Locke 1990: 269; Locke 1997: 302, 303). In the case of the natural (or moral) law the law-maker is God, and the divine law is 'the only true touchstone of *moral Rectitude*' (*Essay* II. xxviii. 8). For Locke this dependency on God was fundamental. 'The origin and foundation of all law', he wrote, 'is dependency. . . . If man were independent he could have no law but his own will, no end but himself. He would be a god to himself, and the satisfaction of his own will the sole measure and end of all his actions' (Locke 1997: 328–9). Locke did not think society could be erected on such a basis.

One consequence is that for Locke the state has a strong interest in upholding religion in general, even though it has no authority to impose particular forms of belief or worship. What this meant in practice he did not spell out, though there is nothing to suggest he would have any time for the kind of civil religion one finds in Spinoza. Locke's aim, above all, was to limit the role of the civil power in religious affairs, and in this he differed profoundly from Hobbes and Spinoza, both of whom gave a thoroughly secular state extensive powers to order and regulate religious worship. Locke's state was more secular in that it was restricted to securing civil goods, but less secular in that its ultimate foundations were religious.

# III: BAYLE

Locke's conviction that atheism undermines the foundations of morality would have been accepted by almost all of his contemporaries, but it was not shared by Pierre Bayle. Bayle is the most enigmatic and difficult to interpret of the philosophers discussed here, and three centuries after his death there is still no agreement as to what he really believed. There is, however, no dispute that he was deeply opposed to religious persecution from whatever quarter it came, including his fellow Protestants. His most extensive discussion of toleration was in the *Commentaire philosophique*, the first two parts of which were published in October 1686, a year after the revocation of the Edict of Nantes. Although much of this was taken up with arguing that the words 'compel them to come in' in the parable of the wedding feast (Luke 14: 23) should not be interpreted as meaning that Christ was giving the apostles, and hence the church, the power to compel anyone, Bayle was not solely concerned with scriptural exegesis. As the title of his work indicates, he sought to provide philosophical arguments as well.

These arguments were based on what might be called the primacy of conscience. Although Bayle was often inclined to indulge in loose talk about the 'rights of conscience', his argument rests ultimately not on rights but on duties, and in particular on the duty to obey one's conscience. For Bayle the fundamental principle, on which the whole argument rests, was that 'everything done against the dictates of conscience is a sin' (OD II 422b). The key word here is *everything*. Others might deny the principle altogether, as Hobbes did (*Lev* 168), or qualify it by restricting it to properly instructed consciences, but for Bayle it was unconditional and applied as much to false consciences as to true ones. He also rejected the widely accepted distinction between errors of fact, which may sometimes excuse, and errors of law (*droit*) which do not: in his eyes all errors excuse if made in good faith (OD II 429b). Since all this applies just as much to theological errors as to any other kind, he concluded that heretics are just as much under a duty to follow their consciences, even if these are erroneous, as the orthodox are to follow theirs.

One potential difficulty with this, as Bayle's critics were quick to point out, was that on his principles if persecutors believed themselves obliged by their consciences they too must be obliged to persecute. Bayle saw the difficulty, which he subsequently described as the 'most embarrassing' for him (OD II 540a). He was ready to concede that the obligation was real enough: 'I do not deny that those who are actually persuaded that they must, to obey God, extirpate the sects are obliged to follow the promptings of that false conscience, and that in not doing so they commit the crime of disobeying God . . .' (OD II 430b). He did, however, add that although such persecutors are obliged to follow their consciences they are nevertheless still committing crimes. As he himself subsequently acknowledged in the *Additions aux pensées diverses* (1694), when someone is acting in accordance with an erroneous conscience 'it does not follow that his action is exempt from sin; if his error is not invincible he is responsible before God for all the bad (*mauvais*) actions that he did following the dictates of his conscience' (OD III 180a).

Bayle also went on to dismiss a further objection, namely that on his principles a magistrate cannot punish someone who steals or kills when that person is persuaded by his conscience that these are lawful actions. This, he thought, does not follow, 'because the magistrate is obliged to maintain society and to punish those who overturn its foundations, as do murderers and robbers, and in such cases he is not obliged to pay any regard to their consciences. He is only obliged to have such regard in things which do not disturb the public peace' (OD II 431a). The implication of this is that, as in Locke, the duties of the magistrate are based on the need to preserve order and maintain civil society, a need which overrides any plea of private conscience.

Bayle also argued, just as Locke did, that if God were to give the true church the right to coerce heretics, all churches would inevitably claim this right, 'because every church believes itself to be the true one' (OD II 426b). Similarly, he insisted that although coercion is quite capable of producing outward conformity it can neither move the heart nor persuade the mind (OD II 371a). He also emphasized the fallibility of our religious beliefs, observing that although one might pardon intolerance amongst those who could clearly prove their opinions and convincingly answer all objections, it was absolutely inexcusable among those 'who are obliged to say, that they have no better solution to give, than that those are secrets impenetrable to the human mind, and concealed in the infinite treasury of the incomprehensible immensity of God' (*Dict.*, Synergists, rem. B: Bayle 1734–41: IX, 465b).

Like Locke, Bayle believed that the preservation of public order was consistent with a wide range of religious belief, including heretical ones. On this he was uncompromising and was strongly opposed to those he called '*Messieurs les Demi-Tolérans*' (OD II 421a), that is those who were willing to tolerate divergencies within mainstream Christianity but who drew the line at the more extreme heresies, such as Socinianism. The problem with all such halfway solutions, he insisted, is that there is no agreement on what the fundamental doctrines of Christianity actually are, and consequently nowhere that a line can properly be drawn. It was therefore necessary to extend toleration to all forms of religious belief, 'not only to Socinians, but also to Jews and Turks' (OD II 419b).

This might seem to lead to universal and unconditional toleration, but, like Locke, Bayle thought that there had to be some exceptions. One, unsurprisingly, was Catholicism. For Bayle, as for Locke, toleration had to be reciprocal, and should not be extended to those who were unwilling to practise it themselves: 'a party which, if it becomes the stronger, will no longer tolerate the other ... ought not to be tolerated at all' (OD II 413a). As a Huguenot refugee Bayle felt very strongly about this, and in the *Dictionary* he criticized those who were prepared to tolerate Catholicism. Such indulgence was, he thought, mistaken: 'since Popery has been time out of mind the sect which persecutes most, and incessantly torments both the body and soul of other Christians wheresoever it can do it, the most zealous advocates for toleration do chiefly design it's exclusion' (*Dict.* Milton, rem. O: Bayle 1734–8: IV, 223b).

The other exception, or so it would appear, was atheism. In the *Commentaire philosophique* Bayle stated that magistrates 'can and ought to punish all those who offend against the fundamental laws of the state, amongst whom are commonly placed those who take away providence and all fear of divine justice'. An atheist cannot plead that he must obey God rather than man and he therefore 'lies justly exposed to all the rigours of the law' (OD II 431a). On the face of it this might suggest that Bayle's position was similar to Locke's, but in fact their views were very different. Bayle did not think that atheism undermines the whole basis of morality. In his earliest major work, the *Pensées diverses sur la comète*, he argued at considerable length that atheism is far less harmful than idolatry, that it does not lead to a corruption of morals, that atheists often led morally upright lives, and that a society of atheists is possible (Bayle 1939: §§ 133, 161, 172, 174). In support of this he referred to a number of atheists who had lived upright and virtuous lives. Most of his examples were taken from the ancient world, but he also included Spinoza, whom he described as 'the greatest atheist there had ever been' (Bayle 1939: § 181; see also OD III 397a, 399b–400a, 406a). In the *Dictionary* article on Spinoza, Bayle noted that everyone who knew him described him as 'a man of a social disposition, affable, honest, obliging, and very regular in his morals' (Bayle 1734–41: IX, 354).

Such remarks did not go unnoticed, and in the first of the clarifications written for the second edition of the *Dictionary* Bayle tried to rebut the complaints of those who thought he had been unduly favourable to atheists and others of no religion. He obviously felt some conciliatory gestures would be appropriate, and though he continued to affirm that the love and fear of God are for most people less powerful motives than the desire for glory or the fear of death or infamy, he did deny that atheists have real virtues because their actions are not motivated by the love of God. Self-love is their real motive, and their apparent virtues are no more than glittering sins, *splendida peccata*. 'It remains true', he concluded, 'that good works can only be produced within the confines of true religion' (Bayle 1965: 401).

It is, however, clear that Bayle did think that atheists could have an idea of *honnêteté*—that is decency, uprightness, or integrity (Bayle 1939: § 178). Moreover, although they cannot consider themselves bound by conscience if this is conceived of as the voice of God, Bayle certainly thought that atheists could have other grounds for acting in accordance with their consciences. In one of his last works, the *Réponse aux questions d'un provincial*, he distinguished between conscience based on divine commands reinforced by rewards or punishments and conscience regarded as 'a judgement of the mind which leads us to do certain things because they are in conformity with reason' (OD III 986b). An atheist, he thought, could perfectly well have a conscience in this latter sense.

This alternative understanding of conscience does, however, undermine one of the key arguments in the *Commentaire philosophique*, that we must always obey our conscience since this is for us the voice of God and we must always obey God rather than man. If God does not exist or is unknowable, this argument collapses. For an atheist conscience cannot be anything more than moral belief, which is always fallible and all too often mistaken, and it is very hard to see on what grounds he could think that there must always be an overriding duty to obey a conscience so conceived or hold that others should be obliged to respect it. Bayle himself seems to have realized this, and in his later writings he placed considerably less emphasis on the duty to obey conscience and considerably more on the dangers of an erroneous conscience, especially in matters of religion. 'The principle of conscience', he wrote, 'is often the cause of an infinity of crimes, and it is certain that a man who is only moderately vindictive if he has no religion becomes a tiger when false zeal takes over his conscience' (OD III 985a).

This false zeal was, he thought, endemic amongst Christians, and especially amongst the clergy. In the *Additions aux pensées diverses* he had complained that the 'dogma of intolerance' was universally upheld by all Christian sects, except for those which themselves needed toleration, and he added that the stronger sects preached tolerance in countries where they lacked power and intolerance where they possessed it (OD III 179a). By the end of his life he came to think that this was irremediable. It was, he held, inevitable that religion would disturb the public peace so long as it was divided into sects (OD III 1011b). It is difficult to say whether he saw this as a consequence of Christianity itself or merely as a corruption of it, but he took the view that 'all men of good sense would rather live in a society without religion than in a society infected by such a religion' (OD III 985b). The French Protestants, he thought, would be much better off living under a *Roi Spinoziste* (OD III 954a).

All this was very unlike the religious pluralism advocated by Locke. They also differed profoundly on civil disobedience. In the *Nouvelles lettres de l'auteur de la Critique générale*, published early in 1685, Bayle insisted that 'sovereigns have the right to act unjustly towards their subjects since it is not permitted for subjects to oppose them' (OD II 225a). The revocation of the Edict of Nantes did not cause him to change his mind, and he stuck to his principles even after the Revolution of 1688–89. Locke welcomed this wholeheartedly, as did many of the exiled

Huguenots, but Bayle did not. In the *Avis important aux réfugiez* (another anonymous work, though there can be little if any doubt that he wrote it) he denounced the 'so-called [prétenduë] sovereignty of the people', insisting that in all states it is necessary for there to be a supreme tribunal whose commandments all are obliged to obey and which cannot be judged except by God (OD II 594a–595a). On such matters Locke was very much closer to Bayle's bitterest enemy, Pierre Jurieu.

Like many pessimistic sceptics, Bayle was quietist in politics and fundamentally conservative in temperament. It would, he observed, be best to observe existing customs unless the alternatives can be shown to be better (*Dict.*, Spinoza, rem. O). His own religious position remains something of a mystery, but he seems to have drifted away from the Calvinism in which he had been reared and by the end of his life he may well have become an unbeliever. Whether he had already done so by the time he wrote the *Commentaire philosophique* is very hard to say, but much of his argument in that work depends upon a conception of conscience as the voice of God.

# Conclusion

Although Hobbes, Spinoza, Locke, and Bayle were in general men of very different philosophical outlook, they did all share a deep hostility to the combination of clerical intolerance, scholastic philosophy, and pagan superstition that Hobbes labelled the Kingdom of Darkness. All were firmly of the view that the clergy should never in any circumstances wield coercive power. Where they did differ fundamentally was over the powers the civil authorities possessed over religion, especially in its public manifestations.

For Hobbes and Spinoza religion was too disruptive, too dangerous to be left to private judgement. It was therefore essential that the practice of religion in general, and public worship in particular, should be controlled by the civil authorities. Controlled, it must be emphasized, rather than abolished: both men saw religion as a useful way of inculcating political obedience—indeed for them this was its primary function. Hobbes sought to modify Christianity to achieve this particular end, whereas Spinoza hoped to create a post-Christian civil religion which would do this more effectively. They did, however, leave a space for private belief, in that individuals holding (and in Spinoza's case expressing) heterodox opinions should be left unmolested so long as they did not disturb the civil order. For Hobbes the establishment of political order required the union of civil and ecclesiastical power in one (artificial) person, and like Spinoza he was an early advocate of what the French call *laïcité*, of the civil authorities controlling and managing religion for essentially secular purposes.

Locke's views were very different. He was quite ready to prohibit religions whose doctrines or practices were inconsistent with civil society, but he took the view that most religious believers simply wished to worship God as they thought best and would not disturb the civil order provided they were tolerated (Locke 1968: 139–41). So far as church and state were concerned he sought separation, not subordination. He was adamant that the civil authorities could under no circumstances compel anyone to engage in any form of religious worship or punish those who refused to conform. For him freedom of worship was fundamental in a way it was not for Hobbes or Spinoza, both of whom saw religion in instrumental terms. Where he differed most profoundly from them was that his ultimate aims were religious not political.

Bayle's aims are more difficult to assess. Like Locke he had a deeply-rooted abhorrence of religious persecution, an abhorrence sharpened in his case by personal experience. His religious views remain a matter of uncertainty and dispute. He was more pessimistic than Locke and there is some evidence from his later writings that he came to think that a general toleration would lead to sectarian strife and that the civil authorities would have to take steps to prevent this—a view much more like those of Hobbes or Spinoza.

## REFERENCES

AUBREY, J. (1898). *'Brief Lives', chiefly of Contemporaries.* Ed. A. Clark. 2 vols. Oxford.

BAYLE, P. (1734–8). *The Dictionary Historical and Critical of Mr. Peter Bayle.* 2nd edn. 5 vols. London.

BAYLE, P. (1734–41). *A General Dictionary, Historical and Critical.* 10 vols., London.

BAYLE, P. (1939). *Pensées diverses sur la comète.* Ed. A. Prat. 2 vols. Paris.

BAYLE, P. (1965). *Historical and Critical Dictionary.* Ed. R. H. Popkin. Indianapolis.

HOBBES, T. (1656). *Elements of Philosophy, the first section, concerning Body.* London.

HOBBES, T. (1682). *An Answer to a Book published by Dr. Bramhall.* London.

HOBBES, T. (1976). *Thomas White's De Mundo Examined.* Ed. H. W. Jones. London.

HOBBES, T. (1994). *The Elements of Law, Natural and Politic . . . with Three Lives.* Ed. J. C. A. Gaskin. Oxford: Oxford University Press.

KING, P. (1829). *The Life and Letters of John Locke.* London.

LOCKE, J. (1690). *A Second Letter concerning Toleration.* London.

LOCKE, J. (1692). *A Third Letter for Toleration.* London.

LOCKE, J. (1699). *Mr. Locke's Reply To the Right Reverend the Lord Bishop of Worcester's Answer to his Second Letter.* London.

LOCKE, J. (1706). *Posthumous Works of Mr. John Locke.* London.

LOCKE, J. (1967a). *Two Treatises of Government.* Ed. P. Laslett. 2nd edn. Cambridge: Cambridge University Press.

LOCKE, J. (1967b). *Two Tracts on Government.* Ed. P. Abrams. Cambridge: Cambridge University Press.

LOCKE, J. (1968). *Epistola de Tolerantia*. Ed. R. Klibansky, trans. J. W. Gough. Oxford: Oxford University Press.

LOCKE, J. (1990). *Drafts for the Essay concerning Human Understanding, and other Philosophical Writings*. Vol. I, ed. P. H. Nidditch and G. A. J. Rogers. Oxford: Oxford University Press.

LOCKE, J. (1997). *Political Essays*. Ed. M. Goldie. Cambridge: Cambridge University Press.

LOCKE, J. (2002). *Writings on Religion*. Ed. V. Nuovo. Oxford: Oxford University Press.

LOCKE, J. (2006). *An Essay Concerning Toleration and other Writings on Law and Politics*. Ed. J. R. Milton and P. Milton. Oxford: Oxford University Press.

MALCOLM, N. (2002). *Aspects of Hobbes*. Oxford: Oxford University Press.

SPINOZA, B. DE (1928). *The Correspondence of Spinoza*. Ed. A. Wolf. London.

SPINOZA, B. DE (1958). *The Political Works*. Ed. A. G. Wernham. Oxford: Oxford University Press.

SPINOZA, B. DE (2007). *Theological-Political Treatise*. Ed. J. Israel. Cambridge: Cambridge University Press.

WALDRON, J. (1988). 'Locke: Toleration and the Rationality of Persecution', in S. Mendus (ed.), *Justifying Toleration*. Cambridge: Cambridge University Press, 61–88.

# INDEX

9 780199 671649